Human Learning and Memory

This innovative textbook is the first to integrate learning and memory, behavior, and cognition. It focuses on fascinating human research in both memory *and* learning (while also bringing in important animal studies) and brings the reader up to date with the latest developments in the subject. Students are encouraged to think critically: key theories and issues are looked at in detail; descriptions of experiments include why they were done and how examining the method can help evaluate competing viewpoints. By looking at underlying cognitive processes, students come away with a sense of learning and memory being interrelated actions taken by the same human being, rather than two separate activities. Lively and engaging writing is supported by lots of examples of practical applications that show the relevance of lab-based research to everyday life. Examples include treatments for phobias and autism, ways to improve eyewitness testimony, and methods of enhancing study techniques.

David A. Lieberman was an undergraduate at Columbia and received his PhD from Brown. He taught for four years at the University of Illinois, Champaign-Urbana, where he was twice selected as the "most stimulating" teacher in psychology in University polls of graduating seniors. He moved to the University of Stirling in Scotland where his course on learning received the highest student ratings of any course in psychology. He served two terms as Associate Editor of the *Quarterly Journal of Experimental Psychology*, and was one of two psychology members of the SERC panel that awarded research grants in psychology. He is the author of *Learning and the Control of Behavior*, *Learning: Behavior and Cognition*, and *Learning and Memory*.

D1709433

Human Learning and Memory

David A. Lieberman

CAMBRIDGE
UNIVERSITY PRESS

CAMBRIDGE UNIVERSITY PRESS
Cambridge, New York, Melbourne, Madrid, Cape Town,
Singapore, São Paulo, Delhi, Tokyo, Mexico City

Cambridge University Press
The Edinburgh Building, Cambridge CB2 8RU, UK

Published in the United States of America by Cambridge University Press, New York

www.cambridge.org
Information on this title: www.cambridge.org/9780521701396

First published 2012

Printed in the United Kingdom at the University Press, Cambridge

A catalogue record for this publication is available from the British Library

Library of Congress Cataloguing in Publication data
Lieberman, David A.
Human learning and memory / David A. Lieberman.
    p.   cm.
Includes bibliographical references and index.
ISBN 978-0-521-87747-3 (hardback) – ISBN 978-0-521-70139-6 (paperback)
1. Learning, Psychology of.   2. Memory.   I. Title.
BF318.L537   2011
153.1 – dc23   2011041582

ISBN 978-0-521-87747-3 Hardback
ISBN 978-0-521-70139-6 Paperback

For my wife Myra and my grandsons Anton, Rory, and Eli

Contents

Part II) **Memory**

Figures

Acknowledgments

I'd like to thank three individuals who played particularly important roles in the preparation of this text. The first two are editors at Cambridge University Press – Andy Peart, who commissioned the text, and Hetty Marx, who then shepherded it through to publication. Both were helpful, supportive, and encouraging throughout, and I am really grateful to both of them. The third is my wife Myra. Writing a textbook can absorb prodigious amounts of an author's time and emotional energy, and once again Myra encouraged me to proceed despite knowing the unfair burden this would place on her. She did so because she knew how much pleasure writing gives me, and I am more grateful than I can say for her continuing generosity, good humor, and love.

Introduction

CONTENTS

Imagine being born without the ability to form memories. Nothing you experienced would leave any trace: You would not be able to learn to walk or talk, you would not remember anything that happened to you, you would be permanently imprisoned, like a fly in amber, in the mind of an infant. Our abilities to learn and remember are the foundation stones on which we build our lives; we would be lost without them.

Normally, we learn and remember so effortlessly that we take the skills involved for granted. Consider memory. You have stored information about physical skills such as how to walk and write; you remember your experiences with countless friends and acquaintances, the facts you learned in school about subjects such as history and geography, the meaning of 80,000 English words, and so on. Focusing just on vocabulary, you know how to pronounce and spell each of these 80,000 words, and in many cases you also have a vast store of information about the words. In the case of the word *cat*, you know what cats look like, how they like to be stroked, their propensity for attracting fleas, and so on. In the course of your life, you have stored an almost unbelievable amount of information, and yet you usually can access information from this store almost instantly when you need it. It is an astonishing feat, and in this book we will be looking at how you do it.

Human learning?

The eminent learning psychologist Robert Rescorla once published a paper entitled "Pavlovian Conditioning – It's Not What You Think It Is." In a similar vein, the focus of this book both is and isn't what the title suggests. The use of the word "human" might seem to imply that it will be devoted exclusively to research involving humans, with animal research having no place. That is not so. Animal research has played a central role in the development of our understanding of learning, and this research will be covered where appropriate.

Nevertheless, the use of the word "human" does signal a fundamental shift in orientation. Textbooks on learning have traditionally focused on animals, with human applications introduced only as a kind of supplement or "extra." In a chapter on reinforcement, for example, the core of the chapter would be research on how reinforcement affects rats and pigeons; only once this was established might there be supplementary material showing effects on people.

For a reader not familiar with this area, this emphasis on animals might seem peculiar, but learning textbooks focused on animal research for the very good reason that almost all research in this field was carried out on animals. One reason was practical – it is easier to control the environment of animals than people, and this makes it easier to disentangle the contributions of different variables. Another was that animals were thought to have simpler learning systems, and again this makes it easier to understand the fundamental processes involved. And yet a third reason was ideological. For many decades psychology was dominated by behaviorists who – for sound reasons – distrusted explanations that attributed behavior to mental states that couldn't be observed. One advantage of studying animals was that it would be easier to avoid speculations about their mental states and just focus on the variables that controlled their behavior. The end result was that researchers whose real interest was learning in humans nevertheless devoted their careers to studying rats and, later, pigeons.

Over recent decades, this picture has changed substantially. With the rise of cognitive psychology there has been increased interest in the cognitive processes that underlie behavior, leading to far more research on humans and far less on animals. However, this shift has not yet been reflected in textbooks, where the focus has remained very heavily on learning in animals.

In my view, the quantity and quality of human research has reached a point where we no longer need to focus on rats and pigeons – if we want to understand learning in humans, we can do so using research that actually studies humans. One advantage of this approach is that it frees space to cover the new paths that research has taken. Recent years have seen a rapid growth of research on phenomena such as causal learning and evaluative conditioning, research that has been largely ignored in existing texts. A further advantage is that students find it hard to believe that studying the behavior of white rats is the best way to understand people; a textbook that focuses on human research has a far greater chance of capturing their interest and even enthusiasm.

For these reasons, my goal in this text was to explore what we now know about learning and memory in humans, bringing in research on animals only where it was historically important – it would be difficult to talk about classical conditioning, for example, without discussing the crucial contributions of Pavlov – or where it still provides the most illuminating evidence. In working toward this goal, several assumptions about textbook writing guided me, and in the remainder of this preface I will discuss these orienting assumptions. Briefly, I wanted this textbook to be *stimulating, enjoyable, integrative*, and *practical.*

Intellectually stimulating

One of my fundamental goals was to present ideas in a way that would be intellectually rigorous and stimulating. All textbook authors face the difficult problem of how to balance the need for broad coverage against the dangers of superficiality – of losing students in a forest of facts. My own bias is toward depth rather than breadth: I think students gain more from a deep understanding of fundamental ideas than from a superficial familiarity with a much larger set of facts. In writing this text, I have tried to explore the most important issues in learning and memory in depth, rather than to provide shallower coverage of all topics.

One example is the treatment of experimental design. If students are to be helped to think critically, it is vital that they understand the logic of experiments rather than just memorize their conclusions. To encourage this understanding, Chapter 1 provides an introduction to the experimental method: the advantages and disadvantages of experiments, why learning researchers sometimes study animals, and so on. Subsequent chapters build on this foundation by analyzing selected experiments and issues in depth, while providing briefer summaries of other studies. Where this selective approach has meant that coverage of some issues has had to be curtailed, I have provided references that the interested reader can consult for more information.

I have taken a similar approach to presenting theories, concentrating on presenting a small number in detail rather than more superficial coverage of them all. In classical conditioning, for example, I have focused on the Rescorla–Wagner model. Through extensive analysis of this model, I have tried to convey a feeling for how theories can be used to explain known phenomena and to generate novel and sometimes counterintuitive predictions. Similarly, Chapter 11 explores Raaijmakers and Shiffrin's SAM model, using it to show how many of the properties of memory can be explained through just a few simple principles. And the text concludes with an in-depth discussion of neural network models, exploring their potential to explain behavior ranging from classical conditioning in slugs to the acquisition of language in humans.

Enjoyable

No matter how stimulating ideas may be in principle, they will not have this effect in practice unless readers understand them and find them interesting. I have tried very hard, therefore, to present ideas clearly and, where possible, entertainingly; I hope reading the text will feel more like participating in an enjoyable conversation than listening to a formal lecture.

Applications: linking the laboratory and the real world

One way to make ideas come alive is to explore their practical implications, and I have tried to do this throughout the text. Students sometimes find research on learning boring because of an understandable disinclination to believe that experiments on rats can shed much light on human behavior, and similar problems can arise in seeing the value of experiments on the memorization of nonsense syllables. It is not enough for teachers and textbooks to assert that laboratory research is relevant: This relevance has to be demonstrated.

I have done this by interweaving material on laboratory research and practical applications in every chapter. The chapters on classical conditioning, for example, discuss the role of conditioning in generating human emotions such as fear, sexual arousal, and cravings for drugs, and how conditioning principles can be used to treat problems such as phobias and addictions. Similarly, the chapters on reinforcement look at applications such as Lovaas's stunningly effective treatment for autism, and issues such as whether reinforcement undermines intrinsic motivation. The chapter on punishment also contains what I believe to be the most extensive coverage in any text on the use of punishment for children, looking not only at the conditions that determine punishment's effectiveness but also at the possibility of side effects, concluding with an examination of alternatives to spanking such as time-out, response cost, and reinforcement.

The chapters on memory continue this emphasis on practical applications. Applications covered include techniques for improving studying, the accuracy of eyewitness testimony, and the painful issue of whether we should believe adults who suddenly remember having been sexually abused when they were children, despite having no recollection of this abuse in the intervening years.

Integrating learning and memory

Learning and memory are intimately, perhaps inextricably, intertwined. The term *learning* emphasizes the acquisition of information, whereas the term *memory* emphasizes its retention, but both are facets of a single system for storing information about our experiences. You cannot remember an experience unless you first create a record of it (learning), and you cannot learn from this experience unless you retain this record (memory). And yet, despite this intimate relationship, for many years learning and memory were studied separately, with only minimal contact between investigators in the two areas. Research on learning typically focused on the effects of rewards on rats and pigeons; research on memory typically explored people's ability to remember verbal material. The resulting research was published in different journals, and researchers in one area rarely knew much about developments in the other.

One reason for this separation was practical: The almost exponential growth in research made it increasingly difficult for researchers to follow developments outside their own specialty. However, this division was also driven by differences in theoretical orientation. Almost from its inception, research on learning in animals was heavily influenced by associationism and behaviorism: Animal researchers believed that they should focus on visible behavior, rather than speculating about invisible processes that might – or might not – be occurring inside an animal's head, and many also believed that the learning was a fundamentally simple process involving the formation of associations. Memory researchers, on the other hand, were persuaded by the cognitive revolution of the 1950s and 1960s that understanding memory required an understanding of the cognitive processes involved, and that these processes were far more complex than simply the formation of associations. The result was that learning and memory researchers not only studied different behaviors but also adopted radically different approaches to explaining their results, making communication between the two fields difficult.

More recently, this chasm has narrowed. On the learning side, researchers have increasingly recognized the importance of cognitive processes such as memory and attention in even the simplest forms of conditioning – Kamin's research on blocking and Bouton's on extinction illustrate this trend. Learning theorists have also increasingly borrowed ideas that first emerged on the cognitive side – Shiffrin and Schneider's distinction between controlled and automatic processes provides one example, neural network models another.

On the other side of the divide, cognitive theorists have put increasing emphasis on the role of simple associative processes in memory. Raaijmakers and Shiffrin's model of memory, for example, assumes that the creation of a memory record depends on the formation of associations between the elements of a scene and that subsequent retrieval of this record depends on retrieval cues activating some of these elements, with this activation then spreading to the other elements. If so, then understanding memory requires understanding the formation of associations, just as understanding conditioning requires understanding memory. Indeed, the emergence of neural network models has raised the intriguing possibility that associations might lie at the heart of *all* cognition, determining what we think as well as what we remember.

In sum, the gap between associative accounts of learning and cognitive accounts of memory has narrowed remarkably in recent years, to a degree that is perhaps still not fully appreciated. This convergence has opened the path to a coherent and integrated account of learning and memory, and I have tried to convey how close we have come.

Aids to studying

To help readers absorb the sometimes challenging material in each chapter, I have provided Summaries at the end. In addition, each chapter contains Review Questions designed to encourage students to review the material they have read and also to think about it further. If students can answer these questions, they can be confident that they have understood the main themes of the chapter.

Part I Learning

1 Some basic assumptions

CONTENTS

In an early television series called *Dragnet*, police sergeant Joe Friday was forever being confronted by incoherent witnesses to a crime. He would stoically endure their babbling until, his patience finally exhausted, he would interrupt, "We want the facts, Ma'am, just the facts." Psychologists too want the facts, but, with experience, they acquire a certain wary respect for the problems involved in determining facts. What is a fact? Of course everyone knows what a fact is; a fact is . . . , well . . . it's a *fact*, something that everyone knows to be true. Or is it? Was it a fact that the earth was flat because everyone before Columbus believed it to be so? Or that the earth was the center of the universe before Copernicus and Galileo moved it into orbit around the sun? And if we cannot be sure of the truth in cases as obvious as these ("Can't you feel that the earth is still? Can't you see that the sun is moving?"), how much more difficult must it be when the truth is more obscure, and when experts can't even agree among themselves? If one scientist claims that the moon is composed of blue cheese, and a colleague tartly replies, "So's your mother," how are we to decide which of their scientific views is correct?

In older sciences, such as physics and chemistry, disputes over scientific facts are less obvious: Over the years, basic concepts such as the atom and gravity have become firmly established; only after considerable training to learn dispute-free "facts" are new initiates to the profession gradually introduced to the ambiguities and uncertainties of current research. In psychology, which is a relatively new science, these disputes cannot be obscured so easily: The dividing line between "old established facts" and "new controversial hypotheses" is less clear, and there is no comforting bedrock of certainty and accomplishment to support students when they feel overwhelmed by conflicting claims. Consider such a relatively simple problem as the use of corporal punishment: Is corporal punishment an effective and ultimately humane way to eliminate a person's harmful behavior, or is it a barbaric relic of our primitive past? There is evidence to support both views, and it can be more than a little frustrating to try to analyze the polemics of each side, and more than a little tempting to give up in disgust, crying "a plague on both your houses."

In their attempts to resolve such disagreements – to decide what is a fact and what is not – psychologists have relied on several assumptions. These assumptions are now so widely accepted that psychologists rarely question them, but this does not necessarily mean that they are correct. It is perhaps worth emphasizing in advance that the assumptions we will be examining in this chapter really are assumptions, slowly developed over several centuries within a particular cultural and scientific tradition, and indeed not universally accepted even among psychologists. There are good grounds for you to approach these assumptions with a healthy skepticism and to form your own views of their validity. The better you understand these assumptions, however, the better you will understand why research has followed the paths that we will be tracing in subsequent chapters.

One purpose of this chapter, then, is to examine the methodological assumptions that have guided psychological research: Why psychologists rely on experiments to understand behavior, and the logic that guides researchers in designing these experiments. Before considering how to do research, however, we will begin by focusing on an even more fundamental issue: Why study behavior in the first place?

Is behavior lawful?

The most fundamental assumption underlying research into the laws of learning and memory is that there *are* such laws – if people's behavior were simply capricious or random, there would be little point in trying to discover the laws governing it. To clarify the issue, let us begin by defining more precisely what we mean by a law. Within science, a law is essentially a statement of the form "If A, then B." That is, if some condition A exists, we predict that event B will occur. The statement "The sun rises every morning," for example, predicts that if it is morning, then the sun will rise. Similarly, Einstein's famous equation $E = mc^2$ says that if m has a value of 1 and c has a value of 2, then the value of E will be 4 (the real value of c is much greater). The assertion that behavior is lawful, therefore, is essentially a claim that behavior is in principle predictable: Whenever a certain set of conditions arises, the same behavior will always follow.

Determinism versus free will

Most of us believe that at least some aspects of behavior are predictable. However much we might dislike some powerful bully, for example, we don't usually walk over to him and punch him in the nose, because we know very well that his reaction will not be random but intensely and unpleasantly predictable. Opinion varies, however, as to the extent of this predictability or lawfulness.

Determinism

At one extreme, some believe that *all* behavior is predictable. According to the doctrine of **determinism**, people's behavior is entirely determined by their heredity and environment (as used here, the word "environment" refers to past experiences as well as present environment). Your decision to go to college, for example, was probably influenced by factors such as the educational background of your parents, the grades you received at school, the economic advantages of a degree, and so forth. According to determinism, these factors made it inevitable that you would eventually choose to go to college, whether or not you were consciously aware of their influence.

Dramatic advances in physics and chemistry have accustomed us to the idea that nature is inherently orderly, even though our ignorance sometimes makes it appear capricious. But is the behavior of a living organism just as lawful, just as determined, as the orbit of a rocket or the ticking of a clock? Are we really just helpless pawns in the grasp of environmental and genetic forces beyond our control?

Free will

Within Western civilization, strict determinism of this kind has generally been rejected. Humans, according to most Western religions, are fundamentally free: We all have the power to determine our actions; this **free will** makes each of us responsible for our behavior and provides the basis for our concepts of morality and responsibility. Aside from formal religious teachings, however, a deep strain within all of us resents the notion that we are only insignificant links within a causal chain, like billiard balls hurtling blindly through space, propelled by forces we cannot resist.

Why, then, do many research psychologists nevertheless believe in determinism? The reasons are complex, and in the following sections we will consider some of them. As you read this material, some of the arguments might strike you as more philosophical than psychological, and you might wonder why a psychology textbook should be devoting so much attention to this issue. The answer is that a belief in determinism plays an important role in guiding psychological research. If you carry out a study to find a lawful relationship and your effort fails, you are much more likely to persist if you are convinced that there really are laws. As a result, many of the most crucial discoveries about learning and memory have been made by psychologists with a stubborn, even fanatical belief that behavior is lawful. (See, for example, the discussions of Pavlov in Chapter 2 and Ebbinghaus in Chapter 8.) In the sections that follow, we will consider some arguments that have led to this belief.

Neural determinism

One line of evidence supporting the determinist view comes from our rapidly growing understanding of the brain's role in determining behavior. We will discuss the mechanisms involved in more detail in Chapter 2, but in essence the brain consists of a vast network of interconnected cells called neurons, and the transmission of electrical signals through these cells determines our behavior. When we see a friend, for example, the light falling on receptors located at the back of the eye produces electrical signals, and these are then transmitted by means of a series of neurons to the cortex and then ultimately to the muscles that cause us to raise our hand in greeting or to move our lips to say hello. If physicists are correct, and the behavior of all particles in the universe is lawful, then the transmission of these electrical impulses through our brain must also be lawful. (Indeed, neurophysiologists already have a good understanding of the chemical processes that govern the propagation of electrical signals through neurons, and how the arrival of a signal at a neuron's terminal leads to the release of chemicals which then activate the next neuron in the chain.) If these assumptions are right – if our brains control our behavior, and if the brain's operations are lawful – then it logically follows that our behavior must also be lawful. If the operation of any system is lawful, then the output of that system must also be lawful.

We will call this argument **neural determinism**. Its first assumption – that the firing of neurons is governed by laws of physics and chemistry that govern all other materials – is widely accepted, at least within science. The second, though – that our brains control all aspects of our behavior – is more controversial. We will therefore focus on this second assumption, examining the brain's role in three fundamental activities: movement, emotion, and thought.

Movement

Our movements are entirely controlled by the transmission of electrical impulses though our neurons. When we move an arm, for example, this movement is caused by the contraction of muscles within the arm, and these contractions are in turn controlled by neurons. Neurons are connected to every muscle in the body, and electrical impulses arriving at the terminals of these neurons trigger the release of chemicals that in turn initiate muscular contractions. If these neural connections are damaged – for example, if the spine is damaged in an automobile accident so that neural messages can no longer be transmitted from the brain to certain muscles – then we lose the ability to control these muscles. Similarly, the tremors seen in Parkinson's disease are due to degeneration of neurons in the *substantia nigra*, one of the regions of the brain involved in controlling movement, and it is possible to treat Parkinson's by administering L-Dopa, a drug that restores the functioning of the affected neurons. Evidence of this kind makes it clear that movement is entirely controlled by the nervous system.

Emotion

In a similar way, our emotions are controlled by what regions of our brains are active. One early experiment demonstrating the brain's role in emotions was reported by Olds and Milner (1954), who found that delivering a tiny electrical current to certain areas of a rat's brain seemed to produce pleasurable sensations in the rat, as the rat would press a lever as often as 2,000 times per hour to turn on this current. A neurosurgeon, Heath (1963), reported similar effects in humans. One of his patients suffered from narcolepsy, a debilitating condition in which sufferers will suddenly and uncontrollably fall into a deep sleep, even in the middle of a conversation. In an effort to help this patient to stay awake, and thereby retain his job, Heath and his colleagues implanted small electrodes into several areas of the patient's brain. They provided the patient with a control panel that he could use to initiate stimulation of these areas. He described one of the buttons on this panel as his "happy button," saying it gave him a drunk feeling, while another stimulated sexual arousal.

Drugs such as alcohol, heroin, and Ecstasy work in a similar way; by altering chemical activity in the brain, they change the emotions we experience. In both animals and humans, it is possible to produce emotions ranging from rage to euphoria by altering neural activity.

Thought

The suggestion that our brains also control what we think is perhaps the most controversial of these claims. Early evidence for the brain's role in thought came from studies of epilepsy reported by a Canadian neurosurgeon, Wilder Penfield. Epileptic seizures are triggered by abnormal activity in one small region of the brain, and in severe cases it is important to identify the precise region involved so that it can be removed surgically. One way of doing this is to remove part of the skull and use electrodes to stimulate various parts of the brain while the patient is conscious; the patient can then report when they are experiencing the sensations that normally precede their seizures, so that the surgeon can remove the region producing these feelings. (This technique might sound gruesome, but the scalp is anesthetized first, and because there are no pain receptors in the brain, the patient suffers no discomfort.) Penfield discovered that stimulation of some areas would give rise to specific thoughts or images. Depending on the area stimulated, patients reported hearing someone calling their name, waiting at a station for a train, or hearing music. If the stimulation was stopped, the sensation would cease, but it would often return if the same spot was stimulated again (for example, Penfield, 1958). Activity in particular cortical areas thus seemed to control what thoughts a patient experienced.

More recent studies have confirmed the close relationship between neural activity and our thoughts. In one such study by Gelbard-Sagiv *et al.* (2008), tiny electrodes were implanted in the brains of 13 epileptics in order to indentify the source of their seizures. Activity was then monitored while the patients were shown brief film-clips taken from programs such as *Seinfeld* and *The Simpsons*. Then, several minutes later, they were asked to recall the clips they had seen earlier, and to report immediately when one of these clips came to mind. Gelbard-Sagiv and his colleagues found that activity in individual neurons was strongly correlated with recall of particular clips. One neuron, for example, fired whenever the patient remembered the *Simpsons* episode, but not when he recalled other clips. Even more strikingly, activity in these neurons began several seconds *before* the conscious recall. Just as in the Penfield study, activity in certain neurons seemed to be triggering memories.

Similar results were reported in a study by Sheth, Sandkühler, and Bhattacharya (2009). They gave participants difficult problems to solve and asked them to press a key the instant they thought of the solution. The experimenters used EEG recordings to monitor activity in their brains as they worked. (EEG stands for electroencephalogram; electrodes placed on the skin around the head record electrical activity from within the brain.) The recordings revealed that activity in certain regions of the cortex reliably preceded solution – the heightened activity was observed shortly before solution but not otherwise. This finding was particularly striking because the electrical activity was observed up to *eight seconds* prior to the moment when participants became consciously aware of the solution. As in the Penfield and Gelbard-Sagiv studies, conscious experience seemed to be the product of preceding neural activity.

In summary, it appears as if every aspect of our behavior – movement, emotion, and thought – depends on the transmission of electrical impulses within our brains. If this neural activity is lawful, the behavior that it controls must also be lawful.

Examples of lawful behavior

The neural determinism argument claims that behavior *must* be lawful, but that is not quite the same as providing evidence that behavior *is* lawful. There is considerable evidence, though, that our heredity and environment can strongly influence our behavior, and we will look at three examples involving early experience.

Vocabulary development

In an epic study, Hart and Risley (1995) studied 42 children and recorded every single conversation these children heard in their homes during the first three years of their lives. Some of the children came from families where the parents were professionals, others where the parents were working class, and yet others where the parents were on welfare. They found massive differences in their linguistic environments. Whereas children from the professional families heard a total of 45 million words, those from working-class families heard only 26 million, and those from welfare families only 13 million – the children from professional families heard more than three times as many words. There were also surprisingly large differences in how the parents interacted with the children. The professional parents relied far more on encouragement: Hart and Risley recorded a total of 700,000 encouraging comments as against only 80,000 discouraging comments. These ratios were reversed in the welfare families, where children received twice as many negative comments as positive ones. And these differences led to profound differences in the children's development of vocabulary, as the children from professional families used more than twice as many words as those from welfare families. Moreover, these differences at the age of 3 proved to strongly predict children's linguistic ability at the age of 10 – in the authors' words, "We were awestruck at how well our measures of accomplishment at three predicted language skill at nine to 10" (Hart and Risley, 2003). Children's early environment seemed to be having a profound effect on their verbal skills, with all that implies for future jobs and incomes.

Child abuse

A further example of how powerfully our environment can influence our behavior comes from studies of children who are physically or sexually abused. Approximately two-thirds of children who are abused develop serious symptoms, ranging from anxiety and bed-wetting to depression and self-destructive behavior (Kendall-Tackett, Williams, and Finkelhor, 1993). One of the saddest of these after-effects is that many of these children have a greatly increased likelihood of themselves becoming abusers when they become parents. Kaufman and Zigler (1987) reviewed the many studies in this area and concluded, "approximately one-third of all individuals who were physically abused, sexually abused, or extremely neglected will subject their offspring to one of these forms of maltreatment" (p. 190). Conversely, most adults who abuse children were themselves abused as children. In one typical study, Kasper and Alford (1988) studied 125 men who had sexually abused children and found that approximately 85% were themselves abused. The experience of abuse can profoundly influence a child's present and future behavior.

Aggression

One of the consequences of childhood abuse is a 50% increase in the probability that boys will behave violently when they become adults. On the other hand, not all boys who are abused become violent. Why, then, do some boys become violent but not others?

One possibility is genetic. Animal research has shown that an enzyme called monamine oxidase A (MAOA) plays an important role in reducing aggression and that a single gene regulates production of this enzyme. Perhaps, then, the reason that some abused boys are more likely to become violent is that they lack this inhibitory gene.

To investigate this possibility, a team led by Caspi and Moffitt studied males who had been monitored since birth as part of a longitudinal study carried out in Dunedin, New Zealand (Caspi *et al.*, 2002). Accurate records of their childhood experiences were already available, and the authors now tested them to determine if they possessed the MAOA gene that inhibits aggression. To assess violence, Caspi *et al.* used several measures, including convictions for violent crimes.

The results were striking. Males who had been abused as children and lacked the MAOA gene were found to be roughly *six times* more likely to be convicted of violent crimes than were males without these predisposing factors. Moreover, when antisocial behavior was defined more broadly, including measures such as a clinical diagnosis of adolescent conduct disorder, then the results showed that 85% of the boys in this category developed severe antisocial behavior. In other words, just two factors – a history of abuse and the absence of a single gene – were enough to almost completely determine how these boys would behave when they became adults (see also Miles and Carey, 1997).

A second, perhaps surprising, determinant of aggression is nutrition. Several studies have shown that poor nutrition is associated with a wide range of violent and criminal behaviors, and that improving nutrition can substantially reduce this behavior. In one study, 3-year-old malnourished children in Mauritius were enrolled in a program that provided them with healthy meals for two years. Their behavior was then assessed 18 years later, when they were 23, and the authors found that those who had participated in the program had 64% fewer criminal convictions than those in a control group who had not participated (Raine *et al.*, 2003). In another study, Schoenthaler *et al.* (1997) focused on the violent behavior of 13- to 17-year-old inmates in a prison. They all had a long history of violence, and blood measurements revealed that they were also deficient in nutrients such as iron and magnesium. One group was given capsules containing the missing nutrients, while a control group received placebo capsules that looked identical but had no nutritional value. Over the course of 3 months, there was a 92% decrease in violence in the prisoners who received the vitamins, from 131 violent acts to 11; there was no reduction in those who received the placebos. Similar results were reported in a study by Gesch *et al.* (2002), who found that nutritional supplements produced a 26% fall in disciplinary offenses. Taken together, these studies suggest that poor nutrition is a surprisingly important factor in producing aggression, but that simple steps to improve nutrition can reverse this effect.

The feeling of freedom

Findings like these pose a puzzle: If our behavior is influenced so strongly by our heredity and environment, how is it that in our everyday lives we do not experience any sense of being controlled? When you decide what clothing to wear or what to eat for lunch, you have no sense of compulsion that you *must* act in a certain way; quite the contrary, you freely decide. How can our behavior be determined if we constantly feel so free? The answer proposed by determinists is that although we may *feel* free in such situations, our behavior is being controlled just as surely as that of the abused children in the Caspi *et al.* study, who, if they also lacked the MAOA gene, had an 85% chance of becoming extraordinarily violent adults. The difference is simply that in everyday life we are often not aware of the forces that are affecting us.

Advertising

A classic example of how we can be influenced without realizing it is advertising. Most of us believe that we are not taken in by advertisements – we are not seduced by their glitz and instead base our decisions solely on evidence. Some research, however, suggests that we are all more susceptible to advertising than we realize. In one study on this point, Smith and Engel (1968) showed 120 men a picture of an automobile. For half the subjects, the photograph showed only the car, whereas for the other subjects a sexy redhead, dressed in black lace panties and a sleeveless sweater, was standing in front of it. After examining the picture, participants were asked to evaluate the car on several dimensions. Those who saw the car with the attractive female next to it rated the car as significantly more appealing and better designed. They also estimated it to be more expensive (by an average of $340), faster, and less safe. When the authors later asked a subset of the participants if their ratings had been influenced by the presence of the model, however, 22 out of 23 denied it. One respondent claimed, "I don't let anything but the thing itself influence my judgments. The other is just propaganda." Another commented, "I never let myself be blinded by advertising; the car itself is what counts." Thus, although the model's presence clearly altered the participants' ratings of the car, virtually none believed that he had been affected.

Sexual attraction

Another illustration of how the environment can influence us without our realizing it comes from research on sexual attraction. Why is it that we are sexually attracted to some individuals but not to others? Psychologists are still in the early stages of trying to understand attraction, but some interesting evidence has begun to emerge. One early study, by Dutton and Aron (1974), was carried out in an unusual setting for a psychology experiment, a deep river gorge in British Columbia. There were two ways of crossing the river: a narrow, wobbly footbridge located some 230 feet above rapids or a much more substantial wooden bridge only 10 feet above a small rivulet. Males were approached as they crossed either bridge by an attractive female who asked if they would answer some questions for a research project she was conducting. When the interview was over, she gave the males her telephone number in case they later had any questions.

The real purpose of the study was to measure sexual attraction – would the males later phone to ask for a date? Many did, but the study's striking finding was that the proportion asking for a date depended on where the interview took place: Half the men interviewed after crossing the rickety bridge later phoned for a date, compared with only 12% of those interviewed after crossing the solid bridge.

On the surface this result might seem bizarre – why should the location of the interview determine whether males think a female is attractive? Dutton and Aron, however, had predicted precisely this result on the basis of a theory of emotion previously proposed by Schachter and Singer (1962). We will not review the theory in detail, but in essence it proposes that all emotions are characterized by similar states of physiological arousal – increased heart rate, rapid breathing, and so on. Schacter and Singer argued that we therefore need to rely on environmental cues to help us identify what emotion we are experiencing. According to this theory, males would have experienced strong arousal when crossing the high bridge; when they encountered the attractive interviewer, they would have unconsciously thought, "Aha, it must be her beauty that is making me feel so excited." And believing that they were attracted to her, they would have been more likely to ask her for a date.

An alternative explanation might have occurred to you, namely that the results were due to differences in the kinds of men who used the two bridges. Perhaps the higher bridge attracted men who were more adventurous and thus would also have been less timid about asking for a date. To control for this possibility, Dutton and Aron ran a second experiment. Both groups now consisted of men who crossed the high bridge, with one group interviewed while they were on the bridge and the other at least 10 minutes after they had crossed, so that any arousal had time to dissipate. If the earlier results had been an artifact of differences in adventurousness, the two groups should now be equally likely to phone for a date because both consisted of men who chose the high bridge. If the results had been caused by arousal, however, then the group interviewed while still on the bridge should again have been more likely to phone, and this is what the authors found (see also Foster *et al.*, 1998).

The most likely explanation for Dutton and Aron's findings seems to be that the males who crossed the high bridge misinterpreted their arousal, attributing it to sexual attraction rather than to the more prosaic experience of crossing a rickety bridge. When they later decided to ask for a date, they almost certainly believed this to be a free choice, but they were being influenced by factors of which they were entirely unaware.

Political attitudes

A third example comes from a study by Hassin *et al.* (2007), who were interested in how people decide what political party to support. We normally assume that we make decisions as important as these by consciously evaluating the positions of the different parties, but Hassin and his colleagues thought that our choices might be influenced by unconscious feelings of which we are completely unaware. To find out, they asked a group of Israeli citizens to answer questions about their views of the Israeli–Palestinian conflict. The questions were presented on a computer screen but, unbeknown to the participants, a picture was briefly flashed up on the screen before they read each question. For the experimental group, the picture was of an Israeli flag; for the control group, it was a scrambled – and therefore unrecognizable – version of that flag. For both groups, the presentations were very brief, less than 1/50th of a second, and each presentation was followed by a jumbled set of lines called a pattern mask. Previous research had shown that masking stimuli presented under these conditions effectively erase preceding stimuli before subjects can become consciously aware of them. The procedure is thus sometimes referred to as *subliminal* presentation – *limen* is the Latin word for threshold, and the stimulus remains below the threshold of consciousness.

To be sure that the stimuli had not been detected, the experimenters interviewed participants afterwards to see if they had been aware of the flags. None had. As a further precaution, they ran a separate experiment in which a picture of the flag was presented subliminally on half the trials and a control stimulus on the others. Participants were asked after each presentation which stimulus had been presented, and they chose correctly on only 48% of the trials, a result indistinguishable from chance. It was clear that participants had not been aware of the flag's presence; the question was whether it would nevertheless affect how they answered the questions.

It did. The main change was in those whose views were initially close to the extremes, either strongly on the left or right of the Israeli political spectrum. Both groups' views moved strongly toward the center, a movement so pronounced that their views became almost indistinguishable. Even more remarkably, this exposure also influenced how participants voted in Israeli elections held one week later. The authors interviewed participants after the election to find out how they had voted; they found that those who had been exposed to the flag became much more likely to vote for parties in the center. A few brief presentations of a flag that they had not even seen had changed how they voted. (See also Ballew and Todorov, 2007; Rutchick, 2010.)

An obvious question raised by these findings is why exposure to the Israeli flag should have moved attitudes toward the center ground rather than, say, strengthening people in their extreme views. The authors' answer is complex, but in a subsequent study they showed that the arousal of nationalist feelings can have negative effects as well as positive ones. Hassin *et al.* (2009) found that subliminal exposure to the Israeli flag increased Israelis' feelings of prejudice toward Palestinians, and they found comparable effects in the USA. In the American study, conducted in 2008, citizens were asked whether they intended to vote for Barack Obama or John McCain; exposure to an American flag while answering increased support for McCain and decreased support for Obama.

Evaluation

It seems clear that our heredity and environment do influence a wide range of our behaviors, from whom we find attractive to what political parties we support. The fact that our behavior is influenced, however, does not necessarily mean that it is totally determined. Even when under the most intense environmental pressure, it is possible that we still retain some freedom to choose, however circumscribed. Consider again the effects of sexual abuse on children. We have seen that roughly one-third of children who are abused go on to become abusers as adults. By the same token, however, this means that two-thirds of these children do not. Proponents of free will can thus argue that even under the most terrible pressures, each of us retains some capacity to choose our own path.

In the end, it is unlikely that the debate between free will and determinism will ever be resolved conclusively. Not even the most optimistic determinist believes that we will ever be able to predict every aspect of a person's behavior – we would have to know every law and record every moment of the person's life to be able to calculate the cumulative impact of all their experiences. If we can never fully predict behavior, however, then it will always be possible for believers in free will to argue that this lack of predictability reflects an essential inner freedom, whereas determinists claim that it reflects only limitations in our current state of knowledge.

It is thus doubtful whether we will ever know whether behavior is completely lawful. The evidence we have reviewed, however, suggests that environment and heredity do powerfully influence our behavior, whether or not they control it fully.

How should we discover any laws?

If behavior is lawful, at least to some degree, how should we go about discovering these laws?

Introspection

If we want to understand why people behave as they do, one obvious approach is to have them report their thoughts and feelings, a technique called **introspection**. We are all introspective on occasion, and literature abounds with references to people "searching their souls" or "plumbing the depths of their hearts" in an attempt to understand themselves. The first systematic application of this technique, however, was the work of a late nineteenth-century German psychologist, Wilhelm Wundt. The essence of Wundt's technique was extremely simple: Subjects were exposed to a stimulus and then asked to report the sensations aroused by it. In actual practice, however, this technique required long and arduous hours of training. It was important, for example, that a subject report not simply what he or she saw (such as a chair), but the exact sensations the object elicited, the quality and intensity of these sensations, how they changed over time, and so on.

This precise analysis of sensations is not easy. A naive observer exposed to a brightly lighted piece of coal and a dimly lighted paper, for example, will invariably report that the coal appears darker, even though physically it might actually be reflecting far more light. Observers in such cases are reporting not what they actually see but what they expect to see. Wundt's subjects underwent extended training to overcome this and similar errors. Once the observers were properly trained, Wundt hoped to use their reports to analyze the complex patterns of human thought into their constituent elements and then discover the laws by which these elements are combined to produce the richness and variety of mental life.

Though the rigorous demands of Wundt's technique now seem somewhat daunting, the underlying logic has great intuitive appeal. If we want to understand the processes of learning, what better way is there than by studying these processes at work within our own minds? In the end, we must all rely on the judgment of our senses – it is a brave person who strides forward when his or her eyes tell of an abyss ahead. In the same way that our peripheral senses provide us with our most reliable information about the external world, introspection would seem to be the best guide to the world of the mind.

The unconscious

Yet, despite its obvious attractions, introspection gradually fell into progressively greater disrepute, until eventually it almost disappeared from psychology. One reason for this collapse was that, even as Wundt was painstakingly beginning to train his subjects, a Viennese physician named Sigmund Freud was developing his revolutionary theories – theories that, in an offhand way, would ultimately destroy the rationale for introspection. Freud exposed for the first time the Byzantine world of the unconscious, its primitive swirl of emotions hidden from consciousness behind powerful defensive barriers. This metaphor of hidden, subterranean forces had devastating implications for introspection, attacking its very foundation: a faith in the accessibility of all thought to conscious analysis. Unless every aspect of human thought and emotion could be observed and analyzed, introspection could at best provide only an incomplete and fragmented picture of the causal mechanisms of behavior. And Freud's theories suggested that consciousness was but the visible tip of the iceberg, with vast areas of the mind forever hidden in the murky depths of the subconscious.

Freud's theories suggested for the first time that there might be severe limits to the power of conscious analysis, but it seems likely that these limits would have become apparent in any case. Consider, for example, what happens when you try to prove a geometry theorem. You may struggle for minutes or even hours, doggedly searching for a solution, when suddenly the correct answer occurs to you. What happened exactly? How did you suddenly pass from a state of complete and utter confusion to one of confidence in the right answer? Clearly some important mental processes intervened between these two states, but, introspectively, all is a blank, your mind an empty vacuum from which the correct solution emerged as if by spontaneous generation. To take an even more homely example, how is it that we are able to control and coordinate our bodily movements? Try, for example, to introspect as you repeatedly flex your thumb. Concentrate intensely and try to feel every sensation. You might be able to feel your thumb's movement, but can you feel the command that initiates that movement? In fact, to move your thumb, your brain also instructs hundreds of other muscles in your back and legs to contract to maintain your balance, but introspection provides no hint of the intricate and coordinated sequence of movements involved. Our inability to trace the processes involved even in such simple acts as thumb flexing suggests serious limits to the usefulness of introspection in analyzing complex thought and learning.

The problem of confirming reports

Considerations such as these suggest that introspection can at best play only a limited role in helping us understand behavior. It would seem, however, that we should at least be able to use introspection in analyzing that fraction of our experience that is accessible to consciousness. Again, however, critics have raised serious objections to the use of introspection even in this limited domain. The problem, fundamentally, is one of confirmability: How are we to confirm the accuracy of an introspective report when it is based on private events that are inaccessible to any outside observer? If a person says she or he is feeling angry, for example, how do we know whether the person is really feeling anger or fear, or perhaps some subtle combination of the two?

It might seem churlish to question the honesty of such a report (isn't a person the best judge of her or his own feelings?), but studies of perception in other situations suggest a need for greater caution. Just as our visual senses are not flawless – the moon is *not* larger at the horizon, and desert oases glimpsed from afar have a dismaying tendency to recede as we approach – so, too, introspection can yield data that are not necessarily accurate.

The problem of evaluating observers' reports is not, of course, unique to introspection. A person who says he feels hungry is really no different from a scientist who reports seeing a rat or, for that matter, a flying saucer. Each of these statements is simply a report of subjective experience; the fact that the stimulus for one example originated outside the body rather than inside it does not give the former report any greater validity. Whatever the original stimulus for these reports, we are faced with the problem of evaluating their accuracy – that is, evaluating how closely the original events and the verbal reports correspond.

Reports of external events can be confirmed by establishing either their reliability (for example, by comparing the reports with those of other observers in the same situation) or their consistency with other data (for example, radar reports in the case of flying saucers). In the case of introspective reports, however, confirmation is not so easy. To start with, how are we to estimate the reliability of an introspective observer when no other observer can detect the private events on which the report is based? One sensible solution adopted by introspectionists was to expose several observers to the same external stimulus; if they independently reported the same reactions, this would support the view that they were reporting their experiences accurately.

This approach worked well in some situations, but it proved less successful in others. One of its most spectacular failures arose in a controversy over "imageless thought." Some psychologists believed that the meaning of any word was simply the image that it produced – the meaning of the word "chair," for example, would be the image that comes to mind when you think about this word. This approach seems plausible when we consider concrete nouns like chair, but what of more abstract words such as "truth" or "meaning" – do these words also produce images? One influential introspectionist, Oswald Kulpe, reported that when he and his colleagues introspected they could not detect any trace of an image while thinking of such words. Another leading introspectionist, however, insisted that even the most abstract words produced images if you introspected carefully enough. In the case of *meaning*, for example, he reported seeing "the blue-gray tip of a kind of scoop which has a bit of yellow about it (probably a part of the handle) and which is digging into a dark mass of what appears to be plastic material" (Titchener, 1915, p. 519). This image had its origins, he suggested, in injunctions from his youth to "dig out the meaning" of Latin and Greek phrases. Each side insisted that the other was wrong, and there was no way to resolve their disagreement.

Evaluation

The realization that much of the mind's functioning is unconscious, coupled with the difficulty of reliably observing even those areas that ostensibly are conscious, eventually led to the virtual abandonment of introspection as a scientific technique. Do not conclude that introspection is totally without value. It is still a fertile, if informal, technique for generating hypotheses about the causes of behavior, and it can sometimes provide confirmable information that can be highly valuable (see, for example, Lieberman, 1979). For the most part, however, psychologists have abandoned introspection as a systematic technique for acquiring knowledge.

In thus rejecting introspection, we must admit that we seem to be turning our backs on much of the richness and fascination of the mental world – indeed, of the entire world, for what else does any of us directly know or experience besides the workings of our own minds? It is perhaps worth emphasizing, therefore, that this rejection was not prompted by petulance, or by a Calvinistic desire to make psychology seem cold or dreary. The study of the mind originated as a branch of

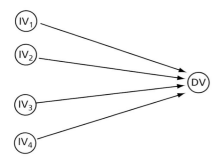

Figure 1.1 Four independent variables (IVs) simultaneously influencing a dependent variable (DV).

philosophy, and for centuries it was concerned exclusively with the nature and determinants of conscious experiences. These genuinely fascinating problems were finally put aside only when psychologists became convinced that direct study of the mind was futile as long as observers could not reach agreement on even its most elementary properties. In domains where agreement is obtainable, introspection can still serve as a useful tool, but for the substantial areas of mental functioning that are unconscious, it can play little role.

The experimental method

As the limitations of introspection became clear, psychologists turned instead to experimentation as a means of discovering the causes of behavior. In outline, the experimental method is very simple: We alter some aspect of the environment, called the **independent variable**, and then see if it affects some aspect of behavior, called the **dependent variable**. A consistent relationship between them – for example, environmental condition A is always followed by behavior B – is called a **law**.

One thing at a time!

If experimentation were really so simple, discovering the laws of behavior would be easy: All we would have to do is manipulate our independent variables, observe their effects, and combine the resultant laws into a comprehensive account of behavior. The problem is that *we must manipulate only one independent variable at a time.* If several independent variables changed simultaneously (see Figure 1.1), then it would be impossible to say which one was responsible for the resulting behavior. The obvious solution is to ensure that only one aspect of the environment changes during an experiment, but in many situations this turns out to be difficult or impossible.

To illustrate this point, suppose that we wanted to find out which of two treatments was more effective for depression. One treatment was psychotherapy – trying to identify the emotional causes of the problem by talking to a trained therapist – and the other was vigorous exercise. To compare their effectiveness, suppose we ran an experiment in which one group received psychotherapy and the other group exercised, and that only participants in the first group improved. If this difference was statistically significant, could we conclude that psychotherapy is more effective?

On the surface, it seems a very simple experiment – the only difference between the groups was in which treatment they received. In fact, however, the groups could also have differed in many other ways. Suppose, for example, that the participants viewed psychotherapy as a much more plausible treatment than exercise; if subjects in the psychotherapy group had a stronger belief that they would improve, this in itself could have alleviated their feelings of depression. In other words, the groups differed not only in which treatment they received but also in how hopeful they were that it would work, and the feeling of hope might have produced the improvement.

Moreover, even if the subjects' expectations of improvement were the same in the two groups, it is possible that the *experimenters'* expectations were different. Perhaps previous research had suggested that psychotherapy was more likely to be effective, so that the experimenters expected participants receiving this treatment to improve more. If so, the greater improvement in this group might be due not to the treatment per se but rather to the fact that the experimenters *expected* them to improve more.

This might at first seem highly unlikely, even silly, but considerable research suggests that experimenters' expectations really can influence the outcome of experiments. In an experiment by Rosenthal (1966), for example, participants were shown pictures of faces and asked to rate whether the pictures appeared to be of successful people. (The rating scale ranged from -10 for faces of people thought to be very unsuccessful to $+10$ for faces of people looking very successful.) Each group of about a dozen participants was read standard instructions and then shown slides of the different faces. The study used different experimenters for the different groups, and these experimenters were led to expect different outcomes. One group of experimenters was told that they were being given a special set of subjects who would probably produce positive scores, whereas a second group of experimenters was led to expect negative scores. In fact, participants were assigned to the experimenters at random. Under these circumstances, could experimenter expectations make any difference? The results were that they did: Experimenters expecting positive results obtained significantly higher scores than did those expecting negative results. Thus, despite the fact that all participants saw the same faces and were read the same instructions, their ratings of the faces were strongly influenced by what their experimenters expected.

Clever Hans

How could an experimenter's expectations affect a subject's evaluation of a picture? We know very little about the underlying processes, but some evidence suggests that subtle cues from the experimenter are involved.

One of the classic examples of such cues is the case of Clever Hans (see Pfungst, 1965). Hans was a horse that lived on a German farm at the turn of the century. Hans wasn't an ordinary horse, though: He was the only horse in Germany that could add! When asked the sum of two plus two, for example, Hans would slowly begin to tap the ground, one, two, three, four... and then stop. Nor was this simply a trick he had memorized, because he could add virtually any numbers, and it didn't even matter who asked the question. Moreover, addition wasn't his only skill: He was equally proficient at subtraction and, incredibly, multiplication and division. An obvious explanation for his prowess was some sort of signal from his master, but when a blue-ribbon panel of experts convened to investigate Hans's extraordinary powers, they found that Hans performed equally well in his master's absence.

In a brilliant series of experiments, German psychologist Oscar Pfungst eventually discovered the explanation for Hans's apparent genius. Pfungst found that Hans's accuracy was considerably reduced if the person who asked the question didn't know the correct answer. Furthermore, the further away the questioner stood, the less accurate was Hans's answer. Finally, putting blinders around Hans's eyes totally destroyed his performance. Clearly, Hans could answer questions only if he could see someone who knew the correct answer. But what possible visual cues could the questioner have been providing? The answer, Pfungst discovered, was that questioners tilted their heads slightly forward as they finished their questions, and this was Hans's cue to begin tapping. As the tapping approached the correct answer, the observers tended to straighten up in anticipation, and this slight tensing was Hans's cue to stop. Hans was extraordinarily sensitive to such cues, responding to the raising of eyebrows or even the dilation of nostrils, and Pfungst was eventually able to control Hans's tapping completely by producing these cues deliberately. Hans truly was an extraordinary horse, but his genius lay more in his powers of observation than in any arithmetic ability.

Let us now return to our depression experiment. Suppose that we redesigned our experiment yet again to ensure that the experimenter who ran the study expected both groups to improve equally, and we again found substantially greater improvement in the experimental group. Now, at long last, would we have proved that building self-confidence is an effective treatment for depression? Yet again, the answer is no. Why not? What other variable could possibly have been present? It is not easy to identify other variables, but the fact that we can't identify alternative explanations doesn't prove that there aren't any. The blue-ribbon panel was unable to find any plausible explanation for Hans's dazzling performance, but that didn't prove that it was the result of a genuine mastery of arithmetic. In a similar vein, for centuries naturalists were unable to explain the mysterious ability of bats to navigate in total darkness, but that didn't prove that it was the result of some occult power. (The discovery of radar in the 1930s eventually led to the solution.) An experiment, in other words, can never prove that a particular explanation is correct because it is always possible that some alternative explanation will eventually be found.

The nature of scientific progress

We started with a seemingly simple experiment, but the more we analyzed it, the more alternative explanations for its outcome we identified. This is always the case. The goal of the experimental method is to change only one independent variable at a time, but this ideal can rarely if ever be fully realized. We can control for the effects of particular variables, such as subject and experimenter expectations, but there are always changes that we cannot control – fluctuations in humidity, the occurrence of sunspots, the death of an earthworm in China! This in turn has important implications for the nature of scientific progress.

Slow . . .

One such implication concerns the slowness and confusion with which science sometimes progresses. A popular image of science has the scientist in an antiseptic white lab coat, progressing inexorably through rigorous analyses. In practice, scientific progress is often much more confused and halting. As we have seen, it is impossible to control for all possible variables; we can only control for those variables that seem important. Our notions of what variables are important, however, are often wrong. For example, one of the most dangerous things a woman in Victorian England could do was enter a maternity hospital; many thousands of women died every year after giving birth. When Joseph Lister suggested that doctors could prevent these deaths if they washed their hands with soap, his proposal was greeted with incredulity: How could washing hands with boiled-down animal fat prevent a woman from dying? Now, with our greater understanding of the existence and nature of germs, his suggestion makes sense, but at the time it seemed utterly preposterous. Similarly, in the case of Clever Hans, few would have believed beforehand that a horse could be so sensitive to minute changes in people's postures.

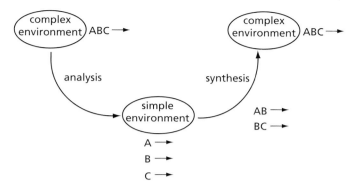

Figure 1.2 Using the experimental method, the experimenter analyzes a complex environment to isolate variables and then combines or synthesizes the variables in progressively more complex combinations.

There is thus a built-in catch-22 to scientific progress: To discover scientific laws, you must control all important variables; unfortunately, you can only identify what variables are important if you already know the laws! This problem is not insurmountable. We just have to plug away, identifying important variables as best we can in experiments that may initially lack important controls. This bootstrapping process means that progress will initially be slow and frustrating as we struggle to identify the important variables.

Artificial

A second implication of our analysis concerns the inherent artificiality of experiments. To isolate the effects of one variable, you need to hold others constant, but the more you control the environment, the less like real life it becomes. The underlying strategy is summarized in Figure 1.2: You start with a complex environment and, by *analysis*, try to break this complex environment into simpler ones so you can study the effects of constituent elements (A, B, C, and so on) one at a time. Then, once you have determined the effects of each variable on its own, you use the method of *synthesis* to begin recombining them, studying what happens when two or more variables act together (AB, ABC, and so on). The scientific method thus proceeds by first analyzing complex environments into simpler ones, then gradually returning to the more complex environment that was the original focus of interest.

In psychology, most research is still analytical, with the result that it is very easy to feel depressed by its artificiality. "It's all so meaningless," you might say. "What does the behavior of a student in an artificial laboratory setting have to do with real life?" The answer lies in the assumptions we have been tracing in this chapter. If behavior is lawful, and if the best way of discovering these laws is through well-controlled experiments, then eventually the principles discovered in these artificial settings will help us understand behavior in the more complex conditions of the real world.

In other sciences, this faith in the experimental method has paid off handsomely. In genetics, for example, Gregor Mendel discovered the principles of genetics by studying how the color of pea flowers determined the colors of their progeny. In one sense, his experiments were highly artificial: Peas and humans would seem to have little in common. By studying the transmission of traits in this simple setting, however, geneticists have been able to identify genetic principles that also apply to the vastly more complex genetic system of humans, an advance that has already made possible test-tube babies, as well as significant progress toward the cloning of humans from single cells. In less than 100 years, we have moved from investigating the garden pea to understanding some of the most profound mysteries of human life.

The use of animals

Having decided to study the laws of behavior, and to do so through careful experimentation, we now come to the question of what species to study. If our goal is to understand human behavior, the answer might seem obvious: We should study humans. Given the blinding clarity of this logic, why have psychologists sometimes studied animals instead?

The advantages of using animals
Control of the environment

The reasons that psychologists study animals are complex, but all are rooted in the problems of experimental control discussed earlier. We said then that one crucial problem in psychological research is to manipulate only one independent variable at a time while holding all others constant. In practice, this requires extensive control over the subject's environment. For both moral and practical reasons, such control is easier to attain with animal subjects than with human subjects.

For example, one problem of considerable importance in human behavior concerns the effects of a child's early environment on her or his development. Freudians have long argued that the first years of life are crucial in determining personality. More recently, educators have suggested that early sensory and social deprivation is an important factor in the poor school performance of some children (particularly from underprivileged homes) and have urged governments to invest in compensatory child-care programs for young children. How are we to determine whether the role of early experience is really so crucial and, if so, which aspects are most important? To determine the importance of early sensory experience, for example, should we run controlled experiments in which half the children are reared normally while the other half are permanently confined to a barren environment, devoid of all stimuli? Similarly, to determine the importance of a mother's role in a child's normal development, should we compare children reared with their mothers and children taken away from their mothers and reared in isolation? Such experiments would hardly be humane or practical. The questions involved are significant, with serious implications for the future structure of our schools and even our families, but the experiments necessary to answer such questions are clearly unacceptable.

Using animals as subjects, however, psychologists have conducted experiments to answer precisely these questions, with often fascinating results. Harry Harlow, for example, reported a series of experiments in which infant rhesus monkeys were reared in varying degrees of social isolation. When taken away from their mothers immediately after birth and reared in total isolation, these infants became highly neurotic, spending much of their time huddled in corners, rocking back and forth and sucking their thumbs. Furthermore, this pattern of disturbed behavior persisted into adulthood, and most were unable to function normally in a group, or even to mate.

These early studies supported the critical role of early experience in social development, and in later experiments Harlow and others isolated some important variables. The presence of the mother, for example, is not necessarily critical; infants taken away from their mothers but reared with other infants show significantly less disturbance (Harlow and Harlow, 1965). Another finding, with poignant social implications for certain humans, is that male rhesus monkeys, which normally play an insignificant role in child rearing, can, if necessary, replace the mother with no apparent ill effects to either child or father (Mitchell and Brandt, 1972).

A similar line of experiments has examined the role of early sensory experience in the development of rats. Some rats were reared in "enriched" environments that included other rats and a variety of toys, platforms, colors, and sounds; other rats were reared in "deprived" environments that lacked these stimuli. Animals reared in the enriched environments developed larger brains (Rosenzweig, 1984), with considerably more complex interconnections among their neurons (Turner and Greenough, 1985). These results suggest that early stimulation plays a critical role in the brain's development and thus in our capacity for learning in later life.

Simpler systems

One advantage of using animals as subjects, then, is that we can more easily control their environments and thus determine which variables are important. A related advantage is studying simpler systems. To isolate the effects of a single variable, one strategy is to control the environment so that few variables will be present; an alternative strategy is to study a simpler system, in which fewer variables exert an influence. Suppose, for example, that you wanted to understand the principles of electronics. You would obviously find it easier to understand these principles if you began by studying a transistor radio rather than a giant computer: The simpler the system, the easier it is to understand its operations. Thus, scientists were able to isolate the fundamental principles of genetics by first studying two lower life forms – the fruit fly and the pea – that possess simpler systems. If, instead, they had first tried to understand these principles in a more complex system – for example, the inheritance of human intelligence, which is almost certainly influenced by many thousands of genes – we would probably understand little or nothing about the principles of genetic transmission.

The simpler the system, the easier it is to determine its fundamental principles. Determining the principles of behavior in animals, however, can help us to understand human behavior only if these principles are similar. Is this assumption justified? Do the principles of learning and memory in animals have any relevance for human behavior?

Are animal and human behavior similar?

Throughout history, the notion that animals and humans are similar would have been met with indignation and disbelief, but in 1859 Charles Darwin published a book that for the first time challenged the complacent view of human beings that they are the unique culmination of creation. Darwin dared to suggest that human beings are not unique, that they are only one of many species of animals on Earth, all shaped by the same environmental forces and evolved from the same common ancestors. It follows that, if humans and other animals are so closely related, important similarities must exist between them.

Biologically, the proof was not long in coming; indeed, much of it had already been assembled. Despite the incredible diversity of animal species (there are now thought to be more than 3 million species, ranging in size from virtually invisible microorganisms to the mammoth blue whale, whose tongue alone weighs more than an elephant), the underlying biological principles are surprisingly similar. Our understanding of human neurophysiology, for example, is built largely on the pioneering work of Hodgkin and Huxley on the giant squid. Similarly, our understanding of human vision is based on Hartline and Ratliff's investigations of the eye of the horseshoe crab, a primitive species almost unchanged from primordial times. And when we begin to examine species more closely related to humans, the similarities become even greater. The basic principles of digestion, vision, respiration, locomotion, and so forth are, for all practical purposes, identical across the various mammalian species. Indeed, modern medicine has been able to develop so quickly precisely because of this fundamental equivalence. The drugs and surgical techniques on which our lives now depend were generally pioneered not with people, but with mice, monkeys, and the famous guinea pig – that much-put-upon rodent whose name has become synonymous with the concept of experimentation.

For post-Darwin scientists, animals and people were clearly similar, at least in physical construction. Behaviorally, on the other hand, this similarity was less obvious. Even if humans had once been simple apes, so the argument went, they had long since begun a unique evolutionary path that left them the only animal capable of thought and symbolic communication. In recent years, however, evidence has accumulated that human beings are not unique even in these areas.

Language?

The most striking evidence has come from research on language. Because chimpanzees are our closest relatives, many psychologists believed that if any animal could master the rudiments of language, it would be chimpanzees. Early attempts to teach chimpanzees to speak, however, met with little success. Hayes and Hayes (1951), for example, reared a chimpanzee named Vicki in their home, but after four years of effort Vicki had learned a grand total of only four words: *mama*, *papa*, *cup*, and *up*. However, subsequent research on the anatomy of the chimpanzee vocal tract revealed that they were not physically capable of producing the full range of sounds required for speech. Vicki's failure could have been because of this physical limitation rather than any deficiency in her intellectual capacity.

To test this hypothesis, Allen and Beatrice Gardner set out to teach a chimpanzee to use a language that did not require speech – American Sign Language for the deaf. The subject for their study was a baby chimpanzee named Washoe, and the results were dramatic. By the time she was 5, Washoe had learned more than 130 signs and was able to use them reliably in a variety of situations. The sign for *dog*, for example, was elicited by a wide variety of dogs, both living and in pictures, and even by the barking of a dog that could not be seen. Washoe also demonstrated some ability to combine signs; when she wanted a refrigerator opened, for example, she signed "open food drink" (Gardner, Gardner, and Van Cantfort, 1989).

When the Gardners' research was published, it provoked intense controversy (see, for example, Terrace, 1985; Pinker, 1994). To some degree, this was because of genuine problems in the methodologies used, but in some cases it probably also reflected difficulty in believing that any animal was capable of language, a skill that for so long had been assumed to be uniquely human. At the heart of the controversy was whether the chimpanzees really *understood* the signs that they were using. If Washoe was hungry and made the sign for banana, did this mean that she understood what this sign meant, or was she simply repeating a movement that had been rewarded with food in the past? A chimpanzee making a sign might be behaving no more intelligently than a rat pressing a bar – both might simply be repeating behavior that had previously produced food.

The key issue was what linguists call *semanticity*, whether when a word was used it was evoking some sort of mental representation of the named object. In our banana example, when Washoe saw this sign, did it evoke some representation of a banana in her brain? Because we cannot observe animals' mental states, there will probably always be some level of doubt. Several studies published since the Gardners' work, however, support the claim that chimpanzees understand the signs that they use, and we will look at two examples.

Washoe's baby

Our first, rather poignant example involves Washoe. After her period of active training ended, she became a mother at the age of 15. Her baby was ill at birth, and Washoe had to be anesthetized so that the infant could be removed for treatment. He recovered and was returned to her, but several weeks later he again became ill, so that a pediatrician again needed to anesthetize her. When she saw the needle, she began to scream and sign "My baby, my baby."

Sadly, the infant died. When Washoe saw her trainer the next day, her first sign was "Baby?" The trainer replied by signing "Baby gone, baby finished." Washoe's response was dramatic:

Washoe dropped her arms that had been cradled in the baby sign position...broke eye contact and slowly moved away to a corner of the cage...She continued for the next several days to isolate herself from any interactions with the humans and her signing dropped off to almost nothing. Her eyes appeared to be vacant or distant.

(Fouts, Hirsch, and Fouts, 1982, p. 170)

This account is anecdotal and therefore must be treated with caution, but it is difficult to read it without feeling that Washoe had some understanding of the meaning of the signs that were used. (For a more formal test of understanding, see Savage-Rumbaugh *et al.*, 1980.)

Kanzi

An alternative strategy for bypassing the limitations of a chimpanzee's vocal chords was developed by Duane Rumbaugh of Georgia State University and was later continued in collaboration with his wife, Sue Savage-Rumbaugh. They, too, believed that it was a mistake to try to teach chimpanzees to speak, but instead of using sign language, they developed a new language using geometrical shapes that they called *lexigrams* as words. The lexigrams were displayed on a keyboard linked to a computer, and subjects could choose words by pressing the appropriate symbol on the board.

The chimpanzees trained in this program soon showed performances very similar to those of Washoe. One of the participants, a female named Lana, developed an intriguing ability to create novel word combinations. Some of the foods that she ate were not assigned lexigrams by the experimenters, and Lana therefore invented her own names to request them. When she wanted a cucumber, for example, she asked for "banana which-is green," and she requested an orange by using the lexigrams for "apple which-is orange (color)" (Rumbaugh and Savage-Rumbaugh, 1994).

Another participant was a bonobo chimpanzee named Kanzi. (Bonobos are one of two chimpanzee species.) Kanzi's mother was one of the early participants in the program, but she proved to be a very slow learner and made little progress. Though Kanzi was present during his mother's training sessions, the experimenters made no effort to train him. Nevertheless, when Kanzi was 2 years old, the experimenters discovered that he understood the meaning of the lexigrams that the experimenters had tried and failed to teach his mother. Simply by watching this training, he seemed to have worked out for himself what the symbols meant. The experimenters then initiated an active training program for Kanzi, and by the time he was $5\frac{1}{2}$, his lexigram vocabulary had increased to 149 words.

At this point, Kanzi astonished the experimenters for a second time when they realized that he had also learned to understand human speech. Again, simply by listening to the conversations of his trainers as they taught him to use the lexigrams, Kanzi had learned the meaning of a number of English words and phrases. In one test of his abilities, he was placed in a room containing twelve objects and given verbal instructions about what to do with these objects. (The experimenter was located in an adjacent room behind a one-way mirror, to avoid inadvertently providing Kanzi with cues through gestures.) One of the instructions, for example, concerned a sponge ball that had eyes, a nose and a mouth; Kanzi was told "Feed your ball some tomato." Even though Kanzi had never been asked to do anything remotely like this, he immediately picked up the ball and tried to place a tomato in its mouth. To provide a baseline for comparison, Alia, the $2\frac{1}{2}$-year-old daughter of one of Kanzi's caretakers, was also tested with the same set of instructions; Kanzi responded correctly to 74%, Alia to 66% (Savage-Rumbaugh *et al.*, 1993; Savage-Rumbaugh, Rumbaugh, and Fields, 2009).

One of the important characteristics of most human languages is that different meanings can be expressed by changing the order of the words in a sentence – the sentence "Tom bit the dog," for example, has a very different meaning from "The dog bit Tom." This characteristic is important because it helps to make possible the richness of human language – by changing word order, we can use a small number of words to express an enormous range of ideas. Savage-Rumbaugh and colleagues also tested Kanzi's sensitivity to word order by giving him instructions in which the same words were presented in different orders – for example, "Put the raisins in the shoe" versus "Put the shoe in the raisins." Again, Kanzi's performance was far above chance, as he responded correctly to 81% of these sentences; Alia was correct on only 64%. Kanzi appears to have learned English simply by listening to the conversations of those around him, and his vocabulary and comprehension seem roughly on a par with those of a $2\frac{1}{2}$-year-old child.

Alex the parrot

One possible reaction to the evidence that chimpanzees can understand and use language might be, "Yes, chimpanzees may be smarter than we thought, but they are the exception; it is unlikely that other species are even remotely as intelligent." A rapidly growing body of research, however, suggests that other species are also more intelligent than traditionally assumed (for example, Pearce, 2008). We don't have the space to review all this evidence here, but one example might hint at what has been found. Mammals, especially primates, are widely believed to be the most intelligent of the vertebrates (species with a backbone), whereas birds are thought to be among the least intelligent – when we refer to someone as a "bird brain," it is not a compliment. Recent years, however, have seen impressive evidence of avian intelligence, including the ingenious use of tools by crows (Weir, Chappell, and Kacelnik, 2002), and the ability of pigeons to form concepts such as *chair*, so that if shown pictures of various objects, they can reliably pick out the ones containing chairs (Herrnstein, Loveland, and Cable, 1976; Zentall *et al.*, 2008). Another example concerns Clark's nutcrackers, a small bird that lives in mountainous terrain. In order to survive the winter they have to bury large quantities of seeds during the summer, and they form incredibly detailed mental maps of their hiding places. These maps contain the location of thousands of food caches – imagine trying to memorize a map like this for yourself – and they are then able to retrieve the buried food in winter even when it is hidden under three feet of snow (Vander Wall, 1982). The most striking evidence, however, has come from the study of a parrot.

Pet owners have long been aware of parrots' skill in repeating what is said to them ("Polly want a cracker?"), but everyone assumed that they were blindly repeating what they heard, without comprehension. Some evidence, however, hinted at greater ability than this image suggested, and so Irene Pepperberg (1993, 2009) acquired an East African gray parrot which she named Alex, and set out to study whether it could learn to talk. She and her assistants talked to Alex and also gave him opportunities to watch people talking to each other. Over the course of 30 years, perhaps the longest experimental study of a single animal, Alex acquired a vocabulary of around 150 words, and he was able to use these words with great accuracy. When shown an object he had not seen before, for example, he could describe its shape and color, and he could say how many objects had been placed in front of him, up to six. He could also say where he wanted to be taken, using the phrase "Wanna go..."; if taken somewhere else, he would squawk in protest. On the basis of her studies, Pepperberg believed that Alex's intelligence was equivalent to that of dolphins and great apes. Alex died in 2007, at the age of 31, and his last words to Pepperberg, the day before he died, were "You be good. I love you."

This research is relatively recent, but it raises the intriguing possibility that language skills may be present in many more species than previously thought possible. (For evidence of similar abilities in dolphins, see Herman *et al.*, 2001.) When we hear animals in a zoo making what sound to us like meaningless noises, might the problem sometimes lie in our lack of understanding rather than in theirs?

More than 100 years ago, Charles Darwin wrote that "The difference in mind between man and the higher animals, great as it is, certainly is one of degree and not of kind" (Darwin, 1920/1871, p. 128). The evidence on this point is not yet conclusive, but it is already clear that animals are far more intelligent than once believed. This does not mean that animals and humans are identical. Every species is unique, and it would be foolish to expect to gain a complete understanding of people from the study of pigeons or white rats. On the other hand, given that animals and humans have shared millions of years of evolution, it would be surprising if there were not also similarities. Just as research with fruit flies and the pea made possible the extraordinary advances in genetics in the last century, so research on animals might help us in understanding our own behavior.

Ethical issues

Because it is possible to exert much greater control of the environment in experiments on animals, such research has the potential to significantly enhance our understanding of basic processes. On the other hand, the very similarity of animal and human behavior that makes research on animals attractive also raises serious ethical issues. If animals are similar to us in intelligence, and presumably also in feelings, how can we justify confining them in cages and, in some cases, subjecting them to painful electric shocks?

One view is that such research cannot be justified, because animals are living creatures with just as much right to life and freedom as humans have. This position is attractive in its strong value for all life, but few people hold it in its pure form. Suppose, for example, that you had a child who contracted rabies, and that the only way to obtain a vaccine to save the child's life required killing a mouse. Would you do it? Very few people faced with this dilemma would not choose to save the child, implicitly valuing a child's life more than that of a mouse.

Rightly or wrongly, then, most people do value human welfare more than that of animals, but this does not imply that animal life is worthless. Thus, the problem remains of deciding whether the benefits of particular experiments with animals outweigh the cost to the animals. To assess this, we need some method of quantifying both the benefits and the costs; in practice, though, this is difficult if not impossible. Suppose, for example, that we wanted to assess the cost to the subjects of an experiment on the effects of punishment. How could we decide how much pain a rat would experience if it were given an electric shock? What if we substituted a fish or a cockroach as the experimental subject? Do they also feel pain? If so, is it more or less than that experienced by the rat?

If it is difficult to find any objective way of assessing the costs of animal research, it can be equally difficult to assess its benefits. In our hypothetical rabies example, we assumed that killing the mouse would save the life of the child, but the benefits of experiments are rarely this predictable. Experiments that seem minor at the time they are performed can eventually have momentous theoretical and practical benefits. In a study by Comroe and Dripps (1977), for example, physicians were asked to rate the ten most important advances in cardiovascular and pulmonary medicine and surgery that had benefited their patients. In total, 663 studies were found to have been crucial in leading to these breakthroughs; 42% of them involved experiments that, at the time they were reported, seemed totally unrelated to the later clinical application. When doing basic research, it is difficult to predict what benefits might eventually be derived from enhanced understanding of a fundamental mechanism.

In deciding whether a planned experiment is justifiable, then, it is difficult to assess either the costs to the animals used or the long-term benefits to humans. There are no simple guidelines; all we can say here is that an assessment of the benefits to be gained depends heavily on the validity of the assumptions discussed in this chapter. If behavior is lawful, if experimental research is the best way to discover these laws, and if animal and human behavior is similar in important respects, then research on animals might play an important role in increasing our understanding of human behavior.

Learning and memory: an overview

Summarizing our discussion until this point, we have suggested that psychological research is based on several assumptions: that behavior is lawful, that the best way to discover these laws is through controlled experiments, and that research on animals can sometimes help us understand human behavior. Before proceeding to examine the research that has resulted from these assumptions, though, we need to address one final question – namely, what this book is about. Of course, you already know that it is about learning and memory, but in this section we will examine more closely what we mean by the terms, and the relationship between them.

Defining learning

Learning is a vast topic. It affects almost everything we do, from making friends to riding a bicycle to learning organic chemistry. As a result, it is impossible to cover every aspect of learning in a single course, and it has become customary to study different aspects in different courses: Courses on developmental psychology deal with one aspect, courses on educational psychology with another, courses on cognition a third, and so on.

Within this division, courses on learning generally concentrate on a particular form of learning called *associative learning*. To explain what associative learning is, we will begin by examining what we mean by the broader term *learning*.

Some stimuli always elicit the same reaction. If you accidentally touch a hot pan, for example, it will make you pull your hand back every time; if a sudden gust of wind hits you in the eye, it will make you blink every time. In cases like this, in which a stimulus always elicits the same response, we call the stimulus–response relationship a **reflex**.

$$\text{Reflex} : S \rightarrow R$$

In many cases, though, how we react to events changes with experience. If you saw a flash of light, you might initially pay attention to it to see if it was important, but if you saw it several times and nothing of interest followed, you would soon begin to ignore it.[1] If the light was then followed by a puff of air hitting your eye, though, and this happened repeatedly, you would eventually begin to blink as soon as you saw the flash, in anticipation of the puff that was to follow. Your reaction to the puff would have changed because of experience, and this would be an example of learning. A simple definition of learning would thus be *a change in behavior due to experience*. As sometimes happens with simple definitions, however, this one quickly runs into difficulties.

One problem is that there are some changes caused by experience that are really not what we mean by learning. If your behavior changed because you had not eaten for several hours, for example, or because you had been paralyzed in an accident, these would not be what we mean by learning. What we really mean are experiences that result in the storage of information in your brain, information

---

[1] Technically, this would be an example of *habituation*, in which our reaction to a stimulus changes because of repeated presentation of that stimulus. Specifically, the response to the stimulus becomes weaker, or habituates.

that alters your capacity to respond, whether or not you actually use it. If you were taught to ride a bicycle, for example, this would be an example of learning, whether or not you later choose to use this skill.

To capture the meaning of learning more precisely, we will redefine **learning** as a change in our *capacity* for behavior, as a result of particular *kinds* of experience. This definition is regrettably more cumbersome, but it comes closer to what we really mean when we talk about learning.

Associative learning

In the case of habituation, learning occurs as a result of the presentation of a single stimulus (however, see Whitlow and Wagner, 1984). A more elaborate form of learning occurs when two events occur together and we learn about the relationship between them. If we use the symbol E_1 to represent one event and E_2 to represent the second event, then in **associative learning** we learn about the association or relationship between the two events:

$$E_1 \rightarrow E_2$$

The two events could potentially be anything: a drop in air pressure warning of a storm to come; a television theme tune announcing *Friends*; a tone of voice signaling annoyance. Learning psychologists, however, have been particularly interested in instances of associative learning where the second event is biologically important – food, say, or bodily injury – and survival might depend on being able to predict this event. Suppose that a lion always visits a watering hole at 4:00 in the afternoon; if antelopes that also use this water could learn this stimulus–stimulus relationship (4:00 p.m. → lion), this would allow them to avoid the area at this time and thereby prolong their lives. Or consider a related situation from the lion's point of view: Suppose that, whenever it stalks an antelope while remaining downwind of it, it is more likely to succeed. If it could learn this response–stimulus relationship (downwind stalking → succulent antelope), then it too would have a longer career.

Classical conditioning

In those cases where an important event is reliably preceded by a stimulus, the stimulus often comes to elicit the same behavior as the event it predicts. If a light is repeatedly followed by a puff of air to the eye, for example, then as we saw earlier the light on its own would eventually begin to elicit a blink. This is an example of **classical** or **Pavlovian conditioning**. Classical conditioning allows us to prepare for forthcoming events; in our eyeblink example, if we blink before the puff arrives, the lid closure can prevent particles from being blown into our eyes.

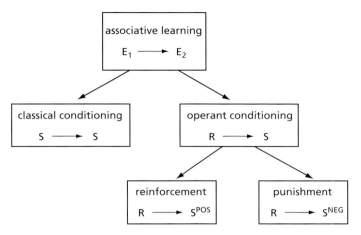

Figure 1.3 Varieties of associative learning. Associative learning involves the detection of relationships between events (E), where the events concerned can be responses (R) or stimuli (S), and the stimuli can be positive (S^{POS}) or negative (S^{NEG}).

Operant conditioning

When an important event follows a response rather than a stimulus, the result is often a change in the response's probability, and this is called **instrumental** or **operant conditioning.** If your parents gave you a sports car every time you received an A for a course, for example, the amount of time you spent studying would be very likely to increase. This example illustrates one of the two subtypes of operant conditioning, reinforcement and punishment, that differ in whether the change in responding is an increase or a decrease. In **reinforcement**, the consequence that follows a response is desirable and the effect is to strengthen it – the use of a reward to increase studying, for example. In **punishment**, on the other hand, the consequence is undesirable and the effect is to weaken the response. Children who burn their hands when touching a hot pan quickly learn not to repeat this behavior.

As summarized in Figure 1.3, the essential distinction between classical and operant conditioning lies in whether an important event follows a stimulus (for example, light → air puff) or a response (for example, touching pan → burn). As we shall see, both forms of conditioning play a major role in shaping our lives. This might not be obvious for classical conditioning because classical conditioning often occurs without our awareness (see Chapter 4). Also, the best-known conditioned responses are salivation and blinking, neither of which would probably make a "top 10" list of critical skills. However, classical conditioning also affects far more important aspects of our behavior, including emotions such as fear and sexual arousal, what foods we like, and the effects of drugs such as heroin and alcohol. Learning psychologists have been able to use an understanding of the processes involved to develop therapies for problems such as phobias, alcoholism, and bed-wetting. We will look at the principles of conditioning, and how they can be practically applied, in Chapter 2.

The importance of reinforcement and punishment is probably more obvious, but even here we tend to underestimate their significance. As in the case of classical conditioning, this is partly because we are not always aware of their effects. Attention from others, for example, can be very reinforcing, and when parents and teachers pay attention to a child who is misbehaving they sometimes inadvertently reinforce the behavior they are trying to eliminate. Also, reinforcement and punishment sometimes appear ineffective because they are not used optimally. Improved understanding of the principles involved has allowed psychologists to develop techniques for reducing children's misbehavior, for teaching convicts to master a year's worth of school in only a month, and for helping autistic children to lead normal lives. We will look at the principles of reinforcement in Chapter 4 and at how they can be applied in Chapter 5.

Memory

We turn now to the meaning of our second fundamental concept, memory. Robert Rescorla (1988) once published an article entitled "Pavlovian conditioning: it's not what you think it is." In the same spirit, this section could have been entitled "Memory: It's sort of what you think it is, but not quite."

Defining memory

The term *memory* is commonly used in one of two senses. One is as a mental record of our experiences. Something happens; later we recall it; memory refers to the record that makes this recall possible. Another meaning focuses on the act of retrieving this record, as when we say that we remember something. Here, we commonly mean that we have a conscious feeling of re-creating or reliving the original experience; memory refers to this conscious reliving of past experiences.

Both of these definitions capture some of what we mean by the term memory, but both have flaws. Consider first memory as a record of experiences. Actually, this is a good definition of one aspect of memory, but in common usage it implies an *accurate* record, resembling a photograph. As we shall see, that is not so. If memory is a photograph, it is one taken by a camera with a distorting lens, resulting in incomplete or inaccurate images. Moreover, when the time comes to retrieve these images, it is as if the person who examines the photograph is also wearing distorting lenses, so that further inaccuracies arise during retrieval. Memory *is* a

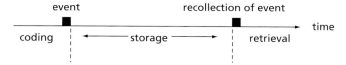

Figure 1.4 Coding, storage, and retrieval of an experience.

record, but a far less accurate record than we normally realize (Chapters 9, 10, and 11).

Turning to our second definition, that of memory as the conscious reliving of experiences, the problem here is that this is true of only some memories. If you were asked what you ate for breakfast this morning, you probably would be able to remember not only what you ate but where you were as you ate it, and so on. Remembering really would resemble watching a video of the scene. If you were then asked where most movies are produced in California, you would again have no difficulty in replying, but this time you would have no sense of reliving a specific moment in time – the answer would just pop up into your head. As we shall see in Chapter 12, memories that involve conscious reliving of specific moments are called **episodic memories**, whereas memories that involve factual knowledge that just "pops up" are described as **semantic memories**. And there is a further class called **implicit memories** in which past events influence us without our realizing it – we don't have a conscious sense of remembering *anything*. Thus, even though remembering sometimes involves reliving an experience, this is not always the case.

Our second definition is thus also flawed, but it does capture an important aspect of memory not covered by the first – that memory is about not just the formation of a record, but also its retrieval or use. In fact, memory theorists talk about three stages in remembering an event: **coding**, **storage**, and **retrieval**. Coding refers to what happens when we experience an event and form a record or code in our brains to represent it. This record then remains in storage until a time comes when we attempt to retrieve it (see Figure 1.4). As we shall, all three stages play a critical role in determining whether we remember our experiences.

To capture all three aspects, we will define **memory** as the processes by which we code, store, and retrieve information about our experiences. This definition is certainly similar to everyday usage, but it emphasizes the importance of all three stages in memory, not just that of coding. Also, as we have seen, these three processes differ in two important respects from our normal assumptions about memory. First, the record that is formed is less accurate – sometimes, much less accurate – than we usually realize. And second, the process of retrieving information can occur at an unconscious level, with the result that past experiences sometimes influence us without our realizing it (Chapter 10).

Learning and memory

With provisional definitions of both learning and memory under our belts, we can now consider the relationship between them. In ordinary usage, learning and memory refer to quite different aspects of behavior. As an illustration, consider a class of schoolchildren that has a lesson on Roman history and is then tested on what they have learned. Suppose that one child does better on the test than another child does, and that the reason is that the second child didn't pay attention during the lesson. The second child's poorer performance would clearly be due to poorer learning.

Now let us focus on a second pair. Suppose that again one does better, but that this time the difference is because the first child was tested an hour after the lesson and the second child was tested a year later. Here we would say that the second child's performance was due to poorer memory. In normal usage, in other words, learning refers to the *acquisition* of knowledge, whereas memory refers to how well we *retain* that knowledge.

This distinction is useful, but it is important to recognize that the processes of acquiring and retaining knowledge are inextricably intertwined, as you cannot study one without also studying the other. If you want to study learning, you must at some point test what was learned, and that inevitably involves memory. And if you want to study memory, you must first expose participants to the material to be remembered, and that involves learning. Thus, although experiments on learning primarily focus on the acquisition of information, and experiments on memory on its retention, any experiment on one inevitably involves the other.

An example might help to clarify this point. In Chapter 2 we will discuss a form of conditioning called taste-aversion learning, in which animals and people develop aversions to foods eaten before they become ill. In an experiment by Etscorn and Stephens (1973), for example, rats were allowed to drink a saccharine solution and then, 24 hours later, they were given a drug to make them ill. The result was that the rats developed an aversion to the taste of saccharin, a result that could only have occurred if, when they became ill, they remembered what they had eaten 24 hours earlier. The formation of this association clearly depended on memory.

Similarly, memory depends on the formation of associations. In a typical memory experiment, participants are given a list of words to memorize and then asked to recall them. On the surface, the procedure is very different from that in our classical conditioning example – the subjects are people rather than rats; the material to be learned is a list of words rather than an association between a taste and illness. As we shall see in Chapter 8, however, associations also play a critical role in the memory experiment. When subjects read the words, they do not try to memorize them in isolation; instead, they look for relationships between the words, and they use these relationships to form associations or connections between them. Moreover, they not only form associations between the words, they also form associations between the words and the experimental context in which they are presented. When the time comes to recall the words, participants rely on these associations to retrieve them: Remembering the context reminds subjects of some of the words, remembering some of the words reminds subjects of others, and so on (see Chapter 11). Memory thus depends on the formation of associations, just as the formation of associations depends on memory.

In this sense, learning and memory are two sides of the same coin. Although one emphasizes the acquisition of knowledge and the other its retention, they are both products of a unified system for coding, storing, and retrieving information about our experiences. The procedures used to study conditioning and memory are very different, but the underlying processes are often the same.

Summary

In this chapter we reviewed some of the assumptions that underlie the research that we will be discussing in later chapters:

- That behavior is lawful, as our environment and heredity jointly determine how we behave. The position that we have labeled neural determinism argues that behavior *must* be lawful. We also looked at examples where environment and heredity do strongly influence us, and evidence that such influence can occur without our realizing it.
- That introspection is of limited value in helping us to understand people's behavior. Experiments allow us to identify which aspects of our environment affect our behavior, but progress is often constrained by the need to manipulate only one aspect of the environment at a time.
- That experiments on animals allow greater control of the environment, making it easier to identify the processes involved. Animals are far more intelligent than once believed, so that an understanding of learning gained in animal research has the potential to help us in understanding learning in humans, but this similarity also raises ethical issues about the use of animals in experiments.

It is important to remember that these are all *assumptions* – it is important to understand the reasoning behind them, but you don't have to accept them.

We also introduced the concepts of learning and memory:

- The term *learning* emphasizes the acquisition of knowledge and skills, and *memory* emphasizes the retention of this information. However, these processes are inextricably intertwined: We can only determine if someone has learned something by seeing if they later remember it, and we can only remember an event if we stored information about it when it occurred.

- Our discussion of learning will focus on associative learning, which involves learning about the relationship between two events. In classical conditioning, we learn about the relationship between two stimuli; in operant conditioning (reinforcement and punishment), we learn about the relationship between a response and its consequence.

A suggestion for studying

As we will see in the chapters on memory, one of the most effective techniques for studying is to review material after you have read it – both immediately and then after a delay. Immediately after reading material we often have the impression that we will remember it because it still resides in our short-term memory and is thus easy to recall. However, that impression can be misleading, as the material may not have been stored in long-term memory – or, at any rate, not stored in a manner that will be easy to later retrieve. One of the best ways to ensure that you really will remember is to pause after each section that you read and try to recall it without looking back at the text, and then to review it again when you finish the chapter. You can use these summary sections to help you – after each item in the summary, try to remember as much as you can of what was said about it in the chapter, and then look back at the earlier sections to see how well you did. If there was material you didn't recall, you can review it and then try to recall it all again. The more you review material in your head – for example, the next day while walking across campus! – the better you are likely to remember it

Incidentally, another technique which is thought to help, though there is only limited evidence, is to think about how you would teach the material to someone else while you review it. The extra thought required can be very useful in ensuring you really understand the material, and thus remember it.

Review questions

1 Is behavior governed by laws? What are the arguments for and against this view?

2 What developments undermined the use of introspection in psychology?

3 In what ways do the views of Skinner and of cognitive psychologists differ? In what respects are they the same?

4 How do experiments control for unwanted variables?

5 What are the strengths and weaknesses of the experimental method?

6 Why do psychologists believe that the results of experiments carried out in highly artificial laboratory settings can tell us anything about behavior in the real world?

7 What are the arguments for and against the use of animals in psychological research?

8 What evidence suggests that animals might be more similar to humans in learning and intelligence than traditionally assumed?

9 How do the concepts of learning and memory differ? Why might it be argued that they represent two sides of the same coin?

2 Classical conditioning

CONTENTS

A dog stands motionless in the middle of a room, immobilized by a leather harness. The room is very quiet, all outside sound blocked by one-foot-thick concrete walls. A bell rings, and the dog turns toward the bell but otherwise shows little reaction. Five seconds later, the dog is presented food powder through a long rubber tube. The silence returns. Ten minutes pass; the bell sounds again and, as before, is followed by food. Ten more minutes pass. Again the bell sounds, but this time the dog begins to move restlessly in its harness, saliva dripping from its mouth. As the trials continue, the dog appears increasingly excited when the bell sounds, with more and more saliva flowing into a tube that has been surgically implanted in the dog's mouth. The saliva flows through the tube into an adjoining room where technicians record the number of drops.

When word of this experiment reached other scientists, the news was greeted with tremendous excitement. Within a few years, virtually every psychologist in the world knew the experimenter, Ivan Petrovich Pavlov. Within a few decades, his research had become perhaps the best known in the history of science, ranking with the legendary fall of an apple onto Isaac Newton's head.

Why all the excitement? What was so interesting about the fact that a dog could be trained to salivate? In this chapter we will try to answer these questions. We will look at what Pavlov discovered and why other scientists thought it so important. And we will consider what subsequent research has revealed about the surprisingly powerful role of conditioning in shaping our lives.

The associative context

Scientists' excitement on hearing of Pavlov's discoveries had its roots in many centuries of effort to understand human behavior. Early explanations were generally religious in character. Human behavior was seen as unpredictable, determined by fate or the whim of the gods. The advent of Christianity produced significant changes in these beliefs, but behavior was still seen as fundamentally unpredictable. Individuals were believed to have free will because they had souls. For almost 1,700 years there were few significant departures from this theme, until the publication in 1650 of *The Passions of the Soul* by René Descartes. Descartes was a brilliant mathematician (Cartesian geometry was named after him), but he was also an outstanding philosopher, of such eminence that he was invited to Sweden to serve as the personal tutor to Queen Christina, then one of Europe's most powerful monarchs. He wanted to decline the queen's invitation politely, but she dispatched a warship to collect him, and he then found the honor too great to refuse. Conditions, however, proved less than ideal: Classes were held at five o'clock in the morning, in the unheated library of the castle. It was apparently an unusually rigorous winter even by Swedish standards, and Descartes died of pneumonia before it ended (Boring, 1950).

The reflex

Aside from its implications for those contemplating careers in philosophy, Descartes's life is important to us because he was the first major figure in Western civilization to offer a detailed, mechanistic explanation for human behavior. According to Descartes, our senses and muscles are connected by a complex network of nerves, and the flow of "animal spirits" through these nerves makes possible the instinctive reactions necessary for survival. If a person were to step into a fire accidentally, for example, the nerves in the foot would be stimulated and would transmit this excitation to the brain. The brain would then release animal spirits into the nerve, which would flow back to the calf muscle and cause it to swell, resulting in the foot's withdrawal from the flame. This simple mechanism – a receptor activating a muscle through a direct, innate connection – Descartes called a *reflex*, and he proposed that reflexes underlie all automatic, involuntary reactions.

The association

Descartes's analysis showed how seemingly complex movements of the body could be explained by the same simple mechanisms that governed machines, but he was not prepared to allow a similar determinism in the operation of the mind. This audacious step was taken some 40 years later by an English physician named John Locke, secretary to the Earl of Shaftesbury. As was the custom of those times, Locke met weekly with educated friends to discuss current issues in areas such as science and theology. At one of these meetings, the disagreements became particularly intense, and it puzzled Locke that intelligent men could hold such different opinions regarding the same basic facts. He resolved to prepare a brief paper for the next meeting analyzing how each of us forms our ideas of the world and why our ideas are so different. Twenty years later, he finally completed this analysis, and it was published as a lengthy book, *An Essay Concerning Human Understanding*. The ideas in this essay were elaborated by later philosophers such as David Hartley and James Mill; together, these ideas form the doctrine that has become known as British Associationism.

The British Associationists

According to the Associationists, thought is simply a succession of ideas, so that the basic unit of all thought is the idea. Descartes had believed many of our ideas to be innate, but Locke argued that our minds at birth are a *tabula rasa*, or blank slate. Any ideas we may have, he said, could only be acquired through experience. Locke suggested that sensations that occur together become associated, so that if one of these sensations recurs it will automatically elicit the other. A stone, for example, produces a variety of visual and tactile sensations, which become associated through repeated pairings. This compound sensation (associated sensations) then forms our idea of a stone.

Ideas, in other words, are nothing more than sensations that have become associated together. This process of association also explains the sequence in which ideas occur to us.

Our ideas spring up, or exist, in the order in which the sensations existed, of which they are the copies. This is the general law of the "Association of Ideas." . . . Of the successive order of our ideas, many remarkable instances might be adduced. Of these none seems better adapted to the learner than the repetition of any passage, or words; the Lord's Prayer, for example, committed to memory. In learning the passage, we repeat it; that is, we pronounce the words, in successive order, from the beginning to the end. The order of the sensations is successive. When we proceed to repeat the passage, the ideas of the words also arise in succession, the preceding always suggesting the succeeding, and no other. Our suggests father, father suggests which, which suggests art; and so on, to the end. How remarkably this is the case, anyone may convince himself, by trying to repeat backwards even a passage with which he is as familiar as the Lord's Prayer.

(Mill, 1829)

The laws of association

The concept of association can thus explain not only the existence of ideas but even the order in which they occur. The strength of an association was assumed to depend on **contiguity**: The closer in time two events occurred, the more strongly they would be associated. In the Lord's Prayer, the word *our* is immediately followed by *father*, and as a result a strong association is formed between them. The word *which* follows soon after, but the time between *our* and *which* is longer than the time between *our* and *father*; as a result, *our* is associated with *father* more strongly with *which*, so that *our* is more likely to make us think of *father*.

A second principle of association was *frequency:* The more often two words occurred together, the more strongly they would be associated. The Lord's Prayer again provides an example: The more often we hear it, the more strongly we associate the words, and thus the better we recall it.

A third principle determining the strength of an association was said to be the *intensity* of the feelings that accompanied the association. If you accidentally burned your hand, for example, the intense pain involved would become strongly associated with the situation, and you would be likely to remember the accident whenever you returned to the place where it occurred.

By the nineteenth century, therefore, the historical groundwork was in place for a theory of human behavior based on associations. Descartes had shown how movements could be explained through associations, or connections, between senses and muscles, and the British Associationists had extended his analysis to the mind, showing how thought could also be explained through associations between ideas and how ideas could in turn be analyzed into associations among sensations. The key to understanding human behavior, therefore, seemed to lie in understanding how associations are formed. On this issue, however, the philosophers were unable to agree. Each philosopher identified a set of factors that might influence the strength of an association, but because the evidence for these factors rested solely on introspection, there was no obvious way to decide which factors were really important and which, if any, were spurious. If only there were an objective method for studying the formation of associations...

Pavlov's conditioned reflexes

Ivan Petrovich Pavlov was born in a small village in Russia in 1849. His early years were spent preparing for the priesthood at the local church school. His plans eventually changed, and in 1870 he walked hundreds of miles across Russia to enroll in St. Petersburg University as a student of physiology. His particular interest was in the physiology of digestion, and he developed ingenious surgical procedures for measuring salivary and gastric secretions in dogs.

Saliva is secreted by special glands within the cheek and then carried by ducts to the cheek's inner surface. By surgically redirecting one of these ducts, Pavlov was able to divert the saliva to the external surface of the cheek, where it could be collected through a connecting tube and then analyzed. Using this surgical preparation, known as a *fistula*, Pavlov found that salivation was an automatic, reflexive response that was elicited whenever food came into contact with the mucous membranes of the mouth.

The discovery of conditioning

After his dogs had been tested for several sessions, Pavlov noticed a strange phenomenon: The dogs began to salivate not only when food was placed in their mouths but also at other times. Many scientists would have either ignored this salivation, considering it irrelevant, or sought actively to prevent it because its occurrence would contaminate their measures of the pure reflex to food. Pavlov, however, was fascinated. If salivation is a reflexive response, lawfully elicited only by very specific stimuli such as the presence of food in the mouth, why should it suddenly begin to occur in the absence of these stimuli?

An associative analysis

In analyzing this "psychic" secretion, which appeared to have no cause, Pavlov noticed a pattern to its occurrences. For example, the dogs were particularly likely to salivate when they saw the experimenter enter the room, or when they heard his footsteps approaching. Was it possible that the dogs had come to associate these stimuli with the delivery of food, and this was why they were salivating? Or, in Pavlov's terminology, that in addition to the innate or *unconditioned reflexes* with which every animal was born, they were able to form new, *conditioned reflexes*?

Stating his hypothesis in physiological terms, Pavlov began by assuming that the presentation of any stimulus would produce activity in a set of neurons in the brain that effectively represented that stimulus (a "center"). When food was presented in a dog's mouth, for example, this would activate the food center in the brain, and activity in the food center would then be transmitted through an innate

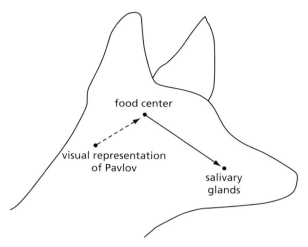

Figure 2.1 Pavlov's view of the neural connections involved in classical conditioning. If the sight of Pavlov preceded food, the neurons in the cortex that were activated by the sight of Pavlov would become connected to the food center (the broken line). Excitement in the food center would then be transmitted via an innate pathway (solid line) to the dog's salivary glands.

connection to the salivary glands, causing salivation (Figure 2.1). If a stimulus such as a tone preceded the food, this stimulus would activate its own cortical center. So far, this analysis conformed closely to physiologists' understanding of the brain's functioning at the time, but Pavlov now introduced a critical new assumption. If two centers of the brain were active at the same time, he suggested, the connection between these centers would be strengthened. In our example, the fact that activity in the tone center was closely followed by activity in the food center would mean that the connection between these centers would be strengthened. The next time the tone was presented, therefore, activity in the tone center would be transmitted to the food center, and from there to the salivary glands.

If this analysis was correct, Pavlov saw that it could have far-reaching implications. As we saw in Chapter 1, behavior depends on the routing of electrical impulses through the brain, and this routing depends on the strength of the connections between individual neurons. If we could understand how the strength of neural connections is altered, we would understand the crucial mechanism underlying the brain's operations. Because of the brain's complexity, however, it is normally extremely difficult to study the formation of new connections. Suppose, for example, that we wanted to study the neural changes that occur as a child memorizes a poem in school. How would we observe changes in connections between individual neurons in the child's brain? And even if we had a technique for doing so, how would we know which of the brain's 100,000,000,000 neurons to monitor? If Pavlov's hypothesis was correct, however, he could monitor the formation of new connections simply by measuring a dog's salivation: The stronger the connection between the tone and food centers, the more electrical impulses would be transmitted to the food center and from there to the salivary glands, resulting in greater salivation. The amount of salivation, therefore, provides a simple index of the strength of this connection. To determine the laws governing the formation of neural connections, therefore, all Pavlov needed to do was to manipulate possible variables and observe their effects on the amount of salivation. If, as he believed, all education and training "are really nothing more than the results of an establishment of new nervous connections" (Pavlov, 1927, p. 26), then studying how dogs learn to salivate might lead to an understanding of the neural mechanisms underlying all learning.

Excited by this possibility, Pavlov abandoned his research on digestion, even though it had already made him world famous and was soon to earn him the Nobel Prize. Instead, he set out to study how new associations were formed by deliberately pairing stimuli with the presentation of food and observing how the conditions of pairing influenced the development of salivation.

Controlling the conditions

Pavlov recognized from the outset that the task was not going to be an easy one: The brain was an enormously complex organ, sensitive to countless stimuli from the outside world, so that the effects in which he was interested might easily be lost in the flood of stimuli constantly washing over his subjects.

Unless we are careful to take special precautions the success of the whole investigation may be jeopardized, and we should get hopelessly lost as soon as we began to seek for cause and effect among so many and various influences, so intertwined and entangled as to form a veritable chaos. It was evident that the experimental conditions had to be simplified, and that this simplification must consist in eliminating as far as possible any stimuli outside our control which might fall upon the animal.

(Pavlov, 1927, p. 20)

To achieve this, Pavlov conducted his initial studies in an isolated room, where no one but the experimenter was allowed to enter. This precaution, however, proved inadequate, as even the slightest movement of the experimenter, such as a blink, was enough to distract the dogs. Pavlov tried placing the experimenter outside the room, but this did not solve the problem, as the dogs continued to be affected by stimuli such as the footsteps of passersby and even a cloud that temporarily reduced the amount of light coming in the window. Finally, Pavlov was driven to designing a completely new laboratory that, with the aid of a "keen and public-spirited Moscow businessman," he had built in St. Petersburg.

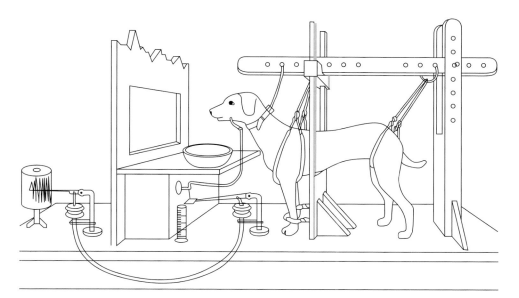

Figure 2.2 Apparatus used in Pavlov's study of salivary conditioning in dogs. Saliva flowed through a tube connected to the dog's cheek and travelled to another room where it could be recorded. (After Yerkes and Morgulis, 1909.)

The laboratory looked like a fort, with walls more than a foot thick, encircled by a trench filled with straw to reduce vibrations from passing traffic. The actual test rooms were widely dispersed through the building to minimize distracting noises. Figure 2.2 illustrates a typical test room. The dogs were strapped into loose-fitting harnesses to reduce movement, and any salivation was carried off through a tube to an experimenter in an adjacent, soundproof room. With the aid of a variety of electrically operated signal devices, Pavlov was now able to control almost completely the external stimuli that reached his subjects, and thus was ready to make a systematic study of how associations are formed.

A typical experiment

We can illustrate the quality of the results Pavlov now obtained with an experiment by one of his students. Anrep (1920) first presented his dogs with a tone by itself and found that it had no effect on salivation. He then paired the tone with food: The tone was sounded for five seconds; then, two seconds later, food was presented. Each of these tone–food pairings was called a **trial**, and Anrep presented a trial every few minutes. (The actual time between trials varied between 5 and 35 minutes.) On an average of once every ten trials, the tone was presented by itself for 30 seconds so the experimenter could measure the amount of salivation elicited solely by the tone.

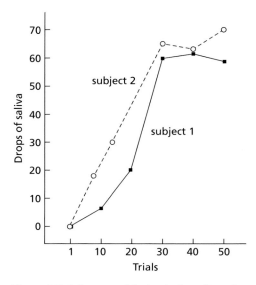

Figure 2.3 Salivary conditioning in dogs. (Data from Anrep, 1920.)

The results for two subjects are shown in Figure 2.3, where we can see that the magnitude of salivation on the test trials gradually increased from 0 drops to a maximum level, or *asymptote*, of about 60 drops after 30 pairings. One striking feature of these results is the smoothness and regularity of the learning curves. It normally requires averaging the results of many subjects to eliminate random variations and produce curves of this smoothness, but because of the extraordinary control Pavlov achieved over the environment, he and his colleagues were able to produce beautifully clear and uniform data even in single subjects. Even more dramatic evidence of the underlying lawfulness of behavior in this situation is the similarity of the learning curves of the two subjects: Even though the subjects were tested separately, their behavior was virtually identical on trial after trial.

Pavlov called the salivation elicited by the food an **unconditioned response** (UR), because no training was necessary to establish it, whereas the salivation to the tone was a **conditioned response** (CR) – that is, a response whose occurrence depended on particular conditions of training. Similarly, the food was an **unconditioned stimulus** (US) for salivation – that is, a stimulus that elicits a response without training. Finally, the tone was called a **conditioned stimulus** (CS) – a stimulus that, through training, elicits a response.[1] (See Figure 2.4.) The entire procedure,

---

[1] Pavlov actually used the term *conditional response* because the occurrence of the response was conditional on previous pairings of the CS and the US. The term was mistranslated as *conditioned response*. Some authors are now returning to Pavlov's original terminology, referring to conditional and unconditional stimuli and responses.

Conditioning

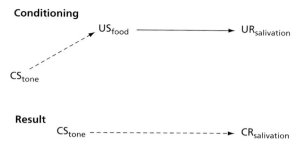

Result

CS_{tone} - - - - - - - - - - - - - - - - - - ▸ $CR_{salivation}$

Figure 2.4 A typical classical conditioning procedure.

in which the pairing of a CS with a US results in an increase in responding to the CS, has come to be known as **Pavlovian** or **classical conditioning**.

Extinction

Pavlov saw conditioning not simply as a useful tool for studying the formation of associations but as a process of fundamental importance in its own right. As we have seen, animals are born with a variety of innate reflexes that allow them to respond quickly to important events – for example, blinking when a gust of air brings the danger of particles being blown into the eye, or lifting a foot when it touches a burning surface. Unlearned reflexes such as these are important in allowing animals to cope with situations that always require the same response. Some features of the environment, however, vary in what response is appropriate, and Pavlov saw classical conditioning as a vital mechanism that allowed animals to adjust their behavior to new circumstances. Grizzly bears, for example, feed on salmon, but rivers contain salmon only during the brief migration season of that fish. If a bear visits a river one day and finds it teeming with salmon, the bear will clearly have a better chance of survival if it can learn that the river is now a good source of food and therefore return the next day.

Once the salmon migration is over, however, a river that was once full of fish might become empty. What happens to an established association when the CS no longer reliably signals the US? The answer is shown in Figure 2.5, which presents the results of an experiment in which a previously conditioned stimulus was presented a number of times without the US. The result was that the conditioned response gradually disappeared, a phenomenon referred to by Pavlov as **extinction**. Although answering one question, this result immediately raised another – namely, why did the response disappear? If a neural connection had been established in the brain between the CS and the US, could this connection have been obliterated simply by presenting the CS by itself a few times?

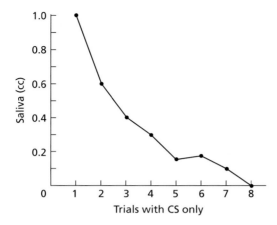

Figure 2.5 Extinction of a conditioned response when the conditioned stimulus is presented by itself. (Data from Pavlov, 1927.)

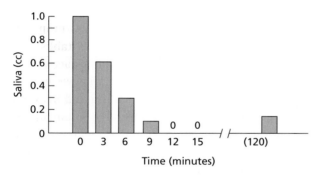

Figure 2.6 Spontaneous recovery of an extinguished response. (Data from Pavlov, 1927.)

To Pavlov, this was implausible. There was no physiological evidence that neural connections suddenly disintegrated in this way, and observations of the dogs' behavior also suggested that the connections formed during conditioning were still present after extinction. If, for example, an interval of time was allowed to elapse after extinction had been completed, and if the CS was then presented again, the previously extinguished response would suddenly reappear. Figure 2.6 shows that after a series of extinction trials in which salivation was progressively reduced to zero, the CS was reintroduced after a lapse of two hours and again elicited a significant amount of salivation. This **spontaneous recovery** of the response was only temporary; with further presentations of the CS, the recovered response would again be rapidly extinguished. The recovery clearly demonstrated, however, that a connection still existed between the CS and the response.

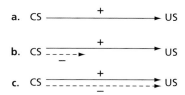

Figure 2.7 Pavlov's view of the development of inhibitory connections during extinction: (a) By the end of conditioning, an excitatory connection has been formed between the CS and the US (solid line). (b) Presentation of the CS by itself produces a new, inhibitory connection (broken line). (c) With repeated presentations of the CS by itself, the inhibitory connection becomes stronger (represented by a longer broken line).

The concept of inhibition

If the CS were still associated with salivation, why had the dog stopped salivating during the earlier extinction trials? The answer, according to Pavlov, was not that the old, excitatory connection had been destroyed, but that the CS had also acquired the capacity to inhibit responding. In an elaboration of Pavlov's ideas proposed by Konorski (1948), pairing of the CS and the US was assumed to establish an excitatory connection between the corresponding brain centers, so that activation of the CS center would be transmitted to the US center. If the CS were then presented on its own, a new, inhibitory connection would be established between the centers so that activity in the CS center would now tend to block or inhibit activity in the US center as well as to excite it. Once the strength of the new, inhibitory connection matched that of the existing excitatory connection, the net input would be zero and no response would be elicited.

During Pavlov's time, no direct evidence was available for the existence of inhibitory connections in the brain, but physiological research since then has confirmed their existence. When an electrical impulse arrives at a neuron's terminal, it causes the release of chemical neurotransmitters that flow across the synaptic cleft to the next neuron in the chain. In excitatory connections, the neurotransmitters produce changes in the cell membrane of the second neuron that eventually cause it to initiate an electrical signal. Different neurons, however, produce different neurotransmitters, and some have the effect of blocking changes in the cell membrane. Thus, if two neurons converge on the same target neuron, and one releases excitatory neurotransmitters while the other releases inhibitory ones, their effects might cancel each other, resulting in no change in the target neuron's electrical activity.

During conditioning, Pavlov suggested, an excitatory connection is established between the CS and the US (Figure 2.7a). During extinction, a parallel inhibitory connection is developed (Figure 2.7b – the length of the line is being used to represent the strength of the association). As the inhibitory connection becomes stronger, it is increasingly effective in preventing the response, until eventually, when the excitatory and inhibitory tendencies are equally balanced, the conditioned response is no longer elicited (Figure 2.7c).

Conditioned inhibition

Direct evidence for the existence of inhibition came from the phenomenon of **conditioned inhibition** – the tendency of a stimulus to block, or inhibit, responding as a result of previous training. The training procedure used by Pavlov was to alternate between trials in which the CS+ (positive stimulus) was paired with food and trials in which the CS+ and the CS– (inhibitory stimulus) were presented together without food. The CS– signaled that food would not be forthcoming and acquired the capacity to inhibit salivation. Suppose, for example, that we conditioned salivation to a metronome, but that on certain trials we presented a whistle at the same time as the metronome and did not present food.

$$\text{metronome} \rightarrow \text{food}$$
$$\text{whistle} + \text{metronome} \rightarrow \underline{\quad}$$

After a series of such trials, subjects would respond vigorously when the metronome was presented by itself, but not when the metronome was presented in conjunction with the whistle. The reason, according to Pavlov, was that pairing the metronome with food had resulted in the establishment of an excitatory connection between the corresponding neural centers, whereas pairing the whistle with no food had resulted in an inhibitory connection between the whistle and food. When the metronome was presented by itself, it excited the food center and thus elicited salivation, but when the whistle was also presented, it inhibited the food center. The excitatory and inhibitory tendencies cancelled each other, with the net result that the dogs didn't salivate on trials when they heard the whistle.

To test this explanation, Pavlov presented the whistle together with another conditioned stimulus, a tactile stimulus that had previously been paired with food:

$$\text{whistle} + \text{tactile stimulus} \rightarrow ?$$

If the whistle were truly able to inhibit salivation, it should now reduce responding to the tactile stimulus in exactly the same way as it had to the metronome. As shown in Table 2.1, this is exactly what happened: When the tactile stimulus was presented by itself, it elicited copious salivation, but when it was combined with the whistle, salivation declined drastically. The whistle really was inhibiting salivation. (For further discussion of inhibition, including the need for appropriate

Table 2.1 A test for conditioned inhibition (data from Pavlov, 1927, p. 77)

Time	Stimulus presented for one minute	Drops of saliva during one minute
3:08 p.m.	Tactile	3
3:16 p.m.	Tactile	8
3.25 p.m.	Tactile + whistle	<1
3:30 p.m.	Tactile	11

control groups, see Williams, Overmier, and LoLordo, 1992, and Cole, Barnet, and Miller, 1997.)

Returning to extinction, most learning psychologists now agree that extinction involves not the destruction of the excitatory association formed during conditioning but rather the formation of a new, inhibitory association. (See Rescorla, 2001, and Bouton, 2004, for reviews.) As extinction trials continue, the inhibitory connection becomes progressively stronger until, eventually, it equals the excitatory tendency in strength and responding ceases.

The renewal effect

More recent research has revealed another aspect of extinction which, because of its potentially important implications, we will also discuss here. In essence, this research has shown that the effects of extinction are to some extent limited to the context in which it occurs. Consider a dog conditioned to salivate to a tone. This effect is quite general: The dog will salivate whenever it hears the tone, whether in the laboratory or outside. Suppose, however, that it is now given a series of trials in which the tone is presented by itself. The response will extinguish, but in this case the effect will be strongest in the training context: The dog will not respond when the tone is presented in the laboratory, but it will still tend to respond when it hears the tone elsewhere. The response elsewhere is weaker than it was at the end of conditioning – if extinction training is resumed, it will extinguish quite quickly – but the effects of extinction do seem to be limited, at least in part, to the specific environment in which the CS was presented.

In one of the first demonstrations of this phenomenon, Bouton and King (1983) gave rats fear conditioning trials in which a tone was followed by an electric shock. This training occurred in a distinctive cage that we will call cage A. Then, in the second phase, the rats received extinction trials in which the tone was presented by itself until it no longer elicited fear. For one group, these extinction trials were carried out in the same cage as conditioning, but for a second group the tone was presented in a different cage (B). Finally, there was a test phase in which both groups were returned to the cage used during conditioning and the tone was again presented by itself:

	Conditioning	Extinction	Test
Group 1:	A	A	A
Group 2:	A	B	A

What behavior would you expect during this final test phase? Because fear was completely extinguished during the second phase, you might think that the tone would not elicit fear in either group. Indeed, that was the outcome in the group trained in cage A throughout. In the ABA group, however, the tone elicited almost as much fear during the test as it had during conditioning – it was almost as if extinction had never occurred. This recovery was not total: As the test continued, the fear extinguished very rapidly, demonstrating that the earlier extinction trials had had a lasting impact. Nevertheless, the rats' fear clearly had returned, or been renewed, when the rats were returned to the original cage, and as a result this phenomenon has been called the **renewal effect**.

Subsequent research established that fear is renewed if the CS is presented in almost any environment other than the one used for extinction (for example, Harris *et al.*, 2000; Tamai and Nakajima, 2000). The renewal effect thus provides further evidence that extinction does not eliminate the connection between the CS and the US; even if the CS stops eliciting fear in the extinction context, it might still do so in other contexts.

You might have noticed the similarity between the renewal effect and spontaneous recovery. In both cases, a response that appeared to have been extinguished later returns. (In the case of spontaneous recovery, it is the passage of time that leads to the response reappearing; in the renewal effect it is a change in the environmental context.) In both cases, to be sure, the recovery is only temporary: If extinction trials resume, the recovered response will usually extinguish quite quickly. Nevertheless, the puzzle remains: Why does a response that has been completely extinguished reappear when conditions change?

One way to think about this is suggested by a theory that we will encounter in Chapter 3, first put forward by Leo Kamin (1969). Kamin suggested that when an important event such as food or shock occurs, we look for an explanation. In the conditioning phase of the Bouton and King experiment, the first time the rats were shocked they would have been surprised (to put it mildly), and they would have searched their memories to identify a possible cause. They would have remembered the tone that preceded the shock, and so formed a tentative expectation that future tones might also be followed by shocks. And this expectation would have hardened into certainty as conditioning continued.

When the tone was no longer followed by shock during extinction, the rats would have been surprised yet again. They knew that the tone had been followed by shock during the conditioning phase, but now, in a different room, it wasn't. Something had clearly changed; could it be that the tone only signaled danger in the original context? When returned to the first room in the test phase, therefore, they would have again been fearful, because in this room the tone had always been followed by shock.

You might be feeling skeptical that rats would engage in reasoning of this kind, and indeed we are not suggesting that the process occurs in quite the conscious or verbal way we have outlined. Rather, the core of the argument is that during extinction, rats (and dogs, and people) learn not just about the CS but also about the general context in which extinction takes place. Put another way, extinction is to some extent context-specific: We learn that shock no longer follows the tone *in this room.* When we encounter the tone in other rooms, therefore, we might again become fearful, because we are not sure whether it will be followed by shock, as it was during conditioning, or not followed by shock, as it was during extinction. (Note: This explanation is derived from ideas proposed by Leo Kamin (1969) and Mark Bouton (2004). It is not identical to either, though, so neither should be held responsible for it in its current form.)

The context-specificity of extinction has potentially important practical implications. Suppose that you developed an intense fear of dogs after being bitten by one. And that to help you overcome your fear, a psychologist exposed you to a very friendly dog at a distance, and then gradually brought the dog closer. The purpose would be to help you overcome your fear through extinction, exposing you to the fearful stimulus but ensuring that harmful consequences no longer followed. Even if your fear disappeared completely, the renewal effect suggests that it could return if you encountered a dog in a different context – in the street, say, rather than in your therapist's office. We will discuss therapies for fear in more detail later, but for now the key point is that while conditioning generalizes widely, extinction tends to be more specific to the context in which it occurs. If the environment changes, the extinguished response may reappear, at least temporarily.

Other phenomena

Pavlov and his colleagues built up an extraordinarily detailed picture of the basic processes of conditioning. Indeed, in the 1950s it could still be argued plausibly that every single major fact about conditioning had been anticipated by Pavlov some 50 years earlier. We cannot convey the richness of Pavlov's work in the space available, but we shall summarize briefly a few of the other phenomena he discovered.

Generalization

Pavlov found that conditioning resulted in salivation not only to the CS presented during training but also to other stimuli that were similar to it. In one experiment, he conditioned salivation to a tone of 1,000 Hz.[2] After conditioning, the dogs salivated not only to the 1,000-Hz tone but also to tones of 1,100 Hz, 1,200 Hz, and so on, with the greatest increase in salivation occurring to the tones most similar to the training stimulus (that is, 900 Hz and 1,100 Hz). This phenomenon was called **generalization**, and to Pavlov it had clear adaptive advantages. In nature, we rarely if ever encounter exactly the same stimulus twice; even a human face is never viewed from exactly the same angle or in exactly the same light. It is crucial, therefore, that a response is not restricted to the precise stimulus encountered on conditioning trials – if you became ill after eating a toadstool, for example, you would be wise to avoid similar toadstools, not just those that were of exactly the same size.

Discrimination

In some situations, however, it might be very important *not* to respond in the same way to similar stimuli. The optimum response to a mushroom, for example, is not the same as to a toadstool. To test whether his dogs could learn to distinguish, or discriminate, between similar stimuli, Pavlov tried pairing a tone with food many hundreds of times, to see if salivation would eventually become more sharply focused on the precise stimulus that was being presented. Simple repetition, however, did not sharpen control much. Pavlov found that a much more effective procedure was *discrimination training* in which conditioning trials with a positive stimulus (CS+) were alternated with presentations of a negative stimulus (CS−).

$$CS+ \rightarrow food$$
$$CS- \rightarrow \underline{\quad\quad}$$

In a typical experiment, a 1,000-Hz tone would be presented and followed by food on half the trials; on the remaining trials, selected at random, a 900-Hz tone would be presented without food. The typical results of such an experiment are shown in Figure 2.8. At first the subjects responded to both stimuli, as responding conditioned to CS+ generalized to CS−. As training continued, responding was

[2] The pitch of a tone is determined by the frequency with which its basic sound pattern is repeated each second. Frequency is measured in units called hertz (Hz), where one Hz equals one cycle per second.

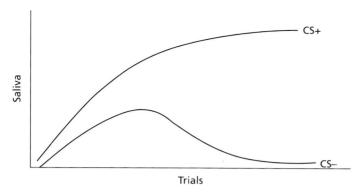

Figure 2.8 Idealized representation of discrimination learning. On half the trials, a tone was followed by food (CS+); on the remaining trials, a different tone was presented which was not followed by food (CS−).

increasingly restricted to CS+. The subjects had learned to discriminate, or respond differentially to, the two stimuli.

As with many other terms in learning, the term **discrimination** can be used in several different ways, although the core meaning is similar in each case. In perhaps the most common usage, we say that someone discriminates between two stimuli if he or she responds differently to the stimuli. However, the term is also sometimes used to refer to the procedure that produces this outcome (repeated presentations of two stimuli, only one of which is followed by the US), or to the process in the brain assumed to generate this behavior. These different meanings are potentially confusing, but in most cases the intended meaning is clear from the context.

Second-order conditioning

Once a response had been conditioned to a CS, Pavlov found that he could then use that CS to condition the response to yet another stimulus. In one demonstration, a dog was first given conditioning trials in which a metronome was paired with food. Then, once the metronome elicited salivation reliably, food presentations were discontinued and a black square was paired with the metronome:

1. metronome $\rightarrow$ food
2. black square $\rightarrow$ metronome

After several trials, the black square also began to elicit salivation, even though it had never been followed by food. Pavlov called this phenomenon **second-order conditioning** and considered it to be the outcome of a double associative chain, from the square to the metronome, and then from the metronome to food. (See Rescorla, 1980a, for an alternative interpretation.)

Counterconditioning

In addition to extinction, Pavlov discovered another way to eliminate a conditioned response, which was to pair the CS that elicited it with a US that elicited a different response. If the new response is incompatible with the old one, so that only one of them can occur at a time, then the more strongly the new response is conditioned the less likely it is that the old response will occur again. This technique has become known as **counterconditioning**. Pavlov provided a particularly dramatic demonstration of its power by showing that it could be used to suppress even unconditioned responses. In one experiment, he used an electric shock that normally elicited violent escape reactions and repeatedly followed it with presentations of food. Provided that the intensity of the shock employed was not too severe, he found that the dogs' normal defensive reactions were eventually suppressed almost entirely. Rather than jumping or showing any signs of discomfort on being shocked, a dog's only visible reaction was "turning its head to where it usually received the food and smacking its lips, at the same time producing a profuse secretion of saliva" (Pavlov, 1927, p. 30).

What behaviors can be conditioned?

We've seen that news of Pavlov's discoveries was greeted with great excitement. Among psychologists, this was because of the hope that conditioning could be used to understand the brain. By studying salivation, it might be possible to understand the processes involved in the formation of neural connections, and in this way to understand the fundamental mechanism that underlies virtually every aspect of human behavior. The public's fascination, though, was not based on the prospect of a better understanding of the brain, and certainly not on any profound (hitherto untapped) interest in salivation. Salivation was interesting not in its own right but because it was an *involuntary* behavior. Descartes was the first to distinguish between voluntary behavior, which he believed was controlled by the soul, and involuntary or reflexive behavior, which was not. If someone asked you to raise your right hand, for example, you could easily do so if you were disposed to be cooperative, but if he asked you to salivate, with the best will in the world you would struggle to comply. And yet here was Pavlov able to make a dog salivate anytime he wished. If his techniques would work with salivation, was it possible that conditioning could be used to control *any* involuntary behavior, or perhaps even voluntary behavior? Could his methods be used to control every aspect of our behavior, every muscle and every gland?

It is this question that we will now examine, as we consider what behaviors can be conditioned. To anticipate a bit, we will see that conditioning does indeed influence a remarkably wide range of our behaviors, and probably plays a crucial role in our lives without our realizing it. As we shall see, though, it does not allow the manipulation of people's behavior in quite the manner initially hoped or feared.

The need for control groups

One of the first attempts to extend classical conditioning to other responses was reported by John B. Watson, the founder of behaviorism. Watson believed that psychologists should be concerned with overt behavior rather than the hidden processes of the mind, and he argued for a greater concern with practical applications. Thus, in 1920, together with Rosalie Raynor, Watson set out to discover whether fear could be classically conditioned in humans in the same way as salivation was conditioned in dogs.

Little Albert

Their subject was a 9-month-old infant; his name was given in their published paper as Albert B., though he was later immortalized as Little Albert. Albert was normally a "stolid and unemotional" infant who almost never cried. As the first step in their experiment, Watson and Raynor presented Albert with a white rat and found that it elicited no signs of fear; Albert's only discernible reaction was an attempt to play with the animal. They then began conditioning trials in which every presentation of the white rat was followed by a loud noise that had previously been found to elicit strong fear. Almost immediately, Albert began to show signs of distress on presentation of the rat, and these signs increased over succeeding trials. When they presented the rat on the eighth trial, they recorded Albert's behavior as follows:

The instant the rat was shown the baby began to cry. Almost instantly he turned sharply to the left, fell over on left side, raised himself on all fours and began to crawl away so rapidly that he was caught with difficulty before reaching the edge of the table.

(Watson and Raynor, 1920, p. 5)

This fear reaction also generalized to similar stimuli that, before conditioning, had been neutral (for example, a rabbit and a fur coat). Albert's fear reaction showed no signs of fading with time and was still present on a test trial given almost a month later. The experiment had to be terminated at this point because Albert's mother ceased working at the hospital where they had been testing him.

The results they obtained were very convincing: After only seven conditioning trials, Albert's reaction to the rat was converted from one of mild curiosity to one of apparent terror. But could the change in Albert's behavior really be attributed to classical conditioning?

The essential element of Pavlov's procedure seems to be that behavior changes because of the pairing of two stimuli, a CS and a US. But was the change in Albert's behavior really due to the pairing of the white rat with the loud noise?

You might be struggling to make sense of this question, because the answer seems so obvious. The rat was paired with the noise, and the result was a dramatic transformation in Albert's behavior. True enough, pairing of these stimuli was followed by a change in behavior, but this doesn't necessarily mean that the pairing was actually the *cause* of that change. If one event is followed by another – if, for example, your turning the page of a book you are reading is closely followed by a bolt of lightning striking your house – this doesn't necessarily mean that the first event is the cause of the second. And similarly in Watson and Raynor's experiment, the fact that pairing of the stimuli was followed by a change in Albert's behavior doesn't necessarily mean that the pairing caused the change. Perhaps some other factor was responsible. And later research established that there really were other possible explanations.

Sensitization

One such explanation is that Albert's fear increased simply because of the repeated presentations of the rat. This might seem very unlikely: If the rat did not elicit fear initially, why should repeatedly presenting it by itself endow it with the capacity to do so? The first point to note is that this explanation is possible even if it doesn't seem very likely. As we saw in Chapter 1, explanations that initially seem wildly implausible sometimes turn out to be correct. In this case, moreover, there is evidence that such effects really can occur. In one experiment by Davis (1974), rats received repeated presentations of a tone. Initially, each tone presentation caused a startle response, but with repetitions this startle response diminished in magnitude (**habituation**). In a second experiment, Davis exposed his rats to exactly the same sequence of tones, but this time with an 80-db. noise present throughout the experiment. Under these conditions the startle response to the tone became *stronger* over trials. Such an increase in the strength of a reflexive response when a stimulus is repeated is called **sensitization**.

Why should the presence of a loud background noise reverse the effects of repeating a tone? For our current purposes, the explanation doesn't really matter – the crucial point is that sensitization can occur – but Groves and Thompson (1970) have proposed an explanation in terms of arousal. When we are asleep, our arousal level is low, and any stimulation will produce only a muted response. When we are awake, we respond to stimuli more strongly, and the greater our arousal, the more vigorously we tend to respond. When a loud noise was added in Davis's experiment, its continuous presence caused a steady increase in the rats' level of arousal, and this in turn amplified their response to the tone. Returning to the Watson and Raynor experiment, if the rat did elicit a small amount of fear initially, it is entirely possible that it was simply the repeated presentations of the rat that increased Albert's fear (perhaps because the experimental situation was itself inducing increasing levels of arousal), not the pairings of the rat with the loud noise.

Pseudoconditioning

Another possible explanation of Albert's fear is that it was caused by repeated presentations of the loud noise. We know that the noise frightened Albert; perhaps Albert became increasingly anxious as training continued, until eventually any unexpected stimulus would frighten him. Albert's fear, in other words, could have been caused simply by repeated presentations of the noise, rather than by the pairing of the rat with the noise. Even if the noise had only been presented on its own, Albert might still have become frightened when the rat was presented.

This may sound implausible, but again there is evidence from other experiments for precisely such effects. In a study of eyeblink conditioning by Kimble, Mann, and Dufort (1955), adults received sixty pairings of a light (the CS) with a puff of air to the eye (the US). A control group received the identical treatment for the first twenty trials, but on trials 21–40 they received only the US. Finally, on trials 41–60 they again received paired presentations.

Trials	Experimental group	Control group
1–20	CS → US	CS → US
21–40	CS → US	US
41–60	CS → US	CS → US

How much should responding to the CS increase during trials 21–40? The experimental group received 20 pairings of the CS and the US during this period, whereas the control group received only the US. If pairing is important, responding to the CS should increase in the experimental group; if presentation of the US by itself can increase responding to a CS, then responding should also increase in the control group. As shown in Figure 2.9, the rather remarkable result was that responding not only increased in the control group, it increased just as much as in the experimental group.

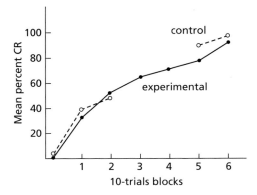

Figure 2.9 Pseudoconditioning. The experimental group received 60 pairings of a light with an air puff; the control group received CS–US pairings on trials 1–20 and 41–60 but only the air puff was presented during the intervening trials. (Adapted from Kimble, Mann, and Dufort, 1955.)

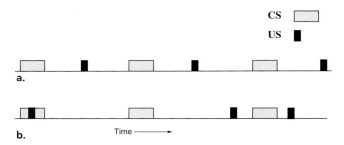

Figure 2.10 Control groups for classical conditioning: (a) the unpaired control; (b) the random control.

An increase in responding to a CS caused by presentations of a US by itself is called **pseudoconditioning**, and it is perhaps not as mysterious as it might seem. In the case of eyeblink conditioning, puffs of air to the eye are likely to dry the eye, making it more likely that subjects will blink whenever any sudden stimulus is presented. (For another possible explanation, see Wickens and Wickens, 1942.)

Returning to the Watson and Raynor experiment, Albert's fear might have been because he associated the rat with the noise, but it also might have been caused by repeated exposure to the rat (sensitization) or the noise (pseudoconditioning). To demonstrate classical conditioning, we need to be sure that any increase in responding is caused by *pairing* of the CS with the US, not just to presentation of one of these stimuli.

One way to satisfy this requirement is to use an **unpaired control** – a group in which the CS and the US are presented at widely separated times (Figure 2.10a). Subjects in an unpaired control receive the same number of CS and US presentations as experimental subjects who receive normal conditioning, but the presentations are arranged so that the CS and US never occur together. If pairing of a CS and a US produces an association, then the experimental group should respond more; if responding is due simply to the combined effects of receiving the CS and US separately, then responding in the two groups will be equal.

Still another possibility is to use a **random control** group – a group in which the CS and the US are presented at entirely random intervals, with no relationship between them. In this group, the US might sometimes precede the CS, sometimes follow the US, and sometimes even occur during the CS (Figure 2.10b). In the random control, therefore, the CS and the US will sometimes occur together, purely by chance. Overall, though, there is no relationship between the two stimuli: The US occurs just as often in the absence of the CS as in its presence.

The analysis we have been pursuing might seem rather technical – does the precise design of the control group really matter? And the short answer is: yes.

Suppose, for example, that a study reported that Aids can be cured through a therapy based on conditioning. It would clearly be vital to know whether the treatment's effectiveness was really due to conditioning, and this could be done only if the study included appropriate controls for other explanations. Most applications of conditioning are not quite this dramatic, but we shall shortly encounter evidence that conditioning influences behaviors as fundamental as fear, sexual arousal, and craving for drugs. To evaluate this evidence, we must know whether the results are truly due to conditioning.

Selecting the right control group, though, is not easy. As discussed in Chapter 1, what control group we use depends on what explanation we are trying to evaluate, and as our knowledge of a phenomenon increases, our understanding of the processes involved inevitably changes. In the case of classical conditioning, it did not occur to early researchers that presentations of the CS or US on their own could affect responding; when these possibilities were recognized, the unpaired control group was developed. Rescorla (1967) then identified another process that might be important in conditioning (see our later discussion of *contingency*), and, because the unpaired control did not control for this process, he advocated replacement of the unpaired control by the random control. The random control was soon widely adopted, but more recent research has made it clear that it too fails to control for some processes, leading some researchers to advocate a return to the unpaired control! (See, for example, Domjan, 2003.) The problem, in essence, is that no one control group can control for all possible explanations; which control group you use depends on which explanation you want to eliminate.

Although this back-and-forth might at first appear rather messy and chaotic, it actually reflects an increasingly sophisticated understanding of conditioning. On the surface a conditioning experiment couldn't be simpler – we just pair a CS and a US – but it turns out that each of these stimuli has multiple consequences, and disentangling the processes involved has proved far from straightforward. (For further discussion see Gormezano, Kehoe, and Marshall, 1983; Williams, Overmier, and LoLordo, 1992; Papini and Bitterman, 1993; Rescorla, 2000.) For the moment, though, let us stop beating this not-quite-dead horse and accept that for our purposes both the unpaired and the random control provide useful tools for assessing conditioning. Armed with these tools, we can now return to the question of what behaviors can be conditioned.

Autonomic and skeletal responses

One way of categorizing responses is by the subsystem of the nervous system that controls them. Two semi-independent systems are involved in transmitting impulses from the central nervous system to other parts of the body. The *skeletal nervous system* controls striped muscles, so called because their alternating bands of dark and light fibers give them a striated, or striped, appearance when examined under a microscope. Most of the muscles we think of when we hear the word *muscle* – biceps, triceps, deltoids, and so on – are actually striped muscles, whose function is to adjust the position of the body in space. The *autonomic nervous system*, on the other hand, controls the smooth muscles and glands, which are involved in regulation of the internal environment. Smooth muscles, as you might imagine, have a uniform or smooth appearance under the microscope; they are responsible for movements within the body. Rhythmic contractions of the smooth muscles lining the gullet, for example, are responsible for the movement of food from the mouth to the stomach (contractions known as peristalsis); glands secrete chemical substances such as adrenaline and saliva.

The skeletal nervous system is thus responsible for coping with the external environment through bodily movement, whereas the autonomic nervous system regulates the internal milieu. The bodily movements controlled by the skeletal nervous system are called **skeletal responses**; the glandular and smooth muscle activities controlled by the autonomic nervous system are called **autonomic responses**. We will begin our discussion by looking at some examples of autonomic behaviors that can be conditioned, and then turn to the possibility of conditioning skeletal responses.

Arousal

When we encounter new or stressful situations, our bodies prepare for action through a complex set of responses known collectively as arousal. The adrenal gland secretes the hormone adrenaline, heart rate increases, blood pressure changes, and so on. One component of arousal is perspiration, and we can measure this component by passing a very small electrical current through the skin and measuring the current that is transmitted. The skin's conductivity defines the galvanic skin response, or GSR, which is thus just a measure of perspiration: The more we perspire, the more readily our skin conducts an electric current. By measuring perspiration, therefore, the GSR gives us a simple index of a person's arousal. (The GSR is also sometimes referred to as the *skin conductance response*, or SCR.)

Because it measures arousal, the GSR has been of considerable interest to psychologists. It can be used to assess concentration – the harder subjects concentrate, the more aroused they might become – and also the presence of emotions. The GSR is used as the main component of polygraph, or lie detector, tests: When people are lying, they tend to become aroused, so that by measuring the GSR we can obtain indirect evidence about whether someone is lying.

(It is important to emphasize, however, that polygraph tests are very far from infallible. The fact that someone becomes aroused when asked an incriminating question does not necessarily mean that the person is lying; the person might just be embarrassed or frightened.)

The important point in the present context is that arousal, as measured by the GSR, is readily conditioned. If a person receives a mild electric shock, for example, arousal occurs; if this shock is preceded by a tone, the tone will also acquire the capacity to elicit the GSR. Champion and Jones (1961) have shown that this increase is genuinely the result of classical conditioning: If the tone and shock are presented separately, in an unpaired control group, the GSR to the tone does not increase.

Blood sugar levels

A central concept in understanding the activities of the autonomic nervous system is **homeostasis.** In order to survive, we have to maintain a stable environment within our bodies. For example, we need to maintain the body's temperature at a constant level; deviations in any direction, either up or down, can have lethal consequences. In a similar way, our bodies act to maintain constant levels of water, energy, and so on. Systems that are organized in this way, to maintain constant environments, are said to be homeostatic.

The autonomic nervous system plays a key role in maintaining stable conditions, and research has suggested that many of these autonomic responses can be conditioned. Instead of waiting until an external stimulus produces potentially dangerous changes within the body, conditioning allows the body to anticipate these changes and initiate processes that will counteract them. One example concerns glucose levels in the blood. Glucose is a form of sugar, and it provides the energy for activity within our cells. It is thus vital that adequate levels of glucose be maintained. To find out if the processes involved could be conditioned, Siegel (1972) gave rats injections of insulin, a hormone that reduces the amount of glucose in the blood. Pavlov had hypothesized that the physical cues associated with the act of injecting a drug would act as conditioned stimuli, with the effects of the drug within the body then becoming conditioned to these cues. To find out if this had happened, Siegel now gave his subjects a test injection of saline, a neutral fluid that normally has no effect.

As predicted, the saline injection elicited a strong conditioned response, but this proved to be an *increase* in blood glucose, rather than the decrease produced by the insulin. Appropriate controls showed that saline on its own does not have this effect; the increase was due to the earlier pairings of the act of injection with insulin.

Why was the conditioned response in this case the opposite of the unconditioned response, when in every other example of classical conditioning we have encountered the two responses were the same? The answer, according to Eikelboom and Stewart (1982), is that the conditioned and unconditioned responses in this situation *are* the same – it is just that we need to identify the unconditioned response correctly. When insulin is injected, it produces a fall in blood glucose below the optimal level; when the body senses this fall, it reacts by increasing glucose levels. It is this *compensatory response* that is conditioned; by taking compensatory action in advance of a disturbance, the body can minimize the disruption that is caused (see also Siegel, 2005).

Pain

Siegel (1975) also investigated whether the effects of morphine can be conditioned. Morphine is one of the most effective painkillers, or analgesic drugs, that we have. With repeated administration, however, morphine loses its potency, a phenomenon known as *tolerance*. The reason for this loss of potency, Siegel suggested, was classical conditioning. As far as a person in pain is concerned, any reduction in pain is highly desirable, but from the body's point of view, the morphine is interfering with the pain system that protects us by ensuring that we *do* react to harmful experiences by feeling pain. Thus, when an injection of morphine reduces pain, the body responds with an increased sensitivity to pain, or *hyperalgesia*, to return sensitivity to its appropriate, homeostatic level. Siegel hypothesized that this compensatory, hyperalgesic reaction would be conditioned to the cues of being injected. Every time the morphine was administered, the conditioned hyperalgesic response would become stronger, and this would explain why the morphine loses its effectiveness: The analgesic effect of the morphine is opposed by the conditioned hyperalgesic response.

To test this hypothesis, Siegel gave rats a series of morphine injections. If a compensatory reaction had been conditioned to the cues of being injected, then a test injection of saline should now cause an increase in the rats' sensitivity to pain, rather than decreasing it as morphine does. To measure pain sensitivity, Siegel used an ingeniously simple technique in which he placed the rats on a moderately hot metal plate and recorded the time until the rats licked their paws; the greater their pain sensitivity, the sooner they would lick their paws. Rats who had previously received morphine, he found, were more sensitive to pain following a saline test injection, and appropriate controls established that this was the result of conditioning. (For comparable results in humans, see Flor *et al.*, 2002.)

Siegel found that this compensatory reaction was conditioned not only to the injection but also to the room in which the injection was given: Pain sensitivity was greater in the room where morphine had been administered than in other rooms. This effect, moreover, can be very powerful. Tiffany, Maude-Griffin, and Drobes (1991) repeatedly injected rats with morphine in a distinctive environment. When they later tested pain sensitivity in that environment following an injection of morphine, they found that rats previously injected in that environment required six times as much morphine as control rats did to produce a set level of analgesia.

Siegel has suggested that the conditioning of compensatory reactions to environmental cues could also explain drug overdoses (for example, Siegel, 2001). As implied by the very term "overdose," it has long been assumed that such deaths are caused by addicts injecting a much larger amount of heroin than they normally use. Post-mortems, however, have shown that levels of morphine in victims' blood are generally no higher than in other addicts (for example, Monforte, 1977). Siegel therefore suggested that the main cause of these deaths might be taking heroin in an unfamiliar setting. He suggested that heroin elicited compensatory reactions as the body tried to defend itself, and that these compensatory responses would be conditioned to the environment in which the heroin is injected. If the addict then takes heroin in a new setting, the conditioned compensatory reaction will be weaker and the effects of the heroin correspondingly magnified.

To evaluate this hypothesis, Siegel (1984) interviewed individuals who had survived heroin overdoses; he found that 70% had taken their heroin in an unfamiliar setting. Additional evidence comes from a study by Siegel *et al.* (1982) in which rats received daily injections of heroin to develop their tolerance and were then given a greatly increased dose. Of the rats given the overdose in the same environment as earlier injections, 32% died. If the overdose was administered in a different environment, however, 64% of the subjects succumbed.

On a perhaps lighter note, the effects of alcohol also seem to be influenced by conditioning. In one study by Remington, Roberts, and Glautier (1997), British college students who consumed alcohol in a novel form – a blue, peppermint-flavored beverage – were far more impaired on subsequent cognitive and motor tasks than students who consumed exactly the same amount of alcohol in a form much more familiar to them, a glass of beer. In the case of alcohol as in the case of heroin, cues associated with consumption may come to elicit reactions that reduce the alcohol's impact. (Should any practical applications of this principle occur to you, you should of course ignore them.)

Skeletal responses

We have reviewed only a small sample of the autonomic responses that have been conditioned. The full list is very long, and it now looks as if a high proportion of the behaviors controlled by the autonomic nervous system, perhaps even all, can be conditioned. What, then, of skeletal responses? Can they also be conditioned?

The answer is yes, but in this case the list is much smaller. The problem is that conditioning requires an unconditioned stimulus capable of eliciting the desired behavior, and the number of skeletal responses that can be elicited in this reflexive way is relatively small. Where a suitable US exists – for example, a puff of air that elicits an eyeblink – then skeletal responses can be conditioned, but most skeletal behaviors – walking, pushing a button, driving a car – cannot. Novels in which the protagonist is conditioned to assassinate the President when he hears a secret word are thus exactly what they seem, fiction.

Conditioning motives and emotions

Conditioning cravings

The skeletal and autonomic responses we have examined so far have all involved relatively discrete, easily specified responses such as salivation, blinking, and per-spiration. In some cases, however, the conditioned response appears to be a moti-vational state that can lead to any of a wide range of responses.

Hunger

To illustrate this distinction between a specific response and a motivational state, consider the following experiment by Weingarten (1983). Seven hungry rats were exposed to repeated pairings of a 4.5-minute tone with the presentation of food. Then, in a test phase, the rats were given continuous access to food so that they were sated. Nevertheless, when the tone was again presented, they immediately began to eat, consuming approximately 20% of their normal daily ration within a short period. A CS that had been paired with food, in other words, seemed to acquire the capacity to elicit hunger, so that the rats would eat whenever the CS was presented.

Similar effects have since been reported in research on humans. In one study, participants were exposed to their favorite snack foods for several minutes and then given an opportunity to eat. Participants' self-reports of how hungry they felt more than doubled following exposure to the snacks, and not surprisingly those who reported the greatest hunger also ate the most (Nederkoorn *et al.*, 2004). You may have experienced a comparable phenomenon in passing a bakery, where the smell of freshly baked bread suddenly made you feel hungry. Simply seeing or smelling a favorite food seems to trigger an urge to eat, a general motivational state that can be satisfied by any of a wide range of specific behaviors, such as buying the bread or hurrying home to prepare a meal.

In addition to influencing when we feel hungry, classical conditioning also affects what foods we choose to satisfy that hunger. We tend to assume that our food preferences are innate, and up to a point this is so – infants, for example, have an innate preference for sweet tastes over bitter ones. In some cases, though, the nutritive properties of food are not signaled by obvious properties such as sweetness, and in these cases learning – and in particular, conditioning – seems to play an important role. As one example, rats have been shown to develop a preference for foods that are high in calories. In one experiment by Capaldi *et al.* (1987), rats were given a liquid with a distinctive flavour and then, 30 minutes later, a meal. The greater the caloric value of the meal, the more the rats preferred that flavor in a later choice test. (See also Tarner, Frieman, and Mehiel, 2004.)

Finally, conditioning can also induce satiety: If a stimulus that has been associated with high-calorie meals is presented to rats while they are eating, they will reduce how much they eat. It thus appears that conditioning influences almost every aspect of eating, from when we feel hungry to what foods we choose to satisfy this hunger to when we stop eating. (For reviews, see Rozin and Zellner, 1985; Capaldi, 1996.)

Sexual arousal

There is also evidence that sexual arousal can be conditioned. Many experiments have demonstrated the conditioning of sexual behavior in animals (see Domjan and Holloway, 1997, for a review), and this research eventually led to attempts to see if sexual arousal could also be conditioned in humans. In one early experiment, Rachman and Hodgson (1968) recruited seven males to serve as subjects. The unconditioned stimuli used to produce sexual arousal were 40 slides of nude women. Each slide was preceded by a CS, a picture of knee-length, black, fur-lined boots. The picture of the boots was projected for 30 seconds, followed by 10 seconds of one of the nude slides. To assess sexual arousal, penile erection was measured by means of a rubber tube whose stretching could be monitored by an automatic recording system.

Initially, none of the subjects showed any sign of arousal to the boots. After only 30 pairings, however, strong arousal had been conditioned in five of the seven subjects, with an erection occurring every time the boots were presented. This response, moreover, generalized to similar stimuli: Three of the subjects also became aroused to brown fur boots, two to high-heeled black shoes, but none to low-heeled black shoes or sandals. At the conclusion of the experiment, sexual arousal to the boots was extinguished by repeatedly presenting the boots by themselves.

This experiment might arouse mixed feelings – the thought of males now being aroused by the sight of black boots is almost sinister in some ways, hilarious in others. On its own, though, it is not conclusive, because there was no control group to confirm that the observed change was due to pairing of the CS and the US. A later study by Plaud and Martini (1999) remedied this defect by including a random control; the results confirmed that sexual arousal can be conditioned in males. This finding was further extended in an experiment by Hoffmann, Janssen, and Turner (2004); the authors showed that sexual arousal can be conditioned in females as well as males, and also raised the intriguing possibility that such conditioning can occur without a person's awareness. The CS was a photograph of the abdomen of a member of the opposite sex, and the US was a 30-second excerpt from an erotic movie. To ensure that participants would not be aware of the CS, it was presented for only 30 ms, a period too short for conscious detection. These brief presentations did seem to prevent awareness – when interviewed later, none of the participants reported having seen the CS. Despite this, over trials there was a significant increase in sexual arousal when the CS was presented in the conditioning group; no such increase occurred in an unpaired control. (See also Hoffman, 2011.)

There are still very few studies in this area, and we thus need to treat this evidence with some caution. If confirmed, though, it could have important implications. If sexual arousal is conditioned to the stimuli present when we become aroused, this could affect what stimuli we find exciting in the future. For example, conditioning of this kind could play an important role in the development of abnormal behaviors such as fetishes. In one case reported by McGuire, Carlisle, and Young (1965), a 17-year-old male saw a girl dressed only in her underwear through a window. Thereafter, he often masturbated while recalling this image and eventually developed a strong sexual obsession with female underwear, which he bought or stole. We don't know whether all fetishes develop in this way, but it is possible that classical conditioning plays a role in channeling our sexual desires.

Cravings for drugs

Further evidence for the conditioning of motivational states has come from research on addictive drugs. For many years, anecdotal evidence suggested that stimuli that are associated with the consumption of drugs can arouse intense cravings for these substances. Cigarette smokers, for example, often report a strong desire to smoke on returning to locations where they typically smoke, and similar effects have been reported in heroin and cocaine users.

To study this phenomenon in a more controlled situation, Bonson *et al.* (2002) studied cravings for cocaine in a laboratory setting. In one session, cocaine addicts were shown a videotape of other addicts taking cocaine, together with items used in taking cocaine, such as a crack pipe and a razor blade. In a second, control session, the addicts saw a videotape about art, together with items such as a paintbrush and paper. At the end of each session, they were asked to rate their craving for cocaine on a scale from 1 to 10, where 1 represented no craving and 10 an extreme craving. The average rating at the end of the control session was 1.4; at the end of the cocaine-cue session it was 5.1. Seeing cues associated with drug use clearly had a substantial impact on craving.

Similar results have been reported for drugs such as alcohol and cigarettes. In one study by Droungas, Ehrman, Childress, and O'Brien (1995), cigarette smokers were shown either a videotape during which participants smoked, a nature documentary, or a film on industrial safety that included material on distressing accidents. At the conclusion of each session, they were asked to rate their moods, and they were then taken to a waiting room where they were given an opportunity to smoke while they believed themselves to be unobserved. Subjects reported a significantly stronger desire to smoke after seeing the smoking video, and when given an opportunity they began smoking much sooner.

If the urge to drink or smoke is in part conditioned, it follows that it should be possible to use extinction as part of therapeutic treatments to help individuals who want to give up drinking or smoking. In one test of this possibility, Collins and Brandon (2002) recruited college students who were moderate-to-heavy drinkers for a study. In the first phase they were asked to sniff a cup containing beer and then to rate their urge to drink. The rating scale ranged from 0 to 6, with 6 representing the maximum possible urge; the average rating was approximately 2.5. Participants were then given 7–10 trials in which they were exposed to the sight and smell of the beer for approximately one minute at a time. They were asked to rate their urge to drink at the end of each trial; by the end of this phase, the average rating had fallen from 2.5 to 1.7. The desire to drink had not been eliminated – not surprising, considering how long the habit had been established – but just a few extinction trials did produce a significant reduction in the urge to drink.

In addition to testing whether the urge to drink could be reduced through exposure to alcohol-related cues, the study also examined the role of contextual cues in this process. In our earlier discussion of extinction we saw that the effects in rats are partly specific to the setting in which extinction occurs. To determine if that would also be the case with humans, the authors asked participants to evaluate their urge to drink one final time. This final evaluation was conducted either in the same room as the extinction trials or in a different room. When the test was in the same room, the urge to drink remained low: Participants rated their desire for a drink as 1.7 in both contexts. When the test was conducted in a different room, however, the urge to drink increased to 2.6, almost the same as it had been before extinction. Confirming Bouton's findings in rats, the effects of extinction seemed to be confined to the room in which it occurred.

In a final, clever twist, the authors also ran a third group which, like the second group, was tested in a new room. However, the test room now contained a distinctive cue that had been present throughout the extinction trials, namely a green plastic clipboard and an unusual pen. (They had been used for completing the rating forms during extinction.) The authors' reasoning was that if the test environment resembled the extinction environment more closely, the effects of extinction would be more likely to generalize, and that was indeed the result: When the pen and clipboard were present, the urge to drink remained low. In practical terms, this study suggests that extinction of cravings could play a useful role as part of a wider program for treating addiction, but that such programs need to ensure that cravings are extinguished not only in the therapeutic setting but also more widely. (For further discussion of the role of conditioning in addiction, see Lowman, Hunt, Litten, and Drummond, 2000; Siegel *et al.*, 2000; Drobes, Saladin, and Tiffany, 2001; MacKillop and Lisman, 2005.)

Conditioning aversions

Just as stimuli associated with attractive outcomes can motivate behavior to obtain these outcomes, stimuli associated with harmful outcomes can arouse motives directed toward avoiding these outcomes.

Fear

One example is fear. If a child is bitten by a dog, encountering that dog again would be likely to arouse intense fear, which would then motivate behavior to get away from it.

To study the processes involved, we first need some way to measure fear, and one useful solution is the GSR. However, the GSR is really a measure of arousal rather than fear per se, so that increases in the GSR don't necessarily indicate fear. Also, for ethical reasons most GSR studies have been restricted to relatively mild aversive stimuli, and the results are thus not necessarily a good guide to how fear would develop in more traumatic situations.

To overcome these limitations, many studies of fear conditioning have used rats as subjects. Fear has been measured using the **conditioned emotional response**

(CER) procedure, a technique developed by Estes and Skinner (1941). The first step in this procedure is to train the rats to press a bar to obtain food. At first, the rats receive a pellet of food for every press, but the proportion of responses that produce food is gradually reduced, until eventually the rats will press the bar steadily, without pausing, for long periods. At this point, the experimenters can present the conditioned stimulus that they want to test. When rats in a confined space are frightened, they tend to freeze, with the result that they are less likely to press the bar. By counting the number of bar-presses made in the presence of the test stimulus, therefore, we obtain a simple and objective measure of the rats' fear.

In practice, a more useful index of fear is obtained by calculating a statistic known as a **suppression ratio**. If a tone is presented for three minutes, for example, we count the number of bar-presses that occur not only during the tone (B) but also during the preceding three minutes (A). The suppression ratio is then defined as

$$\text{suppression ratio} = \frac{B}{A + B}$$

Suppose, for example, that a rat responded 50 times during the period before the tone was presented. If the tone were not frightening, the rat would continue to respond at roughly the same rate in its presence, so that it would also respond 50 times during period B. The suppression ratio would thus be

$$\frac{B}{A + B} = \frac{50}{50 + 50} = 0.5$$

If, on the other hand, the tone elicited fear, the rat would freeze for as long as the tone was on, yielding a suppression ratio of

$$\frac{B}{A + B} = \frac{0}{50 + 0} = 0$$

We thus have a somewhat unusual measure in which a lower score represents greater fear, with 0 representing the maximum measurable fear and 0.50 representing no fear.

Using the CER as a measure, many experiments have demonstrated that fear does become conditioned to stimuli that precede aversive events. To cite just one example, Annau and Kamin (1961) trained rats to press a bar to earn food, and then occasionally presented a 3-minute noise followed by an electric shock. Different groups received shock intensities varying from 0.28 to 2.91 milliamps; Figure 2.11 shows the suppression ratios for the different groups on successive conditioning trials.

The first time the noise was presented, on day 1, it produced no fear in any of the groups (a suppression ratio of 0.50). In the group that received a very mild shock (0.28 volts), this remained the case on subsequent days: Presentation of

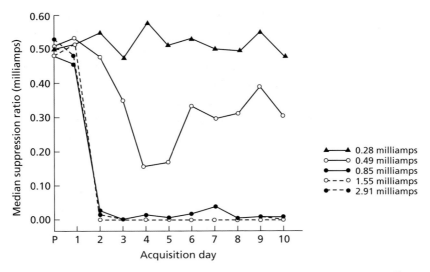

Figure 2.11 Acquisition of a conditioned emotional response (CER) over 10 days. Different groups received electrical shocks ranging in intensity from 0.28 milliamps to 2.91 milliamps. (Annau and Kamin, 1961.)

the noise had no effect on bar pressing, and the suppression ratio remained at 0.50. For subjects receiving 0.49 milliamps, responding was reduced by the noise, leading to a sharp fall in the suppression ratio. As training continued, however, the noise began to have less effect, and the suppression ratio began to increase. A noise paired with a mild shock, in other words, did induce fear at first, but with continued exposure subjects seemed to adapt to the shock and find it less frightening. Finally, when more severe shocks were used, a single conditioning trial was sufficient to suppress responding almost totally (the suppression ratio on trial 2 was close to 0), and it remained suppressed on subsequent trials. These results suggest that more intense shocks produce stronger conditioning of fear, and that this fear is more likely to endure.

Taste-aversion learning

Another situation in which negative states become conditioned involves illness. If you have ever had the experience of becoming ill after eating contaminated food, for example, you may have found that the nausea you experienced became associated with the food, so that tasting or even smelling that food in the future was enough to make you feel ill.

In one of the first experimental demonstrations of such **taste-aversion learning**, Garcia and Koelling (1966) began by offering rats a choice between two water bottles, one of which contained normal water and the other a water solution with a distinctive flavor. Once they had established that the rats had no preference between the two, they ran a conditioning phase in which the rats were allowed to drink the flavored water for 20 minutes and then were exposed to X-rays that would make them ill. After the rats had recovered, Garcia and Koelling again offered them a choice between the two solutions. They found that while the rats were still willing to drink the normal water, consumption of the flavored water that had been followed by illness was substantially reduced. It appeared that the aversive properties of illness had been conditioned to the taste that preceded it. (See the discussion of the adaptive value of preparedness in Chapter 3 for a fuller account of this study.)

In the Garcia and Koelling study, no direct measure of the conditioned response was available; the experimenters could only infer that the flavor made the rats feel ill from the fact that they refused to drink it. In some subsequent studies, however, this assumption has been confirmed more directly. In one dramatic study by Gustavson *et al.* (1974), coyotes were made ill after eating meat; the next time they were offered this meat, they all avoided it and some actually vomited.

These results suggest that the taste of the meat elicited a conditioned state of nausea. Moreover, other results suggest that tastes that are paired with illness can themselves become repugnant. In a survey by Logue, Ophir, and Strauss (1981), 65% of the college students interviewed reported at least one aversion to a food that had been acquired through association with illness, and of this subgroup 83% reported that the food tasted aversive. (See also Berridge, 2000.) Interestingly, many reported disliking this taste even though they knew that their illness had actually been caused by something else, such as the flu. Such results suggest that classical conditioning may not be a conscious or rational process: Even if we are confident that a CS will no longer be followed by a US – that eating a certain food will not make us ill, or that new techniques mean that going to a dentist will not be painful – the CS might still elicit feelings of fear or nausea. We will discuss this possibility further in Chapter 3.

One particularly unfortunate situation in which taste-aversion learning is now thought to play a role is chemotherapy. Many cancer patients who receive chemotherapy lose weight, and it was generally assumed that this weight loss reflected a direct effect on metabolic processes. Bernstein (1978), however, suggested that at least part of this weight loss might be due to classical conditioning. Perhaps, she suggested, the foods eaten before each treatment become aversive through conditioning. As treatment continues, and more and more foods are followed by illness, patients' normal diet may increasingly elicit feelings of nausea, leading to the observed reduction in the amount eaten.

To test this hypothesis, Bernstein gave a group of cancer patients a distinctively flavored ice cream to eat one hour before undergoing chemotherapy. As predicted, they developed an aversion to this flavor. These results suggest that at least some of the weight loss caused by chemotherapy could be due to taste-aversion learning (see also Jacobsen *et al.*, 1993; Schafe and Bernstein, 1996). If so, it may prove possible to reduce this harmful effect in the future by applying conditioning principles – for example, by having patients eat a special diet before treatment sessions, so that conditioning will occur to this food rather than to the normal diet. (See Stockhorst *et al.*, 1998, for a successful application.)

Evaluative conditioning

One interesting aspect of taste-aversion learning is that it does not simply result in the taste eliciting nausea; it also seems to alter perceptions of the taste itself. Coyotes react with seeming repugnance to the taste of a food previously paired with illness, spitting it out; people report that the taste has become repulsive, so that even if they know that the food didn't really make them ill, they still can't stand its taste. Might this be a more general phenomenon? Could it be that whenever a US elicits emotional responses, these feelings become conditioned to the stimuli that are present? Or, put another way, is the CS simply a signal that the US is coming, or does conditioning change our feelings about the CS itself?

Evidence that conditioning does change our feelings about the CS comes from **evaluative conditioning**, a phenomenon in which the *hedonic value* of the US – the extent to which it causes us pleasure or pain – become transferred to stimuli that precede it. In one of the first studies of this phenomenon, Razran (1938) showed people photographs of female college students and asked them to evaluate each woman's beauty, intelligence, and likeability. Two weeks later participants were shown some of the photographs again, but this time while eating a free lunch (see also Razran, 1954). Finally, several hours later they were asked to evaluate the photographs again. The surprising result was that the women who had been seen while the judges were eating were rated as significantly more likeable and attractive.

Although this result provides gratifying support for one bit of folk wisdom – the way to a man's heart really is through his stomach – it is also perplexing. At a rational level it doesn't seem to make sense – surely we shouldn't judge people by whether we are eating when we meet them? It perhaps becomes more comprehensible, though, if thought of as part of a more general tendency to seek out situations where we experience pleasure and avoid situations where we experience pain. If you suffer in a certain environment, for example, it makes sense that you should develop an aversion to that environment and thus avoid it in the future. In this sense evaluative conditioning can be seen as just one more example of the conditioning of emotions; what it adds to earlier research is the suggestion that conditioning can result not just in elicitation of an emotion – feeling excited or fearful about some forthcoming event – but also a change in our liking of the CS itself.

Evaluative conditioning could influence our feelings about a very wide range of stimuli, from what foods we like to what political parties we support. Political parties often have patriotic music or the national flag in the background of rallies and advertisements, and they could be trying to capitalize on evaluative conditioning, with the positive emotions elicited by the music or the flag being subtly transferred to the candidate. (See Fazio and Olson, 2003, and Crano and Prislin, 2006, for further discussion.) However, the evidence for the existence of evaluative conditioning has been challenged. One problem is that the effects observed in the laboratory are often small. On the other hand, the unconditioned stimuli used in these studies are generally quite mild – for example, a picture of an ice cream sundae rather than a real sundae – and the number of pairings small. In real life, especially with more potent stimuli and more frequent pairings, the effects might be much stronger.

A further problem is that the early studies did not employ adequate controls, so that it was not clear whether their results were really due to conditioning – that is, to pairings of a CS with a US. (See Field and Davey, 1999, and Lovibond and Shanks, 2002, for discussions of this problem.) More recent studies have employed tighter controls, and the results have confirmed that changes in participants' evaluations of stimuli have been due to pairings of these stimuli with other, more attractive stimuli (for example, Stevenson, Boakes, and Prescott, 1998; Field and Moore, 2005; Vansteenwegen *et al.*, 2006). Thus while the issue is not yet entirely settled, it does currently look as if evaluative conditioning is a real phenomenon, and potentially an important one. (For a review, see De Houwer, Thomas, and Baeyens, 2001.)

Applications

By studying conditioning in the highly controlled environment of the laboratory, Pavlov and his successors hoped to be able to tease apart the complex processes involved in the formation of associations. The laboratory, though, was not an end in itself – the ultimate goal was always to apply the knowledge gained in the laboratory to helping people in real life. In this section, we will examine two attempts that have been made to apply conditioning principles, to phobias and alcoholism.

Phobias

The first speculations about the possibility of applying classical conditioning principles to practical problems appeared in the Watson and Raynor (1920) study in which they conditioned "Little Albert" to fear a white rat. At the end of their report, they suggested that fear conditioning in children of the kind that they had demonstrated might explain many of the phobias and anxieties found in adults. If so, then it should also be possible to use conditioning principles to eliminate these fears.

Systematic desensitization

One of their suggestions for eliminating fear was to associate the feared stimulus with a pleasurable experience, such as eating or sexual stimulation. The pleasant feelings elicited by these events would be incompatible with fear, they reasoned, so that if these reactions could be conditioned, then fear might be suppressed. This is, of course, the counterconditioning procedure originally described by Pavlov. The first human application of this strategy was in an experiment by Mary Cover Jones (1924). One of her subjects, a boy named Peter, was terrified of rabbits, and, following Watson and Raynor's suggestion, she resolved to introduce the rabbit while Peter was engaged in the pleasurable activity of eating.

She introduced the rabbit only gradually, on the eminently reasonable assumption that simply dropping the rabbit on to Peter's lap while he was eating would not have produced the desired effect. Instead, she introduced the rabbit gradually over a period of days, first keeping it at a distance and then moving it progressively closer to the boy's chair. The result was nothing short of spectacular, as Peter not only lost all fear of the rabbit but actively began to seek out opportunities to play with it.

Despite the impressive success of this treatment, there was little further research for 30 years. The next significant development was not until the mid 1950s, when Joseph Wolpe (1958) reported a therapy he had developed called **systematic desensitization**. Wolpe's technique was similar to that of Jones, except that he used relaxation rather than eating as the response to be conditioned. Also, instead of actually presenting the fear stimuli, he asked his patients to imagine the stimuli. A therapist using Wolpe's technique would ask patients to describe situations that frightened them and then would arrange these stimuli in a hierarchy based on how much fear they produced. A patient who had a fear of snakes, for example, might find the idea of looking at a toy snake to be only somewhat threatening. Other stimuli involving snakes would then be arranged in ascending order according to their fearfulness, until the most frightening situation was reached – perhaps picking up a live snake. The therapist would train the patient in special techniques to encourage deep relaxation (see Wolpe and Lazarus, 1966). Typically, a patient would start with the lowest stimulus in the hierarchy and visualize that frightening scene while trying to relax. Only when the patient reported complete relaxation while imagining that scene would the therapist ask the patient to visualize the next scene, and so on.

Wolpe reported remarkable success with this technique in eliminating phobias, and subsequent studies have largely confirmed his claims. In a study by Paul (1969), for example, students who had severe anxieties about public speaking were treated with either systematic desensitization or insight-oriented psychotherapy (which focuses on identifying the cause of the phobia). When examined two years later, 85% of those given desensitization showed significant improvement relative to pretreatment levels, compared with 50% in a psychotherapy group and only 22% in an untreated control group. The effectiveness of systematic desensitization varies depending on the phobia being treated, but it is one of the most effective treatments currently available for phobias involving specific objects such as snakes or blood, or activities such as flying (Borden, 1992; Thyer and Birsinger, 1994).

Exposure therapy

One limitation to the effectiveness of systematic desensitization is that the conditioned stimulus is imagined rather than experienced directly. In some cases, patients have overcome their fear of an imagined stimulus such as a snake only to find themselves still fearful when they encountered a snake in real life. To overcome this problem, many therapists now use an **exposure** treatment in which patients are exposed to the stimuli that actually frighten them. As in systematic desensitization, exposure is gradual, starting with situations that elicit minimal fear and advancing only gradually to more frightening situations. Patients are still encouraged to relax, but this element of the treatment typically receives less emphasis because of the difficulties of remaining fully relaxed while engaged in physical activities such as moving toward a snake. Exposure is thus closer to straightforward extinction, in contrast to systematic desensitization's emphasis on counterconditioning, but it too has proven very effective (for example, Öst, Stridh, and Wolf, 1998; Barlow, Raffa, and Cohen, 2002).

The origin of phobias

Watson and Raynor suggested that phobias are caused by conditioning, and thus that it should also be possible to eliminate them using conditioning principles such as extinction and counterconditioning. The success of systematic desensitization and exposure therapy has left little doubt about the value of conditioning principles in treating phobias, but there has been continuing controversy about the role of conditioning in *causing* phobias. When phobics have been interviewed to determine the origins of their phobias, some have been able to remember traumatic incidents that triggered their phobias but some have not. In a representative study by Öst and Hugdahl (1981), 58% of the phobics that were interviewed could recall traumatic incidents that triggered their phobias, but 42% could not.

Several explanations have been proposed to account for cases where phobias do not appear to be due to conditioning. In some cases, the cause appears to be *vicarious learning*, in which individuals learn that a stimulus is dangerous because they see someone else being injured. In one such case, a boy developed a severe dental phobia when he accompanied a friend to the dentist and the dentist's drill accidentally punctured his friend's cheek (Öst, 1985, cited by Barlow and Durand, 1995). These cases can be viewed as examples of conditioning, rather than exceptions, if we assume that animals and humans are innately programmed to become distressed when they see another member of their species hurt. If a young monkey sees his mother becoming frightened when she encounters a snake, for example, it would clearly be advantageous for the infant to learn to associate snakes with fear. In the course of evolution, the sight of others' distress could thus have become an unconditioned stimulus for anxiety – indeed, the boy who saw his friend injured became so distressed that he ran from the dentist's office. (For more direct evidence that the sight of others in distress can lead to the conditioning of fear, see Mineka and Cook, 1986, and Gerull and Rapee, 2002.)

What of cases in which phobics cannot recall *any* traumatic incident, whether involving themselves or others? One possibility is that such incidents occurred but were forgotten. This might at first seem implausible – surely someone who experienced a trauma severe enough to produce a phobia would remember it? – but people's memories for painful incidents are surprisingly poor. In one study cited by Loftus (1993), a survey of 1,500 people who had been hospitalized within the preceding year revealed that 25% could not recall this hospitalization! Moreover, memory seems to be particularly poor for incidents experienced when we are young, which is when many phobias develop. (See, for example, Henry *et al.*, 1994.)

The issue of how phobias arise is still controversial, but it does look as if a very substantial proportion of specific phobias – those involving specific stimuli such as snakes and spiders – are due to conditioning. (For divergent views on the possibility of other causes, see Mineka and Öhman, 2002, and Poulton and Menzies, 2002.)

Aversion therapy

A second major application of conditioning principles has been **aversion therapy**, in which the goal is not to eliminate fear but rather to harness it to produce avoidance of a harmful situation. This principle is by no means new, with some of the most imaginative – and gruesome – applications stemming from ancient times. Pliny the Elder, for example, recommended a treatment for alcoholism that consisted of covertly putting the putrid body of a dead spider in the bottom of the alcoholic's tankard. When the drinker would innocently tip the contents into his mouth, the resulting revulsion and nausea supposedly would deter him from ever drinking again. A somewhat more modern example (technically, at any rate) involved the treatment of a 14-year-old boy who wanted to give up smoking (Raymond, 1964). The boy was given injections of apomorphine, a drug that produces intense nausea, and each injection was timed so that it would take effect while the boy was in the middle of smoking.

On the first occasion he was given an injection of apomorphine 1/20g, and after seven minutes he was told to start smoking. At eleven minutes he became nauseated and vomited copiously. Four days later he came for the second treatment, and said that he still had the craving for cigarettes, but had not in fact smoked since the previous session because he felt nauseated when he tried to light one…Two months later he left school and started working. He said he had "got a bit down" at work and wanted to "keep in with the others," so he had accepted a proffered cigarette. He immediately felt faint and hot, and was unable to smoke. It is now a year since his treatment, and his parents confirm that he no longer smokes.

(Raymond, 1964, p. 290)

Although Raymond's results were highly impressive, early attempts to apply his procedures to problems such as smoking and alcoholism were less successful. In retrospect, the main problem in these early studies was probably the unconditioned stimulus used. Raymond used apomorphine; because this is a dangerous drug that requires medical supervision, many of the early follow-up studies used electric shock instead. As we saw in our discussion of preparedness, however, stimuli such as the taste of alcohol or the odor of cigarette smoke are difficult to associate with shock, and this could account for the higher failure rate in these studies (Lamon, Wilson, and Leaf, 1977). Once research on taste-aversion learning in rats made this problem clear, researchers switched to USs that would be easier to associate. For alcoholism, nausea-inducing drugs such as Antabuse are now used.

A further problem in the early studies was that even where treatment was effective initially, patients often relapsed when treatment was discontinued. The cause was probably discrimination learning, as patients would have rapidly learned that whereas drinking alcohol in the clinical setting was followed by illness, drinking in their neighborhood bar or with friends had no such consequences. Rather than learning not to drink, they simply learned not to drink in the presence of the experimenter! More recent studies have therefore incorporated other forms of training to help patients cope with temptation once treatment has ceased.

One approach has been to provide counseling during treatment to teach strategies for coping with the urge to smoke or drink when it arises. Another approach has been to provide posttreatment "booster" sessions to help maintain the aversion established during treatment. In one study using this approach, Boland, Mellor, and Revusky (1978) paired alcohol with lithium during treatment and arranged additional conditioning trials after patients had been discharged.

When they assessed their patients six months after discharge, they found that 50% of the chronic alcoholics in the treatment group were still abstinent, compared with only 12% of the controls.

The use of multicomponent treatments in which aversion therapy has been combined with other approaches has contributed to an improvement in the long-term effectiveness of aversion therapy (Hall, Rugg, Tunstall, and Jones, 1984; O'Farrell *et al.*, 1996). In a review, Elkins (1991) reported that approximately 60% of alcoholics treated with aversion therapy were still abstinent one year after treatment, an impressive result for a problem that is notoriously difficult to treat. However, this does not mean that aversion therapy is always appropriate. The need for hospitalization means that aversion therapy for alcoholism is expensive, and its unpleasant nature leads to higher drop-out rates during treatment. Where milder forms of treatment are possible, therefore, they are preferred. For patients suffering from chronic alcoholism, however, aversion therapy appears to be an effective alternative.

Summary

- The British Associationists proposed that the crucial process underlying human thought is the formation of associations between ideas.
- Pavlov developed a practical technique for studying this, by exposing dogs to pairings of a light with food. The amount of salivation to the light indicated the strength of the association, thereby providing an objective technique for tracking the formation of associations.
- Classical conditioning is defined as a change in behavior that is the result of pairing a stimulus (the conditioned stimulus, or CS) with a stimulus that reliably elicits a response (the unconditioned stimulus, or US). Control groups are needed to establish that learning is really due to pairing of these stimuli.
- Conditioning is not confined to salivation. Virtually all behaviors that can be elicited by an unconditioned stimulus can be conditioned, including autonomic responses such as those controlling blood sugar and pain.
- Conditioning also affects our desires and cravings; examples include hunger, fear, sexual arousal, and cravings for drugs. There is also evidence that conditioning can affect our feelings about the CS itself, a phenomenon called evaluative conditioning.
- Pavlov also found that a conditioned response could be weakened or extinguished by presenting the conditioned stimulus on its own. Extinction involves the formation of a new, inhibitory connection between the CS and the US.
- Among the other phenomena discovered by Pavlov were second-order conditioning, counterconditioning, generalization, and discrimination.

- Practical applications of conditioning principles include the most effective therapies currently available for phobias (systematic desensitization and exposure therapy), and aversion therapy for alcoholism.

Review questions

1 Why did Pavlov's research attract so much attention?

2 What were the laws of association according to the British Associationists?

3 Why did Pavlov attribute extinction to an inhibitory process? What evidence supports his interpretation?

4 What is an unpaired control group? Why is it necessary?

5 What autonomic and skeletal behaviors can be classically conditioned? Why is the CR sometimes different from the UR?

6 What is the difference between an overt response and a motivational state? What evidence suggests that motivational or emotional states can be classically conditioned?

7 When drug addicts are undergoing treatment for their habits, talking about drugs in a therapy group will sometimes elicit withdrawal symptoms. How could this behavior be explained by classical conditioning? (*Hint:* What does homeostasis suggest should happen when a drug is administered?)

8 Suppose you suddenly realized that your supply of a medication you really needed was running low and you wouldn't be able to obtain any more for another day. What could you do to increase its effectiveness in the meantime?

9 Describe the CER procedure and the use of suppression ratios to measure fear.

10 What evidence suggests that a taste paired with illness will itself become aversive?

11 It is often said that the way to a man's heart is through his stomach. What research on conditioning supports this claim? How?

12 How could the Pavlovian concepts of generalization and counterconditioning be used to account for the success of systematic desensitization?

13 Can conditioning principles account for the development of phobias?

3 Conditioning principles and theories

CONTENTS

We have seen that classical conditioning is not just a neat way to get dogs to salivate; it affects crucial aspects of our behavior, including fear, sexual arousal, and drug addiction. Our goal in this chapter, therefore, will be to gain a deeper understanding of conditioning. We will begin by looking at the principles of conditioning: What factors determine how strongly a response will be conditioned? We will then look at theories of conditioning: What is the nature of the learning processes that eventually produce the drops of salivation or the surge in fear? Along the way, we will encounter issues such as whether people can be conditioned without their awareness, why advertising is effective, and why basketball coaches sometimes fundamentally misunderstand their sport!

Principles of conditioning

The British Associationists, sitting in their armchairs several centuries ago, identified a number of laws of association, of which the most important were *contiguity*, *frequency*, and *intensity*. We will begin our survey of the principles of conditioning by considering the extent to which these laws have been supported by experiments.

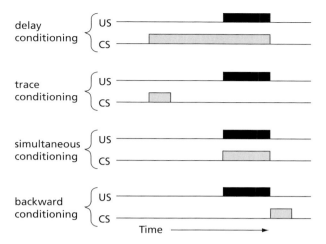

Figure 3.1 Paradigms for four varieties of classical conditioning. The bars on the time line indicate periods during which a stimulus is presented. In simultaneous conditioning, for example, the US occurs at the same time as the CS and for the same duration.

Contiguity, frequency, and intensity

Contiguity

The most important principle of association was thought to be **contiguity**. The very concept of an association – a bond between two events that occur together – implicitly assumes that contiguity is necessary, and considerable effort has been devoted to exploring the role of contiguity in classical conditioning.

As with most other aspects of conditioning, Pavlov was the first to investigate the role of contiguity in establishing a strong conditioned response. He experimented with four different temporal arrangements between the CS and the US (see Figure 3.1). In **delay conditioning**, once the CS came on, it remained on until the US was presented. In **trace conditioning** the CS was terminated before the US began. As the British Associationists would have predicted, Pavlov found that conditioning was much stronger in the delay conditioning paradigm, where the CS and US were on at the same time.

Subsequent research confirmed Pavlov's findings. In a typical study, Moeller (1954) looked at the effects of the CS–US interval on GSR conditioning. He used a trace conditioning paradigm in which a brief burst of white noise (100 ms) was followed after a delay by a weak electric shock, with the interval between the onset of the CS and the onset of the US (the interstimulus interval, or ISI) set at either 250, 450, 1,000, or 2,500 milliseconds (ms). Moeller's results are illustrated in Figure 3.2, which shows that the strength of the conditioned response was greatest in the group with a 450-ms gap, conditioning was weaker with a delay of

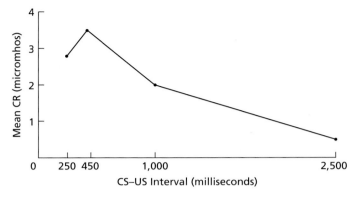

Figure 3.2 GSR conditioning as a function of the CS–US interval during training. (Adapted from Moeller, 1954.)

one second, and virtually no conditioning occurred when the delay was increased to 2.5 seconds. Both the optimum interval and the maximum interval that will sustain conditioning vary somewhat for different responses (see Cooper, 1991, for a discussion of why this might be), but as a general rule the shorter the interval between the CS and US, the better the conditioning.

In Pavlov's third basic procedure, **simultaneous conditioning**, the CS and the US come on at the same time. According to the British Associationists, simultaneous conditioning should be the optimal procedure for producing conditioning – two stimuli can't be any closer than being on simultaneously. That, however, was not at all what Pavlov found: When he presented the CS and the US simultaneously, he found virtually no conditioning, and this result has been confirmed in subsequent experiments. (We've already encountered an indirect example in Figure 3.2 – when the tone and shock were very close, 250 ms, conditioning was actually poorer than when the gap was 450 ms.)

Why should this be? Why, if contiguity is so important, is an association not formed when two stimuli are as close as it is possible to be, occurring at exactly the same time? The perhaps surprising answer seems to be that an association *is* formed, it is just that this association is not translated into a conditioned response (see, for example, Rescorla, 1980b; Matzel, Held, and Miller, 1988). Consider a dog in a delay conditioning procedure/experiment in which a tone comes on first, followed by food. In this condition the tone has predictive value – it warns the dog that food is about to appear. The dog can then prepare for the arrival of this food by salivating, which will allow it to digest the food more efficiently. If the tone and food come on at the same time, however, then the tone has no predictive value – the dog doesn't need the tone to tell it that food is coming, the food has already appeared! In other words, it appears that a CS will elicit a response only if the CS has *adaptive value* – that is, it will allow the dog (or person) to prepare for the forthcoming US. If the CS and the US come on simultaneously, the CS has no predictive value, and it will not elicit a preparatory response.

Something similar seems to happen in Pavlov's fourth basic procedure, **backward conditioning**. In backward conditioning the US is presented first, and only then the CS. As in simultaneous conditioning, backward conditioning does not produce a conditioned response, and again the explanation seems to be that, although an association is formed, the CS does not predict the imminent occurrence of a US, and thus there is no point in responding to it (see Matzel *et al.*, 1988). In fact, because the CS in backward conditioning is normally followed by a long period in which the US does not occur, the CS actually signals a *reduced* likelihood of the US occurring rather than an increased likelihood, and for this reason backward conditioning can lead to a CS acquiring inhibitory properties (e.g., Cole and Miller, 1999). For our purposes, though, the main point is that conditioning really does depend critically on the time between the CS and the US. The closer the two stimuli are (as long as they are not simultaneous!), the stronger the conditioning will be, and conversely if the gap is too long – in the case of GSR conditioning, just a few seconds – then conditioning will not occur at all.

Why, then, doesn't the CS elicit a conditioned response? The most likely explanation is that the CS in this situation has no predictive value. In most conditioning experiments, the CS precedes the US, and the CS thus allows the subject to take preparatory action. If a light is paired with a puff of air to the eye, for example, then subjects blink when the puff is due, thereby protecting their eyes. If a light and an air puff are presented simultaneously, however, there is no time to prepare. As we shall see shortly, conditioning is an *adaptive* process whose purpose is to allow organisms to prepare for forthcoming events. When responding would serve no purpose, as in simultaneous and backward conditioning, it would be pointless to respond, and the processes involved in conditioning seem to have evolved so as to ensure that we respond only in situations where a response would be helpful. (For evidence that excitatory associations can be also formed during backward pairings, even though no response is made, see Albert and Ayres, 1997, and Williams and Hurlburt, 2000.)

Frequency

A second variable that the British Associationists thought determined the strength of an association between two events was the frequency of their pairing. Pavlov's research on salivary conditioning strongly supported this view (see Figure 2.3) and so has subsequent research. In general, the strength of the conditioned response seems to increase most during the early trials of conditioning, with the rate of increase gradually declining as training continues, until performance eventually reaches a stable plateau, or **asymptote**.

Intensity

The third major principle proposed by the British Associationists was that the strength of any association depends on the vividness or intensity of the stimuli involved. Associations involving emotional or traumatic events, for example, were thought to be better remembered. Again, research on conditioning strongly supports this principle. Annau and Kamin (1961), for example, found that the amount of fear conditioned to a tone depends on the intensity of the shock that follows the tone (see Figure 2.11). There is also evidence that the intensity of the CS is of some importance, although this effect appears weaker (see Grice, 1968).

On the whole, then, the armchair speculations of the British Associationists have been impressively confirmed by research under controlled conditions. Associative learning really does depend on the contiguity and intensity of the CS and the US, and on the frequency of their pairing.

Challenges to contiguity

Until 1966, all the available evidence converged on a coherent and satisfying picture of conditioning in which the foundation stone was contiguity: If two events are contiguous, then an association will be formed between them. The strength of this association might be modulated by other factors such as the intensity of the stimuli involved. Fundamentally, though, conditioning appeared to be a simple process in which associations were automatically formed between contiguous events. In 1966, however, two landmark papers were published in *Psychonomic Science*, ironically a relatively obscure journal with a reputation for publishing competent but minor studies. These two papers posed a fundamental challenge to traditional views of the role of contiguity and unleashed an intellectual ferment – revolution would not be too strong a word – that is still continuing.

Contingency

The first of these papers was the work of Robert Rescorla, then a graduate student at the University of Pennsylvania. In his paper, Rescorla suggested that contiguity between two events was not sufficient for conditioning; something more was needed. Specifically, he suggested that a CS must not only be contiguous with a US but must also be an accurate *predictor* of the occurrence of the US. To understand what he meant by this, consider the situations outlined in Figure 3.3, in which a series of tones and shocks are presented. In situation **a**, the shock sometimes occurs while the tone is on, but not when it is off. The tone is thus a useful predictor of the shock; shock is more likely when the tone is on. But now

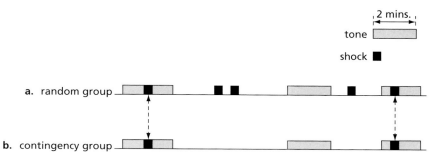

Figure 3.3 An illustration of contingency. The period during which a tone is present is indicated by a shaded bar, and the presentation of a shock is indicated by a solid bar. In situation **a**, a shock is sometimes presented while the tone is on but never when the tone is absent. In **b**, shocks are also sometimes presented during the tone but now shocks are also presented in the absence of the tone. (As indicated by the broken lines, both groups received the same number of shocks in the presence of the CS; they differ only in what happens in the absence of the tone.) In situation **a** there is a contingency between the tone and the shock – the onset of the tone tells you that there is now a greater danger of shock. In situation **b**, there is no contingency between the tone and the shock – there is no relationship between them, and the tone's onset does not signal any greater probability of shock.

consider situation **b**. Again, shocks sometimes occur while the tone is present, but shocks now also occur in the tone's absence. In fact, shocks occur just as frequently when the tone isn't there as when it is. In this situation the tone would have no predictive value, as it would not help you to estimate when you would receive a shock.

What these examples tell us is that the predictive value of a CS can vary quite widely – at one extreme, a tone might be a perfect predictor of shock; at the other, it might have no value. It would be quite useful, therefore, if we had some way of measuring predictive value. In fact, there are several such measures, but one of the most useful is a mathematical statistic called a **contingency**. Because contingencies are defined in terms of probabilities, however, we need to start by quickly reviewing what we mean by a probability.

You may already know that a probability is essentially just a mathematical expression of the likelihood that an event will occur. If there is no chance of an event occurring, the probability is said to be 0; if the event is certain to occur, the probability is said to be 1.0. Suppose that a tone was presented 100 times, and that every one of these presentations was followed by a shock. In that case, the probability of a shock following the tone would be 1.0. This can also be expressed as the probability of a shock occurring "given that" the tone has already occurred, or, in probability notation, as

$$p(\text{shock} \mid \text{tone}) = 1.0$$

Let us further suppose that the shock never occurs in the absence of the tone. The probability of a shock in the absence of the tone would then be 0,

$$p(\text{shock} \mid \text{no tone}) = 0$$

This would be similar to the situation previously outlined in Figure 3.3a – shock would be more likely when the tone was on than when it was off.

Now consider a situation more like that in Figure 3.3b, in which shocks still occurred in the presence of the CS but now also occurred in its absence. Specifically, suppose that the probability of a shock in the absence of the tone was exactly the same as in its presence:

$$p(\text{shock} \mid \text{tone}) = p(\text{shock} \mid \text{no tone}) = 1.0$$

Because the shock would occur just as often in the absence of the tone as in its presence, the tone would no longer help you to predict when shock would occur.

So, even though tone is followed by shock equally often in both of our examples, its predictive value would be very different. One way of capturing this idea is to say that the predictive value of a CS depends on the extent to which the probability of the US *changes* when the CS is present. And that is what a contingency statistic measures. The contingency between a CS and a US is defined as the difference between the probability of the US when the CS is present and when it is absent (Allan, 1980). Or, in probability notation:

$$\text{contingency} = p(\text{US} \mid \text{CS}) - p(\text{US} \mid \text{no CS})$$

If the two probabilities are different, then there is a contingency between the two stimuli, and the CS will be able to help us in predicting when the US will occur.

In a typical conditioning experiment, the CS is closely followed by the US, and the US is never presented in the absence of the CS. The CS and the US are thus contiguous in time, and, because they always occur together, there is also a strong contingency between them. Until Rescorla, everyone had simply taken it for granted that it was the contiguity between the two stimuli that determined the outcome – if a CS and a US occur together, then an association will be formed. Rescorla, however, wondered whether the predictive value of the CS might also be important. What would happen, he asked, if a tone and a shock were presented contiguously, as in most fear-conditioning experiments, but the shock was also presented in the absence of the tone, so that the tone would have no predictive value?

To find out, Rescorla ran several experiments using procedures similar to the ones outlined in Figure 3.3. In one of these experiments (Rescorla, 1968), rats were exposed to a series of tones and shocks. In the random group, there was no relationship between the stimuli; they were presented at totally random intervals. As a result, shock was just as likely in the absence of the tone as in its presence.

In the contingency group, on the other hand, shocks occurred only when the tone was on. The conditions were arranged so that the probability of a shock during a tone was exactly the same in both groups; they differed only in that the random group also received shocks in the absence of the tone.

What should we expect to happen? If conditioning depends simply on contiguity, then conditioning should be equal, since both groups had the same number of tone–shock pairings. The groups differed, however, in terms of contingency: There was a strong contingency between the tone and shock in the contingency group but none in the random group. Insofar as contingency is important, therefore, we should expect stronger conditioning in the contingency group. And that is what Rescorla found. To measure fear, he used a CER test in which he presented the tone while the rats were pressing a bar to obtain food. The rats in the contingency group immediately stopped responding when the tone was presented, indicating strong fear. When the tone was presented to the rats in the random group, however, they carried on as if nothing had happened. Despite repeated pairings of the tone with shock, these rats showed no sign of fear when the tone was presented.

These findings do not mean that contiguity is not important; in GSR condition-ing, for example, we saw that a delay of even 2 seconds could largely prevent conditioning. Rescorla's results, however, suggest that contiguity is not enough; for conditioning to occur, a CS must also be a good predictor of the US. In one sense, this is hardly surprising. If a tone and a shock occur at random intervals, the tone will not signal an increase in the likelihood of shock. There is no rea-son, therefore, why the tone should elicit fear. When viewed from the traditional perspective of contiguity, however, these results are deeply puzzling. According to Pavlov, an association is formed whenever CS and US centers in the brain are active at the same time. But in the random group, the tone and shock occurred together many times; why was no association formed? How could presentations of the shock by itself have prevented conditioning?

We will return to this question later; for now, we simply note that Rescorla's work provided one of the first indications that conditioning is not just a simple process based on contiguity; something rather more complex seemed to be going on. For the first time, the simple picture painted by Pavlov was beginning to unravel.

Preparedness

The second seminal paper of 1966 was by Garcia and Koelling, and they also challenged the assumption that any two events that were contiguous would be associated. In particular, these researchers challenged the idea that it did not matter what stimulus was chosen as a CS. Pavlov had claimed, "Any natural phenomenon chosen at will may be converted into a conditioned stimulus . . . any visual stimulus, any desired sound, any odor, and the stimulation of any part of the skin" (1928, p. 86). Subsequent research almost universally supported Pavlov's position – until, that is, the publication of Garcia and Koelling's paper.

Their experiment had its origins in naturalistic observations of animal behavior – in particular, of a phenomenon in rats called bait-shyness. Rats, it turns out, resist human efforts to exterminate them. When left poisoned bait, they tend to take only the smallest taste at first; if they survive, they rarely if ever touch that food again. Classical conditioning provides a possible explanation for the rats' avoidance of the bait: Ingestion of the poisoned bait produces nausea, and this reaction becomes conditioned to the gustatory and olfactory cues that precede the nausea. On future occasions, the rats avoid the bait because its odor or taste makes them ill. As we saw in Chapter 2, this phenomenon is known as taste-aversion learning.

As plausible as this explanation is, it cannot account for one aspect of the rats' behavior. Although the poisoned rats later avoided the bait, they showed no reluctance to return to the *place* where they had been poisoned and consume other foods there. If associations form between any contiguous events, then we should expect place cues to be associated with illness as readily as taste and odor cues, but this did not appear to be happening. Was it possible that the rats could associate nausea with tastes but not visual cues?

To test this hypothesis under controlled laboratory conditions, Garcia and Koelling allowed rats to taste distinctly flavored water from a drinking tube that was wired so that every lick produced not only water but a brief noise and light flash. Following exposure to this taste–noise–light compound, they received a dose of radiation sufficient to make them ill. Then, on a test trial, the rats were exposed to each of the compound stimuli separately, to determine which ones had become aversive. A lick produced either the flavored water or plain water plus the noise–light compound. As shown in Figure 3.4a, the rats were now very reluctant to drink the flavored water, but they had no such compunctions about the bright–noisy water. As suggested by the naturalistic observations, it looked as if nausea could be conditioned to gustatory cues but not visual ones.

An alternative explanation, however, was possible: Perhaps the noise and light used in the experiment were simply too faint to be detected, so conditioning would not have occurred with any US. To test this hypothesis, Garcia and Koelling repeated their experiment with the same compound CS, but with electric shock as the US instead of X-rays. The results for the suppression test are shown in Figure 3.4b, which illustrates that the audiovisual stimulus produced suppression of drinking while the taste stimulus had no effect. We thus face this strange situation in which nausea cannot be conditioned to a noise, nor fear to a taste, even though each of these conditioned stimuli is easily associated with the other US.

Subsequent research has established that it is possible to associate taste with shock and noise with illness, but it is much more difficult, requiring many more

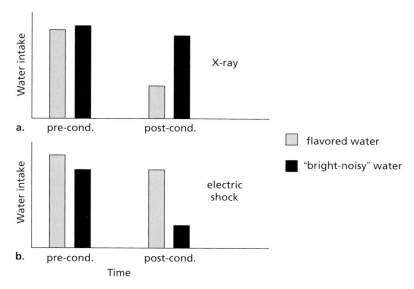

Figure 3.4 Water intake before (pre) and after (post) conditioning: (a) when X-rays were used as the US; (b) when shock was used as the US. The gray bars represent intake of the flavored water; the dark bars represent intake of plain water when licking produced a noise and light. (Based on Garcia and Koelling, 1966.)

trials (for example, Best, Best, and Henggeler, 1977). Seligman (1970) has coined the term **preparedness** to refer to the fact that we seem prepared to associate some CS–US combinations more readily than others.

The evidence for preparedness provided another important challenge to the principle of contiguity. In Garcia and Koelling's experiment, noise and taste were both contiguous with illness, and yet the rats did not develop any aversion to the noise. Contiguity, in other words, is not sufficient for learning to take place. Moreover, subsequent research on taste-aversion learning established that contiguity is not even necessary. In one memorable experiment by Etscorn and Stephens (1973), conditioning occurred despite a delay of 24 hours between eating a food and becoming ill. The irresistible conclusion is that conditioning is not just a simple process of hooking together any events that occur together; some more complex process or processes must be involved.

We will return to the question of what these other processes might be shortly. Before leaving taste-aversion learning, though, we will briefly comment on one other question raised by their results, namely *why* it should be easier to condition nausea to a taste than a noise. To answer this question, it might be helpful to begin by standing back a bit and considering the broader question of why classical conditioning occurs in the first place.

In discussing Pavlov's research, we referred to his view that the process of conditioning evolved because it helps animals survive in their natural environments. Conditioning, in this view, evolved as a means of identifying stimuli that cause or predict important events. If an animal knows where food is available, for example, or which of the other animals in its vicinity is likely to attack it, then it can use this information to guide appropriate action. Culler (1938) expressed this view with some eloquence:

[Without a signal] the animal would still be forced to wait in every case for the stimulus to arrive before beginning to meet it. The veil of the future would hang just before his eyes. Nature began long ago to push back the veil. Foresight proved to possess high survival-value, and conditioning is the means by which foresight is achieved.

(Culler, 1938, p. 136)

Salivary conditioning provides one example of the advantages of foresight: If a dog knows when food is coming, it can begin to salivate beforehand, and this will allow it to consume the food more quickly – not a small advantage when predators or other hungry dogs are around. (See also Zamble *et al.*, 1985; Hollis *et al.*, 1997). In the real world, though, some cues are much more likely to be helpful than others. Consider a rat that became ill after eating rancid meat. If it developed an aversion to all the stimuli that were present when it began to feel ill, it would be as likely to develop an aversion to a bird that happened to be singing as to the rancid meat that it had eaten earlier. And if it thereafter scurried to its burrow whenever it heard a singing bird, it would have been more likely to die of hunger and exhaustion than to prosper. The pressures of natural selection would thus favor rats (and people) that associated illness with preceding tastes, rather than with irrelevant lights or sounds.

Blocking

The 1960s were a difficult time for the principle of contiguity. First, Rescorla showed that temporal contiguity between a CS and a US is not sufficient to ensure conditioning; the CS must also be a good predictor of the US. Then Garcia and Koelling showed that even valid predictors are not always conditioned. In 1969, a third event undermined still further the traditional view of contiguity and suggested an alternative analysis to replace it. That event was the publication of a paper by Leo Kamin.

Kamin (1969) gave rats fear-conditioning trials in which two stimuli, a noise (N) and a light (L), were paired with an electric shock. The noise and the light came on together, remained on for three minutes, and were immediately followed by the shock. To assess conditioning to the light, Kamin used a CER test in which the light was presented while the rats pressed a bar to obtain food. The suppression ratio for the light was 0.05, indicating substantial fear conditioning. (Recall that a suppression ratio of 0.50 indicates no fear and zero indicates maximal fear.)

Kamin was interested primarily in a second group, though. The subjects in this second group received identical pairings of the noise-light compound with shock, but these compound trials were preceded by trials in which the noise by itself was paired with shock.

	Pretraining	Conditioning
blocking group:	N $\rightarrow$ shock	NL $\rightarrow$ shock
control group:		NL $\rightarrow$ shock

For subjects in the blocking group, therefore, the noise already elicited fear when the compound trials began. What effect should we expect this to have on conditioning to the light?

According to a contiguity analysis, fear should be conditioned to the light in both groups, because, in both, the light was repeatedly and contiguously paired with the shock. The results for the two groups, however, proved to be very different. The suppression ratio in the control group was 0.05; the ratio for subjects given preliminary conditioning to the noise was 0.45, a statistic only barely distinguishable from the 0.50 level representing no fear. In other words, prior conditioning to the noise had blocked conditioning to the light. Kamin thus called this phenomenon, in which prior conditioning to one element of a compound prevents conditioning to the other element, **blocking**.

Blocking thus provided yet another case in which pairing a CS with a US did not result in conditioning. The message was becoming overwhelming: Conditioning was more than just a simple process of associating any two events that occurred together; something more must be involved.

Surprise!

To account for blocking, Kamin proposed an intriguing explanation. When an important event such as shock occurs, he said, animals search their memories to identify cues that could help to predict the event in the future. Imagine that a rat foraging for food in a forest is suddenly attacked by an owl. If the rat survives the attack, it will search its memory to identify cues that preceded the attack and thus help it avoid such an event in the future. If the rat had seen the owl in a tree just before the attack, for example, then the next time it saw an owl it would dive for cover.

Kamin's first assumption, then, was that unconditioned stimuli trigger memory searches for predictive cues. His second assumption was that such searches require effort. In taste-aversion conditioning, for example, we have seen that animals may develop an aversion to foods consumed as much as 24 hours earlier, indicating that any memory search must cover events spread over at least this time period. Such a search would require considerable time and effort, and Kamin speculated that, to save energy, subjects would scan their memories only if the US were unexpected or surprising. If the US were expected, then by definition some cue predicting its occurrence must already have been available, so that no further search would be needed.

To see how this analysis can account for blocking, consider first the control group that received only the compound trials. The first shock would have been unexpected and would have triggered a memory search for the cause. The rats would remember the preceding noise and light, and thus both cues would be associated with the shock.

Similarly in the blocking group, presentation of the shock during the preliminary phase would have surprised the rats and thus triggered a memory search in which the rats recalled the noise and associated it with the shock. When the noise was then presented as part of the noise–light compound, the rats would have expected the shock to follow and hence would not have been surprised. As a result, they would not have searched their memories and thus would not have learned about the relationship between the light and the shock.

According to Kamin, then, the reason that blocking occurs is that the US is expected. To test this analysis, he used an ingenious design in which he changed the US used during the compound trials so that its presentation would come as a surprise. As before, a noise was paired with shock during preconditioning, but during conditioning the shock presented at the end of each noise–light compound was unexpectedly followed by a second shock five seconds later:

$$\text{Noise} \rightarrow \text{Shock} \qquad \text{Noise–Light} \rightarrow \text{Shock} \dots \text{Shock}$$

During pretraining, the rats would have learned that the noise was followed by a shock, and thus on the compound trials they would have expected the first shock. The second shock, however, would have been a surprise. The rats should therefore search their memories for possible causes, notice the light, and associate it with the shock. And that is what Kamin found: When the light was later presented on its own, it produced powerful fear in the group that had received two shocks. This result, and those of similar experiments (e.g., Dickinson, Hall, and Mackintosh, 1976), suggests that surprise is one of the key factors in conditioning: Conditioning will occur if and only if the US surprises us.

We suggested earlier that conditioning cannot just be a matter of associating brain centers that are active at the same time; one or more other processes must be involved. And Kamin's analysis now provides us with one possible model of what these other processes might be. According to this analysis, when we experience an unexpected and important event, it triggers an active search through memory for possible causes, a search that can (as in taste-aversion learning) extend to events that occurred many hours earlier. Then, once possible causes have been identified, there appears to be some sort of selection process to choose which is the likeliest cause, or, if not the cause, the best predictor. If you became ill, for example, your brain would be much more likely to identify an earlier meal as the cause, rather than a song you had heard on the radio. This model of conditioning is only provisional, but it does provide us with an intriguingly different framework for thinking about conditioning.

(For other interesting research on the role of memory in conditioning, see Revusky, 1971; Wagner, Rudy, and Whitlow, 1973; Bouton and Nelson, 1998; and Manns, Clark, and Squire, 2002.)

The Rescorla–Wagner model

The evidence for contingency, preparedness, and blocking posed a major challenge to the long-held view that conditioning is essentially a simple process in which brain centers that are active at the same time become associated. In the case of contingency, Rescorla found that animals are sensitive to even small differences in the probability of shock in the presence of a CS and in its absence. If the difference in the two probabilities was 0.4, for example, then conditioning would be stronger than if the difference was 0.2 (Rescorla, 1968). The obvious way to account for this sensitivity is to assume that animals are capable of computing probabilities, but that would imply a remarkable level of sophistication.

Suppose that rats were exposed to alternating periods when a tone was on and when it was off. During the on periods, which lasted 27 seconds, they always received 3 shocks; during the off periods, which lasted 48 seconds, they received 5 shocks. To determine whether shocks were more likely when the tone was on, the rats would first have to count the shocks while the tone was on and also assess how long it was on. They would then need to calculate the probability of the shock by dividing the number of shocks by the time. They would then need to perform a similar calculation in order to determine the probability of shock when the tone was absent. And, finally, they would need to compare these two probabilities to decide whether shocks were more likely when the tone was on. It would be a feat of remarkable complexity for a rat – or a person. Could this really be how it is done?

In 1972 two psychologists proposed an alternative explanation that, by comparison, was almost unbelievably simple. Robert Rescorla and Allan Wagner presented a theory that accounted not only for the effects of contingency but for almost every other aspect of conditioning – the occurrence of conditioning itself, extinction, blocking, and so on. And they achieved all this using only a single, simple equation!

The Rescorla–Wagner model has proved to be one of the most remarkable and influential models in psychology, and we therefore will examine it in some detail. Before we begin, it might be worth noting that some parts of the exposition are difficult and may require careful rereading. This might seem to contradict the claim that the model is simple, but once you understand the model, it really is simple. The catch is that it is stated in mathematical form, so you will have to master unfamiliar symbols and concepts before the model begins to make sense. Mastering this new terminology is not easy, but the potential reward is an insight into how complex behavior can sometimes be explained by remarkably simple processes.

The model

The main impetus for the Rescorla–Wagner model came from Kamin's work on blocking. As we have seen, Kamin used the concept of surprise to account for blocking. If a powerful event surprises us, he said, we search for an explanation, and it is this search process that produces learning.

Rescorla and Wagner took this fundamental insight of Kamin's and modified it in several important respects. In essence, they introduced three major changes:

- They extended the model. Where Kamin had assumed that surprise determines *whether* conditioning occurs, Rescorla and Wagner assumed that the amount of surprise on any trial would also determine *how much* conditioning occurred.
- In order to be able to predict the amount of conditioning, they stated their model in mathematical form.
- They changed the terminology. Kamin couched his explanation in terms of cognitive concepts such as expectations and surprise; Rescorla and Wagner were reluctant to speculate about mental states and so adopted more neutral terminology.

Translating surprise

To explain how Rescorla and Wagner accounted for conditioning, we will start with a hypothetical example. We will first consider how this example could be explained in terms of surprise, and then look at how it would actually be handled by the Rescorla–Wagner model.

Suppose that one night your hands began to itch, and on examining them you discovered a rash. You thought about what might have caused it; there was no obvious explanation, but you remembered that half an hour earlier you had eaten a bowl of chocolate peanut butter ice cream. You had never reacted badly to peanut butter before, but was it possible that you had suddenly developed an

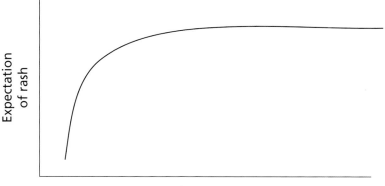

Experiences of eating peanut butter

Figure 3.5 How expectations of an outcome might change with experience. If eating peanut butter was repeatedly followed by a rash, for example, your expectation of illness might increase rapidly until you reached a point where you were 100% certain that you would become ill.

allergy? The next time you ate peanut butter, you would wonder whether you would become ill again; if you did, your belief that peanut butter was the cause would be strengthened. Assuming that your passion for the sensuous delights of peanut butter led you to continue sampling it, and that each act of indulgence was followed by another rash, your suspicion that peanut butter was the cause would eventually approach certainty.

Figure 3.5 plots how your expectation of becoming ill might increase over trials. As you can see, we have assumed that your expectation would increase rapidly at first, but each new experience would produce a smaller change, until eventually your expectation approached a maximum value – in this case, certainty that peanut butter was the cause.

The reason we have assumed that your expectation would change rapidly at first but then more slowly concerns surprise. The first time you noticed the rash, it would have been a complete surprise; you would have searched for an explanation, remembered the peanut butter, and formed a tentative belief that peanut butter was the cause. The next time you ate it, therefore, you would have been half-expecting a rash to follow. When it did, you would not have been nearly so surprised, and as a result you would not have needed to alter your expectation as much. If an expectation is completely wrong, it makes sense to modify it substantially, but the more accurate the expectation is, the less you need to adjust it. As your expectation of illness increased over trials, therefore, you would have needed to modify it less and less, until eventually it reached its maximum value.

This intuition – that how much we adjust our expectations depends on how surprised we are – lies at the heart of the Rescorla–Wagner model. However, Rescorla and Wagner wanted to avoid mentalistic terminology. It is not possible

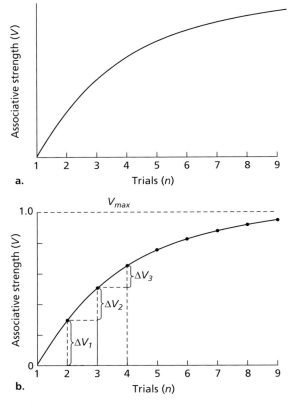

Figure 3.6 How associative strength (V) increases over conditioning trials (n) according to the Rescorla–Wagner model: (a) a typical learning curve; (b) the same curve, showing the change in associative strength on each trial (ΔV) and the asymptotic value of associative strength (V_{max}).

to be certain what a rat is thinking or feeling and – as we saw in Chapter 1, and will see again later – there can also be problems in inferring people's thoughts and emotions.

Rescorla and Wagner therefore chose to express their theory using more neutral terminology. Thus where Kamin had talked of expectations, Rescorla and Wagner simply said that pairing a CS with a US would produce some form of association between them, without speculating about the nature of this association. They used the symbol V to represent the strength of this association.

They assumed that associative strength would increase over trials in roughly the manner shown in Figure 3.6a. As in our previous example, the first trial would produce a large increase in associative strength, the second trial a somewhat smaller increase, and so on. Rescorla and Wagner used the symbol ΔV to represent the change in associative strength on each trial (Δ, or *delta*, is the mathematical symbol for change). The change in associative strength produced by the first trial

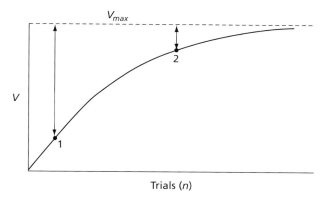

Figure 3.7 The relationship between V and V_{max} early and late in conditioning. Early in conditioning (point 1), the difference between V and V_{max} is great. Later (point 2), the difference is much less.

was ΔV_1, the change on trial 2 was ΔV_2 and so on. As shown in the figure, associative strength is assumed to approach a maximum value; technically, it never quite reaches this maximum, it just keeps getting closer and closer. In mathematics, when a curve approaches but never quite reaches a maximum value, that maximum is called an **asymptote**, and we will use the symbol V_{max} to represent this maximum strength (Figure 3.6b).

We can summarize the model to this point by saying that associative strength increases over trials until it reaches a stable maximum value; in mathematical symbols, V increases by ΔV on each trial until it approaches V_{max}. To predict the strength of association, then, all we need is a formula to predict ΔV! A number of formulas were possible; in choosing one, Rescorla and Wagner started by assuming that the amount of conditioning on any trial, ΔV, would be determined by the difference between V and V_{max}:

$$(\Delta V) \approx V_{max} - V$$

Stated in words, their assumption was that conditioning on any trial would depend on the difference between the associative strength at the beginning of that trial and the maximum possible strength.

To make this more concrete, consider a trial early in conditioning – point 1 in Figure 3.7. Associative strength at the beginning of this trial would still be low, and thus there would be a large difference between V and V_{max}. (This difference is represented by the vertical line in the figure.) Because of this large difference, Rescorla and Wagner assumed that there would be a substantial increase in associative strength on this trial. Now consider point 2 in the figure. Associative strength is now much closer to the maximum possible value; because there is only a small difference, there would be much less conditioning. Conditioning, in other words, would depend on the difference between V and V_{max}.

At this point it might be difficult to see any relationship between this analysis and our earlier account in terms of surprise. The terminology is certainly very different, but if we examine the two versions more closely, the underlying concepts are actually very similar. Consider point 1 again. In the Rescorla–Wagner version, associative strength at this point is far below its maximum; similarly in a surprise analysis, expectation of the US would be far below its maximum value of certainty. And because current strength is far from where it should be, both versions predict that there will be a substantial change in current strength. Later in conditioning, associative strength (*expectation*) will be closer to its maximum, and there will therefore be less need to change. The terminology is different, but both versions assume that how much we change our associations or expectations depends on how far the existing value is from where it should be. In surprise terms, the more our expectations diverge from reality, the more we need to change them. Or, in Rescorla–Wagner terms, the further V is from V_{max}, the more we need to adjust V.

We have used the concept of surprise to introduce the Rescorla–Wagner model, but as we have seen the model is actually phrased in terms of associations, and from this point onwards we will stick to the model's terms. We have already introduced its most important concept – that conditioning on any trial depends on the difference between V and V_{max} – but we now need to add a few details. First, to make it easier to talk about how much conditioning will occur on a particular trial, we will use the symbol n to represent trial number. On trial 1, for example, the associative strength at the beginning of the trial will be V_1; the associative strength at the beginning of trial 2 will be V_2, and so on. Similarly, we will use the symbol ΔV_n to represent the change in associative strength produced by trial n. The change in associative strength produced by trial 1 would thus be ΔV_1, the change produced by trial 2 would be ΔV_2, and so on. Using these modified symbols, our exposition of the model to this point could be summarized as

$$\Delta V_n \approx (V_{max} - V_n)$$

Expressed in words, the model assumes that the change in associative strength on any trial will depend on the difference between the associative strength at the beginning of the trial (V_n) and the maximum possible strength (V_{max}).

The role of parameters

In our presentation of the model to this point, we have talked as if the learning curve shown in Figure 3.6a is the one found in all conditioning curves, but this is not quite right. The overall shape of the curve – increasing over trials, but at a declining rate – is indeed uniform, or at least roughly so, but the asymptotic level of conditioning can vary, and so too can the speed of conditioning. In discussing taste-aversion learning, for example, we noted that such aversions develop very quickly, whereas salivary conditioning generally requires many trials for conditioning to reach its peak. To allow the model to account for variations in the speed of conditioning, Rescorla and Wagner added a constant, c, to their equation. The complete statement of the equation was thus:

$$\Delta V_n = c(V_{max} - V_n)$$

where

V_n = the strength of the association at the beginning of trial n

ΔV_n = the change in the strength of the association produced by trial n

In mathematics, a constant in an equation is called a **parameter**.[1] The Rescorla–Wagner model actually has two parameters: V_{max} and c are both constants. V_{max} determines the asymptotic level of conditioning – the higher the value assigned to V_{max}, the higher will be the asymptotic level of conditioning. The other parameter, c, determines the speed of conditioning – the greater the value of c, the faster conditioning will reach asymptote.

Now that we have the final version of our equation, it might seem a simple matter to test it. All we need do is present a series of CS–US trials, use the equation to predict associative strength, and then see if our predictions are right. Alas, there is a catch: before we can use the formula, we need to know what values of c and V_{max} to enter. According to the model, the value of these parameters depends, at least in part, on the US used, and that means that we might need to assign different values for every possible US. Suppose, for example, that we ran a GSR conditioning experiment in which the US was a 30-volt shock; what values of c and V_{max} should we use?

One way to find out would be to run a pilot experiment using this shock; once we had the results, we could try out different values of c and V_{max} to see which ones yielded the most accurate predictions. Once we knew the appropriate values for this pilot experiment, we could then use the same values in any future experiments involving the same shock.

This approach is called *parameter estimation*, and it turns out to be much more difficult than it sounds. Suppose that we used a particular set of parameter values

---

[1] The value of the parameter V_{max} was assumed to be determined solely by the US used, whereas the value of c was determined by both the CS and the US. In fact, Rescorla and Wagner used two different constants, α and β, to represent the effects of the CS and the US, rather than the single parameter c, and they also used the symbol λ to represent asymptotic conditioning rather than V_{max}. We have altered the symbols to make the exposition of the model easier to follow. Should you read the model in the original, you will find the equation stated as

$$\Delta V_n = \alpha\beta(\lambda - V_n)$$

The value of c in our version of the equation must lie between 0 and 1.

to predict the results of an experiment and our predictions turned out to be incorrect. Obviously something was wrong, but what? Was it the value of c we used that was wrong, or V_{max}, or both, or maybe even the entire theory? The problem is that any theory inevitably involves a number of assumptions, and if the theory's predictions prove to be incorrect it can be very difficult to determine which of these assumptions was erroneous. In the entire history of learning theory there has been only one sustained effort to estimate a theory's parameters in this way (Hull, 1943). When this failed, after more than a decade of effort, it convinced many learning theorists that the field simply wasn't ready for mathematical models; our understanding of the processes involved in learning wasn't advanced enough.

Given this history, Rescorla and Wagner decided not even to try to determine the appropriate values for c and V_{max}; instead, they just used arbitrary values! This use of arbitrary values may seem pointless, to put it mildly, but although this strategy precludes *quantitative* predictions, it turns out that the model can still make some very interesting *qualitative* predictions. That is, although the exact points on the learning curve depend on the values of c and V_{max} used in the equation, and thus will vary with different choices of these parameters, the general shape of the curve turns out to be the same no matter what values are used. Thus although the model does not let us predict the exact number of drops of saliva, it always makes the same qualitative predictions about whether salivation will increase or decrease. This might still seem a waste of time – we hardly need a sophisticated mathematical model to tell us that conditioning will increase over trials – but Rescorla and Wagner were able to show that even simple statements of this kind can lead to interesting and unexpected predictions.

The model's successes

To see how this can happen, we will first consider how the model accounts for relatively straightforward phenomena such as conditioning and extinction. Then, once the basic operations of the model are a bit clearer, we will turn to some of its more striking predictions. To begin, though, let us take a look at how the model accounts for the basic shape of the learning curve during conditioning.

Conditioning

Suppose that we repeatedly paired a tone with food. To see how the model works, we will assume that the value of V_{max} is 1.0, and the value of c is 0.30. How much learning should we then expect? At the beginning of the first trial, the value of V would be zero, because the CS has never been paired with the US before. The amount of conditioning on that trial would then be

$$\Delta V_1 = c(V_{max} - V_1) = 0.30(1.0 - 0) = 0.30$$

Table 3.1 Using the Rescorla–Wagner model to predict conditioning

Trial	V_n	$\Delta V_n = c(V_{max} - V_n)$
1	0.00 Δ	$V_1 = 0.30(1.0 - 0.00) = 0.30$
2	0.30 Δ	$V_2 = 0.30(1.0 - 0.30) = 0.21$
3	0.51 Δ	$V_3 = 0.30(1.0 - 0.51) = 0.15$
4	0.66 Δ	$V_4 = 0.30(1.0 - 0.66) = 0.10$

So, associative strength started at zero and has now increased by 0.30; at the beginning of the second trial, therefore, associative strength would be 0.30. The increase in associative strength produced by this second trial would thus be

$$\Delta V_2 = c(V_{max} - V_2) = 0.30(1.0 - 0.30) = 0.21$$

The predicted values for V on the next two trials are shown in Table 3.1. As you can see, they correspond exactly to the values plotted in Figure 3.1.

Our success in predicting these hypothetical data is perhaps not too surprising (especially when you consider that the calculations were done first and the graph simply plots these calculations!), but it does indicate the capacity of the model to generate learning curves of the shape found in most conditioning experiments. The predicted shape of the curve is the same, moreover, regardless of what values of c and V_{max} are used. These parameters alter the height of the asymptote and the speed with which it is reached, but in all cases the basic shape of the curve remains the same. (You might find it useful to verify this for yourself by working through some calculations using other values. You can use any value for V_{max}, but the value of c must lie between 0 and 1.0.)

Extinction

What about other aspects of conditioning? For example, can the model explain decreases in responding as well as increases? Yes, and it does so using exactly the same equation used to predict conditioning. The key to understanding how one equation can predict diametrically opposite results lies in V_{max}. We have said that V_{max} is the strength of the association that would be produced if a CS and a US were paired repeatedly. In extinction, we know that the level of conditioning reached after extended training is zero. The value of V_{max} on any trial in which a US is not presented, therefore, must also be zero.

To see the implications of this, suppose that after the third conditioning trial in our previous example we began to present the CS by itself. On the first extinction trial, V would have an initial value of 0.66 (see Table 3.1), but as a result of the omission of the US on that trial, its associative strength would be changed by

$$\Delta V_1 = c(V_{max} - V_1) = 0.30(0 - 0.66) = -0.198$$

The strength of the association, in other words, would be decreased by approximately 0.20, and its new strength would be

$$V_2 = 0.66 - 0.20 = 0.46$$

A second extinction trial would decrease its strength by a further −0.14, and so on, until eventually V would approach its asymptotic value of zero. Using only a single equation, therefore, the model can predict extinction as well as conditioning.

Blocking

We can also use the model to explain blocking. Before doing so, however, we need to consider how conditioning is affected if two stimuli instead of just one are present on a trial. We said earlier that conditioning on any trial depends on how surprising the US is, which in turn depends on how much the subject expected the US to occur. Rescorla and Wagner assumed that if two conditioned stimuli, a and b, were presented together, the subject would take both stimuli into account in estimating the likelihood of the US. Specifically, they proposed that the association or expectation at the beginning of a trial would be the sum of the strengths of each of the stimuli present:

$$V_{ab} = V_a + V_b$$

Suppose, for example, that a and b had been paired separately with food and had associative strengths of 0.30 and 0.50, respectively. If the two stimuli were presented together, subjects would assume that food must really be likely. The associative strength of the compound would be

$$V_{ab} = V_a + V_b = 0.30 + 0.50 = 0.80$$

In predicting how surprising a US will be, we need to take into account all the stimuli present. Thus, the amount of conditioning on a compound trial in which a and b occur together would be[2]

$$\Delta V_a = \Delta V_b = c(V_{max} - V_{ab})$$

---

[2] We have assumed that conditioning to a and b would be equal, but that is not necessarily the case. The value of the parameter c depends on the CS used as well as the US, so the value of c for one stimulus might differ from the value of c for another stimulus. If we used a compound of red and green lights as our CS, for example, and if the green light was much brighter, there would probably be more conditioning to the green light.

where

$$V_{ab} = V_a + V_b$$

We are now in a position to explain blocking. Recall that there was an initial pretraining phase in which a noise was repeatedly paired with shock, and then a conditioning phase in which a noise–light compound was paired with shock. During pretraining the associative strength of the noise would have increased until it essentially reached asymptote. If we assume that V_{max} for the shock was 1.0, then by the end of conditioning,

$$V_{noise} = 1.0$$

If the noise were presented with the light, then their combined associative strength would be

$$V_{nl} = V_{noise} + V_{light} = 1.0 + 0 = 1.0$$

The amount of conditioning to the light on this trial would therefore be

$$\Delta V_{light} = c(V_{max} - V_{nl}) = 0.3(1.0 - 1.0) = 0.3(0) = 0$$

In other words, no conditioning would occur, which is exactly what Kamin found.

Overexpectation

There are three main criteria used in evaluating any scientific theory. The first is whether it can account for known phenomena, and we have seen that the Rescorla–Wagner model has had considerable success in this regard, accounting not only for conditioning itself but also for phenomena such as extinction, blocking, and contingency.[3]

A second criterion is the scientific principle of **parsimony**. In essence, this says that where competing theories can account for the same data, preference should be given to whichever of the theories is the simplest. If one theory requires 5 assumptions to explain a phenomenon and another can do it with just two, then we should prefer the theory with the fewer and simpler assumptions. Note that this principle is not, strictly speaking, logically necessary: It is entirely possible that the more complex theory could be the correct one. Scientists, however, have a deep love of simple explanations – there is something beautiful, something deeply satisfying, about being able to explain a wide range of complex phenomena in terms of just a few simple assumptions. And, as it turns out, simpler theories often have proved right. Newton's theory of gravity is one impressive example,

---

[3] We haven't been able to cover their analysis of contingency for space reasons, but a full account is available in Rescorla and Wagner (1972).

as Newton was able to account for an astonishing range of phenomena – the orbits of the planets, the movements of the tides, the fall of an apple – in terms of just one fundamental force. In any case, for better or worse, scientists prefer simpler accounts wherever possible, and the Rescorla–Wagner model is just about the simplest account imaginable – it basically says that almost every aspect of conditioning can be explained by the difference between two quantities, V and V_{max}.

There is, however, a third, even more demanding criterion used to judge scientific theories, and that is its ability to predict new, previously unknown phenomena. So, how well has the Rescorla–Wagner model fared by this more daunting criterion? To assess the model's success in this crucial respect, we will focus on one of its strangest and most counterintuitive predictions, that in some circumstances pairing a CS with a US will result not in conditioning but in extinction!

Suppose that we exposed rats to conditioning trials in which a tone and a light were separately paired with an intense shock:

$$tone \rightarrow shock$$

$$light \rightarrow shock$$

Then suppose that we presented the tone and light together on the next conditioning trial:

$$tone + light \rightarrow shock$$

What effect should this additional pairing have on fear of the tone? Because the tone is again followed by an unpleasant shock, you might expect a further increase in fear, but, according to the Rescorla–Wagner model, the situation is not that simple. As we've already seen, the amount of conditioning in any situation depends not simply on the US but also on the associative strength at the beginning of the trial. Suppose, for example, that only a few trials were given before the compound trial, so fear levels to the two stimuli were only moderate:

$$V_a = V_b = 0.20$$

On the compound trial, V_{ab} would be 0.40. If we assign c the arbitrary value of 0.5, then the change in associative strength on that trial would be

$$\Delta V_a = \Delta V b = c(V_{max} - V_{ab}) = 0.5(1.0 - 0.4) = 0.30$$

In accordance with common sense, in other words, the model predicts an increase in fear conditioning on this trial.

Now suppose that extensive conditioning to the tone and light took place before the first compound trial, with this result:

$$V_a = V_b = 0.9$$

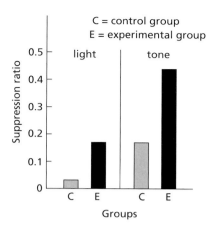

Figure 3.8 Fear elicited by a light and a tone following just conditioning (control group) or following additional trials in which the tone and light were presented jointly, followed by shock (experimental group). Fear was measured with a suppression ratio in which 0.5 represents no fear and 0.0 represents strong fear. The data thus show that additional conditioning trials actually reduced fear. (Based on data from Rescorla, 1970.)

In this case, the associative strength of the compound would be 1.8, so that on the compound trial:

$$\Delta V_a = \Delta V_b = c(V_{max} - V_{ab}) = 0.5(1.0 - 1.8) = -0.40$$

Even though the compound is still being followed by a powerful electric shock, the model now predicts a decrease in fear levels!

Rescorla (1970) tested this prediction. In the first phase, rats were given extensive pairings of both a tone and a light with shock, so that fear conditioning to each would be essentially at asymptotic levels. An experimental group was then given 12 compound trials in which the tone and the light were presented together and followed by the same shock as in training; a control group received no further training. Finally, fear conditioning to the two stimuli was assessed by presenting them separately in a CER (conditioned emotional response) test. (See Chapter 2 for a discussion of the CER test.)

Figure 3.8 shows the results of this experiment. Let us look first at the results for the light: Note that responding was suppressed much more in the control group (suppression ratio of 0.03) than in the experimental group (suppression ratio of 0.17). The initial pairing of the light with shock, in other words, had resulted in strong fear conditioning, but the additional pairings in the experimental group actually reduced that fear. The effect on the tone was, if anything, even more dramatic, with the extra compound trials resulting in an even greater decrease in fear. Indeed, the tone no longer appeared to elicit any fear at all; the observed suppression ratio of 0.44 was virtually indistinguishable from the neutral point of

0.50. Extra pairings of the tone and light with shock not only did not increase fear, as common sense might predict, but actually reduced or even eliminated it! It is a bizarre result, but precisely what the model predicts. This phenomenon is often referred to as the **overexpectation effect**, because it is the result of cues predicting the US more strongly than is justified.

The model's limitations

We have examined in some detail one prediction of the model; other predictions have also been tested and many have been confirmed (for example, Blough, 1975). In some important respects, however, the model's predictions have proved incorrect. We will consider one example here, involving a phenomenon called *latent inhibition*.

In the first demonstration of this phenomenon, Lubow and Moore (1959) gave animals extensive preexposure to a CS before conditioning trials in which the CS was paired with a US. Sheep and goats were repeatedly shown a flashing light. This was followed by conditioning trials in which the light was paired with shock. A control group received the identical conditioning trials but without preexposure to the light.

How should preexposure to the light affect subsequent conditioning? According to the model, these trials should have no effect. In mathematical terms, V_{max} is always zero when no US is presented; if the light is initially neutral ($V = 0$), then

$$\Delta V = c(V_{max} - V) = c(0 - 0) = 0$$

At the beginning of the conditioning phase in Lubow and Moore's experiment, therefore, the light should have had no associative strength in either group, and learning in the two groups should have proceeded identically. Contrary to this prediction, Lubow and Moore found that conditioning was significantly slower in the group preexposed to the light, a phenomenon they termed **latent inhibition** because they believed that the CS becomes inhibitory during the preexposure phase. Subsequent evidence made it clear that the CS is neither excitatory nor inhibitory following preexposure; it is simply difficult to condition (for example, Reiss and Wagner, 1972). To prevent confusion, therefore, many researchers now prefer to use the term **CS preexposure effect** rather than latent inhibition.

Whatever it is called, one possible explanation for this phenomenon is that, when a stimulus is repeatedly presented by itself, we learn to ignore it (for example, Kaye and Pearce, 1987). As simple as this account is, the Rescorla–Wagner model cannot accommodate it because the model does not include any mechanism for changing the amount of attention paid to a stimulus. (See Escobar, Arcediano, and Miller, 2002, for a review of other possible explanations.)

Evaluation

We have seen that there are three main criteria for evaluating scientific theories – the capacity to explain known phenomena, to predict new ones, and to do all this using the simplest possible set of assumptions. By all three criteria, the Rescorla–Wagner model has had impressive success. In addition to explaining a wide range of phenomena using only a single, simple equation, the model has also generated a variety of counterintuitive predictions – for example, that a conditioning trial can reduce associative strength – and many of these predictions have been supported. As researchers have continued to test the model's predictions, however, it has become clear that there are also many phenomena that the model cannot explain. (For a thorough review of the model's weaknesses as well as its strengths, see Miller, Barnet, and Grahame, 1995.)

Other theories have been proposed to try to address some of the model's deficiencies (for example, Mackintosh, 1975; Pearce and Hall, 1980; Wagner and Brandon, 1989, 2001; Van Hamme and Wasserman, 1994; Schmajuk, Lam, and Gray, 1996; Denniston, Savastano, and Miller, 2001). One striking feature of many of these theories, however, is that they incorporate a version of the Rescorla–Wagner model's basic formula; they add other features to address processes such as attention, but the basic formula remains. Thus, although the Rescorla–Wagner model undoubtedly requires modification and extension, many psychologists believe that the insight at its heart – that conditioning depends on the discrepancy between current associative strength and asymptotic strength – captures a fundamental truth about the nature of conditioning.

Theories inevitably evolve, and perhaps this insight will eventually be seen as mistaken and supplanted by a deeper one, as Newton's ideas about gravity were eventually overtaken by Einstein's. Even were that to happen, the model has contributed to a rebirth of interest in mathematical models of learning with its remarkable demonstration of the power of a few simple assumptions to explain a wide range of seemingly complex phenomena. Its impact has been profound: Miller *et al.* (1995) called it "the most influential theory of associative learning to emerge ... over the last 25 years," and Siegel and Allan (1996) wrote that "there have been few models in experimental psychology as influential as the Rescorla–Wagner model." Whatever its ultimate fate, the Rescorla–Wagner model is likely to prove a historic landmark in the evolution of our understanding of learning.[4]

---

[4] We have focused our discussion of theories of conditioning on the Rescorla–Wagner model, because it has been by far the most influential theory. We will use this footnote, though, to briefly describe one alternative, that of Balsam, Drew, and Gallistel (2010). Their account, like that of Rescorla and Wagner, was a reaction to the evidence that conditioning cannot be explained simply

Associative and cognitive theories

The Rescorla–Wagner model provides us with a powerful tool for predicting the strength of the association formed on any trial, but the model is silent about the nature of this association. When a tone is paired with food, for example, what is the nature of the link that is formed between them?

Conditioning in animals

According to one of the earliest cognitive theorists of associative learning, Edward Tolman (1932), the pairing of a CS and a US leads to the formation of an expectation. If a tone is followed by food, for example, then a dog will form an expectation that future tones will also be followed by food. Tolman was not very specific about how this expectation would then be translated into a conditioned response, but the general notion was that the dog would take whatever action was appropriate to prepare for the expected food. Thus, a dog would salivate when it expected food because such anticipatory salivation would help it to digest the food more quickly and efficiently (see Hollis, 1982); a rabbit would blink when it expected a puff of air to its eye because this blink would protect the eye.

---

in terms of contiguity. Rescorla's work on contingency, for example, showed that pairing a CS with shock would result in conditioning only if the CS had predictive value – if the shock was more likely when the CS was present than when it was absent.

As we noted earlier, one possible reaction to this evidence is to assume that animals are able to calculate the probability of events, and thus to judge whether a US is more likely in the presence of a CS than in its absence. Rescorla and Wagner rejected this account, but Balsam and his colleagues embraced it! Specifically, they proposed that both animals and people are exquisitely sensitive to the distribution of events over time, and it is this sensitivity that allows them to assess whether a US is more or less likely in certain situations. To take a homely example, if you were always home when your mail was delivered in the morning, you might eventually form an accurate sense of how likely it was to arrive at various times – unlikely at 9, more likely at 9:20, very likely at 9:30, and so on. And perhaps you'd also notice that delivery times varied depending on which mailman (CS!) was on duty, with one tending to appear a bit later than the other. Balsam *et al.* suggest not that you do all this consciously, but that our brains are very sensitive to the timing of events, and that they build sophisticated temporal maps indicating the likelihood of events at different points in time.

To this point, their notion might seem a bit vague, but they, like Rescorla and Wagner, were able to express it in mathematical terms, so that it is possible to state precisely what the predictive value of any stimulus will be, and how this predictive value will influence conditioning. Their account assumes very sophisticated processing of the distribution of events over time, and it remains to be seen whether they are right – perhaps, as was the case with the Rescorla–Wagner model, it will prove possible to explain seemingly complex behavior in terms of simpler underlying processes. On one point, though, everyone is in agreement – conditioning depends not simply on the contiguity of the CS and US but on how useful the CS is as predictor of the US. What remains to be seen is the best way of capturing this insight.

Stimulus substitution

Pavlov's interpretation was very different. As we have seen, he believed that the CS and the US centers became linked so that activation of the CS center would lead to activation of the US center. The CS would therefore elicit the same behaviors as the US did; in effect, it was as if the CS had *become* the US – hence the term **stimulus substitution**. For Tolman, the CS became a signal that food was coming. (Imagine the dog thinking, "Oh boy, I'm about to get food.") For Pavlov, the CS effectively became a substitute for that food, in that it elicited the same responses. (You can imagine the dog thinking, "Oh boy, what lovely food this is." Note, though, that Pavlov did not actually speculate about what dogs were thinking. His view was simply that the CS would elicit the same response as the food.)

At first, Pavlov's substitution theory might seem silly. A dog may not be a brilliant scholar, but surely it has enough sense to be able to distinguish a tone or a light from food! On closer examination, however, this claim is perhaps not as outrageous as it sounds. The assumption that a dog knows that a light is not food begs the important question of *how* it knows. We tend to think that identifying food is trivially simple; everyone knows, for example, that apples are edible but pebbles are not. Babies, however, do not know this and will often try to ingest objects that are emphatically not edible. This is also true of many other species, which have to learn which objects in their environment are edible. If a visual cue is repeatedly followed by food in the mouth, therefore, it is not inconceivable that a conditioning process might lead us to respond to this cue as food in the future.

But if Pavlov's dogs viewed the light as food, you may be asking yourself, why didn't they try to eat it? The answer is, they did! Pavlov found that when a dog is released from its harness after pairings of a light bulb with food, it eagerly runs over to the light bulb and licks it. The dogs didn't actually chew or swallow the bulb, but this might have been because the bulb's hardness inhibited the dog's swallowing reflexes. In other studies in which the physical characteristics of the CS have been more appropriate, animals *have* tried to ingest the CS. One example we have already encountered is autoshaping, in which a pigeon exposed to pairing of a circular key light with food will begin to peck the key. The existence of this phenomenon is very difficult to explain in terms of expectations: If the key light is simply a signal that food is imminent, why does the pigeon bother to peck it? If the lighted key has been identified as food, on the other hand, this pecking at the key becomes more understandable: The bird is trying to eat it!

Support for this interpretation comes from a classic experiment by Jenkins and Moore (1973), who paired a lighted key with food in one group and with water in another. As we have already noted, a bird's responses to food and water are different. When given food, a pigeon pecks with its beak open; when given water, its beak is almost closed, and the pigeon uses its tongue to pump the water into its mouth. Also, a pigeon pecks water with its eyes open, but it pecks food with its eyes closed. (Food pecking is much more forceful, and the pigeon might close its eyes to protect them from ricocheting stones.) According to the substitution hypothesis, therefore, pigeons exposed to light–food pairings should try to eat the key with an open beak and closed eyes, whereas those exposed to light–water pairings should peck with a closed beak and open eyes. As Figure 3.9 shows, this was exactly what happened. The pigeons seemed to be trying to eat the key paired with food and to drink the key paired with water. (For some striking cases where animals actually *have* eaten stimuli paired with food, see Breland and Breland, 1961.)

Further evidence of the power of the mechanism involved, and of its apparent irrationality, comes from another study by Jenkins (reported in Hearst and Jenkins, 1974), in which the key light was located along one wall of a 6-foot-long box and the food source along another (Figure 3.10). The key light was occasionally presented for 5 seconds, followed by the raising of a grain magazine so that the grain was accessible for 4 seconds. Because of the layout of the box, if the pigeons approached the key and pecked it when the light came on, they could not return to the food dispenser in time to eat all the food. Nevertheless, Jenkins found that his birds would run over to the light as soon as it came on, peck it, and then quickly hurry back to the food magazine. Because of the length of the box, they missed most or all of the food on the trials in which they pecked. Despite this, they continued to peck the key in session after session (see also Williams and Williams, 1969). Pecking the key seemed more important to the birds than eating.

Tolman's expectations

Pavlov's substitution theory thus needs to be taken seriously: In many situations, animals do behave as if a CS paired with food really is food, and they will persist in trying to eat the CS even if it costs them real food. On the other hand, evidence also supports Tolman's view that a CS acts as a signal that the US is coming. One source of support comes from observations of dogs' behavior during salivary conditioning experiments. They do not just salivate; they will also turn toward the food tray and, if released from the harness, approach the tray (Zener, 1937). Their behavior strongly suggests that they expect to find food there, and similar results have been obtained in other experiments. In Jenkins's long-box experiment, for example, the pigeons usually approached the key light when it was illuminated, but in some cases they moved toward the food dispenser instead. (See also Colwill and Motzkin, 1994.)

Figure 3.9 Typical responses of key-pecking during autoshaping trials. The photographs on the left show typical pecking when the US was water; the photographs on the right show typical pecking when the US was food. (Jenkins and Moore, 1973; the photographs were provided by Bruce Moore.)

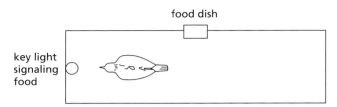

Figure 3.10 Top view of the apparatus used by Jenkins to study autoshaping in pigeons. (Adapted from Domjan and Burkhard, 1986.)

A two-system hypothesis

We now have what seems a distinctly confusing situation in which animals sometimes behave as if a CS paired with food actually is food and try to eat it, but at other times behave as if the CS is simply a signal that food is coming and initiate appropriate action to obtain it (see also Jenkins *et al.*, 1978; Timberlake, Wahl, and King, 1982). One way to resolve this conflict is to assume that both views are correct, and that the reason why the outcome varies is that classical conditioning actually involves two distinct learning systems – an *associative* system in which the CS elicits responses automatically, and a *cognitive* system in which expectations guide responding.

Perhaps the first learning system to evolve was a relatively primitive one in which the CS was simply associated with the US and thus elicited the same responses. In the course of time, a more sophisticated system developed that involved active anticipation of the US; this allowed subjects to select flexibly from a range of preparatory responses, taking into account other information available at the time. Insofar as both systems still coexist in vertebrates, this would explain why animals act sometimes as if the CS is a signal for food and at other times as if it actually is food.

The idea that the brain contains two distinct learning systems has been proposed by a number of theorists over the years (for example, Konorski, 1967; Razran, 1971; Squire, 1992). Each theorist has attributed somewhat different properties to the two systems, but a common theme has been that one system is essentially simple and automatic, whereas the other involves some sort of expectation about the properties of the forthcoming US. We will call the assumption of two systems, one associative and the other more cognitive, the **two-system hypothesis.**

The brain's evolution

Indirect evidence for two learning systems comes from what is known about the evolution of the vertebrate brain. Studies of fossil records and of the brains of living species suggest that the vertebrate brain has changed enormously in the course of evolution. These changes, however, have consisted not so much in the disappearance of old structures – most of the primitive structures of an alligator or rat brain can still be easily recognized, almost unchanged, in that of a human – as in the elaboration of new structures. In particular, there has been a massive increase in the outer covering of the brain known as the *neocortex*.[5] The proportion of the brain devoted to neocortex in humans is 150 times greater than in the tree-shrew-like mammals from which we are thought to have descended, even after adjusting for differences in body weight. The functions of this vastly expanded neocortex include cognitive processes such as thinking and language. The neocortex is also the center of awareness. (If the neocortex is damaged or anesthetized, a person loses consciousness.)

In the course of evolution, the anatomy of the central core of the brain has remained unchanged to a remarkable extent, with emerging cognitive functions concentrated in a massively expanded outer region. Insofar as the older core has retained its old functions as well as structure, a relatively primitive associative system might still be present in vertebrates along with a more advanced cognitive one. Epstein has proposed a similar hypothesis to account for human emotions, suggesting that a largely preconscious system evolved first, and that this system remained when a more rational and analytical system emerged. In his words,

It is inconceivable that, with the advent of language and the capacity for analytical thought, the hard-won gains of millions of years of evolution were summarily abandoned. It can more reasonably be assumed that the same principles ... that apply to nonhuman animal cognitions apply as well to human cognitions, wherein they influence and are in turn influenced by a newly acquired verbal-analytical rational system.

(Epstein, 1994, p. 714)

Two routes to fear

More direct evidence for the existence of two learning systems has come from recent research on the physiological mechanisms underlying fear conditioning. On the basis of this research, LeDoux (1994, 2002) has proposed that the area of the brain primarily responsible for the conditioning of fear is a structure called the *amygdala*. When the amygdala is surgically removed, rats do not learn to fear a tone that signals shock. LeDoux found two different pathways leading from the senses to the amygdala: a direct path that can trigger a fear response very quickly, and an indirect path that goes first to the cortex and only then to the amygdala (Figure 3.11). He suggested that the direct path allows a rapid, automatic response

---

[5] The outer covering of the brain is called the *cortex*. Some form of cortex is present in most vertebrates, but it is expanded considerably in mammals, and the larger, newer section of the cortex is called the *neocortex*. In humans, most of the cortex consists of neocortex.

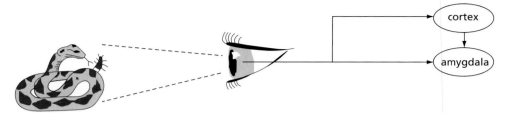

Figure 3.11 Two routes to fear.

to signals of possible danger, whereas the cortical path, although slower, allows subjects to evaluate the signal more carefully and decide whether fear is really appropriate. If you glimpsed a fast-moving object out of the corner of your eye, for example, the direct path might trigger immediate arousal, while the cortical path would allow you to weigh the situation and decide whether the moving object was a dangerous predator or just a harmless bird, and thus whether further action was needed.

Two systems in humans

Summarizing the argument to this point, we have supposed that conditioning involves two separate systems in the brain, a relatively primitive system involving the formation of associations, and a more sophisticated system involving the formation of expectations. We have further supposed that the associative system is located in subcortical structures such as the amygdala, while the cognitive system is located in the cortex. However, in humans the cortex is also known to be the seat of consciousness – if the cortex is selectively anesthetized, we lose consciousness. It thus seems plausible to suppose that the formation of expectations might be a conscious process in which the detection of a CS triggers a conscious expectation that a US will follow. (See also Öhman and Mineka, 2001.) According to this expanded version of our two-system hypothesis, an association would be formed whenever a CS is followed by a US, and, independently, we would also become consciously aware of the relationship between these stimuli. Normally these processes would occur simultaneously, but, as in animals, it might be possible for one to occur without the other. (For a thoughtful exposition of possible relationships between the two systems, as well as alternative views, see Lovibond and Shanks, 2002.)

In most conditioning experiments participants would become aware of the relationship between the CS and the US – it is hard to miss the fact that the presentation of a light is always followed by a puff of air in your eye! If for any reason the cognitive system did not detect this relationship, however, then the two-system hypothesis suggests that conditioning could nevertheless occur without participants' awareness.

Brain damage

How is it possible, you might wonder, for the cognitive system not to notice such an obvious sequence of events? One possibility is brain damage. Suppose that the cortex was severely damaged in a car accident. According to the two-systems hypothesis the brain would no longer be able to form expectations, but conditioning could still occur if subcortical systems were intact.

To test this prediction, Bechara *et al.* (1995) investigated fear conditioning in patients with various forms of brain damage. On each trial a colored slide was presented; whenever the color blue appeared, it was followed by a loud blast of a horn. They used the GSR to assess whether fear conditioning had occurred, and at the end of the conditioning trials they also asked participants to say which color had preceded the horn blast.

One of the participants had a hereditary condition that causes damage to the amygdala. This subject showed no sign of conditioning. When interviewed afterwards, however, this subject knew that the blue slide had been followed by the noise. We thus have a rather unusual situation where even though the subject knew that blue would be followed by an aversive noise, he showed no fear. The cortical system still produced an expectation of an aversive stimulus, but the amygdala was not translating this expectation into fear.

The same procedure was used with a second patient who had suffered accidental damage to the hippocampus, an area of the brain that is known to play an important role in certain kinds of memory. This patient showed normal conditioning, with blue eliciting a stronger GSR than any of the other colors. When asked which color was followed by the noise, however, he had no idea! This participant could not form expectations, but fear conditioning nevertheless proceeded normally. Combined with the results for the first subject, these findings suggest that fear conditioning and expectations can develop independently, with damage to the brain eliminating one without affecting the other (Figure 3.12). (See also Knowlton, Mangels, and Squire, 1996; Morris *et al.*, 2001; LaBar and Phelps, 2005.)

Subliminal presentations

Another way to prevent conscious awareness of the relationship between the CS and the US is to present the CS in such a way that participants will not notice it. In one study exemplifying this approach, Öhman and Soares (1998) presented participants with pictures of either a snake or a spider, followed on some trials by a mild electric shock. A discriminative conditioning procedure was used in which

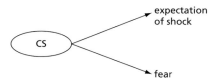

Figure 3.12 Following conditioning, a CS can independently elicit an expectation of shock and fear; one can occur without the other.

one of the stimuli was followed by the shock while the other was not:

$$CS+ \rightarrow shock$$
$$CS- \rightarrow \underline{\quad\quad}$$

To see if conditioning could occur without awareness, each stimulus was presented for only 30 milliseconds (0.03 seconds) and immediately followed by a masking stimulus – in this case, a meaningless jumble of dark and light shapes. Previous research had shown that masking stimuli presented under these conditions effectively erase preceding stimuli before subjects can become consciously aware of them. The procedure is thus sometimes referred to as *subliminal* presentation – *limen* is the Latin word for threshold, and the stimulus remains below the threshold of consciousness.

To check that subjects were genuinely not aware of the CS, the experimenters ran an additional group in which there was a 4-second gap between the CS and the US, and during this gap participants were asked to report whether the picture had been of a snake or a spider. The percentage of correct responses was almost exactly at chance (50.5%), confirming that participants had no idea what stimulus had been presented. And yet, despite this lack of awareness, conditioning occurred normally, as presentations of CS+ eventually elicited substantially higher GSRs than CS−. The CS+ was thus eliciting fear even though participants did not know that it had been presented.

The evidence for conditioning without awareness has not gone unchallenged (for example, Lovibond and Shanks, 2002). All experiments are susceptible to alternative interpretations, but there are particular problems involved in assessing awareness that make research in this area more than usually fraught. Wiens, Katkin, and Öhman (2003), for example, noted a possible alternative interpretation of Öhman and Soares's results. The CS+ and CS− trials in that experiment alternated randomly, but with one restriction, that there could not be three consecutive trials involving the same stimulus (for example, CS−, CS−, CS−). Suppose that participants could not identify the pictures, but that as training continued participants realized that there were never three trials in a row without a shock. If so, then after two trials without shock they would have expected a shock on the third trial, and hence shown more fear. In other words, even though they were unaware of the pictures, they might have had some awareness of the sequence in which shocks were presented, and this partial knowledge could have led to greater fear on CS+ trials than on CS− trials. What looked like conditioning without awareness might have been nothing of the kind: Even though participants were not aware of one predictor of the shock, the pictures, they might have been aware of another, the shock sequence.

This might sound an abstruse and unlikely analysis, but Wiens and his colleagues nevertheless decided to test it. And, perhaps to their surprise, they found that the order in which the trials were presented did affect responding. Other aspects of their findings led them nevertheless to support the original conclusion of conditioning without awareness, but this example illustrates the kinds of subtle problems that can arise in trying to assess awareness. We must, therefore, be cautious in drawing conclusions. On balance, current evidence does suggest that conditioning can occur without a person's awareness, but the issue is not yet closed. (For examples of positive reports, see Olsson and Phelps, 2004; Smith *et al.*, 2005; Weike, Schupp, and Hamm, 2007; for a contrary view, see Lipp and Purkis, 2005.)

Advertising

If conditioning can occur without awareness, this could be a factor in the effectiveness of some advertising. Advertisers have long believed that they can influence the attractiveness of their products by presenting them in conjunction with other, more appealing stimuli. Hotel or tourism campaigns, for example, invariably feature handsome men and attractive women, and commercials for political candidates are often set against a scenic background and accompanied by patriotic music. Could classical conditioning be at work in these advertisements, with our positive feelings about the context being transferred, without our awareness, to the product being promoted?

We have already encountered evidence that our feelings about one stimulus can be transferred to accompanying stimuli in our discussion of evaluative conditioning in Chapter 2. As to whether such conditioning could occur without our awareness, at least some evidence suggests that the answer is yes. In one study by Janis, Kaye, and Kirschner (1965), subjects were asked to read a persuasive message; those who read the message while they were eating were significantly more likely to accept the positions advocated than were control subjects who were not eating. Similarly, Gorn (1982) found that attractive music played during a commercial significantly increased preference for the product. And, as we discussed in Chapter 1, Smith and Engel (1968) found that the presence of an attractive woman standing next to an automobile powerfully influenced subjects' evaluation of that car. In both the Gorn and the Smith and Engel studies participants were interviewed after the experiments were over and almost all denied that their rating of the product had been affected by the accompanying stimuli.

A more recent study by Winkielman, Berridge, and Wilbarger (2005), although not directly on conditioning, provides further evidence of how our emotions can affect us without our realizing it. Participants were shown photographs of faces on a computer screen and asked to rate the gender of each face. As they worked on this task, however, they were also exposed to subliminal presentations of either angry or happy faces. Finally, to assess the effect of this subliminal exposure, they were given a lemon-lime drink to try and asked how much they would be willing to pay for it. Despite the fact that participants were not aware of the faces, those who had been exposed to the happy faces drank substantially more of the beverage and were willing to pay twice as much to buy it! The effect was only temporary, but if even subliminal stimuli can affect us in this way, it does raise the question of how much more powerfully we might be influenced by advertisements in which a product, be it a soap powder or a politician, is paired with emotionally appealing stimuli. (For other work relevant to conditioning and advertising, see Cacioppo *et al.*, 1992; Priluck and Till, 2004; Schachtman, Walker, and Fowler 2011.)

Summary

There is suggestive evidence, then, for the existence of two distinct systems in conditioning: a relatively primitive system based on associations, and a cognitive system based on expectations. If there truly are separate systems, this could help to explain a number of otherwise puzzling aspects of our behavior, including why we sometimes feel anxious but cannot say why. In one clinical case, a woman who had been raped had no conscious memory of the incident, but she nevertheless became extremely upset when returned to the scene of the crime (Christianson and Nilsson, 1989). Another case involved a French woman who suffered from a condition called Korsakoff's syndrome, one consequence of which was that she lost the ability to form new memories. Each time her physician, Edouard Claperede, came to see her, she failed to recognize him, even if their last encounter had been only minutes previously, so that on each occasion he had to introduce himself all over again. (See also the discussion of retrograde amnesia in Chapter 10.) One day, as a test, he concealed a pin within his hand when he greeted her and shook her hand. When he next met her, he again offered to shake her hand but this time she refused, even though she could not say why (Claperede, 1911). As in the case of the woman who had been raped, unconscious associations seemed to be eliciting fear, even though at a conscious level she had no memory of what had happened to be causing this fear.

The suggestion that conditioning involves two separate systems is not universally accepted. Many psychologists who study learning would argue that it would be more parsimonious to assume one system until the evidence for two systems becomes overwhelming, and that we have not yet reached that point (for example, Lovibond and Shanks, 2002). The evidence for two systems thus must be viewed with some caution. I think the balance of evidence does favor the assumption of two systems, but it is important to recognize that this is just one reading of the evidence; the issue is not yet settled.

Causal learning

In previous sections we have traced a gradual shift in psychologists' understanding of classical conditioning. At first, learning theorists saw conditioning as a fundamentally simple process in which associations were formed whenever two centers in the brain were active at the same time. The research reviewed in this chapter, however, led to profound changes in this view. Experiments on contingency, preparedness, and blocking showed that conditioning does not occur indiscriminately to whatever stimuli happen to precede a US. Instead, conditioning becomes focused on the stimuli in the environment that are the best predictors of the US, even if (as in the case of taste-aversion learning) the best predictor occurs many hours before the US. If so, conditioning must involve far more than just the formation of associations between contiguous events; it appears to entail a more sophisticated system for detecting relationships, allowing us to anticipate when important events are going to occur and to take preparatory action (see also Dickinson, 1980).

This shift in perspective was neatly captured in the title of an article by Rescorla (1988): "Pavlovian conditioning: it's not what you think it is." He went on to write, "Pavlovian conditioning is not a stupid process by which the organism willy-nilly forms associations between any two stimuli that happen to co-occur. Rather, the organism is better seen as an information seeker using logical and perceptual relations among events . . . to form a sophisticated representation of its world" (p. 154).

If this perspective is correct, one question that arises is whether we might use this sophisticated system for detecting other kinds of relationships. In our daily lives, after all, we are constantly trying to identify causal relationships between events: Is a friend angry because of something we said? Is our rash an allergic reaction to something we ate? Does underlining passages in a text help us get better grades? In all these cases we try to identify causal relationships; might the processes involved in detecting CS–US relationships also play a role in these other instances of **causal learning**?

Medical diagnosis

Intriguing evidence on this point was reported in a study by Gluck and Bower (1988) designed to simulate the judgments that doctors must learn to make in diagnosing patients. University students were given fictitious medical records of

250 patients. Each patient had some combination of the following symptoms: a bloody nose, stomach cramps, puffy eyes, and discolored gums. On the basis of these symptoms, participants were asked to decide which of two diseases each patient was suffering from – we will call them Bad and Worse. After each diagnosis they were told the actual disease. Finally, after reading all 250 records, subjects were shown each symptom one at a time and asked to estimate the probability that a patient with this symptom had Bad or Worse. In fact, the cases had been constructed so that the symptoms varied in predictive value.

Although the problem was presented as one of medical diagnosis, it can also be viewed as analogous to classical conditioning, with each symptom functioning as a CS and each disease as a US. If a record showed that a patient had a bloody nose (symptom A) and stomach cramps (symptom B), and this was followed by information that the patient had Worse, this can be viewed as a compound conditioning trial in which the compound stimulus AB was followed by Worse:

$$CS_{AB} \rightarrow US_W$$

It is then possible to use the Rescorla–Wagner model to calculate the change in the strength of the association between the symptoms and the disease on every trial. The stronger the association between, say, symptom A and Worse, the more likely subjects should be to expect patients with this symptom to have this disease.

Gluck and Bower found that the Rescorla–Wagner model was remarkably accurate in predicting subjects' probability estimates. And, even more remarkably, the model's predictions proved to be more accurate than those of the main theories of human concept learning that were also tested. The Rescorla–Wagner model, developed to account for the behavior of rats in fear conditioning experiments, thus seemed to be better at predicting human behavior than were models explicitly developed to explain people's ability to learn complex conceptual relationships.

Retrospective revaluation

This result might at first seem so unlikely as to be unbelievable – surely the reasoning that a doctor uses in diagnosing diseases is far more sophisticated than the skills involved in associating a light with a puff of air to the eye? Indeed, there undoubtedly are differences, but from an evolutionary perspective the claim of similarities is perhaps not as outrageous as it first sounds. Studies of evolution have made it clear that evolution generally involves relatively small changes to existing mechanisms, rather than the creation of entirely new systems from scratch. In the case of the brain, once evolution had produced a sophisticated system for detecting relationships between, say, tastes and illness, it would not be surprising if this system was then adapted for use in other areas, and if some of the core principles remained the same.

Gluck and Bower's experiment initiated what soon became a flood of research, as experimenters examined whether the associative principles discovered in research on classical conditioning could also explain more complex forms of decision making such as causal learning. The path of this research proved bumpy, as each newly published experiment seemed to reverse the conclusions of its immediate predecessor. As an example, one line of research has concerned a phenomenon called **retrospective revaluation**. In our earlier discussion of blocking, we saw that the training procedure involves the following steps:

$$(1) \quad A \rightarrow X$$
$$(2) \ AB \rightarrow X$$

The outcome, as we have seen, is that the initial conditioning to stimulus A blocks conditioning to the added stimulus B. In retrospective revaluation experiments, the order of these steps is reversed:

$$(1) \ AB \rightarrow X$$
$$(2) \quad A \rightarrow X$$

In a typical experiment, participants might be told that their task was to figure out what foods were causing a patient to have an allergic reaction. They would then be shown what the patient ate each night, one meal at a time, and for each meal whether it was followed by illness. During stage one, for example, they might be told of some nights on which the patient ate spaghetti (A) and meatballs (B), and that the patient became ill after each of these meals. Then, in stage 2, the list of meals would include ones in which the patient ate only spaghetti (A), and again became ill:

$$(1) \ \text{spaghetti} + \text{meatballs} \rightarrow \text{illness}$$
$$(2) \qquad\qquad\qquad \text{spaghetti} \rightarrow \text{illness}$$

Finally, they would be asked to rate the likelihood that each of the foods encountered in the experiment would make the patient ill.

What should we expect to happen? According to an associative analysis, participants should believe that eating meatballs (B) produces illness, because every time the patient ate meatballs they would become ill. The Rescorla–Wagner model, for example, would say that the AB trials during the first phase should result in A and B both becoming associated with illness. When stimulus A on its own was then paired with illness, this would have further strengthened the association between A and illness. Crucially, however, these added $A \rightarrow$ illness trials should have no effect on conditioning to *B*, because *B* is not present. According to the model, therefore, *B*'s association with illness should remain intact, so that participants should still expect eating meatballs (*B*) to produce an allergic reaction.

That, however, was not what was found. The model's prediction has been tested in several experiments, and in every case participants concluded that while the spaghetti produced illness, the meatballs did not (for example, Dickinson and Burke, 1996; Shanks, 1985).

From an associative perspective this result is puzzling: If eating meatballs is always followed by illness, why is no association formed? The answer that may have already occurred to you is that participants were not just blindly forming associations; they were logically analyzing the evidence. When told in the first phase that meals of spaghetti and meatballs were followed by illness, they would have recognized that both were possible causes. When then told that spaghetti on its own produced illness, however, they would have retrospectively revaluated the earlier evidence: If the patient became ill every time he ate spaghetti, the presence of meatballs during the earlier meals was probably irrelevant. In reaching a conclusion, in other words, participants were not just associating whatever items they heard mentioned; they were thinking logically about what the evidence meant.

Given the success of the Rescorla–Wagner model in explaining conditioning, its failure to account for retrospective revaluation seemed to imply that causal learning and conditioning must involve different processes. In particular, retrospective revaluation seemed to involve much more sophisticated processes of inferential reasoning. Before the obituaries for an associative interpretation could be properly written, however, follow-up experiments (for example, Balleine, Espinet, and González, 2005) showed that retrospective revaluation effects could also be obtained in conditioning experiments with animals! Moreover, several theorists soon showed how, with a simple modification, the Rescorla–Wagner model could account for retrospective revaluation after all (Dickinson and Burke, 1996; Ghirlanda, 2005). A phenomenon that at first seemed compelling evidence that the principles of conditioning and casual learning were different thus began to look like yet further evidence for their similarity.

Dogs and doctors

It is important to emphasize that the issue here is not whether the processes involved are identical. A doctor's diagnosis of a patient unquestionably involves forms of logical reasoning far more sophisticated than whatever associative processes might be at work in the conditioning of an eyeblink. In both cases, however, we try to uncover causal relationships that may be hidden in a large mass of data, and at the moment it does look as if the associative processes that emerged in the course of evolution to help animals detect one class of causal relationships may also help people to detect causes in situations that, on the surface, appear very different (Karazinov and Boakes, 2007; Vadillo and Matute, 2007).

This claim may seem unlikely because we are accustomed to thinking of human decision making as a highly rational and sophisticated process, and conditioning as a very primitive one, but they might not differ as dramatically as this view suggests. We have already seen that classical conditioning is more complex than it appears; conversely, research on human decision making has revealed that our decisions are not nearly as logical as once believed. (We will discuss this further in Chapter 7.) Detecting a relationship between two events is easy in some situations – if you get burned every time you put your hand in a fire, you will learn this relationship with impressive speed. When there is a longer gap between two events, however, and the first is not always followed by the second, then detecting their relationship can be far, far more difficult. Some interesting examples come from professional sports, where coaches with years of experience nevertheless sometimes completely misinterpret the relationship between events. Everyone who has ever played basketball, for example, is aware of the "hot hand," that when a player has hit several shots in a row, they are "hot," and it is worth passing the ball to them again because they are likely to score. All players and coaches know this – it is so obvious as not even to be worth discussion – but, at least at the professional level, it is completely untrue: a professional basketball player's likelihood of scoring a basket is exactly the same whether or not they hit their previous shot, or, say, hit three in a row.

When coaches were told of the relevant evidence, they vehemently rejected it – they were sure that they could not be wrong about something that appeared to them so blindingly obvious. (We'll discuss this further in Chapter 7.) Lest you think this misreading of evidence is atypical, or confined to basketball, exactly the same kinds of mistaken beliefs – also held with unshakeable conviction – have been found in other sports. Statistical analysis has shown that some of baseball managers' strongest beliefs – about whether to walk a good hitter, for example, or the importance of a high batting average – are completely wrong. And again, when managers were shown the evidence, they simply didn't believe it. (For an entertaining account, see Lewis, 2003.)

The problem in both cases is that it can be very difficult to detect predictive relationships between events when they are embedded in a sea of other events, and their relationship is probabilistic – A is not always followed by B. In such cases, it would not be surprising if the unconscious processes we use for detecting relationships are based on – or even identical to? – the processes that evolved over millions of years to help our ancestors detect causal relationships. It is too soon to say for sure, but it is an intriguing thought that the processes that govern a dog's salivation might also play a role in doctors' diagnoses of medical conditions or consumers' decisions about what car to buy. (See also Buehner and Cheng, 2005; Pineňo and Miller, 2007; Shanks, 2007; Shettleworth, 2010.)

Terminology

We have used several terms in this section that can easily be confused, so it may be worth concluding with some notes on terminology. The word *associative* is used in two quite different senses, one descriptive and the other theoretical. In the phrase *associative learning*, the term is used purely descriptively: We employ it to describe any situation in which we learn that one event is followed by another – for example, that thunder is followed by lightning. It doesn't matter how this learning occurs, or whether it is conscious or unconsious; if we learn that one event is followed by another, then this is an instance of associative learning.

The term *associative* is also used, however, to describe a particular *theory* about how associative learning occurs, namely that a connection is formed between event representations in the brain, such that activation of one representation automatically leads to activation of the other. In our thunder example, hearing thunder would automatically activate a representation of lighting. According to a cognitive account, on the other hand, events like these are linked in the form of an expectation, a more complex representational structure. If you expect thunder to be followed by lightning, you could logically combine this knowledge with other information you possess, such as that lighting is dangerous and is more likely to strike tall objects such as trees, in order to generate an action plan – "A storm is coming, I need to move away from this tree." So, learning that thunder is followed by lighting would be an example of associative learning, and we could attribute this learning to the formation of simple links or associations (associative theories), or more complex expectations (cognitive theories).

Finally, we need to distinguish between *associative learning* and *causal learning.* We have used the term *associative learning* to describe situations in which we learn that event A is followed by event B; *causal learning* is a subset of associative learning in which A does not simply precede B but actually causes it. For example, suppose that you noticed that you were more likely to develop a rash on days when you ate nuts. If you simply noticed this pattern, it would be an example of associative learning; if, in addition, you inferred that eating the nuts must have *caused* your rash, then it would also be an example of causal learning.

Summary

- Psychologists initially believed that conditioning was a fundamentally simple process in which any stimulus that preceded a US would become associated with it. The strength of this association would depend on their contiguity, frequency, and intensity.

- This belief was challenged by research on preparedness, contingency, and blocking. Together, they suggested that conditioning depended not simply on whether a CS preceded a US but on whether it was a good predicator of that US.

- To explain blocking, Kamin suggested that conditioning occurred only when a US was surprising. When an unexpected event occurs, we search our memory for possible causes.

- Rescorla and Wagner developed a mathematical model of conditioning that was based on Kamin's work, though it avoided speculation on mental states. The model said conditioning causes the formation of an association between the CS and the US, and that the change in the strength of this association on any trial would depend on the difference between its existing strength and the maximum possible strength. They further assumed that the existing strength would depend on all of the stimuli present.

- Their model was able not only to account for most known phenomena in conditioning but also to successfully predict many new ones. Its success was particularly impressive because of its parsimony – its predictions were based on a small number of very simple assumptions.

- There were also phenomena that the model had difficulty explaining, such as latent inhibition, though the original model has since been modified in order to account for them. Whatever its ultimate success, it is unquestionably the most successful – and influential – model in the history of learning.

- The Rescorla–Wagner model is silent as to the nature of the CS–US association. Pavlov believed that conditioning resulted in the formation of a connection between the CS and US centers in the brain, Tolman that an expectation was formed that the CS would be followed by the US.

- There is evidence to support both accounts, and this has led some theorists to the view that in the course of evolution two fundamentally different systems emerged, first a relatively simple associative system and then a more sophisticated cognitive system. Evidence that conditioning can affect us without our awareness supports the idea that we still have a primitive system within our brains, as well as the more sophisticated cognitive one.

- Many psychologists now view conditioning as a sophisticated system that evolved to detect relationships among events, relationships that were sometimes obscured by the temporal gap between them. The processes involved might also play a role in situations seemingly far removed from dogs salivating in a laboratory, such as doctors trying to diagnose the cause of a patient's illness.

Review questions

1 Why did simultaneous and backward conditioning seem to pose problems for the principle of contiguity? How can these apparent anomalies be explained?

2 The principle of contiguity suggests that contiguity is both *necessary* for conditioning (conditioning will occur only if the CS and the US occur closely together in time) and *sufficient* (if a CS and a US occur together, then conditioning will occur). How did the research of Rescorla, Garcia, and Kamin pose problems for this principle?

3 How did Rescorla disentangle the roles of contiguity and contingency in conditioning?

4 How did Garcia and Koelling show that the conditioning of a stronger aversion to a taste than to a light was not simply the result of greater salience of the taste as a conditioned stimulus?

5 How might classical conditioning contribute to an animal's survival? Why might it be better *not* to associate a US with all the stimuli that precede it?

6 How did Kamin account for blocking?

7 How did Rescorla and Wagner build on Kamin's work? What changes did they make to his explanation of blocking?

8 What equation did they use to predict learning? What does each symbol represent?

9 Why didn't Rescorla and Wagner try to determine the real values of the parameters c and V_{max}? What approach did they use instead?

10 What are the three main criteria usually used to evaluate theories? How does the Rescorla–Wagner model fare on each?

11 Why did the evidence for latent inhibition pose a problem for the Rescorla–Wagner model?

12 Can you figure out how their model could be used to account for the phenomenon of conditioned inhibition?

13 What is the difference between signal and substitution accounts of conditioning? What evidence supports each account?

14 What is the two-system hypothesis? How does it account for the conflicting evidence on whether a CS functions as a signal or a substitute for the US?

15 The two-system hypothesis suggests that conditioning can occur even when we are not consciously aware of the relationship between the CS and the US. What kind of evidence has been used to test this claim, and what has it shown?

16 What might be the role of conditioning in advertising?

17 Conditioning probably evolved as a mechanism to help animals predict (and therefore potentially prepare for) important events such as the imminence of food or predators. In recent years psychologists have speculated that we might now use the processes that originally evolved for this narrow purpose to help us to identify cause–effect relationships in situations seemingly far removed from salivating in anticipation of food. To what extent has research on causal learning in humans supported this claim?

4

Reinforcement

CONTENTS

One of the most obvious ways to encourage a behavior is to reward it. Parents praise children's good behavior; companies pay salespeople bonuses for high output; universities promote productive researchers. There is nothing new or profound about the idea of using rewards to encourage behavior – the principle was probably known and used long before the discovery of fire.

If the principle of reward is so obvious, though, why is behavior often so hard to change? Why do parents find it so difficult to get their teenage children to clean their rooms? Or, to take a more immediately relevant example, why do students sometimes find it so difficult to make themselves study? There are, after all, very powerful rewards for studying: in the short term, good course grades; in the longer term, a better job. Yet students often leave studying until the last minute, and some don't get around to it even then. Similarly, smoking and overeating can take years off our lives, and people are often desperate to give up these habits; yet the habits persist. Why is behavior in these situations apparently so irrational, when rewards as potent as a good job and longer life have little effect? Clearly, the principle of reward cannot be quite as simple as it sounds.

To understand why rewards seem to control behavior in some situations but not others, we will examine experimental research into the principles that determine the effectiveness of rewards. Then, in Chapter 5, we will examine some of the attempts that have been made to apply the principles discovered in the laboratory in real life, and what these attempts have revealed about both the strengths and the weaknesses of rewards as a tool for altering behavior. We will begin, though, with the first experimental study of rewards, by Edward Lee Thorndike.

Thorndike's Law of Effect

Thorndike's research, like Pavlov's, had its roots in the philosophy of Associationism, but its most immediate antecedent was the publication of Charles Darwin's *Origin of Species*. Darwin's theory of evolution had proposed that man was but one animal species among many, and this claim triggered a surge of interest in the intelligence and reasoning powers of animals. If Darwin was right, if we are closely related to other animal species, then the traditional view that animals are dumb brutes becomes far less attractive. After all, if our close relatives were dumb, what might that imply about us?

Are animals intelligent?

To lay the basis for a more realistic judgment, a contemporary of Darwin named George Romanes collected observations of animal behavior from reliable observers around the world. When published, the material in Romanes's *Animal intelligence* seemed to strongly support Darwin's thesis, as anecdote after anecdote revealed impressive powers of reasoning. Thorndike, however, was skeptical of these accounts. For one thing, the observations might not be accurate – observers' memories might have become distorted over time, and anecdotes might have been exaggerated as they were told and retold. Even if an incident was described correctly, it might not have been representative of the species' typical behavior. As Thorndike noted,

Dogs get lost hundreds of times, and no one ever notices it or sends an account of it to a scientific magazine. But let one find his way from Brooklyn to Yonkers and the fact immediately becomes a circulating anecdote. Thousands of cats on thousands of occasions sit helplessly yowling, and no one takes thought of it or writes to his friend, the professor;

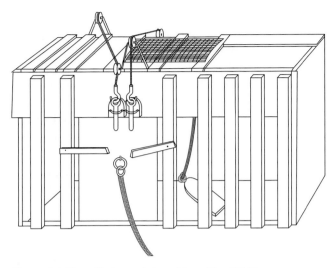

Figure 4.1 Thorndike's puzzle box. (Thorndike, 1911.)

but let one cat claw at the knob of a door supposedly as a signal to be let out, and straightaway this cat becomes the representative of the cat-mind in all the books.

(Thorndike, 1898, p. 4)

The Law of Effect

To remedy these defects, Thorndike argued, "experiment must be substituted for observation and the collection of anecdotes. Thus . . . you can repeat the conditions at will, so as to see whether or not the animal's behavior is due to mere coincidence." To this end, Thorndike began to study learning in animals using an apparatus that he called a *puzzle box*. Basically, it was little more than a wooden crate with a door that could be opened by a special mechanism, such as a latch or a rope (Figure 4.1). Thorndike placed a dish containing food outside the box but visible through its slats, then put the animal to be tested inside and observed its reactions.

When a hungry cat was placed in the box, Thorndike found that it would initially scramble around the box, frantically clawing and biting at the sides of the apparatus to escape and reach the food. After approximately 5 to 10 minutes of struggling, the cat would eventually stumble on the correct response and, finding the door open, would rush out and eat the food. According to Romanes's anecdotes, this success should have led to the immediate repetition of the successful response on the following trial. Instead, Thorndike found that the animal generally repeated the frantic struggling observed on the first trial. When the cat finally did repeat the correct response, however, the **latency** of this response – the time from being put in the box to performing the response – was generally shorter than it had

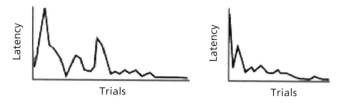

Figure 4.2 Changes in the latency of escape from the puzzle box over trials for two of Thorndike's cats. (Thorndike, 1911.)

been on the first trial, shorter still on the third trial, and so on. Figure 4.2 presents representative records of the performance of two cats. Progress in both cases was gradual and marked by occasional reversals, but on average the time to escape became progressively shorter as training continued.

This slow and irregular improvement did not suggest that the cats had formed any rational understanding of the situation. Instead, Thorndike argued, the food reward was gradually stamping in an association between the box cues and the escape response, so that the box cues gradually elicited the correct response more and more strongly. He repeated this experiment with other responses and also with other species, including chicks, dogs, and monkeys. The basic pattern of the results was almost always the same: a gradual improvement over many trials. This uniform pattern suggested that the gradual strengthening effect of rewards was not confined to a single situation or species but, rather, represented a general law of behavior, which Thorndike formalized as the **Law of Effect**:

Of several responses made to the same situation, those which are accompanied or closely followed by satisfaction to the animal will, other things being equal, be more firmly connected with the situation, so that, when it recurs, they will be more likely to recur . . . The greater the satisfaction . . . the greater the strengthening . . . of the bond.

(Thorndike, 1911, p. 24)

Some controversial issues

When Thorndike's findings were published, they aroused considerable controversy. One focus of debate was his claim that much if not all of animals' seemingly intelligent behavior could be explained by the formation of associations. We will examine this issue in more depth in Chapter 7; we will focus here on two other aspects of his findings that attracted attention.

I can't get no satisfaction

Thorndike was criticized by behaviorists for his use of the term *satisfaction*, which refers to a subjective or mental state. We can't see into the mind of a cat, so how

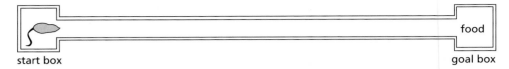

Figure 4.3 A straight-alley maze.

can we know whether it is experiencing satisfaction? This difficulty in assessing satisfaction makes the Law of Effect potentially circular: A response will increase if it is followed by a satisfying outcome, but the only way we know whether the outcome is satisfying is if the response increases! In fact, Thorndike was aware of this problem, and he proposed an independent and objective test for determining whether a consequence was satisfying: "By a satisfying state of affairs is meant one which the animal does nothing to avoid, often doing such things as attain and preserve it" (Thorndike, 1911, p. 245). In other words, if a cat repeatedly tries to obtain food in one situation – for example, by jumping up onto a table where food is kept – then by definition this food must be satisfying, and the Law of Effect now allows us to predict that the food will also be an effective reward for other behaviors, such as escaping from the puzzle box. Meehl (1950) later labeled this property of rewards *transituationality.*

Thorndike's objective definition of satisfaction saves the Law of Effect from circularity, but the term still bothered learning theorists because of its subjective connotation that a reward is emotionally satisfying. An experiment by Sheffield, Wulff, and Backer (1951) illustrates the dangers. To study what events are rewarding, they used an apparatus called a *straight-alley maze*, which consists of a start box and a goal box connected by a long alley (see Figure 4.3). To find out if a stimulus is rewarding, the stimulus is placed in the goal box and the subject in the start box, and the experimenter records how long it takes for the subject to run to the goal box. If the stimulus is rewarding, it should strengthen the response of running, and the speed of running down the alley should thus increase over trials.

The experimenters used male rats as subjects and a receptive female in the goal box as the reward. The normal copulatory pattern in rats consists of a series of 8 to 12 intromissions and withdrawals by the male until it finally ejaculates. When the male reached the goal box, the experimenters allowed it two intromissions, and then abruptly removed it from the goal box. Intuitively, it is not obvious that males would regard this as a satisfying experience, but it proved to be a very powerful reward, as their speed of running down the alley increased over trials by a factor of eight!

Such evidence makes it at least questionable whether all events that strengthen behavior are emotionally satisfying, and it has led learning theorists to prefer the more objective term *reinforcer* to *reward*. A **reinforcer** can be defined as an event that increases the probability of a response when presented after that response. Similarly, we can define **reinforcement** as an increase in the probability of a response caused by the presentation of a reinforcer following that response.

Reinforcement versus conditioning

A further issue arising from Thorndike's work concerned the relationship between the learning he described and that described by Pavlov. The procedures used by the two investigators clearly differed. Pavlov arranged a contingency between two stimuli: food, for example, was presented following a tone but not in its absence. Thorndike, on the other hand, arranged a contingency between a response and a stimulus: Food was presented only after a correct response. If we represent the consequence by the symbol S^*, then we can represent the two forms of learning as follows:

$$\text{Classical conditioning: } S \rightarrow S^*$$
$$\text{Reinforcement: } R \rightarrow S^*$$

Carrying this point a bit further, in classical conditioning the presentation of food depends solely on whether the CS has been presented: Whether a dog salivates has no effect on whether food is given. In reinforcement, on the other hand, the presentation of food depends crucially on the subject's response: No response, no food.

In procedural terms, classical conditioning and reinforcement clearly differ. This, however, does not necessarily mean that the learning processes involved are different. As we suggested in our discussion of classical conditioning and causal learning, a single learning process could be involved in detecting relationships between events, regardless of the nature of the events concerned. Thus, although the *procedures* used in classical conditioning and reinforcement are different, the underlying *processes* could be the same.

If the learning processes were the same, we should expect the principles of classical conditioning and reinforcement to be similar if not identical. Just as classical conditioning depends on how closely the US follows the CS, for example, so the effectiveness of reinforcement should depend on how closely the reinforcer follows the response. As we shall see shortly, contiguity is indeed critical in reinforcement, and many of the other principles of conditioning and reinforcement also turn out to be the same. (For further discussion, see Colwill and Rescorla, 1990; Williams, Preston, and de Kervor, 1990.) For our present purposes, though, the key point to note is the distinction between the two procedures. In both reinforcement and classical conditioning, a response is strengthened because of the presentation of an event such as food: In reinforcement, food is delivered following a response, whereas in classical conditioning the food is delivered following a stimulus.

The reinforcer

One obvious determinant of whether a reward will strengthen behavior is the attractiveness of the reward. As in the classic recipe for elephant stew – where the first step is said to be "catch an elephant" – the first step in using reinforcement effectively is to identify a suitable reinforcer.

Primary reinforcers

The most obvious candidates are stimuli that are necessary for survival, such as food and water. It makes sense that such stimuli would become reinforcing in the course of evolution because an animal that repeats a response that has led to food is likely to have a better chance of obtaining food in the future. Thus, a gene that established food as a reinforcer would be likely to be transmitted to future generations. It therefore came as no surprise when early research demonstrated that stimuli such as food, water, and sexual intercourse were all reinforcing.

In the early 1950s, however, evidence began to accumulate that not all reinforcers were necessary for survival, at least not in the simple physical sense that food is. In an experiment by Butler (1954), monkeys were placed in an enclosed cage with two wooden panels, one painted yellow and the other blue. If a monkey pushed open the blue door, it was allowed to look out into the experimental room beyond for a period of 30 seconds. If it pushed against the yellow door, an opaque screen immediately came down, terminating the trial. Not only did the monkeys quickly solve this problem, learning to push only the blue door, regardless of the side on which it was presented, but they proved remarkably persistent in performing the response. In one experiment in which there was a trial once a minute – that is, a 30-second opportunity to look out into the room, followed by a 30-second blank interval – one subject responded on every single trial for 9 hours without a break. A second subject responded for 11 hours, and a third for an extraordinary 19 consecutive hours.

Visual access to the surrounding room was clearly not necessary for the monkeys' survival in any direct sense, but it proved a remarkably potent reinforcer. As Butler commented, "That monkeys would work as long and as persistently for food is highly unlikely." Visual stimulation now appears to be only one example of a large set of events that Kish (1966) has referred to as *sensory reinforcers*. The most important characteristic of these reinforcers seems to be that they provide variety in our perceptual environment. Rats, for example, prefer to explore complex mazes with many turns rather than to explore simple ones (Montgomery, 1954), and humans confined in a dark room will push a button that turns on a panel of flashing lights, with the rate of button-pushing increasing as the pattern of lights becomes less predictable (Jones, Wilkinson, and Braden, 1961).

The reinforcers we have discussed to this point – food, water, and sensory stimulation – are effective essentially from birth. Reinforcers like this that require no special training to be effective are called **primary reinforcers**.

The Premack principle

The evidence that sensory stimulation can be reinforcing suggests that reinforcers are not all physically necessary for survival. Is there any other characteristic, then, that reinforcers such as hamburgers, sex, and flashing lights share? Perhaps the most useful integrating principle is one suggested by David Premack (1965, 1971). Premack argued that different experiences all have different values for us and that these values can be inferred by observing the amount of time in which we engage in these activities when they are freely available. The common characteristic of reinforcers, said Premack, is that they are all high-probability activities. Is it possible, then, that *any* high-probability activity will reinforce any response that has a lower probability?

Suppose that a group of children were given free access to a number of foods and were found to prefer potatoes to spinach, but to strongly prefer ice cream to both of them. If high-probability responses reinforce lower-probability responses, then – as all parents know – we should be able to use access to ice cream to reinforce eating spinach. However, we should also be able to use access to potatoes to reinforce eating spinach, albeit less effectively, because eating potatoes is also a higher-probability response. Premack (1965) tested predictions like these in a series of experiments involving rats and children, and on the whole the results were positive. The suggestion that more probable responses will reinforce less probable responses thus became known as the **Premack principle**.[1]

A childish application

Homme *et al.* (1963) reported a particularly delightful application of this principle. The subjects were unruly 3-year-olds who repeatedly ignored their nursery

---

[1] A subtle but important elaboration of this principle is known as the *response deprivation hypothesis* (Timberlake and Allison, 1974). This states that whether an activity will serve as a reinforcer depends on whether the current level of the activity is below its preferred level. If a child, given a free choice, will eat two ice-cream bars a day, then access to ice cream will be reinforcing if the child currently has access to fewer than two bars.

school teacher's instructions and, instead, raced around the room screaming and pushing furniture. This kind of behavior can be wearing on even the most patient adults, but it is particularly hard to bear for those responsible for the children's safety. One common reaction of parents in such situations is to lose their tempers and punish the children to get them to do as they are told. Instead, Homme and his co-workers set out to reinforce good behavior through a judicious application of the Premack principle. They reinforced the children's behavior whenever the children sat and played quietly for a specified period of time, with the reinforcer being several minutes of uninterrupted running and screaming! Within only a few days, the children were obeying the teacher's instructions almost perfectly, so that "an observer, new on the scene, almost certainly would have assumed extensive aversive control was being used" (Homme *et al.*, 1963). Later on, new and even better reinforcers were developed through continued observation of the children's behavior, including such decidedly unusual rewards as allowing the children to throw a plastic cup across the room, to kick a wastepaper basket, and, best of all, to push the teacher around the room in a swivel chair on rolling wheels!

The moral to this story is that it is a mistake to think of reinforcers in terms of a restricted list of "approved" stimuli. There is no magic list of reinforcers; the best way to determine what will be reinforcing for someone is to observe that person's behavior.

Secondary reinforcers

In contrast to primary reinforcers, which are effective from birth, some of the most powerful reinforcers affecting our behavior are **secondary** or **conditioned reinforcers**, which have acquired their reinforcing properties through experience. Money, for example, is not at first a very effective reinforcer; showering an infant with dollar bills is unlikely to have any discernible impact on the infant's behavior. As we grow older, though, money becomes increasingly important; in some cases, it becomes an obsession. How, then, do secondary reinforcers, such as money or the word *good*, acquire their reinforcing properties?

The obvious explanation is through pairing with primary reinforcers. Money, for example, can be exchanged for a wide variety of other reinforcers such as food. Somewhat less obvious is the nature of the processes involved. In the case of the word *good*, does it act as a reinforcer because we rationally calculate that someone who is pleased with us is likely to provide other resources that we value, or is the process involved something closer to conditioning, where the positive feelings we have when someone smiles at us become transferred to the word *good* that accompanies this smile? Is the process purely rational, in other words, or is there also some element of emotional conditioning?

Existing research does not allow us to answer this question definitely, but, one way or another, it is clear that the effectiveness of secondary reinforcers does depend on pairing with primary reinforcers (for example, B. A. Williams, 1994, though see also Lieberman *et al.*, 1997). If you wanted to establish the word *good* as a secondary reinforcer for a child, for example, you would want to ensure that this word was followed by other reinforcers such as hugs or candy. And, once *good* had become an effective reinforcer, you would want to continue to pair it with backup reinforcers at least occasionally – as in the case of classical conditioning, repeatedly presenting a secondary reinforcer by itself would be likely to extinguish its reinforcing properties (Warren and Cairns, 1972).

Social reinforcers

A third possible category of reinforcers (one not usually treated separately) is *social reinforcers* – stimuli whose reinforcing properties derive uniquely from the behavior of other members of the same species. In practice, the meaning of this term is clearer than its definition and includes consequences such as praise, affection, and even just attention.

One reason for treating social reinforcers separately is that they are a blend of both primary and secondary reinforcers. Poulson (1983) found that an adult's smile could reinforce behavior in infants as young as 3 months, suggesting that smiling is innately reinforcing. But considerable evidence also indicates that the power of social reinforcers can be altered by pairing them with other reinforcers. The reinforcing properties of the word *good*, for example, can be increased by following it with candy (Warren and Cairns, 1972). Thus, although social reinforcement may have an innate basis, experience also plays an important role.

Our second reason for treating social reinforcers separately is to emphasize their importance. Social reinforcers such as praise and attention are probably the reinforcers we encounter most often in our daily lives, and they play an important – and often underestimated – role in controlling our behavior.

We can illustrate the power of social reinforcers with a study by Allen *et al.* (1964). The subject was a 4-year-old girl, Ann, who had just started nursery school. From the time of her arrival, she spent most of her time interacting with adults rather than playing with other children, and as time went on she developed a variety of behavioral problems. She complained frequently about skin abrasions that no one else could see; she spoke in a low voice that was very difficult to hear; and she spent increasing amounts of time standing by herself, pulling at her lower lip and fingering her cheek.

One possible analysis of Ann's behavior might have been that she was an insecure and unhappy child, and thus needed as much comfort and reassurance as possible to help her adjust to her new surroundings. The authors' analysis, however, was quite different. They noticed that a common feature of all Ann's problem behaviors was that they elicited adult attention. If she stood by herself, for example, a teacher was soon likely to come over to ask what was wrong. If adult attention was reinforcing, the teachers might have been encouraging the very behaviors they were trying to eliminate. The authors' advice to the teachers, therefore, was to change the reinforcement contingencies by paying attention to Ann whenever she played with others but ignoring her when she stood alone. When Ann did talk or play with other children, a teacher would come over to Ann, smile, and talk to her about what she was doing.

The result was a dramatic transformation in Ann's behavior. After just a single day, the proportion of her time spent in social play increased from 10% to 60%, and this higher level was maintained over subsequent weeks. The frequency of reinforcement was then gradually reduced and eventually faded out altogether, but Ann's social play remained at a high level. (As her skills in playing with other children increased, this play probably became its own source of reinforcement.)

Social reinforcers can be very powerful: Even a small shift in adult attention – not money, not candy, but just attention – was sufficient to substantially alter Ann's behavior. Also, as often happens, the crucial role of social reinforcement in directing Ann's behavior was not at first appreciated. Actions such as paying attention to someone are such a common part of our lives that we take them for granted, but, as we shall see again in other applications, social reinforcement can play a very powerful role in controlling behavior.

Negative reinforcers

There is one other class of reinforcers that we need to discuss at least briefly before proceeding. All of the reinforcers we have discussed to this point have been **positive reinforcers**, stimuli whose presentation will strengthen preceding responses. However, there are also **negative reinforcers**, stimuli whose *removal* will strengthen behavior. Suppose, for example, that you had the misfortune to move into an apartment where every night your neighbor played appallingly loud music of a kind you hated. And further suppose that the room also contained a white button mounted on a wall, and you discovered that each time you pushed the button the noise stopped for 1 minute. You would be very likely to develop a real fondness for pushing the button; if so, this would be an instance of negative reinforcement, as the reinforcer would be the removal of an unpleasant stimulus, rather than its presentation. (Another example would be taking an aspirin to relieve the pain of a headache; this behavior would be reinforced by the termination of pain.) To recap, we talk about a stimulus as a positive reinforcer when its presentation strengthens a response, but as a negative reinforcer when it is its removal that is reinforcing.

Note that positive and negative reinforcement are both forms of reinforcement: in both cases the outcome is a strengthening of a response. The term negative reinforcement is sometimes misused to mean punishment, but that is a mistake to try to avoid. If the term reinforcement is used, that always means a strengthening of behavior; in negative reinforcement this is achieved by removing an unpleasant or undesirable stimulus.

In some ways the distinction between positive and negative reinforcement is purely technical – is the result achieved by presenting a stimulus or removing it? – but it is important to use the terms correctly so as to avoid misunderstandings. Also, negative reinforcement is involved in an important form of learning called *avoidance learning.* To return to our hypothetical noise example, suppose that the mysterious button would not only terminate the music when it was on but could also be used to prevent its reappearance when it was off – for example, that pressing the button during the 1-minute period it was off would ensure a 10-minute period of silence before it returned. If you pressed the button while the noise was present, in order to terminate it, it would be termed an **escape response**; if you pressed the button while the noise was absent, to prevent it appearing, it would be called an **avoidance response**.

For many years the learning of avoidance behavior was regarded as a major theoretical puzzle. In our noise example, if you pressed the button while the room was quiet, nothing would happen – the reappearance of the music would be postponed, but the immediate effect would simply be a continuation of the silence. But if nothing happens, how could this act as a reinforcer?

One answer was provided in a cognitive theory of avoidance proposed by Seligman and Johnson (1973). The key to the solution, they suggested, lies in recognizing the role of our expectations in determining our behavior. In our noise example, before learning to press the button you would have experienced many days of noise and so learned to expect it. And when you did press the button, you would have noticed that this was followed by an unusually long period until the noise returned. You would thus now have two expectations: The noise will return soon if you don't press the button, but not if you do. And since you prefer peace to noise, you would naturally decide to continue responding. (For a related account, see Lovibond *et al.*, 2008.)

According to this analysis, avoidance is a purely rational behavior, based on logical weighing of alternative courses of action, and there is evidence to support this (De Houwer, Crombez, and Baeyens, 2005; Lovibond *et al.*, 2008). Research on animals, however, has suggested that emotions such as fear play a greater role in avoidance learning than this purely rational account suggests (e.g., Levis, 1989). As we shall see in Chapter 7, human decision making is often an amalgam of reason and emotion, and it would not be surprising if this was also the case in avoidance. For now, though, the important point is that behavior can be reinforced by the removal of aversive events as well as the presentation of desirable ones, and that the prevention of undesirable events can also be reinforcing.

Delay of reinforcement

Having identified a wide variety of potential reinforcers, we turn now to the question of what determines whether they will be effective in practice.

One of the first variables that psychologists considered was contiguity. Research had already shown that contiguity was critical in classical conditioning, with delays of just a few seconds between a CS and a US often being enough to prevent conditioning. Would the same be true of reinforcement? Would the effectiveness of reinforcement be impaired if there was a brief delay between a response and presentation of a reinforcer?

Research with animals

Research with animals strongly supported this prediction. In a representative study by Dickinson, Watt, and Griffiths (1992), the authors trained rats in an apparatus called an *operant chamber* or, as it is more commonly known, a *Skinner box* (see Figure 4.4). This apparatus was developed by one of the most influential figures in the history of animal learning research, B. F. Skinner, and is essentially a descendant of the puzzle box developed by Thorndike. In Thorndike's box, subjects could make one response per trial: Once they opened the door and obtained food, the trial was over. In a Skinner box, by contrast, animals can respond repeatedly. Rats, for example, are usually trained to press a lever to obtain a small pellet of food; the pellet is delivered into a tray located next to the lever. Because they can press the lever again as soon as they have eaten the pellet, it is possible to earn many reinforcers in a short period of time, making the Skinner box a very efficient apparatus for studying the development of learning.

In the Dickinson *et al.* study, the time between pressing the lever and obtaining food was varied in different groups: Some rats received a food pellet 2 seconds after pressing the lever, others after delays of up to 64 seconds. As shown in Figure 4.5, the delay used had a powerful effect on the rate at which the rats pressed the lever. An increase in the delay of just a few seconds produced sharply lower rates of responding, and responding ceased altogether when the delay reached 64 seconds.

Why should a delay of just a few seconds have such a powerful impact? At first, learning theorists thought it was because rats have poor memories, so that if a reward were delayed, they wouldn't be able to remember the response that produced it. However, later research made it clear that rats can remember their responses for

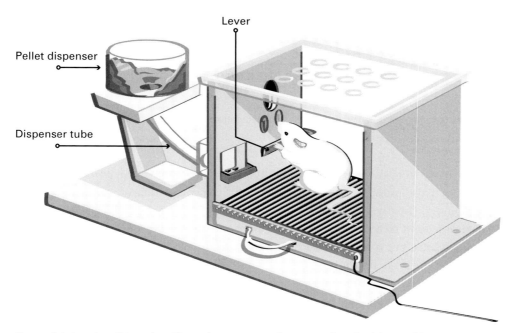

Figure 4.4 A rat in a Skinner box. The rat has a response lever controling the delivery of food, as well as devices allowing different types of stimuli to be produced. (Adapted from Bermudez, 2010.)

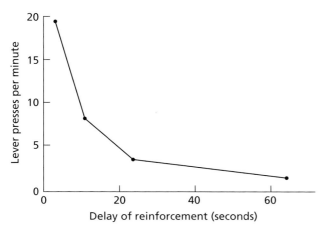

Figure 4.5 Effects of delayed reinforcement on bar-pressing rats. (Adapted from Dickinson, Watt, and Griffiths, 1992.)

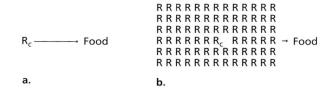

Figure 4.6 A rat's task when reinforcement is delayed, from the perspective of (a) the experimenter, and (b) the rat.

surprisingly long periods – in one study by Capaldi (1971), for 24 hours. It now looks as if the problem is not that rats can't remember their responses, but that they have difficulty figuring out *which* of these responses produced the reward. From our point of view, the correct response in the Dickinson *et al.* study might seem obvious, but from the rat's perspective the situation may have been far more confusing. Prior to finding the food it would have been engaged in a continuous stream of activity – grooming, exploring the cage, and so on – and this behavior would have continued during the delay interval. At any given moment, moreover, it would have been performing many responses simultaneously. As it pressed the lever, it might have been holding its head at a 45-degree angle, breathing rapidly, curling its tail to its left side, and so on. Rather than the simple situation depicted in Figure 4.6a, with just a single response preceding food, the rat would have experienced a situation more like that in Figure 4.6b, with the correct response embedded in a sea of other behaviors. From this perspective, the wonder is not that a delay of a few seconds impaired learning but that the rats managed to learn at all.

Research with humans

What, then, of humans: Will a reinforcer be effective only if it occurs within seconds of the behavior to be strengthened? You will know from your own experience that this is not so: A good grade for an essay, for example, can influence your future behavior even if there was a delay of many days between your writing the essay and receiving the grade. How, then can we reconcile the evidence from animal research with our everyday experience?

One obvious answer is language. Although learning in humans and animals is more similar than you might think – mammals in general and primates in particular are far more intelligent than we sometimes realize – our possession of language makes possible some important differences. If you received a reward without any explanation – think of a mysterious stranger approaching you, silently handing you $500 and then walking away – then you, like the rats in Dickinson *et al.*'s study, might also struggle to understand why you were being rewarded. Indeed, when experiments with humans employ procedures that parallel those used with animals, where rewards are provided without explanation, the results are almost uncannily similar (e.g., Shanks, Pearson, and Dickinson, 1989; Lieberman, Vogel, and Nisbet, 2008). Fortunately for us, the relationship between our behavior and its rewards is rarely this opaque. If a father decides to reward his young daughter for some exemplary behavior, he doesn't just hand her a new toy without a word; he explains what it was for. Language can bridge the gap between a response and a reward symbolically, even when physically they were widely separated in time.

Our possession of language means that a delay in the presentation of a reward need not be nearly as catastrophic for people as for rats. Nevertheless, we are going to suggest that it is still desirable – and sometimes even vital – to reward behaviors as quickly as circumstances allow.

Interfering responses

One problem is that language does not always allow us to fully reinstate the response that we are trying to strengthen. Suppose you were trying to learn tennis and at the end of a point your coach told you that your serve had been excellent; would you always serve perfectly thereafter? If you've ever tried to learn tennis, you know with some certainty that the answer is no. A good tennis serve requires many different movements – you have to bend your knees the right way, throw up the ball correctly, orient your shoulder and elbow properly, and so on. Even if you did finally hit a good serve, you still might find it difficult to know which of your many movements was responsible. And the problem would be exacerbated if you didn't receive feedback until the point was over: You would have continued to move during the delay, and these additional movements would make it harder for you to remember your movements while serving. In situations like this, where the behavior to be learned is complex and thus difficult to remember, immediate reinforcement can still be important[2] (Revusky, 1971; Lieberman *et al.*, 2008).

---

[2] The world is rarely as simple as we might like, and so we need to at least mention a further complication. Psychologists who study motor learning (the learning of physical skills) have suggested that two distinct processes are involved (e.g., Adams, 1971). To continue with our tennis example, to hit a good serve you need to learn the sequence of movements that are required, but you also need to learn what a good serve *feels* like, so that you can recognize whether you are serving correctly and either correct yourself mid-serve or, at any rate, on future serves. Immediate feedback from a coach might help you to identify the correct movements, but while listening to your coach you wouldn't be able to pay as much attention to the physical sensations produced by your serve. Immediate feedback could thus help you with one aspect of the task – learning the correct muscular movements – but interfere with another, that of learning what a correct movement feels like. For complex skills, it is not yet clear what the optimal strategy is for reconciling these conflicting needs. (For two perspectives, see Swinnen *et al.*, 1990, and Lieberman, Vogel, and Nisbet, 2008.)

Delay reduces incentive

A second reason why a delay might be harmful is that rewards tend to be perceived as less attractive when they are delayed. Suppose that you were offered a choice between receiving $100 now or in a year, would you find these options equally attractive? It seems unlikely. In the jargon of the field, a delayed reward is a less attractive **incentive**, and we are less motivated to work to obtain it.

One early demonstration of this effect was reported in a study by Rachlin and Green (1972), using pigeons as subjects. They trained the pigeons in a Skinner box containing two circular plastic disks called keys. If the birds pecked the key on the left, they received 2 seconds' worth of grain immediately, whereas if they pecked the key on the right, they received 4 seconds' worth of food after a delay of 4 seconds:

$$R_1 \longrightarrow \text{2 seconds of food}$$
$$R_2 \longrightarrow \text{4 seconds of food}$$

The time between trials was held constant, so that over the course of a session a bird that always pecked key 2 would receive twice as much food as a bird that always pecked key 1. Despite this, the pigeons pecked key 1 on 95% of the trials. They preferred to receive half as much food rather than wait just 4 seconds for the larger amount.

You might be tempted to dismiss this result as evidence of pigeons' lack of intelligence, but Kirby and Herrnstein (1995) found that humans discount delayed reinforcers in much the same way. To assess the value of delayed rewards, they offered university students a choice between a smaller amount of money to be delivered soon and a larger amount to be delivered later. For example, subjects were asked if they would prefer $12 in 6 days or $16 in 12 days. The students were offered a number of such choices, and, to ensure that they would take these choices seriously, they were told that one of their choices would be selected at random at the end of the session, and they would actually receive the option they had chosen.

Rationally, you might think that the students would have preferred receiving $16 to $12 – as both rewards were substantially delayed anyway, surely it would be better to wait a few more days and receive 33% more money? Apparently not, as most participants preferred the smaller sum that was delivered sooner. Like pigeons, we seem to value rewards less when they are delayed. (See also Kirby, 1997.)

Further evidence on this point was reported in a study by Roll, Reilly, and Johanson (2000). The participants were all heavy smokers, and the study investigated different tactics for encouraging them not to smoke. Every 5 minutes they were offered a choice between having a puff on a cigarette or earning $1. Some

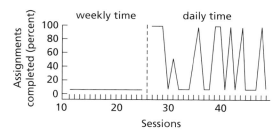

Figure 4.7 Percentage of homework assignments completed by Tom under different delays of reinforcement. (Adapted from Phillips, 1968.)

participants were told that they would receive the money they had earned at the end of the session, others that they would receive it 3 weeks later. The result was that those who had to wait for their money smoked twenty times as much! The reward was the same, but it was far less effective when delayed.

One possible implication concerns behaviors that we normally think of as involving self-control. If someone has difficulty in giving up smoking we usually attribute this to a lack of will power, but another possibility is simply that the rewards he or she can obtain by not smoking – more money, longer life – are too distant to be effective. Even if people know, rationally, that stopping smoking will prolong their life, this consequence may be too far in the future to influence them. We will explore this possibility further when we discuss self-control in Chapter 5.

Reinforcing homework

A study by Phillips (1968) provides a real-life example of the value of providing reinforcement quickly. To improve procedures for treating juvenile delinquents, Phillips established a residential home for boys called Achievement Place. One problem shared by most delinquents is failure in school, which in turn reflects an almost total failure to do any assigned homework. As one component of the treatment program, therefore, Phillips set out to encourage homework completion through the use of reinforcers. Whenever an assignment was completed to an acceptable standard, the boys were allowed to stay up for 1 hour past their normal bedtime on weekends. This reward was known as "weekly time." The effect of this reward on the behavior of one boy, Tom, is shown in Figure 4.7. Over a 14-day period, Tom did not complete a single assignment.

One possible explanation for this failure was that the reinforcer being used was not sufficiently attractive; maybe Tom just didn't value being allowed to stay up late. Another possible explanation was the delay between completing an assignment during the week and being allowed to stay up at the weekend. To find out, Phillips used exactly the same reinforcer in the next phase of the study – one hour of late time for each correct assignment – but now allowed Tom to stay up on the night that an assignment was completed rather than waiting until the weekend. These results are also shown in Figure 4.7, in the section labeled "daily time." We can see that the percentage of homework assignments completed rose immediately from 0 to an average of 50%. Even though the same reinforcer was used in both conditions, its effectiveness varied dramatically depending on the delay in its presentation. Thus, although reinforcers can be effective after a delay, as a general rule they should be delivered as soon after a response as possible if they are to achieve their full potential. Failure to adhere to this principle may be one of the most important reasons that reinforcers are sometimes ineffective.

At the beginning of the chapter, we referred to the puzzle of why students have difficulty studying despite the potent rewards – good grades, a job that pays well – contingent on this behavior. One important reason is almost certainly the delay involved in reinforcement. The reinforcers for studying arrive only after very long delays, whereas those for alternative activities, such as going to a movie or a football game, are essentially immediate.

$$R_{movie} \longrightarrow S^R$$
$$R_{studying} \xrightarrow{\hspace{4cm}} S^R$$

The student who doesn't study might thus be behaving much like the pigeon in the Rachlin and Green study: Both may know that in the long term one response produces much more valuable consequences, but they are nevertheless unable to resist the temptation of immediate gratification. The moral to this section can thus be summarized very simply: *For a reinforcer to be maximally effective, it should be presented as soon as possible after a response.*

Schedules of reinforcement

One of the most important factors determining the effect of reinforcement was discovered by accident. When Skinner was carrying out the research for his PhD, he ran his experiments on weekends as well as during the week, and one Saturday he discovered that his supply of pellets would not last until Monday. Instead of reinforcing every bar-press as he had done in the past, therefore, he decided to reinforce only one per minute. This had two gratifying consequences:

1 His supply of pellets lasted almost indefinitely.
2 The rats continued to respond and, after some initial perturbations, did so at a steady rate.

Over time, Skinner tried several different rules, or **reinforcement schedules**, for deciding which responses to reinforce, and he found that the choice of schedule had important consequences for how his animals responded. We will begin by defining some of the schedules he used and then look at their effects on behavior.

Ratio and interval schedules

The schedules

The simplest schedule is to reinforce a response every time it occurs. This schedule is known, not unreasonably, as a **continuous reinforcement (CRF) schedule**. In the real world, though, behavior is rarely reinforced so consistently. Children, for example, are not praised every time they tell the truth, and factory workers are not paid every time they tighten a screw. Instead, most behavior is reinforced on intermittent, or partial, reinforcement schedules.

Two types of partial reinforcement schedules have been studied most commonly: **ratio schedules** and **interval schedules**. In a ratio schedule, reinforcement depends on the number of responses that have been emitted. In factories, for example, workers' wages used to depend solely on the number of responses they made – for example, the number of dresses made – regardless of how long it took. In an interval schedule, on the other hand, the passage of time since the last reinforcement, rather than the number of responses, determines whether the next response will be reinforced. Whether you find mail the next time you go to your mailbox, for example, will depend on how long it has been since the last time you found mail, not on how often you visited the mailbox in the interim. Note that obtaining reinforcement in an interval schedule *still requires a response*: You do not obtain mail unless you go to the mailbox. The length of the interval determines when reinforcement becomes *available*: a response is still necessary to actually obtain it.

Further complicating matters, ratio and interval schedules can be subdivided according to whether the requirement for reinforcement is fixed or variable. In a *fixed interval* (FI) schedule, the interval that must elapse before a response can be reinforced is always the same, whereas in a *variable interval* (VI) schedule this interval is varied. In an FI 60-second schedule, for example, 60 seconds must always elapse following a reinforcement before a response can be reinforced again, whereas in a VI 60-second schedule, the interval might be as short as 5 seconds or as long as 2 minutes. (The 60 seconds in the schedule's name refers to the average.) Ratio schedules are subdivided in a similar way. In a *fixed ratio* (FR) schedule, the number of responses required for reinforcement is always the same. In a *variable ratio* (VR) schedule, the number of responses required to obtain

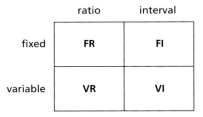

Figure 4.8 Partial reinforcement schedules. The most commonly studied types are *ratio* (where reinforcement depends on the number of responses emitted) and *interval* (where which response is reinforced depends on the time since the last reinforced response). Schedules are further subdivided according to whether the schedule requirement is *fixed* or *variable.*

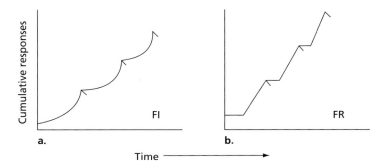

Figure 4.9 Typical cumulative response records generated by two types of schedules: (a) fixed interval (FI); (b) fixed ratio (FR). The short diagonal marks indicate presentations of a reinforcer.

reinforcement varies across successive reinforcements. For example, FR 30 means that every 30th response will be reinforced; VR 30 means that an average of 30 responses (sometimes only 5 responses, sometimes 50, and so on) will be required for reinforcement. A slot machine in a casino is a classic example of a VR schedule: payoffs depend on how many times the machine is played, but the jackpot is made unpredictable to prevent players playing only when a machine has been in use by others for a long time. Figure 4.8 summarizes these four schedules.

Patterns of responding

Learning the distinctions among the various schedules can be tedious, but each schedule has somewhat different effects on behavior, and these differences can be important. Figure 4.9 presents *cumulative records* illustrating the typical patterns of responding obtained under FI and FR schedules of reinforcement. In a cumulative response record, time is plotted along the *x*-axis, and the *y*-axis shows the *cumulative* or total number of responses made since the beginning of the session.

If a rat were to press a lever at a steady rate of one press every second, this would appear on a cumulative record as an ascending straight line. The faster the rat responds, the more steeply the line would rise.

In an FI schedule (Figure 4.9a), reinforcement becomes available only after a fixed period of time has elapsed following the previous reinforcement; each short diagonal mark on the record indicates the occurrence of a reinforcer. We can see that, immediately after reinforcement, subjects respond at a very low rate, but this rate steadily accelerates and reaches a peak just before the next reinforcement is due. Thus, subjects tend to respond in a cyclical pattern.

Because of its appearance when graphed, this positively accelerated response pattern is called an *FI scallop*, and it has important implications for the practical use of FI schedules. For example, if you were a parent who wanted to encourage your daughter to study by praising this behavior, it would be a great mistake to visit her room only at regular, hourly intervals. If your praise were the main reinforcer for studying, it is likely that your daughter would begin to study at regular, hourly intervals. Ironically, psychology professors (including those teaching learning) make exactly this mistake by scheduling exams at predictable, fixed intervals, with the result that students' studying often takes the form of a classic FI scallop: a zero or very low rate of studying immediately after an exam, gradually rising to a frantic peak the night before the next exam! Mawhinney *et al.* (1971) reported evidence that studying really does follow this pattern. To estimate the amount of time students spend studying, they monitored the use of course material in the library. When exams were scheduled daily, students maintained a constant rate of studying of around 60 minutes per day; when exams were scheduled at 3-week intervals, studying immediately after an exam fell to around 15 minutes, and then increased steadily to a peak of almost 2 hours just before the next exam.[3]

Figure 4.9b shows the typical response pattern under an FR schedule. Here, reinforcement is contingent on a fixed number of responses, and the result is generally "pause-and-run" behavior. Subjects pause for a while after reinforcement, but once they begin to respond, they respond steadily until they earn another reinforcer. If the ratio requirement is too great, however, *ratio strain* may be observed: Subjects will begin to respond, then pause, respond a bit more, pause again, and so on. If the schedule requirement is not reduced at this point, subjects soon cease to respond altogether.

In VI and VR schedules, by contrast, the requirement for reinforcement is varied, with the result that a response can be reinforced at any time. The result is that these schedules produce much steadier rates of responding, without such obvious pauses.

---

[3] In this case the effects of an FI schedule on students were almost identical to those on rats and pigeons, but this is not always the case. We will discuss this anomaly further in Chapter 7.

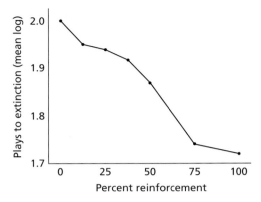

Figure 4.10 The effect of partial reinforcement on responding during extinction. The lower the percentage of reinforcement college students received for playing a slot machine during training, the longer they persisted in playing during extinction. (Adapted from Lewis and Duncan, 1956.)

The partial reinforcement effect

Having described the properties of the five schedules most often studied – CRF, FI, FR, VI, and VR – can we now say which one is best? If our goal were to ensure as strong a response as possible, the obvious answer would seem to be to reinforce the desired response every time it occurred (CRF) – the more often a response is reinforced, the stronger it should be. Indeed, in some respects that is so, but reinforcing every response can sometimes have unintended consequences. Consider the following experiment by Lewis and Duncan (1956). The subjects in this study were college students, and they were given an opportunity to play a slot machine. They were told that they could play as long as they wanted, and that each time they won they would earn 5 cents. The percentage of reinforcement was varied across groups during the first phase: One group was never reinforced; a second group was reinforced once; and so on. Reinforcement was then discontinued, and the experimenters monitored how long subjects continued to play.

You might think that the higher the percentage of reinforcement, the stronger the response, and thus the longer subjects would continue to play. As shown in Figure 4.10, however, that was not the case. Quite the contrary, the lower the percentage of reinforcement during training, the longer subjects played during extinction. This counterintuitive result – that partial reinforcement during training increases responding during extinction – is called the **partial reinforcement effect (PRE).**[4]

---

[4] In the Lewis and Duncan experiment, the no-reinforcement condition (0%) resulted in the highest levels of responding during extinction, but this is not usually the case. The persistent responding in this group was probably caused by the wording of the instructions, which implied that some reinforcement would be given if subjects responded. When this reinforcement was not forthcoming following the first eight plays, participants kept trying.

This effect was so surprising that at first it was called "Humphreys' paradox," after the psychologist who discovered it. Various explanations were proposed, but most learning psychologists now agree that the fundamental cause is the difficulty subjects have in judging whether further responding is likely to produce reinforcement. For subjects who have always been reinforced, the transition to extinction is obvious, and they are likely to quit responding quickly. For subjects who have received reinforcement after long periods of nonreinforcement during training, on the other hand, the transition to extinction is less obvious, and they are more likely to persist in the hope that they will eventually be reinforced.

Tantrum behavior in children provides a real-life example of the partial reinforcement effect. When parents pay attention to a child having a tantrum, their attention can reinforce this behavior. Sometimes parents realize this is the case, so they try hard to ignore the tantrum. If, with great effort, they manage to ignore the child's tantrums 90% of the time, they might then be baffled when the tantrums continue, but this persistence follows directly from the partial reinforcement effect: By reinforcing the behavior on a partial reinforcement schedule (in this case, a VR10), the parents are in fact *increasing* the persistence of the behavior, as the child learns that persistence will eventually pay off. If parents do decide to ignore tantrums, it is very important that they do so consistently, as even one or two reinforcements can dramatically increase the time required for extinction. (See also Chapter 6.)

Choosing a schedule

Let us now return to the question of which schedule is best. Reinforcing every response (CRF) has some important advantages, but it also has some serious disadvantages. One, as we have just seen, is that continuous reinforcement does not encourage persistent responding – if reinforcement is not available for a while, there is a greater likelihood that responding will cease. A further disadvantage is that continuous reinforcement is often costly: In monetary terms, it costs whatever the value of the reinforcer is, but it also requires considerable time and effort of the person delivering the reinforcer to ensure that he or she is always present when the desired response occurs.

Given these problems, the optimum strategy for producing durable responding is usually to begin by reinforcing every response, but then to gradually reduce the rate of reinforcement to the lowest level that will maintain a satisfactory response rate. Schedules with variable reinforcement requirements are generally preferable for this purpose to schedules with fixed requirements because the unpredictability of reinforcement generates more consistent and rapid responding. Our search for the "best" schedule, therefore, has narrowed to two candidates: VR and VI. Which should you use?

The answer turns out to be a bit complicated. A VR schedule normally generates a higher rate of response than a VI schedule because reinforcement on a VR schedule directly depends on the number of responses: If a subject doubles the number of responses he or she makes, that subject will also double his or her reinforcements. On the other hand, if the VR requirement is set too high, subjects will abruptly quit, whereas VI schedules can maintain a low but steady rate of responding even when reinforcement is infrequent. In sum, a VR or a VI schedule is generally the most effective in maintaining persistent responding; a VR schedule will tend to generate higher response rates, but if reinforcement is to be delivered only infrequently, then a VI schedule is more likely to sustain responding.

A criminally successful application

By now, your feelings about schedules might resemble those of the child whose review of a book about penguins began, "This book told me more about penguins than I wanted to know." Learning the technical distinctions among schedules is tedious and might appear pointless. As we suggested earlier, though, different schedules can have very different effects, and, when used imaginatively, schedules can be powerful tools for altering behavior.

In a striking demonstration of the importance of the schedule used, Kandel, Ayllon, and Roberts (1976) used reinforcement as part of a remedial high school education program in a Georgia state prison. The subjects were two inmates, one with a measured IQ of 65, the other with an IQ of 91. To reinforce studying, they were awarded points whenever they passed a test with a score of 80% or better, and these points could then be exchanged for a variety of reinforcers such as cigarettes, cookies, and extra visiting privileges. With 1,000 points, for example, a convict could buy a radio as a present for his family.

The program produced significant progress, but not as much as the authors had hoped. One possible explanation was that the inmates simply were not bright enough to progress any faster. (With IQs of 65 and 91, it was perhaps remarkable that they had progressed as fast as they had.) Another possibility was that the reinforcement schedule did not provide sufficient incentive for the hard work required. To find out, the authors devised a new schedule in which the faster the inmates progressed, the more points they earned. If an inmate completed one grade level in a subject in 90 days, for example, he received 120 points; if he did it in only 4 days, he received 900 points; and if he did it in only 1 day he received 4,700 points. The result was a quite staggering rate of progress. Under the old schedule, one of the convicts, Sanford, had completed ninth-grade English in 3 months – all things considered, not unimpressive. Under the new schedule, he completed tenth-, eleventh-, and part of twelfth-grade English in just 1 week! He often missed recreational periods and stayed up all night to work. As he remarked to one of the instructors, he wanted to "get when the gettin' was good." During the 5 months of the program – standard reinforcement schedule as well as enriched – he advanced 4.6 years in high school arithmetic, 4.9 years in reading, and 6.6 years in language. In other words, he completed almost 5 years of high school in 5 months – roughly 12 times the normal rate. And Sanford was the one with an IQ of 65.

These results have at least two important implications. First, and most relevant to our current concern, they illustrate how powerfully the choice of reinforcement schedule can determine the effectiveness of reinforcement. More generally, they hint at how often we underestimate people's ability to learn and change. Knowing Sanford's criminal record and apparent IQ, few would have believed that he was capable of such progress. But under appropriate learning conditions, all of us – learning disabled as well as gifted, criminal as well as non-criminal – might be capable of far more learning than is commonly assumed. Too often, we blame failure on the learner: "Oh, he's too stupid." "She's just not trying." A much more productive reaction to failure might be to assume that our teaching methods are at fault and to search for better methods. We have now seen two examples in which a critical reexamination of teaching procedures led to dramatic improvements in learning – Phillips's change to immediate reinforcement at Achievement Place, and the Kandel group's imaginative use of a new reinforcement schedule – and we shall encounter others as we proceed. Greater faith in human potential can sometimes pay handsome dividends.

Motivation

Whether you respond to obtain a reward will depend not only on whether you have learned that this response will produce the reward but also on whether you want the reward. You may know that you can buy a cup of coffee from a vending machine, but if you don't feel like a cup of coffee at that moment, you are unlikely to do so.

The first point to note here is that levels of motivation vary: Sometimes we want a certain reward strongly, at other times not at all. As to why motivation to obtain a reward varies, one factor is how long we have been deprived of it (sometimes called *drive*); another is the reward's attractiveness. In our vending machine example, our likelihood of using it would depend not only on how thirsty we are but also on how much we like the drinks it is selling. To use a carrot-and-stick analogy, deprivation acts as a stick to drive us forward, while the quality of the reward acts as a carrot to attract us. The greater our thirst and the more attractive the carrot, the greater the likelihood that we will respond.

On the surface, the concept of motivation is thus simple – the more we want a reinforcer, the harder we will work to obtain it. When this concept is examined

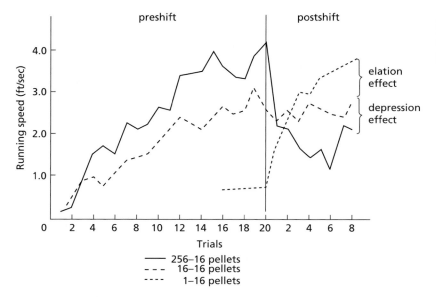

Figure 4.11 Effect of amount of reinforcement on running speed. During the initial phase (left portion of the graph), groups received either 1, 16, or 256 pellets of food on each trial; all groups then received 16 pellets (shown on the right side of the graph). The group previously given 1 pellet ran faster than the group already accustomed to 16 pellets, resulting in an elation effect, or positive contrast. The group previously given 256 pellets ran slower than the group accustomed to 16 pellets, resulting in a depression effect, or negative contrast. (Adapted from Crespi, 1942.)

more closely, though, it turns out to be not quite so straightforward. In this section we will examine two complications: contrast effects and the Yerkes–Dodson law. (For some other complications, see Bolles, 1975, and Dickinson and Balleine, 2002.)

Contrast effects

As noted earlier, the attractiveness of a reinforcer is referred to as its *incentive* value. One determinant of incentive value is the nature or *quality* of the reinforcer – most children, for example, can be relied on to prefer ice cream to spinach – and another is the amount or *quantity* provided. In one examination of the effect of amount, Crespi (1942) trained rats to run down a straight-alley maze to a goal box containing either 1, 16, or 256 pellets of food. The larger the amount, the greater should be its incentive value, and thus the faster the rats should run to obtain it. As shown in the left-hand section of Figure 4.11, that is what Crespi found.

To this point, Crespi's results seem common sense: When a reward is more attractive, rats (and people) will work harder to obtain it. The results of the next phase of the experiment, however, were less obvious. In this second phase, Crespi altered conditions so that all three groups received 16 pellets when they reached the goal box. As shown at the right of the graph, the rats modified their behavior accordingly: Those for whom the reward had been reduced began to run more slowly; those for whom it had been increased ran more quickly. If you examine the graph more closely, however, you will see that running speeds for the three groups differed substantially, even though they were now all receiving the same reward. The group that had previously received 1 pellet now ran the fastest, while the group that had previously received 256 pellets ran the slowest. In particular, the group shifted from 1 to 16 pellets ran faster than the group that received 16 pellets throughout, while the group initially trained with 256 pellets ran more slowly than this group.

Crespi called the overshoot in the group shifted from 1 to 16 pellets (not simply improving, but running faster than the group that received 16 pellets all along) an *elation effect*, implying that the rats were so excited over this improvement in their circumstances that they ran especially fast. On similar reasoning, he labeled the undershoot in the group switched from 256 pellets to 16 pellets a *depression effect*. Other learning psychologists, however, were unhappy with these terms. Aside from the problem of knowing what a rat is feeling – the facial expressions of elated and depressed rats are remarkably similar – the terms *elation* and *depression* imply emotional effects that should disappear as subjects become accustomed to the new levels of reinforcement. In some cases, however, the effects are enduring. (See Flaherty, 1996, for a review.) Psychologists have thus come to prefer the more neutral terminology of **contrast effects** to describe these phenomena, emphasizing that the effect of any reinforcer depends on how it contrasts with reinforcers experienced previously. Crespi's elation effect is now called **positive contrast**, and the depression effect is called **negative contrast**.

Contrast effects suggest that the effects of a reward will depend on people's expectations. If you were expecting a reward of $1, receiving $500 might indeed leave you elated; if you had been expecting $1,000, the more likely effect would be disappointment. The importance of expectations here might remind you of classical conditioning, where we encountered a similar phenomenon in our discussion of the Rescorla–Wagner model. One of their key findings was that the same US could produce either an increase in associative strength or a decrease, depending on the strength of the association (V) at the beginning of the trial – or, in the more cognitive terminology we are now using, on how much subjects expected that US. In both classical conditioning and reinforcement, we seem to evaluate events relative to our expectations, and this comparison or contrast then determines how we react.

We will encounter contrast effects again in Chapter 7, when we discuss the role of reference points in decision making; you can also find more information on contrast effects in Williams (1997).

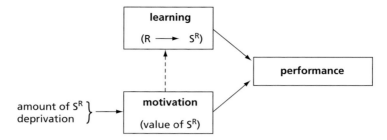

Figure 4.12 If a response is reinforced, future performance of that response will depend on both learning (knowing that the response produces a reinforcer) and motivation (wanting the reinforcer). We shall see later that motivation can affect learning as well as performance (dashed line).

The Yerkes–Dodson law

To introduce our next topic, we first need to clarify the relationship between three related concepts: *learning, motivation,* and *performance.* Suppose that you observed someone entering a room containing a coffee vending machine and wanted to predict whether they would use it to buy a coffee. The outcome would depend in part on whether they knew that you have to insert a coin in order to operate the machine (knowledge that they would have acquired or learned at some point in the past), and in part on whether they actually wanted a cup of coffee. Whether the individual would *perform* the response of inserting a coin, in other words, would depend on both *learning* (knowing that the coin would produce coffee) and **motivation** (wanting the coffee). Figure 4.12 summarizes these relationships.

In our discussion of Crespi's experiment, we implicitly assumed that the amount of food in the goal box affected the rats' motivation, which in turn determined their performance. There is, however, another possibility, namely that the rats' motivation affected learning as well as performance. Consider the rats with the 256 pellets. We know that they ran down the maze more quickly; was this solely because they were more excited at the prospect of obtaining food, or might they also have been quicker to learn that the goal box contained food? Or, to use a human example, suppose that a group of students was promised a large reward for mastering the material in a text. They would be likely to spend more time studying, but might they also be better at absorbing the material that they read? When we are highly motivated, does this have a direct impact on how well we learn?

In a classic experiment to try to answer this question, Broadhurst (1957) trained rats on a visual discrimination in a Y-shaped maze. The maze was flooded with water, and a platform located in one arm of the Y allowed the rats to escape. This is an example of **negative reinforcement**, in which the reinforcer is the termination of an aversive stimulus, rather than the presentation of a desirable one. (Note that negative reinforcement is not punishment: In negative reinforcement as in positive

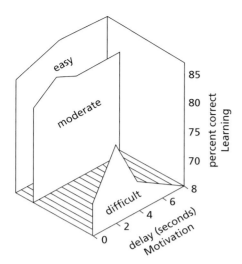

Figure 4.13 The Yerkes–Dodson law. How motivation affected rats' ability to learn the correct path through a maze depended on the difficulty of the problem; motivation generally aided learning on easy and moderate problems, but high motivation impaired learning on a difficult problem. (Broadhurst, 1957.)

reinforcement, behavior is strengthened; the difference between them lies solely in whether this strengthening is the result of presenting a stimulus or removing one.)

The position of the platform in this experiment was shifted randomly over trials, but its current location was always signaled by the illumination of the arms; the brighter of the two arms always contained the platform. To assess the effects of motivation on learning, Broadhurst varied how long the rats were held underwater before being allowed to swim through the maze; the confinement period ranged from 0 to 8 seconds. In addition, he examined the role of problem difficulty by varying the relative brightness of the alleys in different groups. For the easiest problem, the correct alley was 300 times brighter than the incorrect one, whereas for the most difficult problem the illumination ratio was only 15 to 1.

The results for the different groups are shown in Figure 4.13, which plots in three-dimensional form the percentage of correct responses over the first 100 trials as a function of both motivation and problem difficulty. In all three problems, motivation did influence learning, but the optimal level of motivation depended on the difficulty of the problem. On the easy problem, motivation enhanced learning uniformly: The longer that subjects were deprived of air, the fewer errors they made while learning. On the difficult problem, on the other hand, the fastest learning occurred with deprivations of only 2 seconds; increases in deprivation beyond this value resulted in a substantial decrease in learning.

Broadhurst's results suggest that motivation does affect learning, but that the relationship is complex. With relatively simple problems, increasing motivation enhances learning, but on more difficult problems high motivation can actually be harmful. This inverse relationship between task difficulty and optimum motivation – the more difficult the problem, the lower the optimum level of motivation – has been observed in a number of other studies (for example, Hochauser and Fowler, 1975; Bregman and McAllister, 1982). The phenomenon is known as the **Yerkes–Dodson law**, named for the two psychologists who first discovered it.

The reasons that high motivation interferes with the learning of difficult tasks are not fully understood, but the most likely explanation is that motivation affects attention. According to Easterbrook (1959), attention becomes more highly focused when we are aroused; we concentrate more intensely on only a few stimuli while effectively ignoring all others. For simple problems, in which the relevant cues are obvious, focused attention is likely to facilitate learning. For problems in which the important cues are more subtle, however, a subject that focuses attention too narrowly might miss the critical cues and thus take much longer to solve the problem. The result is that high motivation helps subjects to solve simple problems but impairs performance on more difficult tasks. (For experimental support, see Telegdy and Cohen, 1971, and Geen, 1985; for related work, see Beilock, 2008, and Gable and Harmon-Jones, 2008.)

In summary, we have seen that the effectiveness of a reinforcer depends on whether subjects are motivated to obtain it, and this in turn depends on its attractiveness or incentive value (the carrot) and how long subjects have been deprived of it (the stick). In general, stronger motivation produces better performance, but we have also seen two complications – that the incentive value of a reinforcer depends on how it contrasts with previous reinforcers, and that motivation can affect learning as well as performance. As with so many other aspects of reinforcement, the concept of motivation is simple on the surface but rather less so when examined closely.

The role of the stimulus

One aspect of Thorndike's Law of Effect seems little more than common sense, namely the assumption that a response will be affected by its consequences. Thorndike's version, however, is subtly different – it says that a reward will strengthen a response not generally, but in the *particular situation* where the reward was received ("responses . . . followed by satisfaction [will be] more firmly connected with the situation"). To see the importance of this distinction, consider a child praised for cleaning her room. According to Thorndike the effect might be not a general increase in room cleaning, as her parents might fervently be hoping,

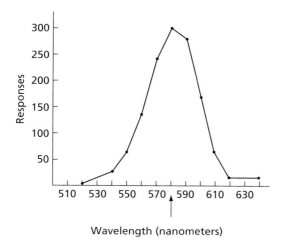

Figure 4.14 Generalization. Pigeons were reinforced for pecking a key illuminated with a 580-nm light (indicated by the arrow). When later tested on other colors, the highest levels of responding occurred to similar stimuli. (Adapted from Guttman and Kalish, 1956.)

but rather an increase only in that situation, perhaps when the parents are present and thus likely to provide further reinforcement.

Stimulus control

Generalization

Thorndike did not systematically test this assumption, but later research was to support it. In one classic study, Guttman and Kalish (1956) trained pigeons to peck at a circular plastic disk, or key, mounted on one wall of a Skinner box. The key was illuminated with a yellowish-orange light of 580 nanometers (nm)[5] and pecks at the key were occasionally reinforced with access to a grain magazine located below the key. To find out what the birds had learned during the training phase, Guttman and Kalish ran a test session in which they varied the color on the key. Sometimes it was illuminated with a green light (550 nm), sometimes with a red light (640 nm), and so on. As shown in Figure 4.14, the birds responded vigorously whenever the key was illuminated with the training stimulus (580 nm), but responding fell off sharply when the test wavelengths diverged from this value. Contrary to our earlier analysis, reinforcement resulted in a general tendency not to peck the key but, rather, to peck the particular stimulus that had been present during reinforcement. Subsequent experiments have extended this finding, showing that even seemingly irrelevant features of the training situation (for example, the appearance of the

[5] A nanometer is a measure of a light's wavelength, which determines its color.

walls, the texture of the floor) can acquire control over the reinforced response, so that subjects respond less when these stimuli are altered (see Balsam and Tomie, 1985).

In Guttman and Kalish's experiment, the response to the training stimulus spread to similar stimuli, a phenomenon known as **generalization**. As the training and test stimuli became less similar, responding declined, and this progressive decline in response is called a **generalization gradient**.

This gradient illustrates the phenomenon of **stimulus control**, in which the probability of a response varies depending on what stimuli are present. In this case, the color of the key acquired control over the birds' pecking, so that changes in this color affected their responding. Similarly, human behavior often comes under the control of stimuli that are present when we are reinforced, sometimes without our realizing it. A businessman, for example, may give generously to charity when in church while behaving ruthlessly at work, and most of us behave quite differently when in the presence of a superior – a parent, a teacher, or an employer – than when we are with friends. We are not quite as consistent as the concept of personality might imply, as our behavior can vary substantially depending on the situation.

Attention

Thorndike was thus right: When a response is reinforced, it will become associated with the stimuli present at the time. But *which* stimuli? Will all the stimuli present acquire control or only some? And if only some, which?

The first question – whether all stimuli will acquire control – proved surprisingly difficult to answer, but when an answer did emerge, it was simple. We are constantly bombarded by stimuli – many thousands of lights, sounds, and odors every second – and we can only attend to a fraction. The inevitable consequence is that only some of the stimuli present when a response is reinforced will come to control it.

One example comes from a study by Rincover and Koegel (1975) involving autistic children. As part of a therapeutic program to help these children learn new behaviors, the authors used rewards to teach them to respond to verbal instructions. For one of the boys, John, training began with the experimenter saying "Touch your chin." The experimenter would prompt the behavior by moving John's hand to his chin, and, once it was there, giving him a piece of candy. The use of the prompt was then gradually reduced, until eventually John would touch his chin without prompting. This training phase was conducted in a treatment room within the hospital where John lived; to test the generality of what had been learned, a new adult took John outside the hospital and again asked him to touch his chin. The instruction was given 10 times, but John did not touch his chin once.

Perhaps he had only learned to respond in the presence of the first experimenter? To find out, they repeated the test, this time with the original experimenter taking him outside, but again John did not respond. Perhaps he had learned to respond only in the room where training was given? Another test, this time with the new experimenter giving instructions in the training room, but again John failed to respond.

John's behavior was now a real puzzle – what, exactly, was controlling his response? – but the experimenters noticed that during the training phase each trial had begun with the experimenter showing John the candy. They therefore ran yet a further test in which the second experimenter took John outside but, instead of asking him to touch his chin, simply held up the candy. John immediately touched his chin. The experimenters had thought that they had been training John to respond to verbal instructions, but instead he had homed in on only one element of the training context, the sight of the candy being held up, and this was the element that now controlled his response.

Attention is not normally quite as narrow as this, but there is always some element of selection in how we perceive our environment. This inevitably leads on to our second question, namely which aspects of the training environment will acquire control? To some extent, the determinants are innate – a sudden loud noise, for example, is far more likely to attract attention than a quiet hum. Learning, however, also plays a role, though the processes involved are complex. To illustrate this, consider the following example drawn from classical conditioning. Suppose that you were exposed to ten pairings of a tone with an electric shock. We know that one likely result would be conditioning of fear to the tone, but might this experience also affect how much attention you paid to the tone in the future? The question might seem silly because the answer seems so obvious – if a tone signaled a painful electric shock, of course we would pay attention whenever we heard it. Indeed, that has been the outcome in some experiments, but in others pairings of a CS and a US have resulted in a *decrease* in attention to the CS (e.g., Kaye and Pearce, 1984). The reason, according to Pearce and Hall (1980), is that when a stimulus reliably predicts an outcome, we no longer need to pay so much attention to it, because we already know what is coming. We would obviously still want to respond when we heard the tone, but the processes involved could become automatic, leaving us free to direct our limited attentional resources to other aspects of the environment. (See also Chapter 7.)

It is striking that even in a situation as simple as this – simply pairing a tone and shock – it can be difficult to predict whether attention to the tone will increase or decrease. We clearly need a theory that can make sense of the discrepant outcomes and predict when we will find an increase in attention and when a decrease, and a theory along these lines has already been advanced (Pearce and Mackintosh, 2010). It will take time for researchers to test the new account, but it looks promising.

Element conditioning   Configural conditioning

Figure 4.15 Elemental versus configural accounts of conditioning. If an AB compound is followed by a US, an elemental account says that two associations will be formed, with A and B forming separate associations with the US. A configural account says that only a single association will be formed, linking the US to the AB compound as a configuration or whole.

Configural learning

In the hypothetical experiment outlined above, the issue was whether pairing a tone with shock would increase or decrease attention to the tone. Suppose, though, that the CS was not just a single stimulus but two or more stimuli presented together – which aspects or components of the stimulus would gain control?

Suppose, to take a very simple example, you saw a red flag immediately before – sorry about this – receiving an electric shock. According to one account, a stimulus like this is best viewed as a set of independent elements (the color red and the shape of a flag), and conditioning might occur to either or both of these elements. According to another account, any stimulus is best thought of as a *configuration* of elements, that is, as a coherent whole, so that a single association will be formed with the entire configuration (Pearce, 2002). As illustrated in Figure 4.15, the issue is whether associations are formed to the individual elements of a situation, or to the situation as a whole.

Evidence for the existence of **configural learning** comes from many experiments; we will focus on one by Bellingham, Gillette-Bellingham, and Kehoe (1985) involving classical conditioning. They gave rats discrimination training involving three kinds of trials, intermixed in an alternating sequence:

$$\text{tone} \rightarrow \text{water}$$
$$\text{light} \rightarrow \text{water}$$
$$\text{tone} + \text{light} \rightarrow \underline{\quad\quad}$$

Not surprisingly, the rats learned to respond at a high rate on trials in which the tone and light were presented by themselves. The more interesting question was how they would behave on trials where the tone and light were presented together. If the elemental account is right, and each element in a compound forms its own association with the US, then presentation of the tone and light together should elicit strong responding, because each stimulus on its own elicits responding. Early in training, that is exactly what happened, but eventually the rats learned to respond to the tone and light when they were presented separately but not when they were presented together. In anthropomorphic terms, they behaved as if they understood that the tone and the light together constituted a unique stimulus – a configuration – and was not just the sum of its parts.

Experiments like these make it clear that we *can* learn to respond to a situation as a whole, but it is also clear that we can learn to respond to the component elements separately. (Recall John's learning to respond only when he saw the candy.) The problem then becomes how to predict when we will find one outcome and when the other, and at present that is not clear. If the truth about stimulus control is thought to reside at the top of the mountain, our journey toward it is arguably still in the foothills. In practical terms, we know that in predicting the results of reinforcement we need to take into account what stimuli are present, but it is sometimes difficult to predict precisely which elements will control responding.

Perceptual learning

We've seen that one possible consequence of exposure to stimuli is a change in how much attention we pay to them. Another, closely related consequence is an improvement in our ability to distinguish, or *discriminate*, these stimuli. If someone with little experience of wines is asked to distinguish a chardonnay and a sauvignon blanc, for example, they are likely to struggle, whereas to an experienced wine taster the differences are like night and day. They can distinguish not only the variety but the region of France in which it was grown, the year, and even whether the sample came from the upper or lower half of the bottle! (Goldstone, 1998.) Similarly, radiographers learn to distinguish X-rays that look identical to the rest of us, and chicken sexers display similar expertise in their more exotic specialty. (Chicks are assessed when they are only one day old, and the differences are apparently exceedingly subtle.) This enhanced ability to distinguish between stimuli, simply as a result of exposure, is known as **perceptual learning**.

As to how perceptual learning occurs, it currently looks as if several processes may be involved, one of which is attention (Goldstone, 1998; Kellman, 2002; Hall, 2008). We seem to learn to pay greater attention to those aspects of similar stimuli that differentiate them, while at the same time learning to ignore features that are irrelevant. Infants, for example, are born with the ability to distinguish a wide range of speech sounds, but by the age of 10 months they can no longer distinguish sounds which are not important in their language, and which they have thus learned can be ignored (Werker and Lalonde, 1988).

One way to enhance perceptual learning is through *easy-to-hard discrimination training*, in which training is first given on problems where the stimuli are easy to distinguish, and only when this is successful are more difficult discriminations introduced. In a representative study by Suret and McLaren (2003), participants

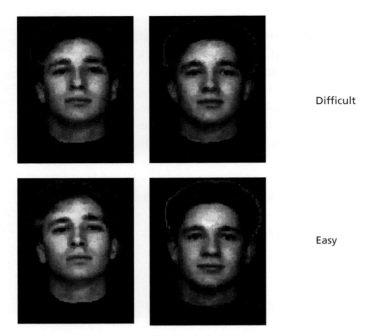

Difficult

Easy

Figure 4.16 Easy-to-hard discrimination training. Suret and McLaren (2003) gave participants a difficult face discrimination problem to solve, but one group was first trained on an easier discrimination. The photographs used in the experiments were similarly blurred.

were given the task of distinguishing pairs of very similar faces, such as those shown at the top of Figure 4.16. One face was presented on each trial, and participants had to indicate which of two categories the face belonged to by pressing one of two keys. As soon as they pressed, they were told if their choice had been correct. Participants were told that the allocation of faces to categories had been arbitrary, and that their task was simply to learn the correct response for each face. And, because the faces were very similar, this required learning to distinguish the similar faces.

For one group the difficult pairs were presented throughout training, while a second group started with 40 trials on easier pairs (such as those shown at the bottom of the figure) before being transferred to the difficult ones. The authors found that the easy-to-hard group were significantly better at discriminating the difficult pairs, despite having had less practice with them. It seems likely that training with the easier pairs taught participants what dimensions were useful in distinguishing the faces, thereby making it easier to discriminate the difficult pairs.[6]

---

[6] Psychologists use the term *dimension* to refer to a set of stimuli which can be arranged in a linear sequence. Color, for example, is a dimension, as colors can be arranged according to their wavelength. Size and brightness are also dimensions, and more specialized continua such as nose

Perceptual learning is also aided if the stimuli to be discriminated are presented simultaneously rather than separately (e.g., Mundy, Honey, and Dwyer, 2007). Again the likely explanation is attention: When stimuli are present simultaneously, it is easier to compare them and thus identify the dimensions on which they differ.

Together, these findings suggest that when something is difficult to learn, it might help to start with a simpler version of the task and only after it has been mastered move on to the difficult one. If a student is having difficulty distinguishing the sounds of a foreign language, for example, it might help to begin with versions that are maximally discriminable, and to present these sounds in close temporal proximity in order to aid comparison. Only when this simpler task has been mastered should training advance to the difficult version.

Practical applications

In some applications involving reward the goal is to have a behavior occur as widely as possible, regardless of the situation. If you were a parent trying to train a child to be honest, you would probably want this behavior to occur very widely. In other situations, however, your goal might be to have a behavior occur only in specific settings. A child, for example, needs to learn to cross a street only when the light is green, not red. In the following sections we will look at what can be done to achieve each of these goals.

Encouraging discrimination

In cases where we want a behavior to occur only in particular settings, one useful technique is to provide **discrimination training**. In this procedure, training is provided not only in the situation where we want the behavior to occur (S+), but also in situations where we do not want it to occur (S−). Presentations of the situations are alternated, and behavior is reinforced only in the positive situation:

$$S+ : R \rightarrow S^R$$
$$S- : R \rightarrow \underline{\quad}$$

We will use a study by Redd and Birnbrauer (1969) to illustrate the methods used in discrimination training, and also their power. The participants were mentally retarded 12- to 15-year-old boys, and the purpose of the study was to examine how the reinforcement contingencies established by adults can shape children's

---

length can also be treated as dimensions. If a set of faces differ in nose length, then learning to attend to this dimension on an easy problem will make it easier to identify differences when the noses are more similar.

behavior. When one of the experimenters was present, the boys were reinforced for playing cooperatively (a typical reward was candy and praise); when the other experimenter was present, the boys were reinforced equally often, but the rewards were delivered at random intervals, regardless of how the boys were behaving. When the boys were later tested, they were far more likely to engage in cooperative play when the first experimenter was present. The experimenters then reversed roles, with the second experimenter being the one who reinforced cooperative play, and the boys altered their behavior accordingly. As a result of discrimination training, cooperative play occurred only in the situation where it was reinforced.

Although the experimenter in this study deliberately arranged discrimination training, we often encounter similar contingencies in real life. If a child's cooperative behavior is praised by a parent but ignored by a teacher, it would not be surprising if the child learned to behave differently at home and in school. Indeed, considerable evidence indicates that our behavior is not as consistent as we think. In one early study by Hartshorne and May (1928), children were given opportunities to behave dishonestly at home, at school, and at play. We tend to think of honesty as a personality trait, and thus expect children who are honest in one situation to also be honest in others, but the authors observed very little correlation between behavior in these settings. As the Redd and Birnbrauer study suggests, when reinforcement contingencies are different in different situations, our behavior sometimes also differs. (For reviews of the evidence that our behavior often depends on the situation, rather than reflecting consistent personality traits, see Mischel, 1984, and Mischel and Shoda, 1995.)

Encouraging generalization

In some cases, our goal is to have a behavior occur widely, regardless of setting. Consider a situation where a little girl admitted stealing a friend's toy and her mother praised her for being honest. The mother's intention might be to encourage a general tendency to be honest, but the effect might be to increase honesty only when a toy is involved, or only when the mother is present. How, then, can we reduce stimulus control to ensure that a reinforced response will generalize widely across situations? The answer, in brief, is to provide training in a variety of settings. To encourage honesty, for example, we would need to reinforce it in different situations – in different places, with different people, and so forth.

At first, this requirement might seem discouraging; people encounter an almost infinite variety of situations in real life, and we could hardly reinforce behavior in all of them. Fortunately, it is not necessary to do so: As long as reinforcement is provided in more than one setting, the reinforced behavior will often generalize quite widely. One example comes from a study by Griffiths and Craighead (1972) in which they trained a severely retarded female to speak more clearly by reinforcing correct articulations. Training was given in a speech therapy room, and her speech improved dramatically. However, the improvement was confined to the training room; elsewhere, she continued to speak unclearly. A second therapist then repeated the training phase, but in an office in the hospital where the woman resided. Her speech improved rapidly, and she now began to speak clearly everywhere.

An understanding of the principles of stimulus control can be very important in practical attempts to use rewards effectively. In trying to eliminate undesirable habits, for example, it can be important to understand the stimuli that are associated with the habit. Consider adults who suffer from insomnia. If they toss and turn for hours before falling asleep, then the stimulus of the bed may become associated with this restless behavior, so that the very act of going to bed will tend to elicit restlessness. To break the link between the stimulus of the bed and worrying, Bootzin (1972) advised an insomniac client to go to bed only when genuinely sleepy and not to engage in any other activities while in bed such as reading or watching TV. If he could not sleep, he was to get up and engage in other activities until he again felt tired. Within a few weeks, the patient was reliably falling asleep within minutes of getting into bed, and subsequent studies have reported similar success (Lichstein and Riedel, 1994).

A preliminary application

To illustrate how the principles discussed in this chapter can be applied, we will use an example reported by Wolf, Risley, and Mees (1964). The subject in this study was a boy named Dicky. Until he was 9 months old, Dicky's behavior was normal, but then he developed cataracts in both eyes, which in turn led to a series of aberrant behaviors. He had difficulty falling asleep, for example, and would cry unless his parents remained by his bedside until he was asleep. Similarly, in other situations in which he didn't get what he wanted, he would have violent tantrums in which he would bang his head, slap his face, and pull his hair. After one of these tantrums, his mother commented, "he was a mess, all black and blue and bleeding" (Wolf *et al.*, 1964, p. 305).

Dicky underwent an eye operation for his cataracts, and his parents were told that he had to wear corrective glasses if his vision was to recover. Despite strenuous efforts, however, they could not get Dicky to wear the glasses. When Dicky was 3 years old, he was diagnosed as schizophrenic and was admitted to a mental hospital for children. The staff there again tried to get Dicky to wear his glasses, but again without success. After 6 months of failure, Dicky's ophthalmologist warned that unless he began to wear his glasses within the next 6 months, he would lose his vision permanently.

At this point, the hospital staff sought the assistance of Wolf, Risley, and Mees. They decided to teach Dicky to wear the glasses using the principles of reinforcement that had been identified in experiments with animals. First, recognizing the importance of immediate reinforcement, they repeatedly paired the noise of a clicker with presentations of candy, so that the noise would become a secondary reinforcer that could then be presented the instant Dicky responded appropriately. Then, since the desired response was one that, to put it mildly, occurred infrequently, they decided to use a learning principle that we have not yet discussed, called **shaping**. Originally developed to teach rats to press a bar, shaping involves first reinforcing whatever aspect of a person's behavior is closest to the desired response. Once this behavior begins to occur more frequently, the experimenter withholds reinforcement until some closer approximation to the desired response occurs, and so on until the desired response has been established.

In Dicky's case, they decided to reinforce him – immediately with the clicker, followed as soon as possible by food – first, simply for picking up the glasses, then for holding them for progressively longer periods, then for moving them toward his head, and so on.

When the authors instituted this program, the result was almost total failure: Although Dicky would hold the glasses, he would not wear them properly on his head. If you had been one of the psychologists involved, what would you have done at this point? One reasonable response would have been to give up, on the grounds that Dicky was simply too psychotic to be treated. The authors, however, believed that reinforcement can work with any individual, no matter how disabled or disturbed; if reinforcement did not work, they believed, then the fault must lie in the way it was being used, rather than in the subject. Specifically, they speculated that the reason Dicky wasn't working to obtain the reinforcer might have been that the incentive value of the reinforcer was not great enough.

To obtain a more effective reinforcer, therefore, the experimenters made bites of meals contingent on appropriate behavior. Dicky still responded poorly at breakfast, and again at lunch. But a third session was given at 2:00 p.m., when Dicky was hungrier, and the shaping program then worked beautifully! Dicky was trained to put his glasses on, then to wear them for longer and longer periods. His eyesight was saved, and over the years a similar training program was used to alter other aspects of his behavior. He learned to talk, to play with other children, and, eventually, to read and write. By the time he was 13, his measured IQ had increased from 50 to 110, and he was enrolled in a class for normal children (Nedelman and Sulzbacher, 1972).

One noteworthy feature of this study was its use of shaping. Although shaping was originally developed for the rather humble purpose of training rats to press levers, the principle can be applied very widely. The insight underlying shaping is that when a behavior is difficult to train, it can help to start with a simpler task and progress only gradually to the more demanding one. In discussing delayed reinforcement, for example, we saw that delays of even a few seconds can prevent learning. If at first reinforcement is given immediately, however, and the delay then lengthened gradually, behavior can eventually be maintained despite delays of minutes or even hours. Similarly, in schedules of reinforcement, abruptly imposing a requirement of 500 responses for reinforcement can result in equally abrupt extinction of the response. If the requirement is introduced gradually, however – first requiring 1 response, then 2, 5, 10, and so on – behavior can be maintained even with quite substantial ratio requirements. The concept of shaping is simple, but it is also potentially very powerful.

Summary

. . . .

- Thorndike found that rewards produce only a gradual strengthening of behavior over trials; the Law of Effect states that a reward stamps in an association between the rewarded behavior and the situation in which it was made.
- Psychologists now prefer the term *reinforcer* to *reward*. In reinforcement, a stimulus such as food is presented following a response; in classical conditioning, it is presented following another stimulus. The procedures are clearly different, but both involve the detection of a relationship between successive events, and the processes involved are probably similar.
- Psychologists sometimes divide reinforcers into three categories: primary, secondary, and social. According to the Premack principle, good reinforcers can be identified by observing what activities individuals engage in when given a free choice: The higher the probability of an activity, the more effective it will be as a reinforcer.

The effectiveness of a reinforcer also depends on:

- Delay. Delays between a behavior and the delivery of a reinforcer make it harder to detect the relationship between them and also reduce the attractiveness of the reinforcer as an incentive.
- Reinforcement schedule. In general, it is best to start by reinforcing a response every time it is made (CRF), but then to reinforce it only occasionally. Partial reinforcement generates high rates of responding and increases the likelihood that responding will persist if there are long periods without reinforcement (the partial reinforcement effect).
- Motivation. The attractiveness of a reinforcer depends in part on how it compares to reinforcers that we have received in the past (contrast effects). Motivation can also affect learning: The Yerkes–Dodson law says that the optimum level of motivation for solving problems is lower for difficult problems.

- Stimulus control. When a response is reinforced, it may be strengthened only in the particular setting where this occurred (or, via generalization, in similar settings). To increase responding generally, it is often necessary to reinforce the response in a variety of settings. Conversely, to ensure that a response occurs only in one situation, it is important to reinforce it in that situation but not others (discrimination training).
- It can be difficult to predict which of the stimuli present when a response is reinforced will come to control it. One issue is whether we will learn about individual stimuli or a group of stimuli as a whole (configural learning). Also, previous experience with a set of stimuli can affect our ability to differentiate or discriminate them (perceptual learning).
- Shaping. When a response is difficult to train, it is sometimes helpful to shape it by first reinforcing a simpler version and only gradually reinforcing closer approximations to the desired behavior.

In outline, most of these principles are very simple, but we don't always appreciate their importance. When reinforcement is used properly, it can be surprisingly powerful.

Review questions

1. Define the following terms: transituationality, sensory reinforcer, social reinforcer, Skinner box, cumulative record, FI scallop, ratio strain, and selective attention.

2. Why didn't Thorndike trust anecdotal observations? What method did he use to study learning instead?

3. What is the Law of Effect? What objections have been raised to it?

4. How do classical conditioning and reinforcement differ?

5. According to Premack, what is the common feature shared by all reinforcers? If the Premack principle is right, what do you think would be effective reinforcers for teenagers?

6. What is the distinction between positive and negative reinforcers?

7. How do escape and avoidance responses differ?

8. Why do even short delays of reinforcement have such devastating effects on learning in animals? Why are delays still sometimes harmful in humans, despite the availability of language to bridge the temporal gap between response and reinforcer?

9. Define the following schedules: CRF, FI, VI, FR, and VR. What are the characteristic effects of these schedules on the rate and pattern of

responding? If your goal were to produce persistent responding, which one of these schedules should you use?

10 If you wanted to encourage a behavior, why would it sometimes be better *not* to reinforce every response?

11 Why does the Crespi experiment suggest that the amount of a reinforcer influences motivation rather than learning? (*Hint*: Suppose that amount influenced only the strength of the association formed between a stimulus and a response. If so, how fast should we have expected the rats to run during the first phase? And, more crucially, how fast should they have run in the second phase?)

12 How are learning, motivation, and performance defined? What is the relationship between them?

13 What does the Yerkes–Dodson law imply about the use of monetary incentives to encourage students to get good grades?

14 Research on attention has shown that only some of the stimuli present when a response is reinforced will acquire control over it, but predicting which stimuli is not easy. What does research on configural learning tell us about this?

15 What about research on perceptual learning? How does experience influence our ability to differentiate stimuli, and what is the likely role of attention in the development of this ability?

16 If your goal was to improve someone's ability to differentiate stimuli, what would be one good way to achieve this?

17 Every vertical mark on the "response" line in the following record represents a response. If response 1 has just been reinforced, what other responses will be reinforced if the schedule is

(a) FI 60 seconds?

(b) VI 60 seconds, with the first two intervals being 30 and 60 seconds?

(c) FR 3?

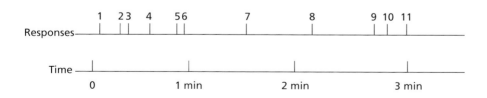

5 Reinforcement applications

CONTENTS

In the introduction to Chapter 4 we considered the paradox that the principles of reinforcement appear so simple, yet in real life behavior is often remarkably difficult to change. One explanation, we suggested, was that the principles of reinforcement might not be as simple as they first appear; in the course of that chapter, we encountered evidence supporting that view. Even brief delays of reinforcement, for example, have far more severe effects on learning than is commonly realized, and our understanding of phenomena such as motivation and stimulus control is still limited. Therefore, we could readily account for our difficulty in using reinforcement effectively by our incomplete understanding of the principles governing its use.

There is, however, another possibility. Even in those cases in which we do understand the principles of reinforcement, it can appear ineffective because we fail to apply the principles in a coherent and systematic way. That is, we might already know enough to use reinforcement more effectively, if only we would apply that knowledge systematically. This, at any rate, was the belief of several learning psychologists in the 1960s, and it led to a major effort, under the rubric of *behavior modification*, to apply the principles of reinforcement developed in the animal laboratory to practical problems of human behavior. In this chapter we will review some of these programs, considering the extent to which they have been successful, and, insofar as they have failed, what these failures can tell us about the remaining gaps in our knowledge. We will begin by looking at some of the attempts that have been made to apply the principles of reinforcement to education.

Three applications

Reinforcement principles have been applied to a wide range of educational problems and institutional settings. We will focus our attention in this section on examples involving schoolchildren, teenage delinquents, and autistic children.

Classroom behavior

One of the most difficult problems for any teacher is children who are severely disruptive in class. By talking, moving around, and so on, they not only fail to learn themselves but also seriously interfere with the work of those around them. To test a reinforcement-based program for dealing with this problem, Hall, Lund, and Jackson (1968) went to a school in a severely deprived urban area. They asked the teachers and principal to identify the children in the school whose behavior posed the most serious problems. One child, a third-grade boy named Robbie, had been in trouble ever since he entered the school. He had received repeated scoldings, been sent to the principal, and even been spanked – all to no avail. A classroom observer found that Robbie spent only 25% of his time on assigned tasks, the remainder of the time being devoted to activities such as talking, snapping rubber bands, drinking milk very slowly and then playing with the carton, and so on. His teacher often urged him to work; indeed, 55% of her contacts with Robbie occurred at times when he was not working.

If you were the teacher in charge of the class, what would you do? One natural reaction would be to punish him, but this had already been tried repeatedly without success. The experimenters' analysis was that the teacher was actually encouraging Robbie's misbehavior by giving him attention when he misbehaved. As we saw in our discussion of social reinforcement, attention from others, even when that attention comes in the form of scolding, can be reinforcing. The experimenters therefore recommended that the teacher use attention to reinforce appropriate behavior. They asked her to ignore Robbie whenever he misbehaved. When he behaved appropriately for one minute, however, she was to come over and praise him, making comments such as, "Very nice, Robbie, you've been working very well."

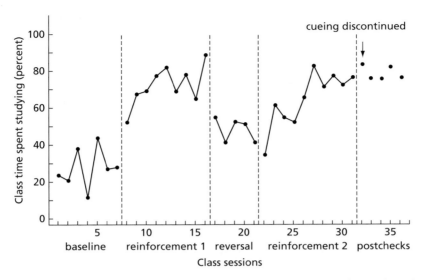

Figure 5.1 Effect of praise on the proportion of class time Robbie devoted to studying. (Hall, Lund, and Jackson, 1968.)

The results are shown in Figure 5.1. When reinforcement was introduced, there was an immediate increase in the proportion of time Robbie spent studying. When the teacher returned to the baseline condition – that is, scolding inappropriate behavior – studying fell; it improved again, however, when reinforcement was reinstated. (The purpose of alternating baseline and treatment phases is to assess whether any improvement is really the result of the treatment, or simply the passage of time; it is called an ABA design.) Moreover, this improvement proved durable: Observations made 14 weeks after the training program had ended revealed that Robbie was still spending 79% of his time working, compared with only 25% during the baseline phase. Not surprisingly, this change in the amount of time spent working also led to a substantial improvement in the quality of Robbie's work. On spelling tests, for example, his performance improved from 57% to 97%.

This improvement was not achieved without effort. To ensure that Robbie would be reinforced immediately when he studied, his behavior had to be monitored constantly. To help the teacher, the classroom observer signaled surreptitiously whenever the criterion for reinforcement was met. In the early stages of the program, therefore, considerable effort was needed to implement it, but in the long term, the improvement in Robbie's behavior meant that he required substantially less of the teacher's attention, and this improvement was maintained when cueing was discontinued. The experimenters obtained similar results with the other children studied. Thus, even a seemingly trivial reinforcer – just a little bit of praise and attention – produced remarkable changes in the behavior of the most severely disruptive children in the school, provided that this reinforcement was both immediate and consistent.

The token economy

This study supports the claim that many failures of reinforcement may be the result of reinforcement's being used in a perfunctory, haphazard way. When reinforcement was used more systematically – and, in particular, when it was immediate and consistent – then even a seemingly minor reinforcer (just a pat on the back) produced dramatic changes in behavior.

It would be misleading, however, to imply that applications of reinforcement principles are always this effective. The "reinforce good behavior, ignore bad behavior" strategy used by Hall, Lund, and Jackson has been found to be effective in many studies, but occasionally students whose disruptive behavior has been ignored have really gone haywire, eventually forcing premature cancellation of the program (for example, O'Leary et al., 1969).

In some of these failures, the problem was that the teachers did not implement the system properly. In the Hall, Lund, and Jackson study, for example, the technique was successful in six of the seven classes in which it was tried. In the one case where it failed, the experimenters found that the teacher had been unable to ignore bad behavior and had continued to become angry and to scold the student whenever he was disobedient.

In other cases, the problem could have been that the social reinforcers used were not effective reinforcers for the students concerned. As we noted in Chapter 5, social reinforcers gain or lose their effectiveness partly through experience; for some children, social reinforcers such as praise and attention are not effective (at any rate, not from their teachers). Where praise fails, a possible alternative is the **token economy**, in which points or tokens are established as secondary reinforcers through pairings with a variety of more potent reinforcers. If children behave appropriately in class, for example, they are immediately given points that can later be exchanged for backup reinforcers such as candy. The advantages of using tokens as reinforcers are these:

1 Because they are easily dispensed, they can be delivered immediately after the child makes a response.
2 Because they are exchangeable for a wide variety of backup reinforcers, they are always likely to be attractive. Even if a child does not want candy at a particular moment, the token might still be desirable because it can also be exchanged for other reinforcers such as toys.

One example of a token economy that we have already encountered is the study by Phillips (1968) in which juvenile delinquents were treated in a residential center called Achievement Place. The boys were given points for appropriate behavior, and these points could be exchanged for reinforcers such as snacks, money, permission to go into town, and so forth. When permission to stay up late was used to reinforce completion of homework assignments, the average percentage completed was 50%; when points were made contingent on completion, this percentage rose to 100%.

Token economies have produced similar improvements in a wide range of settings. In one striking example, a token economy was used to reduce injuries in two mines (Fox, Hopkins, and Anger, 1987). Workers were given trading stamps at the end of each month in which they suffered no injuries, and they received extra stamps if their work group was also injury-free. The stamps could then be exchanged for a wide variety of items at redemption stores. Over a 12-year period, the number of injuries fell by 68% in one of the mines and by 85% in the other. The program was highly cost-effective for the owners: The cost of injuries fell by more than $260,000 a year, whereas the stamps cost only around $12,000. And the program also proved highly attractive to the workers: A union representative at one of the mines even asked that the token program be written into the workers' contracts!

As we shall see, token economies need to be used with some caution. Nevertheless, they provide a potentially useful alternative for situations in which reinforcers such as praise prove ineffective.

Autism

One of the most remarkable practical attempts to apply reinforcement principles has been the work of O. Ivar Lovaas with autistic children. Autism is a psychiatric disorder in which children become totally isolated from their social environment, having neither verbal nor physical contact with other human beings. Typically, autistic children spend much of their days rocking back and forth and fondling themselves, sometimes engaging in bizarre and highly stereotyped gestures. Attempts to treat autism have largely been unsuccessful; in one long-term study of young children with this condition, more than 60% remained severely handicapped and had to be confined to hospitals (Rutter, 1970).

To treat this severely debilitating condition, Lovaas developed a program based almost entirely on the principles of reinforcement we have been discussing. He viewed autism as a set of maladaptive behaviors and so set out to encourage more appropriate behaviors using reinforcement, shaping, discrimination learning, and so on. To train autistic children to talk, for example, Lovaas used a shaping procedure similar to that described in Chapter 4 to train Dicky to wear his glasses; children were immediately reinforced with food whenever they made the desired response, and training started with simple responses such as pronouncing a single word. Their program was based on a technique called **modeling**, in which the teachers first demonstrated or modeled the desired behavior – in this case, pronouncing a word – and then reinforced the children as soon as they repeated it. Once the children had learned to pronounce the desired words, they were given discrimination training to help them to learn how to use it properly – for example, they would be shown a toy and asked its name, with reinforcement given only if they gave the correct name.

Training was a demanding process, spread over many months, but the children did gradually make impressive progress (Lovaas *et al.*, 1973). This preliminary success allowed Lovaas to obtain funds to extend his program. His initial program had been restricted to a small group of children in a psychiatric hospital, but Lovaas was now able to train therapists to work with children in their own homes; the children were all under 4 years of age, and they were assigned therapists who worked with them 40 hours per week for approximately 2 years. The children's parents were also given training in the appropriate use of learning principles, so that appropriate behavior could be reinforced whenever it occurred.

To assess the effectiveness of the treatment program, Lovaas (1987) compared the behavior of the 19 children who participated with that of a control group who were either not treated or else treated only 10 hours per week. The results were quite remarkable. The IQ of the treated group increased by an average of 30 points compared with that of the controls, and 47% of the treated children improved sufficiently to be enrolled in public schools, where their behavior was indistinguishable from that of normal children. In contrast, only 2% of children in the control conditions showed this level of improvement. Lovaas has prepared a film showing the behavior of the children before treatment and after, and the transformation in their behavior is so dramatic that it is sometimes hard to believe that you are seeing the same children.

The results reported by Lovaas and his colleagues are very, very impressive, but his methods proved controversial. One problem was their cost: Treatment requires intensive tuition for an extended period and is thus very expensive. On the other hand, as Lovaas (1987) has pointed out, the cost of one full-time teacher for 2 years is approximately $40,000, "in contrast to the nearly $2 million incurred (in direct costs alone) by each client requiring life-long institutionalization." Another problem concerned the use of punishment. In order to suppress behaviors that interfered with teaching, such as repetitive hand waving, Lovaas made extensive use of punishment, typically in the form of shouting at the children when they misbehaved. This use of punishment proved intensely controversial, and it was eventually found that the treatment could be just as effective without the use of punishment (e.g., Eikeseth *et al.*, 2002).

A further, fundamental issue was whether Lovaas's results could be replicated: Were they reliable, or just a fluke? Replication was not easy – the treatment is intensive and costly, and requires many years – but a number of replication studies have now been reported, and to an impressive extent their results have mirrored those of Lovaas. In a study by Birnbrauer and Leach (1993), for example, four of the nine children in the treatment group approached normal levels of functioning after two years, almost exactly the level of improvement reported by Lovaas. Remarkably similar results were reported by Sallows and Graupner (2005), who found that half of the twenty-four children they treated improved to the point where they could be enrolled in normal classrooms. A particularly encouraging aspect of this study was that for one of the groups the treatment was administered by the children's parents, and the results for this group were almost identical to those for a group treated by trained therapists. (The parents were trained in the methods to be used and also received occasional supervision.) If this finding can be replicated, it would open up the possibility that the Lovaas treatment (also known as ABA or behavioral treatment) could be made available far more widely, at substantially lower cost.

In an authoritative review published in the journal of the American Academy of Pediatrics, the Lovaas or ABA treatment was found to produce "substantial, sustained gains in IQ, language, academic performance and . . . social behavior, and their outcomes have been significantly better than those of children in control groups" (Myers and Johnson, 2007; see also Virués-Ortega, 2010). The best outcomes have been obtained when treatment is intensive (40 hours per week) and starts at an early age (e.g., Howard *et al.*, 2005). Under these conditions, it does look as if the Lovaas treatment has the potential to transform the lives of many children suffering from autism.

The problem of maintaining behavior

When psychologists first attempted to apply the principles of reinforcement to problem behaviors, there was considerable doubt that they would succeed. Could the behavior of delinquents, much less of children with severe learning disabilities or of psychotics, really be altered just by reinforcing them for appropriate behavior? Over the years, it has become clear that the answer is yes: Provided that reinforcement is used in a coherent and systematic way, it can be effective in settings as diverse as elementary schools and universities, prisons and psychiatric wards. It is now well established that behavior can be altered by reinforcement; the greater problem has proved to be maintaining these gains when the reinforcement program is terminated.

The problem of extinction

Consider, for example, the token economy used in Achievement Place. The initial results obtained with this program were highly positive. Boys who participated in this program were found to have substantially lower rates of court appearances during the 2-year period following their participation than did boys with similar backgrounds in a comparison condition, and participants also had higher grades in school (Fixsen *et al.*, 1978). When their behavior was examined over a longer period, however, much of this improvement was lost (Wolf, Braukmann, and Ramp, 1987). When you think about it, this is perhaps not surprising: If delinquents return to the environment that produced their delinquent behavior, it is understandable that they might return to the patterns of behavior that they had previously found to be effective in these environments.

We can see evidence of this effect on a smaller scale in the program used in Achievement Place to encourage boys to study. As noted earlier, when points were made contingent on Tom's completion of homework, the percentage of assignments completed rose to 100%. When points were eventually discontinued, however, the percentage of completions fell back to zero. In other words, when Tom received a reward he valued for studying, he studied; when this reward was discontinued, he stopped studying. After all, why should anyone persist in a behavior if it no longer produces reinforcement?

The implicit assumption in the programs we have been reviewing is that there are sources of reinforcement in the natural environment that will maintain the desired behavior if it can be established initially. A delinquent might need external incentives to learn to read, for example, but once the behavior is established, the inherent pleasure available from reading books, newspapers, and so on should maintain the behavior. In some cases, though, it can take time for these natural reinforcers to develop; if the reinforcement program is to be effective, then, it may be necessary to ensure that the reinforced behavior will continue long enough for the natural reinforcers to assume control.

Tactics for encouraging maintenance

Partial reinforcement

Several of the principles reviewed in the previous chapter can be used to encourage persistence. One such technique is partial reinforcement. As we noted in Chapter 4, the greater the intermittency of reinforcement during training, the longer behavior will persist after reinforcement is terminated. In most reinforcement programs, therefore, continuous reinforcement is used to establish a behavior initially, but the frequency of reinforcement is progressively reduced as training continues.

Reinforcing in a variety of settings

Another technique for maximizing the persistence of behavior is to reinforce it in a variety of settings. According to the principle of stimulus control, reinforcement strengthens behavior most in the particular setting in which training is given. By reinforcing behavior in a variety of settings, however, we can increase the likelihood that it will generalize widely, and thus not extinguish immediately when conditions change (for example, on leaving the classroom in which training was given).

Fading

A third potentially useful technique involves fading out the reinforcement program gradually, rather than terminating it abruptly. In our discussion of shaping, we saw that a reinforced response is more likely to persist if any changes in the reinforcement program – for example, in the number of responses required for reinforcement – are introduced gradually rather than abruptly, and this principle also applies to the termination of the program. In a study by Hall and colleagues (1972), for example, the experimenters were students in a university course on behavior modification. These students carried out projects in their own homes using the principles studied in the course. One such project involved a boy named Jerry, who had started wearing an orthodontic device when he was 8 years old. Jerry was supposed to wear the device for 12 hours a day. In practice, though, he wore it for only a few hours a day because he hated it. After 8 years, four dentists, and $3,300 in bills, Jerry's condition was essentially unchanged.

As a first step toward altering this behavior, Jerry's mother began to keep careful records of how often he wore the device, so she could accurately assess the effects of any treatment. During this baseline period, Jerry wore the device only 25% of the time (see Figure 5.2). To increase this percentage, his mother first tried social reinforcement. She did not reprimand her son when he failed to wear the device, but she praised him when he did. This social reinforcement produced a substantial increase in the desired behavior – he wore the device 36% of the time – but for practical purposes the increase was not sufficient. In the next phase, therefore, his mother tried a more powerful reinforcer: money. If Jerry was wearing the device when his mother checked, he received 25 cents; if he was not, he lost 25 cents. His mother paid him at the end of each month, and the amount of time Jerry spent wearing the device increased to 60%. To increase it still further, his mother changed to immediate reinforcement – Jerry received payment immediately after each inspection – and the wearing time now rose to 95%! As we have seen again and again (and again...), a reinforcer presented immediately is generally far more effective than the same reinforcer presented after a delay.

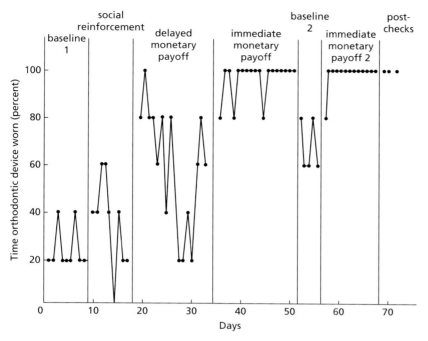

Figure 5.2 Effects of three different reinforcement techniques: social reinforcement in the form of praise, money delivered after a delay, and money delivered immediately. The reinforced behavior was the wearing of an orthodontic device. (Hall *et al.*, 1972.)

At this point, the reinforcement program was discontinued, and the amount of time Jerry spent wearing the device immediately declined to 64%. This still represented a substantial improvement over the original figure of 25%, but the change was still not sufficient to cure Jerry's dental problems. The immediate reinforcement condition was therefore reinstituted, and Jerry returned to wearing the device reliably (the percentage this time was 99%). Instead of terminating the program abruptly, his mother now faded it out gradually. The frequency with which Jerry's behavior was checked was gradually reduced from five times a day to only once every 2 weeks, and the behavior was now maintained. Eight months later, Jerry's dentist told him that he had made great progress and no longer needed to wear the device. By using reinforcement and then fading it out gradually, Jerry's mother was able to establish and maintain a behavior that years of scolding and nagging had proved powerless to influence.

Harmful effects of reinforcement

The material reviewed in the previous sections testifies to the beneficial effects that reinforcement can have when used properly. When encouraged to use reinforcement more frequently, however, parents and teachers sometimes react with suspicion, especially when the proposed reinforcer is a material one such as tokens or money. In this section, we will consider some of the reasons for this suspicion and the extent to which it might be justified.

Moral objections

Bribery

One common objection to the use of reinforcement is that it seems to be a form of bribery. Why should a child be offered money or other rewards to mow the lawn or do other chores? Many people perceive these tasks as a duty; if so, a material inducement is nothing more than a bribe.

This view has some appeal: There is something disturbing about offering a reward to get someone to do something they should be doing anyway. However, we need to consider this issue in the context of available alternatives. There is no problem if children accept responsibility, but what alternatives are available if they do not? We could admonish them to do their duty, or threaten them with punishment if they disobey, and these strategies might be appropriate in some circumstances. In at least some situations, however, these disciplinary techniques are ineffective as well as unpleasant. Consider the examples we have already seen: Robbie's teachers tried punishment to eliminate his misbehavior without success, and 8 years of reprimands had no effect on getting Jerry to wear his orthodontic device. In both cases, however, the introduction of reinforcement led to a rapid and substantial improvement in behavior, which was then maintained even after reinforcement was discontinued. These examples do not prove that reinforcement is always preferable to punishment, but they do suggest that reinforcement can be more effective than traditional forms of discipline in at least some circumstances, and might avoid harmful side effects that sometimes come with punishment (see Chapter 6). O'Leary, Poulos, and Devine (1972) discuss other issues concerning the relationship between reinforcement and bribery.

Greed

A second objection to the use of rewards – particularly material rewards – is that they promote greed. If children were offered $20 for cleaning their rooms, in this view, they would soon begin demanding money for doing other chores too, rather than accepting the chores as a necessary aspect of cooperative living. In fact, we have already encountered indirect evidence that material reinforcers can have this effect. In Chapter 4, we saw that extended exposure to a particular reinforcer devalues lesser reinforcers: A rat that had previously received 256 food pellets for running down an alley would not run nearly as fast to obtain 16 pellets as a rat that received 16 pellets all along. In other words, it looked very much as if the 256-pellet rat had become greedy!

Similar effects have sometimes been observed in applications involving material reinforcers. In one study, delinquent female adolescents were reinforced with money when they behaved appropriately in class – for example, not talking while the teacher was explaining something. The program was run during classes held in the morning, and it produced a significant improvement in students' behavior. However, disruptive behavior increased during the afternoons, when the program was not in effect. As one student said to the experimenters, "If you don't pay us, we won't shape up" (Meichenbaum, Bowers, and Ross, 1968, p. 349).

To avoid these kinds of problems, most reinforcement programs begin by using relatively mild reinforcers such as social praise. Material reinforcers are used only if these milder forms of intervention prove ineffective.

Undermining intrinsic motivation

A further objection to the use of reinforcers is that they can devalue the activity on which they are contingent. One view is that a person should be directed toward a certain behavior by **intrinsic motivation** – motivation that comes from the activity itself rather than from any consequences that might follow it. In the words of A. S. Neil, a Scottish educator who founded an influential school known as Summerhill:

The danger in rewarding a child is not as extreme as that of punishing him, but the undermining of the child's morale through the giving of rewards is more subtle. Rewards are superfluous and negative. To offer a prize for doing a deed is tantamount to declaring that the deed is not worth doing for its own sake . . . A reward should, for the most part, be subjective: self-satisfaction for the work accomplished.

(Neil, 1960, pp. 162–163)

In practice, it is sometimes difficult to distinguish precisely intrinsic and extrinsic reinforcers. Take eating. Should eating be considered intrinsically motivated because the pleasure derives from eating itself, or is the food an extrinsic reinforcer? In theory, however, the distinction seems reasonably clear: Intrinsically motivated behaviors are those that are relatively independent of external or arbitrary reinforcers.

Support for Neil's view comes from a study by Lepper, Greene, and Nisbett (1973). The purpose of their experiment was to investigate the effects of reinforcement on children's behavior in drawing pictures. In the first phase, the spontaneous level of drawing was determined by providing a nursery class with free access to felt-tip markers and paper and observing how much time they spent in drawing during a 3-hour period. One week later, the children were told that there was a visitor who would like to see what kinds of pictures children draw with markers. A reward group was told that they would receive a Good Player award – consisting of a card with a gold star, a red ribbon, and their names inscribed – if they drew a picture. A control group was also asked to draw a picture, but no reward was mentioned.

To test the effects of the reward, markers were again made available in the nursery one to two weeks later. Children in the control group spent almost exactly the same amount of time drawing as they had during the baseline phase, but the children who had been rewarded spent only half as much time as they had before.

Determinants of undermining

If reinforcement reduces long-term interest in an activity, why was it so effective in the studies reviewed earlier in this chapter, in which changes in behavior were maintained even after reinforcement was discontinued? Clearly, reinforcement does not always reduce interest; the outcome must somehow depend on the particular circumstances in which it is used. In this section we will consider several possible factors suggested by recent research.

Intrinsic or extrinsic?

One obvious difference between the Lepper group study and earlier applications is that the activities reinforced in most of the earlier studies were not all that exciting to begin with. Robbie, for example, hardly derived pleasure from studying, nor did Jerry enjoy wearing his orthodontic device. In contrast, the Lepper study involved reinforcing a very attractive activity – drawing pictures. Perhaps reinforcement reduces interest only when intrinsic interest is high to begin with.

Support for this hypothesis comes from Lepper, Greene, and Nisbett's data. During the baseline phase, most of the children spent considerable time drawing; for these children, as we have seen, reinforcement significantly reduced interest. Some children, however, showed little interest in drawing initially, and these children became *more* interested in drawing following the reward. In practical terms, if a child hates lawn mowing, there is probably little danger that his or her interest will be reduced by the offer of a reinforcer; in fact, the pleasure derived from earning money and feeling grown-up might actually enhance interest. However, for those children who already enjoy mowing lawns – a rare and much prized species – the offer of a reward might be more likely to prove counterproductive.

Coercion

Lepper (1981) and Deci and Ryan (1980) have suggested that when children are reinforced for engaging in an activity, they may feel that they are being controlled or manipulated. This sense of being controlled is aversive and could be responsible for their subsequent loss of interest in the task. According to this analysis, whether reinforcement will have a damaging effect should depend on whether recipients perceive it as an attempt to control their behavior. To test this hypothesis, Ryan (1982) gave students a number of interesting puzzles to solve. In one group, the experimenter said "Good" whenever the students solved a puzzle; in a second group, the experimenter said "Good, you're doing as you should." As predicted by the control hypothesis, subsequent interest in the task was significantly lower in the second group (see also Feehan and Enzle, 1991). The more we feel controlled, the less we enjoy the task we are being forced to perform.

Competence

We might expect quite different results if reinforcers were delivered in a way that encouraged feelings of competence. If reinforcement was contingent on the quality of performance rather than simply on completing the task, it might be more likely to increase feelings of competence and thus lead to greater enjoyment and interest. In one study supporting this prediction, Enzle and Ross (1978) offered university students $1.50 for working on difficult puzzles. In one group, the reward was promised simply for participating in the experiment; in a second group, it was contingent on achieving a level of competence well above average (this level was not specified, but all the subjects in this group were told that they had attained this high level). As in earlier studies in this area, subjects who were reinforced simply for participation showed significantly less interest in the task after the experiment was over, but subjects reinforced for their skill showed greater interest. When reinforcement implies a greater level of competence, the pleasure we experience is likely to enhance our enjoyment of the task rather than diminish it: "This is something I'm good at; what fun!" (See also Cameron, Pierce, Banko, and Gear, 2005.)

Praise or money?

A consistent finding in the literature has been that the danger of undermining interest is substantially greater when material rewards such as money are used, as opposed to praise or approval (e.g., Cameron and Pierce, 1996; Deci, Koestner, and Ryan, 1999). This may be because material rewards are more likely to be seen as attempts at manipulation rather than as expressions of genuine appreciation, but, whatever the reason, it appears that the use of monetary and other material rewards carries a particular risk. An interesting study suggesting how powerfully – and subtly – money can affect us was reported by Vohs, Mead, and Goode (2006). In one of their experiments, participants were first asked to play a game of Monopoly, and at its conclusion they were given either $4,000 in play money or $200, which they were told they would use later. Then, while on the way to another room to participate in a second task, they encountered a confederate of the experimenter who accidentally spilled twenty-seven pencils. Participants who had been given a large sum were less likely to help than participants given a smaller sum, or not given any. Similar effects were found in other experiments. In one, participants who had been exposed to money were much less likely to contribute to a charity: only 39% contributed, compared to 67% in a control group. In another, participants were given a choice between working on a task on their own or with someone else; those exposed to money were three times more likely to want to work on their own. These results suggest that exposure to money, even just play money, can make people more selfish and self-oriented. We can only speculate as to why this should be, but the work of Voh and her colleagues adds to the evidence that money may have special properties that make it more than just "another reinforcer," and it reinforces the need for caution when considering money as a possible reward. (See also Heyman and Ariely, 2004.)

Evaluation

The discovery that rewards can undermine interest in a task led to a flurry of research, and no little controversy, with behaviorally oriented psychologists tending to emphasize the advantages of reinforcement and cognitive psychologists the drawbacks. (See, for example, Cameron, Banko, and Pierce, 2001; and Henderlong and Lepper, 2002.) As research accumulated, however, the differences narrowed, and there is now broad agreement over the circumstances in which undermining is more likely.

In summarizing this consensus, the first point to note (and emphasize) is that rewards are usually used to encourage behaviors that people don't enjoy, not those that they do. Children, for example, are usually reinforced for engaging in activities they find unattractive – eating spinach, cleaning their rooms, and doing homework come to mind – and in these circumstances there is little danger of undermining interest. The risk is greater when behavior is intrinsically motivated, but even here praise is likely to encourage interest if it leaves a child feeling competent and valued (Cameron and Pierce, 1996; Henderlong and Lepper, 2002). To use a concrete example, suppose that you wanted to encourage children to practice the piano. It would probably be better to praise them for practicing rather than offering a material reward, because praise seems less likely to be perceived as a mechanism of control. Moreover, this praise would be more likely to encourage long-term interest if it emphasized their competence ("That sounds lovely; you've really improved") rather than their obedience ("That's wonderful; you've practiced for an hour just as you were supposed to").

The principle of minimal force

Despite the sometimes spectacular success of applied reinforcement programs such as token economies, parents and teachers often resist the use of reinforcement, and it is now clear that at least some of their concerns are justified. Rewards can encourage greed and lead to a sense of being controlled, which could reduce long-term interest in the reinforced activity.

These difficulties do not mean that we should never use reinforcement. When a task is unattractive, reinforcement can be a far more pleasant – and effective – technique than are alternatives such as threats or admonitions to be good. To minimize the problem of harmful side effects, however, current evidence suggests that when reinforcement is used, it is best to follow what might be called the principle of minimal force – that is, to use the least powerful reinforcer that is likely to be effective (see Lepper, 1981). In general, it is best to start with relatively mild reinforcers such as praise, turning to material reinforcers only if praise proves ineffective. Whatever the reinforcer chosen, wherever possible it should be administered in a way that encourages feelings of competence rather than mere obedience.

Promoting autonomy

No one likes to be manipulated or controlled, and the more reinforcement is perceived as part of a caring or supportive relationship, the more likely it is to be effective. One way to encourage this feeling of cooperation rather than coercion is to have the potential recipient of a reward involved in the design of the program – choosing the goals, the reinforcers to be used, and the contingencies. An interesting example comes from a study by Ludwig and Geller (1997). Although the study did not involve reinforcement, it nicely illustrates the importance of individuals participating in the design of programs affecting their behavior. The study focused on a pizza firm's desire to reduce accidents involving their drivers. One group of pizza deliverers were assembled for a meeting to discuss the importance of coming to a full stop before joining the main road outside their store; they decided for themselves what targets to set for the percentage of occasions on which drivers should behave in this way, and they then received feedback for several weeks on the group's success. A group at another store was treated similarly, except that their managers specified the targets. (The targets were set to match those chosen by the first group.)

The drivers' behavior was monitored without their knowledge, not only during the 4 weeks of the program but for $5\frac{1}{2}$ months after it ended. Both groups showed similar behavior in meeting the explicit target of coming to a full stop, but drivers who had participated in the target setting were found to also improve in other

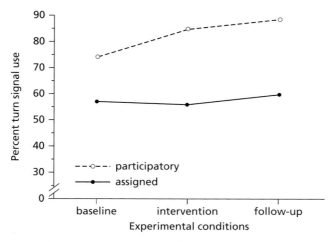

Figure 5.3 Percentage of turn signal use by pizza-delivery drivers who participated in the setting of goals or who had the goals assigned. (Adapted from Ludwig and Geller, 1997.)

safety behaviors not mentioned in the program. Figure 5.3 shows the percentage of occasions on which drivers signaled before turning onto the main road. The subjects in the participatory group improved substantially on this behavior, and the improvement was maintained even after the program was terminated. The performance of subjects who had been assigned targets, however, if anything deteriorated and was indistinguishable from that of control subjects who were never asked to change their safety behavior.

All attempts to change others' behavior can potentially be seen as coercive, and much depends on exactly how these programs are implemented. The more individuals feel that they are valued, and their needs and wishes are being considered, the more likely it is that they will cooperate in changing their behavior over the long term. (See also Grolnick and Ryan, 1989.)

Self-control

We have seen that the greatest weakness of reinforcement programs lies not in establishing behaviors initially but, rather, in maintaining them when the program is discontinued. If no reinforcement is provided, the response may simply extinguish. Also, in cases where the reinforcement program is seen as coercive or manipulative, interest in the task can actually be lower than it was originally.

A potential solution to both of these problems is to encourage **self-control** – that is, training people to control their own behavior rather than relying on reinforcement from external sources. Before considering how we might help people to exercise greater self-control, though, we need to discuss what we mean by this term.

The concept of self-control

To understand self-control, let us start with a concrete example. Suppose that a man named Tom wants to lose weight, but every time he tries to diet he fails. He has a particular weakness for chocolate bars and eats several every night before going to bed. Each time he diets he vows that he will give up these chocolates, but when he goes to bed he just can't resist eating them.

Willpower

How can we explain Tom's inability to diet? The conventional explanation for failures like this is poor willpower – Tom just doesn't have the self-control or willpower to make himself adhere to his diet. But what does it really mean to blame his failure on lack of willpower? The term willpower implies that we have a will that we can use to make ourselves do what we want, but is there really one part of our mind that forces other parts to obey its bidding? If so, and if some people have stronger wills than others, we should expect that individuals with strong wills would be uniformly good at making themselves perform difficult tasks, but this does not appear to be the case. For example, you might know people who are very good at making themselves study, but cannot resist cigarettes or overeating. (See also Mischel and Mischel, 1977.)

Another problem with the concept of willpower is that it seems to leave us helpless. If some people have greater willpower than others, what can people like Tom, who are deficient, do to suddenly endow themselves with more?

Difficulties like this have persuaded some psychologists that the concept of willpower is not really useful in explaining self-control – indeed, that it is simply an explanatory fiction that we invoke to explain behaviors that we don't understand. If Tom has difficulty dieting, we attribute his difficulty to poor willpower, but we have no independent evidence that willpower exists – we can't see it, and even Tom can't feel it. The explanation is circular: We attribute Tom's failure at dieting to poor willpower, but the only way we know that he lacks willpower is that he is having difficulty in dieting. It is a bit like the medieval belief that people who behaved strangely were possessed by demons – the strange behavior was attributed to demons, but the only evidence for the existence of demons was the strange behavior. Both explanations might make us feel better because they seem to provide an explanation for behavior that would otherwise be mysterious, but they are really only pushing the mystery a step further away. In the case of willpower, lack of willpower seems to explain Tom's difficulty in dieting, but we don't then consider what willpower really is, and why Tom has less of it than others have.

The claim that willpower doesn't exist might strike you as obviously mistaken because we have all been exposed to this concept for so long that we simply take it for granted. Suppose for the moment, though, that the claim were correct and willpower really did not exist – how then could we explain why some people succeed at dieting or giving up smoking, but others fail?

Reinforcement contingencies

Behavioral psychologists such as B. F. Skinner (1953) and Howard Rachlin (1974) have proposed one possible explanation. They argue that difficulties in self-control arise not from a lack of willpower but, rather, from reinforcement contingencies that favor immediate gratification over our long-term interests. Consider again Tom's problems with eating chocolate. If he eats a chocolate bar before going to bed, he obtains immediate reinforcement from its taste. If he leaves it uneaten, he will lose some weight, but the amount he loses will be so small as to be undetectable. Only if he diets for an extended period will he lose enough so that he can begin to see the difference in a mirror, or to feel healthier. In other words, although there are strong reinforcers available for dieting, they are substantially delayed. Given a choice between eating a chocolate bar and not eating it, Tom may chose to eat it because he obtains a small but immediate form of reinforcement for doing so; dieting produces greater reinforcement, but only after a much longer delay:

$$S_{night} : R_{eat} \longrightarrow S^R_{chocolate}$$
$$R_{diet} \xrightarrow{\hspace{4cm}} S^R_{weight\ loss}$$

The situation is much like that faced by the pigeons in the Rachlin and Green experiment that were given a choice between a small amount of food immediately or a large amount after a delay, or students who have to choose between studying and going to a movie (see Chapter 4). And unfortunately for Tom, the outcome is also the same – the small but immediate reinforcer exerts greater control.

In this view, choosing between eating chocolate or abstaining is no different from choosing whether to have a hamburger or a hot dog for lunch, or what clothing to wear to a party. They are all simply choice situations in which we choose between alternative responses, and the choice we make largely depends on the reinforcement available for each. As to why some people are better at refusing chocolate, one factor might be differences in the reinforcement contingencies affecting them. If Tom faces greater-than-average stress, for example, then the soothing properties of chocolate may make it a more powerful reinforcer for Tom than for others, thereby increasing the likelihood of his eating. Also, people who are good at dieting may have learned coping or self-control responses that help them in these situations.

A painful example

To illustrate the concept of self-control responses, we will use an experiment by Kanfer and Seidner (1973). To measure self-control, they asked one group of subjects to keep one hand in a bucket of ice water for as long as they could stand it. The water was very cold, and the average immersion time was only 57 seconds. A second group, however, was given access to a slide projector containing pictures of holiday scenes, and they were allowed to look at these images while their hands were in the water. The subjects in this group were able to keep their hands immersed for an average of 149 seconds, almost three times as long as those in the control group. Note that this result cannot be explained by willpower – because subjects were assigned to groups at random, the levels of willpower in the two groups would have been roughly equal. The reason that subjects in the slide group could keep their hands in the water was that they had a response they could perform – looking at pictures – that allowed them to distract themselves from their pain.

In this analysis, *self-control* is viewed simply as a set of responses that individuals can perform to alter their own behavior. This might at first seem contrary to the principle of determinism that we discussed in Chapter 1: If all behavior is determined, you might wonder, how can people be said to control their own behaviors? Skinner (1953) suggested a solution to this apparent paradox. His argument was that behavior is indeed controlled by the environment, but that an individual's behavior can also alter that environment. An individual can thus perform a response now to alter his or her environment and thereby indirectly alter the probability of his or her future behavior. In the Kanfer and Seidner experiment, for example, when subjects turned on the slide projector they changed their visual environments, and this helped them to reduce the amount of attention they paid to their pain. The greater self-control of individuals in the slide group was thus not because of greater willpower but, rather, because they used a specific response that allowed them to modify the situation.

Self-control techniques

Stimulus control

In considering how you can change your behavior, one useful principle that we have already encountered is that of stimulus control. We saw in Chapter 4 that when a response is reinforced, this usually results not in a general increase in the probability of the response but rather in an increase in the specific situation in which it was reinforced. The idea is that the stimuli present when a response is reinforced become associated with the response, so that the response is more likely to occur when these stimuli are present.

This principle turns out to have several useful applications in programs for changing behavior. One example we have already encountered in Chapter 4 was Bootzin's work on insomnia. To help clients who had difficulty falling asleep at night, Bootzin (1972) advised them to get up from bed whenever they had difficulty in sleeping, so that the stimulus of being in bed would not become associated with their restless behavior and thereby come to elicit it. This treatment, as we have seen, proved very effective.

Another interesting application of stimulus control was reported by Stuart (1967), as part of a program he developed for treating obesity. As one part of his program, Stuart asked his patients not to eat while engaging in other activities such as reading or watching television. The purpose was to break the association between these stimuli and eating, so that there would be fewer situations that elicited this behavior. This program proved to be remarkably effective – his eight patients lost an average of 38 pounds in one year, making it one of the more successful dieting programs ever reported. Subsequent studies using his techniques have largely confirmed this success, but, as in most other diets, participants often find it hard to maintain their weight loss after the program has ended (Wadden, Foster, and Letizia, 1994). Because of the very powerful reinforcement that food provides, it is not easy to change eating behavior, but the principle of stimulus control does seem to help and can contribute to impressive weight losses over periods of at least a year. (See also Levy, Finch, Crowell, Talley, and Jeffrey, 2007.)

Self-reinforcement

We have suggested that one of the main reasons that reinforcement is sometimes ineffective is the delay between response and reinforcer. Consider the behavior of studying. There are a number of powerful reinforcers for studying – good grades, parental approval, improved career prospects, and so on – but these reinforcers are delayed for weeks, months, or even years. To take a wildly hypothetical example, imagine a college student who has to choose between reading a psychology text and going out on a date. The reinforcement for the date is relatively immediate; the reinforcement for studying is delayed days or weeks. From a reinforcement perspective, it is hardly surprising that many students have difficulty studying under these conditions.

When the environment does not provide immediate reinforcement for a behavior, one possible strategy is for individuals to reinforce themselves. If you wanted to increase the amount of time you spent studying, for example, you could reinforce your own studying behavior by, say, allowing yourself a 15-minute break whenever you completed reading 20 pages of a text. But would this technique really work? If you found it difficult to study, would you really wait until you had completed a difficult assignment before taking a break, or would you just give up and take the break anyway?

The answer, according to Skinner, would depend on your past history. As we have seen, Skinner viewed self-control simply as a set of responses, with the same properties as other responses. In particular, he argued that self-control responses are learned in the same way as other behaviors, through a combination of reinforcement and punishment. Whether children will learn to reinforce themselves – for example, with candy, or more likely with praise ("I've been such a good girl") – will depend on whether such behavior is in turn reinforced by others. When children praise themselves appropriately, others may in turn praise them. (Tommy: "I did a good job cleaning my room, didn't I, Mommy?" Mother: "Yes, Tommy, you did it beautifully.") If they cheat, on the other hand, they might be reprimanded. Provided that we get enough appropriate feedback, we eventually learn to praise ourselves only when such praise is merited, and this self-praise can then help to maintain our behavior.

Developing self-control

To illustrate how a behavior such as self-reinforcement might be learned, we will use an example reported by Drabman, Spitalnik, and O'Leary (1973). The subjects were 10-year-old boys in a class for children with academic and emotional problems. Eight of the most disruptive boys in the class were selected for special training, and a token economy was established in which the boys were given points on a 5-point scale for good behavior and for completing assignments; at the end of each lesson, the points could be exchanged for cakes, candies, or pennies.

The program was highly effective: The frequency of disruptive behavior fell by two-thirds, and the average number of assignments completed rose from 83 to 130. It was not possible, however, to maintain the token economy indefinitely. What, then, could be done to ensure that the gains would be sustained once the program was withdrawn?

Because a teacher could not always be available to provide reinforcement, Drabman and his colleagues decided to train the children to reinforce themselves. At the end of each lesson, the boys were to award themselves points on the basis of how they had behaved, with these points then being exchanged for other reinforcers in the usual way. To ensure that the boys would reinforce themselves appropriately, the researchers instituted a training program in which the teacher

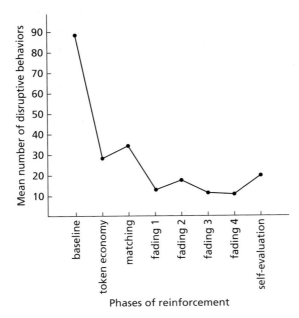

Figure 5.4 Mean number of disruptive behaviors in successive phases of a self-control program. (Adapted from Drabman, Spitalnik, and O'Leary, 1973.)

initially reinforced the boys for accurate self-reinforcement. Once this behavior had been learned, the frequency of checking by the teacher was progressively reduced.

Specifically, the teacher monitored the boys' behavior during the self-reinforcement phase, and at the end of each lesson the boys' self-ratings were compared with the teacher's ratings. If the boys' ratings were within one point of the teacher's, they received the points they had given themselves; if the ratings matched accurately, the boys also received a bonus point, but if they had deviated from the teacher's ratings by more than a point, they received no points. To reduce the likelihood that the checking would be seen as a form of control, the experimenters explained that being selected for checking was a privilege because only those boys who were checked would have the chance to earn bonus points.

Over days, the proportion of boys selected for checking was gradually reduced, until all the boys were receiving whatever points they had awarded themselves without any formal checking. On days when their self-ratings exactly matched the teacher's, though, the teacher strongly praised them.

The results are shown in Figure 5.4. During the final phase, in which they received whatever points they had awarded themselves, their behavior was not only maintained at the levels achieved when the teacher controlled reinforcement, but, if anything, actually exceeded those levels.

Returning to our studying example, the reason that some students spend more time studying than others could be, in part, because they obtain immediate secondary reinforcement when they complete an assignment, in the form of a feeling of pride. And the source of this pride could be that they were differentially reinforced when they were younger for sticking to commitments – praised when they did, but not when they didn't. This analysis is speculative, but the results of the Drabman *et al.* study suggest that children can learn to reinforce their own behavior if the appropriate use of self-reinforcement is itself reinforced. (See also Wood and Flynn, 1978.)

More broadly, it appears that self-control procedures can be very powerful if they are backed up by occasional monitoring and support from others (for example, Ward and Carnes, 2002). In the case of obesity, self-control procedures have been very effective in helping people lose weight, but participants usually regain this weight once treatment is terminated. To counter this problem, Latner *et al.* (2002) tried incorporating external sources of reward and punishment into a self-control program. For example, participants were told that they would be dropped from the program if they did not adhere to the regulations during the first few months. This combination of self-control methods with external consequences has produced the most impressive results to date, with participants maintaining losses of more than 15% of their body weight for more than five years.

Improving your studying

To summarize some of the self-control principles we have been discussing, we will conclude by briefly considering how you can use self-control principles to increase the amount of time you spend studying. According to several successful programs (for example, Goldiamond, 1965; Fox, 1966), your first step should be to find a quiet spot where you can work with minimal disturbance – for example, an isolated desk in a library. Begin by setting yourself a modest target for how long you will study, and then reinforce yourself (self-reinforcement) when you reach your target (the reinforcer could be coffee, a break with friends, or even just a notation on a special record card – an accurate record of progress can be a surprisingly powerful reinforcer). Then, over days, gradually increase your target (shaping).

For this strategy to work, it is important to choose an effective reinforcer. Some evidence suggests that a public declaration of both your goals and your progress – for example, posting a graph of your studying time where your friends can see it and thus encourage you – can also be important (see Hayes *et al.*, 1985). Also, you need to set goals that are realistically attainable. If you have difficulty concentrating, you might need to set your initial goal at only 15 minutes, or even 5 minutes, and then increase your target gradually.

To maximize the probability that your desk will become a cue for studying and not for other behaviors, ensure that studying is the only activity you engage in while there. If you feel an uncontrollable urge to daydream or have a snack, leave immediately, and return only when you feel able to resume concentrating on your work (stimulus control). These are by no means the only useful techniques for improving studying habits. (For some other techniques, see Fox, 1966; Weinstein and Meyer, 1986.) However, if you do want to improve your studying, you may find this approach a helpful component of a broader program based on careful reading, reviewing what you have read as soon as you finish a section, and other basic study skills (see the discussion of studying in Chapter 12).

Throughout our discussion of self-control, we have used an analytical framework first proposed by Skinner. There are, of course, other ways of thinking about self-control, and in recent years some of these alternative perspectives have received greater experimental attention. If you'd like to investigate some of these other approaches, you can find useful introductions in Gollwitzer and Sheeran (2006) and Baumeister, Vohs, and Tice (2007).

Summary

- When reinforcement principles are used properly, they can be surprisingly effective. Examples include reducing classroom misbehavior, increasing homework and miners' safety, and treating autism.
- When reinforcement is discontinued, the behavior that was rewarded may extinguish. To provide more time for reinforcers in natural environment to take over, useful techniques include using partial reinforcement in training, reinforcing behavior in a variety of settings, and fading out the use of reinforcement gradually.
- Reinforcement can sometimes have harmful side effects. If material rewards such as money are used, there is a danger of encouraging greed. Also, when children are reinforced for activities that they enjoy, this can paradoxically undermine interest, particularly if the child feels coerced.
- To minimize side effects, the "principle of minimal force" should always be applied: Start by using the mildest reinforcer that is likely to be effective (in most cases, praise).
- One way to reduce people's feelings of being controlled by others is to encourage self-control. According to Skinner, self-control is simply a set of learned behaviors, acquired because they change the probability of future behaviors and thereby shorten the time to reinforcement. Self-control in this view is a matter not of willpower but of learning effective strategies such as stimulus control

and self-reinforcement. These techniques have proven very effective in helping people to lose weight and increase the time they spend studying.

Review questions

1 The "principle of minimal force" suggests starting with relatively mild reinforcers such as praise whenever possible. Can social reinforcers such as praise really modify difficult behaviors? If they fail, what other reinforcers can be used?

2 What can be done to increase the likelihood that behaviors will persist long enough after a reinforcement program is terminated to allow natural reinforcers to acquire control?

3 What are the potentially harmful effects of reinforcement? In what situations are these most likely to occur?

4 What are some of the techniques by which people control their own behavior? How can they be applied to studying?

5 How does Skinner explain self-control? How does his account differ from that of willpower? What does each approach say about variability in self-control? In other words, should a person who shows strong self-control in one situation (for example, giving up smoking) also have above-average self-control in other situations (for example, studying)?

6 Punishment

CONTENTS

Of several responses made to the same situation . . . those which are accompanied or closely followed by discomfort to the animal will, other things being equal, have their connection with the situation weakened, so that, when it recurs, they will be less likely to occur.

(Thorndike, 1911, p. 244)

We are gradually discovering – at an untold cost in human suffering – that in the long run punishment doesn't reduce the probability that an act will occur.

(Skinner, 1948a)

Punishment is one of society's oldest techniques for controlling behavior, and also one of its most controversial. Does it really work? If we spank a child for disobeying an order or send an adult to prison for stealing, will the treatment really be effective? Or are we only building up a reservoir of hostility and bitterness that will lead to even more antisocial behavior in the future?

Principles of punishment

Methodological issues

Definitions

Before discussing the evidence, we need to define some terms. Broadly, **punishment** refers to a reduction in the likelihood of a response caused by an aversive consequence. However, psychologists have distinguished between two types of punishment, *positive punishment* and *negative punishment*, which differ in whether the aversive state is brought about by presenting a stimulus or removing it. In positive punishment – normally just called punishment – suppression is due to the presentation of a stimulus; in negative punishment, to its removal. A spanking would be an example of positive punishment, as it involves the presentation of an aversive stimulus. A parking fine, on the other hand, would be an example of negative punishment, as the aversive state is caused by taking away money. In both cases the outcome is suppression; they differ simply in whether this is achieved by presenting a stimulus or by removing it.

As we saw in Chapter 4, a similar distinction is made in the case of reinforcement, where positive reinforcement refers to a strengthening of behavior achieved by presenting a stimulus, and negative reinforcement refers to a strengthening achieved by removing a stimulus. You may find it easier to remember the meaning of all these terms if you distinguish between the method used – is a stimulus presented or removed? – and the outcome – is a behavior strengthened or weakened? Reinforcement involves strengthening a response and punishment involves weakening it; the terms positive and negative indicate whether this is achieved by presenting a stimulus or removing it.

You can test your understanding of these distinctions by answering the following question: *Is negative reinforcement a form of punishment?*

The correct answer is no. Negative reinforcement is still reinforcement; the qualifier negative simply means that this strengthening is achieved by removing a stimulus. If you answered this incorrectly, you might take some comfort from the fact that this mistake is very common, and even appears in some textbooks. To avoid it, just remember that reinforcement always refers to strengthening, and punishment always refers to weakening.

Observation versus experiment

There has been no lack of debate over the effectiveness of punishment, but rarely can either side produce unequivocal evidence to support its position. This is perhaps not surprising. How, after all, can we evaluate the long-term effects of punishment?

Consider spanking as an example: It might seem easy enough to compare the behavior of children who are spanked with those who are not, but in practice such data are often difficult to interpret. In a study by Eron *et al.* (1963), for example, parents of 451 schoolchildren were interviewed to find out what kinds of punishment they used in different situations. If their children were rude, for example, they were asked whether they would say, "Young men (ladies) don't do that sort of thing," or "Get on that chair and don't move until you apologize," or would spank the child until he or she cried. The researchers found that the harsher the punishment chosen by the parents, the more likely the children were to be aggressive at school. Punishing aggression, in other words, seemed to increase the frequency of this behavior rather than reduce it.

As we shall see later, there is some support for this conclusion, but this study nevertheless poses serious problems of interpretation. First, even though the parents said they would have used a certain form of punishment, this does not necessarily mean that they would actually have done so. And even if they did, we cannot be sure that it was their use of this punishment that made their children aggressive. Might not some other aspects of the parents' behavior – a lack of love or concern, for example – have produced both the punitiveness and the aggression? Or perhaps the causal relationship is reversed: Perhaps the children's persistent aggression and disobedience, produced by other causes, progressively forced the parents to use punishments of ever-increasing severity. The fact that punishment and aggression are correlated, in other words, does not necessarily mean that punishment has caused the aggression. Thus, although studies based on questionnaires or on more direct forms of observation can be an important source of hypotheses about causal relationships, it is difficult to reach unequivocal conclusions by observing behavior in a complex social environment.

Animals versus humans

The obvious alternative is experimentation under the controlled conditions of the laboratory. For punishment, though, this raises serious problems. For obvious reasons, psychologists are extremely reluctant to use severe punishment in studies that involve human subjects. If punishment is to be studied in the laboratory, therefore, we must either use very mild punishments, such as verbal rebukes, or else employ animals as our subjects.

Each of these alternatives has its drawbacks. It is certainly useful to know how a child will react to being told "No, that's wrong" by a stranger, but this might not be a reliable guide to the effects of being spanked by an enraged parent. So, what are the drawbacks to using animals as experimental subjects? As we have already seen, there are many similarities in the laws of learning across different species; by no stretch of the imagination, however, could a human being be described simply as a very large rat.

In trying to determine the effects of severe punishment, then, is it better to extrapolate from the effects of mild punishment in humans or severe punishment in animals? In practice, psychologists have resolved this dilemma by using both approaches; in this chapter we will look at the results obtained with each, and at the extent to which they have contributed to a unified picture of the effects of punishment. We will begin by examining the effects of punishment on the punished response and consider whether punishment really produces long-term suppression of behavior. We will then consider the effects of punishment on other behavior; that is, even in situations in which punishment does suppress the punished response, might it have side effects that would make its use inadvisable? Finally, we will consider the implications of this research for what parents and teachers should do when children misbehave.

Is punishment effective?

We have argued that, by studying punishment under controlled conditions, it should be considerably easier to determine its effects. What, then, does this research tell us about whether punishment is effective?

Bar pressing in rats

The early evidence was largely negative, suggesting that punishment had little or no effect on behavior. Thus, although Thorndike had accorded punishment equal status with reinforcement in his first statement of the Law of Effect, his own research subsequently convinced him that punishment led to no permanent reduction in behavior. Similarly, B. F. Skinner (1938) was persuaded by his research with rats that the effects of punishment were at best only temporary. In one of these experiments, a group of rats was first trained to press a bar to obtain food, then presentations of the food were discontinued. This is known as an *extinction* procedure; the typical result is a gradual decrease in responding, until subjects eventually stop responding altogether. To evaluate the effects of punishment, Skinner divided his subjects into two groups during the extinction phase, with subjects in one of the groups being punished every time they pressed the bar during the first 10 minutes of extinction. The punishment consisted of a slap on the rat's paw.

Figure 6.1 shows the cumulative number of responses made during extinction. Initially, the punishment contingency appeared highly effective; subjects stopped responding for as long as it was in effect. After the punishment period ended, however, they gradually began to respond again, until by the end of the second session they had emitted the same total number of responses during extinction as

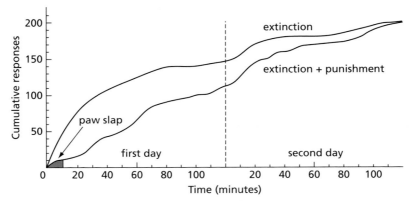

Figure 6.1 The effect of punishment on responding during extinction. Bar-presses during the first 10 minutes of extinction were punished in the extinction + punishment group but not in the extinction group. The figure plots the cumulative number of responses during extinction, so that a horizontal line indicates a period without responding. (Skinner, 1938.)

the control subjects who had never been punished. Punishment, in other words, seemed to suppress responding only temporarily, leading Skinner and others to conclude that it was an ineffective and undesirable technique for changing behavior.

This conclusion, however, was based on very little evidence. Because of their reluctance to inflict pain, most experimenters either avoided punishment altogether or chose relatively mild stimuli as their punishers. As we have mentioned, Skinner used a slap on the paw to punish his rats, and Thorndike's conclusions were based on experiments with humans using the word "wrong" as the aversive event. Only in the past few decades have experiments using more intense punishers been reported in any number, and the effect has been to reverse dramatically the earlier negative conclusions: At least insofar as the white rat is concerned, compelling evidence now indicates that punishment can produce powerful and enduring suppression of behavior. Boe and Church (1967), for example, repeated Skinner's bar-pressing experiment but used electric shock as the punishing event rather than a slap on the paw. To evaluate the importance of punishment severity, they varied the intensity of the shock for different groups from 0 to 220 volts.[1]

With mild intensities of shock, their results resembled Skinner's, as Figure 6.2 shows. The brief period of shock at the end of training produced little enduring reduction in the number of responses emitted during extinction. As the intensity

---

[1] Although the shock used in this study was undoubtedly aversive, it was not as intense as it sounds. The aversiveness of a shock depends on the amount of current passing through the body rather than on the shock voltage; under the conditions of this study, the shocks were intense but not physically harmful.

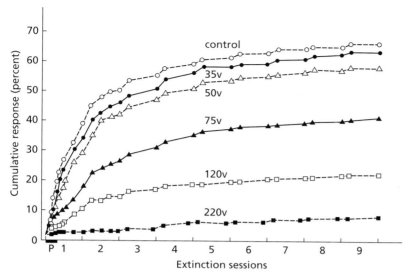

Figure 6.2 The effect of shock intensity on responses during extinction. Different groups received shocks ranging in intensity from 0 volts (the control group) to 220 volts during a 15-minute period at the beginning of extinction, marked *P* on the *x*-axis. The measure of responding was the cumulative number of responses during extinction, expressed as a percentage of responding during the last session of training. In the 220-volt group, for example, the total number of responses during extinction was less than 10% of responses during the final session of reinforcement. (Boe and Church, 1967.)

of the shock was increased, however, the effect on subsequent responding became increasingly pronounced, until, in the 220-volt group, responding was not only suppressed during the punishment period but showed virtually no signs of recovery over nine subsequent sessions. When the punishment used was of sufficient severity, in other words, even a brief period of punishment resulted in profound and enduring suppression of behavior.

Self-injurious behavior in humans

Are the effects of intense punishment on humans the same as those observed on animals? For obvious reasons, the data on this point are limited, but the evidence we do have suggests a number of similarities. In a clinical study reported by Bucher and Lovaas (1968), for example, electric shock was used to treat self-injurious behavior in autistic children. (See Chapter 5 for a discussion of autism.) One of the most horrifying manifestations of this syndrome is self-injurious behavior, in which children repeatedly and viciously attack their own bodies. In the case of a 7-year-old boy named John, the resultant physical damage was so serious that he had to be hospitalized and kept in complete physical restraint 24 hours a day. "When removed from restraint he would immediately hit his head against the crib,

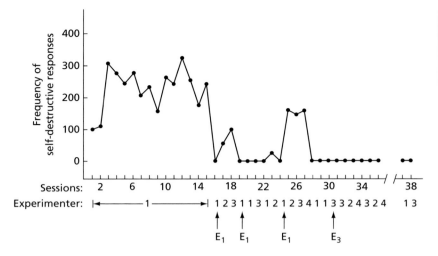

Figure 6.3 The frequency of self-destructive behavior before and after punishment. The experimenter present during each session is indicated; experimenter 1 (E₁) or experimenter 3 (E₃) administered shocks during the sessions marked by an arrow. (Adapted from Bucher and Lovaas, 1968.)

beat his head with his fists, and scream . . . He was so unmanageable that he had to be fed in full restraints; he would not take food otherwise. His head was covered with scar tissue, and his ears were swollen and bleeding" (Bucher and Lovaas, 1968, p. 86).

Because of the risk of permanent physical damage resulting from continued confinement, it was vital that some way be found to eliminate this behavior as quickly as possible. One technique that had previously been found to be effective consisted of ignoring the self-injurious behavior (thereby eliminating adult attention as a possible source of reinforcement) and simultaneously rewarding incompatible behaviors such as hand-clapping or singing songs. Because of the particular circumstances involved, however, this approach was not feasible, and Bucher and Lovaas decided instead to use punishment. This might at first seem to be a bizarre choice of treatment because John's behavior suggested that, if anything, he enjoyed being hurt. Nevertheless, once a day John was taken to a special room where his restraints were removed, and he was given an immediate electric shock every time he hit himself. The results are shown in Figure 6.3, which plots the number of self-destructive responses observed during successive treatment sessions. During the first 15 baseline sessions, the experimenters did not administer punishment, and John hit himself an average of almost 250 times during each session. When punishment was introduced in session 16, however, this behavior disappeared almost immediately.

To see if this suppression would prove lasting, the experimenters did not use punishment in some subsequent sessions, and John's self-injurious behavior began to reappear. When this behavior was again punished, it was again suppressed, and it now remained suppressed. Using a total of only 12 shocks, Bucher and Lovaas were able to eliminate a response that had occurred previously at a rate of several thousand times a day for more than 5 years. Similar results were obtained with the other children treated.

Principles

Results such as these have made it clear that punishment can suppress behavior under at least some conditions. What, then, determines whether punishment will be effective?

Intensity

Boe and Church's experiment showed that the effectiveness of a punishment in animals depends on its intensity, and similar results have been reported in humans. In a study by Williams, Kirkpatrick-Sanchez, and Iwata (1993), for example, the subject was a profoundly retarded young woman who engaged in self-mutilating behaviors such as hitting and biting her body and gouging her eyes. Initial treatment with a relatively mild form of shock was ineffective, but when her therapists switched to more intense shock, her self-injurious behavior was very rapidly suppressed, and staff were later able to maintain this suppression solely by using reprimands that had previously been paired with the shock. (This procedure, in which a stimulus paired with an aversive event itself becomes aversive, is called *secondary punishment*.)

Given that punishments are more effective when they are intense, it might seem that anyone considering using punishment should opt for the strongest punishment possible. As we shall see shortly, however, punishment can also produce undesirable side effects, and the stronger the punishment, the greater the danger. One obvious solution would be to use the mildest form of punishment that is likely to be effective, but this can vary from individual to individual (mild punishment is less likely to be effective with individuals accustomed to more severe forms), and from response to response (when powerful reinforcers are maintaining a behavior, the level of punishment required to suppress it will inevitably be greater). It is thus not possible to provide universal guidelines: Choosing the optimum level of punishment comes down, in the end, to trial and error.

Delay

A second important factor determining the effectiveness of punishment is the delay between the response and the punisher. In an experiment by Solomon, Turner, and

Lessac (1968), dogs were offered a choice between two foods, one highly preferred and the other less so. The foods were presented in two dishes, located on either side of the experimenter's chair. If the dogs approached the dish that contained the less preferred food, they were allowed to eat freely, but if they began to eat the preferred food, the experimenter would hit them on the snout with a rolled-up newspaper. The delay interval between the moment when the dogs started eating and the time they were punished was either 0, 5, or 15 seconds for different groups.

Regardless of which delay was used, all the subjects learned quickly, requiring an average of only three or four punishments before avoiding the preferred food entirely. To determine the extent to which these punishments had resulted in an enduring change in behavior, the dogs were deprived of food and exposed to a daily series of 10-minute temptation trials. During these tests, the hungry dogs were returned to the room in which they had previously been trained, but with the experimenter now absent; one food dish contained 500 grams of the preferred food, and another dish contained only 20 grams of the nonpreferred food. The question was, how long would the hungry dogs be able to resist the temptation of eating the preferred food?

For the group that was punished with a 15-second delay during training, the answer was about 3 minutes. The dogs that had been punished after a delay of 5 seconds, however, resisted eating for 8 days, and those that had been punished immediately went without eating for 2 weeks. A delay of only a few seconds in punishing a response, therefore, can have profound implications for the effectiveness of punishment – in this case, resisting eating for 3 minutes versus 2 weeks.

To find out if delay of punishment is so critical in humans, Aronfreed (1968) used a procedure very similar to that developed by Solomon. Instead of offering dogs a choice of food dishes, Aronfreed asked schoolchildren to choose one of two toys and then to describe the chosen toy to the experimenter. One of the toys was highly attractive, the other much less so. If they selected the unattractive toy, the children were allowed to describe it, but if they chose the attractive toy the experimenter would punish them by saying "No" and taking away a candy from a pile they had been given previously. For some of the children, this punishment took place as soon as they began to reach for the attractive toy, but for others it was delayed for either 2, 6, or 12 seconds. This procedure was then repeated for each of 10 different pairs of toys, with choices of the attractive member of each pair always being punished.

As in Solomon's study, the delay of punishment had little apparent effect on initial learning; virtually all the children learned to avoid the attractive toy after only two or three punishments. Again as in Solomon's study, however, the effect of the delay interval proved more dramatic when behavior was measured in the experimenter's absence. During this testing phase, when the experimenter finished laying out a new pair of toys, he would explain that he had suddenly remembered something he needed to do elsewhere and would leave the child alone with the toys for 10 minutes. Of those children who had been punished immediately during training, only half made any attempt to play with the attractive toy, and the majority of these children waited at least 5 minutes before doing so. Of the children whose punishment had been delayed for even 6 seconds during training, however, almost all transgressed during the temptation period, and most did so within less than a minute of the experimenter's departure. Thus, delays of even a few seconds seemed to reduce substantially the effectiveness of punishment.

The effects of delaying punishment in children, therefore, seem remarkably similar to the effects in animals, with punishment proving far more effective when administered immediately. We have less evidence concerning the role of delay in adults, but an interesting study by Wagenaar and Maldonado-Molina (2007) suggests that delay may also be important here. They examined the effects of punishment on the behavior of drivers who were caught driving while intoxicated. Specifically, they compared states in the USA that impose an immediate suspension of a driver's license when a driver fails an alcohol breath test with states where suspension did not take effect until conviction in a court. The punishment was thus the same, but there was a substantial difference in how soon it took effect. In the states where punishment was immediate, the authors found that it led to a substantial decrease in subsequent accidents and convictions, leading to a 5% reduction in fatal crashes and saving 800 lives per year. In states where suspension was delayed, on the other hand, it had no effect at all on drivers' subsequent behavior. As we saw in our discussion of reinforcement, punishment seems to be much more effective when it is immediate.

Schedule

The effects of punishment also depend critically on the schedule used. In an experiment by Azrin, Holz, and Hake (1963), for example, pigeons were trained to peck a key to obtain food, and once this behavior was established key-pecks also began to produce electric shocks. The shock schedule varied from FR 1 (every response punished) to FR 1,000 (only one response in 1,000 punished). Punishment of every response resulted in total suppression of pecking, but as the probability of punishment was reduced, responding was much less affected.

Again, similar results have been reported in experiments on humans. In an observational study, Larzelere et al. (1996) asked mothers to keep diaries of when their children misbehaved and whether they were punished. The researchers found that the higher the proportion of disobedient acts that mothers punished, the less likely their children were to disobey. Similarly, Brennan and Mednick (1994) found that the effectiveness of punishment for criminal behavior depends on the consistency with which this behavior is punished: The higher the proportion of an individual's arrests that led to punishment, the less likely the individual was to reoffend. As common sense would suggest, punishment is more likely to be effective if it is delivered immediately and consistently.

Stimulus control

Another important factor in determining the effectiveness of punishment is the similarity between the conditions during training and testing. If the dogs in Solomon's study had been tested in the training room with the experimenter still present, for example, it seems likely that they would have resisted eating even longer, whereas if they had been tested in a totally different room, without any experimenter and with different dishes, they would probably have given in to temptation much sooner.

Support for this prediction comes from an experiment by Honig and Slivka (1964), who looked at the effects of punishment on key-pecking in pigeons. During preliminary training, a plastic key was illuminated with one of seven alternating colors, varying in wavelength from 490 to 610 nanometers (nm), and pecking was reinforced in the presence of each. When the rate of pecking to each color was roughly equal, Honig and Slivka began to selectively punish responding in the presence of the 550-nm stimulus by presenting an electric shock whenever this color was pecked.

The results of this selective punishment are illustrated in Figure 6.4, which shows the rate of responding to each stimulus recorded over 9 days of punishment train-ing. Punishment of responding to the 550-nm stimulus was highly effective from the outset, because the birds almost immediately stopped responding whenever this color appeared on the key. The extent to which responding was suppressed in the presence of the other colors, however, depended on their similarity to the punished stimulus. Responding to the 530- and 570-nm stimuli, for example, was also strongly suppressed, but as the test stimuli became increasingly dissimilar to the punished stimulus, the amount of suppression decreased. (Note that what is generalizing in this case is *inhibition* of responding, rather than responding: The weaker the inhibition, the more likely subjects are to respond. That is why response levels increase as the test stimulus becomes less similar to the training stimulus, rather than becoming lower, as in the generalization gradients we have encountered previously.)

As training continued, and the birds learned that punishment occurred only in the presence of the 550-nm wavelength, their rate of responding to the non-punished wavelengths progressively increased. In other words, if punishment is delivered in one situation, its effects may generalize at first, but if subjects repeat-edly find that responding in other situations is safe, then responding may eventu-ally be suppressed only in the setting in which it is actually punished.

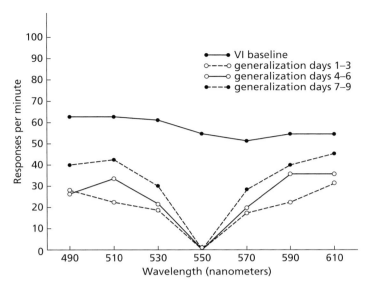

Figure 6.4 Generalization of a punished response. During the baseline condition, key-pecking was reinforced in the presence of each of seven different colors. The remaining curves show the changes in responding to each of these colors following the introduction of punishment in the presence of the 550-nm stimulus. (Honig and Slivka, 1964.)

Remarkably similar results were obtained in the Bucher and Lovaas study discussed earlier. John's self-destructive behavior was punished for the first time in session 16, when experimenter 1 was present, and the result was virtually immediate suppression (Figure 6.3). To determine the extent to which self-injurious behavior would be suppressed in other situations, the authors arranged for different experimenters to be present in the test room on different days. Only the first experimenter ever punished hitting, and whenever this experimenter was present, self-destructive behavior remained at very low levels. When the other experimenters were present, however, there was a perceptible increase in its frequency (though still far below baseline levels), and as testing continued it began to rise alarmingly. As with the pigeons in the Honig and Slivka experiment, John seemed to be learning that punishment occurred only in a particular situation, and, as a result, suppressed his self-destructive behavior only in that situation. During session 30, therefore, experimenter 3 was also instructed to use punishment whenever John hit himself, and thereafter there were no further recurrences of this behavior, regardless of which experimenter was present in the room.

One important implication of this finding is that if you want to eliminate a response entirely it might not be sufficient to punish it in only one situation. Suppose, for example, that you wanted to train young children not to play in the street. Ideally, an explanation of the dangers involved would be sufficient, but suppose this failed and you decided to use punishment. If the children were punished only when you were nearby, they might very well learn a discrimination: If a parent is nearby, playing in the street is dangerous; if a parent is not nearby, then it's perfectly safe! To ensure that behavior is suppressed more generally, you would ideally want to arrange for this behavior to be punished in different settings – for example, for playing in different streets and, if possible, when no adult appeared to be present, so that the children would learn that playing in any street is dangerous, regardless of whether anyone appears to be watching.

Verbal explanation

To this point, the results of punishment research in humans seem almost uncannily similar to those obtained with animals. As we argued earlier, however, the fact that the principles of animal and human learning are sometimes similar does not necessarily mean that they are identical. In particular, it would be very strange indeed if the cognitive and linguistic capacities of humans did not play some role in determining how we react to punishment.

This point is neatly illustrated in Aronfreed's experiment. In addition to the immediate and delayed punishment groups that we have described, Aronfreed included another delayed punishment group in which children were not only punished when they picked up an attractive toy, they were also given an explanation for why they should not do so. This toy was difficult to tell about, they were told, and was therefore only for older children. The children in this group were subsequently found to be significantly more likely to resist temptation than were those not given an explanation.

Similar findings have been reported from field studies in which parents have been interviewed to determine what sorts of punishment they used. In a study by Sears, Maccoby, and Levin (1957), for example, mothers who made extensive use of reasoning reported punishment to be far more effective than did those who reported using punishment alone. Similarly, in the Larzelere et al. study described earlier, the authors assessed the immediate effects of punishment in young children by calculating the average time interval separating successive instances of misbehavior such as fighting and examined how this was affected by the mother's reaction to each incident. The data revealed that punishment on its own had no effect: Following a fight, the average time until another fight was the same whether or not the child was punished. When the punishment was accompanied by an explanation, however, the average time until the next fight increased by almost 40%.

Why should the addition of even a few words of explanation make punishment so much more effective? One possibility is that an explanation helps to clarify what behavior is being punished. If a child were punished in the evening for something he did that morning, for example, without an explanation he would have no way of knowing what he was being punished for. In addition, explanations can provide children with justification for why they are being punished. In Aronfreed's experiment, the children were not only being told which behavior to avoid (playing with the attractive toy), but why (because it was only appropriate for older children). If the explanation helped the children to perceive the punishment as fair, it might have reduced their resentment and thus increased their willingness to cooperate.

To assess the effects of clarification and justification, Cheyne (1969) repeated Aronfreed's experiment but varied the explanations used. One group of children were simply told "That's bad" when they chose the attractive toy. A second group received an additional phrase to clarify what behavior was being punished: "That's bad, you shouldn't play with that toy." As expected, the clarification group deviated significantly less in a later temptation situation, suggesting that the effectiveness of delayed punishment does depend on how clearly the punished response is identified. The least deviation of all, however, occurred in a third group of children, who were told not only which response was forbidden but why: "That toy belongs to someone else." If a punishment is perceived as fair or reasonable, in other words, it is more likely to be effective.

Cheyne found that the effectiveness of justification depended on the age of the children. Telling children "That toy belongs to someone else" increased compliance in third-grade children, but it had no effect on those in kindergarten. This suggests that, as children grow older, their behavior increasingly comes under the control of generalized moral codes or rules. Thus, although punishment may play a role in establishing these rules with younger children, as the children grow older it may be increasingly possible to rely on verbal appeals to these ethical codes, rather than on the direct elicitation of fear.

Hoffman (1989) has suggested that explanations can also play an important role in children's moral development. When a child misbehaves in a way that involves harm to others, he says, it is important to explain the consequences for the other person, rather than simply to say, "Stop that." Children who receive such explanations seem to be more likely to develop empathy for others and accept responsibility for their own behavior.

Summarizing the evidence to this point, it appears that punishment is most effective when it is immediate, firm, consistent, delivered in a variety of settings, and accompanied by a clear (and fair) explanation. Used under these conditions, punishment can be a powerful technique for suppressing behavior.

Side effects of punishment

Insofar as we confine our attention to the effects of punishment on the response being punished, it is clear that Thorndike was right – punishment can suppress behavior. But does this necessarily mean that we should use it? In addition to weakening the response that it follows, punishment may produce damaging effects on other aspects of behavior, so that we need to weigh the advantages of punishment against its disadvantages before deciding whether to use it. In this section, we will examine evidence about punishment's side effects.

Fear

The problem is that aversive stimuli have a variety of effects. We have seen that one effect is to suppress preceding behavior, but aversive events can also elicit powerful emotions such as fear and anxiety, and these emotions could have a variety of undesirable consequences.

Reduced interest

Suppose, for example, that a teacher publicly criticized a schoolchild for poor performance. For some children, such criticism might act as a spur to greater effort, but for others the consequences might be less benign. If schoolwork were repeatedly associated with failure and punishment, studying might eventually become a source of fear rather than pleasure, so that the child would begin to avoid studying (and school) whenever possible. In one experimental analogue of this situation, Martin (1977) gave 6-year-old boys a series of tasks to perform. On some tasks, the boys were praised when they worked; on others, they were reprimanded when they did not work; on a third set of tasks, they were ignored regardless of their behavior. On the surface, the reprimands seemed to be effective, in that the boys worked the hardest on tasks where they were reprimanded for not working. However, when they were given an opportunity to perform the tasks when the experimenter was not present, Martin found that the children never chose the tasks that had been associated with reprimands.

Impairment of attention

Even in situations where the fear of punishment makes us work harder, this anxiety can lead to poorer performance. In our discussion of the Yerkes–Dodson law, we noted that increases in motivation can result in a narrowing of attention, so that highly motivated subjects actually do worse on complex tasks (for example, Zaffy and Bruning, 1966). If children are punished for doing poorly on a difficult task, therefore, their anxiety could result in even poorer performance.

Indirect evidence that punishment can interfere with attention comes from a study by Cheyne, Goyeche, and Walters (1969). Using a situation similar to that developed by Aronfreed, the researchers asked children to select one of two toys. If the children selected the wrong toy, a buzzer was sounded; the intensity of the

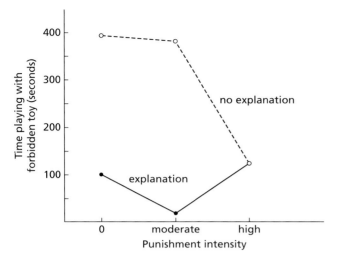

Figure 6.5 The effect of punishment intensity and explanations on a child's obedience to instructions. Intense punishment produced greater obedience than moderate punishment in children not given an explanation, but intense punishment was less effective for children who did receive an explanation. (Based on data from Cheyne, Goyeche, and Walters, 1969.)

buzzer was 0, 88, or 104 decibels (db) for different groups of children. In addition, half the children were then given a verbal explanation of what they had done wrong. To measure the effectiveness of the punishment, the experimenters observed how much time the children spent playing with the forbidden toy during a subsequent temptation test. If no explanation was given, more intense punishment reduced playing time (Figure 6.5). For children who received an explanation, however, the 104-db buzzer produced *less* obedience than the weaker buzzer.

On the surface, this result is bizarre: Why should an intense punishment be less effective than a mild one? This result, however, is exactly what an attentional analysis would predict: The anxiety aroused by the more intense buzzer would interfere with children's attention to the explanation, leading to poorer performance. Supporting evidence for this interpretation comes from comparing the behavior of the children who received an explanation with the behavior of those who did not. Adding an explanation increased obedience for children in the 0- and 88-db groups but had no perceptible effect on children who received the 104-db buzzer. The children in this group, in other words, behaved as if they had not heard what the experimenter was saying.

Learned helplessness

The potentially harmful effects of punishment on performance can be exacerbated if behavior is punished often. Returning to our school example, suppose that when a child is punished for doing poorly on an assignment, the anxiety this produces makes her perform even more poorly the next time. If the teacher then becomes even angrier ("You're not trying!"), the child might become even more anxious, hence becoming even more likely to fail, and so on, in a vicious circle. Eventually, if the child fails often enough, she may conclude that it is not worth even trying, even though she may actually have the ability to do well.

The first evidence that punishment can lead to individuals giving up came from a very influential series of experiments by Seligman, Maier, and Overmier. In the first of these experiments, Seligman and Maier (1967) trained dogs in a rectangular shuttle box with a shoulder-high barrier set in the center. A 10-second warning light was occasionally presented, followed by a 50-second shock delivered through the floor of the cage. If the dog jumped over the barrier while the shock was on, the shock was immediately terminated; if it jumped before the shock was presented, the light was terminated and the scheduled shock was canceled. The dogs could thus either escape the shock or avoid it altogether if they jumped across the barrier when the light came on.

Naïve dogs learned very quickly: after just one or two experiences of shock, the dogs began to jump over the barrier as soon as the shock was presented, and within a few more trials they learned to avoid almost all shocks. A second group, however, behaved very differently. These dogs were given pretraining in which they were confined in a harness and given 64 shocks that they could neither escape nor avoid. When these pretrained subjects were transferred to the avoidance task, their behavior was initially similar to the first group, as they ran about the cage when they received the shock. After about 30 seconds, however, they typically lay down on the floor and remained there, whining quietly, until the shock was terminated. In other words, it looked very much as if they had given up, and most of these subjects showed no signs of learning over successive trials.

There was, moreover, another puzzling feature of the behavior of these dogs. On most trials, as we have seen, they made little or no effort to escape, but occasionally one would jump over the barrier and thereby terminate the shock. In naïve dogs, a single success was usually enough to firmly establish the jumping response, so that the dogs would repeat it on all subsequent trials. But the dogs given inescapable shock during pretraining showed no sign of learning from a successful escape; on the trial following a successful escape, they immediately reverted to the pattern of passive acceptance shown earlier.

To explain these results, Overmier and Seligman (1967) suggested that during pretraining the dogs had learned that they were helpless – no matter how hard they struggled, they could not escape the shock. When they were transferred to the shuttle box, therefore, they made no effort to escape the shock because they had learned that such efforts were futile. And on those occasions when they did escape, they did not repeat the response because such apparent successes during pretraining had always proved to be illusory. If on one pretraining trial a dog had lifted its paw just as the shock was terminated, for example, it would have found repeating this response on subsequent trials had no effect.

This **learned helplessness** hypothesis provoked considerable controversy – would dogs really think in such complex ways? – and subsequent research has suggested that other processes may also be involved. (See Maier, 1989, and LoLordo and Taylor, 2001, for reviews.) At present, however, it does look as if part of what animals learn when they are exposed to inescapable shock is that they are helpless, so that there is no point in even trying to escape.

Carol Dweck and her colleagues have suggested that learned helplessness can also occur in schools. Children who repeatedly fail at math, for example, might conclude that they are helpless and thus stop trying. In an experimental analogue of this phenomenon, Dweck and Repucci (1973) had two teachers give fifth-grade children a series of problems. One of the teachers always gave the children solvable problems, and the other presented only insoluble ones. When the second teacher finally gave the children some solvable problems, they failed to solve them, even though they had solved exactly the same problems earlier for the first teacher. (See also Dweck and Licht, 1980; Peterson, Maier, and Seligman, 1993.)

It is important to emphasize that effects of this kind are not inevitable. Children differ widely in their reactions to anxiety: For some, a particular punishment can be incapacitating; for others, the same punishment can be an incentive to greater effort. The available evidence, however, suggests that the use of punishment can pose special dangers in education, where it can lead to dislike of the subject and even deterioration in learning.

Aggression

Pain-elicited aggression

Another possible consequence of presenting an aversive stimulus is that it can elicit aggression. This effect is known as **pain-elicited aggression**. In a study by Ulrich and Azrin (1962), pairs of rats from the same litter were placed in a test cage and given electric shocks through the floor of the cage. The authors reported that the rats responded to the shocks by rearing up on their hind legs and beginning to push each other. If the shocks were very intense, and continued long enough, the rats would begin to bite each other.

In subsequent experiments, Ulrich and his colleagues reported similar results with virtually every species tested, including species as diverse as cats, raccoons, monkeys, and alligators. In other words, it appears as if the tendency to attack when hurt is one of the most powerful and universal of all animal instincts (though see also Blanchard, Blanchard, and Takahashi, 1977).

For obvious reasons, there has been little direct research on pain-elicited aggression in humans, but some research suggests that we too behave more aggressively when we are hurt. In one experiment by Berkowitz, Cochrane, and Embree (1981), university women were asked to act as teachers and either reinforce or punish a partner who was engaged in a learning task. Some of the "teachers" had one of their hands in a tank of cold water; others had one of their hands in a tank of warm water. Teachers whose hands were in cold water were significantly more likely to be punitive toward their partners than were teachers whose hands were in warm water (see also Berkowitz, 1989).

Modeling

There is evidence that the use of punishment can also serve as a model for aggressive behavior. Children, after all, are highly imitative, particularly when the model is important or influential in their lives (Rosenthal and Bandura, 1978). If a parent frequently uses physical force to control a child, therefore, the child may learn to imitate this behavior. In an early study on imitation by Bandura, Ross, and Ross (1963), nursery school children were exposed to an adult model who punched and kicked a large inflated doll. When the children were later left alone with the doll, they proved significantly more likely to attack the doll than were children in control groups who had not seen the model.

You might think that the measure of aggression used in this study was highly artificial: Does the fact that a child is more likely to attack a doll really tell us anything about the likelihood that the child will punch a friend? A field study by Leyens *et al.* (1975) suggests that the answer might be yes. In their study, adolescents at a Belgian residential center for juvenile delinquents were exposed for two weeks to one of two sets of recreational films; one set emphasized physical violence, including films such as *Bonnie and Clyde* and *The Dirty Dozen*. To determine the effect of these films, the experimenters recorded the frequency of aggressive behavior during morning and evening play periods. (Aggression was defined as "physical contact of sufficient intensity to potentially inflict pain on the victim" and included hitting, slapping, choking, and kicking.) The result was that the adolescents exposed to the violent films became significantly more likely to attack one another, with the frequency of such attacks almost tripling from the first to the second week of the treatment period. Adolescents exposed to the non-violent films, on the other hand, showed a significant decrease in aggression over the same period.

This effect is not confined to juvenile delinquents. In a study by Josephson (1987), boys in a Canadian elementary school were shown either a 14-minute excerpt from a television program involving violence (a police SWAT team ambushing and shooting a gang of killers) or an equally exciting film without violence (a bike race with dramatic stunts). The boys were then given an oppor-tunity to play floor hockey, and the experimenters observed levels of aggression during the game – for example, how often the participants pushed or elbowed their opponents. They found that the boys who had just seen the violent film engaged in almost 50% more acts of aggression. (See also Wood, Wong, and Chachere, 1991; Bushman and Huesmann, 2001.)

Long-term effects

If exposure to a single violent film could have such a substantial effect, it seems at least possible that repeated exposure to violence from a model as influential as a parent might play a major role in determining a child's aggressiveness. In accordance with this prediction, research has shown that children who are severely punished by their parents are far more likely to be physically aggressive toward their peers (Eron *et al.*, 1963), to later become juvenile delinquents (Glueck and Glueck, 1950), and, when adults, to develop emotional problems such as depression, alcoholism, and spousal abuse (Straus and Kantor, 1994). Moreover, more recent evidence suggests that these effects are not confined to severe punishment – even milder forms such as spanking are correlated with increases in aggression. In a representative study by Strassberg *et al.* (1994), parents of 273 young children were interviewed to determine the methods of discipline they used. To separate the effects of spanking from more violent forms of punishment, the authors focused on a subgroup of parents who reported using spanking but not more severe forms such as hitting. The researchers then observed the children of these parents in kindergarten and recorded how often these children behaved aggressively toward other children – for example, hitting or bullying them. They found that children who were spanked were roughly twice as likely to behave aggressively as those who were not.

Similar results have emerged from studies which have looked at the long-term effects of exposure to violence on television or in video games. In one such study, Huesmann *et al.* (2003) measured how much televised violence children watched and then assessed the effects, if any, on their behavior 15 years later. They found that children who had watched substantial amounts of violence on television were much more likely to behave violently when they became adults. For example, children in the high-exposure group were almost twice as likely to push their spouses if they later married (42% vs. 22%), and they were also more likely to have punched another adult and to have a criminal conviction for violence.

A critical problem for such studies is separating causation from correlation. In this case, was it watching programs containing violence that made children more aggressive, or was it simply that children who are aggressive are more likely to watch such programs? To disentangle these possibilities, the authors used a statistical technique called structural modeling. If watching violent programs makes children more aggressive, then how many hours they watched should be a good predictor of their behavior as adults. If, on the other hand, aggressive children are more likely to watch violent programs, and aggressive children then become aggressive adults, then children's level of aggression should be the best predictor of their behavior as adults, with the number of hours watched adding little to our ability to predict their behavior. In fact, the former proved to be the case: by far the best predictor of adults' aggressive behavior was how many hours of violent programs they had watched while children, not how aggressive they were at the time.

The authors concluded that watching violent programs on television really does increase the likelihood of aggression. The effect was particularly strong, moreover, when the children identified with the aggressor, or the aggressor was rewarded for their aggression. If so, watching films such as *Dirty Harry* or *The Terminator* would be particularly likely to encourage aggression.

We have cited only a few studies here, but there is now overwhelming evidence of a correlation between the use of physical punishment in childhood and the development of aggression. We need to be cautious, however, in interpreting this correlation. One problem is that a correlation between punishment and aggression does not necessarily mean that punishment causes aggression. The true relationship could actually be the reverse, with high levels of aggression leading to greater use of punishment. If a child is very aggressive or disobedient, this could gradually push a parent into using stronger punishment, as milder forms prove inadequate. The fact that punishment is correlated with aggression, therefore, doesn't necessarily mean that punishment causes aggression (Muller, 1996; Hipwell *et al.*, 2008).

A further problem is that even if there is a causal relationship between punishment and aggression, this does not mean that all forms of punishment are equally likely to lead to aggression. There is evidence that whether punishment produces harmful side effects depends on many factors, including the intensity of the punishment and the extent to which parents provide explanations for its use (Larzelere, 1986; Strassberg *et al.*, 1994). Another important factor seems to be whether punishment is used in a reliable and consistent way, so that children know what will happen if they break rules. Punishment is much more likely to produce serious side effects when parents behave unpredictably, blowing up one minute over a relatively minor problem and then ignoring much more serious misbehaviors (Patterson, Reid, and Dishion, 1989; see also Turner and Muller, 2004).

The relationship between punishment and aggression is thus not simple, and it would be misleading to conclude that the use of punishment inevitably leads to aggression. On the other hand, the consistency with which researchers have observed a correlation between corporal punishment and aggression, and the

Figure 6.6 The problems of punishment. © The New Yorker Collection 1991 / Jack Ziegler / cartoonbank.com. All rights reserved.

experimental evidence that exposure to violence can lead to aggression – recall the effects of seeing a violent film on children's aggression during a game of hockey – suggest a genuine link between the two. Physical punishment may not always produce aggression, but it does seem to produce a strong impulse in this direction.

Conclusions

The evidence we have reviewed in the preceding sections seems to point to diametrically opposed conclusions. On the one hand, we have seen that punishment, if used properly, can be very effective in suppressing behavior. On the other, we have seen that intense forms of punishment can elicit fear and pain, potentially leading to such undesirable effects as a dislike of school and increased aggression (see Figure 6.6). What, then, should we conclude about the use of punishment?

The first point that needs to be emphasized is that the fact that punishment can cause harmful side effects does not necessarily mean that it will always do so. When electric shock has been used to suppress self-injurious behavior in autistic children, for example, researchers have reported no signs of harm in some cases (Risley, 1968) and reported beneficial side effects in others (Lovaas, Schaeffer, and Simmons, 1965). Whether side effects will occur seems to depend on several factors, including the intensity of the punishment and its social context – as we have seen, parents who are loving and make extensive use of reasoning consistently report punishment to be more effective. Indeed, Baumrind (1991) has observed that the healthiest children – friendly, cooperative, and self-reliant – often come from families where parents use punishment, including spanking, to enforce rules consistently, but these parents also go to great lengths to explain the rules and (especially as the children grow older) to involve their children in setting them.

Baumrind's research suggests that when mild punishment is used in a consistent manner to enforce clear rules, and in the context of a loving and supportive family, it need not have damaging effects. On the other hand, the danger of side effects suggests that it is worth minimizing the frequency and severity of punishment wherever possible.

Alternatives to punishment

We have seen that punishment can be effective, but the danger of side effects suggests that it is worth trying to avoid the use of corporal punishment in situations where this is possible. In this section we will consider several alternatives to corporal punishment for dealing with children's misbehavior.

Reinforcing good behavior

Instead of punishing children when they are bad, a possible alternative is reinforcing them when they are good! In one investigation of this approach, Madsen *et al.* (1970) compared the effectiveness of reinforcement and punishment in getting first-grade children to stay in their seats during lessons. In the first phase, observers in the classroom recorded how often the children got out of their seats at times when they shouldn't during a 6-day period. The teachers were then asked to punish the children for standing by ordering the children to sit down whenever they got up. As you might expect, the immediate effect of this command was that the children sat down, so that from the teacher's point of view the command might have appeared highly effective. When the frequency of inappropriate standing was measured over the course of the entire day, however, the introduction of punishment was found to produce an overall *increase* in standing (see Figure 6.7). The fact that the teacher paid attention to the children when they stood up, in other words, seemed to be reinforcing this behavior.

After repeating the baseline and punishment phases to establish the reliability of this result, Madsen and colleagues asked the teacher to stop punishing standing and instead to reinforce incompatible behavior. Specifically, they asked the teacher to praise the children or smile at them whenever they were sitting down and working. As Figure 6.7 shows, this proved highly effective: For the first time, the frequency of standing fell significantly below its baseline level.

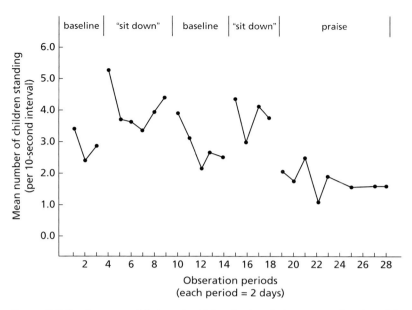

Figure 6.7 The frequency of first-grade children leaving their seats as a function of the teacher's reaction. (Adapted from Madsen *et al.*, 1970.)

The punishment used in this study was a relatively mild reprimand, and a stronger form of punishment might well have been more effective. On the other hand, we have already encountered evidence that even stronger forms of punishment are sometimes not as effective as reinforcement. In Chapter 5 we discussed the Hall, Lund, and Jackson (1968) study of children in an elementary school who had been identified as having the most serious disciplinary problems. Years of scolding and even corporal punishment had proven ineffective in reducing the disruptive behavior of children such as Robbie, but the introduction of praise for good work produced rapid and dramatic transformations.

Further evidence that reinforcement can be more effective than punishment in the classroom comes from a study by Tulley and Chiu (1995). They asked 135 student teachers to recall which disciplinary incidents in the previous month they felt they had handled the most successfully and which the least successfully. Three behaviors proved to be particular problems – disruption, defiance, and inattention. Strong punishment, in the form of yelling or corporal punishment, proved to be the least effective strategy for dealing with these problems, as they were reported to be effective on only 4% of the occasions on which they were used. Milder forms of punishment such as detention and loss of privileges were somewhat more effective, working 53% of the time. Providing an explanation of the desired behavior was more effective still – this approach was effective 78% of the time. By far the most effective strategy, however, turned out to be reinforcement, as praising or rewarding more appropriate behavior was successful on 92% of the occasions where it was used.

The use of reinforcement in this way can require considerable effort and imagination. When children misbehave, and especially when they seem to be deliberately disobeying instructions, a parent's or teacher's first reaction is often anger. It is far easier to yell at children in these situations than to stop and think, "I wonder how I could reinforce good behavior instead." The available evidence, however, suggests that the effort involved might be worthwhile: Reinforcement is not only more enjoyable than punishment, in some situations it is also more effective.

Using minimal force

As attractive as reinforcement might be as an alternative to punishment, there are some situations where reinforcement on its own does not seem to be sufficient. Gerald Patterson, for example, established a project to help parents of children with serious antisocial behavior, a project that eventually involved hundreds of families. At first, they relied on reinforcement, training parents to reinforce positive behaviors such as cooperation and compliance. In a summary of this work, Patterson, Reid, and Dishion (1989) wrote: "This approach simply did not work. Even though the children became slightly more cooperative, they still hit others and had temper tantrums" (p. 2).

To produce lasting changes in this behavior, Patterson and his colleagues found that parents needed to use a combination of consistent reinforcement for appropriate behavior with mild forms of punishments. In this section we will look at three such alternatives to the use of corporal punishment: extinction, time-out, and response cost.

Extinction

Where misbehavior is being maintained by reinforcement, one way of eliminating it is simply to withhold the reinforcer. In one application of this approach reported by C. D. Williams (1959), the subject was a 2-year-old boy who had been seriously ill for the first year and a half of his life. Even after he recovered physically, he continued to demand special attention and to throw tantrums whenever he did not get his way. On going to bed, for example, he insisted that both his parents stay with him until he was asleep, and if either of them left the room – or even tried to read – he would cry bitterly until they returned to the room and resumed giving him attention. Falling asleep typically required from 30 minutes to 2 hours, so his demands became a considerable strain on his parents, and they consulted Williams for advice.

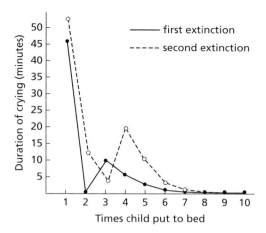

Figure 6.8 Extinction of a child's tantrum behavior. (C. D. Williams, 1959.)

One analysis of the boy's behavior might have been that he had suffered severe psychological trauma as a result of his earlier illness, and now needed all the love and attention he could get. Williams, however, felt that he had simply become used to receiving attention during his illness, and that his tantrum behavior was now being maintained by the attention it produced. To eliminate this behavior, therefore, Williams recommended that the parents simply ignore any crying that took place after they put the child to bed. On the first night, the child screamed and raged for 45 minutes before finally falling asleep (Figure 6.8, solid line). The parents did not go in, however, and on the following night he didn't cry at all. Crying reappeared briefly on a few subsequent nights, but within a week it had disappeared completely.

One week later, the boy's aunt baby-sat for him so his parents could have a night out. When she put him to sleep, he again began to cry, and she went in to him. As shown in Figure 6.8 (broken line), this single reinforcement was enough to trigger another massive burst of crying on the following night, but the parents again refused to go in, and within a week the crying had disappeared again, this time permanently. Simply by ignoring his tantrums, therefore, his parents were able to eliminate this behavior within a matter of days, and follow-up observations 2 years later suggested that he had become a friendly and outgoing child, with no sign of any harmful after effects.

Procedurally, **extinction** is clearly different from punishment, involving the withholding of a reinforcer rather than the presentation of a punisher. Psychologically, however, it is probably more realistic to think of extinction as a relatively mild form of punishment rather than as an alternative. When a response is not reinforced after a long history of reinforcement, this is an aversive event, and it can lead to feelings of frustration and, like punishment, aggression. Herbert and colleagues reported a particularly dramatic example (1973). To reduce deviant behavior, the researchers advised the mothers of six deviant children to ignore them when they misbehaved. When the children discovered that they were no longer receiving attention, however, they became furious: Four of the six children assaulted their mothers, and one kicked out a window of the room in which training was being given!

Thus, although extinction is normally a relatively mild form of punishment, it can produce powerful side effects in some circumstances. (Frustration probably also explains why the boy in the Williams study cried so long the first night that his parents ignored his tantrums.) Also, extinguishing a response can require many trials; in situations where it is important to suppress a behavior immediately – for example, where a child is in danger of injuring himself – then other forms of punishment might be more appropriate.

Time-out

A second, relatively mild form of punishment is **time-out**, a procedure in which children are removed to a less reinforcing environment when they misbehave. A very mild form of time-out is being required to sit at the edge of a group and allowed to watch the others play but not participate (White and Bailey, 1990); more aversive forms include sitting in a chair facing a corner, or having to go to a bare room.

A study by Rortvedt and Miltenberger (1994) provides a nice example of how time-out can be used. The study focused on two 4-year-old girls who frequently refused to comply with their parents' requests. During an initial observational phase carried out in the home, one of the girls, Morgan, failed to follow 87% of her mother's instructions, despite her mother's pleading and scolding. When the time-out phase was initiated, her mother was asked to praise her whenever she complied with a request; if she refused, she was taken to another room and told to sit quietly facing the wall for 1 minute. If she was sitting quietly at the end of the minute, she was allowed to leave the chair, but if not, the time-out period was extended until 10 seconds elapsed without noise. Figure 6.9 shows that this procedure resulted in an immediate improvement in Morgan's behavior, and after only seven sessions she was complying with every single instruction. This improvement was still present when her behavior was observed again 6 weeks later, and the other girl showed similar gains.

Time-out might seem to involve little more than the classic punishment of sending children to their rooms, and indeed this is a form of time-out. The classic version, however, suffers from at least two defects. First, a child's room is usually a fairly reinforcing environment because of the toys it contains, reducing its effectiveness as a form of punishment. Second, children who are sent to their

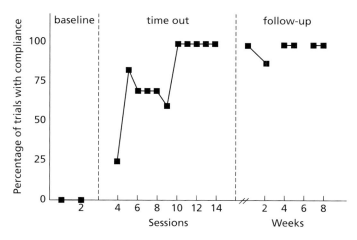

Figure 6.9 The percentage of her mother's instructions that Morgan followed. Compliance is shown for a period before training, during a time-out phase in which noncompliance resulted in having to sit in a chair in the corner, and during observations 6 weeks after the termination of training. (Adapted from Rortvedt and Miltenberger, 1994.)

rooms often have to stay there for extended periods, but research with time-out has shown that even quite brief periods in a chair, sometimes just 1–2 minutes, can be equally effective (Brantner and Doherty, 1983).

Time-out has proved to be effective with a very wide range of problems and children, but difficulties can sometimes arise. One is where a child refuses to cooperate and attempts to leave the chair. A variety of approaches have been tried for dealing with this problem, ranging from gently holding the child in the chair to a quick spank, but it is not yet clear which of these approaches is most effective (Roberts and Powers, 1990; McNeil, Clemens-Mowrer *et al.*, 1994; Reitman and Drabman, 1996). A further limitation is that time-out is inappropriate as a punishment for certain kinds of behavior. Suppose, for example, that a child repeatedly creates a disturbance in class to escape from work that she finds difficult. In this case, using time-out would only make matters worse, as it would allow her to succeed in her aim of escaping from work (Taylor and Miller, 1997). In most of the situations where time-out has been tried, however, it has proven highly effective.

Response cost

Response cost is a form of negative punishment in which a reinforcer is taken away whenever the target response occurs. The reinforcer that is removed is often points or money – a typical example would be a parking fine in which $50 is lost whenever a car is parked illegally.

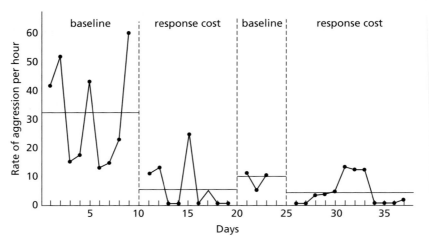

Figure 6.10 The rate of aggressive behavior per hour exhibited by Randy. During baseline periods, aggression was not punished; during response cost phases, aggression resulted in the loss of "smiley faces," which in turn canceled later access to reinforcers such as snacks. (Reynolds and Kelley, 1997.)

Reynolds and Kelley (1997) have reported an imaginative treatment for aggression using response cost. The subjects were four preschool children who displayed high rates of aggression. For example, Randy, the 4-year-old son of two psychology professors, engaged in aggressive acts such as throwing toys or destroying structures built by classmates. During the baseline phase, he was observed to behave aggressively more than 30 times per hour. To reduce this behavior, a blue chart with five yellow smiley faces attached with Velcro was posted in the classroom at the beginning of each day. Each time Randy behaved aggressively, his teacher briefly explained what he had done wrong and removed one of the smiley faces. If he still had at least one smiley face on his chart at the end of the period, then he was allowed to choose an attractive reward such as a special snack or being allowed to be the teacher's helper. (He had helped to select the rewards at the beginning of the study, when the teacher had also explained the procedure that would be followed.) In addition, if he earned a reward on at least 4 days during the week, then at the end of the week he was allowed to choose a small toy.

The effect on Randy's behavior can be seen in Figure 6.10. When the response cost procedure was initiated, his average rate of aggression fell from 31 incidents an hour to only 6. When the baseline condition was reinstated, his level of aggression rose somewhat, but quickly fell when response cost was reinstated. Similar results were obtained for the other participants, and when interviewed all said that they had enjoyed it. (Randy expressed disappointment when the treatment ended.) The teachers reported that they had found the treatment easy to use, and all four sets of parents asked the experimenter to help them set up similar programs in their homes. A further positive feature, relative to time-out, was that the children did not have to be removed from the class, so their education was not interrupted. Combining punishment with enhanced levels of reinforcement was clearly very effective.

Summarizing our discussion, there are strong grounds for avoiding severe forms of punishment wherever possible, and milder forms can still be very effective. Where milder forms don't work, however, developmental psychologists disagree about whether it is appropriate to use corporal punishment. Punishments such as spanking can increase short-term compliance, but it is not clear whether these short-term benefits outweigh long-term costs such as increased aggression and selfishness (Gershoff, 2002). If you would like to find out more about this issue, you can find articulate statements of the cases for and against corporal punishment in papers by Larzelere and Kuhn (2005), and Gershoff and Bitensky (2007).

Summary

- When punishment is immediate, firm, and accompanied by a clear (and fair) explanation, and when it occurs in a variety of settings, it can be very effective in eliminating undesirable behavior. However, punishment can also produce harmful side effects.
- One potential side effect is the conditioning of fear and anxiety. Anxiety narrows attention, so punishment for poor school work can lead to even poorer performance, until eventually the child stops trying, a phenomenon known as learned helplessness.
- Another possible side effect is aggression. Painful experiences elicit aggression, and an adult's use of punishment can also serve as a model for using force to get what you want.
- The principle of minimum force suggests using the mildest form of punishment likely to be effective. Possible alternatives to corporal punishment include extinction, time-out, and response cost.
- In some situations reinforcing good behavior is more effective than punishing bad behavior.

Review questions

1 Define *secondary punishment* and *pain-elicited aggression*.
2 Why is caution necessary in interpreting the results of observational studies?

3 What are the advantages and disadvantages of studying the effects of punishment in animals? In humans?

4 What determines whether punishment will be effective?

5 Why do explanations enhance the effectiveness of punishment?

6 What are the possible harmful effects of punishment? What conditions make these harmful effects more likely?

7 What are the advantages and disadvantages to reinforcement as an alternative to punishment?

8 What other alternatives are there to the use of punishment? What is the evidence on their effectiveness?

7 Theories of reinforcement

CONTENTS

From the very beginning of the study of reinforcement, there has been conflict between two fundamentally different interpretations. The first, exemplified
by Thorndike, is that reinforcement is essentially a very simple process. When
Thorndike placed his cats in the puzzle box for the first time, they struggled frantically to escape and reach the food dish outside. Eventually, after 8–10 minutes
of scrambling about, a cat might accidentally contact the release mechanism and
escape. If the cat formed a rational appreciation of the situation, he argued, it
should repeat this response immediately on subsequent trials:

If there were in these animals any power of inference, however rudimentary, however
sporadic, however dim, there should have appeared among the multitude some cases when
an animal, seeing through the situation, knows the proper act, does it, and from then on
does it immediately upon being confronted with the situation. There ought, that is, to be a
sudden vertical descent in the time-curve.

(Thorndike, 1911, p. 73)

In all the scores of animals Thorndike tested, not once did he observe sudden and
enduring improvement of this kind. In most instances, improvement over trials
was a slow, gradual affair. (See Figure 4.2 for some representative records.)

To Thorndike, this gradual improvement in performance, with its occasional reversals and failures, did not at all resemble the behavior of a rational animal fully aware of the relationship between the latch and the door:

> The gradual slope of the time-curve...shows the absence of reasoning. They represent the wearing smooth of a path in the brain, not the decisions of a rational consciousness.
>
> (Thorndike, 1911, p. 74)

Reinforcement, he concluded, caused the formation of an association between the rewarded response and the stimuli that were present at the time, so that thereafter these stimuli would elicit the response automatically.

European psychologists such as Wolfgang Kohler proposed a very different view. The apparent stupidity of animals in the puzzle box, Kohler argued, reflected not so much their lack of intelligence as Thorndike's! The problem, according to Kohler, was that the construction of the box meant that the causal relationship between behavior and outcome was concealed. The physical relationship between the release mechanism and the door was not visible in most cases, and thus the animals could not perceive why pressing a latch *here* should have any effect on a door *there*. If the relationship had been visible, Kohler suggested, animals would have behaved far more intelligently.

In one test of this prediction, Kohler (1927) provided a chimpanzee with a stick in her cage and then placed a bunch of bananas outside the cage just beyond her reach:

> She grasps at it, vainly of course, and then begins the characteristic complaint of the chimpanzee: she thrusts both lips – especially the lower – forward, for a couple of inches, gazes imploringly at the observer, utters whimpering sounds, and finally flings herself on the ground on her back – a gesture most eloquent of despair...Thus, between lamentations and entreaties, some time passes, until – about seven minutes after the fruit has been exhibited to her – she suddenly casts a look at the stick, ceases her moaning, seizes the stick, stretches it out of the cage, and succeeds, though somewhat clumsily, in drawing the bananas within arm's length...The test is repeated after an hour's interval; on this second occasion, the animal has recourse to the stick much sooner, and uses it with more skill; and, at a third repetition, the stick is used immediately, as on all subsequent occasions.
>
> (Kohler, 1927, pp. 32–33)

This abrupt change in behavior, Kohler concluded, revealed a sudden *insight* into the nature of the problem, rather than the gradual strengthening of an association.

So, two similar situations in which animals were faced with food tantalizingly out of reach, but with dramatically different outcomes. The situation was summarized with some amusement by the eminent British philosopher Bertrand Russell:

> animals that have been carefully observed have all displayed the national characteristics of the observer. Animals studied by Americans rush about frantically, with an incredible

display of hustle and pep, and at last achieve the desired result by chance. Animals observed by Germans sit still and think, and at last evolve the solution out of their inner consciousness.

(Russell, 1927, pp. 32–33)

Which view is right? Is reinforcement a simple process involving the formation of associations, or a more sophisticated process involving rational calculation and planning? In this chapter we will look at several controversial issues concerning how reinforcement works; we'll see that the issue of simplicity versus complexity is one that surfaces again and again.

Association or expectation?

We will begin by considering precisely what is learned when a response is reinforced. We will start with Thorndike's account and then trace how psychologists' views have evolved since then.

The emergence of two theories

S–R theory

When a cat escaped from the puzzle box and ate the food, Thorndike believed that the resulting pleasure stamped in an association between the impulse to make the response and the sense impressions that accompanied it. This associative account differed markedly from the mentalistic interpretations of animal behavior that preceded it, but in one respect it was still not sufficiently radical for early behaviorists such as John B. Watson (1913). The problem, for Watson, was that Thorndike still assumed that associations were formed between *sensations* and *impulses* – mental events inside the animal's head. The stamping in of an association, moreover, was attributed to the feelings of *pleasure* that followed it. But how could anyone know what sensations or emotions were going on inside an animal's head? And what value is there in explaining an animal's behavior in terms of its mental states if there is no way of determining the accuracy of these explanations?

The essence of the scientific method – the quality that distinguishes it from other intellectual pursuits such as literary criticism or philosophy – is that scientific debates are settled by evidence. If a physicist makes what on the surface seems a totally absurd claim – for example, that no object can move faster than the speed of light, and that no matter how much energy is invested, this maximum speed cannot be exceeded by even 1 millimeter per second – then this claim is evaluated solely by how it fits with evidence, rather than whether it sounds plausible. This emphasis on evidence rather than on opinion allows science to progress, rather than becoming bogged down in unresolvable differences of opinion. Watson argued that mental explanations do not allow this evidence-based approach, because we cannot know what an animal is thinking or feeling.

Injunctions to avoid all references to the mind were hard enough to accept with animal behavior, but Watson went further and argued that the same prohibition should apply to explanations of human behavior. The problem is fundamentally the same: We can observe other people's behavior – we see them smiling, for example – but we cannot directly observe their emotions, and the inferences we make about these emotions might be very wrong. (As Shakespeare's Hamlet warned, "one may smile, and smile, and be a villain.") Any explanation that attributes people's behavior to their thoughts or feelings, therefore, is untestable because we cannot be sure what these feelings are.

Watson therefore argued that behavior should be explained in terms of *visible* events, because only explanations stated in these terms could be objectively tested. Applying this analysis to reinforcement, Watson agreed with Thorndike's emphasis on associations but rejected the assumption that these associations were formed between mental events. Where Thorndike spoke of a sense impression or sensation, Watson and other behaviorists substituted the visible object in the environment that gave rise to it – the *stimulus*. And when Thorndike spoke of mental impulses to respond, behaviorists substituted the muscular movements that resulted from these impulses – the *response*. Reinforcement, in their view, strengthens an association between an environmental stimulus and a response, and for this reason this view became known as **stimulus–response** or **S–R theory**.

A cognitive rejoinder

Early cognitive psychologists vehemently disagreed with this behaviorist analysis. Even if mental states were sometimes difficult to observe, they play a crucial role in determining our behavior, and it would thus be folly to ignore them. A vivid statement of this view came from William McDougall, a social psychologist and contemporary of Watson's. In the course of an entertaining and sometimes caustic debate with Watson, staged in 1929, McDougall asked his listeners to imagine the following scene:

I come into the hall and see a man on the platform scraping the guts of a cat with hairs from the tail of a horse; and, sitting silently in attitudes of rapt attention, are a thousand persons who presently break out into wild applause. How will the Behaviorist explain these strange incidents: How explain the fact that vibrations emitted by the cat-gut stimulate all the thousand into absolute silence and quiescence; and the further fact that the cessation of the stimulus seems to be a stimulus to the most frantic activity? Common sense and psychology agree in accepting the explanation that the audience heard the music with keen pleasure and vented their gratitude and admiration for the artist in shouts and hand clappings. But the Behaviorist knows nothing of pleasure and pain, of admiration and gratitude. He has relegated all such "metaphysical entities" to the dust heap, and must seek some other explanation. Let us leave him seeking it. The search will keep him harmlessly occupied for some centuries to come.

(Watson and McDougall, 1929, pp. 68–69)

One of the most influential of the early cognitive theorists was Edward C. Tolman, and his explanation of how animals learn differed markedly from that of S–R theorists. Tolman argued that learning was a far more complex, thoughtful process than simply forming associations. He said that animals did not blunder about responding blindly to the stimuli they happened to encounter; instead, they actively sought to understand the world around them and responded to this world purposefully, choosing the course of action best suited to achieving their goals. In the case of Thorndike's cats, Tolman would have said that the cats formed an **expectation** that pressing the latch would open the door, and that they pressed the latch with the deliberate intention of obtaining food.

Convergence: intervening variables

At this point the positions of the two sides were about as far apart as they could be, with behaviorists arguing that it was not possible to discuss mental events and cognitive psychologists arguing that it was not possible to ignore them. Over time, however, the positions of the two sides moved much closer. Tolman played a particularly influential role in this convergence. Although his work emphasized the role of mental or cognitive processes in behavior, he was also, perhaps surprisingly, a behaviorist. He was familiar with introspectionists' efforts to study the mind through introspective reports (see Chapter 1), and, like Watson, believed that these efforts had failed. Too much of the mind's workings was unconscious, and even when introspectionists were able to report on their experiences, their reports were often contradictory. The fact that we cannot observe other people's mental states directly, however, does not mean that we cannot have *theories* about what these processes might be.

To understand Tolman's approach, it may help to begin by considering the role of theories in other sciences. Consider Newton's theory of gravity. No one has ever seen gravity, but this did not prevent Newton from putting forward a theory about the properties of this invisible force. His theory specified the precise effects gravity would have on visible objects such as apples and planets, and it was the fact that these predictions could be tested, and when tested proved correct, that led to the theory's rapid acceptance. The fact that something cannot be seen, in other words, is not a barrier to creating a theory about it, *provided* that the theory leads to testable predictions.

This requirement of testability is crucial. The characteristic of science that distinguishes it from other approaches is that explanations are judged by evidence. In religion, for example, one person may believe passionately in religion A and another in religion B, and there is no way to prove which is right. In science, by contrast, theories are judged by the accuracy of their predictions. If theory A predicts behavior more successfully than theory B, then we must prefer theory A – at least until some more accurate account comes along.

One implication of this approach worth emphasizing, because it is so counterintuitive, is that it does not really matter whether a theory is plausible – all that matters is its success in accounting for known phenomena and predicting new ones. In physics, for example, some current theories are so counterintuitive as to verge on the bizarre. Einstein's theory of relativity posits that space is curved, even if that space is totally empty, and one of the key assumptions of quantum physics is that a particle can be in two places at the same time. These theories may not make sense, but they have proved extraordinarily successful in predicting characteristics of the universe, and for this reason are now widely accepted.

Applying this logic to psychology, Tolman proposed that psychologists should also be able to create theories about mental events that they could not see, provided that their theories led to testable predictions. He used the term **intervening variable** to describe any internal event X that intervened between the presentation of a stimulus and the eventual occurrence of a response:

$$S \rightarrow [X] \rightarrow R$$

It was acceptable to theorize about the existence of such intervening variables, he said, provided that the theory was stated clearly enough to predict whether the presentation of stimulus S will trigger X, and whether the occurrence of X will in turn lead to response R. Provided that these relationships are stated clearly, we can then evaluate the theory by seeing if the stimulus really does lead to the predicted response.

Behaviorists initially opposed the discussion of mental events, but evidence for phenomena such as *latent learning* and *learning without responding* (for reviews, see Goldstein, Krantz, and Rains, 1965; Lieberman, 2004) convinced S–R theorists that they too would need to posit the existence of internal processes if they were to explain behavior[1] (e.g., Hull, 1943).

---

[1] One notable exception was B. F. Skinner, who believed that behavior should always be explained in terms of the environmental and genetic factors that give rise to it, rather than through mental states (e.g., Skinner, 1950). Skinner did not deny the existence of mental states; he simply believed that any practical science of behavior would ultimately have to focus on the environmental variables that shape behavior, and that theorizing about mental states would distract psychologists from this focus. A full discussion of Skinner's views would take us too far afield, but we should note that many psychologists still accept his view, and that his emphasis on the practical

Both sides thus came to share the view that any successful account of reinforcement would need to consider what was going on inside the brain when a reinforcer was presented. They still differed sharply, however, in their views of what these internal processes were.

For S–R theorists, learning was still an essentially simple process involving the formation of associations, even if some of these associations might not be observable. For Tolman, learning involved much more sophisticated processes such as expectations. In the case of the puzzle box, for example, S–R theorists believed that food would stamp in an association between the response of pressing the latch and the box stimuli that were present, so that the box would thereafter elicit the correct response automatically:

$$S_{box} \rightarrow R_{press}$$

Tolman, on the other hand, believed that the cats learned that the door would open when they pressed the latch, and so pressed the latch in order to obtain the food. Thus where S–R theorists saw animals pressing the latch blindly, without knowledge of the consequences, Tolman believed that the cats pressed because they knew that doing so would open the door and provide access to food. So, which view was right?

Testing the two theories

To find out, both sides devised experiments to test their theories.

We cannot trace all the experiments that followed – there were literally hundreds – but we will focus on two to give a flavor of the how the dialogue evolved.

Where's my banana?

Tolman, as we have seen, believed that animals form expectations. But if we cannot see inside an animal's head, how do we know whether it has an expectation? The key to answering this question is to understand that Tolman was no longer using the term expectation in its conventional sense, as a conscious state. For Tolman an expectation was now a *theoretical* entity, something whose existence was hypothesized in order to explain visible behavior. Tolman was using the term in exactly the same way that a physicist might use the term *atom* or *quark*. No physicist has ever seen an atom, but they hypothesize the existence of atoms

---

determinants of behavior has been exceptionally productive – many of the applications discussed in Chapter 5 stemmed in whole or in part from Skinner's work. Most psychologists, though, now believe that theories about mental states can enrich our understanding of behavior rather than act as an impediment. (For one presentation of this view, see Lieberman, 1979.)

in order to explain the properties of the visible world. Similarly, Tolman was postulating the existence of expectations in order to help him explain behavior.

But how do we know if his theory was right? How do we know if a cat or other animal expects something to happen? Tolman proposed several behavioral measures. One was **disruption**. The idea here is that if an animal has an expectation and it is not met, this will lead the animal to behave differently; there will be some form of disruption or disturbance of its normal behavior.

We can illustrate this concept with an experiment by a psychologist with one of the most splendidly euphonious names in the history of psychology, O. L. Tinklepaugh. Tinklepaugh (1928) trained monkeys to reach under one of two cups to retrieve a reward that they had seen the experimenter place there earlier. On some trials, the reward was a banana; on others, a piece of lettuce – a food that monkeys consider less desirable but will normally eat readily. On test trials, after baiting the cup with a banana, Tinklepaugh would reach under the cup while the monkey wasn't looking and replace the banana with lettuce. Tinklepaugh reports the monkey's typical reaction when he told it to "come get the food":

She jumps down from the chair, rushes to the proper container and picks it up. She extends her hand to seize the food. But her hand drops to the floor without touching it. She looks at the lettuce but (unless very hungry) does not touch it. She looks around the cup and behind the board. She stands up and looks under and around her. She picks the cup up and examines it thoroughly inside and out. She has on occasion turned toward observers present in the room and shrieked at them in apparent anger. After several seconds spent searching, she gives a glance towards the other cup, which she has been taught not to look into, and then walks off to a nearby window. The lettuce is left untouched on the floor.

(Tinklepaugh, 1928, p. 224)

Observations of this kind might not prove that the monkey expected a banana, but it is difficult to think of any other explanation. (For equally compelling evidence of expectations in rats, see Colwill and Rescorla, 1985.)

Masochistic rats

At this point you might be convinced that animals form expectations, but S–R theorists were also able to marshal evidence in support of their view. In one particularly striking study, Fowler and Miller (1963) trained two groups of rats to run down a straight alley to a goal box containing food. One group received just the food, but the second group also received a brief electric shock. According to a cognitive analysis we should expect the shocked rats to run more slowly – if you expect to receive a painful shock when you reach your goal, your enthusiasm for being there is likely to be diminished. The result, however, was that the shocked rats actually ran faster. Moreover, rats that received a 75-volt shock to their hind paws ran faster than those that received only 60 volts: The stronger the shock, the greater the rats' apparent eagerness to obtain it.

From a cognitive perspective, this result is bizarre – if the rats knew that they were going to receive a shock in the goal box, surely they should have run more slowly? – but it was precisely the outcome that an S–R analysis had predicted. The first point to note is that when rats are shocked on their hindpaws, they react by jumping forward. As this is an unconditioned response, it should be conditioned to whatever cues are present. As training continues, therefore, the cues of the goal box should begin to elicit a tendency to jump forward. And, since the rest of the maze is similar in appearance to the goal box – painted the same color, and so on – this tendency to jump forward should generalize to the rest of the maze. Every part of the maze would thus begin to elicit a tendency to jump forward, the net result being an increase in the speed of running.

An alternative explanation may have occurred to you – perhaps the rats did realize that the shock awaited them in the goal but actually enjoyed being shocked, or perhaps they just wanted to get it over with as quickly as possible. To find out, Fowler and Miller ran a third group, one in which the rats were again shocked in the goal box, but this time the shocks were delivered to their forepaws rather than their hind paws. Just as shocks to the hind paws elicit a tendency to jump forward, shocks to the forepaws elicit a tendency to recoil, or move backwards. According to a conditioning analysis, therefore, the cues of the maze should now elicit a tendency to move backward rather than forward, leading the rats in this group to run more slowly. If, on the other hand, the rats enjoyed shock, the rats in this group should run down the alley just as enthusiastically as those in the hind paw group.

As shown in Figure 7.1, it was the S–R prediction that proved correct: While the rats in the hind paw group ran faster than the control group, those in the forepaw group ran slower. Rats, in other words, do *not* enjoy being shocked; shock increased running only when it was delivered to the hind paws.

Overall, these findings do not support a cognitive analysis. If the rats had expected to be shocked, both of the shocked groups should have run more slowly, but instead the effect depended on where on the body the shocks were administered. Just as Thorndike's cats had shown no sign of thought in their frantic efforts to escape the puzzle box, so the rats in this study seemed to be controlled solely by the stimuli immediately in front of them, without apparent awareness of the consequences that would follow.

The two-system hypothesis

In reviewing the conflict between S–R and cognitive theories, we have now seen persuasive evidence for both views. S–R theorists could point to the enthusiasm

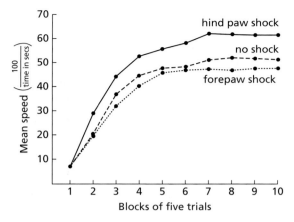

Figure 7.1 Mean speeds of rats running down an alley to a goal box containing food. When the rats reached the goal box, they received either a shock to the forepaws, a shock to the hind paws, or no shock, depending on the group to which they belonged. (Adapted from Fowler and Miller, 1963.)

with which rats ran to a box where they would be shocked, a behavior that hardly seemed to reflect a keen appreciation of consequences. On the other hand, the fury of Tinklepaugh's monkeys when they failed to find a banana provided equally compelling support for the claim that animals have expectations. We could continue to cite evidence supporting each side, but the fundamental dilemma would remain the same: By the mid 1960s both sides could point to considerable evidence supporting their views, making it very difficult to decide which was right. Why? Why after decades of effort and hundreds of experiments was it still so difficult to say which theory was correct?

The ambiguity problem

One reason is that the theories were too vague. We have seen that both sides had agreed that theories could incorporate unobservable processes, *provided* that the resulting theories led to clear, testable predictions. Neither theory, however, was able to meet this criterion. Consider first Tolman's account. He accepted that expectations could not be observed directly but argued that the presence of an expectation could nevertheless be inferred from what happened if the expectation was not met. If Tinklepaugh's monkeys were expecting a banana, then their behavior would be disrupted when they found lettuce instead. But *what* disruption? Would the monkeys hurl the lettuce leaf to the floor and shriek, as some in fact did, would they search for the missing banana with quiet dignity, or, perhaps, just gaze mournfully at the experimenter while silently contemplating the untrustworthiness of humans? Tolman's theory gives us no clue. No matter what the outcome, it would not have shaken Tolman's belief in the existence of expectations. But if a theory can explain any possible outcome, then there is no way to disprove it; it has become untestable.

Similar problems existed for S–R theory. In order to predict behavior, S–R theorists largely relied on well-established principles of learning such as conditioning and reinforcement, but what if these principles predict different outcomes? In Fowler and Miller's experiment, for example, we have seen that S–R theory predicted that shock to the hind paws would increase the speed of running, because the shock would elicit a tendency to jump forward. However, S–R theory also assumes that a response that is followed by an aversive event will be punished. If the rat ran faster, that would have been consistent with S–R theory because of classical conditioning, but if they ran slower that would also have been consistent because of punishment! Again, no matter what the outcome, S–R theory would have emerged unscathed. And that is one powerful reason why the dispute between S–R and cognitive theory proved so difficult to resolve – the vagueness of the two theories meant that each could explain almost any result that was obtained.

Two systems?

One reason for the difficulty in testing the two theories, then, was their vagueness. There is, however, another explanation that, if correct, would readily account for the difficulty in establishing which was correct: Perhaps they both were. Until now we have implicitly assumed that there is only one learning system, the only issue being whether this system is associative or cognitive. There is, however, no logical reason why there couldn't be two systems. Perhaps, as we suggested in our analysis of classical conditioning, a relatively primitive system evolved first in which stimuli were simply associated with responses, eliciting them automatically. With the development of the neocortex, a more sophisticated system might have emerged that allowed animals to anticipate the consequences of these responses. Each system could have important advantages, with the associative system allowing rapid and automatic responses in simple or dangerous situations, and the cognitive system allowing more sophisticated planning in situations where there is time to consider the consequences of alternative courses of action, and to integrate information from different sources. In planning how much to study tonight, for example, you could take into account a forthcoming exam, your work in other subjects, a birthday party of a friend, and so on.

Over time, the view that reinforcement can give rise to expectations as well as habits attracted increasing support, to the point where it is now widely accepted. (See, for example, Bolles, 1972; Mackintosh and Dickinson, 1979; Rescorla, 1987; Öhman and Mineka, 2001; Hall, 2002; Schwartz, Wasserman, and Robbins, 2002; Mazur, 2006; Bouton, 2007; Pearce, 2008.) After decades of theoretical warfare, it was as if a truce had been declared, with both sides agreeing that the other had a good case after all, and everyone getting together for drinks and a barbeque.

This consensus is genuinely gratifying, suggesting that years of theoretical conflict were not in vain. Some differences, however, still remain. Not all learning theorists would agree with the particular version presented here, which attributes the formation of associations and expectations to fundamentally different underlying systems; it is also possible to view them as different outputs of a single system. Also, while there is now impressive agreement on fundamental concepts, shadings of the earlier split still exist, and this is reflected in continuing differences in terminology. For example, Rescorla (1987), who describes himself as an "unreconstructed associationist," still prefers to use the language of associations in describing learning: Instead of talking of *expectations*, he uses the term *response–reinforcer* or *response–outcome* (R–O) association. In some respects, the distinction is purely linguistic because what Rescorla means by a response–outcome association seems almost identical to what Tolman meant by an expectation: a link between a response and an outcome that allows subjects to anticipate what will occur. A case can be made, however, that the choice of terms to describe this unit, whether associative or cognitive, has potentially important implications.

The advantage of the term *association* is that its meaning is more clearly defined: Two events are associated when one elicits or activates the other. Thus, the term avoids some of the excess (and ambiguous) theoretical baggage that the term *expectation* brings with it from its use in everyday discourse. On the other hand, for precisely this reason the term *expectation* might be preferable because its richer (albeit ambiguous) meanings allow it to explain behavior that a strictly associative account has considerable difficulty with. The searching behavior of Tinklepaugh's monkeys is much easier to understand if we assume that they had learned to expect a banana under the cup, rather than simply forming a response–banana association.

Some differences, then, remain, but compared to the yawning gap that separated learning theorists in the past, the current differences are blissfully small. Whatever we call them, there is now considerable agreement that reinforcement can result in something approximating expectations as well as simpler associations. After decades of experimentation and struggle, associative and cognitive theorists have converged on remarkably similar accounts of what is learned.

Is reinforcement automatic?

A second major area of controversy has been whether rewards can strengthen people's behavior automatically, without their awareness. As with so many other issues concerning reinforcement, this question was first raised by Thorndike. In his research on cats, he found that learning was surprisingly slow: His cats might escape very quickly on one trial, only for this apparent evidence of insight to be followed by much longer latencies on the next trial. To explain the slow and uneven nature of their improvement, he proposed that reinforcement stamps in associations automatically, without conscious thought or deliberation:

[A reward] does not pick out the "right" or "essential" or "useful" connection by any mystical or logical potency. It is, on the contrary, as natural in its action as a falling stone…It will strengthen connections which are wrong, irrelevant or useless, provided that they are close enough to the satisfier.

(Thorndike, 1935, p. 39)

Superstition

Skinner's pigeons

Thorndike's claim that a reinforcer acts automatically suggests that a reinforcer should strengthen whatever response happens to precede it, even if this response played no role in producing it. Striking support for this view came from an experiment by B. F. Skinner (1948b). Skinner placed pigeons in a box and gave them grain to eat once every 15 seconds. The birds did not have to perform any response to obtain the grain; it was presented every 15 seconds regardless of their behavior. Most of the birds nevertheless developed highly stereotyped behaviors, which they repeated over and over during the interval between reinforcements. One repeatedly turned around in circles, another brushed its head along the floor, a third tossed its head as if lifting an invisible bar, and so on.

The explanation for these strange behaviors, Skinner suggested, lay in the automatic nature of reinforcement. When the food was first presented, it would have strengthened whatever behavior the bird happened to be engaged in at the time. As a result, the bird would have been more likely to repeat this response, and if one of these repetitions happened to coincide with the next presentation of food, it would have been strengthened further, and so on. This process, in which the accidental conjunction of a response and a reinforcer results in strengthening of the response, is called *adventitious reinforcement*. Not all of the repeated responses would have been immediately followed by reinforcement, of course, and on some occasions food might have followed another response and strengthened it instead. In the end, however, Skinner found that six of his eight birds acquired highly stereotyped responses, even though these behaviors played no role in producing food.

Skinner called these response patterns **superstitions**, and speculated that adventitious reinforcement might also be responsible for superstitious behavior in humans. A tribe sacrifices a goat and it rains; a bowler twists his body as his ball rolls down the alley and gets a strike; a basketball coach wears his lucky tie and his team wins. In each case, a response is closely followed by a desired outcome, and the result is that we mistakenly interpret the response as the cause. Once a response like this gets established, moreover, partial reinforcement can maintain it indefinitely. Your team may not always win when you wear your lucky tie, but if you are always wearing it when you win, then the impression that the tie was responsible can seem overwhelming. (For research on superstitions in humans, see Ono, 1987; Wagner and Morris, 1987; Matute, 1995.)

Thomas's rats

In Skinner's experiment, responses were strengthened even though they did not produce food. In an even more remarkable study by Thomas (1981), responses were strengthened even though they *reduced* the probability of food. In this study rats were placed in a Skinner box and given a pellet of food every 20 seconds. As in Skinner's study, the food was free, but there was also a bar in the cage, and if the rat pressed the bar during a 20-second interval it would immediately receive the food that had been scheduled for the end of that interval. However, this response also cancelled the pellet scheduled to occur at the end of the *following* 20-second interval. Suppose, for example, that a rat pressed the bar 5 seconds after being placed in the box. It would immediately receive the pellet that had been scheduled for 20 seconds, but it would lose the pellet that had been scheduled for 40 seconds. And if it responded again at 50 seconds – half way through the interval after that – it would receive the pellet that had been scheduled for 60 seconds but lose the one scheduled for 80 seconds. If a rat responded frequently, in other words, it would receive only half as much food, one pellet every 40 seconds instead of one every 20 seconds. Despite this, Thomas's rats not only learned to press the lever but did so at very high rates, and this behavior continued session after session. Figure 7.2 shows the rate of responding and the number of reinforcements earned for one of these rats. Once it began to respond, the rate rapidly increased to roughly one response per second, even though this meant that it earned only half as many reinforcements.

This behavior may seem remarkably short-sighted, something only animals would do, but similar results have been reported in comparable experiments with humans (Wasserman and Neunaber, 1986). When two events occur in rapid succession, we have a very strong tendency to see the first as causing the second. (See also Michotte, 1963.) Or, put another way, we are very sensitive to events that follow a response immediately; we seem much less sensitive to long-term consequences.

In the real world this sensitivity to short-term consequences is often beneficial, because it helps us to detect causal relationships. When one event causes another they do usually occur in quick succession – when we strike a match, it

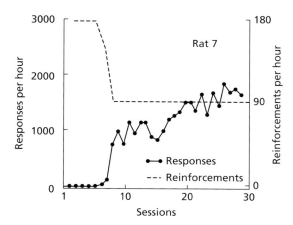

Figure 7.2 Superstition in rats. The graph shows the number of responses made by one rat over successive sessions (solid line), and also the number of reinforcers it earned (dashed line). The rat's rate of responding increased substantially over successive sessions, even though this had the effect of halving the number of reinforcers it received. (Adapted from Thomas, 1981.)

immediately bursts into flame. On some occasions, though, our insensitivity to long-term consequences can lead us to perceive causal relationships where none exists – we will return to this issue shortly.

Reinforcement without awareness

The existence of superstitions is consistent with Thorndike's view that reinforcers will strengthen whatever behaviors happen to precede them. In itself, however, this does not prove that reinforcement is automatic. When a coach wears a lucky tie on game days, this does not necessarily mean that he is unaware of either his behavior or the victories that follow, it is just that he has misinterpreted their relationship. In claiming that a reinforcer acts automatically, what we really have in mind is whether it can affect a person without their realizing it. So, could this happen? Could a reward change your behavior without your knowing?

Thumb twitches

To answer this question, Hefferline, Keenan, and Harford (1959) ran an experiment in which participants were told that the purpose was to study the effects of stress on body tension. They were told that they would be exposed to randomly alternating periods of harsh noise and soothing music, and the effect of the noise would be measured through electrodes attached to their bodies. Except that, unknown to them, the duration of the noise was not random: It was terminated whenever they contracted a very small muscle within their left thumbs, a contraction so small that it could not be observed visually and could be detected only by an electrode mounted above the muscle. As the session progressed, there was a dramatic increase in the frequency of this muscle's contraction. When interviewed afterward, however, all the subjects "still believed that they had been passive victims with respect to the onset and duration of the noise, and all seemed astounded to learn that they themselves had been in control" (p. 1339).

The double agent

Further evidence for reinforcement without awareness was reported in an ingenious experiment by Rosenfeld and Baer (1969). Participants were told that the study was about social attitudes and they were asked questions about topics such as the Vietnam war. The interviewer – a graduate student recruited by the authors to carry out the study – was told to observe the participants to see if they engaged in any distinctive mannerisms and then to try to reinforce one of these behaviors by nodding his head whenever the behavior occurred.

The first subject occasionally rubbed his chin as he talked, so the interviewer, in consultation with the authors, decided to reinforce this behavior. Thereafter, whenever the subject rubbed his chin, the interviewer would nod his head. What the interviewer didn't know, however, was that the "subject" was actually a confederate of the experimenter: He pretended to be naive, but he had been instructed in advance to rub his chin whenever the interviewer said "yeah." In other words, while the interviewer was trying to reinforce the "subject" for rubbing his chin, the "subject" was using his chin rubbing to reinforce the interviewer!

Figure 7.3 shows the results. During the baseline phase, the interviewer used the word "yeah" only occasionally. When the "subject" rubbed his chin following each "yeah," this behavior increased almost immediately; when reinforcement was discontinued (baseline 2), it stopped. This result was replicated in subsequent sessions: Whenever "yeah" was followed by chin rubbing, its frequency increased; whenever reinforcement was discontinued, its frequency decreased. Chin-rubbing was clearly reinforcing the interviewer's verbal behavior, but he seemed unaware of it. When he was eventually told how his behavior had been manipulated, his reaction was one of stunned incredulity. (The procedure, incidentally, is neatly summarized in the title of Rosenfeld and Baer's 1969 report: "Unnoticed verbal conditioning of an aware experimenter by a more aware subject: the double-agent effect.")

Implicit learning

Evidence for learning without awareness has also been found in other kinds of learning. One of the tasks commonly employed in this research has involved

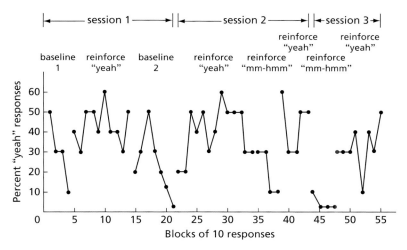

Figure 7.3 The effect of a desired outcome (the interviewee's rubbing his chin) on the interviewer's saying "yeah." During different phases of the experiment, the interviewee rubbed his chin at random (baselines), after the interviewer said "yeah," or after he said "mm-hmm." (Rosenfeld and Baer, 1969.)

something called *serial reaction time*. We can illustrate it with an experiment by Nissen and Bullemer (1987). They asked participants to press a key as soon as an asterisk appeared on a computer screen in front of them. The symbol could appear at any of four locations on the screen, and there was a key located beneath each of the four positions. When the asterisk appeared, participants were to press the key that was beneath it as quickly as they could. For one group, the position where the asterisk appeared on each trial was selected at random. For a second group there was a pattern, though participants were not told of its existence. On the first trial the asterisk appeared at the fourth position, then at the second position, then at the third, and so on. If we represent the four possible positions by the numbers 1 to 4, then over the first 10 trials the sequence was 4231324321, and this pattern was then repeated over and over across subsequent trials.

Figure 7.4 shows how reaction times changed as the experiment progressed. Reaction times in the random group essentially remained constant, but reaction times in the pattern group became substantially faster. This improvement suggests that the pattern group had learned where the asterisk would appear – because they could anticipate where it would appear, they could respond faster when it did. But was this knowledge conscious or unconscious?

To find out, Willingham, Nissen, and Bullemer (1989) interviewed participants after the experiment was over and asked them if they had noticed any pattern to where the asterisk appeared. They then analyzed separately the data of those who had not been aware of any pattern; despite not having noticed a pattern, their performance had improved significantly. As a further test of whether they were

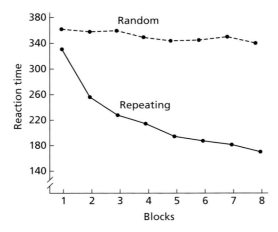

Figure 7.4 Implicit learning. Changes in reaction time when the stimulus requiring a response appeared at random positions on a screen and when it appeared in a 10-item sequence. (Adapted from Nissen and Bullemer, 1987.)

truly unaware of the existence of a pattern, they were then given additional trials in which at the conclusion of each trial they were asked to predict where the asterisk would appear on the next trial. Had they possessed any conscious knowledge of the sequence, they should have had some ability to predict the asterisk's location, but they were unable to do so. Thus despite no conscious knowledge of a pattern – they said they had not noticed it, and when asked to predict the asterisk's next appearance they couldn't – their performance had steadily improved.

This kind of improvement without conscious knowledge is called **implicit learning** – the learning is occurring, but it is implicit in the sense that it is not accessible to conscious awareness. But if participants had no conscious knowledge of where the asterisk would appear, how were they able to respond more quickly as training progressed? The fact that they responded faster than the control group indicates that they knew something about where the asterisk would appear, and yet when asked to predict its position they couldn't. How could they know where the asterisk was going to appear (as shown by faster responding) and yet not know?

The key to resolving this paradox lies in recognizing that information stored in our unconscious can influence us without our realizing it. In our discussion of conditioning without awareness, for example, we saw that a subliminally presented picture of a snake could provoke fear even though at a conscious level participants didn't know that it had been presented. Information stored in our brains often rises to the level of consciousness before we use it, but it appears that it is also possible for our decisions to be guided by knowledge and emotions which we don't know we possess.

Evaluation

We've seen that in a wide range of situations people learn that one event is followed by another without realizing that they have done so. They have learned that contractions of their thumb terminate noises, that saying "yeah" changes how others behave, and that there is a pattern to where symbols appear on a computer screen, all without knowing that they possess this knowledge. On the surface, this evidence seems to provide compelling support for learning without awareness, but it has not gone unchallenged (e.g., Shanks, 2005; Mitchell, De Houwer, and Lovibond, 2009). The arguments are complex, but in essence the issue revolves around how to assess awareness. Consider a participant in Hefferline *et al.*'s experiment who, when asked if she thought that movement of her thumb terminated the noise, said no. Can we really accept this answer at face value? Perhaps she suspected that her movements were having an effect but, because she wasn't sure, didn't want to say so. Or perhaps she was genuinely unaware of the role of her thumb but nevertheless had noticed that the noise stopped when she thought about an upcoming exam – something which, as it happens, she did while holding her head in her hand, thereby contracting her thumb. If so, she did realize that she was controlling the noise, albeit not the precise muscle involved, and it would be wrong to conclude that learning had occurred in the total absence of awareness.

Problems like these make it difficult to reach unequivocal conclusions about learning without awareness. On balance, though, I think the evidence does suggest that reinforcement can affect us without our realizing it. (See also Svartdal, 1995; Dienes and Altmann, 1997; Lieberman, Connell, and Moos, 1998.)

But, hypothetically speaking . . .

On the whole, the evidence we have reviewed so far has strongly supported Thorndike's claim that rewards will automatically strengthen whatever behavior happens to precede them. However, there is also evidence that reinforcement does *not* always work in this automatic way, and we turn now to a particularly striking example reported by Levine (1971).

Testing hypotheses

Levine's study concerned how people learn concepts, and it may help you to understand his experiment if we start with some background material on concepts and how psychologists study them. The definition of a concept can be tricky, but roughly speaking a concept is a set of objects or events, usually a set whose members all share certain common features. The concept *square*, for example, consists of all four-sided objects whose sides are of equal length and meet at right angles. Concepts such as *food*, *human*, and *justice* lie at the heart of our ability to understand the world and think about it, and thus the question of how we learn concepts has attracted considerable attention.

In a typical experiment, participants are shown pictures of shapes, one at a time. They are told that some of the shapes are members of a concept and others are not, and that their task is to figure out which shapes are members. On the first trial, for example, they might be shown a large red triangle and asked if it is an example. At first, of course, they would have no way of knowing and would have to guess. They would be told whether they were correct and then shown another shape, and so on. If the concept was a simple one such as *red*, for example, they would be told they were correct whenever they selected a shape containing this color.

To explain how participants solve problems like this, cognitive theorists proposed that they formulate hypotheses about the solution and then systematically test these hypotheses (for example, Bruner, Goodnow, and Austin, 1956; Trabasso and Bower, 1968). On the first trial, for example, a subject might guess that the concept was triangle, and therefore say yes whenever a triangle was presented. When this hypothesis led to an error, she would abandon it and select a new one for testing on the next trial.

Marvin Levine proposed a formal theory of how people test hypotheses in situations like this. (Similar models were proposed by other theorists such as Trabasso and Bower, 1968.) Levine's theory was based on three simple assumptions:

- Participants start any problem with a set of hypotheses about the solution.
- On each trial, they select one hypothesis for testing and base their response on this hypothesis.
- If the hypothesis is correct, they retain it for testing on the following trial; if it is incorrect, they abandon it and select another hypothesis from those remaining in the set.

As simple as this theory is, it leads to a number of interesting predictions about people's behavior while solving problems. One concerns what happens if a participant's initial set of hypotheses does not contain the correct hypothesis. If the set is small – say, 5 to 10 hypotheses – participants will soon realize that none of the hypotheses in this set is correct, and they should then generate a new set of hypotheses for testing. If their set of hypotheses is very large, however, they will continue to select hypotheses from it. If we now add the assumption that participants learn only about the hypotheses they are testing, the theory predicts that if participants start a problem with a very large set of hypotheses that does not include the solution, they should fail to solve the problem, no matter how simple.

To test this prediction, Levine asked college students to select the letter *A* or *B* on every trial. Whenever they said *A*, the experimenter told them that they were correct; whenever they said *B*, the experimenter told them that they were wrong. The problem was thus unbelievably simple: All participants had to do was to learn to say *A*. Not surprisingly, participants in a control group required an average of only three trials to solve the problem. To see what would happen if participants did not include the correct solution in their hypothesis set, Levine gave a second group pretraining in which the correct letter on each trial was determined by a complex alternation sequence. The basis of solution for a typical problem was the sequence *AABAAABABB*, a sequence that was repeated over and over. If a participant did not solve the problem within 115 trials, the experimenter verbally explained the solution and then presented a new problem, again involving a complex alternation sequence. In all, participants received six such problems during pretraining.

When transferred to the test problem, how should these participants perform? Despite the utter simplicity of the problem, Levine predicted that participants would find it insoluble. On the first pretraining problem, they might begin by testing relatively simple hypotheses such as "*A* is always correct," but as simple hypotheses of this kind repeatedly proved inadequate, they would turn to more complex hypotheses. By the end of pretraining, Levine suggested, their hypothesis set would consist exclusively of such complex hypotheses. When transferred to the test problem, therefore, they would be unable to solve it, because their hypothesis set would not contain the simple hypothesis "*A* is correct."

Levine found that 81% of the participants failed to solve the problem, even when given 115 trials to do so. Indeed, there was no sign of *any* improvement. On trials 91–100, for example, only 53% of their responses were correct, a figure statistically indistinguishable from chance. Thus, even though the response of saying *A* was reinforced every time it occurred, it never increased in strength.

A two-systems interpretation

This result is markedly different from that of Hefferline *et al.* discussed earlier. In the Hefferline experiment reinforcement led to an immediate and substantial increase in the strength of the muscle twitch that preceded it. In Levine's study, by contrast, the correct response showed not even the slightest signs of becoming stronger. So again we face a potential problem: Why does reinforcement strengthen behavior automatically in some situations and yet have no effect in others? And you may also have anticipated our proposed solution: that these different results are the product of different learning systems.

To explain the discrepant findings, we need to add only one assumption to our earlier statement of the two-systems hypothesis: that when the cognitive system is active, it can suppress activity in the associative system. In the Hefferline experiment, participants believed that the noise was presented randomly. When it came on or went off, therefore, they would not have searched for an explanation, and with the cognitive system inactive responding would have been controlled by the automatic system. In the Levine study, on the other hand, participants were told that there was a problem to solve. The cognitive system would therefore have begun to formulate and test hypotheses, and with responding under its control participants would not have noticed that "*A*" was always reinforced. (For discussion of how people's hypotheses can influence how they react to reinforcement schedules, see Lowe, Harzem, and Bagshaw, 1978, and Hayes and Ju, 1998.)

Controlled and automatic processes

The idea of two systems seems to keep popping up, and not just in research on learning. At the same time that researchers in animal learning were converging on the view that reinforcement might involve two learning systems, remarkably similar views were emerging in other areas of psychology (Evans, 2008). Researchers in almost every area of cognition – memory, attention, thought, and decision making – were independently coming to the conclusion that all human thought might involve two fundamentally different kinds of processing.

Different theorists proposed different variants of this idea. Some distinguished between processes based on intuition and those based on more careful reflection; others between processes that were conscious and those that were unconscious; still others between judgments based on reasoning and those based on emotion. (For some representative views, see Epstein, 1994; Sloman, 1996; M. D. Lieberman, 2000; Kahneman, 2003; McClure *et al.*, 2004; Reber and Allen, 2009; Petty and Briñol, 2008.) Although the details varied, a common theme was that one system involved deliberate, conscious consideration of alternative courses of action, while the other was more automatic, operating below the level of consciousness. In one expression of this view, McClure *et al.* (2004) wrote:

these studies suggest that human behavior is often governed by a competition between lower level, automatic processes... and the more recently evolved, uniquely human capacity for abstract... reasoning and future planning.

(McClure *et al.*, 2004, p. 506)

One version of this distinction has proved particularly influential, and so we will examine it a bit more closely. In two papers published in 1977, Shiffrin and Schneider proposed that all cognitive processes can be thought of as either *controlled* or *automatic* (Schneider and Shiffrin, 1977; Shiffrin and Schneider, 1977). Loosely speaking, a **controlled process** is one that requires attention to be executed. An **automatic process**, on the other hand, can be carried out automatically, without conscious monitoring.

One example involves learning to drive a car. At first, driving is very difficult and requires a great deal of concentration. Drivers are slow in making decisions – "Should I begin to slow now?" "Should I turn on my turn signal?" – and their intense need to concentrate makes it difficult or impossible to engage in other activities such as talking. With practice, however, driving gradually becomes automatic, until eventually drivers can easily converse while they drive. Driving thus starts as a conscious process requiring attention, but with practice it becomes largely automatic, a process called **automatization**. (See also Chapter 9.)

Shiffrin and Schneider (1977) developed a formal theory to capture the distinction between these two kinds of processes. They used the term **controlled processes** to describe operations that require attention in order to be executed. Because the total amount of attention available at any one time is limited, only a small number of controlled processes can be performed at the same time. In **automatic processes**, on the other hand, a stimulus elicits a response automatically, without any need for attention. As a result, many automatic processes can be carried out simultaneously, without interfering with each other. Automatic processes can also be carried out very rapidly, because a stimulus can trigger its associated response immediately, without any need for reflection.

This distinction between controlled and automatic processes is almost identical to the distinction between S–R habits and expectations discussed earlier. An S–R habit is an automatic process, as the stimulus elicits its associated response automatically, without thought. An expectation, on the other hand, is a controlled process in which we consciously consider the likely outcomes of responses before deciding how to proceed. Shiffrin and Schneider's analysis also provides a possible framework for understanding the events that occur at the moment a reinforcer is presented, as it either strengthens the preceding response automatically or else triggers a conscious process of evaluation and hypothesis formation.

Summary

As we have traced the evolution of psychologists' understanding of reinforcement, we have seen a number of twists and turns, but the broader picture has been one of considerable convergence. Many psychologists now believe that the brain relies on two fundamentally different modes of processing to carry out its functions. In one, a stimulus elicits a response automatically; in the other, we consciously consider alternatives before deciding on a course of action. The suggestion that these processes are embedded in different systems is speculative, but the fact that researchers in so many different areas have come to a similar view suggests that it might capture an important truth about how the brain functions.

Choosing a response

Having looked at how people learn whether a response will produce a reward, we turn now to what they do with that information. That is, assuming that people know that a behavior will be rewarded, will they engage in that behavior?

This might at first seem a strange question – if a response produces a desirable reward, surely it will be made? – but the outcome depends crucially on what other responses (and rewards) are available. A student may know that studying an extra hour each night will produce a better grade, but this doesn't necessarily mean that he will do so – it will depend on what other activities are available to him, and how rewarding these activities are. Put another way, we rarely face a situation in which only one response is possible; we almost always have a choice between alternatives, each with its own source of reinforcement. How, then, do we choose?

Background

Expected utility

The first serious theory of how people make choices was the work of two seventeenth-century French mathematicians, Pascal and Fermat. They were both interested in gambling and wanted to assess which gambles were worth making and which weren't. Their solution was the concept of *expected value*. To illustrate this concept, suppose that you went to a horse race with a friend and, because she had bought more tickets than she had intended and was a generous sort of person, she offered to let you have one. One of her tickets was for horse A and the other for horse B. If horse A won you would receive $30 and if horse B won you would receive $20. So far it sounds as if you should take ticket A, but suppose you also knew that the chances of horse A winning were only 40%, while the chances of horse B winning were a more encouraging 55%. Which ticket should you accept?

What Pascal and Fermat realized was that you could calculate the value of a bet by multiplying the probability of winning by the amount that would be won. In the case of horse A, the probability of winning is 0.40, while the amount won would be $30. The expected value of the bet would thus be:

$$\text{Expected Value} = \text{probability} \times \text{amount} = 0.40 \times \$30 = \$12$$

This means that if you were fortunate enough to have the opportunity to make this bet over and over, you would win an average of $12 each time. Applying the same reasoning to horse B, the expected value of that ticket would be

$$\text{Expected Value} = 0.55 \times \$20 = \$11$$

In other words, you would be better off with ticket A. It wouldn't necessarily be the better ticket each time – sometimes, after all, horse B would win – but in the long run you would earn more with ticket A than with ticket B.

Calculating expected value is the best way to predict the long-term outcome of a gamble, but philosophers eventually realized that it is not an accurate description of how people actually make decisions. To see this, suppose that you were living in poverty and suddenly discovered that a distant relative had died and left you a million dollars. You would undoubtedly be ecstatic. But now suppose that the next day you learned of the demise of yet another relative, who had also left you a million dollars. You would undoubtedly be pleased, but would you be as excited as the day before? Almost certainly not. Going from nothing to a million dollars is enormously exciting; going from one million to two million, while welcome, is not quite as heart-stopping. The point is that the value of money to us does not depend simply on the amount involved; the impact of winning a million dollars can be different in different contexts.

To accommodate this feature of human nature, another eminent mathematician, Daniel Bernoulli, suggested that in calculating the value of a bet we need to take into account not the amount of money won but rather the psychological pleasure, or utility, that it would bring us. Specifically, the **expected utility** of a bet would be the average amount of pleasure or utility that it would be likely to produce:

$$\text{Expected utility} = \text{Probability of outcome} \times \text{Utility of outcome}$$

In choosing between any two responses, this model suggests that we should calculate the expected utility of each and then choose the one that, in the long run, will produce the better outcome.

Heuristics

It might seem that we have arrived at the optimum method for choosing between alternative courses of action – just pursue the one that is likely to maximize pleasure or utility – and indeed for several centuries philosophers and economists did believe that human decision making was based on such calculations. This view was fatally undermined, however, in a series of papers by two Israeli psychologists, Amos Tversky and Daniel Kahneman (e.g., Tversky and Kahneman, 1974; Kahneman and Tversky, 1979). In a brilliant series of experiments – experiments for which Kahneman eventually won the Nobel Prize in Economics, a prize he would certainly have shared with Tversky had Tversky not died prematurely – they showed that human decision making did not obey some of the key assumptions of expected utility theory. Outlining the nature of these assumptions, and why they were flawed, would take us too far afield, but we can illustrate the problems with a relatively simple example. Suppose that you wanted to buy a car but weren't sure which one to get. How would you decide?

Assessing the value of a car is not quite as simple as the value of a bet because cars differ in many dimensions. One car might be faster, another cheaper, a third more attractive, and so on. In this situation, expected utility theory calls for assessing the utility of each car along each possible dimension, multiplying by the relevant probability, then weighting the product by its importance, and, finally, summing the relevant amounts in order to calculate the overall utility of each car. This is actually not quite as bad as it sounds, but for the sake of simplicity let us assume that each outcome is certain, so that we can ignore the probability component. Suppose that car A costs $10,000, that it is the best car in the group in terms of fuel mileage, but that you don't find it as aesthetically attractive as its competitors. According to expected utility theory, you should begin by assigning a utility to the car's value along each of these dimensions. If you rated utility on a scale from 1 to 10, you would assign a utility to the car's cost (let's say 8 out of 10), its mileage (10 out of 10), and its appearance (5 out of 10). You would then need to weight each of these different utilities by their importance to you. Perhaps appearance is very important to you but mileage and cost aren't. If so, then clearly you would want to give greater weight to appearance in reaching a decision. Suppose appearance was twice as important to you as mileage or cost. You would then assign a weight of 2 to appearance and 1 to mileage and cost. Using U to represent utility, the overall utility of this car for you would then be

$$\text{Car utility} = (2 \times U_{appearance}) + (1 \times U_{mileage}) + (1 \times U_{cost})$$
$$= (2 \times 5) + (1 \times 10) + (1 \times 8)$$
$$= 10 + 10 + 8 = 28$$

You would then go through the same series of calculations for the second car you were considering, the third, and so on. And, finally, you would select the car that had the highest utility overall.

Do you think you – or anyone – would carry out all these calculations in deciding which car to buy? It seems a safe bet that you wouldn't. In the jargon of the field, expected utility theory is an excellent *normative* model – one that tells us how people *should* behave – but less persuasive as a *descriptive* model, one that tells us how people actually behave. But if we don't engage in the elaborate calculations prescribed by expected utility theory, how *do* we make decisions?

Tversky and Kahneman proposed that we use a variety of simplifying short cuts, which they called heuristics. A **heuristic** is a rough rule of thumb, a tactic which will not produce a perfect outcome but will nevertheless usually lead, with much less effort, to a good or at least acceptable outcome. They proposed a number of such short cuts or heuristics, and in the sections that follow we will examine several. As you will see, psychologists have now identified an impressively large number, so to provide some structure for our account we will divide these heuristics into three categories: those used in estimating the probability of outcomes, in assigning utilities to these outcomes, and, finally, in combining all this information to make decisions.

Estimating probability

With sufficient exposure to events, both animals and people turn out to be remarkably good at estimating how often they occur. Suppose that a rat could earn food by pressing either of two levers, each of which produced reinforcement on a VI schedule. If the VI schedule on one lever provided food twice as often as the VI schedule on the other, then eventually the rat would respond almost exactly twice as often on the first lever. The rat's behavior, in other words, would be exquisitely sensitive to the precise rate of reinforcement obtained on each lever. This matching of response rate to probability or rate of reinforcement was discovered by Herrnstein (1961), and is known as the *matching law*. (For a fuller account, see Mazur, 2006.) Similarly, if human participants are given trials in which one of two lights is illuminated on each trial, and they are asked to predict which light will come on by pressing a button underneath that light, then they too will distribute their responses in proportion to the probabilities of the two lights. If the first light is illuminated on 70% of the trials, then participants will push the corresponding button on almost exactly 70% of the trials. With sufficient exposure, in other words, animals and people are very accurate in estimating the probability of events.

In many situations, though, we don't have sufficient exposure to events to estimate probability with this precision. In research on probability learning, participants receive extended practice, typically hundreds of trials or many hours. Moreover, this practice is concentrated in time, so that it is relatively easy to remember what happened on previous trials and thus to begin to make sense of any fluctuations. In real life, conditions are not always so favorable – if a child is praised for cleaning his room only occasionally, each experience may be separated by days or weeks, and it may be much harder for the child to assess the likelihood of earning this praise. How, then, do we estimate probabilities when information is limited?

Availability and representativeness

Tversky and Kahneman identified two heuristics that they believed people use to estimate probabilities. They called the first **availability**. To illustrate it, first try to answer the following question: *Do you think more words begin with the letter **k** or have **k** as the third letter?*

In answering, you probably tried to think of as many words as you could in each category. And, if you are like the participants in an experiment by Tversky and Kahneman (1974), you concluded that more words begin with the letter *k*. If so, you would have been mistaken: More words in English have *k* as the third letter. When we are trying to think of words, though, the first letter is a more effective retrieval cue, and so we find it easier to think of words such as *kitchen* or *killer* than *lake* or *likeable*.

Similar findings were reported in an experiment by Lichtenstein *et al.* (1978), in which participants were asked whether more people die from homicides than suicides. Most said homicide, but again this is incorrect. Because there is much greater coverage of homicides in newspapers and television than of suicides, we find it easier to recall homicides, but suicides are actually far more common.

Availability, then, refers to how easily we can think of instances of some event. In our examples, the availability of an event in memory proved to be a misleading indicator of that event's frequency in the real world, but that is not always the case. Quite the contrary – the ease with which we can think of examples of an event is normally quite a good indicator of how often it occurs. (See, for example, Gigerenzer and Selten, 2001.) Availability is thus usually a good guide to probability, but like other heuristics it is only a rough rule of thumb, and in some situations it can lead us astray.

Tversky and Kahneman's second suggestion for how we estimate probability was **representativeness**. This heuristic is a bit more complicated, but in essence it involves judging whether an event is a member of a category by its similarity to a typical member of that category. Suppose, for example, that you glimpsed a bird through the leaves of a tree. If it looked more like a robin than a crow, than you would undoubtedly decide that it was a robin. Stated in these terms, the concept of representativeness – judging whether something is a member of a category by its similarity to a typical or *representative* member – may seem obvious, even trivial, but again this heuristic can sometimes mislead us. Tversky and Kahneman (1983) provided what has become a classic example. Consider the following description:

Linda is 31 years old, single, outspoken and very bright. She majored in philosophy. As a student she was deeply concerned with issues of discrimination and social justice, and also participated in anti-nuclear demonstrations.

Given this description, which of the following do you think are most likely to be true of Linda:

1 Linda is a teacher in an elementary school.
2 Linds works in a bookstore and takes yoga classes.

3 Linda is active in the feminist movement.
4 Linda is a psychiatric social worker.
5 Linda is a member of the League of Women Voters.
6 Linda is a bank teller.
7 Linda is an insurance salesperson.
8 Linda is a bank teller and is active in the feminist movement.

Consider options 6 and 8 – which did you think was more likely, that Linda is a bank teller or a bank teller who is a feminist? If you chose the latter, you would have had considerable company – so did the majority of the participants in this study. But you would have been wrong. From Linda's description, it certainly sounds as if she might be a feminist, but she might not be. Because the category of bank teller includes all tellers, whether or not they are feminist, it has to be more likely to include Linda. (If this is not clear, consider having to decide whether someone was a driver or a truck driver – the broader description has to be more likely.)

Why, then, did participants believe the narrower description to be more likely? Tversky and Kahneman's explanation is that they judged Linda's membership of each category by comparing their image of her to their image of a typical member of each category. Linda did not especially sound like a bank teller – we probably think of tellers as responsible, careful, middle-of-the-road types – but seemed much closer to our image of a typical feminist. Because she most clearly resembled a typical member of that category (or at least our stereotype of that category), she was judged to be a member. As with our bird example, her membership of a category was judged by how closely she resembled a typical member.

As with our discussion of availability, the point here is not that representativeness is always or even usually misleading. In the real world we often don't have all the information we need to make a decision, or the time to fully analyze the information that we do have. Heuristics are shortcuts that allow us to bypass some of these limitations and make decisions quickly and – usually – effectively, but like all shortcuts they can sometimes lead us astray.

The hot hand

A further example may help to clarify the meaning of these heuristics. All basketball fans are familiar with a phenomenon sometimes referred to as the "hot hand," that shooters tend to score in streaks. When a player is hot, or on a hot streak, they are more likely to score than when they are cold. This is so obvious to basketball fans that it hardly seems worth discussing, but Gilovich, Vallone, and Tversky (1985) nevertheless decided to examine it more closely. The professional baskbetall team the Philadelphia 76ers keeps detailed records of all the shots taken by its players, and the authors were given access to those records. The idea of a hot hand implies that if a player is on a streak – if they have hit several shots in a row – then they will be more likely to score on their next shot than if their previous shots were misses. So Gilovich *et al.* examined the probability of players scoring after previous hits or misses. On average, players scored on 52% of their shots; the percentage of baskets following a previous score was 51%, following two in a row it was 50%, and after three in a row it was 46%. If anything, the probability of scoring went *down* after making a basket! In fact, these differences were not significant: The important finding was that the probability of making a basket was almost exactly the same whether players had scored on their previous shots or missed.

This result was so counterintuitive that the authors tried other ways of testing the hot hand. For example, it could be argued that players do tend to shoot accurately in streaks, but that when a player is hot they tend to take more difficult shots, or defenders guard them more closely, and that these factors mask the fact that their shooting has become more accurate. So the authors examined free throws, shots which are taken at the identical point on the court and without any defender. And the result was exactly the same: The overall probability of hitting a free throw was 0.75, and this was the case whether the player had made his previous free throws or missed them.

When professional coaches and players were informed of these results, they were uniformly dismissive. Bobby Knight, one of the most successful coaches in the history of college basketball, said "there are so many variables involved in shooting the basketball that a paper like this really doesn't mean anything." Similarly, Red Auerbach, longtime coach of the Boston Celtics and probably the greatest professional coach of all time, said "Who is this guy? So he makes a study. I couldn't care less." (Quotes from Gilovich, 1991.) So why are both fans and professionals so convinced of the reality of the hot hand, when a massive data set indicates that it is not true?

It is likely that availability and representativeness both play a role. Starting with availability, when a player scores several times in a row, that is often an exciting – and therefore very memorable – event. We thus tend to remember occasions on which a player scored three times in a row more vividly than those in which he scored twice and then missed. To give an example from my own experience, when I was an undergraduate at Columbia I attended a home basketball game between Columbia and Princeton. Princeton was led by a truly great player, Bill Bradley, and I and the rest of the crowd went wild every time the Columbia player guarding Bradley pressured him and made him miss. Our defender did an incredible job – Bradley missed again and again – and I could not believe it when I read the newspaper the next day that discovered that he had had a great night and scored more than 30 points. It was his misses that I and the other Columbia fans found most exciting, and so I remembered those misses far more vividly than his successes.

Turning to the role of representativeness in the hot hand, it may help to start with a situation involving coin tosses. Suppose that you tossed the coin 15 times in a row and it came up heads every single time. If you tossed it again, do you think the next toss would be more likely to be a head or a tail?

The correct answer is neither. Assuming that the coin is fair, then the probability of a head is always 0.5, regardless of what happened on previous tosses. This feels counterintuitive – when a coin produces a head so many times in a row, surely the laws of chance say that a tail is now due? This belief is so common that is has its own name, the *gambler's fallacy*, but it is wrong: The probability of a head is always the same, regardless of the outcome of previous trials. A coin has no memory, and is not affected by what happened on previous trials.

The underlying problem here is that we have mistaken assumptions about what a chance sequence looks like. If two events occur at random, and are equally likely, we expect any sample to contain roughly equal numbers of each – in this case, heads and tails. This sounds plausible, and if the sample was very large, there would indeed be a roughly equal number. However – and this is where our intuitions about chance go wrong – this is not true for a small sample. A small sample will not necessarily have all the characteristics of the population from which it is drawn. If the population has exactly 1 million heads and 1 million tails, for example, the number of heads and tails in a small sample can differ substantially. Applying this analysis to our basketball example, the problem is that 3 or 4 baskets in a row does not look to us like a random sequence – we feel intuitively that some causal process must have been at work to produce so many consecutive baskets. But that isn't so – if a player takes 20 shots in a game, and hits an average of 50%, then purely by chance sequences of 4, 5, or even 6 shots in a row will actually be quite common (Gilovich, 1991). The problem is that the representativeness heuristic leads us to expect a random process to generate sequences that look random (to be "representative" of the population), but in a small sample that may not be the case.

In sum, our belief in the hot hand may be due at least in part to our reliance on the availability and representativeness heuristics to estimate the likelihood of events. Availability leads us to remember consecutive baskets vividly, and representativeness leads us to believe that sequences like this could not have arisen by chance. The net result is a tendency to see a causal relationship where none exists.

This tendency may also play an important role in the genesis of the superstitions discussed earlier. A basketball coach wears a new tie on the day that his team wins and wonders if the tie was responsible. He continues to wear the tie and his team wins most of its games. He can't believe that this conjunction of events could have arisen by chance: He sees that his team wins almost every time he wears his lucky tie and concludes that the tie must have been responsible. Similarly, people come to believe that animal sacrifices bring rain, that burning witches eliminates plagues, that homeopathic medicines are effective, or that horoscopes predict their future. (The former two beliefs are now sufficiently discredited that they may not require further comment, but if you are surprised by the inclusion of homeopathy and astrology in a list of superstitions, you can find entertaining discussions of these beliefs in Myers, 2010, and Goldacre, 2007, 2008.) In all these situations, the fact that one event is closely followed by another can lead us to suspect a causal relationship; if it happens often enough, our belief may become unshakeable.

Assigning utility

We've suggested that in deciding whether to respond to obtain a reward we take into account both its probability and its utility; we turn now to factors influencing utility. There are many thousands of events that we find rewarding – movies, books, songs, money, food, sports, conversations with friends, and on and on and on. How do we rank this multitude of possible activities and decide which to pursue?

It's all relative

To try to answer this question, Kahneman and Tversky (1979) developed a preliminary account which they called **prospect theory**. The theory is based on a number of assumptions; we will examine two of the most important here.

One was that the utility of a reward is not determined solely by what it is – contrary to the poet Gertrude Stein, a rose is not necessarily a rose, and $10 is not necessarily worth $10. Specifically, their claim was that people evaluate rewards not in isolation but rather relative to some reference point. Suppose that when you were a teenager you were offered $100 to mow a neighbor's lawn. If you only had $10, the offer of $100 might have seemed very attractive; if you already had $10,000, probably not. The attractiveness of a monetary reward, in other words, would depend not simply on the amount involved but on how much money you already had. Similarly, the attractiveness of a hamburger would depend on how hungry you were, and so on. In all these cases, we judge the attractiveness or utility of a reward against some reference point.

In one experimental demonstration of the importance of reference points, Tversky and Kahneman (1981) asked participants to imagine that they were in a store buying a calculator. The salesman told them the price – one group was told that it was $15, another that it was $125 – and then added that they could save $10 by driving to another branch where it was on sale. Those told that the price was $15 said that they would be willing to drive to the other store; those told that it was $125 said that they would not. The saving was identical in both cases – $10 – but its attractiveness depended on the price to which it was compared.

Similarly, people often evaluate their salaries by comparing them to those of others. In one study students and staff at Harvard were asked to imagine two states of the world, one in which they would be paid $100,000 while others earned $200,000, and another in which they would be paid half as much, $50,000, but others would earn even less, $25,000. They were further told that the purchasing power of money in the two worlds would be the same, so that choosing the smaller salary would mean a lower standard of living. In effect, they had to decide which was more important to them, a high standard of living or earning more than others. And the result, perhaps surprisingly, was that approximately half preferred the world in which they would earn more than others, even though this meant receiving only half as much money (Solnick and Hemenway, 1998).

These studies illustrate a crucial point about rewards, that their value depends on our point of reference: $100 might seem a very attractive reward or one of almost no value; it depends crucially on what we compare it to. One way to express this idea is to say that we evaluate rewards not in isolation but rather as *gains* relative to some reference point. Similarly, we evaluate negative outcomes as *losses* relative to a reference point. If the idea of a reference point sounds familiar, it may be because we encountered the same concept in our discussion of contrast effects in Chapter 4. In the case of contrast effects, the effectiveness of a reward depended on how it contrasted with rewards earned previously. In Kahneman and Tversky's version, the set of possible reference points is broader, including the current financial situation and the rewards earned by others, but the basic idea is the same.

The first key assumption of prospect theory, then, was that we evaluate outcomes as gains or losses relative to some reference point. A second was that we react to losses much more strongly than we do to gains. To see this, imagine that you were offered a chance to play a game in which the outcome depended on the toss of a coin. If the coin came up heads, you would win $60; if it came up tails, you would lose $50. Would you play?

In purely logical terms, this might seem an attractive gamble, as if you tossed the coin many times you would win much more than you would lose. Despite this, participants said they wouldn't play. The reason, Kahneman and Tversky suggested, was that we are more sensitive to losses than to gains. The prospect of winning $60 is certainly appealing – note that this is the origin of the term prospect theory – but it would be outweighed in our minds by the more upsetting prospect of losing $50.

Kahneman and Tversky proposed a mathematical function to capture this idea that losses affect us more than gains. Figure 7.5 presents a modified version,

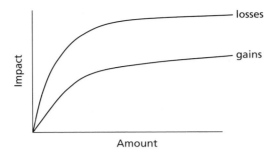

Figure 7.5 The psychological impact of gains and losses, according to Kahneman and Tversky (1979). They propose that a loss of, say, $10 gives us more pain than a gain of $10 gives us pleasure.

showing the psychological impact of different gains and losses. For our purposes, the key feature is that the curve for losses rises more steeply than that for gains, so that a loss of, say, $50 would have a larger impact on us than a gain of the same amount.

The desire to avoid losses is called *loss aversion*, and one interesting consequence is something called the **endowment effect**. The basic idea is that once we acquire something our aversion to losses makes us very unwilling to give it up. One demonstration was inspired by observation of the passionate attachment of Duke University students to their basketball team – as it happens, typically one of the best in the country. Because the basketball stadium is not big enough to hold all the students who want to attend games, Duke has developed a system in which students have to demonstrate their commitment by spending a long time waiting on line for a chance to buy tickets – for a really big game, the wait can be as long as a week! And, as if this weren't bad enough, for these important games students don't even obtain a ticket when they reach the head of the line but only a lottery number, with the winning numbers posted later (Ariely, 2008).

According to the endowment effect, once students obtain tickets the value they attach to these tickets should increase. To test this, Carmon and Ariely (2000) contacted students who had won the lottery and asked them at what price they would be willing to sell their tickets. Similarly, they contacted students who had lost and asked them how much they would now be willing to pay to buy one. Remember that before the lottery result was announced both groups had been equally keen to acquire tickets; it was pure chance whether or not they had obtained a ticket. Nevertheless, the value the two groups now attached to the tickets proved very different. Those who didn't have a ticket were prepared to pay $170 to buy one, whereas those who possessed a ticket would sell it only for $2,400! The simple fact of possession had transformed the psychological value of the ticket. Once we own something, we hate to lose it.

Temporal discounting

Another factor influencing the utility of rewards is the delay until we receive them. In self-control situations, for example, people must choose between the immediate pleasures provided by, say, smoking and the long-term benefits of stopping, including longer life and better health. (See Chapter 5.) Even though the long-term benefits of stopping are vastly greater, people find stopping difficult, and one way to understand their apparent preference for the smaller reward is to assume that rewards become less attractive when they are delayed. The rewards of stopping appear far greater than those of smoking, but because they are delayed their psychology utility might actually be smaller.

In one of the first experiments to study this in humans, Kirby and Herrnstein (1995) presented participants with a variety of hypothetical choices – for example, would they prefer $12 delivered in 6 days or $16 in 12 days? To ensure that participants considered their choices seriously, they were told that they would actually receive one of the choices they had made. It might seem obvious that everyone should have preferred $16 – surely a delay of another six days should not matter that much? – but as the delay to the larger reward was increased, participants began to switch their preference to the smaller one.

Subsequent studies looked in more detail at how the utility of money changes when it is delayed. The methods used have been somewhat technical, but in essence they involve determining how much money people would want now before they would give up the option of a larger amount in the future. Suppose that a participant was told that they could have either $1,000 in a month or $800 right now, and they said that they would be equally happy with either; this would imply that $1,000 in a month has the same utility as $800:

$$\text{Utility (\$1,000 in a month)} = \text{Utility (\$800)}$$

Using a series of questions like this one, it is possible to determine the utility of money after different delays, and Figure 7.6 shows the typical outcome. Utility falls off quite sharply at short delays, and then more gradually as the delay continues to increase. This fall in the utility of a reward when it is delayed is known as **temporal discounting** – the reward's value is reduced or discounted when it is delayed.

People differ quite substantially in how strongly they discount delayed rewards, and these differences could explain many (otherwise puzzling) aspects of behavior. Why, for example, do some people find it so much harder to diet or give up smoking? The answer could lie in how much they discount future consequences. In the case of dieting, it would obviously be harder to succeed if you give more weight to the immediate pleasures of that piece of chocolate cake than to its long-term effects on your appearance. Similarly, individuals who discount more

Learning

Figure 7.6 A theoretical model of temporal discounting. Research suggests that the utility of a reward (the value we attach to it) falls as the time to receive it increases. Value falls particularly rapidly at short delays, and becomes more stable at longer delays.

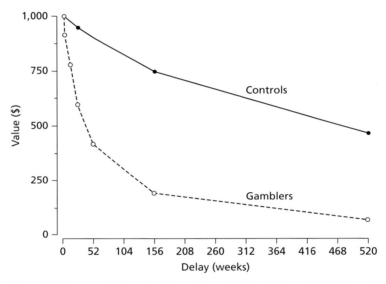

Figure 7.7 Temporal discounting by gamblers. Pathological gamblers had much less tolerance of delays in receiving money – it had much less value for them – than nongamblers. The gamblers appear to require immediate gratification; they cannot tolerate delays. (Adapted from Dixon, Marley, and Jacobs, 2003.)

steeply than normal could be more susceptible to drug addiction, as they would give less weight to the future consequences of taking drugs. As predicted by this analysis, researchers have found that drug addicts do discount future rewards more steeply than non-addicts. Figure 7.7 shows the results of one such study, involving pathological gamblers (Dixon, Marley, and Jacobs, 2003). They were given choices involving $1,000, to see how the utility of this sum changed when it was delayed. As shown in the figure, utility fell far more sharply over time for the gamblers than for a control group who didn't gamble. If the $1,000 was to be delayed for a year, for example, its value for the controls fell to around $800, but for gamblers it was worth only about half as much. Similar results have been reported for individuals with a wide range of other addictions, including cigarettes, alcohol, and heroin. (For a review, see Green and Myerson, 2004.) Addicts seem to be far less tolerant of delays: They require immediate gratification.

The meaning of this relationship between addiction and temporal discounting is not clear. It is possible that individuals who are poor at delaying gratification are more likely to become addicts, but it is also possible that it is the addiction which develops first and eventually leads to steeper discounting. In the case of gambling, for example, the financial problems created by gambling might make gamblers more reluctant to think about the future – what might be called the head-in-the-sand strategy for dealing with problems. Whatever the causal relationship, it is striking that individuals with such a wide range of addictions share this tendency to discount long-term consequences.

Making a decision

We've looked at how people estimate the probability of events and decide their utility. We turn now to how they combine this information in order to make a decision.

Intuition versus deliberation

Kahneman and Frederick (2002) have proposed a possible framework for understanding this. Building on Kahneman's earlier work with Tversky, they start with a distinction – by now, possibly familiar – between two fundamental systems in the brain for processing information. They suggest several possible names for these systems; we will refer to them as the *intuitive system* and the *reasoning system*.

In the intuitive system, decisions are made rapidly and automatically, at an unconscious level. The output of this system, a feeling or intuition about the best course of action, then rises up into consciousness. In most situations, we simply act on these intuitions, but in some situations we may then engage in a slower, more deliberative analysis of our options. This deliberative system can modify the intuitive decision or even override it entirely.

Figure 7.8 shows one way of thinking about the relationship between these systems. Whenever we have to make a choice, the intuitive system will always be activated in the unconscious; its output will then rise to the level of consciousness in the form of an intuition. The deliberative system will normally simply accept or rubber stamp this intuitive judgment, but it some cases it will become more actively involved and take control.

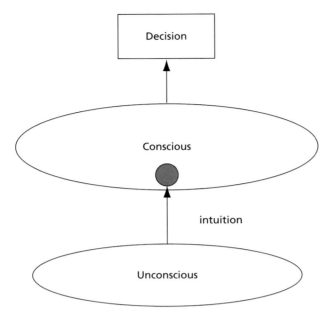

Figure 7.8 Two systems in decision making. Kahneman and Frederick (2002) suggest that decision making starts at an unconscious level, and that the outcome, an intuition, then rises to consciousness, where it sometimes receives further review before a final decision is made.

Intuition's vices

This reliance on intuition can sometimes lead to poor decision making, in part because we tend to have too much confidence in its validity. An interesting example comes from a study by Einhorn (1972) of decision making by doctors. The study involved 193 patients suffering from a form of cancer known as Hodgkin's disease, and the question was how well doctors would be able to assess the severity of their condition, and thus how long they would live. Three doctors, one an international expert, selected 9 characteristics that they believed were relevant to survival, they then rated the patients on each characteristic, and then finally they provided an overall assessment. In effect, the doctors used their long experience in the field to intuitively combine the available information and reach an overall judgment of how ill each patient was.

Quite separately, Einhorn developed a mathematical formula to combine the same information. Using the data from roughly half of the patients, he developed a formula to predict severity. If characteristic 1 proved to be a better predictor of longevity than characteristic 2, for example, then characteristic 1 would be weighted more heavily in the formula.

Einhorn's formula proved to predict longevity far better than the doctor's intuitive judgments – in fact, the doctors' predictions proved to be worthless, as there was no correlation between their assessments of severity and how long each patient actually lived. This result is particularly striking because Einhorn and the doctors were using exactly the same information, the doctors' own ratings of the 9 characteristics. The problem was that the doctors were not able to combine the information about the 9 characteristics effectively, whereas Einhorn's formula did.

One noteworthy feature of this study was doctors' reactions when the results became available. Robyn Dawes, an expert in the field of decision making, once described this study to a group of doctors (Dawes, 1971). The dean of a prestigious medical school was in the audience, and he commented that the problem was that the doctors used in this study had not been sufficiently expert – if only the study had used Dr. X, the world's leading expert in this field, the results would have been far better. Dawes couldn't say so, but Dr. X had actually been one of the participants! As we saw in our earlier discussion of buying cars, it can be very difficult to combine multiple bits of information, and intuition, even the intuition of experts, can be much poorer than we sometimes realize.

One reason that our intuitive judgments sometimes mislead us is that they can be strongly influenced by our emotions, in ways that are not always appropriate. One example comes from a study in which participants were asked how much they would be willing to donate to save migrating birds from drowning in ponds contaminated by oil. Different groups were told that their donation would save either 2,000, 20,000, or 200,000 birds. If the goal was to save birds, a condition in which 200,000 birds would be saved would seem to merit a much larger donation than one in which only 2,000 birds would be helped, but that is not what happened – the suggested donation was virtually identical in all three conditions (Desvousges, Johnson, Dunford, Hudson, Wilson, and Boyle, 1993). To explain this, Kahneman, Ritov, and Schkade (1999) argued that participants' decisions had been based not on a rational analysis of the situation – how much is each saved bird worth? – but rather on participants' emotional reactions to the birds' plight. Kahneman *et al.* suggested that the description used would have conjured up an image of exhausted birds covered in oil, and that it was this emotional image that then guided decisions about how much to give, rather than any rational analysis of what the donation would achieve.

In a conceptually similar study, participants were asked how much they would be willing to pay for airline travel insurance. For one group the policy was described as covering death from "terrorist acts"; for a second group, death from "all risks." Again, a rational analysis would suggest that a policy covering all risks is worth more than a policy covering only terrorism, but the outcome was actually the opposite, with participants willing to pay more for the policy that only covered terrorism (Johnson *et al.*, 1993). It was the emotive word terrorism that seemed to be governing participants' reactions, not a careful analysis of what risks were covered.

Intuition's virtues

From the examples covered so far it might seem that decisions based on intuition are invariably worse than those based on reason and logic, but that isn't always the case. Intuitive decisions are not only much faster, in some situations they can actually be superior. Two studies by Timothy D. Wilson illustrate the point. In one, participants were asked to taste five jams and decide which they liked best. There was a gap of several minutes until they were asked to give their evaluations, and during this gap the experimental group were asked to analyze their feelings about each jam while the control group performed an unrelated task. The quality of both groups' judgments was then analyzed by comparing them to those of a consumer magazine which had used a panel of experts to rate the same jams. The results for the control group correlated well with those of the experts, but those for the group that had analyzed their feelings before deciding did not. Pondering the decision seemed to actually *reduce* its quality (Wilson and Schooler, 1991).

In a related study, participants were asked which of several posters they liked best. As in the jam study, one group analyzed their feelings before deciding, and both groups were then given whichever poster they selected. Finally, they were contacted several weeks later to find out how satisfied they were with the poster they had chosen. Those who had analyzed their feelings were found to be significantly less content; again, thinking too much seemed to have led to poorer decisions (Wilson *et al.*, 1993).

In at least some situations, then, the quick judgments we make intuitively can be superior to those we make after lengthy reasoning. The trick, of course, is to know when to trust our intuitions and when to analyze situations more carefully – and on this point, alas, the literature is as yet silent. (Though see Dijksterhuis *et al.*, 2006, for one view.)

Framing

Our decisions can also be affected by the precise way in which the alternatives are presented to us, a phenomenon called **framing**. In one demonstration, McNeil *et al.* (1982) asked participants to choose between two possible treatments for cancer – for example, radiation or surgery. One version of the question read as follows:

Of 100 people having surgery, 10 will die during treatment, 32 will have died by one year and 66 will have died by five years. Of 100 people having radiation therapy, none will die during treatment, 23 will die by one year and 78 will die by five years. Which treatment would you prefer?

Before continuing, think about this – given this information, which treatment would you prefer?

Other participants were given the following question instead:

Of 100 people having surgery, 90 will survive the treatment, 68 will survive for one year and 34 will survive for five years. Of 100 people having radiation therapy, all will survive the treatment, 77 will survive for one year and 22 will survive for five years. Which treatment would you prefer?

Again, which treatment would you prefer? Because you have seen both questions in quick succession – the participants in the original study did not – you may have realized that the questions actually use exactly the same data; the only difference is in whether outcomes are phrased in terms of living or dying. Concerning death during treatment, for example, the first version says that 10 of 100 people will die during surgery; the second version says that 90 will live. Though phrased differently, the content is exactly the same, but this seemingly minor difference in phrasing had dramatic effects on which treatment was preferred. For one of the conditions in which the participants were patients with medical problems not involving cancer, 68% said that they would prefer the first treatment when the outcome was phrased in terms of living, but only 31% when it was phrased in terms of dying. The same information, but a very different outcome. And even more surprisingly, McNeil *et al.* found similar effects when they put the same questions to doctors – again, doctors' choice of treatment depended on whether the outcome was phrased in terms of living or dying.[2]

Framing effects have been found in a wide variety of contexts – for example, people have more positive reactions to ground beef that is described as 80% lean than as 20% fat (Johnson, 1987). A closely related phenomenon concerns whether people are asked to consider options separately or together. In one study by Kahneman and Ritov (1994), participants were asked how much they would be willing to donate to save endangered dolphins or to provide free medical checkups

---

[2] If you are wondering why preferences were influenced by whether outcomes were stated in terms of living or dying, given that individual questions used the same format for both treatments – for example, in the living version, both surgery and radiation outcomes are phrased in terms of living – the answer is that previous research by Kahneman and Tversky (1979) had shown that people are more sensitive to differences in some percentage ranges than others. For example, a difference between 0 and 10% strikes people as more important than a difference between 90% and 100%. When a 90% chance of living after surgery is compared to a 100% chance of living after radiation, this difference does not seem very large. When a 10% chance of dying after surgery is compared to a 0% chance of dying after radiation, on the other hand, then radiation seems far preferable.

for farm workers. When the options were presented separately, participants offered to donate substantially more to save the dolphins, but when the options were presented together they preferred to help the farm workers. What seems to have happened is that when the options were presented separately the dolphin option elicited a stronger emotional reaction, leading to a greater willingness to give. When the options were presented together, however, the fact that one donation helped people and the other helped animals became more salient, and people felt that they should be more generous to the farm workers. Again, the precise way in which options were presented had a significant impact on the eventual decision. (See also Milkman, Rogers, and Bazerman, 2008.)

Evaluation

We have seen that the process of making decisions, even simple decisions, can be surprisingly complex. We started with expected utility theory, which assumes that people multiply the utility of an outcome by its probability in order to calculate the expected utility of each option, and that they then choose the option with the highest score. Tversky and Kahneman challenged this view, arguing that in most situations we have neither the time nor the processing capacity to carry out all the calculations that it would require. They suggested that we rely instead on simplifying shortcuts called heuristics. To assess the probability of an event, we use the ease with which we can think of examples as a cue (availability), and also its similarity to known members of the category in question (representativeness). To assess the event's utility, we evaluate it in terms of gains or losses relative to some reference point, giving greater weight to losses. Finally, when the time comes for combining all this information, we may either engage in a conscious, deliberative process that can have some of the characteristics recommended by expected utility (for examples, see Payne, Bettman, and Johnson, 1988, and Simon, Krawczyk, and Holyoak, 2004), or else rely on intuition. For centuries, human reason was seen as dominant over our baser instincts and emotions, but many decision theorists now believe that it may be the intuitive dog that wags the rational tail (Haidt, 2001).

Our emotions play an important role in the formation of these intuitions, and this can sometimes lead to poor decisions. On the other hand, intuition allows us to make decisions rapidly instead of always being bogged down in lengthy weighing of every possible option, and in some situations these quick judgments can be a better reflection of our true preferences and feelings. (For more evidence on the positive role of emotions in decision making, see Bechara and Damasio, 2005. For more material on decision making in general, see Kahneman, 2003; LeBoeuf and Shafir, 2005; and Newell, Lagnado, and Shanks, 2007.)

The evidence that emotions as well as reason play a role in decision making fits with the broader theme of this chapter, that the effects of reinforcement depend on the interplay between two different systems, which we have labeled associative and cognitive. As researchers continue learning about reinforcement, the assumption of two systems will undoubtedly need elaboration. We will shortly be turning to research on memory, where we will see that where memories were once seen as processed and stored in a single, vast repository, later evidence suggested a division into two stores, one for short-term memories and one for long-term memories, and then this division was in turn elaborated, with short-term memory seen as having several components and long-term even more. Research has a way of revealing complications as well as, eventually, the beautifully simple processes that sometimes underly them – think of Newton's magisterial organization of so many phenomena in terms of gravity, or Einstein's integration of the laws of physics in terms of relativity. It is thus difficult to predict how our understanding of learning will evolve. It is striking, though, that theorists from so many different areas have found it necessary to posit the existence of two fundamentally different systems, and for now it offers us a useful framework for understanding how reinforcement works.

Summary

- Theories of reinforcement were initially dominated by a clash between two views, known as S–R theory and cognitive theory. Evidence supporting both views eventually led many theorists to the conclusion that in the course of evolution two different learning systems evolved, a relatively primitive associative system in which a stimulus elicits a response automatically, and a more sophisticated cognitive system based on the formation of expectations.
- One line of evidence for an automatic system comes from research on superstition, in which a reinforcer strengthens whatever behavior precedes it, even if that behavior actually reduces the probability of reinforcement. Another comes from research showing that reinforcement can strengthen people's behavior without their awareness. On the other hand, research on problem solving has shown the important role of conscious hypotheses.
- One way of reconciling this evidence is to distinguish between two fundamentally different kinds of processes, controlled and automatic. In controlled processes, attention is required for execution; automatic processes do not require attention, so that many responses can be performed simultaneously and rapidly.
- In most situations we have a choice between actions, each of which has its own history of reinforcement. An early theory proposed that choice in such situations is an essentially rational process in which we choose whichever behavior has the

highest expected utility. Calculating utility, however, can be a very demanding process, and a more recent approach emphasizes the role of mental short-cuts called heuristics. Heuristics don't always produce the optimal response but usually allow us to choose a good response with much less effort.

- In estimating the probability of reinforcement, we may rely on heuristics such as availability (how easily can we think of past examples) and representativeness (we expect a member of a category to have all the typical characteristics of that category).

- In deciding on the value or utility of that reinforcement, we compare it to other reinforcers we have experienced, and we also reduce or discount its value if there is going to be a delay in obtaining it.

- In combining information on the probability and utility of a reward, we sometimes rely on intuition rather than conscious, rational evaluation. Intuitions are often based on emotions, and, like other heuristics, they can sometimes lead to serious errors.

- Our choices can also be influenced by the way in which alternatives are presented to us, a phenomenon called framing.

Review questions

1 Define the following terms: *adventitious reinforcement*, *intervening variable*, and *heuristic*.

2 In what way did Thorndike's cats and Kohler's chimpanzees behave differently?

3 How did Thorndike and Watson contribute to the development of S–R theory? Why did cognitive theorists disagree with them?

4 In what ways was Tolman's approach similar to that of behaviorists such as Watson? In what ways did it differ?

5 In evaluating scientific theories, how important are testability and plausibility?

6 How did Tolman say we could determine whether an animal has an expectation? How did Tinklepaugh's research support the existence of expectations?

7 What evidence supports an S–R account?

8 Why was it so difficult to decide whether S–R or cognitive theories of learning are correct?

9 What is the two-system hypothesis? How does it account for the conflicting evidence?

10 What evidence supports Thorndike's claim that reinforcement will automatically strengthen whatever behavior happens to precede it? What evidence contradicts it?

11 In humans, the question of automaticity can be addressed by asking people whether they were aware of the relationship between their behavior and reward. What does the evidence tell us? Can people's behavior be reinforced without their awareness?

12 How could the distinction between controlled and automatic processes be used to account for the conflicting evidence on whether reinforcement strengthens behavior automatically?

13 What is expected utility? How did Tversky and Kahneman's work on heuristics pose a challenge to this idea of essentially rational decision making?

14 What are the availability and representativeness heuristics? How do we use them in estimating the probability of events such as reinforcement?

15 What is the phenomenon of the "hot hand"? How might availability and representativeness contribute to it?

16 Prospect theory suggests that we evaluate the utility of rewards relative to some reference point. What evidence supports this view? What evidence suggests that we value losses differently than gains?

17 What evidence suggests that we discount the value of a reward when it is delayed?

18 What is the role of intuition in decision making? What are its advantages and disadvantages?

19 What is framing? How does it influence decision making?

Part II | Memory

8 | Memory: an introduction

Memory: an introduction

CONTENTS

In Chapter 1, we noted that learning focuses on the acquisition of knowledge or a skill, whereas memory refers to our capacity to later recall it. We also noted, however, that the two concepts are intimately, perhaps inextricably, intertwined. Learning necessarily involves memory: To show that you have learned a king's name during a history lesson, you must be able to remember the name. Conversely, memory depends on learning: You can only remember the king's name if you learned it in the first place! In essence, learning and memory are two sides of the same coin – that certain experiences have enduring effects on our behavior – and which term we use depends largely on whether we are emphasizing the initial impact of the experience (learning) or its subsequent effect (memory). Having emphasized the first aspect in the preceding chapters, we now turn our attention to memory.

We are so good at remembering things that we tend to take this achievement for granted. If someone asks you your telephone number or what you ate for breakfast, you could answer immediately, and the ease with which you do so can make it hard to see what a remarkable phenomenon this is. In the course of your life, you have stored a huge amount of material in your brain – a vast number of experiences with families and friends, the meaning of perhaps 80,000 English words, the physical movements required to ride a bicycle or talk, and so on. Given this enormous number of stored memories, how do we retrieve the information we want so effortlessly?

The importance of memory becomes obvious when it is impaired for any reason. As we grow older, for example, we tend to become forgetful, and you may have observed the distress of older relatives when they can't remember where they left their eyeglasses, or when they realize that they forgot to turn off the oven before going out, with potentially dangerous consequences. Similar problems can arise when the brain is damaged through illness or injury. One dramatic case discussed by Baddeley (1997) concerns a musician named Clive Wearing, who developed encephalitis, a disease that damages brain tissue. As a result, he lost the ability to form new memories. When his wife came to visit him in the hospital, he invariably expressed great joy, but if she left the room for a few minutes and then returned, he would again become excited, announce that he hadn't seen her for months and ask how long he had been unconscious. He was aware only of the present, with experiences of even a few minutes before lost in a black hole from which not even a glimmer of awareness emerged. Understandably, he was convinced that he had been conscious for only a few moments and would become furious if anyone suggested otherwise – how could he possibly have been conscious, if no record existed in his memory?

Anecdotes such as this highlight the crucial role of memory in normal functioning, and in this and succeeding chapters we will examine the processes underlying our seemingly effortless feats of memory. In this chapter, we'll introduce some of the key concepts that have guided research on memory, and in subsequent chapters we will examine them more closely. Along the way, we will look at some of the practical implications of our growing understanding of memory. When studying a textbook, for example, what can you do to increase your chances of being able to recall the material during an exam? Also, how accurate are people's memories? If you were a juror in a criminal trial, for example, how much faith should you put in the testimony of an eyewitness to a crime, or in that of a woman who claims to suddenly remember having been abused as a child, even though in the intervening years she had no memory of this abuse?

Ebbinghaus's memory

We will begin, appropriately enough, at the beginning, looking at the very first experimental study of memory, and then tracing how psychologists' understanding of memory has evolved during a century of research.

A lot of nonsense

The scientific study of memory began with one heroic figure, the German scholar Hermann Ebbinghaus, born in 1850. After obtaining his doctorate, he travelled in France, and while browsing in a second-hand bookshop in Paris he chanced upon a text by another German psychologist, Gustav Fechner. In it, Fechner demonstrated how perception could be studied using the experimental procedures of the physical sciences. Fechner's findings convinced Ebbinghaus that other aspects of mental functioning should also be susceptible to objective, experimental study, and so Ebbinghaus decided to investigate memory in this way.

Ebbinghaus had no support of any kind – no university position, no laboratory, no participants – and so he was forced to use himself as his one and only participant. He wanted to study memory for material such as words, but he didn't want to use actual words: If he used words, he knew that he would be memorizing material that he had already encountered many times previously, rather than studying the formation of memories from the earliest stages. He therefore decided to create and then memorize *nonsense syllables*, meaningless material which he would never have seen before. (The syllables were arranged in consonant–vowel–consonant sequences, also called CVC trigrams.) His method consisted of reading aloud a list of nonsense syllables and then immediately trying to repeat the list in the correct order. If he could not do so, he read and tested the list again, and then again, and so on, until he reached the criterion of a single perfect recitation.

Once he had learned the list, Ebbinghaus could examine how memory faded over time. Twenty-four hours after memorizing a list, for example, he might reread it and then retest himself; if he couldn't repeat the list perfectly, he would go through the process of learning it all over again, recording how many trials he needed. Typically, fewer trials were needed to learn the list the second time than the first, and Ebbinghaus would then calculate a savings score as a measure of how much he had retained from his initial study. If a list required 10 repetitions to learn the first time, for example, but only 3 trials the second time, this represented a savings of 70%.

On study trials, Ebbinghaus read the words on a list very rapidly, at a rate of 2.5 syllables every second. The purpose of this high speed was to prevent himself from adopting any conscious strategy for memorizing the syllables – he wanted to study memory in its purest, simplest form, without elaboration. Learning even a single list of nonsense syllables under these conditions was a daunting task: A typical list contained around 15 syllables, and the list had to be repeated many times before it could be repeated perfectly. In a more recent study, Tulving explored the difficulty of this task by asking a group of participants to memorize just a single list using Ebbinghaus's procedure; the result was that "2 of the 6 participants became visibly upset and distressed after their performance deteriorated, and I had to terminate

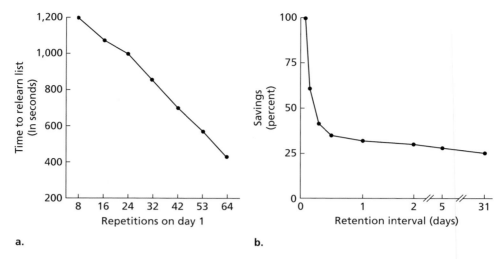

Figure 8.1 Ebbinghaus's memory. (a) The amount of time required to relearn a list on day 2 as a function of how often it was practiced on day 1. (b) Forgetting as a function of the length of the retention interval. (Adapted from Ebbinghaus, 1913/1885.)

[the experiment] for the sake of values higher than those of psychological science" (Tulving, 1985, p. 487). And yet Ebbinghaus memorized not just one list under these conditions but thousands; in the course of just one of his studies, he memorized 350 different lists, involving a total of 189,501 repetitions! You may not be altogether surprised to learn that Ebbinghaus himself referred to his procedure as "tiresome," and that he suffered from severe headaches and exhaustion.

Learning

Despite these difficulties, Ebbinghaus (1913/1885) persisted, and in the end he was able to discover a remarkable number of the principles governing memory. One important determinant, as you might expect, proved to be practice. In one study he repeated a list between 8 and 64 times on one day, and then 24 hours later he determined how many trials he needed to relearn the list. As shown in Figure 8.1a, the results were beautifully regular: The more he repeated a list on day one, the less time he needed to relearn it on day two.

The finding that practice enhances memory is not exactly groundbreaking, but some of Ebbinghaus's other findings were less obvious. For example, he found that memory depended not just on the frequency of practice but also on how this practice was distributed over time. In one experiment, he compared the effects of 36 repetitions of a list on a single day with 12 repetitions on each of 3 days; recall proved to be substantially better when practice was distributed.

Ebbinghaus also examined the effects of extended practice. As the amount of practice on a list increased, he found that the amount of forgetting fell off sharply. In one study illustrating this, he relearned the same list on each of 6 days. On the second day, he needed 39 trials to relearn the list to the point of perfect recitation, but on each successive day the number of relearning trials required fell, until on the sixth day he needed only 3 trials. Extrapolating from these results, he speculated that with sufficient practice material would effectively be remembered permanently, with no loss over time.

Forgetting

Ebbinghaus also studied how memory for learned material deteriorated with the passage of time. In a typical experiment, he would practice a list until he could recall it perfectly. He would then allow a fixed period to elapse before testing himself to see how many of the syllables he could recall. The results of one such experiment are presented in Figure 8.1b, which shows retention (plotted as a savings score) as a function of the length of the retention interval. Forgetting was very rapid over the first hour, but then declined only very gradually over subsequent days.

Practice makes perfect

You may feel some skepticism about the importance of these results: Does the ability of one German to memorize a list of meaningless nonsense syllables really tell us anything about real-life problems such as the best way to study for an exam? As we shall see, Ebbinghaus's pioneering experiments hardly provided the full story, and subsequent research has considerably expanded and deepened our understanding. Nevertheless, it is important to emphasize that Ebbinghaus's findings have proved highly reliable over a wide range of situations – they are not simply laboratory curiosities.

The spacing effect

Consider his claim that memory depends on how practice is distributed over time. This principle has been investigated many times, in a wide range of situations, and on the whole the results have strongly supported Ebbinghaus: Practice is much more effective when it is spaced than when it is massed. In a review of this literature, Dempster (1996) concluded that the **spacing effect** – this is another term for the finding that practice is more effective when it is distributed – is "one of the most dependable, robust, and ubiquitous phenomena in the entire psychological literature" (p. 338).

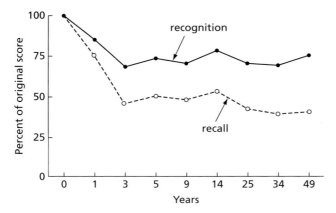

Figure 8.2 Retention of Spanish vocabulary learned in high school, as measured by both recall and recognition. (Adapted from Bahrick, 1984.)

Permanent memory?

Particularly impressive evidence concerning the importance of practice in real-life situations has come from studies by Harry Bahrick and his colleagues, who have examined the ability of adults to recall experiences from high school – for example, the names of their classmates, or facts from algebra lessons. In one study, Bahrick (1984) tested adults' memory for Spanish vocabulary they had learned in high school as much as 50 years earlier, and which they had had little or no opportunity to practice in the intervening years. He used several procedures to assess their memory. In a **recall** test, participants were shown English words and asked to recall their Spanish translations; in a **recognition** test, they were shown possible Spanish translations – some correct, some not – and asked if the translations were accurate. As in virtually all studies that have compared recognition and recall, participants were much better at recognizing material than at recalling it spontaneously (Figure 8.2). Less predictable, however, was the very high level of retention shown by participants. There was a significant amount of forgetting during the first three years following high school, but performance then stabilized, and virtually no further forgetting occurred over almost 50 years. By analogy to the Arctic phenomenon of permafrost, which refers to the fact that ground several feet below the surface remains frozen even in the height of summer, Bahrick suggested the term *permastore* to refer to this seemingly permanent memory; it appears that well-learned memories may melt (be forgotten) up to point, but thereafter may be preserved permanently.

As Ebbinghaus had predicted, then, it appeared that under some circumstances memory can be virtually permanent (see also Conway, Cohen, and Stanhope,

1991). Moreover, Bahrick provided evidence that this impressive retention was due to the principles that Ebbinghaus had identified some 100 years earlier – above all, frequency and distribution of practice. Bahrick compared participants who had taken one, three, or five Spanish courses on their memory for elementary vocabulary – material that would have been learned in the first course – and found substantially better performance in participants who had taken more courses. He estimated that the level of permanent recall in participants who had taken only one course was virtually zero, rising to about 30% after three courses, and over 60% after five courses. The more students practiced their vocabulary – even at a stage where they might have thought they already knew it well – the better they later remembered it.

Bahrick also investigated the effects of spacing practice. In one study, Bahrick and Phelps (1987) compared the performance of students who learned 50 Spanish words in lessons spread 1 day apart with that of students who received the same number of lessons but separated by 30 days. When tested 8 years later, the students who had distributed their practice recalled almost twice as much, even though the total amount of time the two groups had spent studying was identical. (See also Bahrick *et al.*, 1993.)

Long-term memory seems to depend crucially on extensive practice – in studying a foreign language, students repeat the same vocabulary over and over again – and, perhaps equally important, on people having the opportunity to review or refresh their memories at periodic intervals.

To summarize our discussion of Ebbinghaus, he has unquestionably proved to be one of the giants in the history of psychology. After centuries in which our only knowledge of how the mind works was based on armchair speculation, he showed that the principles of memory could be investigated empirically. With only one participant and no support, he invented procedures that guided research on memory for almost a century, and he used these techniques to discover principles that are still valid (for example, Rubin and Wenzel, 1996; Meeter, Murre, and Janssen, 2005). Inevitably, later research suggested new principles, but it was Ebbinghaus who provided the foundation for this research. (For further discussion of his contributions, see Kintsch, 1985; Slamecka, 1985; Gorfein and Hoffman, 1987.)

From association to cognition

Ebbinghaus's primary goal was to determine the empirical conditions that determine how well we remember our experiences, and he made a remarkable start.

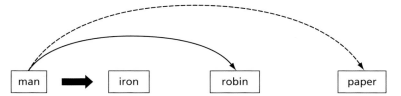

Figure 8.3 Ebbinghaus's view of the importance of temporal contiguity. If the words *man, iron, robin,* and *paper* were presented sequentially, Ebbinghaus believed that *man* would be associated most strongly with *iron*, because they were the most contiguous; less strongly with *robin*, and least strongly with *paper*.

However, he also wanted to understand the mental processes underlying this improvement. Why, for example, does repeating a list make it more memorable?

An associative analysis

Ebbinghaus's analysis was basically associative: When he read a list, he believed that associations were formed between each successive syllable, and it was the strengthening of these associations that eventually allowed him to recall the syllables in correct order. In addition to direct associations, he suggested that associations were also formed between syllables that were not contiguous – he called these remote associations.

Suppose that you were asked to remember a sequence such as *Man, iron, robin, paper.* Ebbinghaus believed that *Man* would be strongly associated with the following word, *iron*, but that weaker associations would also be formed between *man* and *robin*, *man* and *paper*, and so on (Figure 8.3). The greater the distance between the words – and thus the less the temporal contiguity – the weaker the associations should be, and in a series of clever experiments he was able to confirm this prediction (Ebbinghaus, 1913/1885).

Ebbinghaus thus not only discovered a number of the empirical principles that determined memory, he suggested that his findings could be explained by simple principles. Memory seemed to depend on the formation of associations, with the strength of each association depending on the *contiguity* of the units and the *frequency* of their pairing. (Does this sound familiar?)

Although Ebbinghaus's interpretation was sometimes questioned over subsequent decades (for example, Bartlett, 1932), most memory theorists followed in his associative footsteps until the early 1950s. Evidence then began to appear that fundamentally challenged his approach and gave rise to an entirely new framework for understanding memory. In the following sections, we will examine two of the most influential challenges.

Giraffe, milkman, eggplant, Amos, Gerald, typist, baboon, parsnip, garlic, florist, zebra, Byron, plumber, panther, rhubarb, Oswald, wildcat, Jason, diver, radish, leopard, Otto, drugist, melon

Figure 8.4 Words used in Bousfield's (1953) experiment.

Organization

Clustering

One challenge to the associative tradition began with the publication of a seemingly innocuous experiment by Bousfield (1953). He used a procedure known as **free recall**, in which participants are presented a list of words one at a time, as in Ebbinghaus's experiments, but instead of having to recall the words in the order in which they were presented, they are free to recall them in whatever order they choose. Some of the words Bousfield used are shown in Figure 8.4 and before reading the next paragraph you might like to try memorizing the list yourself, to see if you can anticipate Bousfield's discovery. Just read the list of words once and then write down as many words as you can remember, in any order you want.

As you probably noticed, the words are related; in fact, all the words are drawn from four categories: animals, names, professions, and vegetables. The words from the four categories were scattered randomly through the list, but when participants recalled the words, they showed a significant tendency to recall the words from a category together, a phenomenon Bousfield called **clustering**. This clustering suggested that participants had detected the categorical relationships among the words and then used these relationships to organize them into groups.

It turned out, moreover, that this tendency to reorganize material is not confined to lists involving categories. Tulving (1962) presented participants with a list containing words selected entirely at random, and he then looked at the sequence in which they recalled these words. Participants read the words on the list and then recalled them; they then received a second trial in which the same words were presented but in a new random order, and they then recalled them again; and so on. Despite the fact that the words were unrelated and were presented in a different random order every time, Tulving found that participants imposed their own orders on the list, and began to recall certain words together, with the same groupings occurring on one recall trial after another. Tulving called this phenomenon *subjective organization*. It suggested that no matter what words participants are given, they look for relationships among the words and then use these relationships to rearrange the list.

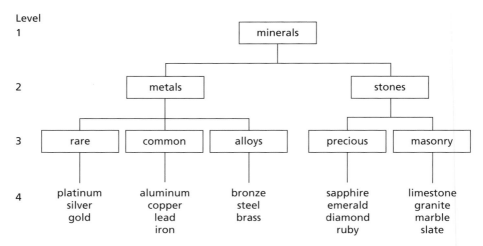

Figure 8.5 The importance of organization. The hierarchically organized list of words used by Bower *et al.* (1969); a control group saw the same words but rearranged randomly.

Moreover, subsequent research revealed that organizing lists of words in this way can substantially enhance our ability to remember them. One nice example comes from a study by Bower *et al.* (1969). They showed one group of participants diagrams of the kind illustrated in Figure 8.5, containing words drawn from several subcategories of minerals. A second group was shown the same set of words, but rearranged randomly within the hierarchical structure: The category name "mineral," for example, might appear in the middle or at the bottom of one of the branches instead of the top. Participants shown the random arrangement could later recall only 18% of the words, whereas those shown the organized version recalled 65%. (See also Hirst, 1988.)

Implications

Evidence for clustering and others forms of organization is contrary to a simple associative analysis, which assumes that participants associate words in the order in which they are presented. Associative analyses do not have to be simple, however, and a more sophisticated version can account for clustering by accepting the importance of hierarchical structures but then assuming that a hierarchical structure is itself no more than a network of associations. If the words *table* and *chair* appear in a list, for example, *table* might remind participants of the superordinate category *furniture*, which would in turn remind them of *chair*, *bed*, and so on. The reason for this is that participants would have experienced these words together many times in their lives, so that strong associations would already exist between them before the experiment began. (It was precisely to avoid such complications that Ebbinghaus invented nonsense syllables.) One prediction that follows from this analysis is that clustering should be found in any list containing words that are strongly associated, even if they are not drawn from the same category (for example, *bed* and *dream*), and this prediction has been confirmed: The stronger the associations among the words on a list, the more clustering is obtained (Marshall, cited in Cofer, 1965).

The occurrence of clustering, therefore, is not necessarily contrary to an associative analysis, because the organizational processes involved can themselves be interpreted in associative terms. (For further discussion of the problems involved in separating associative and organizational accounts, see Cofer, 1965, and Tulving, 1968.) Nevertheless, the evidence for organization suggests that the behavior of participants in memory experiments is far more complex than earlier accounts had implied. Even if we adopt an associative framework for interpreting this evidence, it is clear that participants are not simply associating words in the order in which they are presented. At a minimum, they are associating words with categories and categories with words, but even this is not all: Before participants can use categories, they must notice that some words share these categories in the first place. (If participants don't notice the categories – for example, because the words drawn from a category are spaced too far apart – clustering is much less likely to occur; see Hall, 1971.) The evidence for clustering thus raised the possibility that participants in memory experiments might be playing a much more active role than associative theorists had previously assumed. Rather than simply associating words on a list in the order in which they were presented, participants were displaying a disconcerting tendency to stand back and analyze the lists, looking for strategies that might help them to simplify the task. If psychologists were to understand memory, they might need to understand the cognitive processes involved, processes that might prove far more complex than simply the formation of associations.

Grammar

Chomsky's deep structure

The evidence for organization posed a serious problem for associative theories of memory, but the most devastating challenge began in 1959 with the publication of a massively influential paper by Noam Chomsky. Chomsky was a linguist, and in this article he argued that psychologists' attempts to account for the complexities of human language in simple terms were woefully inadequate. Most of his attack was focused on B. F. Skinner, who had recently published a book attempting to explain

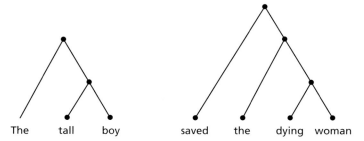

The tall boy saved the dying woman

Figure 8.6 The hierarchical structure of a typical sentence, indicating how the words are divided into phrases.

verbal behavior (Skinner, 1957), but Chomsky's criticism went beyond Skinner, and his article persuaded many psychologists that they had not sufficiently appreciated the complexity of language.

Consider a relatively simple sentence such as

The tall boy saved the dying woman.

According to an associative analysis, we remember a sentence like this by associating the words in the order in which they occur: *The* is associated with *tall*, *tall* with *boy*, and so on. Chomsky argued that the processes involved in understanding and thus remembering a sentence are far more complex. Comprehension of a sentence, he suggested, involves at least two levels of analysis. In the first, we analyze the surface structure of the sentence, which is essentially the phrase structure long taught in classes on grammar. Our target sentence, for example, would initially be divided into a noun phrase, *The tall boy*, and a verb phrase, *saved the dying woman*, and these phrases would then themselves be further decomposed. *The tall boy*, for example, can be divided into *the* and *tall boy*, and so on (Figure 8.6). Once the surface structure of the sentence has been established, Chomsky said that it would be further analyzed for its underlying or *deep structure*. Any idea can be expressed in a number of different wordings; for example, compare the following:

The tall boy saved the dying woman.

The dying woman was saved by the tall boy.

The surface structure of the two sentences is different, but both express the same idea. Chomsky said that the deep structure of a sentence is essentially a representation of this central idea, and that this deep structure can be expressed in any of a number of different surface forms. He went on to propose linguistic rules governing how a sentence's deep structure can be transformed into its surface structure, but for our purposes the key point is that when participants read a sentence they do not simply associate words; they carry out a complex analysis of the syntactic and semantic relationships among the words. (*Syntax* refers to the order in which words occur; *semantics* to the meaning of the words.)

Memory for meaning

It took a while for psychologists to begin to test Chomsky's ideas, but evidence gradually began to appear that supported his distinction between the surface structure of a sentence and its deeper meaning. One experiment nicely illustrating this distinction was reported by Jacqueline Sachs (1967). We have seen that the deep structure of a sentence is essentially a representation of its meaning, and Chomsky suggested that the surface and deep structure are represented separately. If so, it is reasonable to think that participants might recall one without the other – for example, they might remember the meaning of a sentence (its deep structure) but not its precise wording. To test this, Sachs played her participants a tape recording of a story about the discovery of the telescope and occasionally interrupted the tape to show them a test sentence and ask whether it was identical to one of the sentences heard previously. For example, one of the sentences in the passage was

He sent a letter about it to Galileo, the great Italian scientist.

The test sentence was either an exact copy or a modified version such as

1 *He sent Galileo, the great Italian scientist, a letter about it.* (meaning preserved)
2 *Galileo, the great Italian scientist, sent him a letter about it* (meaning altered)

If the test sentence was presented immediately after the original, participants were able to recall the exact wording and reject any alternative. If testing was delayed until many other sentences had been presented, however, participants were no longer able to detect changes in surface structure – they were as likely to accept the altered version in sentence 1 as the original. Modifications that changed the meaning, however, were still rejected. Sachs's results thus suggest that we store the words and the meaning of a sentence separately: At first, we may remember both, but as time passes the exact wording may be lost whereas memory for meaning is preserved.

Memory for surface structure is not always as fleeting as in Sachs's experiment (Anderson and Paulson, 1977; Keenan, MacWhinney, and Mayhew, 1977), but there is now little doubt that we sometimes remember the meaning of a passage even when we have forgotten the words in which it was originally expressed (for example, Kintsch and Bates, 1977; Gernsbacher, 1985). Indeed, this dissociation is quite common: We often remember the general theme or gist of conversations, lectures, and so forth, even though we can't remember the details. As commonplace as this experience may be, it provides devastating evidence against an associative account of memory. More strongly than any of the evidence we have reviewed, research on language suggested that participants reading verbal material cannot simply be associating words in sequence; something far more complex seems to be going on. (For further discussion of what this might be, see Chapter 10.)

Summary

Ebbinghaus developed and used nonsense syllables to minimize the role of past learning, thereby allowing him to study the formation of memories from the beginning.

However, when subsequent researchers moved on to investigate memory for words – in pairs, in lists, and, even more dramatically, in sentences – they quickly encountered the crucial role that meaning plays in memory. Participants do not simply associate words in the order in which they are presented; rather, they look for meaningful relationships among these words and then use these relationships to help them remember the material. When asked to remember a list of unrelated words, participants look for relationships between them, then use these relationships to reorganize the words into a more coherent and easily remembered structure. And when asked to remember sentences, participants use their knowledge of grammar to extract the sentence's deeper meaning. In all these situations, participants are not directly associating words but, rather, developing structures to organize them into groups, structures ranging from membership of the same categories (*animals*, *vegetables*) to complex grammatical rules.

We have suggested that at least some of this evidence can be assimilated into an associative framework (language poses the greatest problem in this regard), but even within this framework, it became clear that participants were doing far more than associating contiguous words – at a minimum, they were also forming associations between words that were separated by many other words, and in the case of categorized lists these categorical links seemed to affect recall far more than associations between contiguous words. Such evidence suggested that psychologists would have to focus on the processes going on between the time a word was presented and the time it was recalled, for participants were clearly active during this period, pursuing a variety of strategies to help them remember. In other words, investigators became convinced that they needed to focus more on the *cognitive* processes inside people's heads – that is, the processes involved in perceiving, storing, and ultimately using information about the external world. The effect was to give birth to an entirely new discipline within psychology, *cognitive psychology*, whose purpose was to understand the mental processes involved in thinking. Instead of a largely behavioral approach, in which experimenters studied the external conditions that influenced memory, cognitive psychologists were more concerned with the mental processes involved. This emphasis did not preclude an interest in practical applications (for example, Neisser, 1978). Nevertheless, the evidence for the importance of organization and grammar led to far greater emphasis on internal processes, and we will now turn our attention to this cognitive approach.

An information-processing framework

Sachs's experiment suggests that what is stored in memory can be very different from the event as originally experienced in the real world – in the case of a sentence read on a page, what is stored is not the pattern of light and dark reaching the eye, but some sort of representation of the *meaning* of the squiggles on the paper. One of the goals of cognitive psychologists was to understand the processes involved: to trace, step-by-step, how an experience in the real world is eventually transformed into a permanent record or representation in the brain.

Cognitive psychologists' thinking about how to do this was guided initially by a theoretical perspective or framework known as **information processing**. This had its origins in the 1940s in the field of engineering, where scientists were developing a strange new machine called a computer. The early computers were pathetically slow by modern standards, and incredibly bulky – in 1949, the magazine *Popular Mechanics* optimistically forecast that computers might someday weigh less than 1.5 tons! Nevertheless, the development of these gargantuan machines profoundly influenced the emerging discipline of cognitive psychology. To understand that influence, we will begin by briefly considering the properties of computers.

The computer analogy

Computers

Despite their remarkable achievements, computers are fundamentally primitive machines that can perform only a few simple operations. To add the numbers 5 and 3, for example, a computer first stores the numbers in separate cells in its electronic memory, along with instructions, or a *program*, that tells it how to add them. Using these instructions, the computer then retrieves the stored numbers from its memory and transfers them to a central processing unit (CPU) where they are added together. The computer then transfers the sum obtained to another memory cell and stores it there. Finally, it conveys the result to us by printing it on paper or displaying it on a screen.

This summary is something of an oversimplification – the steps just outlined would be broken down into tens or hundreds of separate operations. Nevertheless, it does accurately convey the way in which computers solve problems by breaking them down into small steps. Each of these steps is extremely simple (for example, adding 3 and 5), but by executing them at almost unimaginable speed, computers can solve problems of staggering complexity. As this ability of computers to solve problems became clear in the 1940s and early 1950s, psychologists became increasingly fascinated by the mechanisms involved. If computers could solve complex problems by breaking them down into simpler steps, was it possible that human thinking might be based on the same strategy?

At first, many psychologists were skeptical: Could the rather elementary operations of a computer really provide a meaningful analogy to the richness and complexity of human thought? Computers, after all, could solve problems only if given extremely detailed, step-by-step instructions for doing so, and even with such instructions could only solve problems requiring rote, repetitive calculations. In essence, they seemed to be little more than glorified calculating machines. Over time, however, it became clear that these limitations were not as serious as they first appeared. For example, it turned out that computers could be programmed to learn from experience: Given the broad outlines of a problem, they could try out different strategies for solving the problem and then use whatever strategy proved most effective in solving future problems. Furthermore, it became clear that computers need not be confined to rote calculations; they can be programmed to use the same kinds of flexible, goal-oriented strategies used by humans, and in many areas can use them more effectively. Thus, computers have already beaten human world champions at games such as checkers, and on August 31, 1994 – a date that may yet go down as one of the pivotal moments in human history – a computer beat Gary Kasparov, who was the reigning world champion, at chess.

Successes such as these do not prove that people and computers solve problems in identical ways, but they do make it more plausible that the extraordinary abilities of the human brain could be based on processes that, if considered in isolation, might seem absurdly simple. Psychologists thus became increasingly interested in computers as a possible model for human thought, and the concepts and terminology of computer programming had an important influence on the emerging discipline of cognitive psychology.

Sequential processing

One influence was the belief that problem solving can be understood as a sequence of simple operations, in each of which the output of the preceding stage (for example, the sum 8 from our earlier example of $5 + 3$) is participant to one further process or modification (in this case, storage in a memory cell). This sequential analysis has aspects in common with both the cognitive and the associative approaches to learning discussed in the preceding chapter. It is most obviously similar to the cognitive approach in its emphasis on understanding internal processes, but it also strongly resembles associative theories in some respects. Consider, for example, the following quote from Newell and Simon, two of the most influential of the early information-processing theorists:

It looks more and more as if problem solving is accomplished through complex structures of familiar simple elements. The growing proof is that we can simulate problem solving in a number of situations using no more than these simple elements as the building blocks of our programs.   (Newell and Simon, 1963, p. 402)

This belief in the possibility of synthesizing complex behaviors from simple building blocks should be familiar because it is virtually identical to that expressed by S–R theorists such as Clark Hull and also manifested in later associative theories such as the Rescorla–Wagner model. Information processing thus combines the cognitive emphasis on internal processes with the associative belief that these processes are fundamentally simple, and its ability to synthesize these approaches was almost certainly a major factor in its growing popularity (see also Hintzman, 1978).

Terminology

Computer technology also influenced the terminology used to describe the stages of processing. In the case of memory, psychologists noted that, where a computer has to remember information, it does so in three stages: *coding* the input, *storing* it, and then *retrieving* it when it is needed. When a computer is presented with information, the first thing the computer does is to transform, or code, the input into a form that it can process. If the numbers to be added are typed into the computer, for example, the pressure on the keys is transformed into electrical signals, and these signals are then translated into a binary code (a series of 0s and 1s). This transformation process – from pressure on a key to electrical signals to a binary representation – is known as **coding** or encoding. Once the computer has developed a code for the input, the code is stored in the computer's memory. (In older computers, this was done by changing the magnetic states of memory cells.) This process is known as **storage**. Finally, when the stored information is needed for some purpose such as addition, it is retrieved from its location in memory and copied into the computer's central processing unit, where any required arithmetic operations can be carried out. This is known as **retrieval**.

Information-processing theorists began their analysis of memory by similarly conceptualizing memory as a sequential process of coding, storing, and retrieving information. To provide a concrete focus for our discussion of these processes, imagine that as you were walking down a street, a stranger approached and handed you a piece of paper containing the single word *cat*. If you later told a friend about this strange encounter and your friend asked what the word had been, you would probably have no difficulty in recalling it, but how would you do it?

What processes would have occurred in your brain to allow you to store this word when you first saw it and then subsequently retrieve it?

Cognitive psychologists wanted to understand these processes. If you stop to think about it, the goal is an audacious one. We could measure the light from the page that reached your eye, and we can observe whether you respond correctly when asked to repeat the word, but how can we say anything about the invisible processes that went on in your brain during the period in between? Existing technology does not allow us to trace the transmission of activity from one neuron to another in a living person's brain; how, then, can we say what processes occurred?

Two clues to a model of memory

As it happens, at just about the same time that research on organization was convincing psychologists that they needed to understand cognitive processes better, important clues were emerging about the nature of these processes. We will look at two of the key pieces of the jigsaw that was to eventually lead to a model of how memory works.

Rapid forgetting

One critical clue came from experiments reported by Brown (1958) at Birkbeck College in England and by Peterson and Peterson (1959) at Indiana University in America. The two experiments were very similar; we will focus on the one reported by the Petersons.

Previous research, from Ebbinghaus onward, had shown that people can remember verbal material (arrangements of words) for long periods – hours, days, or even years. In virtually all these studies, however, participants were allowed to continue thinking about the material during the retention interval, so that the observed recall was, potentially, the fruit of extended practice. The Petersons wondered how long material would be remembered if participants were not given an opportunity to practice it. To find out, they gave participants a consonant trigram (for example, CHJ) and then, after a delay of between 3 and 18 seconds, asked them to recall it. To ensure that participants did not practice the trigram during the retention interval, the Petersons asked them to count backward by three's from a number such as 793. (Counting backward requires a considerable amount of concentration, so that participants would have little time to think about whatever trigram they had heard.)

On the surface, the task was almost ridiculously easy: Participants were being asked to remember three letters for only a few seconds. However, as Figure 8.7 shows, it proved remarkably difficult. After only 3 seconds, 20% of the participants could no longer recall the trigram, and within 15 seconds, the trigram had been

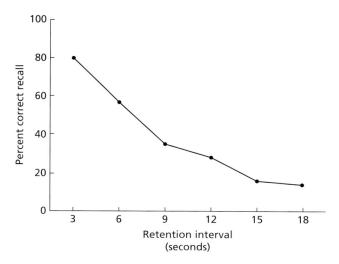

Figure 8.7 Short-term memory: Forgetting when material cannot be rehearsed. (Adapted from Peterson and Peterson, 1959.)

forgotten by almost everyone. Thus, when participants are prevented from repeating or practicing material, it appears that forgetting occurs incredibly quickly, within a matter of just seconds (see also Chapter 11).

Memory span

A second clue came from a phenomenon called memory span.

To experience this phenomenon for yourself, try repeating the following set of digits after reading it only once:

8096

Now try the following set:

517022849375

Most people find repeating the first set easy, but find the second set difficult if not impossible. The number of items that we can remember after a single exposure is known as the **memory span**. Most people can remember between five and nine digits after a single exposure, a range that Miller (1956) immortalized as "the magical number seven, plus or minus two."

That most people can remember only about seven digits may not surprise you – you have probably had more experience than you wanted with looking up a telephone number and then forgetting it before you could dial. This limitation is more paradoxical, though, if you consider how many tens and hundreds of thousands of facts and experiences you have stored in your memory. Given what is clearly the vast storage capacity of human memory, why should it be so difficult to remember a piffling ten or twelve digits?

A preliminary model

Why is forgetting so rapid in the **Brown–Peterson procedure**? And why can we remember only about seven digits after hearing them once? In both cases, there appears to be a striking difference between our ability to recall very recent events – those that occurred just seconds ago – and those that occurred further in the past. First, they differ in speed of forgetting. The Petersons' data suggested that newly formed memories are very fragile – unless we can continue to pay attention to new information, we seem to forget it within just seconds. This contrasts with longer-term memories where, once a memory has lasted more than an hour, we typically remember it for days or even years. Moreover, the number of events that we can store also seems very different for recent memories and older ones. For recent memories, research on memory span suggests that we can store only about seven recent events at any one time. Again, this contrasts sharply with our capacity to store older memories, which is vast. Even if we confine our attention simply to vocabulary, most English-speaking adults know about 20,000 words together with their meanings, suggesting that we can store hundreds of thousands of older experiences, against just seven new ones.

The Atkinson–Shiffrin model

These differences in the properties of older memories and recent ones – in speed of forgetting and in capacity – suggested to a number of psychologists that we may possess two memory stores rather than one. The first, called **short-term memory** or **STM**, was assumed to be a temporary storage system that holds material just long enough for it to be processed; the capacity of this temporary store is very small. Once processing in this first store is completed, the coded material would be transferred to a more permanent store called **long-term memory**, or **LTM**.

Following publication of the Brown and Peterson papers, and one by Miller (1956) drawing attention to memory span, a number of psychologists proposed theories of memory based on the assumption of two separate stores (for example, Broadbent, 1958; Waugh and Norman, 1965). Atkinson and Shiffrin (1968) were the authors of one of these models, and it explained the existing data so successfully that it soon dominated the field and became known as the *modal model*. (In statistics, the mode is the most common score in a data set; here, the

Atkinson–Shiffrin model nicely captured the shared or common features of the various models that had been proposed.)

Because of its importance, we will be examining this model in some detail, but to simplify our discussion we will begin by considering just some of its features. In Chapters 9 and 10, we will complete our survey of the model and consider how its assumptions have been modified following subsequent research.

STS and LTS

Atkinson and Shiffrin called the temporary store the *short-term store* (STS), and the permanent store the *long-term store* (LTS). The purpose of the short-term store was to allow preliminary processing of information. Items held in the short-term store decay rapidly over time; Atkinson and Shiffrin estimated that all trace of a word placed in STS will normally be lost within 30 seconds. For as long as an item resides in STS, however, there is a tendency to transfer it to the long-term store; the longer an item is resident in STS, the greater the likelihood that a copy will be transferred to LTS. And once information is transferred to LTS, it is likely to be held there permanently. (Forgetting, in this view, is not caused by loss of material from LTS but, rather, by difficulty in locating it – for further discussion, see Chapter 11.)[1]

Control processes

Atkinson and Shiffrin suggested that a number of different operations can be carried out on material while it is being held in STS. Some of these processes are automatic, in the sense that they are beyond an individual's ability to deliberately initiate or prevent. (See also Chapter 7.) Other processes were assumed to be under voluntary control, and Atkinson and Shiffrin called these **control processes**.

One important control process identified by Atkinson and Shiffrin was what they called *coding.* This refers to a change in the code assigned to an item – for example, trying to remember the word cat by forming a mental image of a cat. It might have been better if they had referred to this process as *recoding* rather than coding because any word will already have been assigned a code by the time it reaches STS. As we shall see in Chapter 9, if you read the word *cat*, your brain analyzes the patterns of light and dark that reach your eye and, in effect, says,

---

[1] Atkinson and Shiffrin distinguished between short- and long-term stores (STS and LTS) and short- and long-term memories (STM and LTM). The term short-term memory refers to memory for recent events, while long-term memory refers to memory for older events. STS and LTS, by contrast, refer to the stores in the brain where these memories are thought to be held. We will discuss this distinction further in Chapter 9.

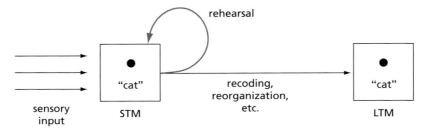

Figure 8.8 A simplified outline of the Atkinson–Shiffrin (1968) model.

"Ah hah, that must be the word *cat*." What is stored in STS is this interpretation or code; if you then form an image of a cat, this is changing the existing code, or recoding.

In any case, Atkinson and Shiffrin suggested that control processes such as coding and organization can increase the chances that material will be remembered once it has been transferred to LTS. However, applying these control processes takes time, and because material in STS decays rapidly, this time is limited. To increase the period available for recoding, they suggest that we use another control strategy, *rehearsal*. By repeating a word, we effectively refresh the word's trace in STS, thereby prolonging the time it is held there. Suppose, for example, that an unrehearsed word would normally decay completely within 25 seconds. If the word is rehearsed before it has disappeared – say at 20 seconds – then this rehearsal will return the word to full strength and thereby initiate another period of 25 seconds before the word is lost. Material can be transferred to LTS for as long as it is in STS, so rehearsing a word not only keeps it active in STS but also makes it more likely that a permanent trace will be formed in LTS (see Figure 8.8).

Implications

As we've seen in earlier chapters, one important test of a theory is its ability to explain known phenomena; another is its ability to predict new phenomena. One reason for the popularity of the Atkinson–Shiffrin model was its success in both, and we will look at three examples.

Rapid forgetting

One phenomenon for which the model offered a simple explanation was the rapid forgetting observed by Peterson and Peterson. (This was the experiment in which participants were shown a trigram and then asked to count backward to prevent rehearsal.) The model's explanation is straightforward. When the trigram is presented, participants initially store it in STS. When they are then asked to count backward, however, this prevents them from rehearsing the trigram. As a result, the code for the trigram decays rapidly, producing a similar decline in recall.

Memory span

Similarly, the model can easily account for the fact that memory span is only about seven digits. According to the model, the limited capacity of STS arises from the fact that we can only rehearse one item at a time. Suppose, for example, that you read the number 683 and wanted to maintain this number in an active state in STS. To prevent the number from decaying, you could rehearse the 6 first, then the 8, then the 3. After finishing the 3, you could return to the 6, and repeat the entire sequence as often as necessary. If the list of digits to be remembered was too long, however, then the first digit would have faded from memory before you could return to rehearse it. It is rather like the plate-spinning act in a circus, where the juggler runs from one plate to the next, giving each a reviving spin (rehearsal) as he goes. Each new spin returns the plate to its original state of activity, but if the juggler tries to maintain too many plates at once, the first plate will have fallen to the table by the time he reaches the last one. In the case of memory span, it appears that we can keep only about seven digits active at one time.

Primacy and recency

As a final example of the model's ability to explain known phenomena, we will consider its account of two important characteristics of memory that we have not yet discussed, the *primacy* and *recency effects*. In experiments on free recall, we've seen that participants are given lists of words to read and then allowed to recall them in any order they want. You might think that participants would be equally good at remembering words from all parts of the list, but this turns out not to be the case. If the probability of recalling a word is plotted as a function of the word's position in the list – this is known as a *serial position curve* – the result usually resembles the curve shown in Figure 8.9. As shown in the figure, the probability of recall is greater for words from the beginning of the list than for words in the middle, and greater still for words from the end. The heightened recall of words from the beginning of the list is known as the **primacy** effect, and the improved recall of words from the end is called the **recency** effect. The obvious question is why recall should be greater for words from the beginning and end of the list.

Let's consider first how the model accounts for the recency effect. If participants are asked to recall a list immediately after they finish reading it, the last words in the list will still be in STS. All participants have to do is to recall these words first, while they are still relatively fresh in STS, and they will obtain high scores for the words at the end of the list. Moreover, if they begin by recalling the last

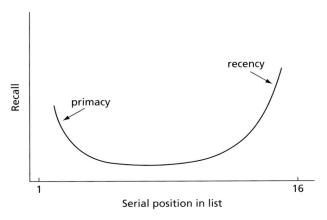

Figure 8.9 A typical serial position curve, showing the likelihood of recalling a word from a list as a function of its position in the list.

word and work backward, then earlier words will continue to decay as they say the later ones, thus accounting for the fact that the last word is recalled best, then the next-to-last word, and so on. As predicted by this analysis, participants do in fact begin by recalling the words from the end of the list first (Welch and Burnett, 1924).

The model explains the primacy effect largely by rehearsal. When the first word in the list is presented, participants can devote all their rehearsal capacity to it, increasing the likelihood that it will be transferred to LTS. When the second word is presented, participants are likely to rehearse both words; the extra rehearsal for the first word will further increase its chances of being transferred to LTS, but the second word will be rehearsed less often and thus will be less likely to be remembered. As each new word is presented, the limited amount of rehearsal time will be spread over more words, reducing the amount of rehearsal that each receives. The cumulative result is that words at the beginning of the list are rehearsed more often than words in the middle or end, resulting in improved recall for the early words.

The model thus offers a simple account for both primacy and recency effects, but how do we know if this account is correct? Do participants really rehearse words in the manner suggested by the model? To find out, Rundus (1971) asked participants to rehearse out loud – that is, to continuously report whatever words they were thinking of, rather than repeating them silently. He counted the total number of times each word in the list was rehearsed, and Figure 8.10 shows the number of times each word was rehearsed (dashed line) together with the probability that these words were later recalled (solid line). For most of the words, the frequency with which a word was rehearsed correlated almost perfectly with how well it was recalled. The exception was words from the end of the list, where, as we have

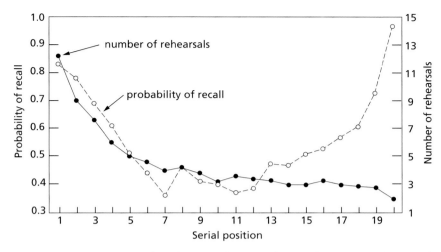

Figure 8.10 The probability of recalling a word in a list of 20 words, together with the number of times the word was rehearsed. (Adapted from Rundus, 1971.)

already suggested, participants were probably recalling words from STS rather than LTS. If we confine our attention to material recalled from LTS, Rundus's results provide striking confirmation of the model's prediction that the likelihood of recalling a word would depend on how often it was rehearsed.[2]

Summary

- The scientific study of memory began with one extraordinary figure, Ebbinghaus. By memorizing lists of nonsense syllables, he demonstrated the importance of variables such as the frequency and spacing of trials. He also showed that forgetting occurs rapidly at first but then much more slowly; subsequent research confirmed that material that is remembered for several years may enter a kind of permastore, where it resides almost permanently.
- Ebbinghaus analyzed his findings in terms of the formation of associations, but when psychologists began to study the memorization of more meaningful material they found that a purely associative analysis was no longer adequate. Even when given lists of unrelated words, we reorganize them (clustering), and when given textual material we abstract and store the underlying meaning – we

---

[2] Rundus's results illustrate the usefulness of distinguishing between STS and STM. Rundus tested his participants' recall immediately after they had finished reading the list, so their recall was, by definition, an example of short-term memory. However, it seems likely that words from the beginning of the list were retrieved from LTS, whereas those from the end were retrieved from STS.

may remember the meaning of a passage long after we have forgotten the specific words in which it was expressed.

- To better understand these more sophisticated processes, psychologists adopted an information-processing framework in which they set out to trace the step-by-step processes by which information is coded, stored, and retrieved.

- Important clues came from two discoveries: that participants can remember only about seven new items at one time, and that in the absence of rehearsal these items are forgotten within seconds.

- To explain these results, Atkinson and Shiffrin proposed that information is initially held in a temporary or short-term store; this store has a limited capacity, and material is forgotten very rapidly if it is not rehearsed. Their model accounts not only for rapid forgetting and memory span, but also for the fact that we remember words from the beginning and end of a list better than from the middle (the serial position effect).

Review questions

1 Why did Ebbinghaus memorize nonsense syllables rather than, say, novels? What are the possible advantages and disadvantages of this approach?

2 Ebbinghaus found that memory for nonsense syllables depended on both the amount and the spacing of practice. What has subsequent research, with different material, revealed about the effects of these variables?

3 What is clustering? Why did its discovery pose a challenge to associative analyses of memory?

4 How did Chomsky's distinction between the surface and deep structure of a sentence lead to an even more powerful challenge to a purely associative analysis of memory?

5 How did the development of the computer influence psychologists' thinking about the operation of the brain?

6 How did research on rapid forgetting and the memory span contribute to the development of the Atkinson–Shiffrin model? What are the main assumptions of this model? How does it account for rapid forgetting and the memory span?

7 According to the Atkinson–Shiffrin model, what is a control process? What are the main control processes carried out on material while it is held in the short-term store?

8 What is the serial position effect? How does the Atkinson–Shiffrin model account for it?

9 Sensory and working memory

CONTENTS

We've seen that associative approaches dominated early thinking about memory, but that growing problems with this approach convinced most theorists that memory was not based simply on the formation of associations; other processes would have to be considered. The Atkinson–Shiffrin model provided a preliminary framework for understanding these processes, but the research it spawned gradually led to important changes. In this chapter and the following one, we'll look at some of the most important changes. We'll begin here by focusing on how sensory input is coded – that is, what happens from the time we receive sensory input to the time a representation of that input is stored in long-term memory. Then, in Chapter 10, we'll consider what happens to material once it reaches that long-term store.

Sensory memory

We have described the Atkinson–Shiffrin model as a two-store model, but they actually postulated three stores. When we perceive the written word *cat*, for

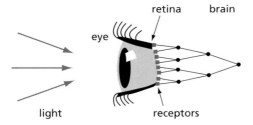

Figure 9.1 A simplified outline of the visual system, illustrating how a large number of neurons at one level converge on a single neuron at the next level.

example, extensive processing must occur before we recognize the lines on the page as representing this word, and Atkinson and Shiffrin suggested that during this preliminary processing material is held in a temporary store that they called **sensory memory**. In this section, we will outline the early stages in sensory processing and discuss the role of sensory memory in facilitating this processing.

From features to grandmothers

The first step in forming a memory of an experience occurs at the senses, where physical energy from the external environment is transformed into electrical activity. To continue with our *cat* example, when you're shown the word on a piece of paper, the reflected light reaches each eye, where it is focused on an area at the back of the eye called the *retina*. Visual receptors located in the retina contain chemicals that are sensitive to light, and the resulting chemical activity eventually produces an electrical signal. As shown in Figure 9.1, these receptors are connected to neurons in the next level of the visual system, which are in turn connected to neurons at a third level, and so on, until eventually the electrical activity generated in the receptors of the eye is conveyed to neurons in the cortex of the brain. The question is how this transmission of electrical signals through a series of neurons eventually makes it possible for you to recognize objects such as letters.

Consider the letter E. In reading printed and handwritten material, you encounter this letter in an almost infinite variety of forms, differing in shape, size, and orientation. How, then, does your brain manage to recognize all these variants as manifestations of the same letter?

The most likely explanation is that your brain simplifies the task by analyzing stimuli by their component *features*. All printed Es, for example, are composed of one long line and three shorter lines, with these lines arranged in certain spatial relationships. If the visual system could analyze a complex visual scene into such component features and extract information about the relationships between them, then it could use this information to identify the letter E whenever it was presented, regardless of its exact size, orientation, and so on.

In fact, physiological studies of the visual system suggest that pattern recognition does begin with analysis of simple features. In one early study done with frogs, tiny wires called microelectrodes were inserted into single neurons in the frog's visual system, and electrical activity in these neurons was recorded as the neurons responded to different visual patterns presented to the frog's eye (Lettvin *et al.*, 1959). The researchers found that different cells were sensitive to different kinds of physical stimuli: Some cells responded only when the external stimulus contained regions of light and dark divided by a sharp edge – in effect, these cells detected the presence of lines or boundaries. Other cells responded only when the line was moving; and still others only when the level of illumination was reduced. In other words, each of these cells seemed to be specialized to detect one feature of the visual input – an edge, movement, or a change in illumination. The most intriguing of these cells, though, were what appeared to be "bug detectors," cells which responded whenever a small, dark, circular object moved into the frog's field of view. (Frogs have an especially keen interest in flying insects, as these insects provide, however reluctantly, the bulk of the frog's diet.)

The frog's visual system is far simpler than that of humans, but studies of cats and monkeys, whose brains resemble ours much more closely, suggest that the human brain also recognizes complex stimuli by first analyzing their component features (Hubel and Wiesel, 1962, 1979). For example, some neurons within the monkey's visual system respond only when horizontal lines are presented, others respond only to vertical lines, and so on. Suppose that the horizontal-line detector and the vertical-line detector are both connected to a single neuron at the next level in the visual system, and further suppose that this neuron fires only if it receives inputs from both the horizontal and the vertical detectors. If so, this higher-level neuron would effectively register the fact that both a horizontal and a vertical line are present somewhere in the visual field.

This example illustrates how sequential processing could allow the visual system to detect features and then combine them into increasingly complex shapes. Starting at the earlier levels and working upward, the visual system might start by detecting a horizontal line, then a combination of lines representing an E, then a combination representing the word "the," and so on. Similarly, the system could recognize faces by first decomposing each face into a set of component features and then combining these features into progressively more complex patterns, until eventually a single cell in the cortex would become active whenever a certain face was present – for example, a "grandmother cell" which would become active whenever you saw your grandmother! And strange as this notion may seem, physiological studies of monkeys' visual systems have suggested that such grandmother cells may actually exist – Gross, Bender, and Rocha-Miranda (1969) found individual cells that would respond whenever a monkey was presented with a picture of another monkey's paw held in a certain orientation, and Perrett *et al.* (1994)

TAE CAT

Figure 9.2 Top-down mechanisms in visual perception. (Adapted from Selfridge, 1959.)

discovered cells that responded only to pictures of monkey's faces. And more recent evidence has suggested similar specialization in the human brain – Quian Quiroga *et al.* (2005) found "Hale Berry" cells that would respond to pictures of her face but not those of the other actresses shown.

The notion of grandmother cells has been controversial, in part because it seems unlikely that any concept could be represented by just a single neuron – if you possessed a cell representing your grandmother and it was damaged or died, would you no longer be able to recognize her? One way or another, many cells must be involved, and some theorists now believe that objects may be represented by a pattern of activity within a large network of neurons, rather than just by activation of a single neuron. (See the discussion of neural networks in Chapter 13.) Nevertheless, it is clear that sequential processing of information plays a vital role in allowing our brains to make sense of the staggeringly large amount of information reaching our senses – 100 million receptors just in a single eye – and this processing may sometimes reach its climax in something not unlike a grandmother cell. (For a vigorous statement of the case for grandmother cells, see Bowers, 2009.)

Top-down processing

Our discussion to this point has implied that perception is a **bottom–up process** that begins at the senses and then continues in a linear fashion from one neuron to another, until information eventually arrives at the highest level of the cortex. Perception, however, also involves **top-down processing** in which information available at higher levels is used to guide processing at lower levels. For a simple illustration, look at the words in Figure 9.2. You probably had no difficulty in reading the words, but your success becomes more impressive when you consider that the central letter in the two words is exactly the same, and yet in one case you automatically read it as an *H* and in the other as an *A*. How did you manage to interpret the same shape so differently in the two cases?

The obvious answer is that your perception of the ambiguous shape was based not simply on its own properties but on those of the letters that surrounded it. In analyzing a word such as *THE*, what seems to happen is that you process each of the letters separately – or, in computer terminology, in *parallel*. Once your brain decides that the first letter is *T* and the final letter is *E*, it then uses this information to decide that the slightly funny-looking shape in the middle must be an *H*. Information from the highest levels of processing thus feeds back to lower levels, to help us decide how to interpret ambiguous features. In this view, recognition of an object requires a combination of bottom-up processing (from individual features to complex shapes) and top-down processing (from knowledge of a shape to recognition of its features).

A further illustration of the importance of contextual cues in identifying a stimulus comes from an experiment by Warren (1970). The participants in this study listened to a tape containing the sentence "The state governors met with their respective legislatures convening in the capital city." However, the section of the tape containing the first *s* in *legislatures* had been cut out beforehand and replaced by the sound of someone coughing. Despite the fact that the *s* was not present, 19 of the 20 participants reported hearing every single part of the sentence distinctly. Even when they were told that one segment of the sentence had been removed, they still were unable to identify which segment was missing. In this situation, it appeared that the words preceding the missing letter led participants to expect the word to be *legislature*, and this expectation was so strong that it led participants to interpret the noise as the expected letter, and so to hear a sound that was not there.

This evidence suggests that perception is not simply a bottom-up process in which the features of a stimulus progressively determine our perception of it; we also use contextual information to decide what a stimulus is likely to be, and we may base our conclusions as much on these expectations as on the actual features of the stimulus. It might seem strange for perception to be influenced so heavily by expectations, to the point where you see and hear things that are not there, but this strategy may make more sense if you consider how impoverished the sensory information available to you often is. Your eyes absorb information at an astonishing rate – objects around you may be moving rapidly, and even if they are stationary, your eyes jump from one fixation point to another as often as four times a second to ensure that important details in a scene are focused on the center of your retina, where receptors are most densely packed. The result is that you normally have very little time to process one stimulus before shifting your attention to another and must base your perceptions on very limited information. Using previous stimuli to form expectations allows you to interpret this fragmentary information more accurately.

You are engaging in this process right now, as you read this sentence. A skilled reader takes in approximately 250 words per minute, and at this rate there simply isn't time to analyze every feature of every letter. Instead, readers process a subset of these features – for example, the contour of a word, and the words that precede it – and then use this information to guess what the word must be. We can illustrate this with the simple sentence "I love Paris in the the spring" – did you notice that a word was repeated? If not, this is another example of how we sometimes see what we expect to see, rather than what is there.

Perception, then, does not involve copying the world but rather interpreting it. We extract as many features as circumstances (and our limited processing capacity) allow, and we then use this fragmentary information to construct a model of the world. This model is normally very accurate, giving us the impression that we are seeing objects directly, rather than making guesses about what they are likely to be. Nevertheless, our conscious perceptions are only the final stage of an extended process in which fragmentary information is collected and analyzed, and the conclusion – our conscious perception – can be totally wrong.

If this notion of perception as a constructive process based on incomplete information still seems strange to you, perhaps a further example will help. Warren and Warren (1970) asked participants to listen to sentences such as the following:

1 *It was found that the *eel was on the axle.*
2 *It was found that the *eel was on the orange.*

In both cases, the section of the tape marked by the * was replaced by a noise. The same noise was used in both cases, but this did not prevent participants who heard the first sentence from hearing the word *wheel*, and those who heard the second sentence from hearing the word *peel*. As in Warren's original experiment, participants were hearing not what was actually there but what they expected to be there; the striking finding in this case is that their perceptions were based on evidence presented several words later. Thus although participants were convinced that they had heard each word as it was presented, in fact processing continued long after the word had ended, and later words led to a retrospective reinterpretation of sounds heard earlier. Perception is a *constructive* process based on our expectations as well as sensory data, and it does not always reproduce reality accurately.

Storing the evidence

We have seen that in identifying a stimulus we consider not only its features but also its context, and the Warren and Warren study makes it clear that this process takes time: We sometimes need to analyze sensory material for an extended period before we can decide what external event generated it. To allow enough time for this processing to be completed, sensory material is initially held in a *very* brief store called sensory memory.

The first evidence that material might be held in a temporary store even before reaching STS came from research by a doctoral student at Harvard, George Sperling. He was interested in how much information people could see if a scene was visible only briefly. If you are in a moving car, for example, and you catch a brief glimpse of someone walking down the street, how well would you be able to describe that person's clothing?

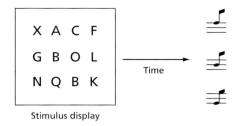

Stimulus display

Figure 9.3 Procedure used by Sperling (1960). An array of letters was shown very briefly; after a delay, either a high, a medium, or a low tone was presented to tell participants which row of the array to recall.

In one early study of this phenomenon, Hamilton (1859) tested how many marbles he could count in a brief glance if a handful were thrown down before him; the answer proved to be about 6. Sperling returned to this question using more modern technology, namely a device called a *tachistoscope* that allows pictures to be presented for short durations. He presented his participants with an array of letters similar to the one in Figure 9.3; the array was presented for only 1/20th of a second, and participants then had to name as many of the letters as they could. Sperling's results proved to be almost identical to those of Hamilton almost 100 years earlier: Sperling's participants could identify about 4 or 5 of the 12 letters in the array, an average of only 37%.

One possible explanation for this relatively poor performance is perceptual: Because the letters were presented so briefly, participants did not have enough time to process them all. There is, however, another possibility: Perhaps participants perceived all the letters initially, but then forgot them very quickly. By the time they reported four or five letters, they had already forgotten the remaining ones.

It is not immediately obvious how you can decide whether a participant did not see something, or saw it but then forgot it almost immediately. To answer this question, Sperling (1960) devised an ingenious *partial report procedure* in which participants were asked to report only some of the letters in the array. Each presentation of an array was followed by one of three tones: If a high-pitched tone was presented, participants were to report the letters in the top row; if a medium-pitched tone, the letters in the middle row; and if a low tone, the letters in the bottom row. If the perceptual interpretation was correct, and participants can process only about 37% of the material in the array, then we should expect participants in the partial report condition to be able to report only 37% of the letters in each row. Performance, however, proved far better than this: Regardless of which row participants were asked to report, they reported an average of 76% of the letters correctly.

Participants did not know in advance which row they would be asked to report, so the fact that they could report 76% of whatever row was requested implies

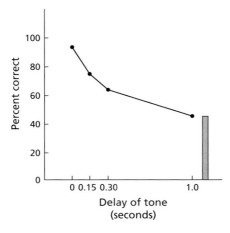

Figure 9.4 Sensory memory. Percentage of letters recalled from one row of an array, as a function of the delay to the recall signal. The vertical bar to the right indicates the percentage recalled when participants tried to recall all of the letters, rather than just those signaled by the tone. (Adapted from Sperling, 1960.)

that they could identify 76% of the whole array, a result far better than the 37% obtained when they tried to report all the letters. To explain this result, Sperling suggested that when visual material is processed, it is initially held in a temporary visual store. This store is assumed to hold a relatively large amount of material, but only very briefly. If participants try to report all the letters in the store, then before they can finish their report some of the material in the store will have faded. If they are asked to report only a small subset of the store, however, they can concentrate their attention on this subset, and effectively "read out" its contents before it can fade.

Sperling tested this fading-trace interpretation in a follow-up experiment in which he varied the time interval between termination of the array and presentation of the tone. The results are shown in Figure 9.4. If the tone was presented immediately, participants could report almost 80% of the requested material, but the longer it was delayed, the fewer letters they could report, until after one second they could report only 38%, which is almost exactly the level found when participants are asked to report all of the letters. These results support the view that visual material is initially held in the form of a visual image or *icon*, and that participants can report details from this icon almost as if they are examining a photograph. The icon fades very quickly, however, so that, after about a second, participants can report only the material that they had time to transfer to STS within that second. Similar results have been reported with auditory stimuli, suggesting that most or all sensory material is held in a brief sensory store initially, to give us time to make sense of it (Massaro and Loftus, 1996).

Short-term memory?

Once an object has been recognized in sensory memory, the Atkinson–Shiffrin model assumed that the sensory code would be transferred to the short-term store where it would receive the processing necessary to convert it into a permanent memory. Some of the model's assumptions about this short-term store, however, proved controversial, and in the remainder of this chapter we will be examining these assumptions more closely. We will begin with the most fundamental question of all, whether the short-term store actually exists.

Before we begin, a quick note on terminology, and specifically on the distinction between short-term and long-term *stores* (STS and LTS), and short-term and long-term *memories* (STM and LTM*)*. Short-term memory and long-term memory are empirical terms, referring to how long memories have been in existence – short-term memories are memories for events that occurred recently, usually within the last few seconds or minutes, while long-term memories are memories for older events. Short-term and long-term *stores*, on the other hand, are theoretical terms that refer to the places in the brain where these memories are believed to be held. In the Atkinson–Shiffrin model, the short-term store is a temporary store where incoming information is held for processing before some of it is transferred to a more permanent, long-term store.

These distinctions are potentially important because when you remember a recent event your memory could have been retrieved from either the short-term store or the long-term store. For example, suppose that you were asked to remember a sentence that you had read a minute ago and were able to do so. This would be an example of short-term memory – that is, a memory for an event that happened quite recently. However, the fact that you could remember the sentence does not tell us where this memory was stored during that minute. Perhaps it remained in STS throughout this period – you might have kept it there by actively rehearsing it – or perhaps it was stored in STS initially but then transferred to LTS, and you then retrieved it from LTS. STM is thus an empirical term defined by how long a memory has been in existence, whereas STS refers to the place where the memory is believed to have been stored. Later theorists have not always preserved this distinction, and the term short-term memory is now sometimes used to refer to recent memories and sometimes to the store in which these memories were initially held.

Two stores or one?

The issue. The extraordinarily rapid forgetting observed by Peterson and Peterson – memory for a trigram faded within seconds when rehearsal was prevented – was one of the key findings that persuaded Atkinson and Shiffrin that there must be a short-term store in which material is held temporarily before being transferred to a more permanent long-term store. Some theorists, however, argued that there was no need to assume two stores, as the Petersons' results could be explained with the far simpler assumption of just one store (for example, Melton, 1963). According to this analysis, coded representations of all experiences are deposited in this single store, and how long they are held there depends simply on how often they are practiced. In the Brown–Peterson procedure, forgetting is very rapid because the counting task prevents rehearsal; as a result, the trigram is repeated only once and forgotten very quickly. Had participants been able to rehearse the material longer, then, as Ebbinghaus showed, they would have remembered it longer.

According to this view, the Petersons' results and those of Ebbinghaus lie on a continuum, where how long we remember an event – from seconds to years – depends simply on how often we encounter it. There is no need to assume different memory stores with different properties; there is just a single store in which retention of all memories depends on how often they are practiced.

So, it is possible to account for the Petersons' findings by assuming either one memory store or two: Which explanation is right? If we possess two memory systems with different properties, then we might expect some variables to affect these systems differently. For example, one condition might strongly interfere with the functioning of STS, but – because the properties of STS and LTS are different – have little or no effect on LTS. In principle, therefore, it should be easy to determine whether we have two memory stores or one, but in practice it has proved difficult. Whenever two-store theorists identified a variable that seemed to affect the two stores differently, one-store theorists would counter with sometimes ingenious explanations of how this evidence was compatible with the existence of a single store. The debate has continued, and there is still no consensus about which view is right. (For contrasting views, see Suprenant and Neath, 2009, and Thorn and Page, 2009.) Both sides, however, agree that the strongest evidence for the existence of two memory stores has come from research on amnesia, and we now turn to this evidence.

Evidence from amnesia

The term **amnesia** comes from a Greek word meaning "without memory" (*amnesty* comes from the same root). The two main forms are *retrograde* and *anterograde*. In *retrograde amnesia*, patients have difficulty in remembering events that occurred before the onset of their condition – this is the condition often depicted in movies, where someone suffers a traumatic shock and then cannot remember who he or she is. In *anterograde amnesia*, in contrast, patients can still remember events that occurred before the onset of their condition, but they cannot form lasting memories for new experiences.

The first case of anterograde amnesia to be studied systematically involved a patient identified in the literature by the initials HM. He suffered from a severe form of epilepsy, and, in an effort to relieve his incapacitating symptoms, his doctors decided to remove the temporal lobes of his cortex and the hippocampus. One unforeseen and devastating result was that he lost the capacity to form new memories. When told that his uncle had died, for example, he experienced intense grief, but he shortly forgot the news and thereafter often asked when his uncle would come to visit. Each time he was told that this uncle was dead his reaction was one of surprise, and his grief was as intense as on the first occasion (Milner, 1966).

Surprisingly, other aspects of HM's memory were unaffected. He could still remember clearly events that had occurred before the operation, and he could converse normally with others, suggesting that he could remember what a person was saying long enough to understand it and formulate a reply. To test whether HM's short-term memory was genuinely normal, Milner tested his memory span, and the results confirmed that his short-term memory was unimpaired. In other words, HM's short-term memory was intact, but he appeared to have lost the ability to convert temporary memories into permanent ones. (See also Baddeley and Warrington, 1970, and Carlesimo *et al.*, 1996.)

A patient referred to as KF was found to have the opposite problem – it was his short-term memory that was affected by brain damage, while his long-term memory functioned normally. The left hemisphere of his brain was damaged in a motorcycle accident, and this had a dramatic effect on his short-term memory: Whereas most people can recall 7 digits after hearing them once, he could now recall only 2. His long-term memory, however, was still normal. When tested on a free-recall task, for example, his ability to recall words from the beginning and middle of the list was excellent; it was only words from the end of the list – those thought to be held in short-term memory – that he had difficulty remembering (Shallice and Warrington, 1970). The results for KF thus complement those for HM: For HM, it was only long-term memory that was affected; for KF, only short-term memory. This pattern of results is difficult to explain if all memory is held in a single store – how could brain damage affect one kind of memory without also affecting the other? This pattern is much easier to understand if memories are held in two separate stores, so that damage could effectively wipe out one while leaving the other unscathed. In short, it does currently look as if short- and long-term memories are held in different stores. (For an opposing view, see Jonides *et al.*, 2008.)

STM as activated LTM

While KF's case supports Atkinson and Shiffrin's assumption of the existence of two stores, it also raises troubling questions about the *relationship* between these stores. They had assumed that words must be rehearsed in STS before they can

Memory

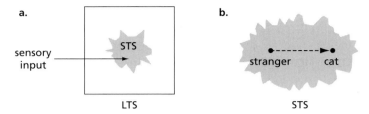

Figure 9.5 STS as active memory. (a) LTS consists of all the nodes in the cortex representing past experiences, and STS is the subset of these nodes that are currently active. (b) Creating a long-term memory of an event requires strengthening connections between nodes (for example, *cat* and *stranger*) while they are simultaneously active; rehearsal can prolong the duration of activity.

be transferred. Our ability to form long-term memories, therefore, should depend on the capacity of the short-term store: The smaller the store, the less material we can rehearse, and thus the less we will be able to transfer. In KF's case, however, a reduction in the capacity of his short-term store from 7 digits to 2 had no impact on his formation of long-term memories. How could this be? If material must be rehearsed in the short-term store before it can be transferred, how could the virtual elimination of the short-term store have no effect?

Problems like this led several theorists to propose a simpler way of thinking about the relationship between the short- and long-term stores (for example, Shiffrin and Schneider, 1977; Jonides, Lacey, and Nee, 2005; Davelaar *et al.*, 2005). Instead of conceptualizing STS as a storage system in which material is held before reaching LTS, Shiffrin and Schneider (1977) suggested that STM could be more usefully conceived as a subset of LTS, consisting of *the items in LTS that are currently in an active state.* Consider again reading the word *cat.* As we saw earlier, light reaching your eye from the page would trigger a series of processes that would eventually result in the activation of the region of your brain that contains your knowledge about this word. Shiffrin and Schneider called the set of neurons involved a **node**, and they assumed that every word has its own node in the brain, which is activated whenever that word is perceived. When you read the word *cat*, the node in LTS that represents this concept would be activated. STS, in this view, is simply the set of LTS locations or nodes that are active at any one time (Figure 9.5a). Thus, rather than viewing STS as a separate storage area which precedes LTS, the "active memory" metaphor interprets STS as a subset of items within LTS, namely those that are currently active.

In Shiffrin and Schneider's model, seeing or hearing a word produces only temporary activation of a node in the brain, and once this activity ceases all trace of the word's occurrence is lost. To form a permanent record of a word's occurrence, we must associate the word with the context in which it occurs. In our *cat* example, you would have to associate the word with other cues present at the time – for example, the appearance of the stranger who handed you the piece of paper. Then, when later asked to recall what you had read, remembering the stranger would help to remind you of what had been written on the paper. (Without such cues, you would have no way to distinguish this experience of *cat* from the thousands of other occasions on which you have undoubtedly encountered this word.) In this model, then, forming a long-term memory is a matter not of transferring an item to a long-term store but, rather, of forming new connections between those nodes in LTS that are in an active state (Figure 9.5b).

In summary, whereas the Atkinson–Shiffrin model views STS as a memory store that precedes LTS, the Shiffrin and Schneider model interprets STS as a subsystem *within* LTS. It is not yet clear whether these two ways of thinking about STS are fundamentally different or whether they are just alternative metaphors for describing the same system. The active-memory metaphor, however, provides a simpler account of the relationship between STS and LTS, and we will use this framework from now on.[1]

Working memory

Atkinson and Shiffrin sometimes used the term **working memory** to refer to the short-term store. Their assumption was that STS is not simply a place for holding information while it is on its way to more permanent storage, but an area where items already in storage can be brought for further processing. For example, suppose that you wanted to multiply 87×6 in your head. You would start by multiplying 6×7; you would then have to remember the product, 42, while going on to multiply 6×80. Finally, you would have to combine the two products. Working memory is where you would both carry out the multiplication and store the sums while you worked.

The mental workbench

Klatzky (1980) has compared working memory to a workbench in a carpentry shop, where wood and other raw materials are held while they are being transformed into

---

[1] Note that when you see your grandmother, you do not simply activate a generic stored representation of her face, you see her face as it is in front of you now. A more precise statement of what is in the temporary store, therefore, would be some amalgam of the sensory information reaching you now with information you had already stored in long-term memory. The key change from the Atkinson–Shiffrin model is that, rather than assuming that sensory information is rehearsed in the short-term store before any contact is made with the long-term representation, sensory information is sent directly to the long-term store, where it can activate associated information; what is then rehearsed would be this enriched representation. If you saw the word *cat*, for example, this would activate information you had previously stored about cats, and it would be this expanded or enriched version that would then be rehearsed.

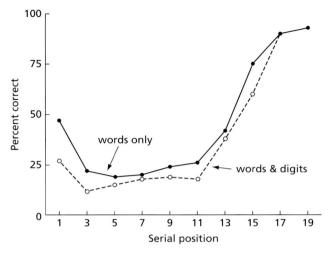

Figure 9.6 The effect of maintaining a 6-digit number in short-term memory on memorizing a list of words. (Adapted from Baddeley and Hitch, 1974.)

new objects such as a cabinet. The materials and tools to be used are brought from storage in the shop and held on the workbench so that they can be easily reached during construction. Similarly, working memory is our mental workbench, where new information can be combined with material already in long-term memory to form a new product.

If the short-term store functions as a mental workbench for carrying out other cognitive tasks, then if this store were filled by one task we should find it very difficult to carry out other tasks that require access to stored information. If you were trying to remember a long list of words, for example, you should find it very difficult to simultaneously solve a multiplication problem. A number of studies were carried out to test this prediction, and the results did show the predicted impairment. However, the degree of impairment proved to be surprisingly small. In a study by Baddeley and Hitch (1974), for example, participants were read a list of 16 words and then asked to recall them. One group, however, was asked to memorize a series of numbers at the same time as they listened to the words. Each number was presented only briefly, and after a 4-second delay participants had to write down the number they had just seen. You might think that having to remember numbers in this way would seriously interfere with their ability to simultaneously memorize words, but this wasn't the case. As shown in Figure 9.6, recall for the words was indeed poorer when participants had to remember numbers than in a control condition where they did not, but the effect was quite small. (See also Parkin, 2000.)

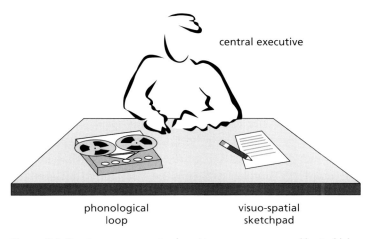

central executive

phonological
loop

visuo-spatial
sketchpad

Figure 9.7 The three components of working memory proposed by Baddeley and Hitch (1974).

Three components

According to the Atkinson–Shiffrin model, filling the short-term store with digits should make it impossible to carry out other tasks such as memorizing words. The fact that there is only minimal interference strongly suggests that working memory cannot rely solely on the short-term store – one or more other memory stores must be available. To account for these results and others like them, Baddeley and Hitch (1974) proposed that working memory consists of three distinct subsystems: what they called a *phonological loop*, a *visuo-spatial sketchpad*, and a *central executive* (Figure 9.7). We will look at each of these components in more detail shortly, but the core idea is that working memory contains two specialized subsystems for storing material. One subsystem stores the sounds of words (you can think of it as a small tape recorder that can hold the sound of a voice saying roughly 7 words), and one stores visual material such as pictures. These "slave systems" are specialized to hold material until it is needed; the central executive decides what material to place in these stores and when to retrieve this material for use in other tasks.

The phonological loop

Baddeley and Hitch proposed that the **phonological loop** holds speech-based information such as the sounds of pronounced words. Any words that you hear are immediately placed on the loop, which holds about 2 seconds' worth of speech. Material on the loop normally fades rapidly, but it can be refreshed if you repeat it to yourself silently, a process called *subvocal rehearsal*.

Why did Baddeley and his colleagues posit the existence of such a seemingly eccentric subsystem? Their proposal was driven by a number of findings, one of which involved people's memory span for words. In a typical memory-span experiment, participants listen to a list of words and then are asked to repeat them; their memory span is the number of words they can reproduce without error in the correct order. Most people can repeat about 7 words after hearing them once, but it turns out that the exact number depends on precisely how long it would take to pronounce each word. In one interesting demonstration of this *word-length effect*, Ellis and Hennelly (1980) assembled participants who could speak both English and Welsh and gave them memory span tests in both languages. The words were chosen to have the same number of syllables, but words spoken in Welsh generally have longer vowels than words in English, and thus take longer to pronounce. The result was that memory span was shorter when Welsh words were used. At the other end of the continuum, speakers of Chinese have the fastest articulation times yet identified, and the memory span for Chinese participants is an impressive 9.9 – the memory span for English speakers, by contrast, is a relatively puny 6.6 (Hoosain and Salili, 1988). Does this mean that Chinese brains are 50% better than English brains? Perhaps, but Baddeley and Hitch's more prosaic interpretation was that the phonological loop can only hold about 2 seconds of spoken material. The faster words are spoken, the more words can be recorded on the loop, and this allowed the Chinese speakers to store more words.

The existence of a phonological loop would also explain Baddeley and Hitch's finding that remembering numbers does not interfere with people's ability to simultaneously memorize a list of words. Participants could store the digits on the phonological loop, leaving the rest of working memory free to process the words.

You may have had the experience of conversing with someone and not really listening to what they were saying because you began thinking about something else. Then, when they noticed your inattention and challenged you to repeat what they had just said, you were able to surprise them (and yourself) by doing so. You succeeded because you had stored their recent utterances on your phonological loop, and thus were able to replay it and effectively read out the words, even though you really hadn't been paying attention.

As illustrated by this example, the main function of the phonological loop seems to be to hold speech-like material, giving us more time to analyze it. If you read a complex sentence in which the meaning doesn't become clear until the very end of the sentence, for example, storing the early part of the sentence on the loop could eventually make it easier to understand the whole. If so, one possible implication is that children who have larger loops might find it easier to learn to speak and to read. Indeed, increasing evidence indicates that this is so. In one study, the size of young children's phonological loops was estimated by seeing how many non-words such as "bamdap" they could repeat after hearing them once. The size of their loops proved to be the best predictor of how many words the children would learn during their first year of school, better even than their measured intelligence

(Gathercole and Baddeley, 1989). Conversely, children with small loops have been found to be much more likely to develop problems such as dyslexia (Miles and Ellis, 1981; Jeffries and Everatt, 2004). Although we tend to think of children who have trouble reading or spelling as unintelligent, this is generally not the case, and in at least some cases the problem may be with what might at first seem like a minor component of memory, the phonological loop. (See also Alloway, 2010.)

The visuo-spatial sketchpad

Although our discussion so far has focused almost exclusively on memory for words, we also need to remember many other aspects of our experience, including the visual appearance of friends, the location of stores, and so on. In fact, our memory for visual events is rather impressive. In one study, participants were shown 10,000 pictures one at a time and allowed to look at each one for only 5 seconds. Two days later they were given a recognition test in which they were shown pairs of pictures and asked which ones they had seen during the study phase; they chose the correct picture 83% of the time (Standing, 1973). Considering the thousands of pictures that had been presented, and the brief exposure to each, this accuracy is remarkable.

Other research suggests that there is some truth to the adage that a picture is worth a thousand words. The ratio is not quite that high, but our memory for pictures does seem to be better than our memory for words, a phenomenon called the *picture superiority effect*. If one group is shown pictures of various objects, for example, and another group is just told the names of the objects and allowed to study the names for the same amount of time, the group shown the pictures will recall more of the objects (for example, Defeyter, Russo, and McPartlin, 2009).

To give us time to process visual material so effectively, Baddeley and Hitch (1974) proposed that working memory incorporates a specialized subsystem called the **visuo-spatial sketchpad**. This system holds visual material not only while it is being processed initially but also when it is later retrieved from long-term memory. In a series of experiments, Baddeley and others provided evidence that the sketchpad and the phonological loop are independent systems, thus making it possible for us to simultaneously listen to a conversation and look at a painting, without one activity interfering with the other (for example, Allport, Antonis, and Reynolds, 1972).

The central executive

The **central executive** performs a number of functions. It controls the operations of its two slave systems, it retrieves material from these systems and from long-term memory, and it plays a central role in further processing of this information in tasks such as reasoning and understanding language. This array of functions is clearly complex, and somewhat vague – what exactly doesn't the executive do? – but an experiment by Baddeley *et al.* (1986) may give you a clearer sense of the executive's functions. The authors compared the performance of two groups of elderly people, a normal group and a group suffering from Alzheimer's disease. (Alzheimer's disease attacks the brain, causing a progressive deterioration in a wide range of cognitive functions.) The researchers trained their groups on two tasks, one that was intended to fill the phonological loop, the other the visuo-spatial sketchpad. Then, in the test phase, they asked participants to carry out the two tasks simultaneously.

Participants in the normal group had relatively little difficulty in coping with this, and their performances when the tasks were combined were similar to their performances when the tasks had been presented separately. Performance in the Alzheimer's group, however, deteriorated sharply. The authors suggest that this deterioration reveals a deficit in the central executive; the Alzheimer's patients could perform each task on its own, but the central executive had great difficulty in coordinating alternation between the tasks (see also Baddeley *et al.*, 1991).

Despite this research, the central executive is still the least investigated, and thus least understood, component of working memory. For this reason, we will not discuss it further, except to point out a potential danger in how we conceptualize it. It is tempting to conceive of the central executive as, literally, a person or executive located within you that makes decisions on your behalf. To do so, however, would be to rob the concept of any explanatory value. If the executive is effectively a person within our brains, is there still another person within the executive that makes decisions on its behalf? If so, is there yet another person within that person, and so on, in an infinite regress? There is no value in explaining a person's behavior in terms of yet another person; to do so only pushes the problem back out of sight, rather than confronting it. To avoid this danger, any hypothetical structure in the brain must be assigned sufficiently clear properties that we can predict in advance how it will function in various situations. Baddeley is fully aware of this difficulty (for example, Baddeley, 1998), and one of the problems for future research in this area will be to specify the properties of the executive clearly.

Before ending our discussion of working memory, we should note that it is a relatively new concept and thus very much still under development. Baddeley himself has proposed that working memory may actually contain four components rather than just three, and he has called the fourth component the **episodic buffer** (e.g, Baddeley, 2003, 2007). In essence, it is a store where we can combine information from the phonological loop, the visuo-spatial sketchpad, and long-term memory. If you were at a party, for example, you might need to integrate information about where people were located in the room, what they were saying, and what their words meant, and the episodic buffer is where you would combine all this stored information. Other theorists have also proposed modifications to Baddeley's model (for example, Barrouillet, Bernardin, and Camos, 2004; Cowan, 2005), and it is not yet clear how many components working memory contains or how they all interact. What is clear is that the older view of short-term memory as an area for the temporary storage of information has been superseded by an emphasis on its role in interpreting and using that information – not just storage memory but working memory.

From STM to LTM

One change to the Atkinson–Shiffrin model, then, has been a shift from viewing short-term memory as a storage area to a mental workbench. Another has concerned their assumptions about how material is transferred from its temporary store to long-term memory.

Levels of processing

According to the original model, rehearsal maintains material in the short-term store in an active state. The longer the material is rehearsed in this way, the greater the likelihood that a permanent memory will be formed.

Rehearsal revisited

To test this assumption, Glenberg, Smith, and Green (1977) devised a clever procedure based on the Brown–Peterson paradigm. Participants were shown a 4-digit number to remember and then, to prevent rehearsal, they were given a filler word and asked to say it repeatedly for the duration of the retention interval. The retention intervals varied from 2 to 18 seconds, with the result that each filler word was repeated between 3 and 27 times. After 60 trials, each involving a different filler word, participants were unexpectedly asked to recall as many of the filler words as they could. Because some filler words had been repeated nine times as often as others, the Atkinson–Shiffrin model predicted that these words would be remembered far better. In fact, there was no difference (see also Craik and Watkins, 1973). This evidence suggests that simply rehearsing a word has little effect; to form a long-term memory, something more seems to be necessary.

Depth

Craik and Lockhart (1972) had previously proposed a theory about what this something else might be. They said that in processing sensory material such as a word, we start by analyzing the word's features at a relatively shallow level, we then combine these features to identify the word, and, finally, we analyze the word at a deeper level based on its meaning. To this point, Craik and Lockhart's analysis was based fairly closely on what was already known about perception, but they now added the crucial assumption that our brains store information about whatever level of analysis is reached, and that the deeper the level, the easier it is to later retrieve these traces. Suppose, for example, that you were shown the word *cat*. If you only analyzed the word sufficiently to identify its letters – for example, because you had very little time – then according to their analysis you would not remember the word as well as if you had also been able to analyze its meaning. The deeper the level of processing, the better the resulting memory.

In one test of this **levels-of-processing** model, Craik and Tulving (1975) showed participants a series of words and asked them to answer a question about each word's properties. For some words, participants were asked to say whether it was written in upper case or lower case (for example, table versus TABLE). Answering this question was presumed to require only a very shallow level of processing of the word's visual appearance. For a second set of words, they were asked to make rhyme judgments – for example, does *hat* rhyme with *mat*? Because participants would have to analyze what the word sounded like as well as the typeface in which it was printed, this was assumed to require a deeper level of processing. Finally, for a third set of words, participants were asked to make a judgment based on the word's meaning – for example, would the word *meal* fit into the sentence "The man ate his ___"? Analyzing a word's meaning was assumed to require the deepest level of processing.

The three conditions were presented in random sequence, so that judgments of visual appearance, sound, and meaning were intermixed. Once all the words had been presented, Craik and Tulving gave participants a recognition test. According to the model, deeper levels of processing should produce better memory, and that is what Craik and Tulving found: The proportion of words recognized was 17% in the case condition, 37% in the rhyme condition, and 65% in the sentence condition. The more deeply a word was processed, the better it was remembered.

Elaboration

Subsequent research broadened the notion of what different levels of processing might entail. In particular, this research suggested that our memory for words depends not only on how *deeply* we process them but also on how *elaborately*. *Depth* refers to a continuum from shallow sensory processing to a fuller analysis based on word meaning; *elaboration* involves the extent to which we consider not only the meaning of a word on its own but its relationship to other words. Where depth can be viewed as a vertical dimension, from shallow to deep, elaboration can be thought of as more of a horizontal dimension, stretching from a single word in isolation to one connected to many others.

We can illustrate the concept of elaboration with an experiment by Stein and Bransford (1979). They presented participants with sentences that had either a simple idea (for example, "The fat man read the sign") or an idea that was elaborated in a manner that was relevant to the theme ("The fat man read the sign warning about thin ice"). When participants were later asked to recall adjectives from the sentence – in this case, was the man fat? – the adjective was recalled correctly 42% of the time for the simple sentences and 74% of the time for the sentences with relevant elaborations, even though the elaborated sentences contained more words. These results suggest that when we elaborate an idea – that is, connect it in a meaningful way to other words or ideas – we remember it better.

Bower and Clark (1969) provided another illustration of how elaboration can improve memory. Participants were asked to memorize lists of unrelated words. One group was simply asked to remember the words, without further guidance, whereas a second group was encouraged to create a story to integrate the words (for example, "The *policeman* ate the *cheese* sandwich while..."). Both groups were given the same amount of time to study the lists, and after memorizing 12 lists they were asked to recall as many of the words from the lists as they could. Participants in the control condition could only remember 13% of the words, whereas those who had embedded the words in meaningful narratives recalled a remarkable 93%. In other words, memory for words does not depend simply on practice: Both groups studied the words for exactly the same time, but the group that used meaningful relationships to organize the material remembered more than 7 times as many words.

A further example of how elaboration can aid memory comes from a study by Nairne, Pandeirada, and Thompson (2008) in which they asked participants to memorize words using a variety of elaborative strategies, all of which had previously been shown to be effective. However, they also included a new condition in which participants were asked to evaluate words in the context of a survival scenario. Specifically, the experimenters asked them to imagine that they were stranded in a deserted area of grassland, so that in order to survive they would need to find food, water, and means of protecting themselves from predators. They were then asked to rate each word in terms of its potential relevance to survival in this situation. On a subsequent recall test, the percentage of words recalled in the survival condition was roughly 50% higher than in any of the other conditions, yielding the best performance yet seen for any memorization strategy. One possible interpretation is that survival has special emotional significance for us – it is *really* important – and thus we evaluate concepts potentially linked to survival in a more thorough and perhaps emotionally charged fashion, leading to better subsequent recall. (See also Nairne and Pandeirada, 2008.)

The concept of levels of processing is not without its problems – for one thing, the definition of depth is somewhat vague, so that it is not always obvious in advance which of two conditions should be expected to produce deeper processing (Baddeley, 1978; Lockhart and Craik, 1990). Nevertheless, how we process material in STM clearly does play a crucial role in how well we later remember it. In particular, the more you think about material you are reading, the more likely you are to recall it. You may have already noted the possible implications of this statement for studying – don't just read a text passively, actively think about its contents – and we will return to this theme in Chapters 10 and 11, where we will discuss it in greater depth.

Consolidation

In our introduction to this section, we noted that the Atkinson–Shiffrin model assumes that the longer information is held in short-term memory, the greater the probability that it will be preserved permanently. One way of explaining this goes back more than 100 years (Müller and Pilzecker, 1900) and is called **consolidation theory**. The basic idea is that the formation of a memory trace takes time, and that strengthening or consolidation of this trace continues for some time after an experience has ended. This idea was translated into neural terms by Hebb (1949) and McGaugh (1966), who proposed that the formation of a permanent memory trace depends on the strengthening of synaptic connections between neurons. They assumed that consolidation of this trace would be completed within seconds or minutes; if consolidation was interrupted, then a permanent memory trace would not be formed.

A study by Lynch and Yarnell (1973) illustrates some of these assumptions. They interviewed football players after they had suffered concussion during a game and been substituted. When the players were interviewed 30 seconds after the injury, they could accurately recall the circumstances. ("[I was hit] from the front while I was blocking on the punt.") When interviewed 5 minutes later, however, they could no longer remember what had happened. ("I don't remember what play it was or what I was doing. It was something about a punt.") Concussion seemed to have interrupted the consolidation processes needed to convert their temporary memories into permanent ones.

Evidence like this strongly confirmed the central assumptions of consolidation theory, that the formation of a memory trace requires time, and that this trace remains fragile until the process has been completed (for example, McGaugh, 2000). These assumptions fit very nicely with the Atkinson–Shiffrin model if we assume that consolidation is the physiological process that allows short-term memories to be converted into long-term ones. Other aspects of consolidation theory, however, proved more problematic. The assumption that consolidation is completed within

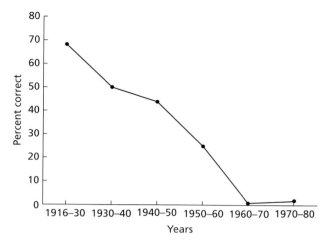

Figure 9.8 Retrograde amnesia gradient for patient PZ. Accuracy of his memories was assessed using his autobiography. (Adapted from Butters and Cermak, 1986.)

minutes, for example, seems to apply in some situations but not others. In our football example, concussion affected only recent memories, but more serious cases of brain damage can affect memories for events that occurred years before the injury. If brain damage affects memories for events that occurred years earlier, this suggests that these memories were not yet fully consolidated, and thus that consolidation is a process that can continue for years.

A particularly dramatic example concerns a patient identified only as PZ. He had been a distinguished scientist, sufficiently eminent to have written and published an autobiography. However, he later became an alcoholic and developed a condition called *Korsakoff's syndrome*. (This condition is not caused by alcohol per se, but rather by poor diet – alcoholics obtain most of their calories from drinking rather than eating. The resulting thiamine deficiency can cause serious brain damage.) One symptom of Korsakoff's syndrome is retrograde amnesia, and PZ had difficulty remembering events that occurred before he became ill. Butters and Cermak (1986) were able to use the material in his autobiography to assess how well he remembered events from different periods. As shown in Figure 9.8, he was very good at remembering events that occurred when he was young, but he was unable to recall almost anything that happened during the last 20 years. Moreover, the improvement over time was gradual – the more time had passed since an event, the greater the likelihood that he would recall it. This suggests that these memories were actually becoming stronger as time passed, in the sense that they became more resistant to the effects of brain damage. And this strengthening process apparently continued for more than 40 years!

How, then, can we integrate the evidence that in some cases consolidation seems to be completed very quickly – football injuries not affecting memories for events several minutes earlier – while in others it continues for years? One possibility suggested by several theorists (for example, McClelland, McNaughton, and O'Reilly, 1995; Eichenbaum and Cohen, 2001; Dudai, 2004) is that we may need to distinguish between two kinds of consolidation. One, the classic kind, probably involves the strengthening of synaptic connections between neurons. This kind of consolidation is relatively rapid, and if it is interrupted the memory being consolidated will be lost. Our concussed football players are a paradigmatic example – even after they recovered, they could not remember the preceding play.

The second kind of consolidation seems to continue much longer and somehow makes memories easier to retrieve. As to how this is achieved, one possibility is that over time we occasionally retrieve memories, and as we think about them they are further strengthened or *reconsolidated*, making them easier to retrieve in the future. An interesting study bearing on this possibility was reported by Linton (1975, 1978), who maintained a detailed diary of her experiences over a 5-year period. She would occasionally select items from her diary at random and judge whether she could recall them. Because the selection was random, she might retrieve a memory more than once during the 5-year period, and this allowed her to evaluate whether the number of times a memory had been retrieved previously affected its current ease of recall.

Her results are shown in Figure 9.9, which plots her success at recalling items as a function of how often she had recalled them previously. During the first 2 years her success rate for all items was very high, around 80%. As time passed, however, recall began to decline, and it was at this point that the number of previous retrievals began to be important. If a memory was retrieved only once during the 5-year period, then her ability to recall it at the end of this period was essentially 0. If the item had been retrieved 4 or more times, on the other hand, her rate of success was far more impressive, averaging over 60%. Even a few retrievals of a memory seemed to strengthen it substantially, making it more resistant to forgetting. (This also fits nicely with Bahrick's suggestion of a permastore, discussed in Chapter 8, where we saw that often-studied material may remain in memory almost indefinitely.)

We will not focus on the practical implications of memory research until Chapter 12, but you might want to add retrieval practice to any mental list you have been building of the factors that might influence exam success – spreading studying over a period of time rather than cramming, actively thinking about the material you are studying rather than just reading it passively, and now reviewing material at some point after reading it. For a variety of reasons, many students find themselves trying to cram as much information into their heads as they can the night before an exam. Cramming is undoubtedly better than not studying at all, but memory research suggests that we are likely to remember more – sometimes far more – if study sessions are spread over time, involve critical

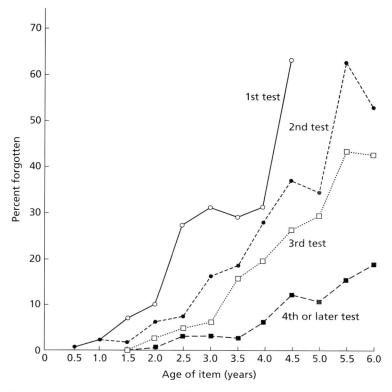

Figure 9.9 Forgetting as a function of how often an item is recalled during the period from acquisition to the final test. The more often an item is recalled, the lower the rate of forgetting. (Adapted from Linton, 1978.)

thinking about the material being studied, and are later followed by attempts to recall the material.

Our understanding of how the brain consolidates memories is increasing rapidly, and recent findings include evidence that sleep enhances consolidation (Rasch and Born, 2008), and that memories that are undergoing reconsolidation are particularly malleable, opening up the possibility that it may be possible to eliminate memories (for example, of traumatic battlefield experiences) during this stage (Doyère *et al.*, 2007). (More general reviews of this burgeoning literature can be found in Wang and Morris, 2010 and Hardt, Einarsson, and Nader, 2010.)

Attention

So far, we have concentrated on what happens during the processing of a single stimulus such as the word *cat*. In real life, of course, the problem we confront is much more difficult. We are bombarded by stimuli – thousands of lights, sounds, and odors every second. We clearly cannot attend to all of the stimuli that reach our senses – imagine trying to read a physics text while listening to a psychology lecture – and so we must select some subset for processing. The term **attention** is used to describe the processes by which we allocate our limited processing resources across competing demands. Formal definitions vary, but its essence was famously captured by William James, in one of the first-ever psychology texts:

Attention . . . is the taking possession by the mind, in clear and vivid form, of one out of what seem several simultaneously possible objects or trains of thought. Focalization, concentration of consciousness are of its essence. It implies withdrawal from some things in order to deal effectively with others.

(James, 1893, pp. 403–404)

In this section we will examine some of the processes by which we manage this selection.

Theories of attention

The cocktail party. Suppose you were at that party, talking to one of the other guests. To what extent would you be able to simultaneously monitor other conversations going on around you? You could do so in a trivial sense simply by switching attention – listening to one conversation for a few seconds, then listening to another, and so on – but the question of interest here is to what extent could you simultaneously take in information from two or more conversations?

To answer this question, Cherry (1953) devised a procedure called **dichotic listening**. Participants wore headphones, and different messages were played in each ear. In one ear, for example, they might hear a speaker talking about Abe Lincoln, while in the other ear, the speaker discussed birds. Cherry wanted participants to concentrate fully on one message, so that he could then measure how much information they simultaneously absorbed from the other ear. To ensure full concentration on the first ear, he asked participants to repeat out loud the words they heard in that ear as quickly as they could, a technique called **shadowing**. (The repeated words follow the original message after a short delay, in much the same way that our shadows follow us as we walk.) If participants could repeat the message accurately, this provided evidence that they were maintaining attention to that ear.

When the session was over, Cherry asked participants what they could remember about the message in their second ear. The answer proved to be very, very little. Participants knew whether they had heard speech (in some conditions, a pure tone was played instead), and they could also say whether the speaker was male or

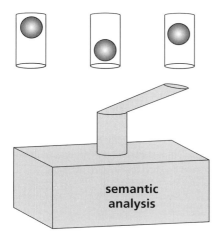

Figure 9.10 A simplified version of Broadbent's filter theory. Sensory input is organized into channels, and each stimulus can be thought of as a ball falling through a tube (channel). All stimuli receive initial processing, but the filter allows the content of only one channel to proceed to more thorough analysis. Stimuli not allowed through the filter decay and are lost.

female. Beyond these relatively simple, physical characteristics of the message, however, they could report little. They could not repeat any of the words, nor even report what language they were in, English or German. In a subsequent experiment by Moray (1959), one word was repeated 35 times in the second ear, but participants were still unable to report what it had been. (See also Wood and Cowan, 1995.)

Filter theories

To explain these results, an English psychologist, Donald Broadbent, proposed what he called a filter theory of attention. Broadbent (1958) suggested that incoming sensory stimulation is organized into channels – as a simple example, visual stimuli might be transmitted along one channel and auditory stimuli along another. He suggested that the stimuli in each channel receive only preliminary processing to determine their physical characteristics. In the case of auditory signals, for example, you would analyze them only enough to establish whether they involved human speech, and, if so, whether the speaker was male or female. The output of this analysis would then be fed into a filter, which would select whatever channel seemed to have the most promising content. This information would be allowed through the filter to receive further processing – in the case of speech, to determine what words these sounds represented. Information on the other channels would not be allowed through and would quickly decay and be lost (Figure 9.10). According to Broadbent's model, therefore, all sensory information receives preliminary

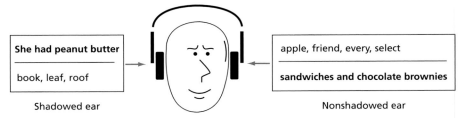

Figure 9.11 Treisman's (1960) procedure. Different messages were presented to the two ears, and participants tried to shadow one of them. At some points, a message that started in one ear was switched to the other ear; the point of switching is indicated by the horizontal dividing line in each message.

processing, but only information in one channel is allowed through the filter for more intensive analysis.

This model neatly accounts for the results of Cherry's experiment and similar studies. Other evidence, however, quickly posed serious problems for the model. In one of Moray's conditions, for example, one of the words presented to the second ear was the participant's name, and many participants did later report having heard it. This is clearly adaptive – it is important that we not be so focused on one task that we cannot detect important events such as someone calling our name – but from the perspective of Broadbent's filter theory, it is deeply puzzling. If information from the second ear is not allowed through the filter, how could participants have known that their names had been presented?

Treisman (1960) reported similar findings. In her study, participants shadowed a coherent story presented to one ear, while a string of largely unrelated words were presented to the other ear. At some points, however, the two messages were switched, so that a sentence that started in one ear was completed in the other ear (Figure 9.11). According to Broadbent's model, participants should have continued to shadow the words presented to the first ear – because the message presented to the second ear was blocked by the filter, participants would have had no way of knowing that the content in that ear was now relevant.

In fact, however, participants did switch to shadowing the second ear when the message was switched there. Here, as in Moray's experiment, the strong implication is that participants were aware of the content of the second message, so that when relevant material was presented, they would switch their attention appropriately. They could only have done this if they had been analyzing the meaning of the messages in both ears, not just in one (see also MacKay, 1973).

By the early 1960s, therefore, the evidence concerning attention had become somewhat confusing. All sides agreed that we cannot fully process all the information reaching our senses, but it was far from clear where in the processing system selection occurred. According to Broadbent, filtering occurred early in processing, before participants had analyzed the meaning of any words they heard. The evidence from Moray and Treisman, on the other hand, suggested that filtering did not occur until a later stage, after at least some semantic analysis had been completed.

Pool-of-resources theories

One framework for reconciling this conflicting evidence was suggested by Kahneman (1973). Instead of thinking of attention as a fixed filter, he suggested that we view it more as a pool of resources that can be allocated flexibly across competing tasks. If two tasks are difficult, so that each requires considerable attention, we might be able to perform only one at a time. If the tasks are easy, on the other hand, then we might be able to perform them simultaneously. The outcome, in other words, depends on how difficult each task is, and thus how much attention it requires from the available pool.

One real-life example concerns the ability of drivers to converse with passengers while driving. If the drivers are experienced, this normally is not difficult: The reason is that both activities are well practiced, and so require relatively little attention. If a car in front of a driver suddenly swerved, however, then the driver would have to concentrate intensely on taking evasive action, and conversation would become impossible. In contrast to Broadbent's filter model, which assumes that we can only carry out one task at a time, Kahneman's pool-of-resources model allows for the possibility of performing several tasks simultaneously, as long as the attention required by each task is modest, and thus the total pool of resources is not exhausted.

Johnston and Heinz (1978) extended Kahneman's theory, and also provided a clever way of testing it. Their version of the theory built on existing evidence that perception is a sequential process. In our *cat* example, we saw that we start by analyzing the physical properties of the stimulus (what features are present), and then move on to interpreting these features (what word is formed by the letters, and what does the word mean). Figuring out the meaning of a word thus requires more processing than simply determining its physical properties. Johnston and Heinz therefore proposed that a task that required semantic analysis would leave less processing capacity available for carrying out other tasks.

To test their theory, they asked one group of participants to listen to a tape recording of a male and a female simultaneously reading two lists of words. One speaker read a list of cities, the other a list of occupations, and the participants were instructed to shadow one of the lists by repeating the words. Because the lists were read by different voices, this task was expected to be relatively easy – to decide which words to repeat, all the listeners had to do was to focus on the voice that was reading them.

A second group performed a similar task, except that for this group both lists were read by the *same* voice. In this condition there were no simple physical cues to indicate which words should be repeated, so the listeners would have to analyze the *meaning* of the words to decide which ones to repeat. As analyzing meaning requires more processing than simply detecting whether the speaker is male or female, Johnston and Heinze predicted that shadowing would now require more attention, leaving less for other tasks.

To find out, they asked both groups to carry out a second task at the same time as shadowing the words. In this subsidiary task a light occasionally appeared, and participants had to push a button as fast as they could whenever the light was presented. If a semantic analysis requires more attention than distinguishing voices, participants in the second group should have had less attention available for detecting the light and thus should have responded more slowly. This is what Johnston and Heinz found. The average response latency for the first group was 433 msec, whereas the average latency for the second group was 482 msec. Even more strikingly, the groups also differed in how well they executed the shadowing task: Participants in the first group made errors in repeating 5% of the words, whereas those in the second group made errors on 21%. As predicted by a pool-of-resources model, it appears that we can potentially perform more than one task at a time, but the more attention is required for one of these tasks, the less will be available for the others. (See also Lavie, 2005.)

Attention as a spotlight

A useful metaphor for thinking about attention is as a spotlight in a theatre. In Broadbent's original conception, there was just one spotlight: We could pay attention (shine our spotlight) on one part of the stage, but everything else would remain shrouded in semi-darkness. To accommodate the evidence for attention as a pool of resources that can be allocated flexibly, we can instead think of a theatre with many spotlights, each capable of illuminating a different part of the stage. All of these spotlights, however, are connected to a single electric generator, so that the total amount of light available is fixed. We could, if we wanted, illuminate several areas of the stage simultaneously, but because the total amount of light available is fixed, providing more light to some areas would necessarily mean less light for others. In the Johnson and Heinz study, participants were able to carry out two tasks at the same time, but the more attention they devoted to the words, the harder they found it to detect the light. Similarly in the Cherry study, because the shadowing task was very demanding, there was little attention left for other tasks, and only the most salient stimuli – a person's name – would attract attention.

One study that fits nicely with the spotlight metaphor – indeed, it inspired it – was reported by Posner, Snyder, and Davidson (1980). To understand their study, consider the properties of spotlights. One such property is that a spotlight is heavy, and thus it takes time to shift its beam from one part of a stage to another. If a stagehand knows in advance where an actor will appear, however, the spotlight can be pointed at that spot in advance, and thus turned on instantly when it is needed. The question Posner and his colleagues asked was whether we can orient our mental spotlight in a similar way, so that when we know beforehand where an event is going to occur we can mentally focus on that place and thus detect the event more quickly.

Posner and his colleagues tested this prediction by asking participants to look at a computer screen and focus on a fixation point at its center. Following a warning stimulus, a letter appeared to either the left or the right of the fixation point, and they were to press a button as soon as they saw it. Crucially, on some trials the warning stimulus was an arrow that pointed to the side where the letter would appear. If attention functions as a spotlight, the arrow should have allowed participants to focus on where the letter would appear and thus respond faster, and that is what happened: Reaction times were significantly faster on trials in which participants knew where the letter would appear. Moreover, a subsequent study by Lu and Dosher (1998) showed that participants were also better at detecting the properties of the stimulus when it did appear. The stimulus they used was a vertical pattern tilted slightly to either left or right, and participants had to indicate the direction of tilt. Because the tilt was small and the pattern was presented only very briefly, the task was difficult, but participants who knew where the pattern would appear proved to be better at it. As a spotlight analogy would suggest, knowing where a stimulus will appear allows us to prepare for it and thus process its features more effectively.[2]

Other predictions from the spotlight metaphor have also been tested, and many have been confirmed. Some, however, have not fared so well. One example concerns the focus of attention. In the case of vision, the spotlight metaphor implies that attention is focused on particular places in the environment, so that we see whatever is located at that position, but in some situations we seem to focus on *objects* rather than places. To understand this distinction, imagine that a picture of a man standing next to a woman was briefly flashed on a screen in front of you. If you focused on the man's face, you would be more likely to notice a watch

---

[2] You may have noticed a possible flaw in this analysis. Perhaps when a warning stimulus was provided participants simply redirected their gaze from the fixation point to the spot where the test stimulus would appear – if so, there would be no need to invoke a mental spotlight; the effects could all be explained in terms of eye movement. Posner and other researchers were aware of this possibility and took steps to eliminate it. In Lu and Dosher's study, for example, the test stimulus followed the warning stimulus so quickly that there wasn't enough time for eye movement. The observed effects really were due to mental preparation, not physical – our brains can process sensory information more efficiently when we are prepared for its arrival.

that he was wearing than a necklace worn by the woman next to him, even if the necklace was actually closer to the man's face. It appears that we sometimes focus on objects rather than places, and that this focus increases attention to all aspects of the object (O'Craven, Downing, and Kanwisher, 1999). Problems such as this mean that the analogy between attention and a spotlight should not be pushed too far, but the spotlight metaphor does still provide a useful way of thinking about attention. (For a review of the similarities and differences, see Cave and Bichot, 1999.)

The effects of practice

We've seen that activities can vary in how much attention they require – deciding whether two voices are the same, for example, is less demanding than figuring out what they are saying. How much attention any task requires, however, depends in part on how much experience we have had with performing it. As we saw in Chapter 7, when a task is practiced extensively – driving a car is the classic example – it becomes increasingly automatic, and thus requires less attention. Shiffrin and Schneider codified this insight with their distinction between *controlled processes*, which require attention for their execution, and *automatic processes*, which don't. Because automatic processes don't require attention, many can be performed simultaneously without interfering with each other.

Automatization

The process by which a controlled process in converted into an automatic process through practice is known as automatization. One example that we have all experienced is learning to read. At first, children find it very difficult to learn to read the squiggles on a page that we call letters. After extensive practice, the process becomes increasingly automatic, until eventually they can instantly recognize these patterns as words.

This automatization of reading not only allows us to read faster, it also helps us to remember what we read. One example comes from research on memory span, which is measured by our ability to repeat a sequence of items after hearing them just once.

As we saw earlier, most people have a memory span of around 7 items, and few can remember more than 9. To experience this for yourself, try repeating the following sequence after reading it just once: *nscitonutoti*. And now try the following: *constitution*. It seems a fairly safe bet that you were able to remember many more letters in the second sequence – in fact, all of them, even though the letters in the two sequences were the same. The reason is that, with practice, reading the letters of a word becomes automatic – instead of having to activate 14

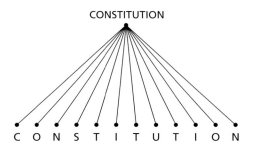

Figure 9.12 Chunking. When we first learn to read, each letter of a word activates its own representation. With practice, we learn to associate all these letter nodes with a single, higher-level node that represents the entire word. As a result, we only have to rehearse a single node when the word is presented in tasks such as memory span.

separate nodes in your brain to represent the letters in constitution, you learn to represent this combination by a single node (see Figure 9.12).

This process of combining separate units into a single representation is called **chunking**, and the suggestion is that eventually an entire word becomes a unit in the same way that a single letter was initially. One prediction that follows from this analysis is that we should be able to remember 7 words just about as easily as 7 letters, and this is largely the case: The average memory span for words is approximately 5. In the present context, the important point is that, with practice, we learn to respond to the letters of a word by automatically activating the word's representation in the brain.

Once a stimulus comes to elicit a response automatically, it can be difficult for us to override this and prevent the response occurring. A classic example is the **Stroop effect**, named after John Stroop, who first discovered it. In a typical experiment, participants are asked to read words printed in different colors; their task is to name the color of each word as quickly as they can. If you were shown the word BOOK printed in red ink, for example, you would be able to name the color as red very quickly. If you were shown the word BLUE printed in red ink, on the other hand, you would found it much harder, and take far longer to respond. Although you would still see the color clearly, reading the word BLUE would elicit a strong tendency to say blue, a tendency that you would have to suppress before you could finally give the correct response. Once a response becomes automatic, it can be difficult to suppress. (See also Shiffrin and Schneider, 1977; MacLeod, 1991.)

Applications

With sufficient practice, people are capable of quite remarkable feats of automatization. In a study by Spelke, Hirst, and Neisser (1976), for example, participants were asked to read a story while writing down a list of words that were being dictated to them. As you can imagine, performance was initially very poor. After 85 sessions of practice, however, participants were able to combine the two tasks effortlessly: Their scores when they performed the tasks concurrently were as good as when they performed them separately.

Chase and Ericsson (1982) reported an even more remarkable illustration of the effects of practice. The single participant in this study, identified as SF, initially had a normal memory span, about 7 digits. With practice, however, his span began to increase – at first to 8, then to 10, and so on. Eventually, after a massive 200 practice sessions spread over 2 years, his digit span had increased to more than 80. Because this feat is so extraordinary, it is perhaps worth spelling it out: After listening to a sequence of 80 digits presented rapidly just once, he could recall the entire sequence perfectly.

You might think that this improvement was due to a general increase in his memory capacity, but this proved not to be the case: If tested on material other than digits, his memory span was exactly the same as it had been at the outset. Instead, his improvement was due to chunking. SF was a long-distance runner, and as he practiced the digit task he hit upon the strategy of recoding number sequences into running times. If presented with the sequence 3492, for example, he might recode it as 3:49.2, a near record for the mile. With practice, these numerical sequences became chunks for SF, in the same way that letters of a word become chunks for the rest of us. Similar effects of automatization underlie many forms of skilled behavior, including the ability of chess masters to remember complex chess positions (a skill that enables some masters to simultaneously play more than 30 opponents while blindfolded), and the ability of skilled waiters to remember 20 complete orders, down to such details as the salad dressing and whether the steak should be well done. (See Ericsson and Kintsch, 1995, for a review of the evidence, together with a theory of how such skills are acquired.)

Change blindness

We will conclude our survey of attention by discussing evidence that we take in much less information about the world than we realize, even about objects that do fall within the beam of our attentional spotlight. One striking example comes from research on **change blindness**, a phenomenon in which observers fail to notice seemingly obvious changes in a scene. In a now-classic study reported by Simons and Levin (1998), one of the experimenters stopped people on a college campus and asked them for directions. During the conversation, two confederates of the experimenter walked between them while carrying a large door. During the few seconds in which the first experimenter was obscured, another experimenter

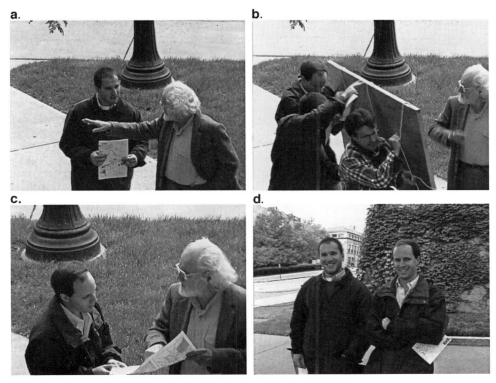

Figure 9.13 Change blindness. Frames from a video made during the Simons and Levin (1998) experiment. (a) The first experimenter asks a passer-by for directions. (b) Two men carrying a door walk between them. (c) The second experimenter continues the conversation. (d) The two experimenters, for comparison. (Simons and Levin, 1998.)

took his place, and the second experimenter then continued the conversation! (See Figure 9.13.) After a few minutes, the experimenter explained that this was actually a psychology experiment and asked whether the participant had noticed anything unusual around the time that the door passed. The remarkable result was that only about half of the participants had noticed the change in experimenters. (See also Simons and Rensink, 2005.)

On the surface, this finding is bizarre, but in a sense it only confirms what we have already seen in other settings. In discussing Sachs's (1967) experiment on memory for sentences, we noted that people generally do not retain verbatim copies of the sentences they have read in long-term memory. Instead, they extract the underlying ideas or *gist*, and it is this abstracted information that is retained. The Simons and Levin experiment suggests that something very similar happens with vision. Although we have the impression that we see the world in great

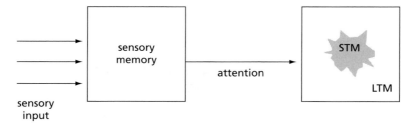

Figure 9.14 One possible integration of current theories of memory. Note that although attention has been shown as occurring between sensory memory and short-term memory, selection probably occurs at many points during processing. Also, the diagram does not include processes such as organization and rehearsal.

detail, in fact we see – and remember – only a small proportion of our sensory input, just enough to allow us to respond appropriately. When we encounter strangers, we don't need to remember every detail of their appearance, and the Simons and Levin experiment reveals in dramatic fashion how little we actually take in.

We've now traced the evolution of theories of attention from a filter that would allow only a small amount of sensory information to be fully processed, to a pool of resources that can be allocated flexibly. Because attention is now arguably one of the most investigated topics within cognitive psychology, our survey has had to be very brief, and we have focused on those aspects that seem particularly relevant to memory. If you'd like to know more about attention, more comprehensive reviews are available in Luck and Vecera (2002), Logan (2004), and Styles (2006).

Looking back over the material covered in this chapter, psychologists have clearly moved a long way from Ebbinghaus's original conception of memory as a single store, to a tripartite division into sensory memory, short-term memory, and long-term memory. (See Figure 9.14 for one view of how these components might be related.) Moreover, as we shall see in the next chapter, there are strong grounds for believing that long-term memory is further subdivided into multiple subsystems. This proliferation of memory systems can be confusing, but if you consider the complexity of the brain – billions of neurons carrying out a wide range of functions – it is not surprising that the brain contains multiple subsystems or modules to execute these functions. We might seem to remember our experiences almost effortlessly but this apparent ease is deceptive, as the formation of a memory depends on sophisticated systems for coding and analyzing sensory data. Memory is a bit like a swan seen gliding across a lake: seen from a distance, all effortless grace, but underneath the surface paddling away furiously. We will continue our exploration of the hidden processes involved in memory in

Chapter 10, where we will examine what happens to a code once it reaches long-term memory.

Summary

• Coding of sensory input begins with analysis of the features of objects. This bottom-up processing is supplemented by top-down processing in which our expectations about a forthcoming stimulus are used to help us analyze its features.

• To allow time for this processing, sensory input is held very briefly in sensory memory.

• Once an object has been recognized and assigned a code, that code is held in a short-term store, where it can receive the additional processing required to form a permanent memory.

• The existence of separate short- and long-term stores has been supported by research on amnesia: Some forms of brain damage selectively impair short-term memory, while others affect only long-term memory.

• Many theorists now view short-term memory as the set of items in the long-term store that are currently in an active state.

• The short-term store is not just where we hold incoming material from the senses; it is also where we hold information retrieved from long-term memory which we require for activities such as problem-solving. To reflect this larger role, short-term memory is now usually referred to as working memory.

• Baddeley has proposed that working memory has three components: the phono-logical loop, the visuo-spatial sketchpad, and the central executive.

• Processing of a word in working memory can vary in depth. The levels-of-processing hypothesis proposes that deeper and more elaborate processing leads to better memory.

• Consolidation theory suggests that the formation of a long-term memory depends on strengthening synaptic connections between neurons, a relatively brief process that is disrupted by brain damage. When we retrieve a memory, this may produce further consolidation.

• We cannot fully process all the stimuli that bombard our senses. Capacity theories of attention suggest that we have considerable flexibility in how we allocate processing capacity; attention is like a mental spotlight that can focus brightly on a narrow area, or more broadly but shallowly on a wider range of inputs.

• With practice, processes can become automatic, so that they no longer require attention.

- Another feature of attention is that we take in far less information than we normally realize; change blindness provides a particularly striking example.

Review questions

1 Define the following terms: *features, partial report procedure, icon.*

2 What are grandmother cells? Do they exist?

3 What is the difference between top-down and bottom-up processing? What evidence suggests that perception involves both?

4 How does Sperling's research suggest the existence of a temporary visual store?

5 How has research on amnesia supported the claim that there are separate short-term and long-term memory stores?

6 Atkinson and Shiffrin viewed short-term and long-term stores as separate systems, but some theorists now view short-term memory simply as the nodes in the long-term store that are currently active. How did research on KF contribute to this altered view?

7 How did Baddeley and Hitch's (1974) research suggest that we need to view STM as being composed of separate subsystems? According to Baddeley, what are the three main subsystems?

8 What evidence points to the existence of a phonological loop?

9 What is the central executive? What is the potential danger in postulating such concepts?

10 What evidence suggests that the formation of a long-term memory requires more than just rehearsal? How did Craik and Lockhart account for this evidence?

11 What is the difference between depth of processing and elaboration? What evidence suggests that elaboration is important in helping us to remember what we read?

12 What is consolidation theory? What evidence suggests that it needs to be modified?

13 How did early research on dichotic listening provide the basis for Broadbent's filter theory? How did subsequent research on dichotic listening undermine this theory?

14 How do capacity theories of attention differ from filter theories? What evidence suggests that the more attention is allocated to one task, the less is available for other tasks?

15 In what respects is attention analogous to a spotlight?

16 When we focus our attention on something, we have the impression that we perceive it in considerable detail. How has research on change blindness challenged this assumption?

17 How are the concepts of chunking and automatization related?

10 Long-term memory

CONTENTS

In Chapter 9, we traced the coding of a word from its detection by our senses to its processing in sensory and then working memory. In this chapter, we'll complete our tracking of the word's journey by looking at what happens to information about a word once it reaches long-term memory.

Memory systems

At roughly the same time as Baddeley and his colleagues were suggesting that short-term memories are formed in separate subsystems, evidence was mounting that the same is true of long-term memories. The nature of the systems in long-term memory, however, was a matter of considerable theoretical dispute. You can obtain a sense of how widely the theories differed if we simply list some of the terms that theorists have used to describe these systems: *conscious* and *unconscious memory* (Kelley and Lindsay, 1996), *implicit* and *explicit memory* (Graf and Schacter, 1985), *procedural* and *declarative memory* (Squire, 1987), *episodic* and *semantic memory* (Tulving, 1972, 2001), and *perceptual* and *conceptual processing* (Roediger and McDermott, 1993; Schacter and Tulving, 1994). Despite this dazzling – or daunting – proliferation of explanations, the differences between

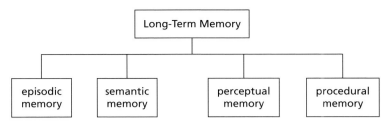

Figure 10.1 Proposed systems of long-term memory.

the theories have narrowed over time, to the point where the two most influential accounts – those of Schacter and Tulving (1994) and Squire (2004, 2009) – are almost identical, differing more in terminology than in basic assumptions.

Our approach in this chapter will be based on a blend of these two accounts, illustrated in Figure 10.1. We will be assuming that long-term memory is composed of four main subsystems, which we will be labeling *episodic memory*, *semantic memory*, *perceptual memory*, and *procedural memory*. Although we will be looking at each in detail as the chapter unfolds, it might be helpful to define them briefly at the outset. *Episodic memory* refers to memories for personal experiences (for example, what you ate for breakfast this morning), while *semantic memory* refers to memories for facts (Paris is the capital of France). *Perceptual memory* refers to improvement in our ability to process sensory input with experience – the more we are exposed to an object, the better our brains become at recognizing it quickly. And finally, *procedural memory* refers to changes that occur on the output side – once having recognized a stimulus, we become faster at deciding how to respond and then in initiating that response. So, memory for personal experiences and facts, for stimuli and responses. It could be that all of these different kinds of memories are just stored together in a great big jumble in long-term memory, but as we shall see there is reason to think that each is processed and stored in a different way.

Episodic and semantic memory

When we talk about memory, we usually have in mind recalling something that happened to us at a particular moment in time. We remember what someone said to us in the morning, where we left our keys, and so on. And, when the memory comes back to us, it usually includes a sense of when and where the event happened. ("I was about to leave the house, and I put my keys down on the table while I answered the phone.") Tulving (1972) called this kind of memory **episodic memory** because it involves remembering a particular moment or episode in our lives.

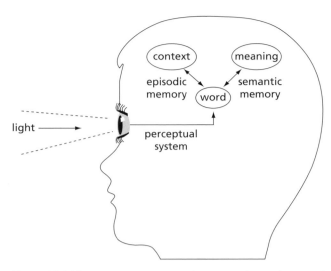

Figure 10.2 Three memory systems. When we read a word, processing in the perceptual system would eventually result in activation of a node in the brain representing that word. Activation might then spread to nodes representing the word's meaning or its context. If the word and its context became associated, this would provide the basis for an episodic memory; if the word became associated with other information already in semantic memory, this would provide the basis for a new semantic memory.

Tulving went on to distinguish episodic memory from what he called **semantic memory**. The latter refers to memories for facts or other kinds of knowledge. Suppose, for example, that while you were in high school you learned that the tongue of a blue whale weighs more than a full-grown elephant. You might still recall this remarkable fact years later (semantic memory), even though you could no longer recall where or when you had learned it (episodic memory). Thus, whereas episodic memories are tied to particular times and places, semantic memories involve more general kinds of knowledge that you just "know."

Two systems

One way of thinking about the relationship between these two kinds of memory is illustrated in Figure 10.2. If someone read the word *cat* in a text, light reflected from the page would trigger a sequence of perceptual processing stages, culminating in activation of the node in the brain that represents this word (see Chapter 9). Activation of the *cat* node would effectively mean that the reader had recognized the word, and this recognition could in turn trigger other processes, depending on the reader's goals at the time. One possibility is that the reader would think about the word's meaning – that is, activation of the *cat* node would spread to the regions of semantic memory that hold information about cats. Or perhaps the reader would focus on the relationship between the word and the context in which it was encountered – for example, the room in which she was sitting.

Either way, we will assume that one result would be a strengthening of neural connections within the brain. If activation of the *cat* node were accompanied by activation of nodes representing the word's context, for example, then the connections between these nodes would be strengthened. As discussed in Chapter 9, this linkage between a word and its context is what makes it possible for us to later retrieve the word: When we think of the context, it reminds us of the events with which it is associated. ("What was the word that I read while sitting in this chair 10 minutes ago? Oh yes, *cat*.") Conversely, if a word or other experience is not linked to a context, we have no way of knowing when we encountered it. The word might seem familiar, but we would have no basis for judging whether this was because we read it minutes or days earlier.

Translated into Tulving's terms, an association between an event and its context provides the basis for episodic memory. If we later reactivate the event together with its context, we effectively re-create the moment when we originally experienced them.

In a similar fashion, if activation of a word's representation led to activation of its meaning, this might lead to the formation of new connections within semantic memory. If you read the sentence "Blue whales have massive tongues," activating the meaning of the words would allow the formation of new links between them, and this would effectively store the new information in semantic memory. (We will examine how this happens in more detail in the next section.)

Are they really different?

Tulving believed that episodic and semantic memories are created in separate systems (see also Schacter and Tulving, 1994; Tulving, 2002). Other theorists, however, were not convinced. Episodic and semantic memories undoubtedly involve different kinds of information, but this does not necessarily mean that these memories are processed and stored in different systems (Roediger, 1990, 1993). After all, we also learn different facts in history and geography – does this mean that there are separate history and geography systems in our brains? Or that, within history, we have separate systems for processing European and American history? Theorists were worried by the possibility of an endless proliferation of memory systems based on nothing more than differences in the content of different memories.

At the heart of this dispute lay the question of what is meant by a memory system. In biology, the term *system* implies a physical structure that carries out a set of processes devoted to a single end. The digestive system, for example, is centered on the stomach and involves the secretion of gastric acids to digest food, whereas the respiratory system is centered in the lungs and involves the extraction of oxygen from the air. These systems are clearly different, and Tulving believed that episodic and semantic memories differ in similarly fundamental ways. An alternative interpretation is that episodic and semantic memories are simply different kinds of information stored within the same system. In this view, the processing of episodic and semantic information is analogous to the digestion of bananas and hamburgers within the stomach; the content might be different, but the digestive processes that operate on them are fundamentally the same.

So, are episodic and semantic memories the products of a single system or of two separate systems? One way to resolve this issue would be to determine where in the brain these memories are formed. If they were formed in different regions, this would support the claim that they are produced by different systems.

Evidence that episodic and semantic memories are indeed formed in different areas has come from studies of *amnesia*, in which individuals have problems in storing or retrieving information, usually as a result of brain damage. Rosenbaum *et al.* (2005) described one such patient identified as K.C. K.C.'s brain was seriously damaged in a motorcycle accident, and this led to a complete loss of episodic memory – he could not remember a single personal experience he had ever had. For example, his brother, with whom he had been very close, had died several years earlier, but K.C. had no memory of being told of his death. Similarly, he had no memory of the events of 9/11; every time he is told, he reacts with shocked horror. Remarkably, however, his semantic memory was virtually intact. Tulving (2002) reported that K.C.'s memory for subjects such as history and geography was normal, and he even could explain the geological distinction between stalactites and stalagmites! The damage to his brain had obliterated his memory for personal experiences, but left his memory for facts largely unaffected.

Nor was K.C.'s case unique. Spiers, Maguire, and Burgess (2001) reviewed 147 cases of amnesia involving damage to an area of the brain known as the *hippocampus*. In almost every single one there was substantial, often dramatic loss of episodic memory. The effects on semantic memory, on the other hand, were more variable and generally smaller. Damage to the hippocampus seemed to affect episodic memory far more than semantic memory.

This is an example of what psychologists call a **dissociation**, a situation in which a variable has a strong effect on one aspect of behavior but little or no effect on another, seemingly similar aspect. When two behaviors are separated or dissociated in this way, it raises the possibility that they are products of different processes – were they products of the same process, we would expect any damage to this process to affect both equally. (For a discussion of possible pitfalls in applying this logic, see Schacter and Tulving, 1994.)

Even more dramatic evidence for a dissociation between episodic and semantic memory comes from a study by Fareneh Vargha-Khadem and her colleagues (1997). Two of the participants in this study suffered hippocampal damage at an early age – one, Beth, was injured at birth, and the other, Jon, at the age of 4. As a result, both had great difficulty in remembering their experiences – they could not recall telephone conversations, holidays, and so on. And yet, despite this apparent inability to store any of their experiences in memory, both children acquired language normally and performed well in school. (For a similar case, see Verfaellie, Koseff, and Alexander, 2000.)

Intuitively, this result is very hard to understand – if the children were unable to remember having a lesson at school, how could they possibly remember anything taught during that lesson? The result begins to make sense, though, if interpreted through the model of episodic memory presented earlier, summarized in Figure 10.2. We suggested that when a word such as *cat* is presented, it can enter into two kinds of associations. In one, it becomes associated with the contextual cues present at the time (in this case, things like the appearance of the teacher and the room); in the other, it becomes associated with other information previously stored in semantic memory. The first process results in the formation of an episodic memory, containing information about when and where the word was heard; the second results in the storage of new factual information in semantic memory. To explain Beth's and Jon's experiences, all we need to do is add the assumption that the hippocampus is the area of the brain where we form associations between events and their contexts, a process that cognitive psychologists call *binding*. When the hippocampus was damaged, Beth and Jon lost the ability to associate events with their contexts, and thus to form episodic memories. Their ability to form associations within semantic memory, however, remained intact, so that they could still learn new facts. Put another way, they were still able to acquire semantic information; they had simply lost the ability to remember the context in which they encountered that information.

Summarizing the material in this section, we can say that there is considerable evidence that damage to the hippocampus affects episodic memory more than semantic memory, and this supports Tulving's view that these memories are formed in different systems. (See also Murphy *et al.*, 2008; Knight and O'Hagan, 2009.) However, not all amnesics show the kinds of dissociation between episodic and semantic memory that we have been discussing, and even where they do, it is possible to explain these dissociations without assuming that they are products of different systems (for example, Toth and Hunt, 1999; Weldon, 1999; Burianova, McIntosh, and Grady, 2010). We will discuss why such evidence can be difficult to interpret shortly, in the section on procedural issues; for now, we will summarize our discussion by saying that there are persuasive grounds for thinking that episodic and semantic memories are products of different systems, but the evidence is not yet conclusive. (For a more thorough analysis of the criteria that must be satisfied before postulating a memory system, see Schacter and Tulving, 1994.)

Implicit memory

Episodic and semantic memories can be consciously accessed – we can consciously remember what we ate for breakfast or the capital of France. Also, we can describe the contents of these memories verbally, and for this reason they are sometimes referred to as **explicit** or **declarative memories**. Other memories, though, can affect our behavior without being brought back into consciousness. Such memories are referred to as *unconscious* or **implicit memories** – they operate at an entirely unconscious level, affecting us even though we are not aware of their existence. We have already encountered one example in Chapter 4, where we discussed a woman who had been raped but had no conscious memory of the incident. When she was taken back to the scene of the crime, though, she became extremely upset. She had no conscious memory of the rape, but it was clearly affecting her (Christianson and Nilsson, 1989).

Such behavior is perplexing: If someone doesn't remember an experience, how could it affect her behavior? We know that memories can be held in storage without our being able to access them, but how could they influence us while they remain in this unconscious state? In this section, we will consider two kinds of unconscious memories, *procedural memories* and *perceptual memories*, and try to understand the processes involved.

Procedural memory

In 1911, a Swiss psychiatrist named Edouard Claparède observed that some patients with amnesia remained capable of certain kinds of learning. In one test, he concealed a pin in his hand as he shook hands with one of his female patients, so that she experienced a sharp prick. The next morning the woman refused to shake hands with him, even though she could not remember their previous encounter (Claparède, 1911).

Some 50 years later when psychologists studied HM, they observed a similar phenomenon. As we saw in Chapter 9, HM was almost totally incapable of consciously recalling his experiences, but he too was found to perform normally on some learning tasks. In one study by Milner (1962), HM was given training on a mirror-drawing task that involved tracing a pattern with a pencil. He could see the pattern only through a mirror suspended above it, and this made the task quite difficult – if the line appeared to slant upwards, for example, he needed to move his pencil downward. Every time HM was tested, he stated that he could not remember having done the task before, but despite this, his performance improved dramatically. He clearly had retained some record of previous sessions, even though he had no memory of having participated in them. Similar results were reported in studies of other amnesics, showing that they were capable of improvement on a wide range of learning tasks, from classical conditioning to solving jigsaw puzzles (Weiskrantz and Warrington, 1979; Spiers *et al.*, 2001).

A common characteristic of these tasks is that improvement does not require conscious recall of prior experiences; it is possible to improve simply by forming an association between a stimulus and a response. In recognition of this characteristic, Winograd (1975) introduced the term *procedural learning* to describe such learning; the suggestion is that these tasks involve learning procedures for carrying out a response, rather than forming conscious memories of the kind that can be expressed in words. Other examples of procedural learning include learning to type and to drive a car.

We don't normally think of skills such as typing as involving memory, but clearly, we must store information about our experiences if we are to improve. The term **procedural memory** has been used to describe such memories. Procedural memory is often distinguished from episodic memory on the basis that procedural memory involves knowing *how* to do something, whereas episodic memory involves knowing *that* something happened. If you remembered that you had a driving lesson yesterday, that would be an example of episodic memory; if, as a result, you became a better driver, that would be an example of procedural memory. The evidence that amnesics with poor episodic memories often have normal procedural memories is another example of a dissociation, and it again suggests that these memories are formed in different systems.

Perceptual memory

Procedural memory involves an improvement in how we overtly respond to a stimulus or situation, as in driving a car. In addition, there is evidence that with practice we can also become better at recognizing the stimulus, an effect that we will refer to as a **perceptual memory**. (Schacter and Tulving [1994] called the underlying system the *perceptual representation system*.)

In one of the first studies to show this improvement, Howes and Solomon (1951) used a device called a tachistoscope to present words very briefly. By varying the length of the presentation, they could assess how long a word had to be presented before participants could reliably recognize it. They found that the more often a word appeared in print in sources such as books and newspapers, the faster participants were able to recognize it. In a similar study by Jacoby and Dallas (1981), words were presented very briefly, for 35 ms, and each presentation was followed by a pattern mask – in this case, a row of asterisks. This mask stopped further processing of the words at the retina, and by reducing the time available for processing made it harder for the participants to recognize the words. They found that common words were recognized twice as often as uncommon words – 65% of the common words were recognized as against only 33% of the uncommon words.

These findings suggest that the more experience we have with a word or other stimulus, the better we become at processing it. In our discussion of "grandmother cells" in Chapter 9, we discussed how recognition of a visual stimulus is the result of transmission of electrical signals between a series of neurons, starting at the eye and eventually reaching the node in the cortex that represents the object; it is activation of this cortical representation that leads to the feeling of recognition. With practice, the connections between these neurons apparently become stronger, leading to faster transmission of the signals and thus more rapid recognition.

The perceptual memories we have described so far have involved permanent changes in our ability to process sensory information. In addition to these long-term changes, cognitive psychologists have found that presentation of a stimulus can cause a *temporary* improvement in processing. In one of the experiments in the Jacoby and Dallas study participants were given a list of words to read. Then, in a second phase, they were given a word recognition test using the procedure already described – each word presented very briefly and followed by a pattern mask. As we've seen, this procedure makes it difficult to recognize the words, and on average only 65% of the words were recognized. If the test word had appeared on the list presented earlier, however, then the rate of recognition improved to around 80%. Earlier exposure to the words, in other words, made it easier to recognize them, a phenomenon known as **repetition priming**. (See Kristjansson and Campana, 2010, for a review.)

Results like these make it clear that exposure to a stimulus can change how we process it, and this in turn means that our brains must have kept some kind of record or memory of the experience. This brings us to the question of why we should consider perceptual memories as the product of a separate memory system. The answer, once again, is dissociation – some variables affect perceptual memories differently than they do episodic and semantic memories.

A nice example comes from a study by Graf, Squire, and Mandler (1984). Its purpose was to assess the effects of anterograde amnesia by comparing the performance of amnesics with normal controls. Both groups were shown a list of words and then given a memory test. For one group, this was a *cued-recall* test in which they were given a clue in the form of the first letters of each word and then asked to recall the whole word. One of the words on the list, for example, was *strap*, and on the cued-recall test participants were shown STR__. (Note that this stem could be completed by many other words such as *strip* and *stroke*. If participants didn't remember the original words, the chances of producing the correct word by guessing were thus low.) A second group was given a *word-stem completion* test. Participants were shown the same stems as the first group, but instead of being asked to recall the word shown earlier they were simply asked to respond with the first word that came to mind.

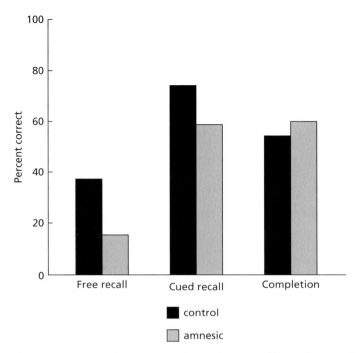

Figure 10.3 Memory in amnesics and normal control subjects. The control subjects did much better on free-recall and cued-recall tests, but the amnesics did better on a word-completion task. (Adapted from Graf, Squire, and Mandler, 1984.)

According to the analysis of priming presented earlier, when participants read a word in the first phase, this should have activated or primed its representation in their memory. When they read the word *strap*, for example, this would have activated the node representing *strap*. If this node was still in an excited state when the word or a fragment of the word was encountered again, then the new input would combine with the existing level of activation, making it more likely that participants would think of *strap*. When asked to complete the stem, in other words, participants should have been more likely to do so using words that they had seen previously.

The results are shown in Figure 10.3. As we would expect from other research on amnesia, the amnesic group were worse than the control group when asked to recall the words. On the word-stem completion test, however, the amnesics not only performed as well as the normals, if anything they performed better! This difference in performance on the two tests is particularly striking given that the stimuli presented in the tests were identical. Both groups, for example, were shown the letters STR; the only difference was in the instructions, whether they were asked to deliberately recall an earlier word or just respond with the first word that popped into their heads. We thus have a paradoxical situation in which participants who deliberately tried to remember a word had difficulty doing so, and yet they retrieved the word effortlessly if they simply said the first word that came to mind!

Recall and word-stem completion are examples of **explicit** and **implicit tests of memory** (Graf and Schacter, 1985). In an explicit test, participants are explicitly asked to retrieve information about an earlier event. ("Was this word on the list you saw earlier?") In an implicit test, on the other hand, memory is measured only indirectly. Participants are not asked to remember anything – indeed, the test is presented as if it has nothing to do with memory, as in word-stem completion where participants are simply asked to think of a word. The results of the Graf *et al.* study – soon confirmed in other experiments with both amnesics and normals – showed that performance on explicit and implicit tests of memory is often unrelated – people can do well on one and yet poorly on the other (see Roediger and McDermott, 1993, for a review).

On the surface, this dissociation is puzzling: If someone has no memory of seeing the word *strap*, why should they think of this word when shown the first few letters? Again, however, this dissociation becomes understandable if we assume that implicit and explicit memories are produced by different systems. In the case of perceptual memories, we have suggested that they are the result of improved processing in the perceptual system, so that detection of a word at the retina is more likely to activate its representation in the cortex. Episodic memories, on the other hand, are the product of processing in the hippocampus that associates words with their contexts. Damage to the hippocampus thus interferes with the formation of episodic memories, involving context, but not the formation of perceptual memories.

In summary, the reason that amnesics do better on word-completion tests than on recall tests could be that the brain has separate systems for processing perceptual and episodic memories. When amnesics read a word during the study phase, they would have processed the word normally in their perceptual systems, and the resulting perceptual memory would have made it more likely that they would think of the word if shown some of its letters. Once the cortical representation of the word was activated, however, they would have had difficulty in associating the word with its context. If they later tried to recall the word, thinking of the context would not activate the word's representation, and the retrieval search would fail. (For related proposals, see Roediger, 1990, and Schacter, 1994.)

Unconscious influences

The evidence we have reviewed shows that previous experiences can sometimes influence us even when we have no conscious memory of their occurrence. This has potentially far-reaching implications, and in this section we will consider two examples, involving prejudice and attraction.

Prejudice

Consider people's attitudes toward cats. During our lives, we encounter cats in a wide range of situations – we read about them, we encounter them in friends' homes, and so on. From these experiences, we gradually assemble a set of attitudes and beliefs about cats – for example, that they are proud, like to be stroked, and will bite if handled roughly. We form similar beliefs about the characteristics of social groups, and in this case our beliefs are called *stereotypes*. Insofar as they are accurate, stereotypes can be very useful – in the case of cats, it is important to know that most cats will become aggressive if handled roughly – but inaccurate stereotypes can cause serious harm. In the 1930s and 1940s, for example, Hollywood movies tended to portray African Americans as lazy and shiftless, and this stereotype undoubtedly contributed to racial prejudice.

For many years social psychologists believed that racial stereotypes were largely conscious – individuals might not want to publicly admit that they were racists, but they were certainly aware of their own attitudes. More recently, however, influenced by cognitive research on unconscious memory, social psychologists have investigated the possibility that racial stereotypes can also influence us at an unconscious level (see, for example, Greenwald and Banaji, 1995, and Macrae and Bodenhausen, 2000). According to this view, exposure to a black face automatically activates or primes stereotypical beliefs about this group, and this stereotype can then influence our behavior without our necessarily being aware of it.

In one test of this hypothesis, Bargh, Chen, and Burrows (1996) showed people pictures of black faces. To ensure that any effects were truly unconscious, they presented the faces subliminally: Each face was shown on a computer screen for approximately 20 milliseconds, followed by a random pattern called a mask. (Pretesting had confirmed that the faces were not detected – not only could individuals not identify the pictures, they did not even realize that any had been presented.)

The faces were presented as participants worked on an exceptionally boring task in which they judged whether pictures contained an odd or an even number of circles. When they finished, they were told that the computer had failed to save the data, and that they would have to do it again. Participants who had been exposed to the black faces reacted to this request with significantly greater hostility than did members of a control group who had been exposed to pictures of Caucasian faces. (See also Chen and Bargh, 1997.)

In a related study, Graham and Lowery (2004) had police officers read a brief account of a crime and then answer questions about the perpetrator. Before reading the account, half were subliminally exposed to words related to *black* such as *Harlem* and *homeboy*. The officers in this priming group were significantly more likely to regard the perpetrator as responsible for his actions, and to recommend a harsh punishment.

Attraction

A second example of how memories can influence our behavior without our awareness has come from research on the *mere exposure effect* (Zajonc, 1968). This refers to the fact that exposure to a neutral stimulus can increase our liking for it. Rats, for example, normally have no preference between the music of Mozart and Schoenberg – if music by the two composers is played in adjacent cages, the rats will spend equal time in each cage. If rats are exposed to music by Mozart while being reared, however, then as adults they strongly prefer Mozart (Cross, Holcomb, and Matter, 1967). Similarly, people who are repeatedly exposed to neutral stimuli such as nonsense syllables and tones begin to find them attractive. In one study by Kunst-Wilson and Zajonc (1980), participants saw pictures of polygons that were flashed on a screen subliminally. When subsequently asked to identify the shapes they had seen in a recognition test, they could not do so, but when asked to rate the attractiveness of these shapes, they rated the shapes they had seen earlier more positively.

The mere exposure effect is so counterintuitive it might be worth citing one final example. Moreland and Beach (1992) arranged for four women to attend a university course on personality psychology. Before the course began, pictures of the women were shown to students in a different course and the women were rated to be equally attractive. The women then attended either 0, 5, 10, or 15 sessions of the personality course. Finally, at the end of the course, students were shown pictures of the four women and asked to rate their attractiveness; the women who had attended the most lectures were now seen as significantly more attractive. This effect occurred even though the class was a large one, with 200 students, and the women had sat quietly during lectures so as not to draw attention to themselves. Even this minimal exposure was apparently enough to significantly increase their perceived attractiveness.

One possible interpretation of results like these is that when a stimulus is familiar, it seems safer and thus more comfortable (Zajonc, 1998, 2001). Whatever the precise mechanism, it seems that familiarity can influence our perceptions of attractiveness without our awareness. (See also Alter and Oppenheimer, 2008.)

Procedural issues

In the introduction to this section, we referred to the remarkable proliferation of theories concerning the components of long-term memory. We have now reviewed evidence concerning four candidates: episodic, semantic, perceptual, and procedural. So, are there really four divisions, and, if so, have we correctly identified their properties?

The short answer is: We don't know. Although most memory theorists now agree that long-term memory is not a unitary system, there are still disagreements about the precise nature of the subdivisions. To some degree, such disagreements are inherent in science – there are always alternative ways of explaining data, and the development and testing of competing theories is a normal part of the scientific method. However, the number of competing theories about the structure of memory – and, as important, the difficulty of deciding which view is right – is arguably greater than in most other areas of cognitive psychology.

Process purity

One reason for this difficulty concerns the tasks that have been used to measure memory. For example, we have assumed that recognition tests provide an index of episodic memory – if someone recognizes a word, this means that he or she remembers having seen it previously. However, although episodic or conscious memory is probably the main determinant of performance on a recognition test, it is not necessarily the only determinant. One influential theory of recognition argues that recognition of a word can result from either of two processes, *recollection* or *familiarity* (Mandler, 1980; Jacoby, 1991). Recollection involves having a specific, conscious memory of having encountered an item before. If, for example, seeing the word *cat* on a recognition test reminded you of seeing it during the study phase, this would be an example of recollection.

However, another possibility is that the word would not remind you of a particular experience but would instead produce a general feeling of familiarity – the word would just "ring a bell." You might conclude that this means that you saw the word earlier, and thus that it must have been on the study list. When you recognize a word, in other words, this could be either because you remember the moment when you saw it, or simply because the word seems familiar (see also Yonelinas, 2002).

As to why some words seem familiar, this could be the result of perceptual memory. If you saw *cat* earlier, processing it would now be easier, and this *perceptual fluency* could be the source of your feeling that it is familiar. (For a clever test of this hypothesis, see Whittlesea, Jacoby, and Girard, 1990.) So, correct recognition of a word could be based on a conscious episodic memory, but it could also be based on an unconscious perceptual memory. The fact that someone does well on a recognition test, therefore, does not necessarily mean that his or her episodic memory system is intact.

Similar problems arise with other tests of memory, with each test potentially reflecting the influence of multiple processes. Under these circumstances, it becomes very difficult to determine how many processes are involved – imagine trying to study the effects of heat if thermometer readings were influenced by the shape and color of objects as well as their temperature.

If you are feeling confused at this point, you shouldn't worry about it – it just means that you have understood how difficult it is to disentangle the processes involved in memory. If every task provided a "pure" measure of a single underlying process, understanding the processes underlying memory would be straightforward, but cognitive psychologists now believe that most if not all memory tasks reflect contributions from multiple processes. Larry Jacoby was the first psychologist to identify this problem, and he suggested an ingenious procedure to overcome it (Jacoby, 1991). Alas, other psychologists identified possible flaws in his approach, and its validity is not yet clear. (For contrasting views, see Curran and Hintzman, 1995; Brainerd, Reyna, and Mojardin, 1999; Rouder et al., 2008.)

Converging operations

The difficulties involved in trying to understand memory are frustrating but not, perhaps, surprising. The brain is composed of billions of neurons organized to carry out hundreds if not thousands of processes, and this makes it very difficult to figure out how many processes are involved, and what each one does. The task of a psychologist trying to understand the brain in some ways resembles that of a child trying to understand the inner workings of a television set by observing the pictures it produces. If you cannot observe what is happening inside a complex system, how do you figure out how it works?

Fortunately, psychologists have some powerful tools not available to the child. The first is the ability to intervene experimentally. Where the child can only observe whatever pictures the television set happens to produce, psychologists can systematically vary the environmental input to the brain. By observing the relationship between different inputs and different outputs, researchers can identify the rules that govern the system's operations, and this in turn allows theorists to produce models of the kind of system that would generate these patterns.

If you want to understand how a system works, though, there are obvious advantages to being able to examine its inner workings directly. In the case of memory, one valuable technique that we have already discussed is studying patients with brain damage. These studies have been enormously useful, but they also have their limits. In the cases of Beth and Jon, damage to their brains was confined almost entirely to the hippocampal region, and this allowed psychologists to clearly separate episodic and semantic memory. In most cases, though, damage is not confined to a single anatomical region, and this makes it harder to identify the function of each area.

Recently, psychologists have gained a more sophisticated tool for studying the brain with the development of brain scanning procedures that allow activity in different regions of the brain to be monitored with unprecedented accuracy. One example is a procedure called a *positron emission topography* (PET) scan. Radioactive material is injected into the blood, which then carries it to the brain. Careful measurement of this radioactivity allows scientists to monitor blood flow and thus determine which areas of the brain are currently most active.

If participants are asked to solve a mathematical puzzle, for example, we can observe increased neural activity in one area of the cortex, and if they are then asked to think of a musical tune, we can see this activity shift to a different region.

Again, this technique has limitations – one area of the brain may become *more* active during puzzle solving, but many other areas will also be involved. If the puzzle is presented visually, for example, then, at a minimum, there will be increased activity in areas involved in visual perception as well as in solving puzzles. And the more regions that are active, the harder it is to assess the role of any one of them.

Individually, therefore, each of these techniques has its limitations, but together they can provide valuable converging evidence on how the brain works. We can illustrate this point with some recent research involving Jon, the patient who lost the ability to form episodic memories when he was 4. One puzzling aspect of his condition was that although he did poorly on recall tests, his performance on recognition tests was normal. Both tests are normally assumed to measure episodic memory, so this dissociation surprised researchers.

We have already encountered a possible explanation, that performance on recognition tests can be based on perceptual memories rather than episodic ones. Perhaps Jon wasn't really recognizing the words he was shown but just responding on the basis that they felt familiar. How, though, do we know whether this explanation is correct?

One line of evidence has come from behavioral studies using *the remember/know* paradigm. In this procedure, participants are shown a list of words and then given a recognition test. If they report recognizing a word, they are then further asked whether this is because they actually remember seeing the word on the study list or because they just know that it occurred, without a specific memory. Gardiner (1988) found that participants reported remembering some words but only knowing others, supporting the claim that performance on recognition tests can be based on a general feeling that a word is familiar. (See also Yonelinas, 2002.)

Converging evidence on this point has come from electrophysiological studies that have measured *event-related potentials* (ERPs). In this procedure, electrodes on the surface of the head are used to measure changes in electrical activity following the presentation of a stimulus. When individuals read words that they later report feel familiar, their brain waves while reading the word show a distinctive change after about 400 milliseconds. When they read words that they later report that they know, on the other hand, there is no change at 400 milliseconds but there is one at around 600 milliseconds (Düzel *et al.*, 1997). Physiological evidence thus confirms the behavioral finding that different processes within the brain produce feelings of remembering and knowing.

There are strong grounds, therefore, for believing that Jon's strong performance on recognition tests could have been based on a general feeling that the words were familiar, rather than on any specific memory of having seen them. To find out whether this was actually the case, Düzel *et al.* (2001) measured Jon's brain waves as he read a list of words. They found no change at 600 milliseconds, indicating that Jon was not processing the words in the form that normally produces conscious memories. They did, however, find the change at 400 milliseconds produced by words that are later judged to be familiar. Behavioral and physiological evidence thus converge to suggest that Jon had lost the ability to form episodic memories. When he says that he recognizes a word, he seems to base this judgment on a general feeling that the word is familiar, rather than on a conscious memory of having seen it.

Organization of semantic memory

We have seen that individuals suffering from anterograde amnesia have great difficulty in creating new memories. Harvard psychologist Daniel Schacter (1996) described one poignant case involving a man in the early stages of Alzheimer's disease. Frederick was referred to Schacter because of problems with his memory, and, to get to know Frederick better, Schacter arranged to play a game of golf with him. On one hole, Frederick hit an excellent tee shot and excitedly discussed what club he would use for his next shot.

Schacter then hit his own tee shot and began to move down the fairway. When he looked back, however, he saw that Frederick was still standing on the tee. When Schacter asked why, Frederick replied that he was waiting to hit his tee shot; he had no memory of having done so only a minute or two earlier. And when Schacter picked Frederick up a week later for another game, Frederick commented that he was a bit nervous because he had never played with Schacter before; Schacter didn't have the heart to correct him.

Using the terminology introduced in the previous section, Frederick's ability to form new episodic memories was clearly impaired: Once he stopped doing something, all traces of the experience were rapidly lost. His semantic memory, however – or at any rate his ability to retrieve semantic information stored before the onset of dementia – was still excellent: He was articulate, he understood terms such as birdie and dogleg, he knew the rules of golf, and so on. In other words, while Frederick had difficulty in remembering personal experiences or episodes, he retained extensive knowledge of the world within which his personal odyssey took place – if you like, the stage on which his part was acted out. This store of general knowledge about the world, or semantic memory, includes such disparate forms of information as the meaning of words, the names and faces of people we know, the capital of France, the correct way to behave in a restaurant, and so on.

Conceived in this way, semantic memory must be vast. Consider just the component devoted to the meaning of words: For speakers of English, this means the store must hold on the order of 20,000 words, together with their definitions (Miller and Gildea, 1987). Moreover, for each of these words we often possess a substantial amount of other information. In the case of *cat*, we know what cats look like, what they like to eat, how they like to be stroked, their propensity for fleas, and on, and on, and on. Semantic memory is not simply large, it is staggeringly large.

How, then, do we organize this vast array of facts to allow us to quickly retrieve information we need? This question will be the focus of this section, as we try to understand how we store and retrieve information about the world. In particular, we will focus on verbal material – for example, conversations with friends or material in a textbook. When you read a sentence in a text like this, how do you store it in memory so that you will be able to retrieve it in an exam?

Concepts

We will start with the question of how you store individual words, before moving on to consider how you store more complex material such as sentences. Suppose that you read the word *dog*: How might you store this word in your semantic memory?

The first point to note is that a word such as *dog* is a **concept**; it is an abstract representation of a class of objects, rather than just a single member of that class. The concept *dog* refers to all dogs, not just a particular dog you might have had as a child.

Our ability to form such concepts is at the heart of our ability to make sense of the world around us. One way to see this is to imagine a child born without the ability to group events into conceptual categories, so that he reacts to every new stimulus as if it was unique. If he encountered a dog, for example, he would not recognize it as similar to dogs he had encountered in the past, and thus would have no basis for deciding whether it was likely to be a friendly companion or a mortal danger. Indeed, he would not even be able to recognize this dog as one he had seen just moments earlier because its perceptual properties would be different every time he encountered it – its limbs would be in a different position, it would be at a different distance and angle, and so on. If every stimulus is unique, this child would have no basis for knowing how to react to it; it would be lost in a sea of other unique events. It is our ability to group similar events together in concepts that allows us to impose coherence on the turbulent stream of our perceptions.

So, concepts are clearly vital, but what exactly are they? The classical view, going back to Aristotle, was that a concept is a set of objects whose membership is defined by rules. The concept *triangle*, for example, consists of all shapes whose boundaries are three straight lines joined at their ends; *squares* are four lines of equal length joined at right angles, and so on. Indeed, some concepts can be defined in this kind of clear, precise way, but many of the concepts that we encounter are not nearly so straightforward. Consider again the concept *dog*. This might at first seem simple to define – for example, "A dog is a four-legged animal with a tail, fur, and so on." As you think more about such definitions, however, they quickly begin to break down. Most dogs have four legs, but some may be born deformed, with only three; although some dogs have tails, others do not; and so on. Another way to see this difficulty is to form mental images of different breeds such as dachshunds, Saint Bernards, poodles, and bulldogs. What is it that unites these very different animals, yet distinguishes them from similar species such as a cat or a fox? There does not seem to be any clear rule that defines category membership.

Prototype theories

If the concept *dog* cannot be given a precise definition, how do we decide whether an animal that we encounter is a dog? One answer to this question was pioneered by a philosopher, Ludwig Wittgenstein (1953), and later elaborated by a psychologist, Eleanor Rosch (1975, 1978). They noted that although examples of a concept do not all share the same features, there is nevertheless a clear *family resemblance* between them. That is, just as members of a family may resemble each other even though there are no features that they all share, so too instances of a concept such as *dog* share broadly similar features. In this view, membership of a category is determined not by a precise rule but rather by the degree to which a candidate possesses the features characteristic of existing members; the more of these features a candidate possesses, the more likely it is to be a member. Concepts, in this view, are "fuzzy"; they are not demarcated by clear boundaries. For example, would you consider a tomato a fruit? When a group of 30 subjects was asked this question, 16 said that it was a fruit and 14 that it was not. And, even more remarkably, when interviewed a month later, 8 of the 30 subjects had changed their minds (McCloskey and Glucksberg, 1978). Although the concept *fruit* might at first seem clear, when examined closely its boundaries prove surprisingly fuzzy.

If concepts have no clear boundaries, this brings us back to the question of how we decide whether a new instance is a member. One suggestion is that as we encounter members of a concept, or *exemplars*, we begin to build a picture of what an average or typical member looks like. This representation of the average member is called its **prototype**. If you hear the word *bird*, for example, you may think of a typical example such as a robin; if you hear the word *chair*, you may think of a typical chair, and so on. According to prototype theory, we average together the features of exemplars of a concept to form a prototype, and we then decide whether a new instance is a member by judging its similarity to this prototype (Posner and Keele, 1968; Rosch, 1975). In our dog example, you would decide whether an animal is a dog by judging its similarity to a typical dog.

One implication of this analysis is that the ease of deciding whether a candidate is a member of a concept should depend on the candidate's similarity to the prototype – the greater the resemblance, the easier the decision. To test this, Rosch (1973) began by determining what the prototypical member of various concepts looked like. She asked people to rate the extent to which various exemplars of a concept seemed typical; if an exemplar was seen as highly typical, this would suggest that the prototype must be quite similar. For the concept *bird*, for example, she found that robins and sparrows were judged to be highly typical birds, whereas chickens and ostriches were rated as much less typical. Then, having established the likely form of the prototype, Rosch asked a second set of participants to decide whether various exemplars were members of the category. They were shown sentences such as "A robin is a bird" and "A chicken is a bird," and asked to push a button marked "true" or "false" as quickly as they could. (They also read false sentences such as "A robin is a vegetable.")

According to the classical view of concepts, membership of a category is defined by rules. As robins and chickens both meet the definition of a bird, they should be equally easy to assess as possible exemplars. Suppose, however, that Rosch is right, and that we judge whether a candidate is a member of a category not by rules but by the candidate's similarity to a prototype. If so, then we should be faster at categorizing members of a concept that are typical, because their similarity to the prototype will be more obvious. And that is what Rosch found: Participants responded significantly faster when an exemplar was typical of a concept than when it was not.

This finding is called the **typicality effect**, and it supports the view that we classify stimuli by comparing them with prototypes. (See also Rosch, Simpson, and Miller, 1976.)

Further evidence for the existence of prototypes comes from a study by Solso and McCarthy (1981). They began by creating faces that would serve as the prototypes for three categories, and then generated exemplars of each category by varying some of the prototypical face's features. They then showed participants all of the exemplars – importantly, *not* including the prototype – and then later tested their memory for these faces. The test included faces that had been shown earlier and also faces that had not, and participants were asked to rate their confidence that

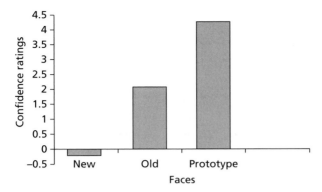

Figure 10.4 Enhanced recognition of prototypes. Participants were shown faces generated from a prototype face, and then shown a new set of faces and asked how confident they were that they had seen them earlier. The ratings for faces seen previously were substantially higher than for faces that had not been seen, but the highest ratings were for the prototypes, even though they had not been presented. (Data from Solso and McCarthy, 1981.)

they had seen each face on a scale from −5 to +5, where +5 represented certainty that they had seen it.

The results are shown in Figure 10.4. The average rating for the old faces – those presented in the first phase – was +2, while the average rating for the new faces was around 0; as you would expect, participants were more confident that they had seen a face when it had actually been presented. The crucial result, though, was for the prototype faces. Even though they had not been presented, participants were very confident that they had seen them – indeed, they were actually *more* confident than for the faces they had actually seen, with average ratings around +4. The implication is that when participants were shown the exemplars during the study phase they formed prototypes for each of the categories and stored these prototypes in memory. Then, when the actual prototypes were presented in the test phase, they seemed very familiar, because they closely resembled the prototypes that the participants had created for themselves.

Exemplar theories

On the surface, results like these seemed to provide compelling evidence for the creation and use of prototypes in memory. It later became clear, however, that this evidence could also be explained without appealing to prototypes (for example, Medin and Rips, 2005). Consider again the typicality effect. The reason that typical instances of a concept are easier to recognize could be because they are similar to the prototype, but it could also be because typical instances are likely to be similar to many other members of the category. A robin, for example, is similar to many other birds, whereas a chicken – or, even worse, an ostrich – is not. If we are asked to categorize an animal that we have never seen, we do it by searching our memories for animals that resemble it. A bird like a robin will remind us of many birds (wrens, crows, etc.), suggesting that it too must be a bird. A bird resembling a chicken, on the other hand, will be less likely to remind us of other birds, and so we will be more hesitant to conclude that it is a member of this category.

Exemplar theory, as this approach is known, assumes that classification of stimuli is based on a comparison with previously stored exemplars, rather than with prototypes. Given that prototype and exemplar theories can both explain the typicality effect, can we say which account is right? There is considerable evidence to support each, and the current view is that both are probably right. There is no doubt that we store exemplars – you remember individual dogs you have encountered, not just a typical dog – but in some circumstances it looks as if we also average together exemplars in order to form a prototype, which is also stored in memory (Smith and Minda, 1998; Ashby and Ennis, 2006).

Semantic networks

To simplify our discussion a bit, let's for a moment suppose that a concept is represented in the brain simply by a prototypical example. In the case of a dog, our prototype would possess characteristic features such as 4 legs, a tail, and so on. Until now, we have treated this prototype as if it was simply a bundle of unrelated features, but if examined more closely it quickly becomes clear that this cannot be right. Pursuing our dog example, a dog cannot simply be an animal that has 4 legs and a tail, there must be a certain *relationship* among these features. If you encountered an animal with 4 legs and a tail but the tail was located at the front rather than the back, and the legs were attached to the top of the body rather than the bottom, it is unlikely that your first thought would be "Ah, a dog." A concept, in other words, cannot just be a random collection of features, there must be some structure or organization to indicate how all of these features are related.

A hierarchical model

One of the first proposals as to what this organization might be was the work of a graduate student in computing science, M. Ross Quillian. His goal was to develop computers that could answer questions. To achieve this, he found that the computer needed a large store of conceptual information, and so he developed proposals for how this store should be organized. After his thesis was completed, he began to work with a cognitive psychologist, Allan Collins, and they eventually published a modified version of his model that they hoped would provide a framework for understanding how the brain accomplishes the same task.

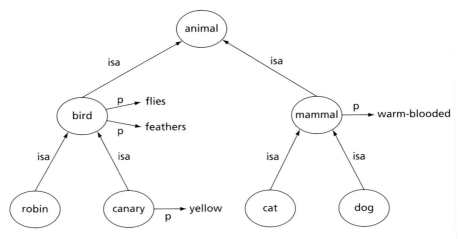

Figure 10.5 Collins and Quillian's (1969) semantic network model. Concepts are organized hierarchically, reflecting category membership, and each concept is connected not only to its superordinate category but also to its distinctive properties. A canary, for example, is a bird (*isa*), and has the property (*p*) of being yellow. In this simplified version of the model, only a small number of concepts and properties are illustrated.

Collins and Quillian (1969) assumed that each word in semantic memory is represented by a set of neurons called a *node*, and that these nodes are connected to each other by pathways called *links*. Figure 10.5 provides an illustration of how such a system might be organized. This particular section of the network contains nodes for concepts such as *canary* and *bird*, and each node contains various links. Consider the concept *canary*. As shown in the figure, a *canary* has properties such as being yellow, and the node for *canary* contains links to these features. In addition, a *canary* is an example of a *bird*, and so the nodes for *canary* and *bird* are also linked.

One noteworthy feature of this **semantic network** is that concepts are connected by different kinds of links. Specifically, the network contains two kinds of links. One kind connects a concept to what is called a superordinate concept – that is, a higher-level concept of which it is a member. A canary, for example, is an example of a bird, and a bird in turn is an example of an animal. This kind of link is sometimes called an *isa* link, as in "A canary is a bird." In addition, there are property links, which are used to connect concepts to their features or properties. Thus, a *canary* is linked to the feature *yellow* by a property link that indicates that yellow is a property of canaries. (It is the existence of such property links that allows us to capture relationships between features such as "the tail is at the back.")

A second important feature of the network is that it is organized hierarchically: A bird is an example of an animal, and hence comes beneath it in the hierarchy, and similarly a canary is an example of a bird. This hierarchical organization is used to allow the network to store information efficiently. Consider the case of a canary. In principle, you possess an enormous amount of information about canaries – not only that they are small and yellow, but that they produce eggs, they have hearts and lungs, the lungs extract oxygen from air, and so on. If all this information were stored with every single bird, the network would be almost unimaginably large, with a massive number of interconnections between nodes. To avoid unnecessary duplication, Collins and Quillian proposed that a feature would be stored with a concept only if it was a distinctive characteristic of that concept – in our example, that a canary is yellow. Information that was characteristic of all members of a class – for example, that all birds have wings – would be stored with the superordinate category *bird* and would not be duplicated for each and every bird. If you want to know whether a canary has a heart, all you would need to do is check the properties stored at the next level up in the hierarchy, or, if necessary, at a still higher level. (The property that birds need oxygen to breathe, for example, would be stored at the level of *animal*, rather than *bird*.) This aspect of the model is known as *cognitive economy*; it assumes that features are stored at the highest level in the hierarchy that is appropriate.

It is all very well to posit that the brain stores information in a hierarchical network such as this, but how do we know whether this claim is correct? If our knowledge of the brain's physiology doesn't yet allow us to say where particular concepts are stored – and it doesn't – then how do we know whether the model is right?

Collins and Quillian used an ingeniously simple procedure to test the model, called the *sentence verification* task. They asked participants to read a series of sentences such as "A canary is a bird" and "A canary has wings," and to say whether or not each sentence was true. (To ensure that participants did not simply respond yes to every sentence, they also included false sentences such as "A canary is a fish.") They realized that participants would have little difficulty in answering these questions, so that there was little point in using a measure such as percentage correct to evaluate performance. Instead, they measured reaction times – how long it was from the time a sentence was presented until participants pushed a button to indicate whether it was true or false. The longer the reaction time, they reasoned, the more mental processes must be involved in evaluating the sentence.

Consider the sentences "A canary is a bird" and "A canary is an animal." Which sentence do you think participants would be able to verify more quickly? Intuitively, it might seem that both questions are equally easy, and thus reaction times should be the same, but Collins and Quillian predicted a very different outcome. According to their account, when you read the word *canary*, this should activate the corresponding node in your semantic network, and this activation should then spread through the links emanating from this node. Because the node

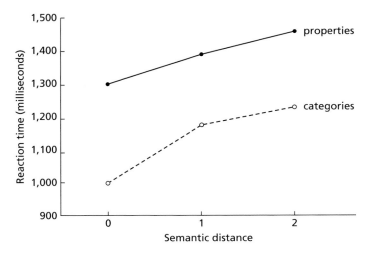

Figure 10.6 Average time to verify sentences as a function of semantic relationships. The solid line shows reaction times for sentences that stated properties of the subject (for example, "A canary can fly"), and the dashed line shows data for categorical sentences (for example, "A canary is a bird"). Semantic distance was measured by the number of links that had to be traversed in Collins and Quillian's semantic network to connect the subject and the predicate. (Adapted from Collins and Quillian, 1969.)

for canary is directly linked to the node for bird, participants should be able to verify that a canary is a bird very quickly. In the case of "A canary is an animal," on the other hand, activation would have spread first to the *bird* node and then to the *animal* node before the relationship could be confirmed. Two nodes would have to be traversed rather than one, so verification should take longer.

A second prediction of the model concerns sentences involving properties. Consider the sentences "A canary is yellow" and "A canary can fly." Again, intuition might suggest that these sentences should be equally easy to confirm, but the model suggests that the first sentence should be easier to verify than the second. According to the model, yellow is a distinctive property of canaries and, hence, will be stored at the same level. Being able to fly, on the other hand, is a general property of all birds and, hence, will be stored with the concept *bird*. Verifying that canaries can fly thus requires moving up the hierarchy, so should take longer.

The results for the experiment are shown in Figure 10.6. As predicted by the model, the time to verify categorical statements depended on the number of links that had to be traversed: The greater the number of links, the more time participants needed to respond. And the predicted relationships involving property sentences were also confirmed: When a property was stored at a higher node in the network, reaction times were significantly longer. These results thus support two key assumptions of the model: That concepts are arranged hierarchically, and that properties are stored at the highest level within this hierarchy where they would be valid.[1]

Subsequent research, however, did not always support the model's predictions (for example, Conrad, 1972; Smith, Rips, and Shoben, 1974). For example, the model assumes that reaction times for categorical statements should depend solely on the number of nodes that have to be traversed during verification. Robins and ostriches are both birds, and so the time to verify "A robin is a bird" and "An ostrich is a bird" should be the same. As we saw in our earlier discussion of the typicality effect, however, this is not the case: Typical instances of a category are verified faster than atypical ones. This is clearly contrary to the assumption that all instances of a concept should be equally easy to verify. To paraphrase George Orwell's satirical novel *Animal Farm*: All birds are equal, but some seem to be more equal than others.

To handle problems like this, Collins and Loftus (1975) developed a revised version of the model. The new version contained several modifications; we will focus on the one designed to let the model account for the typicality effect. The change was simple: Instead of assuming that *isa* links are equal in strength, they proposed that some are stronger than others. For example, because we encounter robins more than ostriches, the link between *robin* and *bird* should be stronger than the link between *ostrich* and *bird*. Figure 10.7 illustrates how the relationships between birds could be represented in the revised model. Strong links are represented by short lines, and weaker links by long lines. Because the *robin–bird* link is stronger than the *ostrich–bird* link, the model now predicts that statements such as "A robin is a bird" will be verified more quickly because activation will be transmitted from *robin* to *bird* more quickly.

Spreading activation

One key assumption in the Collins and Loftus model, as in its predecessor, is that activation of any node will spread out to other nodes in the network through the links connecting them. Activation of *robin* would spread to *bird*, activation of *bird* would spread to *animal*, and so forth. If there were no limits to this spread, the presentation of a single word could eventually result in activation of every other node in the network – something like having everyone in the world talking to you simultaneously – so to prevent this the model sets limits on how activity spreads. It assumes that activity will decrease as it fans out through the network, and also that it will decay over time. If activation spread from *robin* to *bird*, for example,

---

[1] You may be wondering why property statements that involve a single link ("A canary is yellow") take less time to verify than category statements that also involve a single link ("A canary is a bird"). The answer, according to Collins and Quillian, is that it takes less time to move within a level (here, from canary to yellow) than to move up a level (from canary to bird).

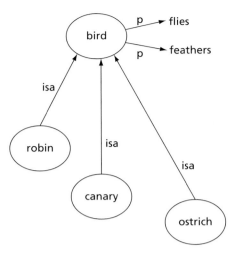

Figure 10.7 A simplified version of the Collins and Loftus (1975) semantic network model. Some instances of a concept are linked to their superordinate category more strongly than other instances, and this is reflected in the length of the lines connecting them.

the *bird* node might be strongly activated at first but this activity would decrease as time passed.

The assumption that activity spreads through the network is known as **spreading activation**, and it allows the model to make some interesting predictions. Suppose that the word *robin* was presented shortly before the word *bird*. Reading *robin* would activate the node that represents it, and activity would spread from there to the node for *bird*. When the word *bird* followed, therefore, its node would have already been partially activated, so that less time should be needed to activate it fully.

To test this prediction, Meyer and Schvaneveldt (1971) used a *lexical decision task* in which participants were shown strings of letters and asked to decide, as quickly as they could, if the strings represented real words. (The term *lexicon* derives from the Greek word meaning *dictionary*; in a lexical decision task participants must consult their mental dictionaries to decide whether a string of letters is a word.) Two strings were presented on every trial, one above the other, and participants were asked to push buttons to indicate whether they were words. On some trials, both strings were words, and Meyer and Schvaneveldt varied the semantic relationship between these words. For example, in one condition the words were *bread* and *butter*, and in another the words were *nurse* and *butter*. According to the spreading activation model, reading the word *bread* should activate or prime the node for *butter*, making it easier for participants to recognize *butter* when they read it. If the first word was *nurse*, on the other hand, activation would be less likely to spread to *butter*, and so the decision time on this trial should be longer. The results neatly confirmed these predictions, as lexical decisions were significantly faster when the words were closely related in meaning. (See also McNamara, 1994.)

This phenomenon is called **semantic priming**, as presentation of a word seems to partially activate or prime the representations of words with similar meanings. This provides powerful support for the claim that words are organized in networks in which words of similar meaning are linked together.

The Collins and Loftus model has been criticized for being, in a sense, *too* successful: Because of the number of assumptions the model makes, and the general form in which these assumptions are stated, the model can explain almost any data, and this makes it difficult to disprove (Smith, 1978). The model's successes, however, suggest that something like semantic networks really do exist, even if our theories about them need further elaboration.

Propositions

Semantic network models focus on how individual words are stored in memory, and in particular on the relationships between these words. In real life, though, we rarely encounter words in isolation; we usually experience them in extended sequences such as conversations or texts. This kind of material poses special challenges, and to explain how we store such material cognitive psychologists have focused on a more sophisticated unit, the *proposition*.

An abstract proposition

To introduce the concept of a proposition, we will start by returning to the seminal work of Sachs (1967) discussed in Chapter 9. She asked participants to read passages discussing topics such as the development of the telescope. If participants were tested immediately after reading a passage, they could remember not only the ideas that had been presented but also the precise words in which these ideas were expressed. As time passed, however, verbatim memory was lost: Participants could still recall ideas accurately but not the original wording. When we read texts or listen to conversations, in other words, we do not store the words that we read – or, at any rate, we do not store them for very long. Instead, we somehow extract the underlying meaning that was expressed in the words, and it is this abstract meaning that we retain.

Another example comes from a study by Brewer (1977). He asked participants in his study to read 92 sentences and he then gave them a cued-recall test to see how well they remembered them. For example, one of the sentences was

> *The hungry python caught the mouse.*

On the cued-recall test, he provided the initial noun phrase ("the hungry python") as a cue, and asked the participants to recall the rest of the sentence. Participants recalled some of the sentence accurately, but 26% of the responses incorporated *implications* of the original wording rather than the wording itself. For our python example, some participants remembered the sentence as

The hungry python ate the mouse.

Why should participants have misremembered the sentence in this way? One plausible explanation is that when they read the sentence they automatically tried to understand it, and that as part of this process they accessed their knowledge about pythons and mice. They would have realized that the python was chasing the mouse in order to eat it, and that once it caught the mouse this would indeed have been the outcome. (The claim is not that participants did all this consciously, rather that this kind of search for meaning is performed automatically whenever we have to decipher verbal material.) What they then stored in memory was not only the words they'd read but also this *interpretation* of what the words meant. When later asked to recall the sentence, some participants apparently remembered the implication of the sentence rather than the wording, leading them to remember a sentence that hadn't been presented.

The Sachs and Brewer studies suggest that while at first we may remember sentences verbatim, over time the details fade, and what remains in memory is the essence of the sentence, its meaning or gist, rather than the words (Goldsmith, Koriat, and Pansky, 2005; Kleider *et al.*, 2008). If we don't store ideas in the form of words, though, then in what form *do* we store them?

Mausoleums and squares

One possibility is **propositions**. Several theories about what propositions are, and how they are formed and used, have been proposed (for example, Kintsch, 1998; Anderson *et al.*, 2004), but a useful starting point is a definition proposed by John R. Anderson (for example, Anderson, 2010). According to Anderson, a proposition is *the smallest unit of knowledge that can be viewed as either true or false.* The word *cat*, for example, is not a proposition because it doesn't make much sense to assert that it is either true or false. The sentence "John's cat is black," on the other hand, is a proposition: It could be true or false.

Proposition can be represented in the form of a diagram, and Figure 10.8a shows a propositional representation of the sentence "The jelly was sweet." The node, labeled A, represents the proposition as a whole, and in this case the proposition has two components: a subject (jelly) and a relation (sweet). This is the simplest possible form of a proposition. Propositions can also be more elaborate, capturing more complex relationships. Figure 10.8b shows a proposition representing a slightly more complex sentence, "The jelly was on the table." As you can see, the proposition now has four components instead of two: The subject of the

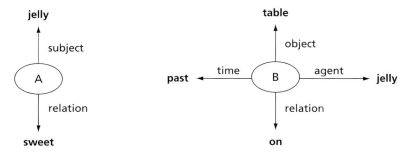

Figure 10.8 A graphic representation of two propositions.

sentence (now called the agent) is *jelly*; it bears the relationship *on* to the object, *table*, and the time is in the *past*.

One important feature of propositions like this is that they are abstract, in that they represent the *meaning* of a group of words, rather than the words themselves. Consider the following sentences:

> *Galileo sent a letter.*
> *A letter was sent by Galileo.*

Despite the differences in their wording, they both express the same basic relationships (Galileo, send, letter), and for this reason they would be represented by the same proposition. Propositions thus have exactly the properties we need to allow us to represent the meaning of a sentence separately from its words.

Although we didn't label them as such, we encountered propositions earlier in our discussion of semantic networks. In Figure 10.5, for example, one of the links was "robin *isa* bird," and that is just the kind of propositional statement that we are examining now. Theories of propositions are thus closely related to earlier theories of semantic networks, but they incorporate a number of modifications. For our purposes, the most important of these changes has been that propositions can include links to the context in which the proposition was encountered, thus making it possible to store declarative as well as semantic memories. As we saw earlier, these forms of memory differ in that declarative memories include a sense of when and where information was acquired, so that when we retrieve a declarative memory we have a sense of replaying or reliving an earlier experience. Because propositions can include this kind of contextual information, they allow the storage not only of semantic memories ("Paris is the capital of France") but also declarative memories ("In school today our teacher told us that Paris is the capital of France").

We've now seen that propositions *could* be an appropriate vehicle for storing memories, but that doesn't mean that they are the format that our brains actually use.

Evidence that we do store our experiences in propositional form – or at least something resembling propositions – has been reported in several studies, and we will focus on one by Ratcliff and McKoon (1978). They asked participants in their study to read sentences such as

The mausoleum that enshrined the tsar overlooked the square.

Then, to assess participants' memory for these sentences, the experimenters presented pairs of words and asked the participants to press a button as quickly as possible if they believed that the words had come from one of the sentences they had read earlier. (Some of the words had appeared earlier, others hadn't.) For example, during testing some participants saw the pair

mausoleum square

while others saw

tsar square.

The question was, which of these pairs would be recognized faster?

You could be forgiven if you found this question difficult to answer – since the words in both pairs had been presented earlier, shouldn't they have been equally easy to recognize? The answer is no, or at least not if you take into account spreading activation. Suppose that when participants read the sentences in the first phase they formed associations between the words. For our mausoleum example, they might have formed associations between *mausoleum* and subsequent words such as *square*. If they then read the word *mausoleum* in the test phase, activity would have spread from its node to the node for *square*. If the next word in the pair actually was *square*, its node would already have been in a state of partial activation by the time they read it, so that less time would be needed to activate it fully. When participants reached the word *square*, in other words, they should have recognized it faster.

This analysis suggests that the time required to recognize *tsar–square* and *mausoleum–square* should depend on how strongly the words in each pair are associated: The stronger the association, the faster the second word should be recognized. So, which pair would have been associated more strongly? A contiguity analysis (and common sense) would suggest *tsar–square*. This is easier to see if we repeat the sentence with the key words in bold:

*The **mausoleum** that enshrined the **tsar** overlooked the **square**.*

Tsar is clearly closer to *square*, so we should expect them to be associated more strongly than *mausoleum* and *square*. In the later test, therefore, the word *square* should be recognized faster after *tsar* than after *mausoleum*.

An analysis in terms of propositions leads us to a very different prediction. The mausoleum sentence is actually a compound of two more basic propositions:

> *The mausoleum enshrined the tsar*

and

> *The mausoleum overlooked the square.*

If participants coded this sentence in the form of propositions, *mausoleum* and *square* would have been in the same proposition, while *tsar* and *square* would have been in different propositions. Since activation should spread more easily between nodes if they are linked in a proposition, activation should have spread more easily from *mausoleum* to *square* (same proposition) than from *tsar* to *square* (different proposition). Participants should thus have recognized *mausoleum–square* faster, and that is what Ratcliff and McKoon found.

It was, in its own way, a dramatic finding: Despite the fact that *mausoleum* and *square* occurred at opposite ends of the sentence, the fact that they were part of the same proposition led to the formation of a strong bond between them. It is a powerful reminder that we do not remember textual material simply by forming associations between successive words; we instead seem to engage in sophisticated processing to uncover the underlying meaning of the sentence, and we then store that meaning in the form of a proposition. (See also Kintsch, 1998; Traxler and Gernsbacher, 2006.)

We should emphasize at this point that we are not suggesting that propositions are the only form in which sentences are stored. As Sachs found in her original study, verbatim records are also stored under at least some conditions. Also, though our discussion has focused on how we store meaning, we store perceptual information as well as more abstract semantic knowledge. If a child learns that Paris is the capital of France in a geography lesson, the child may remember the sound of the teacher's voice and what she was wearing as well as what she said about Paris, and this perceptual information is probably stored in a format other than a proposition. Propositions are thus not the only format we use for storing information, but it does look as if propositions, or something very much like them, play an important part. (For suggestions as to possible alternatives, see Rubin, 2006, and Barsalou, 2008.)

Schemas

We have seen that we often remember the meaning of a passage even when we have forgotten the words in which it was expressed. Indeed, this dissociation is quite common: We usually remember the general theme or *gist* of conversations, lectures, and so forth, rather than the exact words. We have further suggested that we use propositions to store this abstract meaning. How, though, do we extract that meaning in the first place, so that we know what needs to be stored? The wording of some sentences is unambiguous, but more commonly their wording allows more than one interpretation, and we must use our knowledge of the world to infer which meaning is intended. To see this, consider the following short passage (adapted from Charniak, 1973, and Medin, Ross, and Markman, 2005):

Jane heard the jingling of the ice cream truck. She ran to her piggy bank and began to shake it.

You probably had no difficulty in understanding that Jane was excited by the prospect of buying ice cream, that she ran to get money to pay for it before the truck went away, and that she shook her piggy bank to retrieve the money that was stored there. None of this information, though, is stated in the passage; you had to bring considerable knowledge of the world to bear to understand even this simple passage. Somehow, our knowledge of the world must be stored in a form that allows us to make such inferences.

One of the first suggestions for how we do this came from the English psychologist Sir Frederick Bartlett. Bartlett (1932) found that people remembered new material through mental structures that he called **schemas**. A schema is a knowledge structure that is based on a set of similar past experiences; it captures the common features of these experiences. For example, you have probably visited department stores many times, and as a result you have abstracted their common features: large, well-lit spaces, counters with sales assistants behind them, escalators to take you to higher floors, and so on. Similarly, you probably have a schema representing a meal at a restaurant, starting with the waiter seating you and then taking your order. You can use these abstract schemas to help you make sense of new experiences. If when you sit down in a restaurant your waiter stands patiently next to your chair, for example, you understand that he is waiting to take your order rather than hoping to be invited to join you.

Filling slots

Some theorists view a schema as a *frame* with *slots* for particular information (for example, Minsky, 1975; Schank and Abelson, 1977). Your schema for buying ice cream might include slots for the kind of ice cream purchased and the method of payment. If you bought chocolate ice cream and paid in cash, these values would be entered into the preexisting slots in your schema. Each slot would have a *default value* – that is, a standard value that would be assumed unless some other value was specified. Perhaps the default value for buying ice cream would be vanilla. When you buy ice cream or read a story about buying ice cream, schema theories assume that you fill the slots with the appropriate values and then store the resulting schema + values in your memory.

This account leads to some interesting predictions about memory. Whenever you encounter a new situation, you would search for an existing schema to help you interpret it, and you would store the resulting schematic record in memory. Suppose, though, that you could not find an appropriate schema. According to the theory, this could make it harder for you to understand the situation, and thus to remember it. To experience this for yourself, try reading the following paragraph and then, without looking back, recall as much as you can.

The procedure is actually quite simple. First, you arrange items into different groups. Of course, one pile may be sufficient depending on how much there is to do. If you have to go somewhere else due to lack of facilities that is the next step, otherwise you are pretty well set. It is important not to overdo things. That is, it is better to do too few things at once than too many. In the short run this may not seem important but complications can easily arise. A mistake can be expensive as well. At first, the whole procedure will seem complicated. Soon, however, it will become just another facet of life. It is difficult to foresee any end to the necessity for this task in the immediate future, but then one never can tell. After the procedure is completed one arranges the materials into different groups again. Then they can be put into their appropriate places. Eventually they will be used once more and the whole cycle will then have to be repeated. However, that is part of life.

(Bransford and Johnson, 1972, p. 722)

Difficult, wasn't it? Certainly one group of participants in the Bransford and Johnson experiment thought so: Of the 14 main ideas expressed in the passage, they were able to recall only 4. A second group was given the title of the passage – "Washing clothes" – after they had read it. With this title, the passage suddenly made sense, but this group still had great difficulty in recalling what they had read. A third group was given the title *before* reading the passage, and they remembered more than twice as much. If you can use past experience to help you understand a situation – in this case, the actions involved in washing clothes – this gives you a framework for tying together or integrating the new material, and thus to remember it better.

This idea has potentially important implications for education. There has long been a conflict between two approaches to education, one emphasizing the promotion of understanding and the other the memorization of facts. Supporters of memorization argue that education cannot only be about understanding, that it is also important to use rote memorization to ensure that students remember factual material. Research on schemas, however, raises the possibility that in at least some situations this dichotomy may be false, as teaching that helps students to understand how facts fit together can also help them to remember those facts (Mishra and Brewer, 2003).

Schemas can influence not only *how much* information we remember but also *which* information. Schemas usually identify some aspects of a situation as particularly important or central, and others as more peripheral. When eating in a restaurant, for example, the contents of the menu are usually more important to us than the typeface in which they are printed. We should thus expect people to pay more attention to the contents and remember them better.

In order to test this prediction, Brewer and Treyens (1981) started by determining people's schemas about the contents of an office. They asked a group of students what items they would expect to find in a graduate student's office. The students rated items such as a desk, pencils, and textbooks as highly likely to be present; at the other end of the scale, they considered a sewing machine distinctly unlikely. Having established which elements of an office schema were seen as central and which as peripheral, the authors then recruited a second group of students and told them that they would be participating in a psychology experiment. As each student arrived, he or she was asked to wait in the experimenter's office until another student finished the experiment. After only 35 seconds in the office, they were taken to a second room and asked to recall the contents of the office in which they had just been waiting.

According to schema theory, we should expect the students to have focused on those aspects of the office that were central to their schema, while paying less attention to more peripheral details. As predicted, students' memories for features regarded as typical – for example, a desk and a chair – was excellent, as 29 out of 30 recalled these items. Bulletin boards, on the other hand, are less typical, and only 8 out of 30 recalled that the office had a bulletin board. More strikingly, many students recalled seeing items that had not been there. For example, 9 of the 30 students recalled having seen books on the bookshelves, even though none had been present. This, of course, is exactly what an analysis based on schemas would lead us to expect: Because schemas have default values, in this case the presence of books, then unless we specifically notice that the default value is wrong, and therefore override it in the record we are creating, then our record of the experience will include the default value. When students retrieved their memory of the room, for many of them it would have included the default value of books, leading them to remember having seen books. And, even more strikingly, a subsequent study by Lampinen, Copeland, and Neuschatz (2001) suggested that students were not just assuming that books must have been present; they reported actually remembering the books, and in some cases their memories were "clear and vivid." (See also Lampinen and Odegard, 2006.)

Memory as a sketch

This finding points to a fundamental truth about the nature of memory. We all know that our memories are fallible in the sense that we sometimes can't remember things, but on those occasions where we do remember an event clearly, that memory feels to us like an accurate reproduction – a photograph or video – of the original experience. The evidence we have encountered in this and earlier chapters, however, points to a very different picture of memory. When we discussed sensory memory and attention in Chapter 9, we saw that we take in far less information about the world around us than we realize. (The most dramatic example was the Simons and Levin study in which people didn't notice when a stranger who was asking them for directions was replaced by someone else.) Similarly in our discussion of propositions, we saw that people often remember not the exact wording of a sentence but rather its central meaning or gist, and that this can result in falsely remembering elements of the sentence (a python eating a mouse rather than catching it). And now, in the Brewer and Treyens study, students vividly recalled books that weren't there. Putting all these findings together, it looks as if we take in far less information than we realize, fragments rather than the whole, and that what we then store in memory is our *interpretation* of these fragments, rather than the fragments themselves. Memory in this sense is much more like a rough sketch of a scene than a photograph; it is our interpretation of an experience rather than an exact record.

If you'd like to experience this for yourself, in just a small way, then after completing this sentence close your eyes and try to remember what the palm of your right hand looks like. Could you remember clearly the relative lengths of your fingers, the position of each of the knuckles, or the location of the lines crossing your palms? You've probably looked at this palm thousands of times in your life, and yet you may have found that your memory of it is remarkably sketchy. (For an experimental demonstration of the skimpiness of our visual memories, you can consult a paper by Rosielle and Scaggs [2008], with the evocative title "What if they knocked down the library and nobody noticed: the failure to detect large changes to familiar scenes.")

The fact that our memories are more sketchy than we realize is bad enough; more worrying is that these sketches can be seriously distorted, not only missing some details but falsely inserting others. This has important practical implications for areas such as eyewitness memory, implications we will examine in greater depth in Chapter 12.

Scripts

One kind of schema that has attracted particular attention is called a **script**. First proposed by Schank and Abelson (1977), scripts are schemas that deal with stereotyped action sequences such as going to restaurants. To explore the properties of scripts, we will focus on a classic study by Bower, Black, and Turner (1979).

Eating at a restaurant

Bower and his colleagues began by asking people to identify the most common actions involved in activities such as going to a restaurant or attending a lecture. In the case of going to a restaurant, 15 actions were identified by most respondents. These included being seated, looking at the menu, ordering the meal, eating, paying, and leaving. The experimenters then created stories built around these scripts, with each story containing 6 main actions. The researchers gave these stories to a different group to read and then, 20 minutes later, asked them to recall the stories. Participants recalled an average of 3 of the 6 main actions, but the more striking finding was that they also recalled one of the script actions that had not been mentioned, such as paying the bill. As in the Brewer and Treyens study, schemas were leading people to remember events that had not occurred, and the frequency of this error was remarkably high.

It is difficult to tell in this case whether the error arose during storage or retrieval. One possibility is that, as participants read the stories, they automatically made inferences about what was happening based on the relevant script. These inferences were then stored in memory together with actual events, and during the recall phase participants could no longer distinguish the events that had occurred from the ones they had inferred. Alternatively, the errors could have arisen during the recall phase. If participants could not recall all the details, they might have used their restaurant script to reconstruct the stories, leading them to remember events that were in the script but had not actually occurred. For our current purposes, it is not crucial whether the error occurred during storage or retrieval; the key point is that the results demonstrate yet again the powerful influence of schemas in shaping what we remember.

Ecological validity

One final comment. Psychological research is sometimes criticized on the grounds that it is artificial. According to this view, the conditions used in experiments are not really representative of conditions in the real world, so that the results lack *ecological validity* – you cannot assume that the behavior observed in the laboratory will be representative of that in the real world. (For two contrasting views on this issue, see Neisser, 1978, and Banaji and Crowder, 1989.) It is thus perhaps worth noting that the effects of schemas observed in the laboratory have also been observed in real-life situations. In one study, psychologists interviewed Dutch citizens 10 months after an air crash in which 43 people had been killed. When participants were asked whether they had seen the television film of the crash, more than half said that they had – even though no such film existed. Moreover, when asked detailed questions about what had been shown in the film – for example, the plane's speed – most participants not only answered but did so with considerable confidence (Crombag, Wagenaar, and van Koppen, 1996). This behavior is susceptible to alternative interpretations, but it seems likely that those interviewed had seen films of other crashes and used their schematic knowledge of what happens during crashes to infer what happened in this case. The most worrying aspect of this result is the confidence with which people remembered events that had not happened; again, we will consider the implications of such overconfidence in Chapter 12.

A meaningful summary

We've discussed a number of attempts to understand how information is stored in semantic memory – concepts, semantic networks, propositions, and schemas – and on the surface it might appear as if they are all quite different. They are, however, strongly related, and each can be seen as an elaboration of the one discussed before it. When dealing with individual words, we focused on concepts. Then, in semantic networks, we looked at how different concepts might be linked to each other in hierarchically organized networks, in which information is stored efficiently so as to avoid endless duplication. (A robin breathes, a crow breathes, a mountain lion breathes...) The links connecting concepts ("a robin *isa* bird") are equivalent to propositions, and a semantic network can thus be seen as a hierarchically organized set of propositions. These propositions allow the storage of semantic memories (Paris is the capital of France), but they can also be used to store declarative memories, by linking new information to the context in which it was acquired ("In school today my teacher said that Paris is the capital of France"). In order to create propositions, however, we sometimes need to use contextual information to infer the intended meaning of a sequence of words, and we can then call on schemas, which are organized representations of common sequences of events or actions. Putting aside for the moment all the details, it should be clear that remembering even a simple sentence can involve impressively sophisticated processing, and that what is most likely to remain in memory is the abstracted meaning of a communication rather than the particular words used to convey it. Or, condensing this message even further, *meaning is at the heart of memory.*

Summary

- Theorists have suggested that long-term memory is composed of several separate memory systems, each involving different processes and structures within the brain.

- Tulving distinguished between episodic and semantic memory systems. The episodic system stores information about particular moments or episodes; the semantic system stores general knowledge. Both kinds of memories are explicit, in the sense that they can be stated in words.

- Later theorists added two implicit memory systems, which retrieve memories largely without our awareness. Procedural memories are memories for actions which allow us to respond more quickly; perceptual memories are memories for stimuli which allow us to recognize them more quickly.

- The fact that implicit memories are unconscious means that past experiences can sometimes influence us without our awareness; examples include unconscious feelings of prejudice and greater liking for familiar faces.

- Evidence that these four kinds of memory are the products of different memory systems has come from studies of dissociations in which damage to the brain impairs one kind of memory but not the others.

- Knowledge in the semantic system is stored in several different forms, including concepts, semantic networks, propositions, and schemas.

- A semantic network is a collection of concepts organized hierarchically. Properties of concepts are typically stored at only one level within the hierarchy, to avoid duplication (cognitive economy).

- The relationship between an object and its properties is represented in propositions; a semantic network can thus also be seen as an organized array of propositions.

- More broadly, propositions have been defined as the smallest units of knowledge that can be either true or false. When we read sentences, we typically store their underlying meaning as well as the words in which this meaning is expressed, and this meaning is stored in the form of propositions.

- Understanding a sentence often requires knowledge not stated explicitly in the sentence. Such background knowledge is stored in schemas, which contain information about typical events; one form of schema is a script, which stores information about a sequence of events, such as the actions involved in buying an ice cream. Scripts have been described as frames that have slots for each of the events within the sequence.

- Schemas help us in interpreting and then storing our experiences; they also guide us in deciding what aspects of a scene require attention. This selective function can lead to errors, such as remembering something that was part of the typical script but, in this case, didn't actually happen.

Review questions

1 What is the difference between episodic and semantic memory? What evidence suggests that these memories are formed in different systems?

2 How do procedural and episodic memories differ? What evidence suggests that they are the products of different memory systems?

3 What is perceptual memory? What evidence suggests that perceptual and episodic memories are the products of different memory systems?

4 How do explicit and implicit memories differ?

5 What evidence suggests that feelings of prejudice and attraction can be the products, at least in part, of implicit memories, which influence us without our awareness?

6 Why is it so difficult to decide how many memory systems there are, and how does the use of converging operations address this problem? Specifically, how have converging operations helped us to understand why Jon was able to perform well on recognition tests even though his ability to recall these words was poor?

7 How does the typicality effect support the claim that concepts are organized around prototypes?

8 What are exemplar theories of concepts, and how do they account for the typicality effect?

9 What were the main features of Collins and Quillian's semantic network model? What evidence supported it?

10 Why did the typicality effect pose problems for Collins and Quillian's model? How did Collins and Loftus modify the model in order to accommodate this effect? And how did research on semantic priming support their revised model?

11 An attractively simple model of memory would be that, when we read sentences, we form a record consisting simply of each of the words. What evidence suggests that we don't store sentences in the form of words – or, at any rate, not just in the form of words?

12 What are propositions? How does the Ratcliff and McKoon study support their existence?

13 We've suggested that we store the meaning of sentences rather than (or in addition to) the words in which this meaning was expressed. How do we use schemas to help us to infer the intended meaning?

14 What evidence suggests that schemas can help us to remember our experiences? And what evidence suggests that they can also lead to distortions in what we remember?

15 Why is it useful to think of memory as resembling a sketch rather than a photograph?

16 What is the relationship between concepts, semantic networks, propositions, and schemas?

11 Retrieval

CONTENTS

You're taking an exam and the first question is "What was the name of the infant conditioned by Watson and Raynor (1920) to fear a white rat?" You had read the section on fear conditioning a few weeks earlier and reread it just the night before. You *know* that you know the infant's name, it feels as if it's on the tip of your tongue, but you just can't retrieve it, no matter how hard you try. Why? If you'd been asked the question shortly after reading the text, you would have been able to answer it effortlessly, so there can be no doubt that you did store the name. Why, then, can't you retrieve it?

Why do we forget?

The most obvious cause of forgetting is the passage of time: The more time that passes following an event, the harder it becomes to recall it. What is it about the passage of time, however, that causes forgetting?

Decay

One possibility is that the memories or records stored in our brain deteriorate or **decay** as times passes. In this view, forming a memory is similar to writing a name in the sand on a beach – as time passes, wind erodes the message, until eventually no trace remains. Memory seems very similar – when memories fade over time, it feels very much as if whatever records were in our brain have been erased. The more time that passes – that is, the longer the retention interval – the greater the decay.

There is, however, another possibility: Perhaps it is not time per se that causes forgetting but, rather, how we spend this time. In essence, the suggestion is that we form new memories as time passes, and these new memories **interfere** with our ability to recall older ones. So, which explanation is correct: Is forgetting due simply to the passage of time, or to interference from new memories formed during this time?

Long-term memory

One way to evaluate these theories would be to manipulate the number of memories formed during the retention interval. According to an interference analysis, forgetting is the result of events that occur during this interval, and the more events that occur, the greater the interference. According to a decay analysis, on the other hand, forgetting is caused simply by the passage of time; the number of memories formed during the retention interval should not matter.

To test this hypothesis, we need to be able to control how many new memories are formed during the retention interval, but how could we possibly control how many ideas people have? Jenkins and Dallenbach (1924) devised an ingenious solution: To reduce the number of memories formed during the delay, they said, have participants sleep! In the first phase of their experiment, two participants memorized a list of nonsense syllables. (These, you will recall, are meaningless syllables such as *rab*.) Then, after a delay of between 1 and 8 hours, they tried to recall these syllables. In one condition, they remained awake during this retention interval, engaging in their normal daily activities. In the other condition, they memorized the lists at night, immediately before going to bed, so that they spent most of the retention interval asleep.

If forgetting is caused by decay, forgetting in the two conditions should be the same because the delay is the same. If forgetting is caused by interference, on the other hand, we should expect more forgetting when the participants remain awake, because they will be more likely to form new memories. As shown in Figure 11.1, the results supported the interference prediction. When the retention interval was 8 hours, for example, participants could recall approximately five syllables when

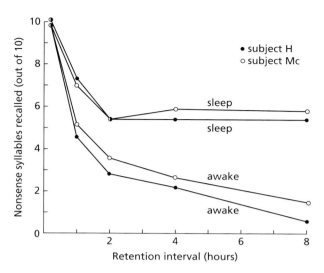

Figure 11.1 The number of nonsense syllables recalled after intervals spent either awake or asleep. (Jenkins and Dallenbach, 1924.)

they had slept during the retention interval, whereas they could recall only one when they had been awake. What happened during the retention interval clearly had a powerful effect on how much was forgotten.

Jenkins and Dallenbach's results suggest that interference is an important cause of forgetting, but it does not necessarily follow that interference is the only cause. In particular, could forgetting be due to decay as well as interference? If you look more carefully at Figure 11.1, you will see that forgetting occurred even in the sleep condition, as decay theory would predict. However, most of this forgetting occurred in the first two hours. If we suppose that the participants did not fall asleep the instant they finished studying the list – a not unreasonable assumption – then interference can also account for the forgetting during the first two hours, and it can more easily explain why virtually no forgetting occurred after this time.

The results of the Jenkins and Dallenbach study, then, support the view that interference is the main cause of forgetting, perhaps even the only cause. On its own, the study is not decisive: As with any experiment, alternative interpretations are possible (for example, Hockey, Davies, and Gray, 1972). Subsequent research, however, has supported the conclusion that interference is the main cause of forgetting. One simple example comes from a study by Baddeley and Hitch (1977). The authors were English, and they asked members of two local rugby teams to recall the names of the teams they had played that season. As you would expect, players had more difficulty recalling teams they had played early in the season than teams they had played more recently. The critical feature of this study, however, was that players often missed games because of injury or other commitments.

For a game that occurred a month earlier, for example, some players might have played three games during the interim, whereas other players might have played just one or two. Through statistical analysis, the experimenters were thus able to assess whether forgetting was caused by the time since a game was played or by the number of other games played during this interval. The results showed that the passage of time per se caused very little forgetting. For example, players were excellent at recalling the last team they had played, whether this game occurred a week or a month earlier. Much more important was the number of games played during the retention interval: The more games played during a season, the harder players found it to recall games played at the beginning of the season. As in the Jenkins and Dallenbach study, forgetting seemed to be caused not by the passage of time but by the events that occurred during this time.

You have probably had similar experiences, though you may not have thought of them in these terms. To illustrate the point, try to remember what you ate each night for the last week. You will probably have little difficulty in recalling your last meal, but it will become progressively harder as you try to remember earlier meals. Of course, this forgetting could be due to the passage of time rather than to the meals you ate during the intervening period. To disentangle the two, now try to remember what you ate on your last birthday. Even though this was probably weeks or months ago, you will probably find it easier to remember than what you ate a week ago. If so, forgetting cannot be caused simply by the passage of time: It seems to depend critically on our experiences during this time.

This example not only illustrates the importance of interference but also provides preliminary evidence for an important principle of interference, that the degree to which memories interfere with each other depends on their *similarity*. Eating a meal seems to interfere with our ability to remember similar meals, but not meals eaten in very different circumstances, such as at a restaurant or for a birthday. Thus, the meals you ate this week will interfere with your memory for meals eaten last week, but not for meals eaten under very different circumstances months or even years ago. Similarly in the rugby example: Whether players participate in one rugby game during a month or four, they will form many, many other memories during this month. The fact that only the latter group forget the game suggests that forgetting is caused not simply by the formation of new memories but, rather, by new memories that are similar to the target – in this case, playing a rugby game.

Short-term memory

The studies we have examined so far have concerned forgetting over relatively long periods – hours or weeks. Over long periods such as these, it appears that forgetting is largely caused by interference. If we consider forgetting over shorter periods, however, it seems plausible that decay might play a greater role. You have

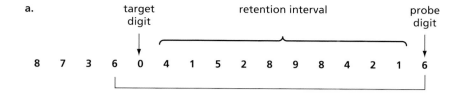

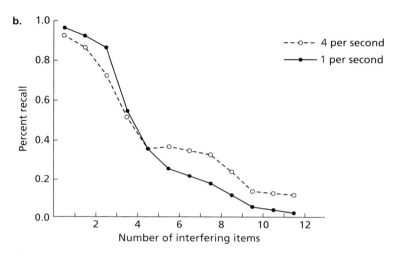

Figure 11.2 Waugh and Norman's (1965) probe-digit procedure. (a) Participants listened to a string of 16 digits; when they heard the last digit, they had to recall the digit that had followed it when it was presented earlier. (b) The percentage of digits recalled correctly as a function of the number of other digits presented during the retention interval. Digits were presented at a rate of either 1 or 4 digits per second.

probably had the experience of looking up a telephone number and then, when you started to dial it, finding that you had already forgotten it. If only a few seconds elapsed, it is hard to see how this forgetting could have been caused by interference from other events. Even here, however, there is evidence that interference really is the cause. In one study by Waugh and Norman (1965), participants listened to lists of 16 digits. The last digit in each list was the same as one of the digits presented earlier; when participants heard this probe digit, their task was to repeat the digit that had previously followed the probe (see Figure 11.2a). Suppose, for example, that a list contained the sequence 690. If the digit 9 was presented for a second time at the end of the list, participants were supposed to recall the digit that had previously followed it, namely 0. This *probe technique* was very demanding – participants had to concentrate hard to remember the exact sequence in which the digits had been presented – but it provided a useful baseline for measuring short-term memory.

For one group in this study, the digits were presented at a rate of one per second. The solid line in Figure 11.2b presents the results for this group. According to an interference analysis, presenting more digits during the retention interval should lead to poorer recall, and this is what happened: The probability of recalling a digit fell sharply as the number of digits presented during the interval increased. Note, however, that this result could also be explained by decay theory: Because digits were presented at a constant rate, trials where more digits were presented during the interval were also trials where the delay was longer. The observed decrease in recall could thus have been caused by decay.

To distinguish the two accounts, Waugh and Norman ran a second group in which digits were presented four times every second instead of once. Because the digits were presented faster during the retention interval, the interval became shorter. According to decay theory, this should have helped recall because there would have been less time for the memory trace to decay. As shown in the figure, however, recall in the two groups was virtually identical. Reducing the length of the retention interval, in other words, had no effect on forgetting; the rate of forgetting depended not on the passage of time but simply on the number of digits presented during this time.

Whether we examine forgetting over long periods or short ones, therefore, the primary cause of forgetting seems to be interference from memories formed during the retention interval. It is possible that decay also plays some role, but it currently looks as if the main cause of forgetting is interference. (See also Oberauer and Lewandowsky, 2008; Berman, Jonides, and Lewis, 2009.)

Interference

As the importance of interference became obvious, psychologists increasingly wondered why the formation of new memories should interfere with our ability to recall older ones.

Retroactive interference

To determine the processes involved, researchers developed a new procedure for studying interference. In its simplest form, it involves two groups that both learn the same material – perhaps memorizing a list of words we will call list 1. The experimental group then memorizes a second list of words, list 2, while the control group does nothing. Finally, both groups are tested for their ability to recall the material from the first list:

	Study		*Test*
experimental group:	list 1	list 2	list 1
control group:	list 1	—	list 1

If recall of list 1 is poorer in the experimental group, this would suggest that the material in list 2 was interfering with recall of list 1. Because the interference produced by list 2 would be acting backward, or retroactively, on memory for list 1, the effect is called **retroactive interference (RI)**.

In one early study using this procedure, McGeoch and McDonald (1931) investigated the role of similarity in interference. Participants first memorized a list of adjectives and then, 10 minutes later, tried to recall them. A control group simply rested during the delay interval, but five experimental groups memorized material that varied in similarity to the original list. At one extreme, one experimental group memorized numbers, material that would seem to have very little in common with adjectives; at the other extreme, another group memorized synonyms of the words used in the first list. (If, for example, the first list had contained the word *priest*, the second list might have contained the word *minister*.) The results confirmed the importance of similarity. The control group was able to remember an average of 4.5 adjectives from the original list; the group that learned numbers remembered 3.7; but the group that learned synonyms remembered only 1.3. The more similar the second list was to the first, the more difficulty participants had in remembering the original.

Proactive interference

Extensive research was carried out to determine the principles of retroactive interference, and attempts were also made to form a coherent theory of why these effects occur (for example, McGeoch, 1942; Postman and Underwood, 1973). The emerging theories were able to account for many of the findings, but some were puzzling. One of the most perplexing findings was also one of the simplest: If participants memorize a list of nonsense syllables until they can recall them perfectly, then are tested 24 hours later, they have considerable difficulty in recalling the syllables. On the surface, this might not seem surprising, but it is very difficult to explain by interference. As we have seen, interference is greatest when material is similar, but it was highly unlikely that participants encountered other nonsense syllables during the 24 hour retention interval. If they didn't encounter similar material, however, why was there so much forgetting?

Benton Underwood, one of the most prolific researchers and influential theorists in this area, provided an ingenious answer. He and other memory researchers often used the same undergraduates in different experiments, so that a single individual might participate in many experiments involving nonsense syllables. Was it possible, then, that participants were forgetting material in an experiment because of material they had learned before that experiment? To find out, Underwood (1957) examined his records and those of colleagues to determine whether the number of studies in which students participated before an experiment affected

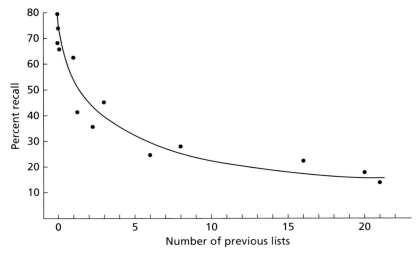

Figure 11.3 Proactive interference. Recall of a list learned 24 hours earlier as a function of the number of lists learned previously. (Adapted from Underwood, 1957.)

how quickly they forgot the material learned in that experiment. As shown in Figure 11.3, he found that recall did fall as the number of previous experiments increased.[1] In some ways this is a bizzare result: If you were trying to recall something that happened an hour ago, for example, why should events that occurred days or weeks ago interfere? Nevertheless, Underwood's data provided clear evidence that this happens, and interference caused by material learned previously is called **proactive interference**, or PI.

The discovery of proactive interference potentially allowed theorists to explain another puzzling finding discussed earlier, namely the extraordinarily rapid forgetting that occurs in short-term memory. When you look up a telephone number and then forget it within seconds, it is difficult to conceive how enough events could occur during this brief period to produce such massive interference. Moreover, we have now seen that interference is largely caused by the occurrence of similar events: Because it is unlikely that you were thinking about other numbers during the retention interval, it is even harder to see how forgetting a telephone number could be caused by interference. Could the explanation, then, be proactive interference from events that occurred *before* you looked up the number?

---

[1] Note that this forgetting cannot be attributed to students becoming increasingly bored as they participated in more experiments. Boredom might lead to their not trying as hard, and thus taking longer to memorize material. In each of these studies, however, training continued until performance had reached a high criterion – typically, perfect recall of the list. Thus, although boredom could explain why participants might take longer to learn the lists, it does not explain why, once having done so, they should then forget the lists faster.

This explanation may not seem much more plausible than one based on retroactive interference, but Keppel and Underwood (1962) nevertheless decided to test it. To measure short-term memory, they used the procedure developed by Peterson and Peterson (1959) a few years earlier. In this procedure participants are given consonant trigrams to remember and then asked to count backward during a retention interval. The Petersons found that memory for the trigrams faded very rapidly – after 18 seconds, it was almost zero. The participants in this study had not participated in similar studies in the past, so it was not immediately obvious how proactive interference could have affected their performance, but Keppel and Underwood noted that the reported results were averages derived from many trials. Was it possible that forgetting did not occur on the first trials, and emerged only gradually as the number of trials increased?

To find out, Keppel and Underwood repeated the Peterson and Peterson experiment but examined how performance changed over trials. Keppel and Underwood found that on the first trial participants recalled the trigrams almost perfectly; only after several trials did signs of forgetting begin to appear. In other words, the rapid forgetting typically observed in this situation is caused at least in part by material learned on previous trials. On the first trial, there is no previous learning and so there is no forgetting; only as trials continue, and interference from earlier trials increases, does forgetting begin to occur.

This result might seem hard to believe – could previously learned material really cause such rapid forgetting? – but this finding was repeatedly confirmed in subsequent studies. In one series of experiments by Wickens (1972; Wickens, Born, and Allen, 1963), participants were given four trials using the Peterson and Peterson procedure. On the first three trials, the nature of the material to be remembered was the same, but on the fourth trial it was changed. If the task on the first three trials was to remember a word, for example, then on the fourth trial it would be to remember a number. Figure 11.4 shows the typical results obtained with this procedure. As in the Keppel and Underwood study, recall is excellent on the first trial and gradually declines on trials 2 and 3. When the target is altered on trial 4, however, recall returns to almost 100%. Wickens called this phenomenon **release from PI**, and it provides further evidence for the crucial role of similarity in interference. If we learn material that is similar to previous material (as on trials 2 and 3), the earlier material interferes with recall; if the new material is dissimilar, however (as on trial 4), there is no interference.

Summing up, evidence for proactive interference suggests that we can forget material not only because of material that we learn subsequently but also because of material learned previously. If you have two similar memories, each makes it harder to recall the other, and it does not seem to matter greatly whether the interfering memory was formed before or after the memory we want to retrieve.

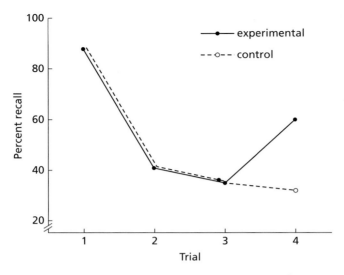

Figure 11.4 Release from PI. Percent recall when the type of material to be remembered is the same on every trial (control group) or changes on the fourth trial (experimental group). (Adapted from Wickens, 1972.)

Erasure or loss?

For the moment, let us confine our attention to the phenomenon of retroactive interference. Why should the formation of new memories cause us to forget older ones?

One possibility is that the formation of new memories leads to the erasure of existing ones. This hypothesis has gone under different names – one early version was called *unlearning*; a more recent variant has been called *overwriting* – and the details have also varied somewhat (see Anderson and Neely, 1996, for a review). A common theme, though, has been that forgotten material is truly destroyed. It is as if our memories can hold only a limited amount of material, so that the creation of new memories results in the modification or destruction of older ones. (A lovely example concerns an elderly professor of ichthyology who, it is said, lamented that every time he learned the name of a new student he forgot the name of a fish!)

Unavailable or inaccessible?

The concept of unlearning was widely accepted for many years, but evidence gradually accumulated that much of the material that appears to have been forgotten is actually still present in our memories. The most influential advocate of this position was Endel Tulving, then a psychologist at the University of Toronto. In one of his early studies, Tulving and Psotka (1971) asked participants to memorize lists of 24 words, where each list contained words drawn from 6 categories. For example, if one of the categories was animal names, the list would have included 4 words such as *cat*, *dog*, *lion*, and *bird*. After participants had had an opportunity to study this list, they were given a recall test. They then memorized several other lists, with a recall test after each study period. Finally, they were asked to recall the words from all the lists.

In accord with previous studies, Tulving and Psotka found retroactive interference: The more lists intervened between a target list and the final test, the fewer words participants could recall from this target list. According to the overwriting hypothesis, this was because memorization of the new lists destroyed records of older ones. To see if this was really the case, the experimenters now ran a further test in which they showed participants the names of the categories that had been used and then again asked them to recall all the words. Recall improved dramatically, and the number of words recalled from each list on this final test was the same as on the tests given immediately after each study period. In other words, although learning new lists had made it harder to recall earlier material, this was not because the earlier material had been destroyed. The words from these lists were still present in memory, and when participants were reminded of the categories from which the words had been drawn, they were able to retrieve every single word.

To explain these results, Tulving and Psotka distinguished between the **availability** of material in memory and its **accessibility** (Tulving and Pearlstone, 1966). According to unlearning theories, forgetting occurs because material is no longer available in memory – it is lost. Tulving and Psotka's results, however, suggested that forgotten material sometimes is available; it appears lost only because we have a hard time accessing it. In their study, participants had apparently used the category names to help them remember the words on each list ("I know one of the categories was animals; now, which animals were they?"), and learning new lists made it harder for them to recall all the categories. When reminded of the category names, they were able to use them to retrieve all the words they had stored.

Other evidence supports the conclusion that our memories hold far more material than we can normally access. Indeed, there is so much evidence that it is hard to decide which studies to examine, but we will look at a few examples.

The tip-of-the-tongue effect

Most of us have had the experience of trying to remember a word, feeling that it is just at the tip of our tongues, but not quite being able to recall it. William James beautifully described this tantalizing experience in 1893:

Suppose we try to recall a forgotten name. The state of our consciousness is peculiar. There is a gap therein; but no mere gap. It is a gap that is intensely active. A sort of wraith of the name is in it, beckoning us in a given direction, making us at moments tingle with the sense of our closeness and then letting us sink back without the longed-for term. If wrong names are proposed to us, this singularly definite gap acts immediately so as to negate them. They do not fit into its mould.

(James, 1893, p. 251)

This subjective feeling of knowing strongly suggests that the forgotten material is really still there, but is this feeling trustworthy?

A path-breaking study by Brown and McNeill (1966) suggests that it is. They asked participants questions that they hoped would trigger a **tip-of-the-tongue** experience – for example, "What is the name of the instrument that uses the position of the sun and stars to navigate?" When participants reported that the answer seemed to be on the tip of their tongues, the experimenters then asked detailed questions such as what is the first letter, and how many syllables does the word have? The results showed that participants could typically answer these questions very accurately. When asked the first letter, for example, their answers were correct 57% of the time. Similarly, when asked to provide words that sounded the same, their answers were sometimes astonishingly close. The correct answer to the sample question just given is *sextant*; similar-sounding words provided by the participants included *secant* and *sextet*. (For a review of research on this phenomenon, see Brown, 2008.)

Recall versus recognition

Further evidence that we store far more material than we can normally retrieve has come from studies comparing *recognition* and *recall*. As discussed in Chapter 8, in a recall test participants are asked to reproduce the material they have learned, without any cues or other help from the experimenter. In a recognition test, by contrast, participants are shown material and asked whether they've seen it previously.

In one experiment comparing these two methods, Mandler, Pearlstone, and Koopmans (1969) first asked participants to study a list of 100 words. One group was then asked to recall the words, whereas a second group was given a recognition test in which they were shown a list of 200 words. Half of the words had been on the original list (old words) and half had not (new words); for each word, participants had to say whether it had been on the original list. The recall group was able to recall only 38% of the words, but the recognition group correctly recognized 96%. Moreover, the high recognition score was not due to saying yes indiscriminately: When shown new words, participants responded positively only 7% of the time.

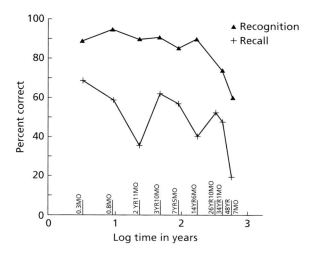

Figure 11.5 Memory for classmates' names over 48 years. When shown yearbook pictures of faces, participants' recognition scores (each face was accompanied by 5 possible names) were consistently higher than those for recall. (Adapted from Bahrick, Bahrick, and Wittlinger, 1975.)

Similar results have been obtained in naturalistic studies which have examined people's memories for their personal experiences, rather than information memorized in the laboratory. In one such study Bahrick, Bahrick, and Wittlinger (1975) examined people's ability to remember the names of their high school classmates. Participants ranged in age from 17 to 74, and the time since graduation varied from a few weeks to a rather impressive 57 years. They were given a variety of memory tests, including cued recall and recognition. In the recall test they were shown pictures of classmates taken from the high school yearbook and asked to give their names; in the recognition test each picture was accompanied by a set of 5 names and they were asked to choose the correct one. As shown in Figure 11.5, performance on the recall test fell sharply over time – after 47 years, participants could recall only around 10% of their classmates' names. Recognition performance, by contrast, was substantially better throughout, and even after 47 years was around 60%. Similar results were reported by Conway, Cohen, and Stanhope (1991) in a study which examined students' ability to remember material learned in a cognitive psychology course. Recall scores were not terribly impressive, but even after 10 years students could still correctly recognize around 65% of the concepts they had learned.

Results such as these have made it clear that people are usually much better at recognizing material than at recalling it. The fact that we cannot recall an event, therefore, does not necessarily mean that we have no record of it: When actually shown the material, we are often very good at recognizing it.

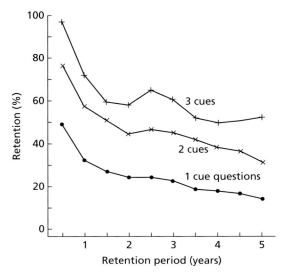

Figure 11.6 The effect of number of retrieval cues on recall. (Adapted from Wagenaar, 1986.)

Wagenaar's diary

Further evidence of how much material we have stored in our memories, even when we can't seem to retrieve it, comes from another naturalistic study, this time by a Dutch psychologist, Willem Wagenaar (1986). Over a 6-year period, he kept a diary in which he recorded one or two of his experiences each day; by the end, he had recorded 2,400 incidents. He then tested his memory for these incidents by using some of the information in each diary entry to see if he could recall the remainder. (A colleague extracted the clues to be used for testing.)

Wagenaar found that his ability to recall his experiences depended on how many cues he allowed himself. For incidents that had occurred one year previously, for example, he found that with one cue he could recall approximately 30% of the remaining information; with three cues, his performance improved to more than 70% (Figure 11.6). This performance was particularly impressive because Wagenaar used very demanding criteria for scoring a memory as correct. One of the test questions, for example, required stating when the incident had occurred, and he scored an answer as correct only if the remembered date was within one week of the actual date.

Considering the number of incidents remembered, and the stringent criteria used for judging an answer correct, Wagenaar's performance is deeply impressive. Nevertheless, he was unable to recall any details about some of his experiences – even when he reread the full diary entries, he could not recall them. Some of these forgotten incidents had involved others, and Wagenaar now consulted the individuals concerned to see if they could provide further information to jog his memory. In every case where they could, their supplementary accounts allowed Wagenaar to recall the forgotten incident, and he was able to recall further details that his informants confirmed. With suitable help, in other words, Wagenaar was able to recall virtually every incident that he had recorded over the course of six years.

We need to interpret these results with some caution – Wagenaar wasn't testing whether he could remember everything that happened to him during these six years, only those events that he had deemed sufficiently important to enter into his diary, and the act of recording them would have involved further rehearsal. Nevertheless, his ability to remember 2,400 incidents (and undoubtedly many more that he hadn't recorded) is impressive.

Savings

The evidence we have reviewed suggests that a surprising amount of the material that enters long-term memory is retained there permanently, and this raises the still more radical possibility that *all* such material is retained. Or, to be clear, that all material that *reaches* long-term memory is retained. As we saw in Chapter 9, there are powerful filtering systems in both sensory and short-term memory that weed out relatively minor aspects of our experiences before they ever reach long-term memory. What, though, of material that – rather like heroic salmon fighting their way upstream – overcomes all the obstacles and finally becomes lodged in long-term memory? Is all this material preserved permanently?

Consider your experiences over the last hour – anything you've remembered this long is probably in long-term memory. If you tried hard enough, you could produce a very detailed account of what you've read during this hour – definitions, concepts, details of experiments, and so on. Evidence even indicates that, one month after reading a passage, you would be able to remember the typeface in which this material was written (Kolers and Ostry, 1974). In addition, you could describe in detail the area where you have been working, and the weather, and, if you talked to others, provide details of your conversations, the clothes they were wearing, and so on. Is it really conceivable that every single one of these details is permanently stored in your memory, as if on a videotape, so that in 30 years every moment would potentially still be available to you? And, by extension, that you retain similarly detailed memories for everything else that has ever happened to you?

Many psychologists as well as lay people find this hard to believe, but it is a very difficult issue to address empirically. If we cannot remember something, how do we know whether the missing material is lost or still stored somewhere, only awaiting appropriate reminders to help us recover it?

Given the implausibility of the latter claim, it is perhaps worth considering one more piece of the evidence that supports it. In a study by Nelson (1978), participants memorized a list of digit–word pairs such as *48–party*. Their memory for this material was tested one month later, and Nelson found that some of the pairs appeared to have been entirely forgotten – participants could neither recall nor recognize these pairs. To test whether some trace might nevertheless still remain, Nelson now used the savings procedure for testing memory pioneered by Ebbinghaus. As discussed in Chapter 8, this involves memorizing material and then, after a delay, relearning it. If learning the material originally required, say, 5 trials, and relearning it requires only 2 trials, then we have evidence that some record of the original experience was retained.

Nelson asked half his subjects to relearn the pairs they had not been able to remember. A control group learned the same material but in different pairings, so that the digit from one forgotten pair was paired with the word from another. If a participant had not been able to remember *48–party* and *26–book*, for example, she might now learn a list containing the rearranged pairs *48–book* and *26–party*. After practicing the material, participants were given a memory test in which they were shown each number and had to remember the word that had followed it. Nelson found that the experimental group could recall 50% of the original pairs, but the control group remembered only 20% of the rearranged pairs. Thus, even though participants had not been able to either recall or recognize some pairs, some trace of these pairs had clearly been preserved.

Summary

We started this section with the question of why we forget, and the first possibility we considered was that memories simply decay over time. This explanation is intuitively appealing, but if decay plays any role in forgetting, current research suggests that it is a small one. In experiments where interference has been controlled – the Jenkins and Dallenbach experiment on sleep, for example, or the Baddeley and Hitch study of memory for rugby – the passage of time per se has turned out to cause surprisingly little forgetting. The main cause of forgetting in these experiments has been interference from preceding or subsequent events.

As to why interfering events cause forgetting, one possibility is that the formation of new memories leads to the erasure of older ones. This explanation is plausible, and some evidence supports it (see Schacter, 1996). However, in many cases where material appears to have been forgotten, it can be retrieved with suitable help, or traces can be revealed with more sensitive measuring procedures. It is thus clear that our memories contain far more material than we normally can recall. In these cases, forgetting is caused by the difficulties in retrieving material, rather than by its erasure.

Retrieval processes

Research on forgetting led to the elimination or discounting of one explanation after another, until eventually we were left with just one explanation as the Mr. Big of forgetting: difficulties in retrieval. In this section, therefore, we turn our attention to trying to understand how retrieval works.

Memory as a warehouse

Storage

To understand retrieval, it can be useful to think of memory as resembling a book warehouse. First, imagine a book warehouse where, as each new book is delivered, it is simply placed on a shelf next to whatever books were delivered before it. Now suppose that the warehouse receives an order for a particular volume. If there are only a small number of books in the warehouse, an employee could easily go through them one by one to find the volume that is needed. As the number of volumes in storage increases, however, this strategy would quickly become impractical – if there were hundreds of thousands of books, it would require days or weeks to complete a search. To have a realistic chance of finding a book, in other words, it is vital that books not be stored simply in order of their delivery; instead, the warehouse must catalog or *organize* books as they arrive, putting cookbooks in one section, mysteries in another, and so on. The better the organization, the easier it will be to find books when they are needed.

The same is true for memory. As we saw in Chapter 8, people rely heavily on organization to help them remember material. If they are asked to memorize a list of words, for example, they remember far more if the material is organized – in the Bower *et al.* (1969) study we discussed then, participants recalled three times as many minerals if they were grouped by type (for example, metals and stones) rather than intermixed randomly. And if a list does not have any structure, containing words selected at random, then people will impose their own structure. Tulving (1962), for example, found that people organize the words on such lists into little groups or clusters, and they then recall these clusters together on trial after trial. We clearly rely on organization to help us remember, and where a suitable organization scheme is not readily available, we develop our own.

Retrieval

A second, closely related factor in facilitating retrieval is the use of appropriate **retrieval cues.** Returning to our book warehouse example, it is not enough to organize material when we store it; when an order comes in, the order must contain sufficient information to direct us to the appropriate area. If we know we are looking for a cookbook, for example, this will obviously limit the search area, and we can limit it even more if we know that it is a book on desserts, or that the author's last name begins with "S." The more retrieval cues are available, the faster the book will be found.

Again, the same could be true of memory. Consider the following example – imaginary, but perhaps not too far from your own experiences. Suppose you're walking down the street and see someone whose face is familiar, but you can't quite remember who he is. Then, a week later, you see the same person in your bank, where he is a teller, and you immediately recognize him and remember a past conversation. Why did you recognize him in the second situation but not the first? One possible answer is that when we have any experience, we store it in memory by forming associations or connections amongst the elements that compose it. When you talk to someone in a bank, you will associate many of the elements that are present – the person's face, the words he speaks, the bank's appearance, and so on. Together, these elements will form a memory *record* or *episode*. If you later see the teller in the street, his face will be associated with this episode, and thus tend to activate it in your memory. However, the association may not be strong enough to activate the record fully – or, at any rate, to activate it more strongly than other memories competing for your attention. When you see the person in the bank, however, there would now be two cues present that were associated with the earlier episode. The total amount of activation reaching the stored episode would therefore be greater and might now be sufficient to bring the episode fully into consciousness.

Retrieval cues

Our analysis to this point has been speculative, but reasoning of this kind led psychologists to investigate the role of retrieval cues experimentally, to see whether they really do have the kind of influence we have hypothesized. In the following sections we will look at examples involving two broad classes of possible cues, external stimuli which come from the surrounding environment, and internal stimuli which come from within our own bodies.

External context

The term *contextual cues* is used to refer to incidental or background stimuli which are present at the time an event occurs. As you read this, your main focus is on the words you're reading, but other stimuli impinging on your senses include the appearance of the room, background sounds, and even the pressure of your chair against your legs. Could any of these background cues become part of the record you're forming of what you're reading, so that exposure to these cues could later help you to remember it?

A study by Smith (1979) suggested that the answer could be yes. He was interested in whether room cues could enhance retrieval, and in the first phase of his study participants memorized a list of 80 unrelated words while sitting in a basement room. Then, one day later, they tried to recall these words. For one group, the test was given in the same room, while for a second group the test was in a room that was perceptually very different. (The basement room contained orange drapes, a carpet, and posters, whereas the other room was a bare, sound-proof enclosure containing computer equipment.) You might think that the location of the test would not matter very much, but Smith found that participants tested in the same room remembered 50% more words. Moreover, he found that even *thinking* about the study room while trying to remember the list enhanced recall, and in fact was as effective as actually being in the room. The room cues had apparently become part of the memory record formed during the study phase, so that the physical or even mental presence of these cues helped to reactivate the episode in memory.

An obvious implication is that if you want to do well on an exam, you should study in the room where the exam will be given. For a number of reasons, though, it is probably not worth sneaking into lecture halls to study. One is that large effects are usually obtained only in studies where the training and test environments differ substantially – one of the largest effects was in a study where the participants were scuba divers; the study phase took place underwater and the test phase was conducted on dry land! (Godden and Baddeley, 1975.) Also, note that the material used in Smith's study was a list of unrelated words. When studying more meaningful material such as textbooks, we focus much more strongly on the relationship between the words, so that the meaning of a passage plays a more prominent role in coding than contextual cues. Thus, although place cues can be very helpful in recalling some experiences, they are less likely to matter in situations where more powerful retrieval cues are available. (For further discussion of this issue, see Smith, 1988; Roediger and Guynn, 1996; and Hockley, 2008.)

Tastes and odors can also serve **as** retrieval cues. Anecdotal evidence for this comes from one of the most famous novels of the twentieth century, Marcel Proust's *Remembrance of Things Past*. The novel opens with the author eating a French pastry called a madeleine. Its taste triggers a flood of associations that eventually carried him through eight volumes and more than 3,000 pages of reminiscences. No laboratory studies have yet produced an outpouring on such an epic scale, but they have confirmed that tastes and odors present during an experience can help us to later remember it. One such study focused on a museum in York, England, that provided visitors with a sense of what York had been like 1,000 years earlier, when it was ruled by Vikings. As part of the experience, visitors were conducted through a street built to resemble a Viking settlement, while simultaneously being exposed to a distinctive odor which evoked, among other things, rotting garbage. Aggleton and Waskett (1999) contacted tourists who had once visited the museum to find out how much they remembered of their visit; a group exposed to this odor as they filled in their questionnaires recalled approximately 20% more than controls given either no odor or one that was equally pungent but not associated with the museum.

Returning to Proust's experience, there is evidence that odors are particularly likely to become associated with emotions, so that reexposure to an odor can trigger powerful emotional memories. Vermetten and Bremner (2003) reported that odors can play a role in post-traumatic stress disorder; if a distinctive odor was present during a traumatic event, later exposures to that odor can trigger vivid and painful flashbacks. Moreover, there is evidence that odors can have effects like this even when presented below the level of awareness, so that people are not even aware of their presence (Zucco, Paolini, and Schaal, 2009).

Internal states

The wide range of contextual cues that have been found to be effective as retrieval cues raises the question of whether *any* stimulus present during an experience can become associated with it, and thus potentially serve as a retrieval cue, and some research supports this. In particular, it appears that internal stimuli – how you are feeling during an experience – can also act as retrieval cues. Anecdotal evidence on this point has come from observations of alcoholics. Clinicians have noted that when alcoholics are drunk, they sometimes hide money or alcohol, but that they then have difficulty in remembering the hiding place when they become sober. The memory returns, however, the next time they become drunk (Goodwin, Crane, and Guze, 1969).

To find out if these anecdotal reports were accurate, Goodwin *et al.* (1969) used a variant of a paired-associate task to measure memory. In the normal version of this procedure, participants learn a list of word pairs such as *table–dog*. After going through the pairs one at a time, they are given a test trial in which they are shown the first word from each pair and asked to say what word followed. In this study, participants created their own pairs: They were shown a list of words, and for each word asked to think of a second word. Then, a day later, they were shown the stimulus words again and asked to recall the word they had generated. During the training phase, one group was given approximately 10 oz of vodka to drink before training – enough to produce intoxication – while a second group remained sober. When memory was tested the followed day, half the participants in each of these groups were intoxicated and half were not.

The results are shown in Figure 11.7. The dependent measure was the number of words correctly recalled, and the figure shows the state of intoxication during

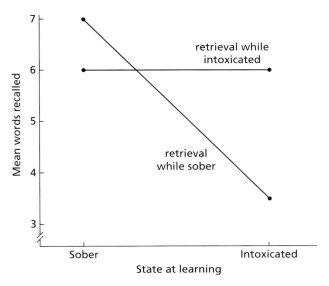

Figure 11.7 State-dependent learning. Mean number of words recalled as a function of the state of intoxication during study and retrieval. (Data from Goodwin, Powell, Bremer, Hoine, and Stern, 1969.)

both training and testing. The first point to note is that the best recall was found when participants were sober during both training and testing; as common sense suggests, studying while drunk is probably not a good idea. The important point in the present context, however, is that recall was consistently better when participants' state during testing matched their conditions during study. Participants who were intoxicated during the study period were more likely to recall the material if they were again intoxicated at test, and similarly, participants who were sober during study did best if they were sober during testing. This phenomenon is called **state-dependent memory**, as our ability to recall an experience depends on our state during coding and retrieval.

Another internal feeling that can act as a retrieval cue is emotion (see, for example, Balch, Myers, and Popotto, 1999, and Ryan and Eich, 2000). If your teacher tells you that you have received a good grade on an exam, the happiness you feel is likely to become a component of your record of this conversation; you will then be more likely to recall this occasion at times when you are again feeling happy. The down side is that this is also true for negative emotions such as anxiety or depression – if you are depressed, you will be more likely to recall earlier experiences which left you depressed. This can lead to a vicious cycle in which people who are depressed keep remembering earlier experiences of failure, with each new memory serving only to deepen their depression. ("I really am worthless, bad things are always happening to me.")

As with the other retrieval cues we have discussed, emotions have been found to have strong effects on retrieval in some experiments while having little or no effect in others. (See discussions in Balch *et al.*, 1999, and Ryan and Eich, 2000.) One possible explanation is that the effectiveness of any one retrieval cue will depend on how many others are present. If there are no other retrieval cues, then adding cue A may substantially enhance retrieval. If cue A is only one of many, on the other hand, its impact is likely to be much smaller.

We cannot cover all of the research that has been done on retrieval cues, but among the cues that have been found to become part of the memory record, and thus to influence later retrieval, are the font in which words are printed (Arndt, 2010), the color of the background against which they appear (Hockley, 2008), and even the clothing worn by the experimenter (Standing *et al.*, 2008). Findings like these suggest that a surprisingly large number of the background stimuli present during an event may become part of the memory record we form. If you talked to a friend while waiting for a class, for example, your record of this conversation might include not only what your friend looked like and the words spoken but more subtle contextual cues such as whether you were feeling tired and the sounds made by passers-by. The more of these cues that were present when you later tried to remember this conversation, the more likely you would be to succeed.

What makes all this difficult is that the environment is constantly changing – not only our external environment but also our internal thoughts and feelings – and this means that the stimuli present during retrieval will inevitably differ from those present during coding. And if these changes are large, they will make it harder for us to locate the information we seek. We began this section with the question of why we forget. One simple answer is that much of the information we store in long-term memory seems to remain there; the problem is that we sometimes lack enough retrieval cues to find it. (See also Jang and Huber, 2008; Lehman and Malmberg, 2009.)

Encoding specificity

In the examples we have considered so far, the contextual cues present during coding became components of the memory record that was formed. If contextual cue A was present at the time of event X, then a compound of these elements, AX, was stored in memory. In some cases, though, contextual cues do more than simply function as background cues, they may change how X itself is coded, producing what might be called an AY compound. One example comes from an experiment by Light and Carter-Sobell (1970) in which they presented participants with sentences that included word pairs such as *strawberry jam*. In a subsequent recognition test, some participants were presented with the same pairs they had seen earlier, while others saw pairs in which the first word was altered – for example, *traffic jam*.

In both cases, participants were asked to say whether the second word (*jam*) had appeared in one of the earlier sentences.

You might think that recognition scores in the two conditions should have been roughly equal – both saw the word *jam* in the first list, and then both were asked whether they had seen it before. In fact, recognition scores for the two conditions were very different: Participants tested with the same pairing recognized 65% of the words, while those tested with altered pairings recognized only 27%. So, why was participants' ability to recognize a word influenced so strongly by what word preceded it?

The explanation lies in the fact that most words have more than one meaning – in our example, *jam* can be a preserve or a traffic snarl-up. In effect, therefore, the two test conditions involved not the same word but two quite different words. It was as if in the first phase all participants were shown a picture of a jar of jam, and in the test phase one group was shown the same picture while a second group was shown a picture of traffic gridlock in a city. It would hardly be surprising if only the first group reported having seen the picture before.

Once thought of in this way, the results make sense, but they illustrate an important principle of memory, that the difficulty of retrieving an experience depends not simply on the nature of the experience – was it particularly interesting or exciting, and therefore memorable? – but on the context in which it occurred, and also, crucially, on the context during retrieval. Endel Tulving and his colleagues at the University of Toronto proposed a specific version of this insight which was to prove very influential in drawing attention to the importance of contextual cues (Tulving and Osler, 1968; Tulving and Thomson, 1973). They called it the principle of **encoding specificity**, and in essence it consists of several intertwined assumptions:

1 There are often alternative ways in which a word or other event can be encoded.
2 The context during coding determines which of these specific codes is assigned.
3 Retrieval depends on whether the context during retrieval again generates this particular meaning or code.

In our example, if *jam* is encoded as a preserve, then retrieval cues will help us to recall it only if they also lead us to think of preserves.

More broadly, the principle of encoding specificity emphasizes yet again the importance of contextual cues in memory. To understand retrieval, we need to take into account the context during both coding and retrieval: The greater the similarity of these contexts, the greater the chances of success.[2]

---

[2] Other theorists have also emphasized the importance of the relationship between the conditions during coding and retrieval. One version is called *transfer-appropriate processing*; it focuses more on the cognitive processes carried out during coding and retrieval rather than on the external

Inhibition

We have examined how retrieval cues help us to locate material lodged in the vast storehouse that is our memory, but so far we have ignored a rather large puzzle implicit in our account, arising from the fact that retrieval cues are often associated with a very large number of targets. If you read the word *cat*, it is probably associated with a very, very large number of memories – facts you learned about cats (their love of fish, enjoyment of stroking, hunting of birds), interactions with individual cats you have known, and so on. When you read the word *cat*, how is it that you are not overwhelmed by a flood of such memories?

One possible answer, developed most vigorously by Michael Anderson, is *inhibition*. His idea, with roots back to Pavlov and beyond, is that our brains rely on inhibitory as well as excitatory processes in order to function effectively. If a retrieval cue elicits multiple memories, there will be a competition between them to determine which will rise up into consciousness, a cognitive version of survival of the fittest. If one memory is far stronger than the rest, the outcome will be decided easily, but if there are multiple contenders, then each may inhibit the others to try to prevent them from winning. If reading the word *cat* reminds you of the time your cat got stuck in a tree, activation of that target memory will simultaneously cause the inhibition of competing memories such as watching a cat playing with string. Out of the ensuing battle in which each activated memory tries to inhibit its competitors, one memory will eventually emerge as the strongest and win the prize of a rise into consciousness. Anderson referred to this phenomenon as **retrieval-induced forgetting** – the idea is that when we retrieve one item from memory, this will cause inhibition of competing memories, making it harder to recall them.

Retrieval-induced forgetting

Anderson's account seems plausible, but is it right? In a clever test, Anderson, Bjork, and Bjork (1994) began by asking participants to memorize word pairs where the first word in each pair was a category such as *tree* or *fruit*, and the second word was a member of that category. Each category was presented 8 times, with a different member each time – in the case of *fruit*, for example, participants saw pairs such as *fruit–banana* and *fruit–orange* (Figure 11.8a). Participants were then given additional practice on half of the exemplars. This was achieved by means of a cued-recall test: If the goal was to provide further practice on *orange*,

stimuli present. Specifically, it says that retrieval is more likely to succeed if the processes carried out at retrieval (for example, thinking about the meaning of a word rather than its appearance) match those carried out when the word was encoded. We will not be able to cover the implications of this idea here, but you can find discussions in Morris, Bransford, and Franks (1977) and Roediger, Gallo, and Geraci (2002).

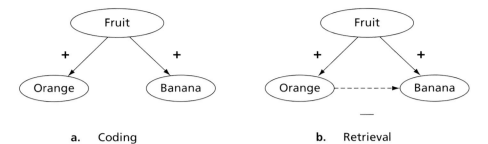

a.   Coding   **b.   Retrieval**

Figure 11.8 Retrieval-induced forgetting. In the first phase, *fruit* was paired with *orange* on some trials and *banana* on others. In the second phase, participants were given additional training on the *fruit–orange* link. Then, in the test phase, they were shown the word *fruit* and asked to recall as many of the fruits they had seen as they could. According to the theory, when we retrieve a memory, our brains inhibit possible competitors to ensure that consciousness is not flooded. Remembering *orange* in the second phase, therefore, would have resulted in inhibition of *banana*, and this would have made it harder to retrieve *banana* in the test phase. In effect, retrieving *orange* would have caused forgetting of *banana*.

for example, participants would be shown *fruit–or__* and asked to fill in the missing fragment with a word seen earlier. Because *fruit* had previously been associated with 8 exemplars, its presentation was assumed to activate all of them, which would trigger a competition in which each would inhibit the others. The fruit that emerged from this completion with the highest level of activation would then rise into consciousness. Continuing with our fruit example, activation of *orange* would have resulted in inhibition of competitors such as *banana*, so that it should now be harder to activate *banana* (Figure 11.8b).

The reasoning is mildly intricate but the conclusion is simple: Practice of one member of a category should inhibit other members, thereby making it harder to access them. If this is not clear, it may help to illustrate how the process would work using hypothetical values for levels of neural activation. Suppose that there is normally some moderate level of activity in a node, even when no stimulus has been presented. (This is called its resting level.) In this case, suppose the normal level of activity in the *banana* node is 10. When the node for *orange* was activated in the second phase, it would have sent inhibitory signals to the *banana* node, and let's suppose that this inhibition reduced the activity level for *banana* from 10 to 5, and that it then remained at this lower level for some period of time. When participants were later asked to recall the fruits they had seen, *banana* would have been at a lower-than-usual level of activity, making it harder to activate. The practical result would have been that participants would have been less likely to recall having seen it.

To test this prediction, the authors gave participants another task to do for 20 minutes and then gave them the category names and asked them to recall as many of the members as they could. Some categories had not been practiced in the second phase, and for these categories participants were able to recall 50% of the words they had seen. When asked to recall *orange*, a word that had received extra practice, the success rate rose to 73%. The crucial result, though, was for words such as *banana*, which were members of a practiced category but had not themselves been practiced; here recall was only 38%. Recalling one word in a category, in other words, seemed to have inhibited access to the others. (Other explanations were also possible but Anderson and his colleagues marshaled persuasive evidence to support their explanation in terms of inhibition. See Anderson and Levy, 2009, for a review.)

One ironic implication of retrieval-induced forgetting is that the act of remembering some things can cause the forgetting of others. To be clear, the suggestion is not that retrieving a memory *always* causes forgetting. Anderson suggests that inhibition will only be necessary when there are strong competing memories, so that some must be weakened in order to allow just one to become conscious (Anderson, 2003). Nevertheless, in at least some situations, remembering some things does seem to cause forgetting of others, and this can have important implications. In a study by Shaw, Bjork, and Handal (1995), for example, participants were told that while attending a student party they had left a jacket containing their wallet in a bedroom, and that when they left they noticed that their wallet was missing. They were then shown photographs of the bedroom and asked to remember as many of the items present as possible, in order to later help the police investigation. The room contained a variety of objects, including 8 college sweatshirts, and in a later interrogation phase they were repeatedly asked questions about 4 of the sweatshirts (for example, "Was there a Harvard sweatshirt on the desk?").

When interviewed again later and asked to recall all of the items that had been present, their recall about objects other than sweatshirts was still good. Their recall of the sweatshirts which were the focus of interrogation was also very good, but their ability to recall the remaining sweatshirts was now significantly worse than that of a control group that hadn't been interrogated (approximately 35% correct, versus 50% for the controls). As in the Anderson *et al.* study, retrieving a memory reduced retrieval of related memories that would have competed with it (in this case, other sweatshirts). If this happened in real life, witnesses who were repeatedly questioned about some aspects of a crime might then forget other aspects, a result that could be serious if those other aspects later proved to be important.

A conceptually similar result was reported by Levy, McVeigh, Marful, and Anderson (2007), who found that remembering a word in one language can impair memory for equivalent words in another language. They recruited participants who were learning Spanish and found that encouraging them to remember the Spanish word for an object made it harder for them to later recall the corresponding word in

English. (I have particularly strong faith in this finding because I've experienced it myself. I learned French in high school and recently have been trying to learn Spanish. The worst thing I can do when trying to remember a Spanish word is to inadvertently think of the French one; my chances of then retrieving the Spanish plummet to near zero.)

Retrieval-induced forgetting might also account for the experience many people have of trying to retrieve a memory and instead repeatedly recalling something which they know is wrong, but not being able to get past it to the memory they actually want. Suppose you were trying to remember the pin number for a new credit card but every time you tried you remembered your old pin instead. Every activation of the old one would further inhibit its competitors, so that your efforts would not only be fruitless they would actually be making the problem worse. The best strategy in this situation is sometimes to just stop trying and let time pass before trying again – the dissipation of inhibition over time, or perhaps the change in context, might then allow you access to the memory really wanted.

Think/don't think!

In the experiments we have discussed so far, inhibition occurred at an unconscious level – had you asked participants whether they were inhibiting weaker memories, they wouldn't have known what you were talking about. Might it be possible, though, for people to *consciously* inhibit memories – for example, to suppress memories that they found painful? Anderson and Green (2001) explored this by first asking participants to memorize word pairs such as *ordeal–roach*. They then presented the first words of some of pairs again, for 4 seconds each. For most of these stimulus words, participants were told to try to remember the second word they had seen earlier and actively think about it, while for some the instructions were to *not* recall the second word – indeed, to do all that they could to prevent this word from rising into consciousness. (The authors called this a **think/no think** procedure – participants were supposed to recall and think about some of the responses, while suppressing thought about others.) Finally, to see if participants' efforts at suppression had been successful, there was a test phase in which the stimulus words were presented yet again and participants were told to recall all the second words, regardless of the instructions received earlier. Figure 11.9 summarizes the procedure.

Some of the stimulus words were presented only in the training phase, and for these words participants recalled around 82% of the responses. For the words which they had been asked to think about, they recalled around 96% – as you would expect, practice during the second phase had strengthened memory for these words. The crucial result, though, was for the responses which participants had been told to forget – here recall was significantly lower, around 75%.

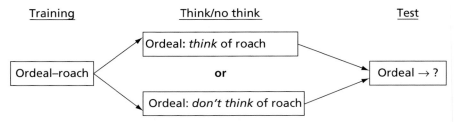

Figure 11.9 The *think/no think* paradigm. Participants learn word pairs such as *ordeal–roach* and are then shown *ordeal* and asked to either think of the second word or avoid thinking of it. In the final phase they again see *ordeal* and are asked what word had followed it.

One possibility that may have already occurred to you is that participants actually did remember these words but were trying to be "good subjects" – realizing that the experimenters expected them to forget these words, they obligingly pretended that they had. To eliminate this possibility, the experimenters ran the experiment again but prior to the final test they told participants that previous research had shown that trying to forget material can paradoxically strengthen it, so that they would probably remember these words better. (Under some circumstances, this actually does happen – see, for example, Wegner, 2009.) If participants were simply trying to be cooperative, recall for "no think" words should now have been better than for "think" words, but it remained poorer. As a further test, the experimenters also ran a condition in which they offered participants a monetary reward for every word that they recalled, but again recall scores were lower for words participants had been told to suppress. Under the demanding conditions of the experiment – staring at a stimulus word for 4 seconds and trying to not allow themselves to think of the second word the entire time, a procedure that was repeated on 16 trials – participants did seem to have learned to inhibit the target word, making it harder to access.

The memories to be suppressed in these experiments were quite mild, involving arbitrarily-chosen words of no special significance. What if the memories to be suppressed were more powerful, involving painful experiences such as rape or battlefield trauma? In post-traumatic stress disorder (PTSD), for example, people often have flashbacks in which they find themselves vividly reliving traumatic experiences, sometimes to the point where they lose all awareness of what is happening around them. Is it also possible to suppress memories of this heightened intensity?

The short answer is that we don't know, though preliminary evidence suggests that we have the capacity to inhibit at least some emotional memories. In one study by Depue, Banich, and Curran (2007), the experimenters used the think/no think procedure developed by Anderson, but instead of words they paired faces with photographs of disturbing scenes such as a serious automobile accident or a badly deformed infant. After repeated exposure to the face-photo pairs, they gave participants practice in thinking about some of the scenes and not thinking about others. Finally, they showed participants the faces again and asked them to verbally describe the scene that each had been paired with. Participants were able to recall 71% of the scenes they had been asked to think about, but only 53% of those they had been asked to suppress. Although the scenes used were not as painful as those involved in truly traumatic memories, these results suggest at least some capacity to suppress emotional memories as well as neutral ones. More broadly, they add to the growing evidence that memories can be inhibited, and thus support the conclusion that inhibition could be one of the reasons why we sometimes forget past experiences.

A model of retrieval: SAM

In previous sections we have discussed some of the factors that determine whether we will remember something. The first determinant is conditions during coding – above all, whether material is organized and practiced. A second important factor is what happens during the retention interval – are other memories formed that could interfere with retrieval? Finally, memory depends on the conditions during retrieval, and whether these conditions match those during storage. Clearly, research has revealed a large number of variables that influence memory; can we now put all the evidence together to create an integrated account of how memory works?

In fact, theorists have proposed a number of theories of memory (for example, MINERVA 2, developed by Hintzman, 1988, and ACT-R, developed by Anderson *et al.*, 2004), but we will concentrate on one, SAM, in order to illustrate what such models can do. Developed by Raaijmakers and Shiffrin (1980; 1981), SAM stands for *search of associative memory*. The theory contains a number of assumptions, which are expressed in mathematical form to allow the derivation of precise predictions. We will not be presenting the full model here, only a few of its core assumptions. As we shall see, however, even in this simplified form the model can account for an impressive number of the characteristics of retrieval.

SAM's assumptions

Coding

The model's assumptions about coding are largely those of the classic Atkinson–Shiffrin model, discussed in Chapter 8. When an item such as a word is presented, its representation in long-term memory is activated, thus effectively placing it in short-term memory. If two items are simultaneously active in short-term memory,

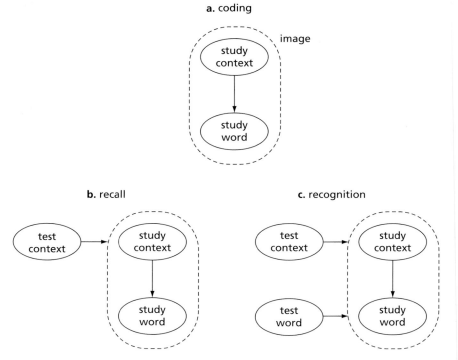

Figure 11.10 A simplified representation of SAM. (a) *Coding.* When we read a word, we form an association between the word and the context in which it is presented; the resulting state in the brain is called an image. (b) *Recall.* If the context during retrieval is similar to the context during coding, it will activate the image. (c) *Recognition.* If the word is present during retrieval, both the word and the context will activate the image, making it more likely that the study word will be remembered.

the association between them will be strengthened. Suppose, for example, that a participant in a memory experiment reads a list of words. As each word is read, its representation in memory will be activated. Environmental or contextual cues will be present at the same time, and so a representation of the context will also be activated. As a result, an association will be formed between the context and the word; in SAM, the resulting structure of a word associated with its context is called an *image* (Figure 11.10a). (If other words are activated in short-term memory at the same time, their representations will also be associated with this word, but we will concentrate on the association between a single word and its context.)

Retrieval cues

Now suppose that participants in this study are asked to recall the words from the list. If the experimental context during this test is similar to that during the study phase, then activation of the representation of the test context will be likely to activate also the representation of the study context, and this will in turn lead to activation of the word's representation (see Figure 11.10b). Retrieval, in other words, is initiated by the presentation of one or more retrieval cues, and the amount retrieved depends on the similarity of this retrieval cue to the stimuli present during encoding.

If participants were instead given a recognition test, there would be two retrieval cues, not only the context but also the word itself. Both of these cues would be likely to activate the record formed during the study phase, leading to stronger activation of this record than in a recall test (Figure 11.10c). The reason that recognition tests usually lead to better retrieval than recall tests, therefore, is simply that recognition tests involve two retrieval cues rather than one. (For a discussion of some situations in which this relationship is reversed, and recall is better than recognition, see Tulving and Thomson, 1973, and Rabinowitz, Mandler, and Barsalou, 1977.)

Cue overload

So far, the assumptions we have discussed are virtually identical to assumptions encountered in previous sections. SAM incorporates an additional assumption that is exceedingly simple but, as we shall see, remarkably powerful. This is simply that the effectiveness of a retrieval cue depends on the number of memories with which it is associated. According to the **cue overload** principle, the more items a cue is associated with, the less effective this cue will be in activating any one of them (Watkins, 1979). If a retrieval cue were associated with only a single event, then exposure to this cue would be very likely to remind you of this event (Figure 11.11a). If the retrieval cue were associated with five events, on the other hand, then this cue would be less effective in activating this memory (Figure 11.11b). It is as if a memory representation contains only a fixed amount of energy, so that the more paths that lead away from this representation, the less activation will be transmitted through any one of them.

SAM's predictions

Our introduction to the model is now complete. We have discussed only a few of its assumptions, but it turns out that these few, simple assumptions can account for a remarkable number of facts about memory. We will consider three examples, simply to illustrate the model's explanatory power.

Organization

As discussed in Chapter 8, one of the most important determinants of how well we remember verbal material is the extent to which the words are structured or

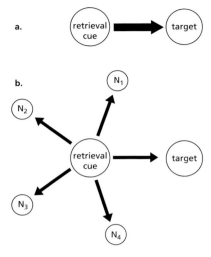

Figure 11.11 Cue-overload. If a retrieval cue is associated with only one other event, it will stimulate the representation of that event in the brain strongly (symbolized by the thick arrow); the more events with which it is associated (represented by N1, N2, and so on), the less it will stimulate any one of them.

organized. One example we discussed was an experiment by Bower *et al.* (1969), in which the task was to memorize a list of minerals. For one group the minerals were organized into subcategories such as common and rare; for another group, the words were arranged in random order. The group that saw the organized list remembered almost four times as many words as the control group did, a remarkable result considering that the two groups had seen the identical words.

We can now explain this result, using the concept of cue overload. To give our analysis a concrete focus, let us assume that a retrieval cue can activate a maximum of 4 memories. For the control group, the words on the list would all have been associated with the experimental context. When asked to recall the list, therefore, this context would have acted as a retrieval cue and it would have activated 4 of the minerals with which it was associated. For the group that saw the hierarchical list, on the other hand, they could have associated 4 category names with the experimental context, and they could then have associated each of these category names with as many as 4 minerals. During the test phase, the experimental context would have reminded them of the subcategories, and each of these subcategories would have reminded them of as many as 4 minerals. If the first category they recalled was common metals, for example, this would serve as a retrieval cue to activate minerals such as copper and lead. If the participants then thought of the second category, this would have reminded them of another 4 minerals, and so on, until eventually they recalled a total of 4 categories and 14 to 16 minerals. (The categories contained different numbers of minerals, so the exact number recalled would have depended on which categories they remembered.)

One reason why organization facilitates memory, in other words, is that organization makes it possible for us to use more retrieval cues. If the experimental context is the only retrieval cue available, we can only recall a small proportion of the words associated with this one cue. As more cues become available, each still leads us to only a few memories, but the total number of accessed memories increases substantially.

Interference

Another powerful influence on retrieval is interference from other memories. The reason memories interfere with each other, according to SAM, is again cue overload. Suppose that a cue is strongly associated with a single event; if so, presentation of this cue will almost certainly activate this memory. If the same cue is associated with many memories, however, then the principle of cue overload says that the cue will be less effective in activating any one of them. The more events occur in the same context, in other words, the harder we will find it to remember any one of these events.

Note that the crucial factor here is simply the number of associations, not when they were formed. Whether an event occurred before or after a memory we are trying to retrieve, the presence of this additional association will make it harder for us to retrieve the memory for which we are searching. Applying this reasoning to our earlier meal example, if you have only ever eaten one meal, you are likely to remember it vividly. The more meals you eat in a particular context, however, the more meals will be associated with this context, and thus the harder you will find it to remember any one of them.

Quantitative predictions

The model we have presented is based on SAM, but is a highly simplified version of this model. The original is not only much more detailed, it is expressed in mathematical form. The use of equations allows SAM to provide not just qualitative predictions – for example, that interference will impair memory – but *quantitative* predictions, stating *precisely* how many words will be recalled. We will not try to trace how these predictions are derived, but we can illustrate the power of mathematical models by considering an experiment by Tulving and Pearlstone (1966) on the role of retrieval cues in memory. Participants first learned lists of words drawn from categories such as *animals* and *birds*. During a subsequent memory test, a control group was simply asked to recall the words, whereas an experimental group was given help in the form of a list of the categories that had

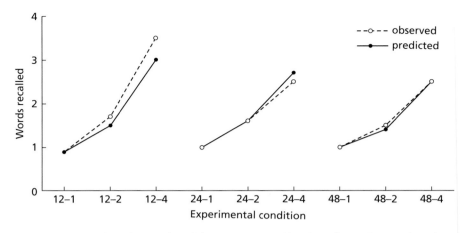

Figure 11.12 SAM's prediction of recall from a categorized list. (Data from Tulving and Pearlstone, 1966.) Lists varied in length and number of words per category; list 12–1, for example, contained 12 words, with only 1 word in each category. (Adapted from Raaijmakers and Shiffrin, 1980.)

been used. Not surprisingly, participants who were reminded of the categories were able to remember more words.

The model we have sketched can easily account for this. Participants in the control had only a single retrieval cue, namely the experimental context, and as a result could recall only a relatively small number of words. Participants in the experimental group, on the other hand, had a much larger number of retrieval cues and thus could recall more words.

The fact that our model can account for this finding is gratifying, but the same assumptions expressed in mathematical form can predict not only that the experimental group will do better but also precisely how many words will be recalled. In this case, the Tulving and Pearlstone experiment included subgroups that varied in the length of the list they were given (they varied from 12 to 48 words) and the number of words in each category (from 1 to 4). Intuitively, it is not immediately obvious how these variations should affect recall, but Figure 11.12 shows that SAM was able to predict the resulting data with astonishing accuracy. The figure comes from a paper by Raaijmakers and Shiffrin (1980), and you can see that the model's predictions, shown by the solid lines, were remarkably close to the actual data, shown by the dashed lines.

Some caution is necessary in interpreting this fit. The problem is that almost any mathematical model can make accurate predictions provided that the model contains enough assumptions. (If a model contains a large number of variables, then if a prediction is inaccurate, all the theorist has to do is keep altering the values of these variables until the model finally produces the desired outcome!) In evaluating a theory, therefore, we have to consider not only the accuracy of its predictions but also how much freedom the theorist had to nudge the predictions in the desired direction. It is too soon to say how well SAM will fare by this criterion – it ultimately depends on how many facts the models can predict using the same assumptions. At present, however, it does look as if SAM can account for an impressive number of phenomena. Thus, although we shouldn't be too overwhelmed by the accuracy of the predictions shown in Figure 11.12, neither should we be too dismissive – the illustrated fit really is impressive. (For further discussion of SAM and other mathematical models of memory, see Raaijmakers, 2008.)

Memory as reconstruction

When people are asked to recall an event, we have been assuming that they search their memories and then reproduce whatever they find. Memory in this view resembles a video recorder: We first accurately record whatever we experience and then, when we need the record, we reproduce it exactly.

We have already discussed evidence that the first assumption – that we record our experiences exactly as they happened – is wrong. In Chapter 9 we saw that we can attend to only some of the stimuli that impinge on us and that we must then use our past experience to interpret this fragmentary evidence. In Sachs's (1967) "Galileo" experiment, for example, she found that participants did not retain verbatim records of the sentences they read. As they read, they extracted the meaning of these sentences, and this meaning was preserved in their long-term memory rather than the exact words.

Our memories, therefore, are not exact records of our experiences, and in this section we will consider the possibility that further distortions can arise in the process of retrieving these memories. In essence, the claim we will consider is that we often cannot retrieve enough detail to reproduce an experience accurately; in these circumstances, we use the details we find to unconsciously reconstruct what must have happened. As with perception, the process is often effective, but it can also lead to errors. Moreover, because the processes involved are unconscious, we can honestly be convinced that our memories are accurate even when they are partially or even wholly wrong.

Reconstructing the past

The War of the Ghosts

A British psychologist, Sir Frederick Bartlett, reported the first evidence that memory involves an active process of reconstruction. In a classic study, Bartlett (1932) asked students to read a Native American (Inuit) folk tale entitled *The War of the Ghosts*. The following is an excerpt:

One night, two young men from Egulac went down to the river to hunt seals, and while they were there it became foggy and calm. Then they heard war-cries, and they thought: "Maybe this is a war-party." They escaped to the shore, and hid behind a log. Now canoes came up, and they heard the sound of paddles, and saw one canoe coming up to them. There were five men in the canoe, and they said:

"What do you think? We wish to take you along. We are going up the river to make war on the people." ... So one of the young men went ...

And the warriors went on up the river to a town on the other side of Kalama. The people came down to the water, and they began to fight, and many were killed. But presently the young man heard one of the warriors say: "Quick, let us go home; that Indian has been hit." Now he thought: "Oh, they are ghosts." He did not feel sick, but they said he had been shot.

So the canoes went back to Egulac, and the young man went ashore to his house, and made a fire. And he told everybody and said: "Behold, I accompanied the ghosts, and we went to fight. Many of our fellows were killed, and many of those who attacked us were killed. They said I was hit, and I did not feel sick."

He told it all, and then he became quiet. When the sun rose he fell down. Something black came out of his mouth. His face became contorted. The people jumped up and cried. He was dead.

(Bartlett, 1932, p. 65)

Bartlett had participants recall the story 15 minutes after reading it, and then again after an interval that varied from a few weeks to months.

Predictably, recall became worse as time passed. What struck Bartlett, however, was that details were not forgotten at random; instead, there was a pattern to how the story changed. Over successive retellings, the story tended to lose its stranger details (from the perspective of British participants) and to move closer to a more "normal" story that fit with their cultural expectations. For example, although the story was entitled *The War of the Ghosts*, the presence of ghosts became progressively less prominent as participants continued to retell the story. Unfamiliar terms became familiar ones (for example, *seal hunting* became *fishing*), and actions that didn't seem to make sense were made more comprehensible through the addition of rationales.

To explain these findings, Bartlett argued that participants used their existing knowledge to interpret the story. As details were lost, participants increasingly used their personal and cultural beliefs – in which ghosts, and black material emerging from mouths, did not play a prominent role – to reconstruct what the original story must have been (see also Bergman and Roediger, 1999).

Remembering Hitler

Subsequent research has supported Bartlett's claim that we reconstruct the past in the light of our current knowledge and beliefs. One nice example comes from a study by Dooling and Christiansen (1977). They gave participants a short passage to read about a ruthless dictator named Gerald Martin. Then, after a delay of either 2 or 7 days, they gave participants a recognition test in which they were shown 14 sentences and for each had to say whether it had been present in the original passage. Immediately before the test, the experimental group was told that the passage had actually been about Adolf Hitler; the control group was not.

One of the test sentences was "He hated the Jews particularly and so persecuted them"; this sentence had not been present in the original passage. When tested 2 days after reading the passage, both groups were very good at recognizing this sentence as false – only around 5% thought that they had seen it previously. When the test was administered after a week, however, almost 25% of the experimental group thought they had seen it. As time passed and they forgot more of the story, they used their knowledge of Hitler to fill in the gaps in their memories.

Hindsight distortion

Further evidence of the role of reconstruction in memory has come from research on **hindsight bias**. In this "I knew it all along" phenomenon, once people know the outcome of an event, they tend to see that outcome as obvious, and to feel that they could have predicted it all along. In a study by Carli (1999), for example, participants read a two-page story about a young woman named Pam and her date with a man named Peter. They first met at a club and enjoyed each other's company, and later arranged to meet again. They went dancing, talked, and had drinks. When Peter drove Pam home afterwards, he said he needed to stop at his apartment for something and Pam went with him. For one group the story ended at this point, for the other there was one additional sentence saying that Peter raped Pam while at his apartment.

One week later both groups completed a questionnaire about the story. Some of the items were about events that actually occurred in the story, and both groups were equally accurate in their answers to these questions. Some of the questions, however, referred to events that had not occurred, but which were judged to be typical of rapes – for example, that the woman had a voluptuous figure, and that they met at a bar. Participants who had been told that the date ended in rape were significantly more likely to remember these (nonexistent) elements of the story. As in the Dooling and Christiansen study, when participants did not fully remember the story, they filled in the gaps with their existing knowledge and beliefs, in this case about the kinds of behavior likely to lead to rape.

A second, more poignant, finding came in answer to questions about Pam's behavior and personality. Those who were told the evening ended in rape were significantly more likely to have a low opinion of her behavior and character. They were more critical of her decisions to kiss Peter and go to his apartment, and more likely to see her as careless, unintelligent, and undependable. In line with the hindsight bias, knowing that the evening ended in rape, participants seemed to have viewed the danger as obvious; Pam should therefore have known this might happen, so that the rape was at least in part her own fault. The Carli study thus illustrates not only how we sometimes reconstruct the past, remembering events that never happened, but also how hindsight sometimes leads us to blame victims for their suffering, mistakenly believing that the danger was obvious and they should have done something to avoid it.

Research has shown that reconstruction errors become more common as the time since an event passes (for example, Dooling and Christiansen, 1977). It appears that as our memories for an experience fade, we increasingly have to reconstruct the past, and inevitably we use our current beliefs in forming these reconstructions. There is not necessarily anything wrong with this – in many cases our reconstructions will be accurate – but problems can arise because the processes involved are often unconscious, and we do not realize the extent to which our memories are based on what are effectively educated guesses.

Source confusion

Bartlett's research was largely ignored for many years, partly because of the casual way in which he carried out and reported some of his experiments, and partly because his emphasis on cognitive processes did not fit well with the behaviorist orientation that then dominated psychology (see Bergman and Roediger, 1999, and Koriat, Goldsmith, and Pansky, 2000). Recent years, however, have seen a sharp increase in interest in research devoted to understanding reconstruction, and why these reconstructions are sometimes inaccurate. Our understanding is still far from complete, but researchers have identified **source confusion** as one major cause of distortion (for example, Johnson, Hashtroudi, and Lindsay, 1993; Mitchell and Johnson, 2009). We have seen that during coding we form associations between current events and the contextual cues that accompany them. If these associations become weaker over time – for example, because other events become associated with the same contextual cues – then we can find ourselves remembering an event but not the context in which it occurred.

A memorable rape

A classic example of source confusion involved Donald Thomson, a prominent Australian psychologist who has published important research on memory (for example, Tulving and Thomson, 1973). One day he was arrested by the police, without explanation, and forced to appear in a lineup. At its conclusion, he was told that he had been identified by a woman as the man who had raped her. Fortunately for Thomson, it eventually emerged that he had an airtight alibi: At the time of the rape, he had been appearing on a live television program – ironically, discussing how people can improve their memory for faces. It turned out that the victim had been watching the program at the time of her assault; she correctly remembered seeing his face, but unfortunately was confused about the source of this memory (Baddeley, 1999).

The misinformation effect

To better understand how such mistakes can occur, memory researchers have developed a variety of procedures for studying source confusion. One of the pioneers in this effort has been Elizabeth Loftus, a cognitive psychologist then at the University of Washington. One of her interests was the accuracy of eyewitness testimony, and whether witnesses' memories of a crime can be altered by the way in which police question them. To find out, Loftus and her colleagues created experimental analogues to what might happen during a police interview. In one such study, Loftus, Miller, and Burns (1978) showed participants a series of slides in which a red sports car stopped at a stop sign, turned, and then hit a pedestrian. Participants were then asked questions about what they had seen. For one group, one of these questions referred to what happened at the stop sign, whereas for a second group the question referred (misleadingly) to what happened at the yield sign. Finally, after a delay of 20 minutes, both groups were shown 2 pictures of the intersection, one showing a stop sign and the other a yield sign, and asked which they had seen.

The control group responded correctly 75% of the time, but the percentage of correct responses in the group asked the misleading question was only 41%. Moreover, when participants in a subsequent study were asked to rate their confidence in their response, their ratings were very high (Loftus *et al.*, 1989). One seemingly innocuous question, in other words, significantly altered witnesses' memory of an incident, and this has been called the **misinformation effect**.

Why did misinformation have such powerful effects in these experiments? One possibility is that participants remembered the original incident but believed that the experimenter would have had no reason to mislead them by referring to a yield sign; they therefore concluded that their recollection must have been wrong. To test this possibility, Zaragoza and Lane (1994) repeated this experiment but before the test warned participants that the questions had contained some inaccurate information. Despite this warning, participants still recalled seeing the yield sign. Similarly, Loftus (1979) found that offering a financial reward for correct answers did not alter participants' answers. It appears that many participants had come to genuinely believe that they had seen a yield sign.

One cause of the misinformation effect appears to be source confusion. When participants are interviewed after a delay, they retrieve information about the yield sign but can be confused about its source – did it come from the original slides, or from the experimenters' question? If they attribute the information to the wrong source, they will conclude, unconsciously, that they saw a yield sign. In another study illustrating source confusion, participants watched a staged crime and then examined mug shots to identify the perpetrator. A few days later, they were asked to identify this person in a lineup. Many participants were successful, but there was a strong tendency to select people whose faces had been seen only in the mug shots (Brown, Deffenbacher, and Sturgill, 1977). As in the Thomson rape case, it seems that it is all too easy for people to become confused about where they have seen a familiar face, especially when their encounter was a brief one and occurred under stressful conditions.

One point to note about Loftus's procedure is that it closely resembles the procedure used in studies of retroactive interference. There, participants learn to associate first one response to a situation, A-B, and then a second response, A-C. Learning the second response often results in forgetting the first, and this is also what happens in Loftus's situation, as information in the question interferes with access to information provided earlier. Also, we should note that the misinformation effect was discovered relatively recently, and there is still some debate about the mechanisms involved. It is likely that several processes contribute; if you want to learn more about this topic, a good summary of the literature is available in Ayers and Reder (1998).

Lost at the mall

In the Loftus, Miller, and Burns study, false information resulted in the modification of an existing memory. In an even more dramatic study reported by Loftus (1993), false information resulted in the creation of a new memory. The focus of the study was a 14-year-old boy named Chris. With the agreement of his parents, Chris's older brother was enlisted to ask Chris if he could remember an incident that happened when Chris was 5 years old and became lost in a shopping mall. At first, Chris couldn't remember it – quite rightly, as it never happened – but his brother prompted him with details, and gradually Chris began to remember. After about 2 weeks, Chris reported having a clear and vivid memory of the incident, and he provided the following account:

I went over to look at the toy store, the Kay-bee toy and uh, we got lost ... I was really scared you know. And then this old man, I think he was wearing a blue flannel, came up to me ... He was kind of bald on top ... he had like a ring of gray hair ... and he had glasses.

(Loftus, 1993, p. 532)

As with other studies of the misinformation effect, it is possible that Chris was only pretending to remember the incident, but other evidence supports the claim that memories implanted in this way feel real. In a study by Hyman and Billings (1998), for example, college students were told that they were participating in a study of memory for childhood events. They were given brief descriptions of various incidents that had happened when they were children (the details were provided to the experimenters by their parents) and asked to add as many details as they could remember. Each of the events was real except for one, which involved them knocking over a punch bowl at a wedding. After this initial interview, participants were interviewed again one day later, supposedly to see if they had recalled any further details. At the first interview, only 3% of those questioned said they could recall the incident, but at the second interview this rose to 27%. Moreover, almost half of this group reported that their memories were clear, and they were able to provide details about what had happened.

This result is bizarre if we think of recall as the accurate reproduction of whatever information we are able to retrieve, but it makes more sense if we as assume that memory involves a process of reconstruction from fragmentary evidence. The less information we retrieve, the greater the need for reconstruction, and thus, the greater the potential for error. In line with this interpretation, experiments have shown that individuals are more likely to accept implanted memories if they are encouraged to form detailed images of the event they are being asked to recall. Hyman and Pentland (1996), for example, found that under these conditions almost 40% of participants recalled details of incidents that had not occurred (see also Garry and Polaschek, 2000). If individuals retrieve highly detailed memories, it is perhaps not surprising that they might have difficulty judging whether the source was a real event or one they had heard about (see also Thomas and Loftus, 2002).

The DRM procedure

You may be finding it hard to understand how people could be fooled so badly, vividly remembering events that never happened. If so, you may find the following demonstration helpful. First, read the following words, spending about 1–2 seconds on each:

Candy, sour, sugar, bitter, good, taste, tooth, nice, honey, soda, chocolate, heart, cake, tart, pie.

This list comes from one used in an experiment by Roediger and McDermott (1995), which in turn was based on an earlier experiment by Deese (1959). Because of its provenance, the procedure is now known as the Deese–Roediger–McDermott procedure, or **DRM** for short. In Roediger and McDermott's version, the experimenters read participants 6 lists of this kind, and then, after a few minutes on another task, asked them to recall as many of the words from each list as they could. You could try this yourself for the single list used here, but it may work if you just answer the following questions, without looking back at the list. Was the word *point* on the list? The word *sour*? The word *sweet*? Now write down your confidence that each of these words was present, using a scale from 1 to 4, where

1 = sure that the word hadn't been present
2 = word probably not present
3 = word probably was present
4 = sure that the word had been present

When Roediger and McDermott did this, 55% of their participants remembered hearing the word *sweet*, even though (you can check this for yourself) it hadn't been present. Moreover, their confidence that it had been present was high, as 58% of those who remembered *sweet* said they were sure they had heard it. In a second experiment, the authors also used the remember-know procedure to assess confidence, asking participants whether they vividly remembered hearing the word, or were sure that they had heard it but didn't have a specific memory. Here, 73% reported a vivid memory, a percentage almost identical to that for words actually on the list. (In some experiments, participants' confidence has actually been higher for *sweet*.) So, why were people so sure they had heard a word that wasn't presented?

The most likely explanation combines two principles, one we encountered earlier (spreading activation) and the one that we are discussing now (source confusion). As you may have noticed, the word *sweet* is associated with many of the words on the list – if you were asked to say the first words that came to mind after hearing *sugar*, for example, *sweet* would be likely to be one of the first words you thought of. When you read the word *sugar*, therefore, activation would spread from its node to that for *sweet*. Similarly, reading *candy* would activate *sweet*, and so on. The node for *sweet* would thus have received spreading activation from most of the words on the list, with the result that it would have itself been strongly activated. In our discussion of short-term memory, we suggested that links are formed between whatever items are active in short-term memory at the same time.

The word *sweet*, therefore, would have been associated with the other words on the list, and so would have ended up as part of your memory of listening to the list. Then, when the time came to recall the list, you might have retrieved *sweet* but – and this is the critical bit – you might not have remembered the source: Were you remembering *sweet* because you heard it, or because it was one of the words you thought of while listening?

Reality monitoring

More broadly, how do we *ever* know whether we are remembering a real event, or just one that we once thought about or imagined? You've probably experienced this problem yourself, perhaps reminding yourself that you had to do something – locking a door, mailing a letter – and then later finding yourself unsure whether you had done it or only thought about it. In situations like this where a memory is not clearly linked to its source, how do we decide whether its source was a real event or one we only imagined?

The most influential figure in investigating this issue – indeed, in raising it in the first place – has been Marcia Johnson. In a series of experiments, she and her colleagues have studied what Johnson and Raye (1981) called **reality monitoring**, the process by which we decide whether a memory represents a real event or an imagined one. Reality monitoring is thus closely related to source confusion: It involves a particular kind of judgement about sources, one in which we must decide whether the source was external (a real event) or internal (a thought or image).

In one study, Johnson *et al.* (1979) showed participants pictures of common objects such as a banana and a clown. On some trials participants saw the actual pictures, but on others they were asked to imagine them. The number of real and imagined exposures was varied – for example, participants might see the clown 2 times but be asked to imagine it 8 times. Finally, they were asked to estimate how many times they had actually seen each picture. The results showed that the more often participants imagined a picture, the higher was their subsequent estimate of how often they had seen it. In other words, they confused real pictures and imagined ones, and the number of imagined pictures influenced their estimate of the number of real ones. Other studies have shown that similar confusions arise in the case of actions – if participants imagine performing an action, they sometimes later recall having actually performed it (for example, Goff and Roediger, 1998; Seamon, Philbin, and Harrison, 2006).

Johnson and Raye (1981) proposed that we use a number of criteria in deciding whether a remembered event was real or imagined (see also Johnson, Hashtroudi, and Lindsay, 1993; Mitchell and Johnson, 2009). The first stage, and normally the most important, is an assessment of the perceptual richness or vividness of the memory. Our memories for real events typically include much more detail than our memories for imagined ones, so that a vivid memory can normally be attributed to a real event with some confidence. This analysis predicts that reality monitoring should be more difficult in situations where an imagined event contains more-than-usual detail, and this prediction has been confirmed in a number of studies. In the Hyman and Pentland (1996) experiment discussed earlier, for example, participants were more likely to accept false memories of a childhood event if they had earlier been asked to generate detailed images of that event. If a memory is vivid, we assume it must be real.

Revisiting the warehouse

On the whole, we trust our memories, believing that they provide us with accurate records of our experiences. We are sometimes frustrated by the fact that we cannot recall as much as we would like, but we have no doubt that, when we do remember an experience, it was real. Starting with Bartlett, however, research on memory has increasingly painted a rather different picture. The records that we store in memory are not exact copies of our experiences – we attend to only a portion of the stimuli that impinge on our senses, and we then engage in extensive processing to infer what objects in the environment must have generated them. Then, when we recall these events, similar constructive processes are required to interpret the information that we have retrieved.

In a sense, retrieval is the second stage in perception. In the first stage we interpret sensory input from the external world – "What is it?" – and store our conclusions in memory. Then, if we are unable to retrieve this record fully, we must again interpret the fragments that we recover – "What was it?" (See also Koriat *et al.*, 2000.) The retrieval of memory traces is thus only the starting point for a reconstructive process that fills in the missing details. Returning to our earlier analogy, we can think of the formation of a memory as equivalent to storing a volume in a book warehouse. This volume, however, does not consist of a collection of photographs of our experiences; it is more like a set of sketches that capture the essence of these experiences, rather than recording all the details. Moreover, while books are in storage they can become corrupted: New experiences can become confused with older ones, as sentences from different sections become intermixed. Reading a stored text, therefore, requires considerable interpretation – what Bartlett called "effort after meaning." With all this interpretation and analysis, it is perhaps no wonder that studying is sometimes exhausting!

Summary

- Forgetting is often attributed to memories decaying over time, but the main cause of forgetting now appears to be difficulty in retrieving memories from storage. This difficulty is caused by interference from memories formed earlier (proactive interference) and later (retroactive interference).

- Forgotten experiences are often still in storage; the problem is that new memories make it harder to find them. It is possible that new memories also sometimes overwrite older ones.

- Whether attempts to retrieve a memory are successful depends on whether the cues present during retrieval are similar to those present during coding. The more retrieval cues, the better the chances of recall.

- Another determinant is cue overload: The more memories are associated with a retrieval cue, the less likely it is that the cue will activate any one of them.

- A third factor is inhibition: When we recall an event, it may inhibit similar memories that are competing with it for access to consciousness. This competition occurs at an unconscious level, but we also seem to be able to deliberately inhibit unpleasant memories.

- Building on these simple assumptions, a model called SAM is able to account for many characteristics of memory, including organization and interference.

- When retrieval fails, we may use the available clues to try to reconstruct the original experience. This process is often unconscious, and this can lead us to overestimate the accuracy of our memories – what feels like a vivid and accurate memory is sometimes a seriously flawed reconstruction.

- One source of error is source confusion, where we remember some aspects of an experience but not the context in which it occurred.

- In reality monitoring, we have to decide whether the source of a memory is something that actually occurred or only something we once thought about. If we often imagine an experience, we may later mistakenly believe that it actually happened.

- The constructive and reconstructive processes involved in first coding and then retrieving an event mean that our memories are sometimes much less accurate than we think they are. A memory is more like a rough sketch than a detailed photograph.

Review questions

1 What is the decay theory of forgetting? What evidence suggests that it is wrong?

2 What is the difference between proactive and retroactive interference? What procedures are used to study them?

3 What evidence suggests that similar memories interfere with each other much more than dissimilar ones do?

4 Some theorists believe that most if not all of the experiences stored in long-term memory remain there indefinitely, and thus that forgetting is

largely the result of problems in retrieving this material. What evidence supports this view?

5 In what ways is memory like a book warehouse? In what ways is this analogy misleading?

6 What evidence suggests that internal as well as external stimuli present during an experience become associated with it, and hence can serve as retrieval cues?

7 What evidence suggests that the context in which a word occurs can subtly influence how we encode it?

8 Anderson has argued that one reason we can have difficulty remembering material is because retrieval cues typically elicit multiple memories, and these memories inhibit each other in a kind of battle to emerge triumphant. How has his research on retrieval-induced forgetting and the think/no think paradigm supported the existence of inhibitory processes in memory?

9 What are the three core assumptions of the SAM model presented in this chapter?

10 How does SAM account for the effects of organization and interference?

11 Remembering an event in some ways resembles watching a video: It feels as if we are replaying an exact record of the original experience. How has research on reconstruction challenged this interpretation?

12 One source of error in retrieval is source confusion, where we remember some aspects of an experience but not the context in which it occurred. Using the terms *rape*, *stop sign*, and *mall* as retrieval cues, discuss cases in which source confusion led people to confidently remember events that never occurred.

13 How are the themes of reconstructive memory, source confusion, and reality monitoring linked? If you had to arrange these concepts in a hierarchy, with each level representing a subcase of the level above it, what would this hierarchy look like?

14 According to Johnson, what factors make it more likely that we will become confused as to whether an imagined event actually happened?

12 | Practical applications

CONTENTS

What's the best way to remember the name of someone you've just met? To memorize vocabulary in a foreign language or remember the material in a textbook?

Or, in the context of the legal system, to know how much confidence to place in the testimony of an eyewitness to a crime? And what if that testimony comes from an adult who has accused her father of sexually abusing her when she was a child, despite having had no memory of the abuse during the intervening years – could someone really forget such a traumatic experience and then suddenly remember it decades later? These are some of the questions we'll try to answer in this chapter as we look at how psychologists have tried to apply the understanding of memory gained in the laboratory to the far more complex and even chaotic conditions of real life.

Mnemonics

Over the centuries, people have developed a variety of techniques for memorizing large quantities of information (for an overview, see Bellezza, 1996). These techniques are called **mnemonic devices**, from a Greek word meaning *mindful* or *remembering*. (Mnemonic is pronounced knee-ma-nick, with the emphasis on the second syllable.) The term *mnemonic* can be used for any memory technique, but it is more often used when discussing techniques for memorizing lists of unrelated facts – for example, a list of things to do, or vocabulary in a foreign language. We'll look at two mnemonic techniques that have proven particularly effective, the **method of loci** and the **pegword system**.

The method of loci

This method is thought to have had its origins some 2,500 years ago in Ancient Greece (Yates, 1966). According to the Greek historian Cicero, a poet named Simonides attended a banquet at which he performed one of his poems. He was called away during the banquet to receive a message, and in his absence the roof of the banquet hall collapsed, killing all those inside. Their bodies were so badly crushed that it was not possible to identify many of the victims. However, Simonides was able to do so by visualizing where each person had been sitting during the banquet. This gave him the idea for a new method for remembering material: To visualize a room or house and then to imagine items placed at different locations within this space. (*Loci* is the Latin word for locations.)

Suppose that you wanted to remember a shopping list. You would start by selecting a location with which you were thoroughly familiar – perhaps the rooms in your house. You would then imagine taking a walk through this space, and as you walked through each room, you would imagine encountering the objects on your list. For example, opposite to the entrance to your house you might see a *carrot* hanging from the wall, on a table in the adjoining living room you might see a *pizza*, and so on. The technique seems to be particularly effective if the images you form are distinctive, and if they embody a strong relationship or interaction between the object and the location. You might want to imagine the pizza hanging over the edges of the table, with the topping dripping on to the carpet below! (See Wollen, Weber, and Lowry, 1972; McDaniel and Einstein, 1990; Richardson, 1998.) Worthen and Deschamps (2008) suggest that humor may also facilitate memory, with more humorous images being more memorable.

As simple as this technique is, it can be remarkably effective. In one experiment by Ross and Lawrence (1968), students memorized a list of 40 words by imagining them located along a walk through their campus. Each word was presented for approximately 14 seconds, and at the conclusion of the session they were able to recall 38 of the 40 words. Over the next 3 days they learned a new list each day, and when tested on all of the lists at the conclusion they could still recall an average of 36.

You might think that this method might be useful once or twice, but that if you kept using it then eventually each spatial location would be associated with so many memories that they would all merge into an indistinguishable blur. Surprisingly, that appears not to be the case. In the Ross and Lawrence study, there was no decrement in performance over days – participants remembered 38.2 words at the conclusion of the first session and 38.4 at the conclusion of the fourth – and similar results have been reported in other studies (for example, Massen and Vaterrodt-Plünnecke, 2006). We cannot rule out the possibility that problems would eventually arise with repeated/extended use, but anecdotal evidence suggests that if problems do arise, they may be minimal. The World Memory Championship, for example, is held every year and includes measures such as how many names of faces can be memorized in 15 minutes, and how many playing cards in an hour. Dominic O'Brian has won 8 times, performing feats such as memorizing a 1,512-digit number in an hour (MSO, 1997). One of the cornerstones of his success has been the method of the loci, and if its effectiveness has diminished over this 8-year period, it has not been apparent. Even more extraordinarily, one individual has used the method of loci to help him memorize a number containing 65,536 digits! (See Raz *et al.*, 2009.) We need more research to be sure, but the phenomenal performance of these experts would suggest that repeated use is not necessarily a problem.

The pegword system

A conceptually very similar mnemonic system relies on words rather than spatial locations to provide bridges between the words to be memorized. In the pegword system, you start by memorizing a set of rhymes such as:

One-bun
Two-shoe
Three-tree
Four-door
Five-hive
Six-sticks
Seven-heaven
Eight-gate
Nine-vine
Ten-hen

If you then wanted to memorize a list of ten words, you would form a mental image linking each target word with one of the "peg" words you have already learned. (You're using the rhyming word as a peg on which to hang the word to be remembered.) If the first word to be memorized was *elephant*, for example, you

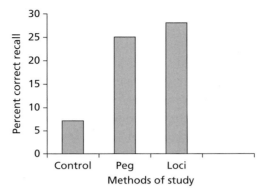

Figure 12.1 The effectiveness of mnemonic systems. The percentage of words recalled from a list after using the method of loci and the pegword systems, compared to a control condition of just thinking about the words. (Adapted from Roediger, 1980.)

might form an image of an elephant in between two hamburger buns, perhaps looking at you – understandably – rather quizzically.

A study by Roediger (1980) compared the effectiveness of several mnemonic techniques with a control condition in which participants were instructed to repeat the words and think about their meaning. When tested at the end of the practice session and also when tested again one day later, the method of loci and the pegword system produced the highest scores. The results for the delayed test are shown in Figure 12.1: The method of loci group still remembered 28% of the words, the pegword group remembered 25%, while the control group remembered only 7%.

Why are they effective?

Deeper processing

In the course of our discussion of memory, we have encountered several principles that determine how memorable an experience will be. One that we discussed in Chapter 8 was *organization*, the idea that material is easier to remember if there is some structure or organization linking the elements involved. The Bower *et al.* (1969) mineral experiment provided one example: Participants found it easier to memorize a list of minerals if they were organized in a hierarchical structure (for example, subdivided into metals and stones) than if they were listed in random order.

Then, in Chapter 9 we discussed the importance of *depth of processing*. If you read a list of unrelated words, you are much more likely to remember them if you analyze each word in depth, focusing on its meaning rather than on more superficial characteristics such as how many syllables it has. We noted that one explanation is that deeper analysis often involves elaboration – rather than analyzing a word solely in terms of its own meaning, deeper analysis often leads us to consider the links with other words. In the experiment by Stein and Bransford (1979), one group read sentences such as "The fat man read the sign," while another group read sentences such as "The fat man read the sign warning about thin ice." Despite the fact that the second sentence was longer, members of this group were almost twice as likely to later recall the adjective *fat*. The elaborated version explained *why* the man's size was important, and thus linked it to a more coherent story. Similarly, Nairne *et al.* (2008) found that asking participants to think about words in a survival context – could the object represented by the word contribute to survival? – produced the best memory ever seen in a memorization test. Again, deeper, more extensive thinking about the meaning of a word was substantially enhancing recall.

We encountered yet another variant of this idea in Chapter 10, when we discussed the role of *schemas* in facilitating memory for prose. In Bransford and Johnson's (1972) "laundry" experiment, participants who knew that the paragraph was about sorting clothes remembered almost 3 times as many of the main ideas as those who didn't. The availability of a schema allowed participants to tie the seemingly unrelated sentences together, greatly facilitating recall.

What these approaches share in common is that instead of coding a word in terms of its sensory features – for example, what it looks or sounds like – they used stored information about its meaning to create a richer, more elaborated representation. As to why this should matter, one possible reason is that a richer representation increases the number of possible retrieval paths. As we saw in Chapter 11, the main cause of forgetting appears to be problems in retrieving material, with success depending on how many retrieval cues are available to activate the target. If we think about an item during coding, we are exploring how it relates to knowledge we already have, and thus the code that we eventually form will contain links to this knowledge. If any of these linked nodes are then activated during retrieval, excitation will spread to the target, making it more likely that it will be activated. Almost everything we have discussed about memory can potentially be understood in terms of this one basic idea – that we create stronger memories if we think deeply about an experience during coding, because this creates links that will help us to later retrieve it.

Figure 12.2 provides an illustration of this idea. Suppose that you had some experience which we will represent by the letter X. One possibility is that you would code it very simply, perhaps just forming an association between X and one aspect of the current environment, stimulus A (Figure 12.2a). If you thought about the experience, though, you might remember similar experiences you had had in the past, or possible implications for the future, and you might end up with

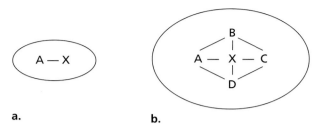

Figure 12.2 Multiple retrieval cues aid recall. If an event X was associated with only one stimulus, A, during coding, later there would only be one cue that could activate the memory of X. If X was associated with multiple cues during coding, there would be many.

a much richer, more elaborated coding such as that shown in Figure 12.2b, where X is now linked to many other elements in your memory, and they are also linked to each other. Now suppose that at some later point you wanted to remember what happened during X. If you had coded it as AX, you would have only one possible cue that could help you retrieve it, A. If you had coded it as ABCDX, on the other hand, you would have many cues, increasing the chances of success.[1]

Our analysis to this point might seem to imply that any code containing multiple elements will facilitate retrieval, but of course this will also depend on the strength of the links between the elements – if elements A and X are linked only weakly, then activation of A will not help much in activating X. So, what factors determine the strength of associations, and in particular the strength of associations between words? Psychologists have used a variety of procedures to study this question, including a technique called **paired-associate learning**. In a typical experiment participants are given a set of word pairs such as *ocean–drink* to learn. Each pair is presented individually for several seconds, and memory is then tested by presenting the first word in each pair and asking participants to provide the second.

In the case of *ocean–drink*, participants would be shown *ocean* and asked what word had followed.

When experimenters first started running experiments like this, they assumed that participants would learn pairs such as *ocean–drink* by associating *ocean* with *drink*. This may seem so obvious as to hardly be worth mentioning, but when experimenters interviewed participants at the conclusion of experiments they

---

[1] To explain why deeper processing enhances memory we have focused on the role of elaboration, the idea that more elaborate representations facilitate retrieval because they have more links to other items in memory. We should note, though, that it is also possible to explain the advantages of deeper processing in terms of *distinctiveness*, the idea that deeper processing leads to more unique or distinctive representations, which are accordingly easier to locate. In our example, ABCDX is likely to stand out more from other memories than AX, because this specific conjunction of elements is likely to be rarer. We will continue to discuss distinctiveness shortly; you can also find relevant material in Gallo *et al.* (2008), and Skinner and Fernandes (2010).

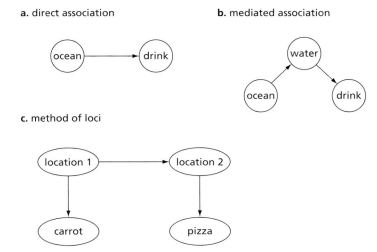

a. direct association

b. mediated association

c. method of loci

Figure 12.3 Mnemonic systems capitalize on existing links. When attempting to form an association between A and B, it is sometimes easier to link A to a mediator, M, and then link M to B; this mediated association can be easier to learn if M already has strong associations with A and B. The method of loci uses this strategy by linking words to familiar spatial locations such as rooms in a house, where we already have strong associations to guide us from one location to another.

were surprised to discover that participants did not always follow this seemingly straightforward strategy. Rather than forming a direct association between *ocean* and *drink* (Figure 12.3a), participants sometimes formed an *indirect* association, using the word *water* to link them: They would associate *ocean* with *water*, and then *water* with *drink* (Figure 12.3b). Water was then acting as a *mediator* to link the words.

On the surface, this seems a peculiar strategy: Why try to remember two associations (*ocean–water* and *water–drink*) when you only have to remember one? Nevertheless, it eventually became clear that participants knew what they were doing – the use of mediators in this way can substantially enhance learning. In one study by Montague, Adams, and Kiess (1966), participants were asked to write down any mediators they used during the training trial. When subsequently tested, they could recall only 6% of the words from pairs where they had not used mediators, but 73% from pairs where they had, a remarkable difference.

One way to make sense of this result is to assume that it is very difficult to form new associations from scratch – because words such as *ocean* and *drink* rarely occur together, their initial associative strength is likely to be low, and this will make it difficult to associate them. To avoid this problem, participants in these experiments were forming indirect associations instead, taking advantage of connections that were already strong and so easier to strengthen. Using a mediator means having to learn two associations rather than one, but it is apparently easier to strengthen two associations that are already strong than to create an entirely new one.

And that is one reason why mnemonic techniques such as the method of loci and the pegword system are effective. In the case of the method of loci, words such as *carrot* and *pizza* rarely occur together, making it difficult to form a new association between them. If we can link carrot to one room in our house and pizza to another, however, then our familiarity with the path between these locations will allow us to get from one to the other almost effortlessly (Figure 12.3c). Similarly in the pegword method, we can use *one–bun* (an easy association to form because of the rhyme) to get to *two–shoe*, so that, provided we have good images linking *bun* and *shoe* to the words to be memorized, remembering one will make it easy to get to the other.

The generation effect

A second reason why these techniques are effective is the **generation effect**, the finding that people are better at remembering material that they generate for themselves rather than just reading. In both the method of loci and the pegword system, users must generate the images that they will use to remember words, and research on the generation effect suggests that this active process of generating material can substantially enhance memory. In the first study to report this effect, by Slamecka and Graf (1978), one group read a list of word pairs while a second group generated the second word in each pair for themselves. If the first group saw the pair *rapid–fast*, for example, then the second group saw *rapid–f__*, and was asked to complete the pair by providing a synonym for *rapid* that begins with f. When the two groups were later given a recognition test, participants who had generated the second word for themselves were much better at remembering the words.

Similar effects have been reported with pictures. In a study by Peynircioğlu (1989), a group given verbal descriptions of scenes and asked to draw them remembered the scenes better than groups that either copied the scenes or just looked at them. This suggests that for pictures as well as words we remember them better if we generate them ourselves. One reason that the method of loci and the pegword system are effective, therefore, is probably that they force us to invest extra effort in creating images. (See also Kinjo and Snodgrass, 2000, and Bertsch *et al.*, 2007.)

Imagery

A third reason why these mnemonics are effective is their use of *imagery*, as people are usually better at remembering images than words. In a study by Bower and Winzenz (1970), for example, participants were asked to memorize pairs of words. One group was shown sentences containing the words (the two target words were capitalized), a second group generated their own sentences, and a third group formed images involving vivid interactions between the words. As predicted by the generation effect, the group asked to create their own sentences remembered more words than the group that was given sentences (11 words instead of 8). The best recall, however, was in the imagery group, whose members recalled an average of 13 words. Thus, even though the sentence and imagery groups both generated their own material, the imagery group did better (see also Richardson, 1998).

A study by Sweeney and Bellezza (1982) demonstrated that imagery can also be used to help remember abstract words that do not lend themselves so obviously to the formation of images. Participants were given a list of abstract words together with short definitions. The word *scurrilous*, for example, was defined as obscene. (A fuller definition would have been obscenely abusive.) To learn the words, one group used a *keyword* system in which the first step was to memorize a keyword that resembled the abstract word in sound (the keyword for *scurrilous* was *squirrel*). Then they formed an image that linked the keyword with the definition. For *scurrilous*, for example, participants were asked to form an image of a squirrel making an obscene gesture! A control group instead practiced sentences that illustrated the correct use of each word. When participants' ability to remember the definitions was tested 4 days later, the keyword group remembered 52% more definitions. This technique has also been found to be effective in learning psychology terms (Carney and Levin, 1998) and foreign vocabulary (Zhang and Schumm, 2000).

One reason why images are easier to remember than words could be that our mental representations of images are more *distinctive* than those of words. Because all words are composed from the same set of 26 letters, in perceptual terms there is not much difference between them; one word does not stand out much – is not highly distinctive – from others. Pictures, by contrast, differ far more from each other, and this could make it easier to locate them during retrieval. A possible analogy would be searching a library for a book: If the book you were looking for was red while all the others were black, it would be easier to find. (See also Weldon and Coyote, 1996, and Hamilton and Geraci, 2006.) Whatever the underlying mechanism, it is clear that imagery can be a powerful aid to memory.

Studying

Mnemonics can be fun, but improving your ability to memorize shopping lists or people's names is possibly not one of your highest priorities. We turn now to one that probably is, the ability to remember material that you study. In previous chapters we have reviewed laboratory research on memory, but how well do the findings from research on nonsense syllables or word lists apply to a student reading a psychology text at 3 in the morning? Could you use the principles discovered in the laboratory to improve your own studying?

Practice

Amount

One of the principles we've discussed is practice. As Ebbinghaus demonstrated so tenaciously, the more time we spend practicing material, the better we remember it. A series of studies by K. Anders Ericsson and his associates suggest that, with sufficient practice, people can attain quite remarkable levels of performance. In one of the first of these studies, Chase and Ericsson (1982) were able to train an individual they identified as SF to increase his short-term memory span from 8 digits to an almost unbelievable 80 – that is, he could repeat a string of 80 digits after hearing it just once! This improvement was the fruit of intensive practice spread over 2 years.

In a subsequent paper, Ericsson and Charness (1994) argued that practice is the basis not only for relatively trivial skills such as memorizing numbers but also for the profound abilities that we label *genius*. To support this claim, they marshaled evidence from domains as diverse as chess, music, and athletics. In every case, they argued, outstanding performers shared three characteristics: They started training at an early age, they were taught by outstanding teachers, and they practiced for at least 4 hours every day. Ericsson and Charness used the term *deliberate practice* to emphasize that the kind of practice they had in mind was not simply engaging in an activity but, rather, disciplined fine-tuning of the skill's components. For example, outstanding tennis players or golfers do not simply play the game for hours; instead, they repeat the identical shot over and over, working to refine the movements involved.

In one study supporting the role of practice, Ericsson, Krampe, and Tesch-Römer (1993) studied outstanding violinists being trained at a music academy in Germany. With the help of the academy's tutors, they divided the students into two groups: those with the potential to become international soloists, and those whose abilities were just below this level. The researchers found that, during the course of their lives, the best students had spent almost 50% more time practicing than had those who were not quite as good.

It is perhaps not surprising that the best performers in any field practice intensively, but we could still argue that what distinguishes a true genius – a Mozart or a Beethoven – is not practice but innate talent. Even here, however, Ericsson and Charness argue that deliberate practice can account for most if not all of the accomplishments of these exceptional figures. Mozart, for example, started practicing at the age of 3, his father was an outstanding violin teacher (he wrote the first book in German on how to teach the violin), and the young Mozart practiced for an astonishing 10 hours every day. Mozart, in other words, not only received all the kinds of training that distinguish all great performers, he experienced them at levels well beyond those of even the most talented musicians.

Thomas Edison, one of the greatest inventors of all time, famously said that genius is 1% inspiration, 99% perspiration, and this is perhaps not so far from Ericsson's view that genius is largely the result of practice. Whether or not Edison is right about the precise proportion of practice and talent that goes into creating a genius, it is clear that all skills, from the mundane to the most sublime, rest on a base of extensive, even gruelling, practice. (See also Ericsson, 2008.)

Spacing

Another important principle of memory discovered by Ebbinghaus was that practice is most effective when it is distributed over time. As anyone who has ever been a student can attest, students have an alarming tendency not to distribute their studying evenly, but instead to concentrate it in the period immediately before an exam. This approach often seems effective because immediately after a practice session the studied material comes to mind readily. However, research has repeatedly shown that the same amount of studying is more effective if spread over a semester rather than crammed into the last week or night. In one study, Bahrick, Bahrick, Bahrick, and Bahrick (1993) examined the ability of members of one family to memorize French and German vocabulary. (You might be able to guess whose family this was.) Some words were studied in sessions separated by 2 weeks, whereas others were studied in sessions separated by 8 weeks. Memory for the words was then tested 5 years later. Given that the number of training sessions in the two conditions had been identical, you might think that they would have produced similar levels of recall, but recall was approximately 50% better in the condition where practice had been spread more widely. This superiority of distributed practice over massed practice is known as the **spacing effect**.

One reason that spacing enhances learning is that it provides learners with more accurate feedback on how they are doing (Bahrick and Hall, 2005; Son, 2010). If you test yourself immediately after trying to learn something, the material may still be in short-term memory, giving you a potentially misleading impression of how well you have learned it (for example, Nelson and Leonesio, 1988). With a longer delay until testing, any retrieval will have to be from long-term memory. This allows you to assess your level of mastery more accurately, and, if necessary, to adjust your studying – perhaps devoting more time to material you've had difficulty remembering, or reading more deeply. (For a discussion of some other possible explanations of the spacing effect, see Greene, 2008.)

We should note that distributed practice is not always better. Whether distributed practice will produce better learning – and, if so, how much – depends on a bewildering array of variables, including the type of material being studied (for example, word pairs versus text), whether spacing is within a session or between sessions (in the case of foreign vocabulary, you could vary how much time elapses before returning to a word within the same session, or how long you leave between study sessions), and whether learning is tested soon after the final practice session or after a substantial delay. (See Dempster, 1996; Raaijmakers, 2003; and Roediger and Karpicke, 2010, for reviews.) In most situations, though, distributed practice does produce better learning, especially if the measure used is long-term retention of knowledge. What is now a large literature can thus be distilled down to one piece of practical advice: Don't cram! Or as Ulric Neisser, one of the founders of cognitive psychology, summarized the situation:

> You can get a good deal from rehearsal
> If it just has the proper dispersal
> (Quoted in Bjork, 1988, p. 399)

Think!

Let's assume that you have decided how much time to devote to studying a subject, and also how you will distribute that practice over time. (The correct answer, of course, is lots of practice, widely distributed.) You would still face one of the most important decisions, namely *how* to study. As we've seen many times, while study time is undoubtedly important, the outcome depends heavily on how this time is used. We've seen that when people read texts, they do not simply form associations between successive words; instead, they extract the meaning of the words and then store this meaning. If you don't understand the text, you will end up storing disconnected ideas, and material that lacks organization is much harder to later retrieve. An example we've encountered several times is Bransford and Johnson's ingenious passage about sorting clothes: Participants who were given the title and thus could understand the passage remembered almost three times as much as those who didn't.

Bower, Karlin, and Dueck (1975) reported a more light-hearted illustration of the same theme. They showed participants pictures that they called droodles – Figure 12.4 shows two examples – and then asked them to draw the shapes from memory. A group that saw the pictures without any labels was able to correctly reproduce 51% of the original pictures. A group given amusing captions, however, recalled 70%. The better we understand material, or can fit it into an existing framework, the better we remember it later.

Applied to studying, this research suggests that the single most important thing you can do to improve your recall of texts is to think about the material as you

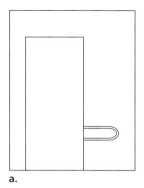
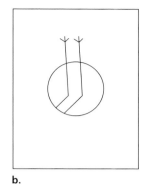

a.   b.

Figure 12.4 Droodles. Bower *et al.* (1975) created cartoons they called "droodles" to stimulate thought about the material to be memorized. (a) A midget playing a trombone in a telephone booth. (b) An early bird that captured a very strong worm. (Adapted from Bower, Karlin, and Dueck, 1975.)

read it, rather than just reading mechanically, without pausing for reflection. When you think about material, you connect it to your existing knowledge, and these connections make it easier to later retrieve the material.

Although this advice might sound reasonable, even obvious, many students don't read in this active, reflective way. The problem is that it is easier to read a chapter straight through than to repeatedly pause to think about its contents. And this difficulty is compounded by the fact that the extra effort just doesn't seem necessary. Immediately after reading a passage we are likely to recall it well because it is still in short-term memory – why pause for thought, and thus prolong your studying, if you already know the material? The problem is that you may not know the material as well as you think, so to ensure long-term retention it is important to think about the material as you read (Nelson, 1999; Karpicke, Butler, and Roediger, 2009).

One interesting tactic for achieving a deeper level of understanding is to imagine, as you read, that you are going to be teaching the material to someone else, and so to periodically pause to think about how you would explain it. Bargh and Schul (1980) found that students who read a passage in this way remembered it significantly better than a control group that did not. (See also Coleman, Brown, and Rivkin, 1997.) It seems likely that we read material more thoughtfully when we expect to have to teach it, making this a simple but potentially effective strategy for improving studying.

Review

A third strategy for improving studying is to review material when you finish reading it – without looking back at the text, seeing how much you can remember.

An obvious benefit is that this allows you to identify areas you haven't understood or haven't remembered, so that you can spend more time on them in future sessions. A less obvious benefit, but one increasingly supported by research, is that it can also strengthen your memory for the material that you retrieve. We usually think of retrieving information from memory as an essentially neutral act that doesn't change the memory, in the same way that retrieving information from a computer doesn't alter what is stored. Current evidence, however, suggests that retrieving a memory *does* change it, perhaps by strengthening existing retrieval pathways or creating new ones. Whatever the reason, the simple act of retrieving a memory can make it easier to retrieve in the future, a phenomenon known as the **testing effect**. Moreover, there is now persuasive evidence that testing yourself on material you are trying to learn can improve retention more than investing the same amount of time in further study.

We can illustrate this with a study by Roediger and Karpicke (2006). In the first phase participants were given two passages to read on topics such as sea otters. For one of the passages this was followed by 7 minutes in which they tried to recall it; for the other passage, they had 7 minutes to reread it. One week later they were tested to see how well they could recall the passages. Perhaps surprisingly, simply recalling the passage proved to be a more effective form of studying than reading it again: Participants who had practiced retrieving the material now remembered 55% of the main ideas, against only 40% for the group that had reread it. This was particularly surprising given that the retrieval group was not given an opportunity to check whether the memories they had retrieved were accurate: The simple act of retrieving a memory was enough to strengthen it.

A subsequent study by Karpicke and Roediger (2010) reported similar effects. The strongest effect, though, was found in groups given an opportunity to check the accuracy of their recall by rereading the passage for 1 minute after each test. Under these conditions, a single review (test plus brief rereading) doubled retention, from 20% to 40%, and if there were three reviews then recall doubled yet again, from 40% to 80%. Just a few attempts to retrieve material, when combined with brief rereading, improved retention from 20% to 80%. (See also McDaniel, Howard, and Einstein, 2009.)

In practical terms, this research suggests that if you want to remember a text well, you should try to recall it as often as possible – perhaps immediately after reading it, at the beginning of your next study session, or even as you are walking through campus to a lecture (see also Berger, Hall, and Bahrick, 1999). The more often you practice retrieval, the better your chances of succeeding under the more stressful conditions of an exam.

We can summarize our discussion of studying using an old joke. A visitor to Manhattan stopped a New Yorker in the street to ask how to get to Carnegie Hall, the famous concert hall. The New Yorker's pithy response was "Practice!"

The advice is undoubtedly sound, though perhaps a bit on the terse side. Effective studying does require practice, but the quality of studying is as important as the quantity. To maximize the chances of remembering what you read, you should space your practice sessions, think about the material as you read, and review it after you have finished. If anyone ever asks you how to get to Carnegie Hall (or better grades), a better answer might be "*Practice*, *Think*, and *Review*!"

Memory and the law

How accurate are our memories? The material we discussed in previous chapters points to seemingly opposite conclusions. On the one hand, we have seen that our memories can be surprisingly good: In Wagenaar's (1986) study of his own memory, he proved able to recall a very large number of his experiences over a 5-year period, sometimes in impressive detail. On the other hand, we have also seen that our memories are far from perfect. We don't always take in as much information as we think we do, and interference can make it hard for us to retrieve the material that we do store. When retrieval is incomplete, we try to reconstruct missing details, and these reconstructions can be inaccurate. In sum, we do retain a surprising amount of information, but the precise amount depends on factors such as how long we are exposed to a situation, the aspects to which we attend, and our experiences before and after the event.

We turn now to an area in which the question of accuracy is particularly important, the criminal justice system. To what extent should juries trust the memories of eyewitnesses?

Eyewitness testimony

Eyewitness testimony plays a crucial role in jury trials. In a study carried out in England and Wales in 1973, the authors identified approximately 900 cases in which police lineups led to the identification of a suspect. Of these, 82% eventually led to a criminal conviction. In almost 350 of these cases, the eyewitness identification provided the only evidence against the accused, but even here the conviction rate was 74% (Devlin, 1976). Clearly, juries put very great weight on the evidence of eyewitnesses. Are they right to do so?

The effect of emotion on memory

In addition to the potential for error present in any memory, particular problems arise when strong emotions are involved. Witnessing a crime, especially a violent crime, will normally produce a strong state of arousal – how does this affect the accuracy of a witness's memory? Does strong emotion enhance memory, by essentially burning the witnessed event into memory, or on the contrary do these emotions interfere with the witness's ability to take in what they are seeing and form a coherent record?

One way to try to answer this question would be to compare crimes involving different levels of stress and see which produce more accurate accounts. For most crimes, however, no other evidence is available to corroborate eyewitness identifications of the perpetrator, making it difficult or impossible to assess the accuracy of these identifications. A witness may confidently report that the criminal was 6 feet tall or had brown hair, but, their confidence notwithstanding, such accounts can be wrong. In one striking case, a man named Herbert Andrews was accused of passing bad checks, and 17 witnesses took the stand to confirm that he was the man who gave them the check. However, subsequent investigations suggested that a second man had actually been responsible, and this second man eventually confessed. Even though many of the witnesses had been completely confident in their identifications, and the two men differed substantially in appearance (the assistant district attorney later said that they "were as dissimilar in appearance as could be"), 17 witnesses had all identified the wrong man (Leach, Cutler, and van Wallendael, 2009).

Because of problems like this, most of the research on the relationship between emotion and memory has been carried out in the laboratory. Literally hundreds of studies have been reported – a review published in 2004 identified 450 (Deffenbacher *et al.*, 2004) – but their results have varied widely, with some finding that emotion enhances memory, some that it hurts, and some that it has no effect. Making sense of this variation has been difficult because of the many ways in which these studies have differed. One obvious difference has been in the methods used to generate emotion. Some have presented arousing stimuli such as loud noises while participants were memorizing a list of words, others had participants view slides of potentially upsetting scenes and then try to recall them, while still others have simulated real crimes (for example, having an actor enter a room during a lecture, steal a bit of equipment and then quickly leave). Studies have also differed in factors such as the population studied, the amount of time the perpetrator was visible, and whether a weapon was present (Neuschatz and Cutler, 2008).

These differences make it difficult to reach unequivocal conclusions, but at present it looks as if two variables might account for much of the variance in the reported outcomes. One is the scope of the questions asked when testing memory, and in particular the extent to which these questions focused on *central* or *peripheral* aspects of the witnessed scenes. As we saw in our discussion of punishment, Easterbrook (1959) proposed that arousal narrows attention, resulting in heightened attention to central aspects of a scene but reduced attention to more peripheral aspects, and this pattern has also been observed in studies of emotion and memory. In a study by Wessel and Merckelbach (1998), for example, spider phobics were shown a bulletin board containing material related to spiders, such as a picture of a spider, and also unrelated material, such as a picture of a baby. On a later memory test, the spider phobics were better than a control group at recalling the material concerning the spider, but worse at recalling the other material. One reason for the divergent results of research on memory and emotion, therefore, could be that studies which assess memory for central details are more likely to find that emotion helps memory, while those that include more questions on peripheral details find the opposite (Reisberg and Heuer, 2007).

A second potentially important factor could be differences in intensity of emotion. Deffenbacher *et al.* (2004) have proposed a distinction between a relatively mild form of emotion that they term *arousal*, and a more intense form that they call *activation*. In arousal, we orient to a novel or potentially dangerous stimulus in order to investigate it; this orienting causes decreases in heart rate, blood pressure, and muscle tone. In activation, on the other hand, we identify the danger as more pressing and prepare for fight or flight; in contrast to arousal, this involves increases in heart rate, blood pressure, and general muscle tone. Deffenbacher and his colleagues analyzed experiments which produced this more intense form of emotion and found that stress impaired memory for *all* aspects of an experience, central as well as peripheral.

Among the studies they reviewed was one by Morgan *et al.* (2004), which produced perhaps the highest level of stress ever seen in an experiment. The investigation was carried out at a US Army survival school that trained soldiers to withstand interrogation. One component of this training involved placement in a mock prisoner of war camp where the soldiers were deprived of sleep and food for 48 hours. They were then subjected to two 40-minute interrogation sessions during which they had to stand while being questioned. One session was conducted under low-stress conditions, and a second under high-stress conditions in which the interrogator stood within 2–5 feet of the soldiers and physically punished them if they did not maintain eye contact with him or answer his questions. (The order in which the sessions were conducted was counterbalanced.) One day later the soldiers were tested to see if they could identify their interrogators. Those who had been interrogated under conditions of high stress performed significantly worse: When asked to identify their interrogator in a line-up, only 30% could do so, compared to 62% in the low-stress condition. Moreover, they were also more likely to mistakenly identify an innocent person as their interrogator, as they chose the wrong person 56% of the time, despite having the option of saying the interrogator was not present. This inability to identify the interrogator was particularly striking given that the interrogation session had lasted for 40 minutes. Under highly stressful conditions involving fears for our personal safety, memory can be remarkably poor.[2] (For a summary of other studies along these lines, see Valentine and Mesout, 2009.)

In summary, while there is still some uncertainty about the precise relationship between emotion and memory, two variables currently seem to play an important role, the intensity of the emotion and the way in which memory is assessed. Milder forms of emotion seem to enhance memory for central aspects of scenes while simultaneously impairing memory for more peripheral aspects, but stronger emotions can have a more uniformly harmful impact. In the context of witnesses to a crime, this suggests that we need to be particularly careful in judging the accuracy of eyewitness testimony if the crime was violent, or for other reasons produced high levels of stress.

Flashbulb memories

Simulations of crime in a laboratory setting have the advantage of allowing us to assess the accuracy of witness's memories, but are the levels of emotion in these studies really equivalent to those produced by witnessing real crimes, especially ones involving violence? In the Morgan study, the answer is almost certainly yes, but very few experiments even approach the level of stress generated in this study. It is difficult to be certain, therefore, whether the results of laboratory studies provide a realistic guide to what happens when someone witnesses a crime in real life.

An alternative method for assessing the effects of powerful emotion on memory was developed by Brown and Kulik (1977). Instead of crime, they asked participants to recall public events that were known to have generated intense emotions. For example, they asked participants what they had been doing when they heard the news of the assassination of President John F. Kennedy 13 years earlier. Despite the long period that had elapsed, they found that 79 of the 80 participants could still remember their experiences vividly – where they were, whom they were with, even what their companions were wearing and precisely what they had said. Given the remarkable detail of these memories, Brown and Kulik compared them to photographs and dubbed them **flashbulb memories**. It was as if the powerful

---

[2] Our analysis of how emotion may influence memory has largely focused on the role of attention, with the implicit suggestion that it is changes in the focus of attention that determine whether emotion helps or hurts memory. Emotion, however, can also affect how memories are consolidated during the time following encoding. In an experiment by Nielson, Yee, and Erickson (2005), participants learned a list of nouns and then later viewed an arousing or nonarousing video; those who saw the arousing video remembered significantly more of the words when tested one day later. Because the video was seen only after the list was learned, it could not have affected attention; instead, it seemed to be influencing how the memory record that had been formed was consolidated. (See also McGaugh, 2004, and Mather, 2007.)

emotions triggered by the shocking news had burned participants' experiences into memory, producing detailed, permanent records.

Subsequent studies have largely confirmed these findings. People do have vivid memories of what they were doing when they heard the news of events that shocked them, such as John Lennon's assassination or the destruction of the Twin Towers on 9/11. But are these memories accurate? Because the studies were retrospective – there was no independent evidence about where people really were when they heard, and exactly what was said – it is difficult to say. To provide clearer evidence, Neisser and Harsch (1992) interviewed 44 college students in January 1986, the day after the American space shuttle Challenger exploded shortly after takeoff, with the loss of seven lives. The researchers asked the students detailed questions about their experiences when they heard the news. Then, 3 years later, Neisser and Harsch interviewed the students again and asked the same questions.

As in the Brown and Kulik study, the students had vivid memories of what they had been doing when they heard the news. However, when the experimenters compared the students' accounts with those given at the time, Neisser and Harsch found that their recollections were often wrong. One student, for example, recalled hearing the news while in her dorm room with a roommate, watching television. When asked to rate her confidence that this memory was accurate, she gave it the highest possible rating. In fact, her original account showed that she had been in a religion class when she heard the news and had watched TV only later. Neisser and Harsch assessed the accuracy of the students' reports on a 7-point scale; the average score was only 3, and 25% of the participants were wrong on every single detail. Interestingly, there was no relationship between how confident people were in their memories and whether these memories were accurate, a surprising result, but one that has been confirmed repeatedly. (See Shaw, McClure, and Dykstra, 2007, for an excellent review.)

Other studies have produced roughly similar results – in some cases, memories have been more accurate (for example, Conway *et al.*, 1994), in others less (for example, McCloskey, Wible, and Cohen, 1988). Surprising and emotionally powerful events do often produce exceptionally strong memories, but rarely of the photographic quality hypothesized by Brown and Kulik (Talarico and Rubin, 2007; Conway *et al.*, 2009).

We began this section with the suggestion that flashbulb memories make it possible to study the effects of emotions that are stronger than those produced in laboratory studies. It could be objected, however, that even events such as hearing about Kennedy's assassination, or 9/11, do not produce the kinds of stress involved in witnessing a violent crime. When emotions are truly intense, according to this argument, our memories will be exceptionally accurate. Other evidence, however, suggests that witnesses to crimes can make exactly the same kinds of mistakes that we have encountered in other settings. One example we have already discussed involved Donald Thomson, the psychologist who was picked out of a police lineup as a rapist because at the time of the rape the victim had been watching a program in which Thomson was being interviewed. The victim had correctly remembered seeing Thomson's face, but unfortunately had become confused about the source of this memory.

Thomson's case is not an isolated one: Studies indicate that eyewitness testimony is often mistaken. One source of evidence has come from studies of police lineups. These lineups usually include individuals known to be innocent, known as fillers, as well as the suspect. In almost 20% of such lineups, eyewitnesses mistakenly identify one of the fillers as the culprit (Wright and McDaid, 1996). Additional evidence has come from cases in which individuals have been convicted of crimes but later shown to be innocent on the basis of DNA tests. In a review published in 2000, Scheck, Neufield, and Dwyer (2000) examined 62 cases in which innocent people were later exonerated on the basis of DNA evidence, including 8 in which the person had been sentenced to death. In 84%, the crucial evidence leading to conviction had come from eyewitnesses. By 2010, the number of cases in which innocent people were later exonerated had grown to 255, and mistaken eyewitness identifications were a factor in 75%. In addition, there were tens of thousands of cases in which DNA evidence led to suspects being cleared before the case came to trial (Innocence Project, 2010).

It would be misleading to leave the impression that eyewitness accounts are always wrong – on the contrary, they are often right. Yuille and Cutshall (1986), for example, interviewed 13 witnesses to a robbery that ended with the thief being shot and killed. Because the thief was shot, considerable forensic evidence was available about his appearance, the car he used, and so on. Witnesses were interviewed at the time of the crime, and then again 4 to 5 months later; they were asked about details such as the robber's appearance, the weapon used, and the sequence of events. The experimenters found that the witnesses recalled between 80% and 90% of the details accurately even months later – they remembered the exact number of shots fired, they could estimate the age of the attacker to within 2 years, and so on (see also Fisher, Geiselman, and Amador, 1989; Odinot, Wolters, and van Koppen, 2009). The point is not that eyewitness accounts are invariably wrong, but rather that the possibility of error has to be taken seriously.

Sources of error

Why are eyewitnesses' memories sometimes flawed? One possible source of errors lies in how events are coded at the time they occur. As we saw in our discussion of attention, we have only a limited capacity for processing information, and we often process and store much less information than we think we do. In the Simons and

Levin (1998) experiment on change blindness, for example, participants engaged in a conversation with one of the experimenters did not notice when a second experimenter took his place while two workmen carried a door in between them. We take in far less information than we realize, especially during brief encounters. Moreover, this problem is likely to be exacerbated if a weapon is used in the commission of a crime. Research on the **weapon focus effect** has shown that people's ability to identify a criminal is impaired if a weapon is present during the crime. There is a natural tendency to focus on the weapon, and this can reduce attention to other aspects such as the criminal's face. (For reviews, and also discussion of other possible explanations, see Pickel, 2007, and Levine and Edelstein, 2009.)

Problems can also arise when the time comes for witnesses to remember what they witnessed. One such problem we have already encountered is the *misinformation effect*. If the police ask a witness questions that imply certain facts – for example, "Did the thief have a scar?" – this can lead witnesses to later become confused about where they acquired this information, and to honestly believe that they saw it themselves.

Source confusion can also occur if witnesses are shown mug shots to identify the criminal. In one study by Brown *et al.* (1977), participants saw a staged crime and then looked at mug shots of possible perpetrators. Several days later, they were asked to identify the criminal in a lineup, and 29% identified innocent individuals whose faces they had seen only in the mug shots. As in the Thomson rape case, witnesses knew they had seen the face before but were confused about where.

If at the conclusion of a lineup a witness is congratulated on having chosen the right person, this can substantially increase the witness's confidence in his or her identification (Wells and Bradfield, 1999). This might at first seem unimportant, but numerous studies have shown that juries put considerable weight on how confident witnesses are when they present their evidence (for example, Wells, Lindsay, and Ferguson, 1979). This is almost certainly a mistake – as we noted earlier, confidence is a very poor predictor of whether a memory is accurate. Nevertheless, juries are strongly influenced by confidence. If the police believe that they have found the right person, their behavior can strongly affect the confidence of witnesses, and this in turn can lead to the conviction of innocent people.

Improving testimony

The research on lineups emphasizes the dangers in accepting eyewitness testimony at face value. As these dangers became more apparent, researchers began to examine whether anything could be done to improve the accuracy of eyewitness accounts, and in this section we will look at some of their findings.

Hypnosis?

One technique that police sometimes use to obtain more accurate information from witnesses is hypnosis. Unfortunately, research has shown that the main effect of hypnosis is not on memory per se, but rather on participants' willingness to talk. In some cases, this can lead to participants volunteering useful information, but it also produces increased output of false memories, and there is no easy way to know which is which (Dywan, 1995; Scoboria *et al.*, 2002). This problem is compounded by the fact that hypnotized individuals are highly suggestible, and will pick up on suggestions made or implied by the person who hypnotized them. In one study by Laurence and Perry (1983), participants were first asked if they had been awakened on any of the nights during the previous week. None had, but when they were then asked under hypnosis whether they had been awoken by loud noises during this period, most said that they had. When interviewed a week later by a different experimenter, 48% repeated they had heard the noises, and even when told that the hypnotist had planted this suggestion, almost half still insisted that their memories of being woken were accurate.

In another investigation of suggestibility, Spanos *et al.* (1991) told participants that under hypnosis they would be returning to a past life. When they were then hypnotized, 83% acted as if they were reliving a past life – when asked their name, for example, giving a name that was not their own, and also specifying a different country of residence. When asked historical questions about the period, however, their answers were almost always wrong – they could not name the country's leader, say whether the country was at peace or at war, or name the currency. In a typical error, one participant said that the year was 1866 and they were living in Germany, even though Germany had not yet become a country at the time.

Because the memories produced by hypnosis tend to be vivid, participants are often confident that they are remembering real events, and this in turn makes their testimony convincing to both police and juries. Nevertheless, evidence now suggests that hypnosis does not increase the accuracy of memory, and in some cases can produce totally spurious results. Summarizing this evidence, one review concluded:

The data clearly indicate that hypnosis is not an aid to memory. On the contrary, hypnosis can reduce the accuracy of eyewitness testimony and create an unjustified increase in confidence in what is remembered. (Mazzoni and Lynn, 2007, p. 33)

Throughout this text, when summarizing evidence we have often had to use qualifiers and warnings of the need for caution, but this is one case where this burden can be shed: Hypnosis is not a reliable technique for improving eyewitness memory.

The cognitive interview

A much more promising technique for improving an eyewitness's memory was developed by Fisher and Geiselman (1992). They used principles of memory derived from laboratory research to develop a new interviewing procedure that they called the **cognitive interview**. The techniques they recommended for improving witness recall included the following:

1 Reinstate the physical and emotional context of the crime as fully as possible, including, where possible, returning to the scene of the crime for the interview.
2 Have witnesses recall events from different perspectives (for example, from that of the victim) and in different orders (for example, backward as well as forward).
3 Have witnesses recall all details, no matter how trivial they might seem.

The common goal of these techniques was to reinstate as many aspects of the original experience as possible. As we saw in our discussion of retrieval cues, the more the environment at retrieval matches that during coding, the greater the likelihood of activating the original memory.

Another important aspect of this method is asking open-ended questions (for example, "What did you see?") and giving witnesses time to answer fully. Although the police do ask some open-ended questions, they are often under time pressure and searching for specific information. In one study of real-life police interviews, when witnesses began to give narrative accounts of what they had witnessed, the police interrupted them, on average, within 8 seconds (Fisher, Geiselman, and Raymond, 1987). This cuts off what could prove to be valuable information and prevents witnesses from remembering aspects that, even though unimportant in themselves, could act as retrieval cues to elicit more critical information.

To test the effectiveness of the cognitive interview, Fisher and Geiselman (1992) showed participants films of real crimes, provided by the Los Angeles Police Department. Then, 2 days later, genuine law enforcement officials interviewed these witnesses. One group was interviewed using standard police procedures, the other using the cognitive interview. Fisher and Geiselman found that witnesses recalled 30 to 35% more detail when the cognitive interview was used, without any increase in erroneous recall. Köhnken *et al.* (1999) reviewed 55 similar studies, and in 53 of the 55 the cognitive interview was more effective, producing, on average, 34% more information. Again, it could be argued that simulation studies in a laboratory do not provide a realistic analogue to what happens in real life, but two studies have been reported in which the police used the cognitive interview in questioning witnesses to real crimes. If anything the results were even better, as the cognitive interview produced 35% more information than standard interviews in one study and 55% more in the other (Fisher, Geiselman, and Amador, 1989; Clifford and George, 1996).

More recent research has focused on ways in which the cognitive interview can be improved so as to produce comparable amounts of information in a shorter time, and the results of these studies have also been promising (Gabbert, Hope, and Fisher, 2009; Dando *et al.*, 2009). On the basis of all this research, versions of the cognitive interview are now widely used by police in Britain, and have also been adopted by the FBI in America (Fisher and Schreiber, 2007).

Improving lineups

Researchers have also explored ways of improving the use of lineups, because they are often critical in determining whether a suspect is brought to trial and then convicted. We cannot cover all the issues raised by the use of lineups here – excellent reviews are available in Wells *et al.* (2000), and Neuschatz and Cutler (2008) – but we will touch on one because of its importance. When witnesses are asked to view a lineup, they typically assume that the police would only have arranged a lineup if they were convinced that they had apprehended the guilty party. On the assumption that the culprit is present, the witness might then identify whichever participant in the lineup most *closely resembles* their memory of the perpetrator, rather than using the absolute standard of whether they are sure that this is the person.

To minimize this possibility, researchers have tried two techniques. The first is to explicitly warn witnesses before the lineup that the perpetrator might not be present. Steblay (1997) summarized the results of 22 simulation experiments that compared lineups where a warning was given with lineups where it was not. She found that giving a warning reduced the number of innocent people who were identified incorrectly by 42%, while having virtually no effect on identifications of the real culprit. A seemingly trivial change in procedure was enough to dramatically reduce false identifications, without impairing correct ones.

The second technique is to present members of the lineup sequentially instead of simultaneously. Witnesses see one person at a time and must make a decision after each one as to whether he or she is the perpetrator; once they identify someone, no other candidates are presented. The rationale for this approach is that if witnesses see only one person at a time, they have to base their decisions on an absolute criterion ("Is this the perpetrator?") rather than a relative one in which they choose whoever resembles the perpetrator the most.

Sequential lineups have been found to be effective in many studies. In one, sequential presentation reduced the rate of mistaken identifications from 43% to 17%, without any decrease in the number of correct identifications (Lindsay and Wells, 1985). Steblay *et al.* (2001) performed a meta-analysis on 23 studies which compared simultaneous and sequential lineups, and found that sequential lineups produced more correct decisions. However, the difference was relatively small (56%

versus 48%), and some researchers have argued that the evidence is not yet strong enough to support its adoption. (For articulate, not to say impassioned, statements of the opposing views, see Malpass, Tredoux, and McQuiston-Surrett, 2009, and Lindsay *et al.*, 2009.) It is clear that warning witnesses that the criminal may not be present substantially reduces false accusations without undermining correct identifications; whether sequential lineups achieve this is not yet clear.

Taken together, the research we have been reviewing showed that eyewitness testimony could be made substantially more accurate with some relatively small changes in procedure, and this success led Janet Reno, then US Attorney General, to convene a special panel to develop national guidelines for the collection of eyewitness testimony. The panel consisted of psychologists, police and prosecutors, and their report was published as *Eyewitness Evidence: A Guide for Law Enforcement* (Technical Working Group for Eyewitness Evidence, 1999). The guide was based almost entirely on psychological research on memory, and it constituted the first-ever national guidelines in the USA for how eyewitness testimony should be collected. Only 25 years had elapsed from the appearance of Elizabeth Loftus's influential paper on the misinformation effect (Loftus and Palmer, 1974), almost certainly the fastest-ever route from the initiation of psychological research on a topic to its acceptance as official government policy. (For an exceptionally interesting account, see Wells *et al.*, 2000.)

Recovered memories

The number of reported cases of child abuse has increased dramatically in recent years, triggering a sometimes fierce debate about whether the incidence of this abuse could really be as great as these reports suggested. Within this broader controversy, there has been an even more impassioned debate about **recovered memories**, cases in which adults have suddenly remembered being abused when they were children, even though they had no recollection of this abuse during the intervening years. Was it really possible for individuals to forget such traumatic and horrifying experiences, and then suddenly remember them many years later?

Two polarized positions rapidly emerged. On one side, some argued that children and adults would not invent such crimes, and to reject their claims – and thus implicitly call them liars – would be to undermine and humiliate individuals who had already suffered too much. On the other side were those who questioned whether it was really possible for such painful and traumatic events to be forgotten. They noted the evidence that false memories can be implanted, as in experiments where detailed and convincing memories were created for invented events such as being lost at a mall and spilling a bowl of punch at a wedding. Given the ease with which such memories can be induced, and the implausibility of the claim that horrific events of abuse could be forgotten for years, was it not more likely that the memories were false? If so, it would clearly be unfair to destroy the lives of decent and loving parents by accepting false accusations.

The conflict between these two views triggered one of the most impassioned controversies in the history of psychology – what the distinguished Harvard psychologist Daniel Schacter called "The Memory Wars" (Schacter, 1996). This conflict continues, but over time a considerable degree of consensus has emerged (for example, American Psychological Association, 1995), and in this section we will outline some of its main elements.

Recovered memories can be real

It has gradually become clear that at least some cases involving recovered memories are genuine. Schacter (1996) describes one such case involving a college professor, Ross Cheit, who entered therapy because of a general sense of dissatisfaction with his life. During this period, he had a dream that reminded him of a counselor at a camp he attended as a child. When he awoke, he suddenly remembered having been molested by this counselor. Distressed, he employed a private detective to help locate the counselor, and eventually they succeeded. Cheit then spoke to his former counselor by phone, a conversation he recorded. In the course of this conversation, the counselor admitted having molested boys, and he said that he had had to leave several jobs because of his activities. Given these admissions, it seems very likely that Cheit's recollection of being abused was accurate.

In most cases of recovered memory, it is difficult to prove whether the abuse really occurred: It is usually the word of the accuser against that of the accused. The strongest evidence has come from a study by L. M. Williams (1994a), who reversed the normal chain of inquiry: Instead of starting from the allegation of abuse and trying to work backward, she started from evidence in childhood that abuse had occurred and then worked forward. She examined hospital records to identify children who had been treated for abuse during the 1970s. She then managed to contact 129 of the women who had been abused 17 years earlier. She discovered that 38% did not remember the particular incident for which they had been hospitalized, and 12% did not remember ever having been abused. Maria, for example, had been abused by her father at least six times when she was 2, but had no memory of it; June had been abused by three cousins over a 2-year period when she was 7, but again as an adult had no memory of it (Williams, 1994b).

The forgetting of abuse in this study was particularly surprising in that most of the women had been between 7 and 12 years old when the abuse occurred, 60%

of the cases had involved vaginal penetration, and 62% had involved violence or physical force. Moreover, the children had been extensively interviewed at the time: They were interviewed by the police for up to 3 hours, they were later referred for a second medical exam, and this was followed by between 1 and 4 visits from a social worker. Despite all this, 38% had no memory of being abused.

In a follow-up study, Williams (1995) interviewed 75 women from her sample who did remember being abused and found that 16% reported long periods during which they had forgotten the abuse. One of these cases involved a woman identified as Kim. When Kim was 7, she was sexually abused by her brother. When interviewed at age 24, she did remember the incident, but reported

> that she forgot about what happened when she was about 12 or 13 and didn't remember again until she was 22. She said that a boyfriend asked if she had been sexually abused, and said her cousin said she had been abused. Kim said, "I don't know." Kim told the interviewer, "that made me start to remember. Then a couple days later I saw [a TV talk show] on sexual abuse and it all came back to me."
>
> (Williams, 1995, p. 665)

Other studies have confirmed Williams' findings. Ghetti *et al.* (2006) interviewed adults who, as children, had testified in trials of their abusers. They had been between 4 and 17 years of age at the time they were abused, and when they were interviewed approximately 13 years later 15% reported a prior period in which they had had no memory of the abuse. When asked about why they had forgotten, typical comments were "I felt afraid, and I did not want to think about it," and "It was so horrible that I pushed it out of my mind" (p. 1017). Similar findings were reported by Geraerts *et al.* (2007). They used newspaper advertisements to recruit women who believed that they had been abused as children, and they then used investigators to search for corroborative evidence of the abuse (for example, someone who had been told about the abuse within a week of its occurrence, or who had been abused by the same person). Of the women who reported that there had been a period in which they had not remembered the abuse, and who had recovered the memory of this abuse on their own – that is, outside of therapy – the investigators were able to corroborate 37% of the accounts. Taken together with the reports by Williams and Ghetti, it seems clear that in at least some cases children do forget serious instances of abuse, only for this memory to return when they become adults.

Recovered memories can be false

It is now also clear that some memories of abuse are false. In one case, a woman who was being counseled recovered memories of being repeatedly raped by her father and then becoming pregnant, only to have her father perform an abortion with a coat-hanger. However, subsequent evidence revealed that the woman was a virgin, and that her father had had a vasectomy before the time of the alleged pregnancy (Testa, 1996, cited in Weiten, 1998). In another case, children at the Little Rascals preschool in North Carolina accused several members of staff of having abused them. One child remembered staff members releasing sharks into a nearby lake to attack the children; another remembered being abducted in a spaceship. Despite the extreme implausibility of some of the accusations, and the fact that some of the accused were mothers of children at the school, two members of staff were convicted of abuse and sent to prison (see Schacter, 1996; Robinson, 2003; and PBS, 1997).

Many cases of recovered memory have involved allegations of satanic rituals (see Nathan and Snedeker, 1995). Despite many thousands of such reports, sometimes involving murder and cannibalism, extensive investigations by law enforcement officials have failed to confirm a single case. One FBI agent investigated 300 cases without finding any corroboration, and the National Center for Child Abuse reported similar results in a survey of thousands of professionals in this area (see Ofshe and Watters, 1994; Schacter, 1996). We cannot conclude that satanic abuse never happens, but it is difficult to believe that so many cases of murder and torture could occur without bodies or other physical evidence ever being found.

Why do so many people remember abuse that never occurred? The most likely explanation lies in our earlier discussion of source confusion and reality monitoring. As we have seen, it is surprisingly easy to become confused about whether an event we remember was real, imaginary, or, perhaps, described to us by others. In the Little Rascals case, for example, it is not difficult to imagine that it all began with one child becoming confused or simply making up a story. This story could have spurred other children to create their own stories, perhaps competing for the story that would create the most excitement, until eventually the children began to genuinely believe that the events they were describing were real. Support for this interpretation has come from evidence that children are particularly susceptible to suggestion. Ceci (1995), for example, reported a variant of the "lost in the mall" procedure in which he and his colleagues interviewed children once a week for 10 weeks. In each session they asked the children if they could remember various incidents, including one false one in which they were taken to hospital because their finger had been caught in a mousetrap. At the end of the 10 weeks, 58% of the children were able to recall the incident, often in great detail. Ceci later showed videotapes of the children's description of this manufactured incident and other, real incidents to psychologists with experience in interviewing children. The children's accounts of the mousetrap incident were so vivid, and described with such confidence, that the psychologists were unable to tell which accounts were true and which were false.

False memories can also arise in the course of therapy, as in the case of the virgin who remembered being raped by her father. If therapists believe that child abuse is a common problem, as many do, then their behavior could unintentionally encourage clients to believe that they were abused, despite the fact that these clients initially had no memory of this abuse (Lindsay and Poole, 1995). This danger could then be increased by therapists' use of hypnosis to help their clients to remember, because hypnotized subjects are particularly susceptible to suggestions made by the hypnotist (Lynn *et al.*, 1997). One example is the phenomenon of *age regression*, in which hypnotized subjects are asked to become children again and relive their experiences. Subjects then begin to talk as if they were children and produce vivid accounts of what happened to them. Their behavior is very convincing, but studies have shown that their regression is not genuine: They behave in ways they *think* children would behave at that age, rather than the way children actually behave. If they are asked to write, for example, regressed subjects do so in a childlike manner, but their spelling is often too sophisticated (for example, Silverman and Retzlaff, 1986). In a study more directly related to the issue of recovered memories, subjects were asked to regress to an earlier life (Spanos *et al.*, 1991). Roughly half came to believe that they had genuinely had an earlier life, and when they were further told that they had been abused during this earlier existence, many also formed clear memories of this abuse.

Another potentially dangerous technique used by some therapists is guided imagery, or visualization, in which clients are encouraged to imagine being abused to help them retrieve genuine memories. As we saw in our discussion of reality monitoring, however, when we create detailed images of an imaginary event, when we later retrieve these images it can be very difficult to distinguish them from memories of real events.

It is very difficult to know how many false memories of childhood abuse have been created using techniques such as hypnosis and visualization. One review concluded that there were "good grounds to fear that tens of thousands of people have developed illusory memories" because of therapy (Lindsay and Poole, 1995), though others have disputed this (for example, Pope, 1996). It is worth noting, however, that in the Geraerts study cited earlier in which attempts were made to corroborate reports of abuse, the authors were able to confirm abuse in 37% of the cases where the women had recovered the memory of abuse on their own; of the 16 cases in which memories of abuse had been recovered in therapy, the authors were unable to confirm a single one (Eich *et al.*, 2008). This does not mean that memories recovered in therapy should never be believed, but it does suggest that the techniques used by some therapists pose serious risks of implanting false memories.

Evaluation

As often happens in psychology and other sciences, what start as substantial differences in expert opinion are often bridged as evidence accumulates. That has certainly been the case concerning recovered memories. There is now substantial agreement that women who have been abused may have long periods in which they do not remember this abuse, though differences remain as to prevalence – how common is such forgetting? – and, even more contentious, the nature of the underlying mechanism. In essence, the debate is whether the forgetting of childhood abuse can be explained in terms of "normal" principles of forgetting, or whether some special mechanism, unique to painful or traumatic memories, must be invoked. Concerning the possibility of normal forgetting, Loftus *et al.* (1994) have written that "there are many reasons why [abuse] might not be recalled . . . Normal forgetting of all sorts of events is a fact of life, but is not thought to involve some special repression mechanism" (Loftus *et al.*, 1994, p. 1178). Similarly, Kihlstrom *et al.* (2005) wrote that "any forgetting is easily accounted for by . . . normal memory processes such as ordinary forgetting" (Kihlstrom *et al.*, 2005, p. 1182).

Against this, proponents of special mechanisms such as Williams (1994b) believe that the pain produced by remembering abuse leads to the active suppression of such memories, rather than simply passive forgetting. In Williams's words:

Likening having no memory of a severe trauma such as child sexual abuse to forgetting to buy a bottle of aspirin on a shopping trip (Loftus *et al.*, 1994) seems to ignore the psychological significance of such events and the resulting distress often experienced by many victims . . . in my view the most reasonable theory suggests that being sexually abused is a qualitatively different life experience from thinking about purchasing a bottle of aspirin, and forgetting is likely to involve different psychological mechanisms.

(Williams, 1994b, p. 1183)

As to the nature of these mechanisms, several theories have been proposed. One is what Freud called repression. Although Freud's views of repression changed over time, his initial belief was that when an experience is deeply traumatic or painful, we may protect ourselves from it by banishing all memories of it to the unconscious, and his daughter Anna further proposed that this suppression is itself an unconscious process that takes place without our awareness (Erdelyi, 2006). Another possibility is what is sometimes called cognitive avoidance. In contrast to what is now cited as Freud's theory of repression, the claim here is that memories are sometimes *consciously* inhibited or suppressed, to avoid the pain they cause. Just as we can learn not to touch a hot pan because avoiding it prevents pain, so too we can learn to avoid thoughts that are painful. In Chapter 11 we discussed Anderson's research showing that our brains will automatically inhibit some memories in order to aid in the retrieval of others, and that this inhibitory process can also be initiated voluntarily. If so, inhibition could play a role in recovered memories, as children who have been abused learn to inhibit memories of this abuse in order to avoid the feelings of distress and anxiety that these memories engender (Smith and Moynan, 2008; Anderson and Levy, 2009).

Many of the comments made by women who have recovered memories are consistent with this idea of voluntary suppression. We quoted two such comments earlier, from women who talked about pushing aside painful memories or not wanting to think about them. Williams (1994b, 1995) has provided similar quotes. One woman said, "I used to think about it for the first two years, then I just blocked it out." And a child, in an especially poignant comment, said, "When I remember about it [the rape] I keep trying to think about good things like Christmas and it goes away" (original in McCahill *et al.*, 1979, p. 44; quoted by Williams, 1994b). The common theme in all these quotes is that the abused children deliberately and consciously suppressed the memories that they found painful.

Whatever the precise mechanisms, there is now substantial consensus that children who have been abused can forget the abuse for long periods, only to recover those memories as adults. There is also growing agreement that active suppression of memories may be one of the causes of this forgetting, even among researchers who have been critical of many of the other claims made about recovered memories (for example, McNally, 2007). However, we have also seen that some recovered memories, perhaps especially those recovered in the course of therapy, are false. The dilemma – and one that has caused heartbreak to tens of thousands of families – lies in knowing whether any particular memory of abuse is accurate. Research on memory has played a vital role in establishing the validity of some recovered memories and in identifying therapeutic techniques that can implant false ones, but we do not yet have a reliable method for determining whether any particular memory is true or false.

Summary

- A variety of mnemonic techniques have been developed to help people remember lists of unrelated facts. The method of loci and the pegword system are particularly effective.
- This effectiveness derives from several memory principles, including providing a structure to link material (organization), the active role of the person in finding connections (the generation effect), and the use of imagery.
- The effectiveness of studying depends not only on the amount of time spent studying but on how this studying is spread over time (spacing); on thinking

actively and deeply about the material while studying it; and on reviewing that material afterwards. *Practice*, *Think*, and *Review*: All have a substantial impact on how much is remembered.

- The principles of memory discovered in the laboratory have also been applied in the criminal justice system. One application has concerned the role of emotion in memory. Early research suggested that strong emotion produces detailed and accurate memories – "flashbulb memories" – but while these memories are vivid, they are not necessarily accurate. Emotion tends to narrow attention, and while this can enhance recall of some details, it can impair recall of others – if a robber uses a gun, attention to the gun can reduce attention to his appearance. Intense emotion is a particular problem, as it can severely impair later recall.

- Hypnosis is of little or no value in improving a witness's memory, but a technique based on memory research has proven very effective. In the cognitive interview, witnesses are questioned in a manner designed to re-create the original scene as fully as possible, thereby maximizing possible retrieval cues.

- Memory research has also been used to improve the effectiveness of lineups. One simple but effective technique is to warn witnesses that the perpetrator may not be present; this substantially reduces false identifications without reducing correct ones. Another, more controversial, technique is to present suspects sequentially rather than simultaneously.

- Research on recovered memories (where adults suddenly recall having been abused as children) has confirmed that some are genuine but also shown that some are false. Techniques such as hypnosis and guided imagery can make it hard for people to tell whether a memory is based on a real event or one that they imagined or heard described.

Review questions

1 What are the method of loci and the pegword systems? What are the three factors that the text suggests may contribute to their effectiveness?

2 According to the text, four factors play a key role in determining the effectiveness of studying. What are they? What evidence points to their importance?

3 Does emotional arousal help or hurt people's ability to remember an experience? What factors seem to influence the outcome?

4 What are flashbulb memories? How accurate are they?

5 Why are eyewitnesses' memories sometimes inaccurate?

6　How effective are hypnosis and the cognitive interview in improving the accuracy of eyewitnesses' memories?

7　What are the two main methods that have been tried to improve lineups? How effective have they been?

8　What are recovered memories? What evidence suggests that some recovered memories are true? What evidence suggests that some are false?

Part III Learning and memory

13 Neural networks

CONTENTS

In previous chapters we encountered examples of learning and memory that varied widely in complexity, from rats learning to press a bar at one end, to humans trying to remember lessons in physics at the other. Ideally, we would like a theory that could encompass all these forms of learning, from rats to humans, from classical conditioning to language learning. In short, a theory of everything.

This might at first seem an outrageous requirement – or, at any rate, one exceedingly unlikely to be fulfilled – but a theory has recently emerged that supporters claim has the potential to meet it. The new theory sets out to explain virtually every aspect of learning, from classical conditioning in animals to language learning in humans. And it does all this using just a single, almost unbelievably simple principle, that when two neurons are active at the same time, the connection between them will be strengthened.

A variety of terms have been suggested to describe this new approach: *connectionist*, *parallel-and-distributed processing*, and *neural network*. We will use the term neural network because it conveys a clearer sense of the assumption at the heart of the model, and in this chapter we will be looking at what this approach is, and how close it has come to achieving its extraordinary goal.

A conceptual introduction

At the heart of this new approach is a belief that psychological theories should be modeled as closely as possible on the known properties of the brain. To understand this view, it may be helpful to begin by contrasting it with the computer or information-processing metaphor that has dominated cognitive psychology for the past few decades.

Brains and computers

As we saw in Chapter 8, the basic structure of a digital computer consists of a central processing unit (CPU) and a memory store: The CPU retrieves items from memory, carries out a sequence of operations, such as addition and subtraction, and then transfers the result back to memory. The computer is capable of carrying out only very simple operations, but by performing them in an appropriate sequence and at extraordinarily high speeds – more than a million operations in a single second – it can solve highly complex problems.

The brain, however, is organized very differently. For one thing, there is no obvious distinction in the brain between the processing of information and its storage; there is only one unit, the neuron, that must somehow carry out both functions. As we saw in Chapter 2, when a neuron is stimulated, it produces an electrical impulse that is transmitted along the long part of the cell called the axon. When this impulse arrives at the axon terminal, it causes the release of neuro-transmitter chemicals that move across the synaptic gap to the next neuron in the chain; the arrival of these neurotransmitters causes the second neuron to produce an electrical impulse, and so on. The brain consists of an almost unimaginably large number of such neurons – between 10,000,000,000 and 100,000,000,000 – and each of these neurons receives inputs from as many as 100,000 other neurons (McClelland, 1999). A densely interconnected network of this kind is called a **neural network**. Figure 13.1 shows a small section of the brain, with some of the connections between the neurons. The complexity of the interconnections is apparent.

In contrast with most computers, then, which carry out only a single operation at a time, the brain contains a vast array of neurons of which many millions or even billions are active at a given moment. In the terminology of electrical circuitry, the brain is a massive parallel system in which an enormous number of circuits operate simultaneously. Unlike most computers, then, the brain is characterized by **parallel processing**.

This difference in architecture has important implications for function: The structure of the brain allows it to easily solve problems that computers find diffi-cult, if not impossible. For example, most people find it easy to read other people's

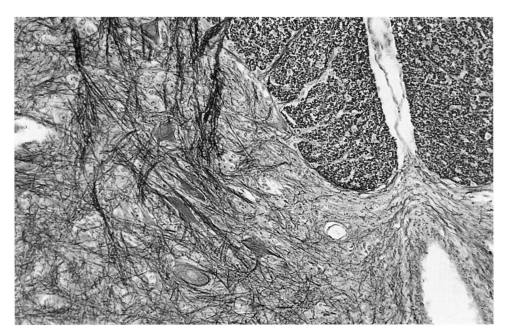

Figure 13.1 An array of cortical neurons, illustrating the dense network of interconections.
© Karl Dolenc/iStockphoto.

handwriting, but this trivial skill is beyond the power of most current computers. Neural network theorists believe that the computer has thus been a partially misleading model for the functioning of the brain and that psychological models should be based instead on the architecture of the brain – that is, they should incorporate neuron-like units that can assume only a limited range of firing states and that are interconnected in dense networks.

Neural networks

In outline, neural network models are surprisingly simple and rest on three basic assumptions:

- *Neural network.* A network consists of a set of interconnected units that we will call neurons. In the simplest form, every neuron is connected to every other neuron.
- *Transmission.* When one neuron in a network becomes active, this activity is transmitted to all the other neurons with which it is connected; how much excitation is transmitted between any two neurons depends on the strength of their connection.
- *Learning.* If two neurons within the network are active at the same time, the connection between them will be strengthened, so that future activity in one will be more likely to produce activity in the other.

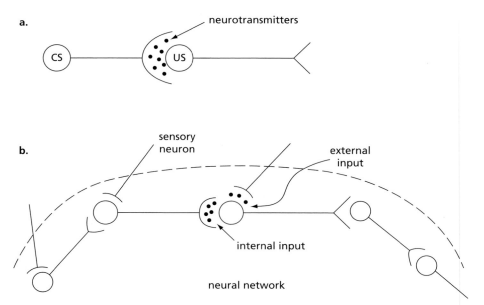

Figure 13.2 Neural connections in a network. (a) A simplified, two-neuron representation of classical conditioning. Neurotransmitters released by the CS neuron stimulate the US neuron. (b) An expanded representation, showing connections between neurons within the network together with sensory input from outside the network.

In essence, these assumptions are virtually identical to those made by Pavlov almost 100 years ago: When two cortical centers are active at the same time, the connection between them will be strengthened. Neural network models, however, incorporate two changes in Pavlov's ideas that have far-reaching implications for these models' ability to predict behavior. First, they assume that the networks involved are quite massive, so that associations will be formed simultaneously among very large numbers of active neurons. Second, they provide a mathematical formula that allows us to calculate exactly how much these connections will be strengthened. Together, these assumptions allow us to make predictions about the brain's functioning in a way that goes far beyond anything Pavlov ever attempted or could have attempted – because of the large number of connections, the model's predictions can be calculated only with the aid of computers.

The delta rule

The predictions of neural network models depend critically on the formula used for calculating how connections are strengthened. A number of formulas or rules have been suggested, but one of the most influential has been the **delta rule**.

To introduce this rule, let us first focus on just two neurons within a network, which we will call the *CS neuron* and the *US neuron* (Figure 13.2a). As we discussed in Chapter 2, stimulation of the CS neuron would generate an electrical impulse that would be transmitted down its axon. When this impulse reached the neuron's terminals, it would cause the release of chemical neurotransmitters that would flow across the synaptic gap to the US neuron. And if a sufficient quantity of neurotransmitters reached the US neuron, then it too would fire.

Of course, these neurons would not exist in isolation. For the CS neuron to fire, for example, it would need to receive input from one or more other neurons. To represent this situation, let us now expand our picture of the network and assume that every neuron in our network also receives inputs from sensory neurons lying outside the network. Suppose, for example, that whenever a tone is presented, a sensory neuron transmits electrical activity from the ear to the CS neuron. Similarly, suppose that whenever food is presented, another sensory neuron transmits activity from receptors in the mouth to the US neuron (Figure 13.2b). If so, the US neuron in the network would receive inputs from two neurons, the CS neuron that lies within the network and a sensory neuron that lies outside it. We will call the excitation that the US neuron receives from within the network the *internal input* – that is, the input from within the network. We will call the excitation that it receives from outside the network the *external input*.

According to neural network models, if the CS neuron is active at the same time as the US neuron, then the connection between them will be strengthened. As to how much it will be strengthened, the delta rule says that the outcome will depend on the relationship between the internal and external inputs. Ignoring some of the complexities of the actual formula, the delta rule in essence states that the change in the internal connection between two neurons (we'll use Δ*Internal input* to represent this change) is proportional to the difference between the internal and external inputs:

$$\frac{\Delta \text{Internal}}{\text{input}} = c \left(\frac{\text{External}}{\text{input}} - \frac{\text{Internal}}{\text{input}} \right)$$

where c is some constant. The greater the difference between the internal and external inputs, the more the interval connection would be strengthened. (This formula is called the delta rule because delta is the name in Greek for Δ, the symbol used in mathematics to represent the change in some quantity. In this case, the change in the strength of the internal connection is determined by the difference between the external and internal inputs.)

This formula has the effect of increasing the internal input to a neuron until it matches the external input. To illustrate this in concrete terms, suppose that in our classical conditioning example the presentation of food results in strong activation of the US neuron. Before conditioning, the connection between the CS and the US neurons is assumed to be weak, so that presentation of the tone does not induce any activity in the US neuron. For purposes of illustration, suppose that the external input to the US neuron has a value of 10 (you can think of this as the release of 10 neurotransmitters), that the internal input has a value of 0, and that the constant c has a value of 0.5. If the tone and food were presented together, the change in the strength of the CS–US connection would be as follows:

$$\frac{\Delta \text{Internal}}{\text{input}} = c \left(\frac{\text{External}}{\text{input}} - \frac{\text{Internal}}{\text{input}} \right) = 0.5(10 - 0) = 0.5(10) = 5$$

In other words, the connection between the CS and the US neurons would be substantially strengthened, increasing from its initial value of 0 to 5.

If the tone and food were now presented together for a second trial, the strength of the connection would be increased again, though not by quite as much. Over a series of trials, the strength of the CS–US connection would continue to be adjusted toward that of the Food–US connection, until eventually the CS neuron would activate the US neuron just as strongly as did the presentation of food. In the case of salivary conditioning, this means that the CS would eventually trigger as much salivation as the US.

The Rescorla–Wagner model

Does any of this seem familiar? As you perhaps have realized already, the delta rule achieves at the neural level exactly what the Rescorla–Wagner model achieves at the associative or behavioral level. Both formulas have the effect of changing an association or connection so as to move it closer to a target value

$$\text{Rescorla–Wagner: } \Delta V = c(V_{max} - V)$$

$$\text{Delta rule: } \frac{\Delta \text{Internal}}{\text{input}} = c \left(\frac{\text{External}}{\text{input}} - \frac{\text{Internal}}{\text{input}} \right)$$

The symbols used are different, but both say that the change in the strength of a connection is determined by the difference between its current value and a target value (V_{max} or External input). This can perhaps be seen more clearly if we change the symbols in the two formulas a bit. First, we've said that both formulas involve a change in the strength of an association, so if we use A to represent the initial strength of the association, and ΔA to represent the change in that association, then the two formulas become:

$$\text{Rescorla–Wagner: } \Delta A = c(V_{max} - A)$$

$$\text{Delta rule: } \Delta A = c \left(\frac{\text{External}}{\text{input}} - A \right)$$

The two formulas use different names to represent the target value (V_{max}, External input), but if we use the same symbol to represent the target, namely T, then the two formulas become:

$$\text{Rescorla–Wagner: } \Delta A = c(T - A)$$
$$\text{Delta rule: } \Delta A = c(T - A)$$

As you can see, in essence the two formulas are identical. In the Rescorla–Wagner model, that target is called V_{max}, in the delta rule it is called the External input, but the difference is purely in the names used. Functionally, the two formulas have exactly the same effect: They change the strength of an associative connection so as to move it closer to a target that is determined by the US used. In practical terms, they both say that pairing of a CS with a US will eventually result in the CS producing the same response as the US.

Indeed, not only is the logic of the two approaches the same, it turns out the formulas used are mathematically identical (see Sutton and Barto, 1981), even though they were developed independently. (The delta rule was developed by Widrow and Hoff, 1960, for use in designing optimal electrical circuits.) That workers in different areas have independently converged on the same rule might just be coincidence. But it could also be an indication that this rule is an optimal solution to the problem of how to modify electrical circuits to make them more adaptive – a solution that not only has been discovered by engineers for the design of electrical circuits, but also has emerged in the course of evolution as the basis for the operation of the brain's neural circuits.

Explaining concept learning

In one sense, then, neural network models are little more than the Rescorla–Wagner model applied not just to two neurons but to many thousands of neurons in a vast, interconnected network. Because the basic principle of the network is that units that are active at the same time have their connections strengthened, it is relatively easy to see how neural networks could account for conditioning: If a CS and a US are presented at the same time, the connection between their cortical representations will be strengthened. But what about more complex forms of learning – could a simple network also account for more sophisticated forms such as the formation of concepts?

Concepts

A **concept** is a remarkably difficult term to define, but a simple starting point is to view it as a set of objects or events sharing common features. *Triangles*, for example, are enclosed shapes formed by the meeting of three straight lines; *squares* are four lines of equal length joined at right angles, and so on. A person is said to understand concepts like these if they can correctly identify which objects are members. Thus, a child is assumed to understand the concept *triangle* if she can distinguish shapes that are triangles from those that are not.

Our ability to form concepts is what makes thought and language possible. Language is created by combining words, but words are simply arbitrary sets of sounds which point to or denote a concept. English, French, and Spanish, for example, use different words to represent the color red (*red*, *rouge*, and *rojo*), but while the sounds are different, they all denote the identical color. Similarly, concepts form the raw material for thought – it is by combining concepts appropriately that we are able to think and reason. ("My new pet is a dog; dogs need food to live, so my dog needs to be fed.") But the fundamental importance of concepts goes even deeper, forming the basis not only of intelligent thought but of our ability to function at all. Imagine a child born without the ability to group objects into conceptual categories. She would have to react to every new stimulus as if it was unique, without any relationship to objects she had encountered previously. If she encountered a dog, for example, she would not recognize it as similar to dogs she had encountered in the past, and thus would have no basis for anticipating how it might behave. Indeed, she would not even be able to recognize this dog as one she had seen just moments earlier because its perceptual properties would be different every time she encountered it – its limbs would be in a different position, it would be at a different distance and angle, and so on. If every stimulus is unique, this child would have no basis for bringing past experience to bear on present problems; the stimulus would be lost in a sea of unique events. The ability to group similar events together in concepts allows us to impose coherence on the turbulent stream of our perceptions.

Concepts are thus at the heart of perception, thought, and language, and for this reason the study of concepts has been one of the most important areas in cognitive psychology. And it has also proven to be one of the most difficult, as even the question of how to define a concept has proven controversial. We said before that a concept could be viewed as a set of objects sharing common features defined by a rule – *a rectangle*, for example, is four lines whose ends intersect at right angles. Many of the concepts that we learn in real life, however, are not so easily defined. Consider the concept *dog.* This might at first seem easy to define – "A dog is a four-legged animal with a tail, fur, and so on." As you think more about such definitions, however, they quickly begin to break down. Most dogs have four legs, but some may be born deformed, with only three; although some dogs have tails, others do not; and so on. Another way to see this difficulty is to form mental images of different breeds such as dachshunds, Saint Bernards, poodles, and bulldogs. What is it that unites these very different animals, yet distinguishes

Figure 13.3 Simulating the effects of wind on airplane wing. If air molecule 1 struck the wing, the computer would calculate the precise force it would exert, and the computer would perform similar calculations for all the other air molecules striking the wing at that moment. By summing the effects of all these molecules, the computer could calculate the overall effect of the wind moment by moment, and how it would change the position of the wing.

them from similar species such as a cat or a fox? There does not seem to be any clear rule that defines category membership.

Given the centrality of concepts to sophisticated human thought, and their complex and elusive nature, it is difficult to imagine how a network consisting of a large assemblage of neurons passing signals back and forth to each other, without any intelligence or purpose, could even begin to form such sophisticated ideas. Moreover, it is difficult to see how we could determine if they were capable of such feats. We could construct a network to see what it could do, but that is easier said than done. Even assuming that we could assemble a collection of neurons and somehow encourage them to form connections with each other, we would still need to provide this network with sensory input to allow it to interact with the outside world. In effect, we would have to build a brain, something far beyond our current ability.

Computer simulation

Two psychologists, Jay McClelland and Donald Rumelhart, came up with a clever way to bypass this problem. Their approach was similar to that adopted by engineers when they want to understand a complex system but are unable to study the system in a laboratory. Suppose you were an aeronautical engineer charged with developing the wing for a new airplane. You wanted to be sure that the wing you were designing would be able to function in difficult conditions such as a thunderstorm, but it would be prohibitively expensive to build an entire airplane just to test if the wing you were designing would really work. One solution would be to build a model of the wing and then test the model in a wind tunnel – you could then *simulate* a storm (create wind conditions that mimic those of a real storm) and see how the wing functioned. Building a physical model, however, can also be expensive, and a possible alternative is to instead create a *computer model* of the wing, and calculate how the wing would react to different wind conditions. Figure 13.3 shows a simplified illustration of how this might work. Suppose that you wanted to test how a particular wing would react in a storm, where the wind was blowing in the direction shown by the arrow. The wind would consist of a huge number of air molecules, but to illustrate how the computer model might work, let's consider what happens when a single air molecule, molecule 1, hits the wing.

If we know the velocity at which the molecule is travelling, we can use Newton's laws of motion to calculate the force with which it would hit the wing, and, also knowing the angle at which it strikes the wing, we can compute the direction in which it would push the wing. (A possible outcome is indicated by the dashed line.) If we repeated the calculations for all the air molecules that were striking the wing simultaneously, we could calculate the overall effect. As the wind continued, we could calculate what the effect would be in the next instant, and the next, as each new wave of molecules struck the wing. In the end we could predict precisely how the wing (and thus the airplane) would move as it passed through the storm. If we know enough about the mathematical laws that govern a phenomenon, in other words, then we can simulate the effects of certain environmental conditions without building a model, by just using a computer to calculate what would happen.

The concept of dog

McClelland and Rumelhart took exactly this approach in order to explore the properties of neural networks. They couldn't construct a real network, so instead they created a model of a network, using a computer to calculate how the network would behave. In one of their studies, they looked at whether a network could form a concept, in particular the concept *dog* (McClelland and Rumelhart, 1985). Using a computer program, they effectively instructed the computer to assume the existence of a very simple network, but to introduce their method we will begin with an even simpler version.

Suppose that there was an exceedingly simple organism whose brain consisted of just 4 neurons, all connected to each other in a primitive neural network. Further suppose that this primitive organism also had 4 receptors in its eye, each of which detected the presence of a single feature in the environment (Figure 13.4). Perhaps one of these receptors was specialized to detect the presence of a tail – anytime a tail was visible in the surrounding environment, the receptor would become active. It would then stimulate neuron 1 in the neural network, which would in turn transmit electrical signals to the other members of the network. Similarly, suppose that receptor 2 (and thus network neuron 2) was sensitive to the presence of 4 legs, so that it would fire whenever it detected the presence of 4 legs, and so on.

Now suppose that a dog walked by. The presence of 4 legs and a tail would cause receptors 1 and 2 to become active, which would in turn activate neurons 1

eye   receptors   brain

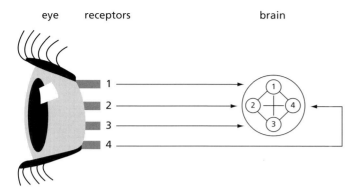

Figure 13.4 A very simple (and hypothetical) animal, with 4 receptors in its eye and 4 neurons in its brain.

and 2 in the network. The fact that these units were active simultaneously would mean that the connection between them would be strengthened, and we could use the delta rule to calculate how much. We could then expose the network to a second dog, again calculate the changes, and so on. In other words, instead of building a real network, we could use a computer to calculate how such a network would respond if exposed to a series of dogs. Would the network somehow form the concept of *dog*?

To find out, McClelland and Rumelhart ran a computer simulation just like the one we have been describing. A network in a real brain would contain many thousands of neurons, but to simplify their calculations McClelland and Rumelhart assumed a much smaller network containing 24 units. To explain their approach, we will simplify the situation still further and talk about a system with just 8 units.

As in our earlier example, suppose that each unit in this small network responds to the presence of a single visual feature. To explore the behavior of the network, we need to expose it to dogs, and so the first step in running the simulation is to create some hypothetical dogs. In real life, dogs share many properties in common – for example, most dogs have 4 legs and a tail – but each dog is also unique. We would thus want our imaginary dogs to also have this property, sharing many features but each also having unique characteristics.

To achieve this, McClelland and Rumelhart assumed that some units in the network would be sensitive to features that are typical of dogs, but others would respond to features that are atypical. In our simplified version, shown in Figure 13.5a, 4 units would respond to features that are typical of dogs: Unit *Legs* would respond to the presence of four legs, unit *Tail* to the presence of a tail, unit *Fur* to the presence of fur, and unit *Ears* to the presence of floppy ears. The other 4 units (N_1, N_2, N_3, and N_4) would be sensitive to features that are less typical of dogs, though some dogs might have them, nevertheless. (Unit N_1, for example, might respond to the presence of a scar.) Thus, if our miniature organism was

a.

b.

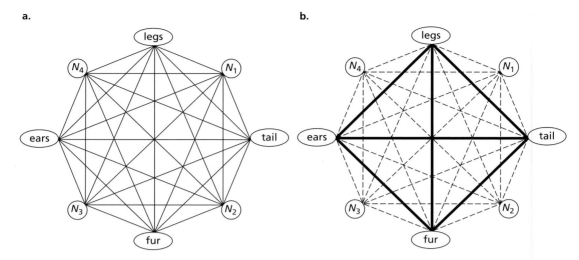

Figure 13.5 A simplified representation of the McClelland and Rumelhart (1985) model. (a) An 8-unit neural network, showing all possible interconnections. Each circle represents a single neuron in the network. (b) The same network after exposure to many exemplars of the concept *dog*. Strong connections involving the prototypical features are shown in heavy lines so that it is clear that these features have become strongly interconnected.

exposed to an animal with a tail, the Tail unit in the network would be activated; if the animal had 4 legs, the Legs unit would be activated; and so on.

To create different dogs, McClelland and Rumelhart first created a prototypical dog that would have all the typical features of a dog – in our simplified model, 4 legs, a tail, fur, and ears. Real dogs, of course, do not have all the features of the prototype: Some have only three legs, some have no tails, and so on. McClelland and Rumelhart therefore created individual dogs by assigning each dog a different combination of these prototypical features. For example, one dog might be assigned the features Legs Fur Ears N_1. It would thus have had three features typical of dogs but also one atypical feature, in the same way that a dachshund has many typical dog features but also unusually short legs. A second dog might have the features Legs Tail Fur N_2, and so on. McClelland and Rumelhart created a total of 50 individual dogs in this way, and then calculated the effect that exposure to each of these dogs would have on connections within the neural network.

One note on terminology before we proceed. We will sometimes say, as a form of shorthand, that a dog was "presented" to the network. It is important to remember that there is no dog, no network, and no presentation! A fuller version of "a dog was presented" would be that the computer was instructed that the units representing this dog's features had been activated, and it was now to use the delta rule to calculate how this would affect the connections between these units. We will sometimes spell this out more fully, but when the shorthand form is used ("a dog was presented") it is important to remember that this simply means that the computer was instructed to calculate changes *as if* a network existed, and a subset of the units within this network had been activated.

Consider now what happens when the first dog is presented. Because this particular dog possessed legs, fur, ears, and one atypical feature, N_1, McClelland and Rumelhart instructed the computer to assume that the corresponding units in the network had been activated, and to calculate how this would affect the strength of the connections between them. For example, because the Legs and Fur units in the network would be activated simultaneously, the connection between them would be strengthened:

$$\text{Legs} \rightarrow \text{Fur}$$

Similarly, the connection from Legs to Ears would be strengthened,

$$\text{Legs} \rightarrow \text{Ears}$$

and the connection between Fur and Ears,

$$\text{Fur} \rightarrow \text{Ears}$$

and so on. Using the delta rule, McClelland and Rumelhart had the computer calculate the changes in each of these connections. They then had the computer calculate the further changes that would occur as a result of exposure to the second dog, and the third, until all 50 of the imaginary dogs had been presented.

The result is shown in Figure 13.5b, in which heavy lines have been drawn only between those units in the network that have become strongly connected. (Because nontypical features also occurred together many times, some of these features also became associated with one another, but these connections were not nearly as strong.) The crucial result stands out clearly: The features that are typical of dogs have all become strongly interconnected, with the result that activation of any subset of these features would be likely to activate the remainder.

This outcome might sound trivial, but it has surprisingly powerful implications. One is that the network can recognize new dogs. Suppose, for example, that the network were presented with a new dog that it had never seen before. Because this new dog would have many typical dog features, these features would activate the entire set of dog features in the network. As a result, the network would respond to this new dog in exactly the same way as it responded to old ones. One way to see this is to imagine that all the dog features in the network were connected to a single output unit – for example, a unit that controls the creature's vocal cords and produces the word *dog*. Whenever a new dog was presented, its features would activate all the typical dog features, which would in turn activate the unit that controls saying "dog." Whether our creature saw an old dog or a new one, it would produce exactly the same response: It would say "dog."

Cats, dogs, and bagels

It is encouraging to see that the network would respond to any dog, old or new, in the same way, but what would happen if it encountered another animal such as a cat? Cats and dogs share many similar features, so would the network call both dogs, or would it be able to discriminate between these concepts and produce the appropriate name for each?

To find out, McClelland and Rumelhart ran a second simulation in which they presented the network with stimuli derived from three prototypes: one of a dog, another of a cat, and a third of an object sharing very few of the dog and cat features, a bagel! The first step, as before, was to create the prototypes for each category. To reflect the similarity of real-life cats and dogs, they made the prototypes for these categories very similar. (Of the 16 features used to represent cats and dogs, 12 were identical.) Because bagels are clearly less similar, the prototype bagel shared only a few features with the prototype dog. They then created 50 exemplars of each category by combining prototypical and atypical features in slightly different ways. Finally, to assess the network's success in categorizing these stimuli, they added units to the network to represent the names of the categories – *cat*, *dog*, or *bagel*.

If a dog was presented on a trial, for example, its presence would be assumed to activate units representing its name as well as its appearance.

The experiment then consisted simply of exposing the network to 50 exemplars drawn from each of the three categories, accompanied in each case by its name. As before, the authors told the computer which units would be activated on each trial and had the computer calculate how this would affect the strength of the connections between these units.

Finally, to find out what the network had learned, McClelland and Rumelhart ran test trials in which they presented the network with new exemplars from the three categories. In each case, they found that the exemplars activated the correct name – if they presented features typical of a dog, for example, activation would spread from the units representing its appearance to those representing its name. Conversely, when they tested the network by activating the features representing the name dog, they found that this activity spread through the network's connections to activate the typical visual features of a dog – in effect, the network produced an image of a typical dog, as it activated the same units that would have been activated had a real dog been present. The network thus behaved remarkably like a child learning the concept *dog*: When presented with a dog, it said "dog";

when presented with the word *dog*, it generated an image of a typical dog. The response to cats and bagels was similarly accurate.

Summarizing the evidence to this point, we have seen that when a network is exposed to exemplars from a category, it forms strong associations between the features that occur together frequently. This has the important effect that activating just some of these features will result in activation of all of them. And this in turn means that the network can respond appropriately to an incomplete or distorted version of a familiar stimulus. If part of a dog is obscured by a tree, for example, the remaining features can still activate the full prototype and thus produce recognition. Similarly, the network can respond appropriately to exemplars that it has never seen before: As long as enough features of the prototype are present, the entire prototype will be activated.

Explaining Life, the Universe and Everything

In *The Hitchhiker's Guide to the Galaxy*, a humorous science fiction novel by Douglas Adams, a giant computer was set the task of determining the meaning of Life, the Universe and Everything. After seven and a half million years, it finally solved the problem (the answer, a bit on the terse side, was 42). The goal of neural network theorists is not quite this audacious, but it doesn't fall far short – to explain virtually every aspect of human thought in terms of the operation of simple neural networks. We have already seen how neural networks account for the formation of concepts, long thought to be one of the highest achievements of the human mind. In this section we'll look at some of the other behaviors that network theorists have tried to explain, and their initial findings.

Conditioning

Because the delta rule is effectively identical to the formula at the heart of the Rescorla–Wagner model, neural network models can account for all the conditioning phenomena that this model explains. Moreover, theorists have developed neural network models that can also explain many of the phenomena that created problems for the Rescorla–Wagner model, such as latent inhibition and occasion setting (see Schmajuk, Lam, and Gray, 1996; Schmajuk, Lamoureux, and Holland, 1998). In short, these models seem to be able to account for almost every aspect of classical conditioning.

As yet there have been fewer attempts to develop neural network models for reinforcement and punishment, but models have been proposed to account not only for basic properties of reinforcement but also for more sophisticated aspects such as the formation of cognitive maps (for example, Brown and Sharp, 1995; Donahoe and Dorsel, 1997; Donahoe, 2002).

Memory

We've seen that neural network models can account for the formation of concepts, but what about remembering experiences with individual dogs? Can a single network not only store common characteristics of dogs but also remember individual dogs?

Episodic and semantic memory

In one test, McClelland and Rumelhart used a computer to simulate the effects of exposing their network to two particular dogs – one named *Rover*, the other named *Fido* – as well as other dogs that were simply called *dog*. When they tested the network by activating the features representing the name *dog*, they found that this activity spread through the network to all the typical visual features of a dog – in effect, the network activated an image of a typical dog. Similarly, when McClelland and Rumelhart activated the features corresponding to the names *Rover* or *Fido*, the network responded by activating the neurons representing the visual characteristics of those dogs. And the network was equally effective in producing names when shown pictures: If, for example, the network was shown a picture of Fido (that is, the network units that represented the appropriate visual features was assumed to be activated), the network responded by activating the features representing its name. The network could thus remember the names of individual dogs as well as the generic term *dog*. (For a more comprehensive model of memory based on a neural network, see McClelland and Chappell, 1998.) In this sense, the network was forming not only semantic memories (the general meaning of the word *dog*) but also episodic memories (representations of specific dogs).

Semantic networks

In addition to remembering the characteristics of individual dogs, networks can also account for some more general aspects of semantic memory. In Chapter 10 we saw that conceptual knowledge is organized in a variety of formats, one of which is called a semantic network (see Figure 10.6). The concept *canary*, for example, is linked to the higher-order concept *bird*, which is in turn connected to the superordinate concept *animal*. Each of these conceptual nodes is also linked to properties of the concept: The node for bird, for example, is assumed to be linked to nodes representing the properties *flies* and has *feathers*. Collins and Quillian (1969) showed that semantic networks of this kind could account for the time

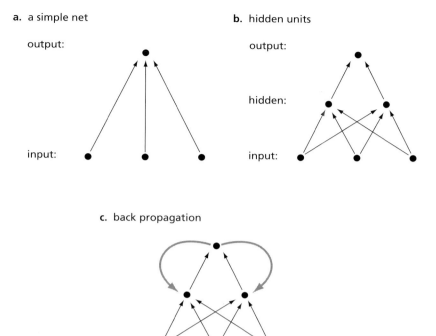

a. a simple net

output:

input:

b. hidden units

output:

hidden:

input:

c. back propagation

Figure 13.6 Hidden units and back propagation. (a) A neural network in which several input units are connected to a single output unit. (b) A network in which a layer of hidden units intervenes between the input and output units. (c) Back propagation: connections from the output units back to the hidden units, allowing the transmission of information about errors.

subjects required to verify sentences such as "A canary is an animal" and "A canary has wings."

Rumelhart and Todd (1993) developed a neural network model that can account for these results. Their model incorporates two features that we have not yet discussed: *hidden units* and *back propagation*. Figure 13.6a illustrates a very simple form of neural network in which several input units converge on a single output unit. Simple networks of this kind can be surprisingly powerful, but they cannot solve some problems, and one way to overcome this weakness is to incorporate so-called **hidden units** (Figure 13.6b). A layer of hidden units intervenes between the input and output units, and though the advantage of having such units might not be immediately obvious, they do substantially increase the power of neural networks to form concepts.

In our discussion of the McClelland and Rumelhart model, we saw that the delta rule is used to adjust the strength of the connections between units: If the input is too high or too low, relative to some target value, then the strength of the neural connection is adjusted accordingly. When hidden units are used, any error at the output level is used not only to adjust connections to these units but also to adjust inputs to the hidden units. Suppose, for example, that the input from hidden unit H_1 to the output unit O is too great; as we saw earlier, this error information would be used to reduce the strength of the connection between H_1 and O. In addition, feedback about this error would be fed back to the H_1 unit (via the gray line in Figure 13.6c) and would then be used to reduce the strength of the connections to this hidden unit. In other words, if too much excitation is reaching the final unit in the network, then connections are modified not only at this level but also at lower levels, and this feedback of information back through the network is called **back propagation**.

Rumelhart and Todd developed a three-layer neural network of this kind to account for behavior on sentence verification tasks. The input units were used to represent concepts such as *robin* and *animal*, as well as relationships such as *isa* and *can*, and the output units were used to represent concepts such as *fly*. If the network was given the sentence "A canary can fly," for example, then the input units representing *canary* and *can* would be activated, as would the output unit *fly*; and the connections between the various units would then be adjusted using the delta rule. The network was given a series of such sentences and then tested on its ability to verify new sentences. The results proved to be similar to those of real subjects. For example, during training the only information provided to the network about sparrows was that they were birds, but during the test phase the network correctly inferred that sparrows have feathers and can fly. The network had absorbed the information in individual sentences and used it to detect common properties – for example, that all birds can fly – and it was then able to use these common properties in evaluating statements about other birds.

Language

In the brief time that neural network models have been in existence, they have proven able to account for a wide range of phenomena in classical and operant conditioning, as well as in the very different domains of memory and concept learning. If this were all these models could do, it would be remarkable enough, but other evidence suggests that they may be able to do much more. The final example we will consider involves their ability to account for many aspects of linguistic behavior. We'll look at two examples, involving the grammatical rules governing pronunciation and formation of the past tense.

Past tense

The most common method of forming the past tense of a verb in English is to add the letters *ed* to the end of the present tense form (jump – jumped, open – opened, and so on). However, many verbs follow different patterns (run – ran, send – sent, and so on). At first, children learn the correct form for all the verbs they know, but then, as their vocabulary grows, they begin to use the *ed* form for all verbs, even ones for which it is inappropriate (*runned*, *sended*, and so on), and for which they previously used the correct form. Finally, they return to using the correct form for all verbs. As complex as this developmental sequence is, Rumelhart and McClelland (1986) have shown that a neural network analysis predicts not only the sequence but also some of its finer details, including which forms are most likely to be confused.

McClelland and Rumelhart's work posed a powerful challenge to existing theories of tense learning, which assumed that children start by learning past tenses essentially by rote, simply memorizing individual forms, but then gradually learn rules such as the use of *ed*. In McClelland and Rumelhart's model, however, there are no rules; the network is able to learn how to form past tenses without using rules, simply by forming neural connections. One advantage of this approach is that it fits with our subjective experiences, as most of us would be hard pressed to verbalize the rules that govern English grammar. (Even in the case of past tenses, this is difficult if not impossible – you may know that *cook* becomes *cooked*, but can you state the rule which says that *run* should become *ran*?) However, as we've seen at many points, our conscious experiences are not necessarily a reliable guide to what is happening at an unconscious level, so the fact that we cannot verbalize grammatical rules does not necessarily mean that they do not exist at some deeper level. In any case, this challenge to existing theories provoked intense controversy, one that is by no means settled. If you'd like to learn more about the issues involved, you can find a readable introduction in a short paper by McClelland and Seidenberg (2000), and contrasting views in papers by Pinker and Ullman (2002) and McClelland and Patterson (2002). A more recent paper by Thomas and McClelland (2008) has argued that the controversy has led to some convergence of the two views: As each side modified their views in response to the other's criticisms, their views moved closer together.

Pronunciation

Network theorists have also addressed how people learn the complex rules that govern English pronunciation. We tend to take our ability to read and pronounce English words for granted, but children, and adults who learn English as a foreign language, can testify to the baffling complexity of the rules governing its pronunciation. Nevertheless, Sejnowski and Rosenberg (1987) explored whether a neural network could learn how to read, in the sense that if shown the spelling of a word, it could instruct a voice synthesizer how to pronounce it correctly. They exposed a neural network to the spelling of 1,000 English words, together with information on how each one should be pronounced. By the conclusion of training it was able to pronounce 95% correctly. And when tested on 20,000 other words that it had never seen before, it was able to pronounce 90% correctly. Given the primitive nature of the network used, and the extraordinary variability of English spelling rules – George Bernard Shaw once pointed out that, on the basis of how its components were sometimes pronounced, the made-up word *ghoti* could be pronounced "fish" – this is a remarkable feat.[1]

Flying!

Perhaps the most striking demonstration of the potential of neural networks to perform sophisticated tasks has come not from computer modeling but from a study of a real network. In order to create it, DeMarse and Dockendorf (2005) began by taking a glass Petri dish and placing a mesh of electrodes along its bottom. Then, on top of the electrodes, they added 25,000 neurons taken from a rat brain. The neurons had been separated from each other, but once in the dish (and kept alive by nutrients) they began to form connections. They would literally reach out, pull back, reach out again, and continue in this way until they made contact with other neurons and established connections. (You can see this happening at http://neural.bme.ufl.edu/page12/page12.html.)

In order to explore the network's capabilities, they decided to see if it could fly a jet plane! They connected two of the electrodes in the dish to a flight simulator for an F-22 jetfighter; one of these electrodes transmitted information from the simulator on the plane's pitch, the other on its roll. (Pitch refers to movements of the plane's nose up or down; roll to movements of the wings which would tilt the plane to the left or right.) The remaining electrodes measured electrical activity in the network and communicated it to a computer which, in turn, processed it into a form which could instruct the simulator to alter the plane's position. If these instructions produced an error – the plane was placed on a trajectory that would have made it crash – then corrective information was fed back to the network.

With practice, the neurons within the network changed their connections in such a way that the network was able to keep the plane level: "The typical performance . . . was within 10 degrees of desired for both pitch and roll" (DeMarse and Dockendorf, 2005, p. 1550). The network's control of pitch was particularly impressive. Figure 13.7 shows the jet's deviation in pitch from the target of zero degrees, which would keep the plane level. As you can see, the network kept the jet remarkably steady, with minimal deviations up or down from the target of level flight. Moreover, the network was able to do this even in conditions simulating

---

[1] "gh" as in enough; "o" as in women; and "ti" as in action.

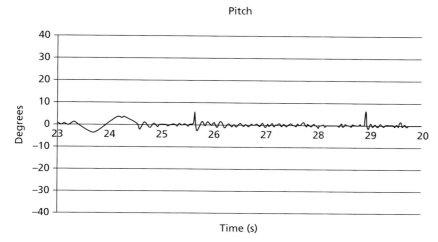

Figure 13.7 Rat neurons flying a jet plane. Neurons from a rat's brain were placed in a Petri dish where they formed connections. When connected to a flight simulator, they learned to fly it. The pitch of a plane refers to the movement of its nose up and down relative to its center; smooth flight requires maintaining pitch at 0 degrees. After training, the neural network learned to maintain pitch almost exactly at 0. (Adapted from DeMarse and Dockendorf, 2005.)

flying through a hurricane! The almost breathtaking conclusion is that a bunch of neurons from a rat's brain, jumbled together in a Petri dish without any pattern or organization, had managed to organize itself into a network which could fly a jet plane.

Evaluation

We have seen that neural network models can account for a wide range of human learning, from classical conditioning at one end to thought and language at the other. The fact that neural network models can account for many aspects of behavior, however, does not mean that it can account for all aspects, nor even that those explanations it can provide are correct. There are other theories which can also account for these behaviors, so the network account is not necessarily correct.

Problems

In addition to these general cautionary notes, there are some specific problems with neural network models in their current form. They have been criticized on several grounds, and we will briefly discuss some of the most important.

Slow learning

In many network models, learning is very, very slow – in the case of concept learning, for example, a simulated network may need to be exposed to exemplars of the concept to be learned many hundreds of times before it really learns them and can categorize new examples correctly. Though slow learning is realistic in some situations – think of someone learning a sport such as basketball or tennis, where thousands of hours of practice can be required – there are also many situations where learning is impressively rapid, sometimes requiring only a single trial. The kinds of network models that we have been discussing cannot handle such rapid learning. This also means that neural network models have difficulty in accounting for episodic memory, in which we remember unique experiences such as what you ate for breakfast this morning. Although we saw earlier that network models can account for the learning of individual facts such as a dog's name, their ability to do so depends on repeated experiences with that name.

To deal with this problem, McClelland, McNaughton, and O'Reilly (1995) suggested that it might be necessary to assume two fundamentally different kinds of brain mechanisms for dealing with episodic and semantic memories. One, based in the medial temporal lobes of the brain, would form memories very quickly, by tying together or *binding* information arriving from the various senses. (If you heard someone saying your name, for example, this auditory input would be bound together with the visual input of what the person looked like, the appearance of the room, etc.) The other system, residing in the neocortex, would involve the more gradual form of learning featured in earlier neural models, in which associations were strengthened gradually. (For a more recent version of this synthesis, see McClelland, 2011.)

Catastrophic interference

A further problem concerns situations in which we learn new material which is similar to material we have learned before. In one experimental procedure used to study this, participants learn one list of paired associates and then learn a second list that uses the same stimuli but different responses – for example, learning a list containing the pair *table–orange* and then learning a second list containing the pair *table–cotton*. Learning the second list does cause some forgetting of the first list, but people can usually still remember about half of the responses from the first list. When neural network models have been used to simulate this task, however, learning the second list produces almost total forgetting of the first list, a phenomenon that has been called **catastrophic interference**. At this point it is not clear whether catastrophic interference represents a fundamental problem for neural network models or simply one that needs to be addressed by appropriate revisions, but we can note that several possible solutions have already been proposed (for example, Kruschke, 1992; McClelland *et al.*, 1995).

Grandmother cells

One of the cornerstones of the neural network model approach is that concepts are represented by the pattern of activity across many neurons, rather than by any one neuron. If a dog were present, for example, it would produce activity in a large number of neurons. There is no one neuron that represents or signals the presence of a dog; you would need to examine the pattern of activity across the entire network to know. This can also be seen in the model's representation of the concepts *dog, cat,* and *bagel*: all three are stored in the same network, and if you recorded activity from just one neuron you would have no way of knowing which was present.

However, there is evidence that in some situations concepts may be represented by individual neurons. In Chapter 9 we discussed evidence for the existence of "grandmother cells," neurons which would fire when and only when a particular object or person – your grandmother – was present. One example we discussed came from a study by Quian Quiroga *et al.* (2005) in which recordings were made from individual neurons in the human brain. Participants were epileptics who had recording electrodes placed in their brains to determine the locus of their seizures. In the course of their treatment they were shown photographs of famous individuals, and the authors discovered that some cells responded selectively to particular people. One cell, for example, responded almost exclusively to pictures of Halle Berry: It fired when shown each of 7 different photographs of her face, but not when shown photos of other actresses. In a follow-up experiment, Quian Quiroga *et al.* (2009) found similar results using pictures of other famous people. One cell, for example, was found to respond almost exclusively to pictures of Oprah Winfrey, increasing its normal rate of firing more than a thousandfold when a picture of her was shown, but not to pictures of other famous individuals such as Whoopi Goldberg. And this cell also fired when the participant saw or heard Oprah's name! This seemed compelling evidence for the grandmother cell hypothesis, as this one cell in the brain really did seem to represent this actress.

However, a reply by Plaut and McClelland (2010) argued that this evidence was far from conclusive. Although this cell and others like it did seem highly specialized, most of the cells recorded in this and similar studies responded to many faces, not just one. And even this cell may not have been responding to "Oprah Winfrey"; there may have been some specific feature that happened to be present in these pictures that wasn't present in others; had a broader range of photographs been used, it might have revealed that this cell was not really responding to Oprah Winfrey at all! The issues raised by the Bowers article are important, but as the exchange of views between the two sides continued, it became clear that the two views – distributed representations versus single-cell representations – were not as far apart as their names would suggest, as both assume that multiple neurons must be involved in representing any object. (If you really had only one cell to represent your grandmother, any damage to this cell would result in your losing your ability to recognize this sweet old lady, a position no theorist finds plausible.) The two views differ in precisely how all these cells are organized, but the views are sufficiently similar that it is currently difficult to marshal evidence that would clearly favor one over the other. The issues are too technical for us to pursue here, but if you'd like to follow a vigorous-but-mutually-respectful exchange of views on the subject, you can consult papers by Plaut and McClelland (2010), Quian Quiroga and Kreiman (2010), and Bowers (2010); they raise deep and important issues about how the brain manages to represent different entities.

But . . .

Together, the challenges we have reviewed have posed real problems for current neural network models. These models may not be able to explain all aspects of behavior, and even those explanations that they can offer are not necessarily superior to those of other available theories. In one sense, the problems that have been identified are critical: If neural network models cannot handle some of the tasks that the brain does almost effortlessly (rapid learning, the ability to preserve old information in the face of new), then the claim that these models tell us something about how the brain actually works is clearly undermined. There is another sense, though, in which the outcome of this debate is almost irrelevant. It could be argued – and will be here – that *of course* current network models are wrong; it could not be otherwise. The networks posited by these models are ridiculously simple, with each neuron connected to every other neuron, and they are trying to explain brains whose structure has been evolving for millions of years. Our brains do not consist of a single, giant network. Instead, evolution has created multiple, highly structured areas which each process certain kinds of information, and information is transmitted in sequence, from one processing area to another, as well as in parallel, with millions of neurons firing simultaneously. It would thus be extraordinary if any of the current models postulating simple, undifferentiated networks were even remotely like our brains.

Your immediate reaction to this declaration could fairly be, "Then what is the point? If these models are almost certainly wrong, why bother with them?" And the answer is, because they have revealed how even simple networks can perform tasks of astonishing sophistication. The importance of current neural network models is not that they are right, but that they suggest how the wonders of the human mind could arise from the operations of massive numbers of neurons acting in concert.

All neurons can do is receive signals from other neurons and then pass them on to yet other neurons. They are either on or off, firing or not firing, and it requires a real leap of imagination to believe that these simple units could give rise to the richness and complexity of human thought. Neural network models provide the first persuasive evidence that such a leap might someday prove justified. They do not tell us how our brains work, but suggest that our brains really *could* work!

The current situation is analogous in some ways to the first flight of an airplane more than 100 years ago. There is only a minimal resemblance between the primitive plane flown by the Wright brothers and the sophisticated planes of today, and in the same way neural network models in 100 years will be far more sophisticated than the primitive models of today. Nevertheless, just as the Wright brothers showed that human flight was possible, so in the future we may feel that McClelland and Rumelhart's work was the first convincing demonstration that human thought could be explained in terms of simple connections between neurons. The brain as a whole is extraordinarily complex, but the basic mechanism might be the simple associative process proposed by Pavlov, that when two areas of the brain are active at the same time, the connection between them will be strengthened.

More than 100 years ago, Pavlov wrote that "Since education and training are really nothing more than the results of an establishment of new nervous connections," then by studying salivary conditioning in dogs we could uncover the key to understanding human thought. It was an extraordinary claim, but his research eventually led to the development of the Rescorla–Wagner model, and their fundamental equation, in the guise of the delta rule, is now at the heart of neural network models. Is it possible that Pavlov was right, and that the study of conditioning did reveal the associative processes that provide the foundation for learning and memory?

It is too soon to say whether the promise of neural network models will be fulfilled, but their solid grounding in the known structure of the brain gives them an inherent plausibility. If they do succeed, the emergence of these models might someday be seen as the single most important step in the evolution of psychology.

Summary

- Neural network models were developed in the belief that theories of cognition should be based as closely as possible on what we know of the actual physiology of the brain. In contrast to the information-processing approach, with its emphasis on sequential processing, neural network models are based on many units being active simultaneously (parallel processing).

- These models assume networks of interconnected units; activity in one unit spreads to all the others, with the spread depending on the strength of their connections.
- Whenever two units are active simultaneously, the connection between them is strengthened. One formula used to calculate such changes is the delta rule; it turns out to be almost identical to the central formula of the Rescorla–Wagner model.
- To explore the capabilities of neural networks, theorists have used computer simulations in which a network is assumed to exist and changes in the strength of all the connections are calculated using a computer.
- These simulations have shown that if networks are exposed to exemplars of a concept, the units representing typical features become very strongly connected. This seemingly simple outcome allows neural networks to form concepts, responding if and only if a member of the concept is present.
- Neural network models can also explain a very wide range of other phenomena, including classical conditioning, the organization of semantic memory, and the learning of grammatical rules governing the formation of past tenses and pronunciation. These achievements are particularly impressive given that the networks that have been studied are simply large sets of units which are all connected to each other, without any kind of structure or intelligence.
- Notwithstanding these successes, neural network models have also encountered problems. Learning is very slow, and the storage of new information can result in serious loss of older information (catastrophic interference).
- Network models are being modified to tackle such problems – past modifications include the inclusion of hidden units and back propagation. Whatever the ultimate fate of these models, they have demonstrated the power of even simple networks to perform tasks of astonishing sophistication.

Review questions

1　How do brains differ from computers in the way that they process information?

2　What are the fundamental assumptions of neural network models? How do these assumptions differ from those of Pavlov?

3　What is the delta rule? In what way is it similar to the formula used in the Rescorla–Wagner model?

4　What is a concept? Why is the ability to form concepts critical to human thought and behavior?

5 What is computer simulation? Why do engineers sometimes use this technique to test theoretical models?

6 How did McClelland and Rumelhart assess the capacity of neural networks to form concepts such as *dog*? What did they find?

7 What is the distinction between episodic and semantic memory? Can neural network models account for both?

8 In order to account for the development of semantic networks, Rumelhart and Todd (1993) had to use a neural network model which incorporated two features not required by McClelland and Rumelhart's model. What were they?

9 How have neural network theorists tried to account for features of language learning such as the ability to master the rules underlying pronunciation and the formation of past tenses of verbs? How have they done?

10 DeMarse and Dockendorf (2005) explored the ability of neural networks to solve difficult problems by assembling a real network, rather than relying on computer simulation. What did they do and what did they find?

11 Neural network models have not been without their problems; what are the three discussed in the text?

12 The text says that the neural network models proposed to date are almost certainly far too simple to account for the complexity of human cognition. Why does it say this? And why does it nevertheless go on to argue that neural network models might someday be seen as one of the most important developments in the history of psychology?

Glossary

accessibility   Material in memory is said to be accessible if it can be retrieved. Forgetting can occur because a memory is not available – it is simply not there – or because it is there but not currently accessible.

amnesia   An impairment in memory caused by brain damage. In *retrograde amnesia*, patients have difficulty remembering events that occurred before the onset of their condition; in *anterograde amnesia*, patients have difficulty in forming new memories.

associative learning   Learning about the association or relationship between two events that occur together.

asymptote   In mathematics, a stable value that a curve on a graph approaches but never quite reaches. As used in learning, it generally describes the level of performance at which improvement ceases, so that further training would produce no additional improvement.

attention   A limited mental resource that is needed for processing some kinds of information. We can control the allocation of attention between competing tasks and also the amount of attention that goes to any one task.

automatic process   A process that occurs rapidly, without any need for attention. Because conscious attention is not required, numerous automatic processes can be carried out simultaneously.

automatization   The process by which a controlled process becomes automatic and thus no longer requires attention for its execution. Automatization usually requires extensive practice, and one result is that an automated task can be carried out at the same time as other tasks without interfering with them.

autonomic responses   Glandular and smooth muscle activities controlled by the autonomic nervous system.

availability   Material is said to be available in memory if it is still in storage, and therefore there is at least the possibility of retrieving it.

availability heuristic   A strategy for estimating the frequency of an event by seeing how easily you can think of examples.

aversion therapy   A procedure for eliminating an unwanted behavior by conditioning fear to stimuli associated with that behavior.

avoidance   A procedure in which an aversive event such as shock can be prevented by a response. This can be distinguished from *escape*, in which a response terminates an aversive event after it has already commenced.

avoidance response   A response that postpones or prevents an aversive event.

back propagation   The transmission of information about errors at one level in a network back to earlier levels. This backward transmission of information helps the network to adjust the strength of connections more effectively, resulting in a closer approximation to the ideal output.

backward conditioning   A procedure in which first a US is presented, then a CS.

behaviorism   The view that the basic datum of psychology should be visible behavior, rather than mental states. There are several different forms of behaviorism, but a common theme is a distrust of introspection as a tool for scientific investigation and a consequent emphasis on explaining behavior in terms of environmental causes rather than mental states.

blocking   A phenomenon in which prior conditioning to one element of a compound reduces conditioning to other elements.

bottom-up processing   Processing of sensory input that is based entirely on the physical characteristics of the stimulus. Also called *data-driven processing*.

catastrophic interference   A problem encountered in some network models in which the learning of new associations results in the almost complete loss of associations learned earlier.

causal learning   Learning that one event is the cause of another. Causal learning can be viewed as a subtype of associative learning. In associative learning, we learn that there is a relationship between the times at which two events occur; in causal learning we learn not simply that there is a relationship but that one event is the cause of the other.

central executive   The component of working memory that controls the allocation of processing capacity to different tasks; it also integrates information held in its slave systems and in long-term memory.

change blindness   A failure to detect a seemingly obvious change in a visual scene.

chunking   The development of a single code to represent several items. One result is that holding all these items in short-term memory uses up no more storage capacity than was originally required to remember just one item.

classical or Pavlovian conditioning   An increase in responding to a stimulus because of its pairing with a biologically important event. The first stimulus is known as a conditioned stimulus, or CS; the second is known as an unconditioned stimulus, or US.

clustering   A tendency to recall related words from a list together, in clusters, even though they were presented separately.

coding   Assigning a code to an event to represent it in memory.

cognitive interview   A set of interviewing procedures designed to increase the accuracy of eyewitness memories and based on principles derived from cognitive research on memory.

concept   A remarkably difficult term to define. One definition is a set of objects or events sharing common features; another is a mental representation of these events, as in a mental representation of a dog. The second definition comes closer to capturing the sense in which we ordinarily use the term concept, but it raises the difficult problem of how to define a mental representation.

conditioned emotional response (CER)   A procedure for measuring fear based on the observation that frightened animals generally freeze. The stimulus to be tested is presented while subjects are responding to obtain a reward such as food. The reduction in their rate of responding to obtain food can be used as an indirect measure of their freezing, and thus of their fear.

conditioned inhibition   A learned tendency for a stimulus to inhibit, or block, the response normally elicited by a CS.

conditioned response (CR)   The response to a conditioned stimulus caused by pairings of that stimulus with a US.

conditioned stimulus (CS)   A stimulus that, through pairing with an unconditioned stimulus, elicits a response.

configural learning   Learning to respond to a compound stimulus in a manner sharply different than to its components – for example, responding much more to the compound than to its elements presented separately. Subjects behave as if they have learned to perceive the compound as a unique stimulus, or configuration, that is more than the sum of its components.

consolidation theory   Assumes that the formation of a permanent memory trace depends on the strengthening of synaptic connections between neurons, and that this process requires time. The more a memory is consolidated, the more resistant it will be to disruption by events such as brain damage.

contiguity   Literally, proximity or closeness. In learning, the principle of contiguity says that the formation of an association between two events depends on their closeness in time. A stronger version is that contiguity is both *necessary* for the formation of an association (the events must be contiguous to be associated) and *sufficient* (any events that are contiguous will be associated).

contingency   A measure of the extent to which two events occur together, or covary, over time. A contingency coefficient is a mathematical statistic determined by two probabilities – the probability that a US will occur in the presence of a CS, and the probability that it will occur in the absence of the CS.

continuous reinforcement (CRF) schedule   Every response is reinforced.

contrast effect   A change in a reinforcer's effectiveness caused by prior experience with other reinforcers.

control processes   In the Atkinson–Shiffrin model, processes that regulate the flow of information and that are under an individual's voluntary control. The main control processes are rehearsal, coding, and retrieval.

controlled process   A process that requires attention to be carried out. Controlled processes are relatively slow, and only a limited number can be carried out at one time. With practice, however, controlled processes can become automatic.

counterconditioning   A technique for eliminating a conditioned response that involves pairing a CS with another US to condition a new response. If the new response is incompatible with the old response, so that only one response can occur at a time, then the new response can replace the old one.

CS preexposure effect   See *latent inhibition*.

cue overload   A reduction in the effectiveness of a retrieval cue in activating an associated memory caused by the cue's association with other memories.

decay   The theory that forgetting is caused by the passage of time.

declarative memory   Memories that can be accessed consciously and described verbally. Episodic and semantic memories are both examples of declarative memory.

delay conditioning   A procedure in which a CS is presented and then continues until a US is presented. (In some experiments the CS terminates when the US starts;

in others, the two overlap.) Some definitions further restrict this term, confining it to situations in which there is also a long interval between CS onset and US onset.

delta rule   A mathematical formula used in neural network models for calculating the change in the strength of the connection between two neurons when these neurons are activated simultaneously. The formula is very similar to the one used in the Rescorla–Wagner model.

dependent variable   The observable behavior that occurs as a result of manipulation of the independent variable during an experiment.

determinism   The belief that all behavior is caused by a combination of environmental and genetic factors.

dichotic listening   A task in which participants listen to two messages simultaneously, one in each ear.

discrimination   Differential responding to two stimuli. In classical conditioning, this can be achieved by discrimination training, in which one stimulus (CS+) is followed by a US but the second stimulus (CS–) is not.

discrimination training   In reinforcement, differential responding to two stimuli can be encouraged by presenting both stimuli but reinforcing responding only in the presence of one. The stimulus that signals that responding will be reinforced is called a *discriminative stimulus* (S^D), or S+; the stimulus that signals nonreinforcement is called S–.

disruption   A term used by Tolman to describe disturbances of behavior when an expected outcome does not occur.

dissociation   A sharp split in the effect of a variable on two aspects of behavior; dissociations provide suggestive evidence that the behaviors are produced by different processes.

encoding specificity   The code that we assign to a word or other event depends on the context in which we encounter it – *jam*, for example, will be coded differently in the phrases *strawberry jam* and *traffic jam*. This in turn means that our ability to retrieve this word will depend on whether the cues present during retrieval are similar to those present during coding, and thus likely to activate the specific code that was stored.

endowment effect   The hypothesis that we value goods we own more than those we don't. One consequence is that once we acquire something, its value for us immediately increases, so that we become disproportionately reluctant to then relinquish it.

episodic buffer A recent addition to Alan Baddeley's theory of working memory, it is postulated to integrate information from different sensory modalities and different sources. Within vision, for example, the episodic buffer is where sensory information about color and shape would be combined to form an integrated image of an object.

episodic memory Memory for autobiographical experiences, including when and where they occurred.

escape response A response that terminates an aversive stimulus that is already present.

evaluative conditioning A change in the attractiveness or hedonic value of a stimulus due simply to its pairing with another stimulus. In a typical classical conditioning procedure, a light paired with food will come to elicit salivation; in evaluative conditioning the focus is on changes in our positive or negative feelings about the light.

exemplar theory A theory of concept learning that assumes that a mental representation of a concept consists of examples or exemplars, and that we decide whether something is a member of this concept by assessing its resemblance to known exemplars. Exemplar theories can be contrasted with prototype theories that assume that concepts are based around prototypes, which are formed by averaging together known exemplars. In exemplar theory, a concept consists of a large number of exemplars; in prototype theory, it consists of a single prototype.

expectation A belief in the present that some event will occur in the future. In everyday usage, expectations are normally assumed to be conscious, but in learning theory the term is typically used when subjects behave *as if* they knew that some event was coming, without assuming that this expectation exists in conscious form.

explicit and implicit tests of memory In an **explicit test,** people are explicitly asked to remember an experience – recognition and recall tests are examples. In an **implicit test,** by contrast, memory is inferred from performance on a task that, on the surface, has nothing to do with memory – an example is a word-fragment completion test in which people are asked to think of the first word that comes to mind when shown some letters.

exposure therapy A treatment for phobias in which phobics are exposed to fear-eliciting stimuli and given an opportunity to learn that these stimuli are no longer followed by traumatic events (extinction). Exposure starts with stimuli that elicit low levels of fear and gradually progresses to more frightening situations.

extinction　In classical conditioning, the weakening of a previously conditioned response when the CS is presented by itself. In reinforcement, the weakening of a previously reinforced response when the response no longer produces the reinforcer. The term extinction can refer either to the procedure (omission of the US or reinforcer) or to the outcome (weakening of the response).

filter theory　A theory of attention that assumes that all aspects of sensory input receive preliminary processing but that only some stimuli can be given enough attention to allow full recognition. Information that is not allowed through the filter will quickly decay and be forgotten.

flashbulb memories　Vivid memories produced by unexpected and emotionally powerful experiences. At one time these memories were thought to resemble photographs in their clarity and accuracy, but this claim is now thought to be exaggerated.

framing　The finding that decisions can be affected by the way in which alternative options are worded or framed.

free recall　In a free recall test, participants are allowed to recall material in any order, rather than being asked to recall it in the order in which it was presented.

free will　The belief that people have the power to determine their own actions, regardless of any external pressures.

galvanic skin response (GSR)　A measure of arousal in which electrodes are placed on the skin, and an electrical current is passed between them. The greater a person's arousal, the more he or she perspires and thus the stronger the current that will be conducted. Also known as the skin conductance response (SCR).

generalization　Responding to a stimulus because of training involving another stimulus. The strength of responding usually depends on the similarity of the two stimuli – the greater the similarity, the greater the generalization.

generalization gradient　The pattern of responding observed when a stimulus is changed along a continuous dimension such as hue or brightness. Responding usually changes gradually, hence the term *gradient*.

generation effect　Enhanced memory for an item that was generated by the memorizer during the study phase rather than provided by someone else.

GSR　See *galvanic skin response.*

habituation　A decrease in the strength of a reflex as a result of repeated presentations of the stimulus by itself.

heuristic   A short cut or rule of thumb that usually leads to a satisfactory decision or solution to a problem. The use of such mental short cuts allows much faster decision making, but it can sometimes lead to decisions that are not optimal.

hidden units   A layer of units in a neural network that intervene between input units and output units. They help networks to extract information about the relationship between features.

hindsight bias   A tendency to recall our earlier feelings and beliefs as being more similar to our current ones than they actually were.

homeostasis   The body's attempts to maintain a stable internal environment.

implicit learning   Acquisition of knowledge that occurs without our awareness. We do not realize at the time that we have learned anything, and the knowledge that we have acquired can later influence our behavior without ever appearing in consciousness. We feel that a certain behavior is appropriate, without knowing why.

implicit memory   A memory that influences us even though it is not present in consciousness.

incentive   The attractiveness of a reinforcer, as measured by how hard we will work to obtain it. The incentive value of a reinforcer is determined by both its quality (ice cream, for example, is widely regarded as more desirable than cod liver oil) and quantity.

independent variable   The aspect of the environment that an experimenter manipulates during an experiment.

information processing   A theoretical framework that views the operations of the brain as analogous to those of a computer, with information being processed in a sequence of simple operations. The main processing stages of memory are coding, storage, and retrieval.

instrumental conditioning   A change in the probability of a response due to the consequence that follows it. Historically, the term *instrumental conditioning* arose in the context of discrete-trial procedures in which the trial terminated as soon as a subject made a response, and the term *operant conditioning* arose in studies where participants were allowed to respond repeatedly without being removed from the apparatus. (An example of a discrete-trial procedure is a rat running down an alley to a goal box to obtain food, and then being removed; an example of the latter is a rat pressing a bar repeatedly to obtain food.) The terms arose in different contexts, but their essential meaning is the same, as both refer to the strengthening of behavior by its consequences.

interference   The theory that forgetting is caused by memories for events that occurred either before or after the event we are trying to remember.

interval schedule   A schedule in which reinforcement of a response depends on how much time has elapsed since the last reinforcement. Note that the requirement for reinforcement is not simply the passage of time but the occurrence of a response after this time.

intervening variable   A variable used in a theory to represent a hypothesized internal state. This state is elicited by a stimulus and helps to determine the eventual response; the state thus intervenes between the independent variable (environment) and the dependent variable (behavior).

intrinsic motivation   Motivation to perform an activity that derives from the attractiveness of the activity itself, rather than from any consequences that might follow the activity.

introspection   A person's examination of his or her own thoughts or feelings.

latency   The time from when a response becomes possible until it actually occurs. In a puzzle box, for example, the latency of the escape response is the time from when the animal is placed in the box until it escapes.

latent inhibition   Slower conditioning to a CS because of previous presentations of the CS by itself. Also known as the CS preexposure effect.

law   A consistent relationship between the independent and dependent variables in which the occurrence of some condition A always leads to outcome B.

Law of Effect   Thorndike's statement that the presentation of a reward would strengthen the connection between the response that preceded it and the stimuli present at the time.

learned helplessness   An impairment in learning to escape or avoid an aversive stimulus such as shock, caused by previous experiences in which the subject could not control the shock. The *learned helplessness hypothesis* attributes this impairment to subjects' learned belief that they are helpless to prevent the shock.

learning   A term devised to embarrass learning psychologists, who tie themselves into knots trying to define it. We have defined it as a change in our capacity for behavior as the result of particular kinds of experience.

levels of processing   A theory that assumes that the more deeply a stimulus is processed during coding – for example, the more attention is paid to its meaning – the better it will be remembered.

long-term memory (LTM)   Memory for experiences that occurred much earlier, or, alternatively, the memory system in which these enduring memories are believed to be stored. (Atkinson and Shiffrin referred to this storage system as the *long-term store*.) There is no agreement about precisely how much time must elapse before a memory is considered to be long-term, but it is often thought to be about 20 to 30 seconds.

memory   The records that we form of our experiences. Or, more broadly, the processes involved in coding, storing, and retrieving those experiences.

memory span   The number of items that can be accurately recalled, in the correct order, immediately after exposure.

method of loci   A technique for remembering a set of items by imagining following a familiar path and encountering the items in successive locations along the way.

misinformation effect   An error in remembering an event caused by subsequently receiving misleading information about it.

mnemonic devices   Techniques for making unrelated facts easier to remember.

modeling   The learning of new behaviors by observing the behavior of others. The individual exhibiting the behavior is called a model, and observational learning is sometimes referred to as *imitation* (which emphasizes the behavior of the observer) or *modeling* (which emphasizes the behavior of the model).

motivation   Subjectively, the desire to obtain a goal. More objectively, a motive is an internal state that influences which goals we try to attain; the stronger the motive to obtain a goal, the harder we will work to obtain it.

negative contrast   A decrease in a reinforcer's effectiveness caused by previous experience with more attractive reinforcers.

negative reinforcement   A procedure in which a response is strengthened by removing an aversive stimulus – for example, by terminating an electric shock. In *positive reinforcement*, by contrast, a response is strengthened by presenting a stimulus such as food. Note that positive and negative reinforcement are both examples of reinforcement, as both strengthen behavior; the difference lies in whether this is achieved by presenting a stimulus (positive reinforcement) or removing one (negative reinforcement).

negative reinforcer   A stimulus (usually aversive) whose termination can reinforce preceding behavior.

neural network   A densely interconnected set of neurons in the brain. Activity in one neuron is transmitted to other neurons within the net.

node   A neuron or set of neurons in the brain that represents a concept or idea, in the sense that the node becomes active when and only when we think of this concept.

operant or instrumental conditioning   These terms refer to a change in the probability of a response as a result of the consequences that follow it.

overexpectation effect   A decrease in the strength of conditioning on compound trials, where the elements of the compound have previously been strongly conditioned separately.

paired–associate learning   In a paired-associate task, items such as words are presented in pairs. At the conclusion of the study period, memory is usually tested by showing participants the first item in each pair and asking them to recall the second.

parallel processing   In the brain, any processes that occur simultaneously. Many of the brain's processes operate in parallel, and neural network theorists believe that this is an important factor in the brain's ability to solve problems, such as reading handwriting, that even the most powerful of modern computers cannot solve. Compare *sequential processing.*

parameter   A constant used in a mathematical formula. The value of a parameter remains the same in successive applications of the equation to the same situation, but different values can be used when the equation is applied to different situations. By assigning different values to parameters, researchers can use the same basic equation to predict a range of experimental results. In the case of the Rescorla–Wagner model, the parameters c and V_{max} determine the speed and asymptotic level of conditioning.

parsimony   A criterion for evaluating theories which states that, where several explanations are possible, we should prefer whichever is the simplest. A theory might be simpler because it involves fewer assumptions, or because those assumptions postulate simpler processes.

partial reinforcement effect (PRE)   The lower the proportion of responses that are reinforced during training, the more persistent responding is during extinction.

Pavlovian conditioning   See *classical conditioning.*

pegword system   A technique for memorizing unrelated words by linking them to pegwords such as "one is a bun" and "two is a shoe." If the first word on the list to be remembered is elephant, for example, the memorizer might form an image of an elephant sitting on a hamburger bun.

perceptual learning   An improvement in the ability to differentiate or discriminate stimuli due to previous experience with those stimuli.

perceptual memory   Improved perception of a word because of previous exposures to that word.

phonological loop   The component of working memory that holds acoustically coded information. Information held on the loop decays rapidly, but it can be refreshed if it is repeated in subvocal speech – in effect, talking to yourself.

positive contrast   An increase in a reinforcer's effectiveness caused by previous experience with less attractive reinforcers.

positive reinforcer   A stimulus whose occurrence can strengthen the behavior that precedes it.

Premack principle   If we assess the probability of activities by the time spent performing them when they are freely available, then the Premack principle says that access to an activity can be used to reinforce any activity of lower probability. If, for example, a child spends more time playing computer games than studying when given a free choice, then access to computer games can be used to reinforce studying.

preparedness   The tendency to associate some CS–US combinations more readily than others. Other terms for this phenomenon include *relevance*, *selective association*, and *associative bias*.

primacy   Improved recall for items from the beginning of a list compared with items from the middle.

primary reinforcer   A reinforcer that requires no special training to be effective; a primary reinforcer will thus be effective for all members of a species from birth.

priming   A temporary improvement in the processing of a word because of an earlier presentation. See also *repetition priming* and *semantic priming*.

proactive interference (PI)   Interference caused by memories for earlier events.

procedural memory   Memory for how to perform actions. Examples include classical conditioning and riding a bicycle.

proposition   The smallest unit of knowledge that can be meaningfully regarded as true or false. In theoretical terms, the abstract format in which this proposition is held in semantic memory.

prospect theory   A theory developed by Kahneman and Tversky to explain how people decide between possible courses of action. It assumes that people evaluate outcomes in terms of gains or losses relative to a reference point, and that in making decisions we put greater weight on avoiding losses than on making gains of equivalent value.

prototype   A typical or average instance of a concept. A robin, for example, is considered a prototypical bird; an ostrich is not.

pseudoconditioning   An increase in responding to a CS as a result of presentations of the US by itself.

punishment   A decrease in the probability of a response because of its being followed by an aversive consequence. Also sometimes used to describe the procedure (attempting to reduce the likelihood of a behavior by following it with an aversive consequence).

random control   A control procedure for classical conditioning in which the CS and US are presented randomly in relation to each other, so that the occurrence of one does not allow an improved prediction about when the other will occur.

ratio schedule   A schedule in which reinforcement of a response depends on the number of responses that have been emitted.

reality monitoring   The processes involved in deciding whether a remembered event really occurred or was only imagined.

recall   In a recall test, people are asked to remember material they have seen without further prompting. See also *free recall*.

recency   Improved recall for items from the end of a list compared with items from the middle.

recognition   In a recognition test, participants are shown material and asked if it is the same as material they were shown earlier. If a participant correctly recognizes a stimulus that was seen earlier, it is called a *hit*; if the participant claims to have seen a stimulus that was not presented, it is called a *false alarm*.

recovered memories   Memories for childhood abuse that are retrieved after a long period in which the individual had no conscious memory of the abuse.

reflex   A stimulus–response relationship in which a stimulus reliably elicits the same response innately, without prior experience.

reinforcement   Presenting a reinforcer following a response, or, alternatively, the typical outcome of this procedure, an increase in response probability as a result of the presentation.

reinforcement schedules Rules that determine when a response will be reinforced.

reinforcer An event that increases the probability of a response when presented after it.

release from proactive interference (PI) A reduction in proactive interference caused by a change in the characteristics of the material being memorized. Interference is greatest when memories are similar, so that if the material currently being learned is not similar to the material learned earlier, the earlier material will be less likely to interfere.

renewal effect The recovery of an extinguished response due to a return to the training context, when extinction had taken place in a different context.

repetition priming A temporary improvement in processing of a stimulus such as a word because of an earlier encounter. This improvement can take the form of faster recognition of the word, a faster decision that it is a word (lexical decision), or an increased likelihood of thinking of the word when given clues such as some of its letters (word-fragment completion).

representativeness heuristic A strategy for assessing the likelihood that something is a member of a category by assessing its similarity to typical (representative) members.

response cost This is a form of punishment in which a reinforcer is taken away following a response. Typically, the reinforcer that is lost is points or tokens.

retrieval The process of finding a code when it is needed for further processing.

retrieval cue A stimulus that helps us to recall an earlier experience, usually because the stimulus was present during the experience, or because it resembles another stimulus that was present.

retrieval-induced forgetting In trying to retrieve one memory, we typically also retrieve others, and to prevent them all flooding into consciousness we inhibit the weaker ones. One result is that for a period thereafter it will be more difficult to retrieve the memories that have been inhibited.

retroactive interference (RI) Interference caused by memories for later events.

retrospective revaluation Broadly, a change in the response to a stimulus due to subsequent experience with other stimuli. One use of the term is in the context of causal learning, where it refers to a change in the belief that one event has been the cause of another because of subsequent experiences involving other possible causes.

SAM   A theory of retrieval developed by Raaijmakers and Shiffrin (1980, 1981); SAM stands for search of associative memory. The theory assumes that contextual cues become associated with a representation of an event during coding (the context and the associated representation are together called an image), and retrieval occurs when one or more of these cues later activates the image.

schema   A knowledge structure that holds information about the common characteristics of a set of objects or events. A schema of a department store might include features such as bright lights and counters with sales assistants behind them.

script   A form of schema containing information about a stereotypical sequence of actions – for example, eating in a restaurant or studying for an exam.

secondary or conditioned reinforcer   A stimulus that acquires its reinforcing properties through experience. In most cases, secondary reinforcers are established by pairing a stimulus with a primary reinforcer.

second-order conditioning   Learning that takes place as a result of pairing a stimulus with a previously conditioned stimulus.

self-control   According to Skinner, the performing of one response to alter the probability of some subsequent response.

semantic memory   Memory for general knowledge, including the meaning of words. Semantic memories are not tied to particular moments – we know the capital of France without necessarily remembering when we acquired the information.

semantic network   A theory of semantic memory that assumes that words are linked in a web of connections based on their meanings.

semantic priming   An improvement in the processing of a word because of an earlier presentation of a word with a similar meaning. This improvement supports the view that words are associated in semantic networks, and that activation of one word in a network spreads to words that have similar meanings.

sensitization   An increase in the strength of a reflex caused by repeated presentations of the stimulus by itself.

sensory memory   A store in which sensory input is held very briefly to allow time to identify it. There are separate stores for holding auditory input (*echoic memory*) and visual input (*iconic memory*); both are thought to hold material for at most a few seconds.

shadowing   Repeating out loud a message heard in one ear while a different message is being presented in the other ear.

shaping A technique for training responses that are initially unlikely to occur. The first step is to reinforce whatever aspect of an individual's behavior is closest to the desired response. As this behavior begins to occur more often, the trainer withholds reinforcement until some closer approximation to the desired response occurs, and so on.

short-term memory (STM) Memory for material presented recently, or, alternatively, the temporary system in which these memories are believed to be held while they are processed. (Atkinson and Shiffrin referred to this temporary system as the *short-term store*.)

simultaneous conditioning A procedure in which a CS and a US are presented at the same time.

skeletal responses Bodily movements controlled by the skeletal nervous system.

source confusion Recalling information correctly but erroneously remembering the context in which this information was acquired.

spacing effect The finding that we remember material better if we distribute or spread our practice of this material over time.

spontaneous recovery An increase in the strength of an extinguished response after a period following the last extinction trial.

spreading activation The theoretical assumption that activation of one node in semantic memory will spread to nodes that are linked to it.

S–R theory A theory that assumes that learning involves the formation of associations between environmental stimuli and the responses made in their presence.

state-dependent memory An improvement in memory that occurs because a person's internal state during retrieval is similar to his or her state during coding.

stimulus control Exists when the probability of a response's occurrence varies depending on what stimuli are present.

stimulus substitution Pavlov's interpretation of the process that occurs during conditioning. He believed that activation of the CS center of the brain would be transferred to the US center and the CS would therefore elicit the same behaviors as the US. To the extent that they elicit the same response, the CS in effect becomes the US.

storage Maintaining a code in memory over time.

Stroop effect The finding that it takes longer to name the color in which a word is printed when the word itself is the name of a different color. The color elicits one response and the written word automatically elicits another, even when we try to ignore it; the competition between them slows responding.

superstition   In Skinner's usage, a behavior that is strengthened because it happens to be followed by a reinforcer, even though it did not actually produce that reinforcer.

suppression ratio   A statistical index used to measure the reduction in responding during a CER test. The index is B/(A + B), where B is the number of responses during the test stimulus and A is the number of responses during an equivalent period immediately before the test stimulus.

systematic desensitization   A therapy for phobias based on counterconditioning. Patients visualize fear-evoking stimuli while relaxing, to associate the stimuli with relaxation instead of fear.

taste-aversion learning   A form of classical conditioning in which a subject develops an aversion for the taste or odor of a food because that food was followed by illness.

temporal discounting   A reduction in the value we assign to an outcome if there is going to be a delay until we receive it.

think/no think paradigm   A procedure in which participants first learn a set of word pairs and are then shown the first words. They are asked to think about the second word for some pairs but to avoid thinking about the second word for others. When later tested on their ability to recall the second words, they are poorer at recalling the words they were encouraged to suppress.

time-out   A form of punishment in which misbehavior results in removal to a less reinforcing environment for a specified period (time-out from reinforcement). Commonly used forms of time-out for children include having to sit in a chair in a corner or having to stay in a bare room.

tip of the tongue (TOT)   An inability to recall something accompanied by the tantalizing feeling that you really do know it and it is just beyond your grasp.

token economy   A systematic procedure for reinforcing behavior in which tokens are made contingent on the performance of desired behaviors; the tokens can later be exchanged for backup reinforcers such as candy. In early applications in mental hospitals, access to the backup reinforcers was restricted so that they could be obtained only with the tokens; this was the basis for the term *economy*.

top-down processing   Processing of sensory input that is based on existing knowledge and expectations. Also called *conceptually driven processing*.

trace conditioning   A technique that involves presenting the CS and terminating it before presenting the US.

trial   In a learning experiment, a discrete opportunity for a subject to learn. In classical conditioning, a single pairing of a CS and a US is called a trial.

two-system hypothesis   A proposal that two different learning systems can be involved when we learn about the relationship between two events: A relatively primitive system that forms an association between the events, and a cognitive system that forms an expectation that the first event will be followed by the second.

typicality effect   The finding that people are faster at deciding if a word is a member of a category if the word is generally regarded as a typical rather than an atypical example.

unconditioned response (UR)   The response elicited by an unconditioned stimulus.

unconditioned stimulus (US)   A stimulus that elicits a response without training.

unpaired control   A control group in which the CS and the US are presented at widely separated times. An unpaired control is sometimes referred to as an explicitly unpaired control.

V In the Rescorla–Wagner model, the strength of the association that is formed when a CS and a US are paired.

visuo-spatial sketchpad   The component of working memory that holds visual material during initial processing and also when it is retrieved from long-term memory in the form of an image. It also holds spatial information about the location of objects in the environment.

weapon-focus effect   The presence of a weapon during the commission of a crime tends to attract attention, and this reduces attention to other elements of the scene such as the perpetrator's face.

working memory   A temporary store in which information is held during initial processing; it is also used for combining and elaborating information already in long-term storage. Baddeley has proposed that working memory has three main components: phonological loop, visuo-spatial sketchpad, and central executive.

Yerkes–Dodson law   An inverse relationship between task difficulty and optimum motivation: the more difficult the problem, the lower the optimum motivation.

References

Adams, J. A. (1971). A closed-loop theory of motor learning. *Journal of Motor Behavior*, *3*, 111–149.

Aggleton, J. P., and Waskett, L. (1999). The ability of odours to serve as state-dependent cues for real-world memories: can Viking smells aid the recall of Viking experiences? *British Journal of Psychology*, *90*, 1–7.

Albert, M., and Ayres, J. J. B. (1997). One-trial simultaneous and backward excitatory fear conditioning in rats: lick suppression, freezing, and rearing to CS compounds and their elements. *Animal Learning and Behavior*, *25*, 210–220.

Allan, L. G. (1980). A note on measurement of contingency between two binary variables in judgment tasks. *Bulletin of the Psychonomic Society*, *15*, 147–149.

Allen, K. E., Hart, B., Buell, J. S., Harris, F. R., and Wolf, M. M. (1964). Effects of social reinforcement on isolate behavior of a nursery school child. *Child Development*, *35*, 511–518.

Alloway, T. P. (2010). *Improving working memory*. London: Sage Press.

Allport, D. A., Antonis, B., and Reynolds, P. (1972). On the division of attention: a disproof of the single channel hypothesis. *Quarterly Journal of Experimental Psychology*, *24*, 225–235.

Alter, A. L., and Oppenheimer, D. M. (2008). Easy on the mind, easy on the wallet: the roles of familiarity and processing fluency in valuation judgments. *Psychonomic Bulletin and Review*, *15*, 985–990.

American Psychological Association (1995). *Can a memory be forgotten and then remembered?* Washington, DC: Office for Public Affairs.

Anderson, J. R. (2010). *Cognitive psychology and its implications* (7th edn). New York: Worth.

Anderson, J. R., Bothell, D., Byrne, M. D., Douglass, S., Lebiere, C., and Qin, Y. (2004). An integrated theory of the mind. *Psychological Review*, *111*, 1036–1060.

Anderson, J. R., and Paulson, R. (1977). Representation and retention of verbatim information. *Journal of Verbal Learning and Verbal Behavior*, *16*, 439–451.

Anderson, M. C. (2003). Rethinking interference theory: executive control and the mechanisms of forgetting. *Journal of Memory and Language*, *49*, 415–445.

Anderson, M. C., Bjork, E. L., and Bjork, R. A. (2000). Retrieval-induced forgetting: evidence for a recall-specific mechanism. *Psychonomic Bulletin and Review*, *7*, 522–530.

Anderson, M. C., and Green, C. (2001). Suppressing unwanted memories by executive control. *Nature, 410*, 131–134.

Anderson, M. C., and Levy, B. J. (2009). Suppressing unwanted memories. *Current Directions in Psychological Science, 18*, 189–194.

Anderson, M. C., and Neely, J. H. (1996). Interference and inhibition in memory retrieval. In E. L. Bjork and R. A. Bjork (eds.), *Memory* (pp. 237–313). San Diego, CA: Academic Press.

Annau, Z., and Kamin, L. J. (1961). The conditioned emotional response as a function of intensity of the US. *Journal of Comparative and Physiological Psychology, 54*, 428–432.

Anrep, G. V. (1920). Pitch discrimination in the dog. *Journal of Physiology, 53*, 367–385.

Ariely, D. (2008). *Predictably irrational: the hidden forces that shape our decisions.* London: HarperCollins.

Arndt, J. (2010). The role of memory activation in creating false memories of encoding context. *Journal of Experimental Psychology: Learning, Memory, and Cognition, 36*, 66–79.

Aronfreed, J. (1968). Aversive control of socialization. In D. Levine (ed.), *Nebraska symposium on motivation* (pp. 271–320). Lincoln: University of Nebraska Press.

Ashby, F. G., and Ennis, J. M. (2006). The role of the basal ganglia in category learning. In B. H. Ross (ed.), *The psychology of learning and motivation* (vol. 46, pp. 1–36). San Diego, CA: Academic Press.

Atkinson, R. C., and Shiffrin, R. M. (1968). Human memory: a proposed system and its control processes. In W. K. Spence and J. T. Spence (eds.), *The psychology of learning and motivation: advances in research and theory* (vol. 2, pp. 89–195). New York: Academic Press.

Ayers, M. S., and Reder, L. M. (1998). A theoretical review of the misinformation effect: predictions from an activation-based model. *Psychonomic Bulletin and Review, 5*, 1–21.

Azrin, N. H., Holz, W. C., and Hake, D. F. (1963). Fixed-ratio punishment. *Journal of the Experimental Analysis of Behavior, 6*, 141–148.

Baddeley, A. D. (1978). The trouble with levels: a reexamination of Craik and Lockhart's framework for memory research. *Psychological Review, 85*, 139–152.

(1997). *Human memory: theory and practice* (rev. edn). Hove: Psychology Press.

(1998). Recent developments in working memory. *Current Opinion in Neurobiology, 8*, 234–238.

(1999). *Essentials of human memory.* Hove: Psychology Press.

(2003). Working memory: looking back and looking forward. *Nature Reviews Neuroscience, 4*, 829–839.

(2007). *Working memory, thought and action.* Oxford: Oxford University Press.

Baddeley, A. D., Bressi, S., Della Sala, S., Logie, R., and Spinnler, H. (1991). The decline of working memory in Alzheimer's disease: a longitudinal study. *Brain, 114*, 2521–2542.

Baddeley, A. D., and Hitch, G. J. (1974). Working memory. In G. H. Bower (ed.), *The psychology of learning and motivation* (vol. 8, pp. 47–89). New York: Academic Press.

——— (1977). Recency reexamined. In S. Dornic (ed.), *Attention and performance* (vol. 6, pp. 647–667). Hillsdale, NJ: Lawrence Erlbaum.

Baddeley, A. D., Logie, R., Bressi, S., Della Sala, S., and Spinnler, H. (1986). Dementia and working memory. *Quarterly Journal of Experimental Psychology, 38A*, 603–618.

Baddeley, A. D., and Warrington, E. K. (1970). Amnesia and the distinction between long- and short-term memory. *Journal of Verbal Learning and Verbal Behavior, 9*, 176–189.

Bahrick, H. P. (1984). Semantic memory content in permastore: fifty years of memory for Spanish learned in school. *Journal of Experimental Psychology: General, 113*, 1–29.

Bahrick, H. P., Bahrick, L. E., Bahrick, A. S., and Bahrick, P. E. (1993). Maintenance of foreign language vocabulary and the spacing effect. *Psychological Science, 4*, 316–321.

Bahrick, H. P., Bahrick, P. O., and Wittlinger, R. P. (1975). Fifty years of memory for names and faces: a cross-sectional approach. *Journal of Experimental Psychology: General, 104*, 54–75.

Bahrick, H. P., and Hall, L. K. (2005). The importance of retrieval failures to long-term retention: a metacognitive explanation of the spacing effect. *Journal of Memory and Language, 52*, 566–577.

Bahrick, H. P., and Phelps, E. (1987). Retention of Spanish vocabulary over 8 years. *Journal of Experimental Psychology: Learning, Memory, and Cognition, 13*, 344–349.

Balch, W. R., Myers, D. M., and Popotto, C. (1999). Dimensions of mood in mood-dependent memory. *Journal of Experimental Psychology: Learning, Memory, and Cognition, 25*, 70–83.

Balleine, B., Espinet, A., and González, F. (2005). Perceptual learning enhances retrospective revaluation of conditioned flavor preferences in rats. *Journal of Experimental Psychology: Animal Behavior Processes, 31*, 341–350.

Ballew, C. C., II, and Todorov, A. (2007). Predicting political elections from rapid and unreflective face judgments. *Proceedings of the National Academy of Sciences, 104*, 17,948–17,953.

Balsam, P. D., Drew, M. R., and Gallistel, C. R. (2010). Time and associative learning. *Comparative Cognition and Behavior Reviews, 5*, 1–22.

Balsam, P., and Tomie, A. (eds.) (1995). *Context and learning.* Hillsdale, NJ: Erlbaum.

Banaji, M. R., and Crowder, R. G. (1989). The bankruptcy of everyday memory. *American Psychologist, 44*, 1185–1193.

Bandura, A., Ross, D., and Ross, D. A. (1963). Imitation of film-mediated aggressive models. *Journal of Abnormal and Social Psychology, 66*, 3–11.

Bargh, J. A., Chen, M., and Burrows, L. (1996). Automaticity of social behavior: direct effects of trait construct and stereotype activation on action. *Journal of Personality and Social Psychology, 71*, 230–244.

Bargh, J. A., and Schul, Y. (1980). On the cognitive benefits of teaching. *Journal of Educational Psychology*, *72*, 593–604.

Barlow, D. H., and Durand, V. M. (1995). *Abnormal psychology: an integrative approach.* Pacific Grove, CA: Brooks/Cole.

Barlow, D. H., Raffa, S. D., and Cohen, E. M. (2002). Psychosocial treatments for panic disorders, phobias, and generalized anxiety disorder. In P. E. Nathan and J. M. Gorman (eds.), *A guide to treatments that work* (2nd edn, pp. 301–335). London: Oxford University Press.

Barrouillet, P., Bernardin, S., and Camos, V. (2004). Time constraints and resource sharing in adults' working memory spans. *Journal of Experimental Psychology: General*, *133*, 83–100.

Barsalou, L. W. (2008). Grounded cognition. *Annual Review of Psychology*, *59*, 617–645.

Bartlett, F. (1932). *Remembering.* Cambridge: Cambridge University Press.

Baumeister, R. F., Vohs, K. D., and Tice, D. M. (2007). The strength model of self-control. *Current Directions in Psychological Science*, *16*, 351–355.

Baumrind, D. (1991). Parenting styles and adolescent development. In J. Brooks-Gunn, R. Lerner, and A. C. Petersen (eds.), *The encyclopedia of adolescence* (pp. 746–758). New York: Garland.

Bechara, A., and Damasio, A. R. (2005). The somatic marker hypothesis: a neural theory of economic decision. *Games and Economic Behavior*, *52*, 336–372.

Bechara, A., Tranel, D., Damasio, H., Adolphs, R., Rockland, G., and Damasio, A. R. (1995). Double dissociation of conditioning and declarative knowledge relative to the amygdala and hippocampus in humans. *Science*, *269*, 1115–1118.

Beilock, S. L. (2008). Math performance in stressful situations. *Current Directions in Psychological Science*, *17*, 339–343.

Bellezza, F. S. (1996). Mnemonic methods to enhance storage and retrieval. In E. L. Bjork and R. A. Bjork (eds.), *Memory* (pp. 345–380). San Diego, CA: Academic Press.

Bellingham, W. P., Gillette-Bellingham, K., and Kehoe, E. J. (1985). Summation and configuration in patterning schedules with the rat and rabbit. *Animal Learning and Behavior*, *13*, 152–164.

Berger, S. A., Hall, L. K., and Bahrick, H. P. (1999). Stabilizing access to marginal and submarginal knowledge. *Journal of Experimental Psychology: Applied*, *5*, 438–447.

Bergman, E. T., and Roediger, H. L. (1999). Can Bartlett's repeated reproduction experiments be replicated? *Memory and Cognition*, *27*, 937–947.

Berkowitz, L. (1989). Frustration–aggression hypothesis: examination and reformulation. *Psychological Bulletin*, *106*, 59–73.

Berkowitz, L., Cochran, S. T., and Embree, M. C. (1981). Physical pain and the goal of aversively stimulated aggression. *Journal of Personality and Social Psychology*, *40*, 687–700.

Berman, M. G., Jonides, J., and Lewis, R. L. (2009). In search of decay in verbal short-term memory. *Journal of Experimental Psychology: Learning, Memory, and Cognition*, *35*, 317–333.

Bermudez, J. L. (2010). *Cognitive science*. Cambridge: Cambridge University Press.

Bernstein, I. L. (1978). Learned taste aversions in children receiving chemotherapy. *Science, 200*, 1302–1303.

Berridge, K. C. (2000). Reward learning: reinforcement, incentives, and expectations. In D. L. Medin (ed.), *The psychology of learning and motivation* (vol. 40, pp. 223–278). San Diego, CA: Academic Press.

Bertsch, S., Pesta, B. J., Wiscott, R., and McDaniel, M. A. (2007). The generation effect: a meta-analytic review. *Memory and Cognition, 35*, 201–210.

Best, P. J., Best, M. R., and Henggeler, S. (1977). The contribution of environmental noningestive cues in conditioning aversive internal consequences. In L. M. Barker, M. R. Best, and M. Domjan (eds.), *Learning mechanisms in food selection* (pp. 371–393). Waco, TX: Baylor University Press.

Birnbrauer, J. S., and Leach, D. J. (1993). The Murdoch Early Intervention Program after 2 years. *Behaviour Change, 10*, 63–74.

Bjork, R. A. (1988). Retrieval practice and the maintenance of knowledge. In M. M. Gruneberg, P. E. Morris, and R. N. Sykes (eds.), *Practical aspects of memory: current research and issues*, vol. 1: *Memory in everyday life* (pp. 396–401). Chichester: Wiley.

Blanchard, R. J., Blanchard, D. C., and Takahashi, L. K. (1977). Reflexive fighting in the rat: aggressive or defensive behavior? *Aggressive Behavior, 3*, 145–155.

Blough, D. S. (1975). Steady state data and a quantitative model of operant generalization and discrimination. *Journal of Experimental Psychology: Animal Behavior Processes, 1*, 3–21.

Boe, E. E., and Church, R. M. (1967). Permanent effects of punishment during extinction. *Journal of Comparative and Physiological Psychology, 63*, 486–492.

Boland, F. J., Mellor, C. S., and Revusky, S. (1978). Chemical aversion treatment of alcoholism: lithium as the aversive agent. *Behavior Research and Therapy, 16*, 401–409.

Bolles, R. C. (1972). Reinforcement, expectancy, and learning. *Psychological Review, 79*, 394–409.

(1975). *Theory of motivation* (2nd edn). New York: Harper & Row.

Bonson, K. R., Grant, S. J., Contoreggi, C. S., Links, J. M., Metcalfe, J., Weyl, H. L., Kurian, V., Ernst, M., and London, E. D. (2002). Neural systems and cue-induced cocaine craving. *Neuropsychopharmacology, 26*, 376–386.

Bootzin, R. R. (1972). Stimulus control treatment for insomnia. *Proceedings of the 80th Annual Convention of the American Psychological Association, 7*, 395–396.

Borden, J. W. (1992). Behavioral treatment of simple phobia. In S. M. Turner, K. S. Calhoun, and H. E. Adams (eds.), *Handbook of clinical behavior therapy* (2nd edn, pp. 3–12). New York: Wiley.

Boring, E. G. (1950). *A history of experimental psychology* (2nd edn). New York: AppletonCentury-Crofts.

Bousfield, W. A. (1953). The occurrence of clustering in the recall of randomly arranged associates. *Journal of General Psychology, 49*, 229–240.

Bouton, M. E. (2004). Context and behavioral processes in extinction. *Learning and Memory, 11*, 485–494.

(2007). *Learning and behavior: a contemporary synthesis.* Sunderland, MA: Sinauer.

Bouton, M. E., and King, D. A. (1983). Contextual control of the extinction of conditioned fear: tests for the associative value of the context. *Journal of Experimental Psychology: Animal Behavior Processes, 9*, 248–265.

Bouton, M. E., and Nelson, J. B. (1998). The role of context in classical conditioning: some implications for cognitive behavior therapy. In W. T. O'Donohue (ed.), *Learning and behavior therapy* (pp. 59–84). Needham Heights, MA: Allyn & Bacon.

Bower, G. H., Black, J. B., and Turner, T. J. (1979). Scripts in memory for text. *Cognitive Psychology, 11*, 177–220.

Bower, G. H., and Clark, M. C. (1969). Narrative stories as mediators for serial learning. *Psychonomic Science, 14*, 181–182.

Bower, G. H., Clark, M. C., Lesgold, A. M., and Winzenz, D. (1969). Hierarchical retrieval schemes in recall of categorized word lists. *Journal of Verbal Learning and Verbal Behavior, 8*, 323–343.

Bower, G. H., Karlin, M. B., and Dueck, A. (1975). Comprehension and memory for pictures. *Memory and Cognition, 3*, 216–220.

Bower, G. H., and Winzenz, D. (1970). Comparison of associative learning strategies. *Psychonomic Science, 20*, 119–120.

Bowers, J. S. (2009). On the biological plausiblity of grandmother cells: implications for neural network theories in psychology and neuroscience. *Psychological Review, 116*, 220–251.

(2010). Postscript: some final thoughts on grandmother cells, distributed representations, and PDP models of cognition. *Psychological Review, 117*, 306–308.

Brainerd, C. J., Reyna, V. F., and Mojardin, A. H. (1999). Conjoint recognition. *Psychological Review, 106*, 160–179.

Bransford, J. D., and Johnson, M. K. (1972). Contextual prerequisites for understanding: some investigations of comprehension and recall. *Journal of Verbal Learning and Verbal Behavior, 11*, 717–726.

Brantner, J. P., and Doherty, M. A. (1983). A review of timeout: a conceptual and methodological analysis. In S. Axelrod and J. Apsche (eds.), *The effects of punishment on human behavior* (pp. 87–132). New York: Academic Press.

Bregman, N. J., and McAllister, H. A. (1982). Motivation and skin temperature biofeedback: Yerkes-Dodson revisited. *Psychophysiology, 19*, 282–285.

Breland, K., and Breland, M. (1961). The misbehaviour of organisms. *American Psychologist, 16*, 681–684.

Brennan, P. A., and Mednick, S. A. (1994). Learning theory approach to the deterrence of criminal recidivism. *Journal of Abnormal Psychology, 103*, 430–440.

Brewer, W. F. (1977). Memory for the pragmatic implications of sentences. *Memory and Cognition, 5*, 673–678.

Brewer, W. F., and Treyens, J. C. (1981). Role of schemata in memory for places. *Cognitive Psychology, 13*, 207–230.

Broadbent, D. E. (1958). *Perception and communication.* London: Pergamon Press.

Broadhurst, P. L. (1957). Emotionality and the Yerkes-Dodson law. *Journal of Experimental Psychology*, *54*, 345–352.

Brown, A. S. (2008). Tip of the tongue experience. In H. L. Roediger III (ed.), *Learning and memory: a comprehensive reference*, vol. 2: *Cognitive psychology of memory* (pp. 377–387). New York: Academic Press.

Brown, E., Deffenbacher, K., and Sturgill, W. (1977). Memory for faces and the circumstances of encounter. *Journal of Applied Psychology*, *62*, 311–318.

Brown, J. A. (1958). Some tests of the decay theory of immediate memory. *Quarterly Journal of Experimental Psychology*, *10*, 12–21.

Brown, M. A., and Sharp, P. E. (1995). Simulation of spatial learning in the Morris water maze by a neural network model of the hippocampal formation and nucleus accumbens. *Hippocampus*, *5*, 171–188.

Brown, R., and Kulik, J. (1977). Flashbulb memories. *Cognition*, *5*, 73–99.

Brown, R., and McNeill, D. (1966). The "tip-of-the-tongue" phenomenon. *Journal of Verbal Learning and Verbal Behavior*, *5*, 325–337.

Bruner, J. S., Goodnow, J. J., and Austin, G. A. (1956). *A study of thinking.* New York: Wiley.

Bucher, B., and Lovaas, O. I. (1968). The use of aversive stimulation in behavior modification. In M. R. Jones (ed.), *Miami symposium on the prediction of behavior: aversive stimulation* (pp. 77–145). Coral Gables, FL: University of Miami Press.

Buehner, M. J., and Cheng, P. W. (2005). Causal learning. In K. J. Holyoak and R. G. Morrison (eds.), *Cambridge handbook of thinking and reasoning* (pp. 143–168). Cambridge: Cambridge University Press.

Burianova, H., McIntosh, A. R., and Grady, C. L. (2010). A common functional brain network for autobiographical, episodic, and semantic memory retrieval. *NeuroImage*, *49*, 865–874.

Bushman, B. J., and Huesmann, L. R. (2001). Effects of televised violence on aggression. In D. G. Singer and J. L. Singer (eds.), *Handbook of children and the media* (pp. 223–254). Thousand Oaks, CA: Sage.

Butler, R. A. (1954). Incentive conditions which influence visual exploration. *Journal of Experimental Psychology*, *48*, 19–23.

Butters, N., and Cermak, L. S. (1986). A study of the forgetting of autobiographical knowledge: implications for the study of retrograde amnesia. In D. Rubin (ed.), *Autobiographical memory* (pp. 253–272). Cambridge: Cambridge University Press.

Cacioppo, J. T., Marshall-Goodell, B. S., Tassinary, L. G., and Petty, R. E. (1992). Rudimentary determinants of attitudes: classical conditioning is more effective when prior knowledge about the attitude stimulus is low than high. *Journal of Experimental Social Psychology*, *28*, 207–233.

Cameron, J., Banko, K. M., and Pierce, W. D. (2001). Pervasive negative effects of rewards on intrinsic motivation: the myth continues. *Behavior Analyst*, *24*, 1–44.

Cameron, J., and Pierce, W. D. (1996). The debate about rewards and intrinsic motivation: protests and accusations do not alter the results. *Review of Educational Research*, *66*, 39–51.

Cameron, J., Pierce, W. D., Banko, K. M., and Gear, A. (2005). Achievement-based rewards and intrinsic motivation: a test of cognitive mediators. *Journal of Educational Psychology, 97,* 641–655.

Capaldi, E. D. (1996). *Why we eat what we eat.* Washington, DC: American Psychological Association.

Capaldi, E. D., Campbell, D. H., Sheffer, J. D., and Bradford, J. P. (1987). Conditioned flavor preferences based on delayed caloric consequences. *Journal of Experimental Psychology: Animal Behavior Processes, 13,* 150–155.

Capaldi, E. J. (1971). Memory and learning: a sequential viewpoint. In W. K. Honig and P. H. R. James (eds.), *Animal memory* (pp. 115–154). New York: Academic Press.

Carlesimo, G. A., Marfia, G. A., Loasses, A., and Caltagirone, C. (1996). Recency effect in anterograde amnesia: evidence for distinct memory stores underlying enhanced retrieval of terminal items in immediate and delayed recall paradigms. *Neuropsychologia, 34,* 177–184.

Carli, L. L. (1999). Cognitive reconstruction, hindsight, and reactions to victims and perpetrators. *Personality and Social Psychology Bulletin, 25,* 966–979.

Carmon, Z., and Ariely, D. (2000). Focusing on the forgone: how value can appear so different to buyers and sellers. *Journal of Consumer Research, 27,* 360–370.

Carney, R. N., and Levin, J. R. (1998). Coming to terms with the keyword method in introductory psychology: a "neuromnemonic" example. *Teaching of Psychology, 25,* 132–134.

Caspi, A., McClay, J., Moffitt, T. E., Mill, J., Martin, J., Craig, I. W., Taylor, A., and Poulton, R. (2002). Role of genotype in the cycle of violence in maltreated children. *Science, 297,* 851–854.

Cave, K. R., and Bichot, N. P. (1999). Visuospatial attention: beyond a spotlight model. *Psychonomic Bulletin and Review, 6,* 204–223.

Ceci, S. J. (1995). False beliefs: some developmental and clinical considerations. In D. L. Schacter (ed.), *Memory distortions: how minds, brains, and societies reconstruct the past* (pp. 91–125). Cambridge, MA: Harvard University Press.

Champion, R. A., and Jones, J. E. (1961). Forward, backward, and pseudoconditioning of the GSR. *Journal of Experimental Psychology, 62,* 58–61.

Charniak, E. (1973). Jack and Janet in search of a theory of knowledge. *IJCAI Proceedings,* 337–343.

Chase, W. G., and Ericsson, K. A. (1982). Skill and working memory. In G. H. Bower (ed.), *The psychology of learning and motivation* (vol. 16, pp. 1–58). New York: Academic Press.

Chen, M., and Bargh, J. A. (1997). Nonconscious behavioral confirmation processes: the self-fulfilling consequences of automatic stereotype activation. *Journal of Experimental Social Psychology, 33,* 541–560.

Cherry, E. C. (1953). Some experiments on the recognition of speech with one and with two ears. *Journal of the Acoustical Society of America, 25,* 975–979.

Cheyne, J. A. (1969). Punishment and reasoning in the development of self-control. Paper presented at the R. H. Walters Memorial Symposium at the Biennial Meeting of the Society for Research in Child Development, Santa Monica, CA.

Cheyne, J. A., Goyeche, J. R. M., and Walters, R. H. (1969). Attention, anxiety, and rules in resistance-to-deviation in children. *Journal of Experimental Child Psychology*, *8*, 127–139.

Chomsky, N. (1959). Review of Skinner's *Verbal behavior. Language, 35*, 26–58.

Christianson, S. A., and Nilsson, L. G. (1989). Hysterical amnesia: a case of aversively motivated isolation of memory. In T. Archer and L.-G. Nilsson (eds.), *Aversion, avoidance, and anxiety: perspectives on aversively motivated behavior* (pp. 289–310). Hillsdale, NJ: Erlbaum.

Claparède, E. (1911). Reconnaissance et moité. *Archives de Psychologie, 11*, 75–90.

Clifford, B. R., and George, R. (1996). A field evaluation of training in three methods of witness/victim investigative interviewing. *Psychology, Crime, and Law, 2*, 231–248.

Cofer, C. N. (1965). On some factors in the organizational characteristics of free recall. *American Psychologist, 20*, 261–272.

Cole, R. P., Barnet, R. C., and Miller, R. R. (1997). An evaluation of conditioned inhibition as defined by Rescorla's two-test strategy. *Learning and Motivation, 28*, 323–341.

Cole, R. P., and Miller, R. R. (1999). Conditioned excitation and conditioned inhibition acquired through backward conditioning. *Learning and Motivation, 30*, 129–156.

Coleman, E. B., Brown, A. L., and Rivkin, I. D. (1997). The effect of instructional explanations on learning from scientific texts. *Journal of the Learning Sciences, 6*, 347–365.

Collins, A. M., and Loftus, E. F. (1975). A spreading activation theory of semantic processing. *Psychological Review, 82*, 407–428.

Collins, A. M., and Quillian, M. R. (1969). Retrieval time from semantic memory. *Journal of Verbal Learning and Verbal Behavior, 8*, 240–247.

Collins, B. N., and Brandon, T. H. (2002). Effects of extinction context and retrieval cues on alcohol cue reactivity among nonalcoholic drinkers. *Journal of Consulting and Clinical Psychology, 70*, 390–397.

Colwill, R. M., and Motzkin, D. K. (1994). Encoding of the unconditioned stimulus in Pavlovian conditioning. *Animal Learning and Behavior, 22*, 384–394.

Colwill, R. M., and Rescorla, R. A. (1985). Postconditioning devaluation of a reinforcer affects instrumental responding. *Journal of Experimental Psychology: Animal Behavior Processes, 11*, 120–132.

(1986). Associative structures in instrumental learning. In G. H. Bower (ed.), *The psychology of learning and motivation* (vol. 20, pp. 55–104). New York: Academic Press.

Comroe, J. H., Jr., and Dripps, R. D. (1977). *The top ten clinical advances in cardiovascular-pulmonary medicine and surgery, 1945–1975*. Final report. January 31, 1977. Bethesda, MD: National Heart, Lung, and Blood Institute.

Conrad, C. (1972). Cognitive economy in semantic memory. *Journal of Experimental Psychology, 92*, 149–154.

Conway, A. R. A., Skitka, L. J., Hemmerich, J. A., and Kershaw, T. C. (2009). Flashbulb memory for 11 September 2001. *Applied Cognitive Psychology, 23*, 605–623.

Conway, M. A., Anderson, S. J., Larsen, S. F., Donnelly, C. M., McDaniel, M. A., McClelland, A. G. R., Rawles, R. E., and Logie, R. H. (1994). The formation of flashbulb memories. *Memory and Cognition, 22*, 326–343.

Conway, M. A., Cohen, G., and Stanhope, N. (1991). On the very long-term retention of knowledge acquired through formal education: twelve years of cognitive psychology. *Journal of Experimental Psychology: General, 120*, 395–409.

Cooper, L. D. (1991). Temporal factors in classical conditioning. *Learning and Motivation, 22*, 129–152.

Cowan, N. (2005). *Working memory capacity.* Hove: Psychology Press.

Craik, F. I. M., and Lockhart, R. S. (1972). Levels of processing: a framework for memory research. *Journal of Verbal Learning and Verbal Behavior, 11*, 671–684.

Craik, F. I. M., and Tulving, E. (1975). Depth of processing and the retention of words in episodic memory. *Journal of Experimental Psychology: General, 104*, 268–294.

Craik, F. I. M., and Watkins, M. J. (1973). The role of rehearsal in short-term memory. *Journal of Verbal Learning and Verbal Behavior, 12*, 599–607.

Crano, W. D., and Prislin, R. (2006). Attitudes and persuasion. *Annual Review of Psychology, 57*, 345–374.

Crespi, L. P. (1942). Quantitative variation in incentive and performance in the white rat. *American Journal of Psychology, 55*, 467–517.

Crombag, H. F. M., Wagenaar, W. A., and van Koppen, P. J. (1996). Crashing memories and the problem of "source monitoring." *Applied Cognitive Psychology, 10*, 95–104.

Cross, H., Holcomb, A., and Matter, C. G. (1967). Imprinting or exposure learning in rats given early auditory stimulation. *Psychonomic Science, 7*, 233–234.

Culler, E. A. (1938). Recent advances in some concepts of conditioning. *Psychological Review, 45*, 134–153.

Curran, T., and Hintzman, D. L. (1995). Violations of the independence assumption in process dissociation. *Journal of Experimental Psychology: Learning, Memory, and Cognition, 21*, 531–547.

Dando, C., Wilcock, R., Milne, R., and Henry, L. (2009). A modified cognitive interview procedure for frontline police investigators. *Applied Cognitive Psychology, 23*, 698–716.

Darwin, C. R. (1859). *On the origin of species by means of natural selection.* London: Murray.

(1920). *The descent of man, and selection in relation to sex* (2nd edn). New York: Appleton (first published 1871).

Davelaar, E. J., Goshen-Gottstein, Y., Ashkenazi, A., Haarmann, H. J., and Usher, M. (2005). The demise of short-term memory revisited: empirical and computational investigations of recency effects. *Psychological Review, 112*, 3–42.

Davis, M. (1974). Sensitization of the rat startle response by noise. *Journal of Comparative and Physiological Psychology, 87*, 571–581.

Dawes, R. M. (1971). *House of cards: psychology and psychotherapy built on myth.* New York: Free Press.

De Houwer, J., Crombez, G., and Baeyens, F. (2005). Avoidance behavior can function as a negative occasion setter. *Journal of Experimental Psychology: Animal Behavior Processes*, *31*, 101–106.

De Houwer, J., Thomas, S., and Baeyens, F. (2001). Associative learning of likes and dislikes: a review of 25 years of research on human evaluative conditioning. *Psychological Bulletin*, *127*, 853–869.

Deci, E. L., Koestner, R., and Ryan, R. M. (1999). A meta-analytic review of experiments examining the effects of extrinsic rewards on intrinsic motivation. *Psychological Bulletin*, *125*, 627–668.

Deci, E. L., and Ryan, R. M. (1980). The empirical exploration of intrinsic motivational processes. In L. Berkowitz (ed.), *Advances in experimental social psychology* (vol. 13, pp. 39–80). New York: Academic Press.

Deese, J. (1959). On the prediction of occurrence of particular verbal intrusions in immediate recall. *Journal of Experimental Psychology*, *58*, 17–22.

Defeyter, M. A., Russo, R., and McPartlin, P. L. (2009). The picture superiority effect in recognition memory: a developmental study using the response signal procedure. *Cognitive Development*, *24*, 265–273.

Deffenbacher, K. A., Bornstein, B. H., Penrod, S. D., and McGorty, E. K. (2004). A meta-analytic review of the effects of high stress on eyewitness memory. *Law and Human Behavior*, *28*, 687–706.

DeMarse, T. B., and Dockendorf, K. P. (2005). Adaptive flight control with living neuronal networks on microelectrode arrays. *Proceedings of the International Joint Conference on Neural Networks*, *3*, 1548–1551.

Dempster, F. N. (1996). Distributing and managing the conditions of encoding and practice. In E. L. Bjork and R. A. Bjork (eds.), *Memory* (pp. 317–344). San Diego, CA: Academic Press.

Denniston, J. C., Savastano, H. I., and Miller, R. R. (2001). The extended comparator hypothesis: learning by contiguity, responding by relative strength. In R. R. Mowrer and S. B. Klein (eds.), *Handbook of contemporary learning theories* (pp. 65–117). Mahwah, NJ: Erlbaum.

Depue, B. E., Banich, M. T., and Curran, T. (2007). Prefrontal regions orchestrate suppression of emotional memories via a two-phase process. *Science*, *317*, 215–219.

Descartes, R. (1650). The passions of the soul. In G. T. B. Ross (trans.), *The philosophical works of Descartes* (vol. 1, pp. 325–404). Cambridge: Cambridge University Press.

Desvousges, W. H., Johnson, R. F., Dunford, R. W., Boyle, K. J., Hudson, S. P., and Wilson, K. N. (1993). Measuring natural resource damages with contingent valuation: tests of validity and reliability. In J. A. Hausman (ed.), *Contingent valuation: a critical assessment* (pp. 91–164). Amsterdam: Elsevier.

Devlin, Lord. (1976). *Report to the Secretary of State for the Home Department of the Departmental Committee on Evidence of Identification in Criminal Cases*. London: Her Majesty's Stationery Office.

Dickinson, A. (1980). *Contemporary animal learning theory*. Cambridge: Cambridge University Press.

Dickinson, A., and Balleine, B. (2002). The role of learning in the operation of motivational systems. In H. Pashler and R. Gallistel (eds.), *Stevens' handbook of experimental psychology* (3rd edn, vol. 3: *Learning, motivation, and emotion*, pp. 497–533). New York: Wiley.

Dickinson, A., and Burke, J. (1996). Within-compound associations mediate the retrospective revaluation of causality judgements. *Quarterly Journal of Experimental Psychology, 49B*, 60–80.

Dickinson, A., Hall, G., and Mackintosh, N. J. (1976). Surprise and the attenuation of blocking. *Journal of Experimental Psychology: Animal Behavior Processes, 2*, 313–322.

Dickinson, A., Watt, A., and Griffiths, W. J. (1992). Free-operant acquisition with delayed reinforcement. *Quarterly Journal of Experimental Psychology: Comparative and Physiological Psychology, 45B*, 241–258.

Dienes, Z., and Altmann, G. T. M. (1997). Transfer of implicit knowledge across domains? How implicit and how abstract? In D. Berry (ed.), *How implicit is implicit learning?* (pp. 107–123). Oxford: Oxford University Press.

Dijksterhuis, A., Bos, M. W., Nordgren, L. F., and van Baaren, R. B. (2006). On making the right choice: the deliberation-without-attention effect. *Science, 311*, 1005–1007.

Dixon, M. R., Marley, J., and Jacobs, E. A. (2003). Delay discounting by pathological gamblers. *Journal of Applied Behavior Analysis, 36*, 449–458.

Domjan, M. (2003). *The principles of learning and behavior* (5th edn). Belmont, CA: Wadsworth.

Domjan, M., and Burkhard, B. (1986). *The principles of learning and behavior* (2nd edn). Pacific Grove, CA: Brooks/Cole.

Domjan, M., and Holloway, K. S. (1998). Sexual learning. In G. Greenberg and M. M. Harraway (eds.), *Comparative psychology: a handbook* (pp. 602–613). New York: Garland.

Donahoe, J. W. (2002). Behavior analysis and neuroscience. *Behavioural Processes, 57*, 241–259.

Donahoe, J. W., and Dorsel, V. P. (eds.) (1997). *Neural-network models of cognition: biobehavioral foundations*. Amsterdam: Elsevier.

Dooling, D. J., and Christiansen, R. E. (1977). Episodic and semantic aspects of memory for prose. *Journal of Experimental Psychology, 3*, 428–436.

Doyère, V., Debiec, J., Monfils, M., Schafe, G. E., and LeDoux, J. E. (2007). Synapse-specific reconsolidation of distinct fear memories in the lateral amygdala. *Nature Neuroscience, 10*, 414–416.

Drabman, R. S., Spitalnik, R., and O'Leary, K. D. (1973). Teaching self-control to disruptive children. *Journal of Abnormal Psychology, 82*, 10–16.

Drobes, D. J., Saladin, M. E., and Tiffany, S. T. (2001). Classical conditioning mechanisms in alcohol dependence. In N. Heather, T. J. Peters, and T. Stockwell (eds.), *International handbook of alcohol dependence and problems* (pp. 281–297). New York: Wiley.

Droungas, A., Ehrman, R. N., Childress, A. R., and O'Brien, C. P. (1995). Effect of smoking cues and cigarette availability on craving and smoking behaviour. *Addictive Behaviors, 20,* 657–673.

Dudai, Y. (2004). The neurobiology of consolidations, or, how stable is the engram? *Annual Review of Psychology, 55,* 51–86.

Dutton, D. G., and Aron, A. P. (1974). Some evidence for heightened sexual attraction under conditions of high anxiety. *Journal of Personality and Social Psychology, 30,* 510–517.

Düzel, E., Vargha-Khadem, F., Heinze, H. J., and Mishkin, M. (2001). Hippocampal damage affects brain indices of episodic but not semantic memory. *Proceedings of the National Academy of Sciences, USA, 98,* 8101–8106.

Düzel, E., Yonelinas, A. P., Mangun, G. R., Heinze, H. J., and Tulving, E. (1997). Event-related brain potential correlates of two states of conscious awareness in memory. *Proceedings of the National Academy of Sciences, USA, 94,* 5973–5978.

Dweck, C. S., and Licht, B. G. (1980). Learned helplessness and intellectual achievement. In J. Garber and M. E. P. Seligman (eds.), *Human helplessness: theory and applications* (pp. 197–221). New York: Academic Press.

Dweck, C. S., and Repucci, N. D. (1973). Learned helplessness and reinforcement responsibility in children. *Journal of Personality and Social Psychology, 25,* 109–116.

Dywan, J. (1995). The illusion of familiarity: an alternative to the report-criterion account of hypnotic recall. *International Journal of Clinical and Experimental Hypnosis, 53,* 194–211.

Easterbrook, J. A. (1959). The effect of emotion on cue utilization and the organization of behavior. *Psychological Review, 66,* 183–201.

Ebbinghaus, H. (1913). *Memory: a contribution to experimental psychology,* trans. H. A. Ruger and C. E. Bussenius. New York: Columbia University, Teacher's College (first published 1885).

Eich, E., Geraerts, E., Schooler, J. W., and Forgas, J. P. (2008). Memory in and about affect. In H. L. Roediger III (ed.), *Learning and memory: a comprehensive reference,* vol. 2: *Cognitive psychology of memory* (pp. 239–260). New York: Academic Press.

Eichenbaum, H., and Cohen, N. J. (2001). *From conditioning to conscious recollection: memory systems of the brain.* Oxford: Oxford University Press.

Eikelboom, R., and Stewart, J. (1982). Conditioning of drug-induced physiological responses. *Psychological Review, 89,* 507–528.

Eikeseth, S., Smith, T., Jahr, E., and Eldevik, S. (2002). Intensive behavioural treatment at school for 4- to 7-year-old children with autism: a 1-year comparison controlled study. *Behavior Modification, 26,* 49–68.

Einhorn, H. J. (1972). Expert measurement and mechanical combination. *Organizational Behavior and Human Performance, 7,* 86–106.

Elkins, R. L. (1991). An appraisal of chemical aversion (emetic therapy) approaches to alcoholism treatment. *Behaviour Research and Therapy, 29,* 387–413.

Ellis, N. C., and Hennelly, R. A. (1980). A bilingual word-length effect: implications for intelligence testing and the relative ease of mental calculation in Welsh and English. *British Journal of Psychology, 71,* 43–52.

Enzle, M. E., and Ross, J. M. (1978). Increasing and decreasing intrinsic interest with contingent rewards: a test of cognitive evaluation theory. *Journal of Experimental and Social Psychology, 14,* 588–597.

Epstein, S. (1994). Integration of the cognitive and the psychodynamic unconscious. *American Psychologist, 49,* 709–724.

Erdelyi, M. H. (2006). The unified theory of repression. *Behavioral and Brain Sciences, 29,* 499–511.

Ericsson, K. A. (2008). Superior memory of mnemonists and experts in various domains. In H. L. Roediger III (ed.), *Learning and memory: a comprehensive reference*, vol. 2: *Cognitive psychology of memory* (pp. 809–817). New York: Academic Press.

Ericsson, K. A., and Charness, N. (1994). Expert performance: its structure and acquisition. *American Psychologist, 49,* 725–747.

Ericsson, K. A., and Kintsch, W. (1995). Long-term working memory. *Psychological Review, 102,* 211–245.

Ericsson, K. A., Krampe, R. T., and Tesch-Römer, C. (1993). The role of deliberate practice in the acquisition of expert performance. *Psychological Review, 100,* 363–406.

Eron, L. D., Walder, L. O., Toigo, R., and Lefkowitz, M. M. (1963). Social class, parental punishment for aggression, and child aggression. *Child Development, 34,* 849–867.

Escobar, M., Arcediano, F., and Miller, R. R. (2002). Latent inhibition and contextual associations. *Journal of Experimental Psychology: Animal Behavior Processes, 28,* 123–136.

Estes, W. K., and Skinner, B. F. (1941). Some quantitative properties of anxiety. *Journal of Experimental Psychology, 29,* 390–400.

Etscorn, F., and Stephens, R. (1973). Establishment of conditioned taste aversions with a 24-hour CS–US interval. *Physiological Psychology, 1,* 251–259.

Evans, J. St. B. T. (2008). Dual-processing accounts of reasoning, judgement, and social cognition. *Annual Review of Psychology, 59,* 255–278.

Fazio, R. H., and Olson, M. A. (2003). Implicit measures in social cognition research: their meaning and use. *Annual Review of Psychology, 54,* 297–327.

Feehan, G. G., and Enzle, M. E. (1991). Subjective control over rewards: effects of perceived choice of reward schedule on intrinsic motivation and behavior maintenance. *Perceptual and Motor Skills, 72,* 995–1006.

Field, A. P., and Davey, G. C. L. (1999). Reevaluating conditioning: a nonassociative explanation of conditioning effects in the visual evaluative conditioning paradigm. *Journal of Experimental Psychology: Animal Behavior Processes, 25,* 211–224.

Field, A. P., and Moore, A. C. (2005). Dissociating the effects of attention and contingency awareness on evaluative conditioning effects in the visual paradigm. *Cognition and Emotion, 19,* 217–243.

Fisher, R. P., and Geiselman, R. E. (1992). *Memory-enhancing techniques for investigative interviewing: the cognitive interview.* Springfield, IL: Charles C. Thomas.

Fisher, R. P., Geiselman, R. E., and Amador, M. (1989). Field test of the cognitive interview: enhancing the recollection of actual victims and witnesses of crime. *Journal of Applied Psychology, 74,* 722–727.

Fisher, R. P., Geiselman, R. E., and Raymond, D. S. (1987). Critical analysis of police interview techniques. *Journal of Police Science and Administration, 15,* 177–185.

Fisher, R. P., and Schreiber, N. (2007). Interview protocols to improve eyewitness memory. In M. P. Toglia, J. D. Read, D. F. Ross, and R. C. L. Lindsay (eds.), *Handbook of eyewitness psychology,* vol. 1: *Memory for events* (pp. 53–80). Mahwah, NJ: Erlbaum.

Fixsen, D. L., Phillips, E. L., Baron, R. L., Coughlin, D. D., Daly, D. L., and Daly, P. B. (1978). The Boys' Town revolution. *Human Nature, 1,* 54–61.

Flaherty, C. F. (1996). *Incentive relativity.* New York: Cambridge University Press.

Flor, H., Birbaumer, N., Schulz, R., Grüsser, S. M., and Mucha, R. F. (2002). Pavlovian conditioning of opioid and nonopioid pain inhibitory mechanisms in humans. *European Journal of Pain, 6,* 395–402.

Foster, C. A., Witcher, B. S., Campbell, W. K., and Green, J. D. (1998). Arousal and attraction: evidence for automatic and controlled processes. *Journal of Personality and Social Psychology, 74,* 86–101.

Fouts, R. S., Hirsch, A. D., and Fouts, D. H. (1982). Cultural transmission of a human language in a chimpanzee mother–infant relationship. In H. E. Fitzgerald, J. A. Mullins, and P. Gage (eds.), *Child nurturance,* vol. 3: *Studies of development in nonhuman primates* (pp. 159–193). New York: Plenum.

Fowler, H., and Miller, N. E. (1963). Facilitation and inhibition of runway performance by hind and forepaw shock of various intensities. *Journal of Comparative Physiological Psychology, 56,* 801–805.

Fox, D. K., Hopkins, B. L., and Anger, W. K. (1987). The long-term effects of a token economy on safety performance in open-pit mining. *Journal of Applied Behavior Analysis, 20,* 215–224.

Fox, L. (1966). Effecting the use of efficient study habits. In R. Ulrich, T. Stachnik, and J. Mabry (eds.), *Control of human behavior* (vol. 1, pp. 85–90). Glenview, IL: Scott, Foresman.

Gabbert, F., Hope, L., and Fisher, R. P. (2009). Protecting eyewitness evidence: examining the efficacy of a self-administered interview tool. *Law and Human Behavior, 33,* 298–307.

Gable, P. A., and Harmon-Jones, E. (2008). Approach-motivate positive affect reduces breadth of attention. *Psychological Science, 19,* 476–482.

Gallo, D. A., Meadow, N. G., Johnson, E. L., and Foster, K. T. (2008). Deep levels of processing elicit a distinctiveness heuristic: evidence from the criteria recollection task. *Journal of Memory and Language, 58,* 1095–1111.

Garcia, J., and Koelling, R. A. (1966). Relation of cue to consequence in avoidance learning. *Psychonomic Science, 4,* 123–124.

Gardiner, J. M. (1988). Functional aspects of recollective experience. *Memory and Cognition, 16,* 309–313.

Gardner, R. A., Gardner, B. T., and Van Cantfort, T. E. (1989). *Teaching sign language to chimpanzees*. New York: State University of New York Press.

Garry, M., and Polaschek, D. L. L. (2000). Imagination and memory. *Current Directions in Psychological Science, 9,* 6–10.

Gathercole, S. E., and Baddeley, A. D. (1989). Development of vocabulary in children and short-term phonological memory. *Journal of Memory and Language, 28,* 200–213.

Geen, R. G. (1985). Test anxiety and visual vigilance. *Journal of Personality and Social Psychology, 49,* 963–970.

Gelbard-Sagiv, H., Mukamel, R., Harel, M., Malach, R., and Fried, I. (2008). Internally generated reactivation of single neurons in human hippocampus during free recall. *Science, 322,* 96–101.

Geraerts, E., Schooler, J. W., Merckelbach, H., Jelicic, M., Hauer, B. J. A., and Ambadar, A. (2007). The reality of recovered memories: corroborating continuous and discontinuous memories of childhood sexual abuse. *Psychological Science, 18,* 564–568.

Gernsbacher, M. A. (1985). Surface information loss in comprehension. *Cognitive Psychology, 17,* 324–363.

Gershoff, E. T. (2002). Corporal punishment by parents and associated child behaviors and experiences: a meta-analytic and theoretical review. *Psychological Bulletin, 128,* 539–579.

Gershoff, E. T., and Bitensky, S. H. (2007). The case against corporal punishment of children: converging evidence from social science research and international human rights law and implications for U.S. public policy. *Psychology, Public Policy, and Law, 13,* 231–272.

Gerull, F. C., and Rapee, R. M. (2002). Mother knows best: the effects of maternal modelling on the acquisition of fear and avoidance behaviour in toddlers. *Behaviour Research and Therapy, 40,* 279–287.

Gesch, C. B., Hammond, S. M., Hampson, S. E., Eves, A., and Crowder, M. J. (2002). Influence of supplementary vitamins, minerals and essential fatty acids on the antisocial behaviour of young adult prisoners: randomised, placebo-controlled trial. *British Journal of Psychiatry, 181,* 22–28.

Ghetti, S., Edelstine, R. S., Goodman, G. S., Cordòn, I. M., Quas, J. A., Alexander, K. W., Redlich, A. D., and Jones, D. P. H. (2006). What can subjective forgetting tell us about memory for childhood trauma? *Memory and Cognition, 34,* 1011–1025.

Ghirlanda, S. (2005). Retrospective revaluation as simple associative learning. *Journal of Experimental Psychology: Animal Behavior Processes, 31,* 107–111.

Gigerenzer, G., and Selten, R. (2001). Rethinking rationality. In G. Gigerenzer and R. Selten (eds.), *Bounded rationality: the adaptive toolbox* (pp. 1–12). Cambridge, MA: MIT Press.

Gilovich, T. (1991). *How we know what isn't so*. New York: Free Press.

Gilovich, T., Vallone, R., and Tversky, A. (1985). The hot hand in basketball: on the misperception of random sequences. *Cognitive Psychology, 17*, 295–314.

Glenberg, A. M., Smith, S. M., and Green, C. (1977). Type I rehearsal: maintenance and more. *Journal of Verbal Learning and Verbal Behavior, 16*, 339–352.

Gluck, M. A., and Bower, G. H. (1988). From conditioning to category learning: an adaptive network model. *Journal of Experimental Psychology: General, 117*, 227–247.

Glueck, S., and Glueck, E. (1950). *Unraveling juvenile delinquency.* Cambridge, MA: Harvard University Press.

Godden, D., and Baddeley, A. D. (1975). Context-dependent memory in two natural environments: on land and under water. *British Journal of Psychology, 66*, 325–331.

Goff, L. M., and Roediger, H. L., III (1998). Imagination inflation for action events: repeated imaginings lead to illusory recollections. *Memory and Cognition, 26*, 20–33.

Goldacre, B. (2007). *The end of homeopathy?* Retrieved from www.badscience.net/2007/11/a-kind-of-magic.

(2008). *Bad science.* London: Fourth Estate.

Goldiamond, I. (1965). Self-control procedures in personal behavior problems. *Psychological Reports, 17*, 851–868.

Goldsmith, M., Koriat, A., and Pansky, A. (2005). Strategic regulation of grain size in memory reporting over time. *Journal of Memory and Language, 52*, 505–525.

Goldstein, H., Krantz, D. L., and Rains, J. D. (1965). *Controversial issues in learning.* New York: Appleton-Century-Crofts.

Goldstone, R. L. (1998). Perceptual learning. *Annual Review of Psychology, 49*, 585–612.

Gollwitzer, P. M., and Sheeran, P. (2006). Implementation intentions and goal achievement: a meta-analysis of effects and processes. *Advances in Experimental Social Psychology, 38*, 69–119.

Goodwin, D. W., Crane, J. B., and Guze, S. B. (1969). Phenomenological aspects of the alcoholic "blackout." *British Journal of Psychiatry, 115*, 1033–1038.

Goodwin, D. W., Powell, B., Bremer, D., Hoine, H., and Stern, J. (1969). Alcohol and recall: state dependent effects in man. *Science, 163*, 1358.

Gorfein, D. S., and Hoffman, R. R. (eds.) (1987). *Memory and learning: the Ebbinghaus Centennial Conference.* Hillsdale, NJ: Erlbaum.

Gormezano, I., Kehoe, E. J., and Marshall, B. S. (1983). Twenty years of classical conditioning research with the rabbit. In J. M. Prague and A. N. Epstein (eds.), *Progress in psychobiology and physiological psychology* (vol. 10, pp. 197–275). New York: Academic Press.

Gorn, G. J. (1982). The effects of music in advertising on choice behavior: a classical conditioning approach. *Journal of Marketing, 46*, 94–101.

Graf, P., and Schacter, D. L. (1985). Implicit and explicit memory for new associations in normal and amnesic subjects. *Journal of Experimental Psychology: Learning, Memory, and Cognition, 11*, 501–518.

Graf, P., Squire, L. R., and Mandler, G. (1984). The information that amnesic patients do not forget. *Journal of Experimental Psychology: Learning, Memory, and Cognition*, *10*, 164–178.

Graham, S., and Lowery, B. S. (2004). Priming unconscious racial stereotypes about adolescent offenders. *Law and Human Behavior*, *28*, 483–504.

Green, L., and Myerson, J. (2004). A discounting framework for choice with delayed and probabilistic rewards. *Psychological Bulletin*, *130*, 769–792.

Greene, R. L. (2008). Repetition and spacing effects. In H. L. Roediger III (ed.), *Learning and memory: a comprehensive reference*, vol. 2: *Cognitive psychology of memory* (pp. 65–78). New York: Academic Press.

Greenwald, A., and Banaji, M. (1995). Implicit social cognition: attitudes, self-esteem and stereotypes. *American Psychologist*, *47*, 766–790.

Grice, G. R. (1968). Stimulus intensity and response evocation. *Psychological Review*, *75*, 359–373.

Griffiths, H., and Craighead, W. E. (1972). Generalization in operant speech therapy for misarticulation. *Journal of Speech and Hearing Disorders*, *37*, 485–494.

Grolnick, W. S., and Ryan, R. M. (1989). Parent styles associated with children's self-regulation and competence in school. *Journal of Educational Psychology*, *81*, 143–154.

Gross, C. G., Bender, D. B., and Rocha-Miranda, C. E. (1969). Visual receptive fields of neurons in inferotemporal cortex of the monkey. *Science*, *166*, 1303–1306.

Groves, P. M., and Thompson, R. F. (1970). Habituation: a dual-process theory. *Psychological Review*, *77*, 419–450.

Gustavson, C. R., Garcia, J., Hankins, W. G., and Rusiniak, K. W. (1974). Coyote predation control by aversive conditioning. *Science*, *184*, 581–583.

Guttman, N., and Kalish, H. I. (1956). Discriminability and stimulus generalization. *Journal of Experimental Psychology*, *51*, 79–88.

Haidt, J. (2001). The emotional dog and its rational tail: a social intuitionist approach to moral judgment. *Psychological Review*, *108*, 814–834.

Hall, G. (2002). Associative structures in Pavlovian and instrumental conditioning. In H. Pashler and C. R. Gallistel (eds.), *Stevens' handbook of experimental psychology* (3rd edn), vol. 3: *Learning, motivation, and emotion* (pp.1–45). New York: Wiley.

(2008). Perceptual learning. In J. Byrne and R. Menzel (eds.), *Learning and memory: a comprehensive reference*, vol. 1: *Learning theory and behavior* (pp. 103–121). Amsterdam: Elsevier.

Hall, J. F. (1971). *Verbal learning and retention*. Philadelphia, PA: Lippincott.

Hall, R. V., Axelrod, S., Tyler, L., Grief, E., Jones, F. C., and Robertson, R. (1972). Modification of behavior problems in the home with a parent as observer and experimenter. *Journal of Applied Behavior Analysis*, *5*, 53–64.

Hall, R. V., Lund, D., and Jackson, D. (1968). Effects of teacher attention on study behavior. *Journal of Applied Behavior Analysis*, *1*, 1–12.

Hall, S. M., Rugg, D., Tunstall, C., and Jones, R. T. (1984). Preventing relapse to cigarette smoking by behavioral skill training. *Journal of Consulting and Clinical Psychology*, *52*, 372–382.

Hamilton, M., and Geraci, L. (2006). The picture superiority effect in conceptual implicit memory: a conceptual distinctiveness hypothesis. *American Journal of Psychology*, *119*, 1–20.

Hamilton, W. (1859). *Lectures on metaphysics and logic* (vol. 1). Edinburgh: Blackwood.

Hardt, O., Einarsson, E. Ö., and Nader, K. (2010). A bridge over troubled water: reconsolidation as a link between cognitive and neuroscientific memory research traditions. *Annual Review of Psychology*, *61*, 141–167.

Harlow, H. F., and Harlow, M. K. (1965). The affectional systems. In A. M. Schrier, H. F. Harlow, and F. Stollnitz (eds.), *Behavior of nonhuman primates* (vol. 2, pp. 287–334). New York: Academic Press.

Harris, J. A., Jones, M. L., Bailey, G. K., and Westbrook, R. F. (2000). Contextual control over conditioned responding in an extinction paradigm. *Journal of Experimental Psychology: Animal Behavior Processes*, *26*, 174–185.

Hart, B., and Risley, T. R. (1995). *Meaningful differences in the everyday experience of young American children*. Baltimore, MD: Paul H. Brookes.

(2003). The early catastrophe: the 30 million word gap by age 3. *American Educator*, *22*, 4–9.

Hartshorne, H., and May, M. A. (1928). *Studies in deceit*. New York: Macmillan.

Hassin, R. R., Ferguson, M. J., Kardosh, R., Porter, S. C., Carter, T. J., and Dudareva, V. (2009). Précis of implicit nationalism. *Annals of the New York Academy of Sciences*, *1167*, 135–145.

Hassin, R. R., Ferguson, M. J., Shidlovski, D., and Gross, T. (2007). Subliminal exposure to national flags affects political thought and behavior. *Proceedings of the National Academy of Sciences*, *104*, 19,757–19,761.

Hayes, K., and Hayes, C. (1951). The intellectual development of a home-raised chimpanzee. *Proceedings of the American Philosophical Society*, *95*, 105–109.

Hayes, S. C., and Ju, W. (1998). The applied implications of rule-governed behavior. In W. T. O'Donohue (ed.), *Learning and behavior therapy* (pp. 374–391). Needham Heights, MA: Allyn & Bacon.

Hayes, S. C., Rosenfarb, I., Wulfert, E., Munt, E. D., Korn, Z., and Zettle, R. D. (1985). Self-reinforcement effects: an artifact of social standard setting? *Journal of Applied Behavior Analysis*, *18*, 201–214.

Hearst, E., and Jenkins, H. M. (1974). *Sign-tracking: the stimulus-reinforcer relation and directed action*. Austin, TX: Psychonomic Society.

Heath, R. G. (1963). Electrical self-stimulation of the brain in man. *American Journal of Psychiatry*, *120*, 571–577.

Hebb, D. O. (1949). *Organization of behavior*. New York: Wiley.

Hefferline, R. F., Keenan, B., and Harford, R. A. (1959). Escape and avoidance conditioning in human subjects without their observation of the response. *Science*, *130*, 1338–1339.

Henderlong, J., and Lepper, M. R. (2002). The effects of praise on children's intrinsic motivation: a review and synthesis. *Psychological Bulletin*, *128*, 774–795.

Henry, B., Moffitt, T. E., Caspi, A., Langley, J. D., and Silva, P. A. (1994). On the "remembrance of things past": a longitudinal evaluation of the retrospective method. *Psychological Assessment*, *6*, 92–101.

Herbert, E. W., Pinkston, E. M., Hayden, M. L., Sajwaj, T. E., Pinkston, S., Cordua, G., and Jackson, C. (1973). Adverse effects of differential parental attention. *Journal of Applied Behavior Analysis*, *6*, 15–30.

Herman, L. M., Matus, D. S., Herman, E. Y. K., Ivancic, M., and Pack, A. A. (2001). The bottlenosed dophin's (*Tursiops truncatus*) understanding of gestures as symbolic representations of its body parts. *Animal Learning and Behavior*, *29*, 250–264.

Herrnstein, R. J. (1961). Relative and absolute strength of responses as a function of frequency of reinforcement. *Journal of the Experimental Analysis of Behaviour*, *4*, 267–272.

Herrnstein, R. J., Loveland, D. H., and Cable, C. (1976). Natural concepts in pigeons. *Journal of Experimental Psychology: Animal Behavior Processes*, *2*, 285–311.

Heyman, J., and Ariely, D. (2004). Effort for payment: a tale of two markets. *Psychological Science*, *15*, 787–793.

Hintzman, D. L. (1978). *The psychology of learning and memory*. San Francisco: Freeman.

(1988). Judgments of frequency and recognition memory in a multiple-trace memory model. *Psychological Review*, *95*, 528–551.

Hipwell, A., Keenan, K., Kasza, K., Stouthamer-Loeber, M., Bean, T., and Loeber, R. (2008). Reciprocal influences between girls' conduct problems and depression, and parental punishment and warmth: a six year prospective analysis. *Journal of Abnormal Child Psychology*, *36*, 663–677.

Hirst, W. (1988). Improving memory. In M. S. Gazzaniga (ed.), *Perspectives in memory research* (pp. 219–244). Cambridge, MA: MIT Press.

Hochauser, M., and Fowler, H. (1975). Cue effects of drive and reward as a function of discrimination difficulty: evidence against the Yerkes-Dodson law. *Journal of Experimental Psychology: Animal Behavior Processes*, *1*, 261–269.

Hockey, G. R. J., Davies, S., and Gray, M. M. (1972). Forgetting as a function of sleep at different times of day. *Quarterly Journal of Experimental Psychology*, *24*, 386–393.

Hockley, W. E. (2008). The effects of environmental context on recognition memory and claims of remembering. *Journal of Experimental Psychology: Learning, Memory, and Cognition*, *34*, 1412–1429.

Hoffman, H. (2011). Hot and bothered: classical conditioning of sexual incentives in humans. In T. R. Schachtman and S. Reilly (eds.), *Associative learning and conditioning theory: human and non-human applications*. Oxford: Oxford University Press.

Hoffman, M. L. (1989). Empathy, social cognition, and moral action. In W. Kurtines and J. Gewirtz (eds.), *Moral behavior and development: advances in theory, research and application* (vol. 1, pp. 275–301). Hillsdale, NJ: Erlbaum.

Hoffmann, H., Janssen, E., and Turner, S. (2004). Classical conditioning of sexual arousal in women and men: effects of varying awareness and biological relevance of the CS. *Archives of Sexual Behavior*, *33*, 43–53.

Hollis, K. L. (1982). Pavlovian conditioning of signal-centered action patterns and autonomic behavior: a biological analysis of function. *Advances in the Study of Behavior, 12*, 1–64.

Hollis, K. L., Pharr, V. L., Dumas, M. J., Britton, G. B., and Field, J. (1997). Classical conditioning provides paternity advantage for territorial male blue gouramis (*Trichogaster trichopterus*). *Journal of Comparative Psychology, 111*, 219–225.

Homme, L. W., deBaca, P. C., Devine, J. V., Steinhorst, R., and Rickert, E. J. (1963). Use of the Premack principle in controlling the behavior of nursery school children. *Journal of the Experimental Analysis of Behavior, 6*, 544.

Honig, W. K., and Slivka, R. M. (1964). Stimulus generalization of the effects of punishment. *Journal of the Experimental Analysis of Behavior, 7*, 21–25.

Hoosain, R., and Salili, F. (1988). Language differences, working memory, and mathematical ability. In M. M. Gruneberg, P. E. Morris, and R. N. Sykes (eds.), *Practical aspects of memory: current research and issues*, vol. 2: *Clinical and educational implications* (pp. 512–517). Chichester: Wiley.

Howard, J. S., Sparkman, C. R., Cohen, H. G., Green, G., and Stanislaw, H. (2005). A comparison of intensive behavior analytic and eclectic treatments for young children with autism. *Research on Developmental Disabilities, 26*, 359–383.

Howes, D. H., and Solomon, R. L. (1951). Visual duration threshold as a function of word probability. *Journal of Experimental Psychology, 41*, 401–410.

Hubel, D. H., and Wiesel, T. N. (1962). Receptive fields, binocular interaction, and functional architecture in the cat's visual cortex. *Journal of Physiology, 166*, 106–154.

(1979). Brain mechanisms and vision. *Scientific American, 241(3)*, 150–162.

Huesmann, L. R., Moise-Titus, J., Podolski, C.-L., and Eron, L. D. (2003). Longitudinal relations between children's exposure to TV violence and their aggressive and violent behavior in young adulthood: 1977–1992. *Developmental Psychology, 39*, 201–221.

Hull, C. L. (1943). *Principles of behavior.* New York: Appleton-Century-Crofts.

Hyman, I. E., and Billings, F. J. (1998). Individual differences and the creation of false childhood memories. *Memory, 6*, 1–20.

Hyman, I. E., and Pentland, J. (1996). The role of mental imagery in the creation of false childhood memories. *Journal of Memory and Language, 35*, 101–117.

Innocence Project (2010). *Facts on postconviction DNA exonerations.* Retrieved from www.innocenceproject.org/Content/Facts_on_PostConviction_DNA_Exonerations.php.

Jacobsen, P. B., Bovbjerg, D. H., Schwartz, M. D., Andrykowski, M. A., Futterman, A. D., Gilewski, T., Norton, L., and Redd, W. H. (1993). Formation of food aversions in cancer patients receiving repeated infusions of chemotherapy. *Behaviour Research and Therapy, 31*, 739–748.

Jacoby, L. L. (1991). A process dissociation framework: separating automatic from intentional uses of memory. *Journal of Memory and Language, 30*, 513–541.

Jacoby, L. L., and Dallas, M. (1981). On the relationship between autobiographical and perceptual learning. *Journal of Experimental Psychology: General, 110*, 306–340.

James, W. (1893). *Principles of psychology* (vol. 1). New York: Holt.

Jang, Y., and Huber, D. E. (2008). Context retrieval and context change in free recall: recalling from long-term memory drives list isolation. *Journal of Experimental Psychology: Learning, Memory, and Cognition, 34*, 112–127.

Janis, I. L., Kaye, D., and Kirschner, P. (1965). Facilitating effects of "eating-while-reading" on responsiveness to persuasive communications. *Journal of Personality and Social Psychology, 1*, 181–186.

Jeffries, S., and Everatt, J. (2004). Working memory: its role in dyslexia and other specific learning difficulties. *Dyslexia, 10*, 196–214.

Jenkins, H. M., Barrera, F. J., Ireland, C., and Woodside, B. (1978). Signal-centered action patterns of dogs in appetitive classical conditioning. *Learning and Motivation, 9*, 272–296.

Jenkins, H. M., and Moore, B. R. (1973). The form of the autoshaped response with food or water reinforcers. *Journal of the Experimental Analysis of Behavior, 20*, 163–181.

Jenkins, J. G., and Dallenbach, K. M. (1924). Oblivescence during sleeping and waking. *American Journal of Psychology, 35*, 605–612.

Johnson, E. J., Hershey, J., Meszaros, J., and Kunreuther, H. (1993). Framing, probability distortions, and insurance decisions. *Journal of Risk and Uncertainty, 7*, 35–51.

Johnson, M. K., Hashtroudi, S., and Lindsay, D. S. (1993). Source monitoring. *Psychological Bulletin, 114*, 3–28.

Johnson, M. K., and Raye, C. L. (1981). Reality monitoring. *Psychological Review, 88*, 67–85.

Johnson, M. K., Raye, C. L., Wang, A. Y., and Taylor, T. H. (1979). Fact and fantasy: the roles of accuracy and variability in confusing imaginations with perceptual experiences. *Journal of Experimental Psychology: Human Learning and Memory, 5*, 229–240.

Johnson, R. D. (1987). Making judgments when information is missing: inferences, biases, and framing effects. *Acta Psychologica, 66*, 69–72.

Johnston, W. A., and Heinz, S. P. (1978). Flexibility and capacity demands of attention. *Journal of Experimental Psychology: General, 107*, 420–435.

Jones, A., Wilkinson, H. J., and Braden, I. (1961). Information deprivation as a motivational variable. *Journal of Experimental Psychology, 62*, 126–137.

Jones, M. C. (1924). The elimination of children's fears. *Journal of Experimental Psychology, 7*, 382–390.

Jonides, J., Lacey, S. C., and Nee, D. E. (2005). Processes of working memory in mind and brain. *Current Directions in Psychological Science, 14*, 2–5.

Jonides, J., Lewis, R. L., Nee, D. E., Lusting, C. A., Berman, M. G., and Moore, K. S. (2008). The mind and brain of short-term memory. *Annual Review of Psychology, 59*, 193–224.

Josephson, W. L. (1987). Television violence and children's aggression: testing the priming, social script, and disinhibition predictions. *Journal of Personality and Social Psychology, 53*, 882–890.

Kahneman, D. (1973). *Attention and effort*. Englewood Cliffs, NJ: Prentice-Hall.

(2003). A perspective on judgment and choice: mapping bounded rationality. *American Psychologist, 58,* 697–720.

Kahneman, D., and Frederick, S. (2002). Representativeness revisited: attribute substitution in intuitive judgement. In T. Gilovich, D. Griffin, and D. Kahneman (eds.), *Heuristics and biases* (pp. 49–81). New York: Cambridge University Press.

Kahneman, D., and Ritov, I. (1994). Determinants of stated willingness to pay for public goods: a study in the headline method. *Journal of Risk and Uncertainty, 9,* 5–38.

Kahneman, D., Ritov, I., and Schkade, D. (1999). Economic preferences or attitude expressions? An analysis of dollar responses to public issues. *Journal of Risk and Uncertainty, 19,* 203–237.

Kahneman, D., and Tversky, A. (1979). Prospect theory: an analysis of decision under risk. *Econometrica, 47,* 263–291.

Kamin, L. J. (1969). Predictability, surprise, attention, and conditioning. In B. A. Campbell and R. M. Church (eds.), *Punishment and aversive behavior* (pp. 279–296). New York: Appleton-Century-Crofts.

Kandel, H. J., Ayllon, T., and Roberts, M. D. (1976). Rapid educational rehabilitation for prison inmates. *Behavior Research and Therapy, 14,* 323–331.

Kanfer, F. H., and Seidner, M. L. (1973). Self-control: factors enhancing tolerance of noxious stimulation. *Journal of Personality and Social Psychology, 25,* 381–389.

Karazinov, D. M., and Boakes, R. A. (2007). Second-order conditioning in human predictive judgements when there is little time to think. *Quarterly Journal of Experimental Psychology, 60,* 448–460.

Karpicke, J. D., Butler, A. C., and Roediger, H. L. (2009). Metacognitive strategies in student learning: do students practise retrieval when they study on their own? *Memory, 17,* 471–479.

Karpicke, J. D., and Roediger, H. L. (2010). Is expanding retrieval a superior method for learning text materials? *Memory and Cognition, 38,* 116–124.

Kasper, C. J., and Alford, J. M. (1988). Redecision and men who sexually abuse children. *Transactional Analysis Journal, 18,* 309–315.

Kaufman, J., and Zigler, E. (1987). Do abused children become abusive parents? *American Journal of Orthopsychiatry, 57,* 186–192.

Kaye, H., and Pearce, J. M. (1984). The strength of the orienting response during Pavlovian conditioning. *Journal of Experimental Psychology: Animal Behavior Processes, 10,* 90–109.

(1987). Hippocampal lesions attenuate latent inhibition and the decline of the orienting response in rats. *Quarterly Journal of Experimental Psychology, 39,* 107–125.

Keenan, J. M., MacWhinney, B., and Mayhew, D. (1977). Pragmatics in memory: a study of natural conversion. *Journal of Verbal Learning and Verbal Behavior, 16,* 549–560.

Kelley, C. M., and Lindsay, D. S. (1996). Conscious and unconscious forms of memory. In E. L. Bjork and R. A. Bjork (eds.), *Memory* (pp. 31–63). San Diego, CA: Academic Press.

Kellman, P. J. (2002). Perceptual learning. In D. Medin and H. Pashler (eds.), *Steven's handbook of experimental psychology*, vol. 2: *Memory and cognitive processes* (3rd edn, pp. 259–299). New York: Wiley.

Kendall-Tackett, K. A., Williams, L. M., and Finkelhor, D. (1993). Impact of sexual abuse on children: a review and synthesis of recent empirical studies. *Psychological Bulletin*, *113*, 164–180.

Keppel, G., and Underwood, B. J. (1962). Proactive inhibition in short-term retention of single items. *Journal of Verbal Learning and Verbal Behavior*, *1*, 153–161.

Kihlstrom, J. F., McNally, R. J., Loftus, E. F., and Pope, H. G. Jr. (2005). The problem of child sex abuse [Letter to the editor]. *Science*, *309*, 1182–1183.

Kimble, G. A., Mann, L. I., and Dufort, R. H. (1955). Classical and instrumental eyelid conditioning. *Journal of Experimental Psychology*, *49*, 407–417.

Kinjo, H., and Snodgrass, J. G. (2000). Does the generation effect occur for pictures? *American Journal of Psychology*, *113*, 95–121.

Kintsch, W. (1985). Reflections on Ebbinghaus. *Journal of Experimental Psychology: Learning, Memory, and Cognition*, *11*, 461–463.

(1998). *Comprehension: a paradigm for cognition*. New York: Cambridge University Press.

Kintsch, W., and Bates, E. (1977). Recognition memory for statements from a classroom lecture. *Journal of Experimental Psychology: Human Learning and Memory*, *3*, 150–159.

Kirby, K. N. (1997). Bidding on the future: evidence against normative discounting of delayed rewards. *Journal of Experimental Psychology: General*, *126*, 54–70.

Kirby, K. N., and Herrnstein, R. J. (1995). Preference reversals due to myopic discounting of delayed reward. *Psychological Science*, *6*, 83–89.

Kish, G. B. (1966). Studies of sensory reinforcement. In W. K. Honig (ed.), *Operant behavior: areas of research and application* (pp. 109–159). New York: Appleton-Century-Crofts.

Klatzky, R. B. (1980). *Human memory: structures and processes*. San Francisco: W. H. Freeman.

Kleider, H. M., Pezdek, K., Goldfinger, S. D., and Kirk, A. (2008). Schema-driven source misattribution errors: remembering the expected from a witnessed event. *Applied Cognitive Psychology*, *22*, 1–20.

Knight, R. G., and O'Hagan, K. (2009). Autobiographical memory in long-term survivors of severe traumatic brain injury. *Journal of Clinical and Experimental Neuropsychology*, *31*, 573–583.

Knowlton, B. J., Mangels, J. A., and Squire, L. R. (1996). A neostriatal habit learning system in humans. *Science*, *273*, 1399–1402.

Kohler, W. (1927). *The mentality of apes* (rev. edn). London: Routledge & Kegan Paul.

Köhnken, G., Milne, R., Memon, A., and Bull, R. (1999). The cognitive interview: a meta-analysis. *Psychology, Crime and Law*, *5*, 3–28.

Kolers, P. A., and Ostry, D. J. (1974). Time course of loss of information regarding pattern analyzing operations. *Journal of Verbal Learning and Verbal Behavior*, *13*, 599–612.

Konorski, J. (1948). *Conditioned reflexes and neuron organization.* Cambridge: Cambridge University Press.

   (1967). *Integrative activity of the brain.* Chicago: University of Chicago Press.

Koriat, A., Goldsmith, M., and Pansky, A. (2000). Toward a psychology of memory accuracy. *Annual Review of Psychology, 51*, 481–537.

Kristjansson, A., and Campana, G. (2010). Where perception meets memory: a review of repetition priming in visual search tasks. *Attention, Perception, and Psychophysics, 72*, 5–18.

Kruschke, J. K. (1992). ALCOVE: an exemplar-based connectionist model of category learning. *Psychological Review, 99*, 22–44.

Kunst-Wilson, W. R., and Zajonc, R. B. (1980). Affective discrimination of stimuli that cannot be recognized. *Science, 207*, 557–558.

LaBar, K. S., and Phelps, E. A. (2005). Reinstatement of conditioned fear in humans is context dependent and impaired in amnesia. *Behavioral Neuroscience, 119*, 677–686.

Lamon, S., Wilson, G. T., and Leaf, R. C. (1977). Human classical aversion conditioning: nausea versus electric shock in the reduction of target beverage consumption. *Behavior Research and Therapy, 15*, 313–320.

Lampinen, J. M., Copeland, S. M., and Neuschatz, J. S. (2001). Recollections of things schematic: room schemas revisited. *Journal of Experimental Psychology: Learning, Memory, and Cognition, 27*, 1211–1222.

Lampinen, J. M., and Odegard, T. N. (2006). Memory editing mechanisms. *Memory, 14*, 649–654.

Larzelere, R. E. (1986). Moderate spanking: model or deterrent of children's aggression in the family? *Journal of Family Violence, 1*, 27–36.

Larzelere, R. E., and Kuhn, B. R. (2005). Comparing child outcomes of physical punishment and alternative disciplinary tactics: a meta-analysis. *Clinical Child and Family Psychology Review, 8*, 1–37.

Larzelere, R. E., Schneider, W. N., Larson, D. B., and Pike, P. L. (1996). The effects of discipline responses in delaying toddler misbehavior recurrences. *Child and Family Behavior Therapy, 18*, 35–57.

Latner, J. D., Wilson, G. T., Stunkard, A. J., and Jackson, M. L. (2002). Self-help and long-term behavior therapy for obesity. *Behavior Research and Therapy, 40*, 805–812.

Laurence, J. R., and Perry, C. (1983). Hypnotically created memory among highly hypnotizable subjects. *Science, 222*, 523–524.

Lavie, N. (2005). Distracted and confused? Selective attention under load. *Trends in Cognitive Sciences, 9*, 75–82.

Leach, A.-M., Cutler, B. L., and Van Wallendael, L. (2009). Lineups and eyewitness identification. *Annual Review of Law and Social Science, 5*, 157–178.

LeBoeuf, R. A., and Shafir, E. B. (2005). Decision making. In K. J. Holyoak and R. G. Morrison (eds.), *The Cambridge handbook of thinking and reasoning* (pp. 243–265). New York: Cambridge University Press.

LeDoux, J. E. (1994). Emotion, memory and the brain. *Scientific American, 270*, 50–57.
(2002). *Synaptic self: how our brains become who we are.* New York: Viking.

Lehman, M., and Malmberg, K. J. (2009). A global theory of remembering and forgetting from multiple lists. *Journal of Experimental Psychology: Learning, Memory, and Cognition, 35*, 970–988.

Lepper, M. R. (1981). Intrinsic and extrinsic motivation in children: detrimental effects of superfluous social controls. In W. A. Collins (ed.), *Minnesota symposium on child psychology* (vol. 14, pp. 155–213). Hillsdale, NJ: Erlbaum.

Lepper, M. R., Greene, D., and Nisbett, R. E. (1973). Undermining children's intrinsic interest with extrinsic rewards: a test of the overjustification hypothesis. *Journal of Personality and Social Psychology, 28*, 129–137.

Lettvin, J. Y., Maturana, H. R., McCulloch, W. S., and Pitts, W. H. (1959). What the frog's eye tells the frog's brain. *Proceedings of the IRE, 47*, 1940–1951.

Levine, L. J., and Edelstein, R. S. (2009). Emotion and memory narrowing: a review and goal-relevance approach. *Cognition and Emotion, 23*, 833–875.

Levine, M. (1971). Hypothesis theory and nonlearning despite ideal S–R reinforcement contingencies. *Psychological Review, 78*, 130–140.

Levis, D. J. (1989). The case for a return to a two-factor theory of avoidance: the failure of non-fear interpretations. In S. B. Klein and R. R. Mowrer (eds.), *Contemporary learning theories: Pavlovian conditioning and the status of traditional learning theory* (pp. 227–277). Hillsdale, NJ: Erlbaum.

Levy, B. J., McVeigh, N. D., Marful, A., and Anderson, M. C. (2007). Inhibiting your native language: the role of retrieval-induced forgetting during second-language acquisition. *Psychological Science, 18*, 29–34.

Levy, R. L., Finch, E. A., Crowell, M. D., Talley, N. J., and Jeffrey, R. W. (2007). Behavioral intervention for the treatment of obesity: strategies and effectiveness data. *American Journal of Gastroenterology, 102*, 2314–2321.

Lewis, D. J., and Duncan, C. P. (1956). Effect of different percentages of money reward on extinction of a lever pulling response. *Journal of Experimental Psychology, 52*, 23–27.

Lewis, M. (2003). *Moneyball: the art of winning an unfair game.* New York: Norton.

Leyens, J. P., Camino, L., Parke, R. D., and Berkowitz, L. (1975). Effects of movie violence on aggression in a field setting as a function of group dominance and cohesion. *Journal of Personality and Social Psychology, 32*, 346–360.

Lichstein, K. L., and Riedel, B. W. (1994). Behavioral assessment and treatment of insomnia: a review with an emphasis on clinical application. *Behavior Therapy, 25*, 659–688.

Lichtenstein, S., Slovic, P., Fischoff, B., Layman, M., and Coombs, B. (1978). Judged frequency of lethal events. *Journal of Experimental Psychology: Human Learning and Memory, 4*, 551–578.

Lieberman, D. A. (1979). Behaviorism and the mind: a (limited) call for a return to introspection. *American Psychologist, 34*, 319–333.
(2004). *Learning and memory: an integrative approach.* Belmont, CA: Wadworth.

Lieberman, D. A., Cathro, J. S., Nichol, K., and Watson, E. (1997). The role of S– in human observing behavior: bad news is sometimes better than no news. *Learning and Motivation, 28*, 20–42.

Lieberman, D. A., Connell, G. L., and Moos, H. F. T. (1998). Reinforcement without awareness: II. Word class. *Quarterly Journal of Experimental Psychology, 51B*, 317–315.

Lieberman, D. A., Vogel, A. C. M., and Nisbet, J. (2008). Why do the effects of delaying reinforcement in animals and delaying feedback in humans differ? A working memory analysis. *Quarterly Journal of Experimental Psychology, 16*, 194–202.

Lieberman, M. D. (2000). Intuition: a social cognitive neuroscience approach. *Psychological Bulletin, 126*, 109–137.

Light, L. L., and Carter-Sobell, L. (1970). The effects of changed semantic context on recognition memory. *Journal of Verbal Learning and Verbal Behavior, 9*, 1–11.

Lindsay, D. S., and Poole, D. A. (1995). Remembering childhood sexual abuse in therapy: psychotherapists' self-reported beliefs, practices, and experiences. *Journal of Psychiatry and Law, 23*, 461–476.

Lindsay, D. S., and Wells, G. L. (1985). Improving eyewitness identification from lineups: simultaneous versus sequential lineup presentations. *Journal of Applied Psychology, 70*, 556–564.

Lindsay, R. C. L., Mansour, J. K., Beaudry, J. L., Leach, A.-M., and Bertrand, M. I. (2009). Beyond sequential presentation: misconceptions and misrepresentations of sequential lineups. *Legal and Criminological Psychology, 14*, 31–34.

Linton, M. (1975). Memory for real-world events. In D. A. Norman and D. E. Rumelhart (eds.), *Explorations in cognition* (pp. 376–404). San Francisco: Freeman.

(1978). Real world memory after six years: an in vivo study of very long term memory. In M. M. Gruneberg, P. E. Morris, and R. N. Sykes (eds.), *Practical aspects of memory* (pp. 69–76). Orlando, FL: Academic Press.

Lipp, O. V., and Purkis, H. M. (2005). No support for dual process accounts of human affective learning in simple Pavlovian conditioning. *Cognition and Emotion, 19*, 269–282.

Locke, J. (1961). *An essay concerning human understanding* (ed. J. W. Yolton). London: Dent (first published 1690).

Lockhart, R. S., and Craik, F. I. M. (1990). Levels of processing: a retrospective commentary on a framework for memory research. *Canadian Journal of Psychology, 44*, 37–112.

Loftus, E. F. (1979). *Eyewitness testimony.* Cambridge, MA: Harvard University Press.

(1993). The reality of repressed memories. *American Psychologist, 48*, 518–537.

Loftus, E. F., Donders, K., Hoffman, H. G., and Schooler, J. W. (1989). Creating new memories that are quickly accessed and confidently held. *Memory and Cognition, 17*, 607–616.

Loftus, E. F., Garry, M., and Feldman, J. (1994). Forgetting sexual trauma: what does it mean when 38% forget? *Journal of Consulting and Clinical Psychology, 62*, 1177–1181.

Loftus, E. F., Miller, D. G., and Burns, H. J. (1978). Semantic integration of verbal information into a visual memory. *Journal of Experimental Psychology: Human Learning and Memory, 4*, 19–31.

Loftus, E. F., and Palmer, J. C. (1974). Reconstruction of automobile destruction: an example of the interaction between language and memory. *Journal of Verbal Learning and Verbal Behavior, 13*, 585–589.

Logan, G. D. (2004). Working memory, task switching, and executive control in the task span procedure. *Journal of Experimental Psychology: General, 133*, 218–236.

Logue, A. W., Ophir, I., and Strauss, K. E. (1981). The acquisition of taste aversions in humans. *Behaviour Research and Therapy, 19*, 319–333.

LoLordo, V. M., and Taylor, T. L. (2001). Effects of uncontrollable aversive events: some unsolved puzzles. In R. R. Mowrer and S. B. Klein (eds.), *Handbook of contemporary learning theories* (pp. 469–504). Mahwah, NJ: Erlbaum.

Lovaas, O. I. (1987). Behavioral treatment and normal educational and intellectual functioning in young autistic children. *Journal of Consulting and Clinical Psychology, 55*, 3–9.

Lovaas, O. I., Koegel, R. L., Simmons, J. Q., and Long, J. (1973). Some generalization and follow-up measures on autistic children in behavior therapy. *Journal of Applied Behavior Analysis, 6*, 131–166.

Lovaas, O. I., Schaeffer, B., and Simmons, J. Q. (1965). Experimental studies in childhood schizophrenia: building social behavior in autistic children by the use of electric shock. *Journal of Experimental Research in Personality, 1*, 99–109.

Lovibond, P. F., Saunders, J. C., Weidemann, G., and Mitchell, C. J. (2008). Evidence for expectancy as a mediator of avoidance and anxiety in a laboratory model of human avoidance learning. *Quarterly Journal of Experimental Psychology, 68*, 1199–1216.

Lovibond, P. F., and Shanks, D. R. (2002). The role of awareness in Pavlovian conditioning: empirical evidence and theoretical implications. *Journal of Experimental Psychology: Animal Behavior Processes, 28*, 3–26.

Lowe, C. F., Harzem, P., and Bagshaw, M. (1978). Species differences in the temporal control of behavior: human performance. *Journal of the Experimental Analysis of Behavior, 29*, 351–361.

Lowman, C., Hunt, W. A., Litten, R. Z., and Drummond, D. C. (2000). Research perspectives on alcohol craving: an overview. *Addiction, 95* (Suppl. 2), 45–54.

Lu, Z., and Dosher, B. A. (1998). External noise distinguishes attention mechanisms. *Vision Research, 38*, 1183–1198.

Lubow, R. E., and Moore, A. U. (1959). Latent inhibition: the effect of nonreinforced pre-exposure to the conditioned stimulus. *Journal of Comparative and Physiological Psychology, 52*, 415–419.

Luck, S. J., and Vecera, S. P. (2002). *Attention.* In H. Pashler (series ed.) and S. Yantis (volume ed.), *Stevens' handbook of experimental psychology*, vol. 1: *Sensation and perception* (3rd edn, pp. 253–286). New York: Wiley.

Ludwig, T. D., and Geller, E. S. (1997). Assigned versus participative goalsetting and response generalization: managing injury control among professional pizza deliverers. *Journal of Applied Psychology*, *82*, 253–261.

Lynch, S., and Yarnell, P. R. (1973). Retrograde amnesia: delayed forgetting after concussion. *American Journal of Psychology*, *86*, 643–645.

Lynn, S. J., Lock, T., Myers, B., and Payne, D. G. (1997). Recalling the unrecallable: should hypnosis be used to recover memories in psychotherapy? *Current Directions in Psychological Science*, *6*, 79–83.

MacKay, D. G. (1973). Aspects of the theory of comprehension, memory and attention. *Quarterly Journal of Experimental Psychology*, *25*, 22–40.

MacKillop, J., and Lisman, S. A. (2005). Reactivity to alcohol cues: isolating the role of perceived availability. *Experimental and Clinical Psychopharmacology*, *13*, 229–237.

Mackintosh, N. J. (1975). A theory of attention: variations in the associability of stimuli with reinforcement. *Psychological Review*, *82*, 276–298.

Mackintosh, N. J., and Dickinson, A. (1979). Instrumental (Type II) conditioning. In A. Dickinson and R. A. Boakes (eds.), *Mechanisms of learning and motivation* (pp. 143–169). Hillsdale, NJ: Erlbaum.

MacLeod, C. (1991). Half a century of research on the Stroop effect: an integrative review. *Psychological Bulletin*, *109*, 163–203.

Macrae, C. N., and Bodenhausen, G. V. (2000). Social cognition: thinking categorically about others. *Annual Review of Psychology*, *51*, 93–120.

Madsen, C. H., Becker, W. C., Thomas, D. R., Koser, L., and Plager, E. (1970). An analysis of the reinforcing function of "sit down" commands. In R. K. Parker (ed.), *Readings in educational psychology* (pp. 265–278). Boston, MA: Allyn & Bacon.

Maier, S. F. (1989). Learned helplessness: event covariation and cognitive changes. In S. B. Klein and R. R. Mowrer (eds.), *Contemporary learning theories: instrumental conditioning theory and the impact of biological constraints on learning* (pp. 73–110). Hillsdale, NJ: Erlbaum.

Malpass, R. S., Tredoux, C. G., and McQuiston-Surrett, D. (2009). Public policy and sequential lineups. *Legal and Criminological Psychology*, *14*, 1–12.

Mandler, G. (1980). Recognizing: the judgment of previous occurrence. *Psychological Review*, *87*, 252–271.

Mandler, G., Pearlstone, Z., and Koopmans, H. S. (1969). Effects of organization and semantic similarity on recall and recognition. *Journal of Verbal Learning and Verbal Behavior*, *8*, 410–423.

Manns, J. R., Clark, R. E., and Squire, L. R. (2002). Standard delay eyeblink classical conditioning is independent of awareness. *Journal of Experimental Psychology: Animal Learning and Behavior*, *28*, 32–37.

Martin, J. A. (1977). Effects of positive and negative adult–child interactions on children's task performance and task preferences. *Journal of Experimental Child Psychology*, *23*, 493–502.

Massaro, D. W., and Loftus, G. R. (1996). Sensory and perceptual storage: data and theory. In E. L. Bjork and R. A. Bjork (eds.), *Memory* (pp. 67–99). London: Academic Press.

Massen, C., and Vaterrodt-Plünnecke, B. (2006). The role of proactive interference in mnemonic techniques. *Memory, 14*, 189–196.

Mather, M. (2007). Emotional arousal and memory binding: an object-based framework. *Perspectives on Psychological Science, 2*, 33–52.

Matute, H. (1995). Human reactions to uncontrollable outcomes: further evidence for superstitions rather than helplessness. *Quarterly Journal of Experimental Psychology, 48B*, 142–157.

Matzel, L. D., Held, F. P., and Miller, R. R. (1988). Information and expression of simultaneous and backward associations: implications for contiguity theory. *Learning and Motivation, 19*, 317–344.

Mawhinney, V. T., Bostow, D. E., Laws, D. R., Blumenfeld, G. J., and Hopkins, B. L. (1971). A comparison of students' studying behavior produced by daily, weekly, and three-week testing schedules. *Journal of Applied Behavior Analysis, 4*, 257–264.

Mazur, J. E. (2006). *Learning and behavior* (6th edn). Upper Saddle River, NJ: Prentice Hall.

Mazzoni, G., and Lynn, S. J. (2007). Using hypnosis in eyewitness memory: past and current issues. In M. P. Toglia, J. D. Read, D. F. Ross, and R. C. L. Lindsay (eds.), *Handbook of eyewitness psychology*, vol. 1: *Memory for events* (pp. 321–338). Mahwah, NJ: Erlbaum.

McCahill, T. A., Meyer, L. C., and Fischman, A. (1979). *The aftermath of rape.* Lexington, MA: Lexington Books.

McClelland, J. L. (1999). Cognitive modeling, connectionist. In R. A. Wilson and F. Keil (eds.), *The MIT encyclopedia of the cognitive sciences* (pp. 137–139). Cambridge, MA: MIT Press.

(2011). Memory as a constructive process: the parallel-distributed processing approach. In S. Nalbantian, P. Matthews, and J. L. McClelland (eds.), *The memory process: neuroscientific and humanistic perspectives* (pp. 129–151). Cambridge, MA: MIT Press.

McClelland, J. L., and Chappell, M. (1998). Familiarity breeds differentiation: a Bayesian approach to the effects of experience in recognition memory. *Psychological Review, 105*, 724–760.

McClelland, J. L., McNaughton, B. L., and O'Reilly, R. C. (1995). Why there are complementary learning systems in the hippocampus and neocortex: insights from the successes and failures of connectionist models of learning and memory. *Psychological Review, 102*, 419–457.

McClelland, J. L., and Patterson, K. (2002). Rules or connections in past-tense inflections: what does the evidence rule out? *Trends in Cognitive Sciences, 6*, 465–472.

McClelland, J. L., and Rumelhart, D. E. (1985). Distributed memory and the representation of general and specific information. *Journal of Experimental Psychology: General, 114*, 159–188.

McClelland, J. L., and Seidenberg, M. S. (2000). Why do kids say goed and brang? *Science, 287*, 47–48.

McCloskey, M. E., and Glucksberg, S. (1978). Natural categories: well-defined or fuzzy sets? *Memory and Cognition, 6*, 462–472.

McCloskey, M. E., Wible, C. G., and Cohen, N. J. (1988). Is there a special flashbulb memory mechanism? *Journal of Experimental Psychology: General, 117*, 171–181.

McClure, S. M., Laibson, D., Loewenstein, G., and Cohen, J. D. (2004). Separate neural systems value immediate and delayed monetary rewards. *Science, 306*, 503–507.

McDaniel, M., and Einstein, G. (1990). Bizarre imagery: mnemonic benefits and theoretical implications. In R. Logie and M. Denis (eds.), *Mental images in human cognition* (pp. 183–192). New York: North Holland.

McDaniel, M. A., Howard, D. C., and Einstein, G. O. (2009). The read-recite-review study strategy: effective and portable. *Psychological Science, 20*, 516–522.

McGaugh, J. L. (1966). Time-dependent processes in memory storage. *Science, 153*, 1351–1358.

(2000). Memory: a century of consolidation. *Science, 287*, 248–251.

(2004). The amygdala modulates the consolidation of memories of emotionally arousing experiences. *Annual Review of Neuroscience, 27*, 1–28.

McGeoch, J. A. (1942). *The psychology of human learning.* New York: Longmans, Green.

McGeoch, J. A., and McDonald, W. T. (1931). Meaningful relation and retroactive inhibition. *American Journal of Psychology, 43*, 579–588.

McGuire, R. J., Carlisle, J. M., and Young, B. G. (1965). Sexual deviations as conditioned behaviour: a hypothesis. *Behaviour Research and Therapy, 2*, 185–190.

McNally, R. J. (2007). Betrayal trauma theory: a critical appraisal. *Memory, 15*, 280–294.

McNamara, T. P. (1994). Priming and theories of memory: a reply to Ratcliff and McKoon. *Psychological Review, 101*, 185–187.

McNeil, B. J., Pauker, S. G., Sox, H. C., and Tversky, A. (1982). On the elicitation of preferences for alternative therapies. *New England Journal of Medicine, 306*, 1259–1262.

McNeil, C. B., Clemens-Mowrer, L., Gurwitch, R. H., and Funderburk, B. W. (1994). Assessment of a new procedure to prevent timeout escape in preschoolers. *Child and Family Behavior Therapy, 16*, 27–35.

Medin, D. L., and Rips, L. J. (2005). Concepts and categories: memory, meaning, and metaphysics. In K. J. Holyoak and R. G. Morrison (eds.), *The Cambridge handbook of thinking and reasoning* (pp. 37–72). New York: Cambridge University Press.

Medin, D. L., Ross, B. H., and Markman, A. B. (2005). Cognitive psychology (4th edn). Danver, MA: Wiley.

Meehl, P. E. (1950). On the circularity of the law of effect. *Psychological Bulletin, 47*, 52–75.

Meeter, M., Murre, J. M., and Janssen, S. M. (2005). Remembering the news: modeling retention data from a study with 14,000 participants. *Memory and Cognition, 33,* 793–810.

Meichenbaum, D. H., Bowers, K. S., and Ross, R. R. (1968). Modification of classroom behavior of institutionalized female adolescent offenders. *Behaviour Research and Therapy, 6,* 343–357.

Melton, A. W. (1963). Implications of short-term memory for a general theory of memory. *Journal of Verbal Learning and Verbal Behavior, 2,* 1–21.

Meyer, D. E., and Schvaneveldt, R. W. (1971). Facilitation in recognizing pairs of words: evidence of a dependence between retrieval operations. *Journal of Experimental Psychology, 90,* 227–234.

Michotte, A. (1963). *The perception of causality* (trans. T. R. Miles and E. Miles). New York: Basic Books (first published 1946).

Miles, D. R., and Carey, G. (1997). Genetic and environmental architecture of human aggression. *Journal of Personality and Social Psychology, 72,* 207–217.

Miles, T. R., and Ellis, N. C. (1981). A lexical encoding difficulty II: clinical observations. In G. T. Pavlidis and T. R. Miles (eds.), *Dyslexia research and its applications to education* (pp. 217–244). Chichester: Wiley.

Milkman, K. L., Rogers, T., and Bazerman, M. H. (2008). Harnessing our inner angels and demons: what we have learned about want/should conflicts and how that knowledge can help us reduce short-sighted decision making. *Perspectives on Psychological Science, 3,* 324–338.

Mill, J. (1878). *Analysis of the phenomena of the human mind* (ed. J. S. Mill). London: Longmans, Green, Reader & Dyer (first published 1829).

Miller, G. A. (1956). The magical number seven, plus or minus two: some limits on our capacity for processing information. *Psychological Review, 63,* 81–97.

Miller, G. A., and Gildea, P. M. (1987). How children learn words. *Scientific American, 257(3),* 94–99.

Miller, R. R., Barnet, R. C., and Grahame, N. J. (1995). Assessment of the Rescorla-Wagner model. *Psychological Bulletin, 117,* 363–386.

Milner, B. (1962). Les troubles de la mémoire accompagnant des lésions hippocampiques bilaterales. In P. Passouant (ed.), *Physiologie de l'hippocampe* (pp. 257–272). Paris: Centre des Recherches Scientifiques.

(1966). Amnesia following operation on the temporal lobes. In C. W. M. Whitty and O. L. Zangwill (eds.), *Amnesia* (pp. 109–133). London: Butterworth.

Mineka, S., and Cook, M. (1986). Immunization against the observational conditioning of snake fear in rhesus monkeys. *Journal of Abnormal Psychology, 95,* 307–318.

Mineka, S., and Öhman, A. (2002). Born to fear: non-associative vs. associative factors in the etiology of phobias. *Behaviour Research and Therapy, 40,* 173–184.

Minsky, M. L. (1975). A framework for representing knowledge. In P. H. Winston (ed.), *The psychology of computer vision* (pp. 211–277). New York: McGraw-Hill.

Mischel, W. (1984). Convergences and challenges in the search for consistency. *American Psychologist, 39,* 351–364.

Mischel, W., and Mischel, H. N. (1977). Self-control and the self. In T. Mischel (ed.), *The self: psychological and philosophical issues* (pp. 31–64). Oxford: Blackwell.

Mischel, W., and Shoda, Y. (1995). A cognitive-affective system theory of personality: reconceptualizing situations, dispositions, dynamics, and invariance in personality structure. *Psychological Review, 102*, 246–268.

Mishra, P., and Brewer, W. F. (2003) Theories as a form of mental representation and their role in the recall of text information. *Contemporary Educational Psychology, 28*, 277–303.

Mitchell, C. J., De Houwer, J., and Lovibond, P. F. (2009). The propositional nature of human associative learning. *Behavioral and Brain Sciences, 32*, 183–198.

Mitchell, G., and Brandt, E. M. (1972). Paternal behavior in primates. In F. E. Poirier (ed.), *Primate socialization* (pp. 173–206). New York: Random House.

Mitchell, K. J., and Johnson, M. K. (2009). Source monitoring 15 years later: what have we learned from fMRI about the neural mechanisms of source memory? *Psychological Bulletin, 135*, 638–677.

Moeller, G. (1954). The CS–UCS interval in GSR conditioning. *Journal of Experimental Psychology, 48*, 162–166.

Monforte, J. R. (1977). Some observations concerning blood morphine concentrations in narcotic addicts. *Journal of Forensic Sciences, 22*, 718–724.

Montague, W. E., Adams, J. A., and Kiess, H. O. (1966). Forgetting and natural language mediation. *Journal of Experimental Psychology, 72*, 829–833.

Montgomery, K. C. (1954). The role of the exploratory drive in learning. *Journal of Comparative and Physiological Psychology, 47*, 60–64.

Moray, N. (1959). Attention in dichotic listening: affective cues and the influence of instructions. *Quarterly Journal of Experimental Psychology, 11*, 56–60.

Moreland, R. L., and Beach, S. R. (1992). Exposure effects in the classroom: The development of affinity among students. *Journal of Experimental Social Psychology, 28*, 255–276.

Morgan, C. A., Gazlett, G., Doran, A., Garrett, S., Hoyt, G., Thomas, P., Baranoski, M., and Southwick, S. M. (2004). Accuracy of eyewitness memory for persons encountered during exposure to highly intense stress. *International Journal of Law and Psychiatry, 27*, 265–279.

Morris, C. D., Bransford, J. D., and Franks, J. J. (1977). Levels of processing versus transfer appropriate processing. *Journal of Verbal Learning and Verbal Behavior, 16*, 519–533.

Morris, J. S., de Gelder, B., Weiskrantz, L., and Dolan, R. J. (2001). Differential extrageniculostriate and amygdala response to presentation of emotional faces in a cortically blind field. *Brain, 124*, 1241–1252.

MSO (1997). 1997 world championships. Retrieved from www.msoworld.com/brain/mental/memory97_2.html.

Müller, G. E., and Pilzecker, A. (1900). Experimentalle Beitrage zur Lehre vom Gedachtnis. *Zeitschrift für Psychologie, 1*, 1–300.

Muller, R. T. (1996). Family aggressiveness factors in the prediction of corporal punishment: reciprocal effects and the impact of observer perspective. *Journal of Family Psychology*, *10*, 474–489.

Mundy, M. E., Honey, R. C., and Dwyer, D. M. (2007). Simultaneous presentation of similar stimuli produces perceptual learning in human picture processing. *Journal of Experimental Psychology: Animal Behavior Processes*, *33*, 124–138.

Murphy, K. J., Troyer, A. K., Levine, B., and Moscovitch, M. (2008). Episodic, but not semantic, autobiographical memory is reduced in amnesic mild cognitive impairment. *Neuropsychologia*, *46*, 3116–3123.

Myers, D. G. (2010). *Psychology* (9th edn). New York: Worth.

Myers, S. M., and Johnson, C. P. (2007). Management of children with autism spectrum disorders. *Pediatrics*, *120*, 1183–1215.

Nairne, J. S., and Pandeirada, J. N. S. (2008). Adaptive memory: remembering with a stone-age brain. *Current Directions in Psychological Science*, *17*, 239–243.

Nairne, J. S., Pandeirada, J. N. S., and Thompson, S. R. (2008). Adaptive memory: the comparative value of survival processing. *Psychological Science*, *19*, 176–180.

Nathan, D., and Snedeker, M. (1995). *Satan's silence: ritual abuse and the making of a modern American witch hunt*. New York: Basic Books.

Nedelman, D., and Sulzbacher, S. I. (1972). Dicky at 13 years of age: a long-term success following early application of operant conditioning procedures. In G. Semb (ed.), *Behavior analysis and education*. Lawrence: University of Kansas.

Nederkoorn, C., Smulders, F., Havermans, R., and Jansen, A. (2004). Exposure to binge food in bulimia nervosa: finger pulse amplitude as a potential measure of urge to eat and predictor of food intake. *Appetite*, *42*, 125–130.

Neil, A. S. (1960). *Summerhill: a radical approach to child rearing*. New York: Hart.

Neisser, U. (1978). Memory: what are the important questions? In M. M. Gruneberg, P. Morris, and R. N. Sykes (eds.), *Practical aspects of memory* (pp. 3–24). London: Academic Press.

Neisser, U., and Harsch, N. (1992). Phantom flashbulbs: false recollections of hearing the news about Challenger. In E. Winograd and U. Neisser (eds.), *Affect and accuracy in recall: studies of "flashbulb memories"* (pp. 9–31). Cambridge: Cambridge University Press.

Nelson, T. O. (1978). Detecting small amounts of information in memory: savings for nonrecognized items. *Journal of Experimental Psychology: Human Learning and Memory*, *4*, 453–468.

  (1999). Cognition versus metacognition. In R. J. Sternberg (ed.), *The nature of cognition* (pp. 625–641). Cambridge, MA: MIT Press.

Nelson, T. O., and Leonesio, R. J. (1988). Allocation of self-paced study time and the "labor-in-vain effect." *Journal of Experimental Psychology: Learning, Memory, and Cognition*, *29*, 1051–1057.

Neuschatz, J. S., and Cutler, B. L. (2008). Eyewitness identification. In H. L. Roediger III (ed.), *Learning and memory: a comprehensive reference*, vol. 2: *Cognitive psychology of memory* (pp. 845–865). New York: Academic Press.

Newell, A., and Simon, H. A. (1963). Computers in psychology. In R. D. Luce, R. R. Bush, and E. Galanter (eds.), *Handbook of mathematical psychology* (vol. 1, pp. 361–428). New York: Wiley.

Newell, B. R., Lagnado, D. A., and Shanks, D. R. (2007). *Straight choices: the psychology of decision making.* Hove: Psychology Press.

Nielson, K. A., Yee, D., and Erickson, K. I. (2005). Memory enhancement by a semantically unrelated emotional arousal source induced after learning. *Neurobiology of Learning and Memory, 84,* 49–56.

Nissen, M. J., and Bullemer, P. (1987). Attentional requirements of learning: evidence from performance measures. *Cognitive Psychology, 19,* 1–32.

O'Craven, K. M., Downing, P. E., and Kanwisher, N. (1999). fMRI evidence for objects as the units of attentional selection. *Nature, 401,* 584–587.

O'Farrell, T. J., Choquette, K. A., Cutter, H. S. G., Brown, E., Bayog, R., McCourt, W., Lowe, J., Chan, A., and Deneault, P. (1996). Cost-benefit and cost-effectiveness analyses of behavioral marital therapy with and without relapse prevention sessions for alcoholics and their spouses. *Behavior Therapy, 27,* 7–24.

O'Leary, K. D., Becker, W. C., Evans, M. B., and Saudargas, R. A. (1969). A token reinforcement program in a public school: a replication and systematic analysis. *Journal of Applied Behavior Analysis, 2,* 3–13.

O'Leary, K. D., Poulos, R. W., and Devine, V. T. (1972). Tangible reinforcers: bonuses or bribes? *Journal of Consulting and Clinical Psychology, 38,* 1–8.

Oberauer, K., and Lewandowsky, S. (2008). Forgetting in immediate serial recall: decay, temporal distinctiveness, or interference? *Psychological Review, 115,* 544–576.

Odinot, G., Wolters, G., and van Koppen, P. J. (2009). Eyewitness memory of a supermarket robbery: a case study of accuracy and confidence after 3 months. *Law and Human Behavior, 33,* 506–514.

Ofshe, R., and Watters, E. (1994). *Making monsters: false memories, psychotherapy, and sexual hysteria.* New York: Scribner's.

Öhman, A., and Mineka, S. (2001). Fears, phobias, and preparedness: toward an evolved module of fear and fear learning. *Psychological Review, 108,* 483–522.

Öhman, A., and Soares, J. J. F. (1998). Emotional conditioning to masked stimuli: expectancies for aversive outcomes following nonrecognized fear-relevant stimuli. *Journal of Experimental Psychology: General, 127,* 69–82.

Olds, J., and Milner, P. (1954). Positive reinforcement produced by electrical stimulation of septal area and other regions of rat brain. *Journal of Comparative and Physiological Psychology, 47,* 419–427.

Olsson, A., and Phelps, E. A. (2004). Learned fear of "unseen" faces after Pavlovian, observational, and instructed fear. *Psychological Science, 15,* 822–828.

Ono, K. (1987). Superstitious behavior in humans. *Journal of the Experimental Analysis of Behavior, 47,* 261–271.

Öst, L. G. (1985). Mode of acquisition of phobias. *Acta Universitatis Uppsaliensis (Abstract of Uppsala Dissertations from the Faculty of Medicine), 529,* 1–45.

Öst, L. G., and Hugdahl, K. (1981). Acquisition of phobias and anxiety response patterns in clinical patients. *Behaviour Research and Therapy, 19,* 439–447.

Öst, L. G., Stridh, B. M., and Wolf, M. (1998). A clinical study of spider phobia: prediction of outcome after self-help and therapist-directed treatments. *Behaviour Research and Therapy, 36,* 17–36.

Overmier, J. B., and Seligman, M. E. P. (1967). Effects of inescapable shock upon subsequent escape and avoidance learning. *Journal of Comparative and Physiological Psychology, 63,* 23–33.

Papini, M. R., and Bitterman, M. E. (1993). The two-test strategy in the study of inhibitory conditioning. *Journal of Experimental Psychology: Animal Behavior Processes, 19,* 342–352.

Parkin, A. J. (2000). *Essential cognitive psychology.* Hove: Psychology Press.

Patterson, G. R., Reid, J. B., and Dishion, T. J. (1989). *A social interactional approach,* vol 4: *Antisocial boys.* Eugene, OR: Castalia.

Paul, G. L. (1969). Outcome of systematic desensitization II: controlled investigations of individual treatment, technique variations, and current status. In C. M. Franks (ed.), *Behavior therapy: appraisal and status* (pp. 62–104). New York: McGraw-Hill.

Pavlov, I. P. (1927). *Conditioned reflexes* (trans. G. V. Anrep). Oxford: Oxford University Press.

(1928). *Lectures on conditioned reflexes* (trans. W. H. Gantt). New York: International Publishers.

Payne, J. W., Bettman, R. R., and Johnson, E. J. (1988). Adaptive strategy selection in decision making. *Journal of Experimental Psychology: Learning, Memory, and Cogntion, 14,* 534–552.

PBS (1997). *Innocence lost the plea.* Retrieved from www.pbs.org/wgbh/pages/frontline/shows/innocence.

Pearce, J. M. (2002). Evaluation and development of a connectionist theory of configural learning. *Animal Learning and Behavior, 30,* 73–95.

(2008). *Animal learning and cognition: an introduction* (3rd edn). Hove: Psychology Press.

Pearce, J. M., and Hall, G. (1980). A model for Pavlovian learning: variations in the effectiveness of conditioned but not of unconditioned stimuli. *Psychological Review, 87,* 532–552.

Pearce, J., and Mackintosh, N. J. (2010). Two theories of attention: a review and a possible integration. In C. Mitchell and M. Le Pelley (eds.), *Attention and associative learning: from brain to behaviour* (pp. 11–39). Oxford: Oxford University Press.

Penfield, W. (1958). *The excitable cortex in conscious man.* Liverpool: University of Liverpool Press.

Pepperberg, I. M. (1993). Cognition and communication in an African grey parrot (*Psittacus erithacus*): studies on a nonhuman, non-primate, nonmammalian subject. In H. L. Roitblat, L. M. Herman, and P. E. Nachtigall (eds.), *Language and communication: comparative perspectives* (pp. 221–248). Hillsdale, NJ: Erlbaum.

(2009). *Alex & me: how a scientist and a parrot discovered a hidden world of animal intelligence – and formed a deep bond in the process.* New York: Harper Paperbacks.

Perrett, D. I., Oram, M. W., Hietanen, J. K., and Benson, P. J. (1994). Issues of representation in object vision. In M. J. Farah and G. Ratcliff (eds.), *The neuropsychology of high-level vision: collected tutorial essays. Carnegie Mellon symposia on cognition* (pp. 33–61). Hillsdale, NJ: Erlbaum.

Peterson, C., Maier, S. F., and Seligman, M. E. P. (1993). *Learned helplessness: a theory for the age of personal control.* New York: Oxford University Press.

Peterson, L. R., and Peterson, M. J. (1959). Short-term retention of individual verbal items. *Journal of Experimental Psychology, 58*, 193–198.

Petty, R. E., and Briñol, P. (2008). Persuasion: from single to multiple to metacognitive processes. *Perspectives on Psychological Science, 3*, 137–147.

Peynircioğlu, Z. F. (1989). Part-set cuing effect with word-fragment cuing: evidence against the strategy disruption and increased-list-length explanations. *Journal of Experimental Psychology: Learning, Memory, and Cognition, 15*, 147–152.

Pfungst, O. (1965). *Clever Hans: the horse of Mr. von Osten.* New York: Holt, Rinehart and Winston.

Phillips, E. L. (1968). Achievement Place: token reinforcement procedures in a home-style rehabilitation setting for "pre-delinquent" boys. *Journal of Applied Behavior Analysis, 1*, 213–233.

Pickel, K. L. (2007). Remembering and identifying menacing perpetrators: exposure to violence and the weapon focus effect. In R. C. L. Lindsay, D. F. Ross, J. D. Read, and M. P. Toglia (eds.), *Handbook of eyewitness psychology*, vol. 2: *Memory for people* (pp. 339–360). Mahwah, NJ: Erlbaum.

Pineño, O., and Miller, R. R. (2007). Comparing associative, statistical, and inferential reasoning accounts of human contingency learning. *Quarterly Journal of Experimental Psychology, 60*, 310–329.

Pinker, S. (1994). *The language instinct.* New York: Morrow.

Pinker, S., and Ullman, M. (2002). The past and future of the past tense. *Trends in Cognitive Science, 6*, 456–462.

Plaud, J. J., and Martini, J. R. (1999). The respondent conditioning of male sexual arousal. *Behavior Modification, 23*, 254–268.

Plaut, D. C., and McClelland, J. L. (2010). Postcript: parallel distributed processing in localist models without thresholds. *Psychological Review, 117*, 284–290.

Pope, K. S. (1996). Memory, abuse, and science: questioning claims about the false memory syndrome epidemic. *American Psychologist, 51*, 957–974.

Posner, M. I., and Keele, S. W. (1968). On the genesis of abstract ideas. *Journal of Experimental Psychology, 77*, 353–363.

Posner, M. I., Snyder, C. R., and Davidson, B. J. (1980). Attention and the detection of signals. *Journal of Experimental Psychology: General, 109*, 160–174.

Postman, L., and Underwood, B. J. (1973). Critical issues in interference theory. *Memory and Cognition, 1*, 19–40.

Poulson, C. L. (1983). Differential reinforcement of other-than-vocalization as a control procedure in the conditioning of infant vocalization rate. *Journal of Experimental Child Psychology, 36*, 471–489.

Poulton, R., and Menzies, R. G. (2002). Non-associative fear acquisition: a review of the evidence from retrospective and longitudinal research. *Behaviour Research and Therapy*, *40*, 127–149.

Premack, D. (1965). Reinforcement theory. In D. Levine (ed.), *Nebraska symposium on motivation* (vol. 13, pp. 123–180). Lincoln: University of Nebraska Press.

(1971). Catching up with common sense, or two sides of a generalization: reinforcement and punishment. In R. Glaser (ed.), *The nature of reinforcement* (pp. 121–150). New York: Academic Press.

Priluck, R., and Till, B. D. (2004). The role of contingency awareness, involvement, and need for cognition in attitude formation. *Journal of the Academy of Marketing Science*, *32*, 329–344.

Quian Quiroga, R., Kraskov, A., Koch, C., and Fried, I. (2009). Explicit encoding of multimodal percepts by single neurons in the human brain. *Current Biology*, *19*, 1308–1313.

Quian Quiroga, R., and Kreiman, G. (2010). Measuring sparseness in the brain: comment on Bowers (2009). *Psychological Review*, *117*, 291–299.

Quian Quiroga, R., Reddy, L., Kreiman, G., and Fried, I. (2005). Invariant visual representation by single neurons in the human brain. *Nature*, *435*, 1102–1107.

Raaijmakers, J. G. W. (2003). Spacing and repetition effects in human memory: application of the SAM model. *Cognitive Science*, *27*, 431–452.

(2008). Mathematical models of human memory. In H. L. Roediger III (ed.), *Learning and memory: a comprehensive reference*, vol. 2: *Cognitive psychology of memory* (pp. 445–466). New York: Academic Press.

Raaijmakers, J. G., and Shiffrin, R. M. (1980). SAM: a theory of probabilistic search of associative memory. In *The psychology of learning and motivation* (vol. 14, pp. 207–262). New York: Academic Press.

(1981). Search of associative memory. *Psychological Review*, *88*, 93–134.

Rabinowitz, J. C., Mandler, G., and Barsalou, L. W. (1977). Recognition failure: another case of retrieval failure. *Journal of Verbal Learning and Verbal Behavior*, *16*, 639–663.

Rachlin, H. (1974). Self-control. *Behaviorism*, *2*, 94–107.

Rachlin, H., and Green, L. (1972). Commitment, choice, and self-control. *Journal of the Experimental Analysis of Behavior*, *17*, 15–22.

Rachman, S., and Hodgson, R. J. (1968). Experimentally induced "sexual fetishism": replication and development. *Psychological Record*, *18*, 25–27.

Raine, A., Mellingen, K., Liu, J., Venables, P., and Mednick, S. A. (2003). Effects of environmental enrichment at ages 3–5 years on schizotypal personality and antisocial behavior at ages 17 and 23 years. *American Journal of Psychiatry*, *160*, 1627–1635.

Rasch, B., and Born, J. (2008). Reactivation and consolidation of memory during sleep. *Current Directions in Psychological Science*, *17*, 188–192.

Ratcliff, R., and McKoon, G. (1978). Priming in item recognition: evidence for the propositional structure of sentences. *Journal of Verbal Learning and Verbal Behavior*, *20*, 204–215.

Raymond, M. J. (1964). The treatment of addiction by aversion conditioning with apomorphine. *Behaviour Research and Therapy*, *1*, 287–291.

Raz, A., Packard, M. G., Alexander, G. M., Buhle, J. T., Zhu, H., Yu, S., and Peterson, B. S. (2009). A slice of pi: an exploratory neuroimaging study of digit encoding and retrieval in a superior memorist. *Neurocase*, *15*, 361–372.

Razran, G. (1938). Conditioning away social bias by the luncheon technique. *Psychological Bulletin 35*, 693.

(1954). The conditioned evocation of attitudes (cognitive conditioning?). *Journal of Experimental Psychology*, *48*, 278–282.

(1971). *Mind in evolution*. New York: Houghton Mifflin.

Reber, A. S., and Allen, R. (2009). Implicit and explicit learning. In A. Cleeremans, P. Wilken, and T. Bayne (eds.), *Oxford companion to consciousness* (pp. 403–407). London: Oxford University Press.

Redd, W. H., and Birnbrauer, J. S. (1969). Adults as discriminative stimuli for different reinforcement contingencies with retarded children. *Journal of Experimental Child Psychology*, *1*, 440–447.

Reisberg, D., and Heuer, F. (2007). The influence of emotion on memory in forensic settings. In M. P. Toglia, J. D. Read, D. F. Ross, and R. C. L. Lindsay (eds.), *Handbook of eyewitness psychology*, vol. 1: *Memory for events* (pp. 81–116). Mahwah, NJ: Erlbaum.

Reiss, S., and Wagner, A. R. (1972). CS habituation produces a "latent inhibition effect" but no active "conditioned inhibition." *Learning and Motivation*, *3*, 237–245.

Reitman, D., and Drabman, R. S. (1996). Read my fingertips: a procedure for enhancing the effectiveness of time-out with argumentative children. *Child and Family Behavior Therapy*, *18*, 35–40.

Remington, B., Roberts, P., and Glautier, S. (1997). The effect of drink familiarity on tolerance to alcohol. *Addictive Behaviors*, *22*, 24–53.

Rescorla, R. A. (1966). Predictability and number of pairings in Pavlovian fear conditioning. *Psychonomic Science*, *4*, 383–384.

(1967). Pavlovian conditioning and its proper control procedures. *Psychological Review*, *74*, 71–80.

(1968). Probability of shock in the presence and absence of CS in fear conditioning. *Journal of Comparative and Physiological Psychology*, *66*, 1–5.

(1970). Reduction in the effectiveness of reinforcement after prior excitatory conditioning. *Learning and Motivation*, *1*, 372–381.

(1980a). *Pavlovian second-order conditioning*. Hillsdale, NJ: Erlbaum.

(1980b). Simultaneous and successive associations in sensory preconditioning. *Journal of Experimental Psychology: Animal Behavior Processes*, *6*, 207–216.

(1987). A Pavlovian analysis of goal-directed behavior. *American Psychologist*, *42*, 119–129.

(1988). Pavlovian conditioning: it's not what you think it is. *American Psychologist*, *43*, 151–160.

(2000). Associative changes with a random CS–US relationship. *Quarterly Journal of Experimental Psychology*, *53B*, 325–340.

(2001). Experimental extinction. In R. R. Mowrer and S. B. Klein (eds.), *Handbook of contemporary learning theories* (pp. 119–154). Mahwah, NJ: Erlbaum.

Rescorla, R. A., and Wagner, A. R. (1972). A theory of Pavlovian conditioning: variations in the effectiveness of reinforcement and nonreinforcement. In A. H. Black and W. F. Prokasy (eds.), *Classical conditioning II: current research and theory* (pp. 64–99). New York: Appleton-Century-Crofts.

Revusky, S. (1971). The role of interference in association over a delay. In W. K. Honig and P. H. R. James (eds.), *Animal memory* (pp. 155–213). New York: Academic Press.

Reynolds, L. K., and Kelley, M. L. (1997). The efficacy of a response cost-based treatment package for managing aggressive behavior in preschoolers. *Behavior Modification*, *21*, 216–230.

Richardson, J. T. E. (1998). The availability and effectiveness of reported mediators in associative learning: a historical review and experimental investigation. *Psychonomic Bulletin and Review*, *5*, 597–614.

Rincover, A., and Koegel, R. L. (1975). Setting generality and stimulus control in autistic children. *Journal of Applied Behavior Analysis*, *8*, 235–246.

Risley, T. R. (1968). The effects and side effects of punishing the autistic behaviors of a deviant child. *Journal of Applied Behavior Analysis*, *1*, 21–34.

Roberts, M. W., and Powers, S. W. (1990). Adjusting chair timeout enforcement procedures for oppositional children. *Behavior Therapy*, *21*, 257–271.

Robinson, B. A. (2003). *The "Little Rascals" ritual abuse case in Edenton, NC*. Retrieved from www.religioustolerance.org/ra_edent.htm.

Roediger, H. L. (1980). The effectiveness of four mnemonics in ordering recall. *Journal of Experimental Psychology: Human Learning and Memory*, *6*, 558–567.

(1990). Implicit memory: retention without remembering. *American Psychologist*, *45*, 1043–1056.

(1993). Learning and memory: progress and challenge. In D. E. Meyer and S. Kornblum (eds.), *Attention and performance* (vol. 14, pp. 509–528). Cambridge, MA: Bradford/MIT Press.

Roediger, H. L., Gallo, D. A., and Geraci, L. (2002). Processing approaches to cognition: the impetus from the levels-of-processing framework. *Memory*, *10*, 319–332.

Roediger, H. L., and Guynn, M. J. (1996). Retrieval processes. In E. L. Bjork and R. A. Bjork (eds.), *Memory* (pp. 197–236). San Diego, CA: Academic Press.

Roediger, H. L., and Karpicke, J. D. (2006). Test-enhanced learning: taking memory tests improves long-term retention. *Psychological Science*, *17*, 249–255.

(2010). Intricacies of spaced retrieval: a resolution. In A. S. Benjamin (ed.), *Successful remembering and successful forgetting: a festschrift in honor of Robert A. Bjork* (pp. 23–47). New York: Psychology Press.

Roediger, H. L., and McDermott, K. B. (1993). Implicit memory in normal human subjects. In H. Spinnler and F. Boller (eds.), *Handbook of neuropsychology* (vol. 8, pp. 63–131). Amsterdam: Elsevier.

(1995). Creating false memories: remembering words not presented in lists. *Journal of Experimental Psychology: Learning, Memory, and Cognition*, *21*, 803–814.

Roll, J., Reilly, M., and Johanson, C. (2000). The influence of exchange delays on cigarette versus money choice: a laboratory analog of voucher-based reinforcement therapy. *Experimental and Clinical Psychopharmacology, 8,* 366–370.

Rortvedt, A. K., and Miltenberger, R. G. (1994). Analysis of a high-probability instructional sequence and time-out in the treatment of child noncompliance. Special issue: Functional analysis approaches to behavioral assessment and treatment. *Journal of Applied Behavior Analysis, 27,* 327–330.

Rosch, E. (1973). On the internal structure of perceptual and semantic categories. In T. E. Moore (ed.), *Cognitive development and the acquisition of language* (pp. 111–144). New York: Academic Press.

(1975). Cognitive representations of semantic categories. *Journal of Experimental Psychology: General, 104,* 192–233.

(1978). Principles of categorization. In E. Rosch and B. B. Lloyd (eds.), *Cognition and categorization* (pp. 27–48). Hillsdale, NJ: Erlbaum.

Rosch, E., Simpson, C., and Miller, R. S. (1976). Structural bases of typicality effects. *Journal of Experimental Psychology: Human Perception and Performance, 2,* 491–502.

Rosenbaum, R. S., Köhler, S., Schacter, D. L., Moscovitch, M., Westmacott, R., Black, S. E., Gao, F., and Tulving, E. (2005). The case of K.C.: contributions of a memory-impaired person to memory theory. *Neuropsychologia, 43,* 989–1021.

Rosenfeld, H. M., and Baer, D. M. (1969). Unnoticed verbal conditioning of an aware experimenter by a more aware subject: The double-agent effect. *Psychological Review, 76,* 425–432.

Rosenthal, R. (1966). *Experimenter effects in behavioral research.* New York: Appleton-Century-Crofts.

Rosenthal, T. L., and Bandura, A. (1978). Psychological modeling: theory and practice. In S. L. Garfield and A. E. Bergin (eds.), *Handbook of psychotherapy and behavior change: an empirical analysis* (2nd edn, pp. 621–658). New York: Wiley.

Rosenzweig, M. R. (1984). Experience, memory, and the brain. *American Psychologist, 39,* 365–376.

Rosielle, L. J., and Scaggs, W. J. (2008). What if they knocked down the library and nobody noticed? The failure to detect large changes to familiar scenes. *Memory, 16,* 115–124.

Ross, J., and Lawrence, K. A. (1968). Some observations on memory artifice. *Psychonomic Science, 13,* 107–108.

Rouder, J. N., Morey, R. D., Sun, D., and Speckman, P. L. (2008). A hierarchical process-dissociation model. *Journal of Experimental Psychology: General, 137,* 370–389.

Rozin, P., and Zellner, D. (1985). The role of Pavlovian conditioning in the acquisition of food likes and dislikes. *Annals of the New York Academy of Sciences, 443,* 189–202.

Rubin, D. C. (2006). The basic-systems model of episodic memory. *Perspectives on Psychological Science, 1,* 277–311.

Rubin, D. C., and Wenzel, A. E. (1996). One hundred years of forgetting: a quantitative description of retention. *Psychological Bulletin, 103,* 734–760.

Rumbaugh, D. M., and Savage-Rumbaugh, E. S. (1994). Language in comparative perspective. In N. J. Mackintosh (ed.), *Animal learning and cognition* (pp. 307–333). San Diego, CA: Academic Press.

Rumelhart, D. E., and McClelland, J. L. (1986). On learning the past tenses of English verbs. In J. L. McClelland, D. E. Rumelhart, and the PDP Research Group (eds.), *Parallel distributed processing: explorations in the microstructure of cognition*, vol. 2: *Psychological and biological models* (pp. 216–271). Cambridge, MA: MIT Press.

Rumelhart, D. E., and Todd, P. M. (1993). Learning and connectionist representations. In D. E. Meyer and S. Kornbum (eds.), *Attention and performance XIV: synergies in experimental psychology, artificial intelligence, and cognitive neuroscience* (pp. 3–30). Cambridge, MA: MIT Press.

Rundus, D. (1971). Analysis of rehearsal processes in free recall. *Journal of Experimental Psychology, 89*, 63–77.

Russell, B. (1927). *An outline of philosophy*. London: George Allen & Unwin.

Rutchick, A. M. (2010). Deus ex machina: the influence of polling place on voting behavior. *Political Psychology, 31*, 209–225.

Rutter, M. (1970). Autistic children: infancy to adulthood. *Seminars in Psychiatry, 2*, 435–450.

Ryan, L., and Eich, E. (2000). Mood dependence and implicit memory. In E. Tulving (ed.), *Memory, consciousness, and the brain: the Tallinn Conference* (pp. 91–105). Philadelphia, PA: Psychology Press.

Ryan, R. M. (1982). Control and information in the intrapersonal sphere: an extension of cognitive evaluation theory. *Journal of Personality and Social Psychology, 43*, 450–461.

Sachs, J. S. (1967). Recognition memory for syntactic and semantic aspects of connected discourse. *Perception and Psychophysics, 2*, 437–442.

Sallows, G. O., and Graupner, T. D. (2005). Intensive behavioral treatment for children with autism: four-year outcome and predictors. *American Journal of Mental Retardation, 6*, 417–438.

Savage-Rumbaugh, E. S., Murphy, J., Sevcik, R. A., Brakke, K. E., Williams, S., and Rumbaugh, D. M. (1993). Language comprehension in ape and child. *Monographs of the Society for Research in Child Development, 58*, 1–221.

Savage-Rumbaugh, S., Rumbaugh, D., and Fields, W. M. (2009). Empirical Kanzi: the ape language controversy revisited. *Skeptic, 15*, 15–33.

Savage-Rumbaugh, E. S., Rumbaugh, D. M., Smith, S. T., and Lawson, J. (1980). Reference: the linguistic essential. *Science, 210*, 922–925.

Schachter, S., and Singer, J. E. (1962). Cognitive, social and physiological determinants of emotional state. *Psychological Review, 69*, 379–399.

Schachtman, T. R., Walker, J., and Fowler, S. (2011). Effects of conditioning in advertising. In T. R. Schachtman and S. S. Reilly (eds.), *Associative learning and conditioning theory* (pp. 481–506). Oxford: Oxford University Press.

Schacter, D. L. (1994). Priming and multiple memory systems: perceptual mechanisms of implicit memory. In D. L. Schacter and E. Tulving (eds.), *Memory systems 1994* (pp. 233–269). Cambridge, MA: MIT Press.

(1996). *Searching for memory: the brain, the mind, and the past.* New York: Basic Books.

Schacter, D. L., and Tulving, E. (1994). What are the memory systems of 1994? In D. L. Schacter and E. Tulving (eds.), *Memory systems 1994* (pp. 1–38). Cambridge, MA: MIT Press.

Schafe, G. E., and Bernstein, I. L. (1996). Taste aversion learning. In E. D. Capaldi (ed.), *Why we eat what we eat: the psychology of eating* (pp. 31–51). Washington, DC: American Psychological Association.

Schank, R. C., and Abelson, R. (1977). *Scripts, plans, goals and understanding.* Hillsdale, NJ: Erlbaum.

Scheck, B., Neufield, P., and Dwyer, J. (2000). *Actual innocence: five days to execution and other dispatches from the wrongly convicted.* New York: Doubleday.

Schmajuk, N. A., Lam, Y. W., and Gray, J. A. (1996). Latent inhibition: a neural network approach. *Journal of Experimental Psychology: Animal Behavior Processes, 22,* 321–349.

Schmajuk, N. A., Lamoureux, J. A., and Holland, P. C. (1998). Occasion setting: a neural network approach. *Psychological Review, 105,* 3–32.

Schneider, W., and Shiffrin, R. M. (1977). Controlled and automatic human information processing: 1. Detection, search, and attention. *Psychological Review, 84,* 1–66.

Schoenthaler, S., Amos, S., Doraz, W., Kelly, M.-A., Muedeking, G., and Wakefield, J. Jr. (1997). The effect of randomized vitamin-mineral supplementation on violent and non-violent antisocial behavior among incarcerated juveniles. *Journal of Nutritional and Environmental Medicine, 7,* 343–352.

Schwartz, B., Wasserman, E. A., and Robbins, S. J. (2002). *Psychology of learning and behavior* (5th edn). New York: W. W. Norton.

Scoboria, A., Mazzoni, G., Kirsch, I., and Milling, L. S. (2002). Immediate and persisting effects of misleading questions and hypnosis on memory reports. *Journal of Experimental Psychology: Applied, 8,* 26–32.

Seamon, J. G., Philbin, M. M., and Harrison, L. G. (2006). Do you remember proposing marriage to the Pepsi machine? False recollections from a campus walk. *Psychonomic Bulletin and Review, 13,* 752–756.

Sears, R. R., Maccoby, E. E., and Levin, H. (1957). *Patterns of child rearing.* Evanston, IL: Row, Peterson.

Sejnowski, T. J., and Rosenberg, C. R. (1987). Parallel networks that learn to pronounce English text. *Complex Systems, 1,* 145–168.

Selfridge, O. G. (1959). Pandemonium: a paradigm for learning. In D. V. Blake and A. M. Uttley (eds.), *Proceedings of the Symposium on the mechanisation of thought processes* (pp. 511–529). London: HMSO.

Seligman, M. E. P. (1970). On the generality of the laws of learning. *Psychological Review, 77,* 406–418.

Seligman, M. E. P., and Johnson, J. C. (1973). A cognitive theory of avoidance learning. In F. J. McGuigan and D. B. Lumsden (eds.), *Contemporary approaches to conditioning and learning* (pp. 69–110). Washington, DC: Winston-Wiley.

Seligman, M. E. P., and Maier, S. F. (1967). Failure to escape traumatic shock. *Journal of Experimental Psychology, 74,* 1–9.

Shallice, T., and Warrington, E. K. (1970). Independent functioning of verbal memory stores: a neuropsychological study. *Quarterly Journal of Experimental Psychology*, *22*, 261–273.

Shanks, D. R. (1985). Forward and backward blocking in human contingency judgement. *Quarterly Journal of Experimental Psychology*, *37B*, 1–21.

　(2005). Implicit learning. In K. Lamberts and R. Goldstone (eds.), *Handbook of cognition* (pp. 202–220). London: Sage.

　(2007). Associationism and cognition: human contingency learning at 25. *Quarterly Journal of Experimental Psychology*, *60*, 291–309.

Shanks, D. R., Pearson, S. M., and Dickinson, A. (1989). Temporal contiguity and the judgment of causality. *Quarterly Journal of Experimental Psychology*, *41B*, 139–159.

Shaw, J. S., Bjork, R. A., and Handal, A. (1995). Retrieval-induced forgetting in an eyewitness-memory paradigm. *Psychonomic Bulletin and Review*, *2*, 249–253.

Shaw, J. S., McClure, K. A., and Dykstra, J. A. (2007). Eyewitness confidence from the witnessed event through trial. In M. P. Toglia, J. D. Read, D. F. Ross, and R. C. L. Lindsay (eds.), *Handbook of eyewitness psychology*, vol. 1: *Memory for events* (pp. 371–397). Mahwah, NJ: Erlbaum.

Sheffield, F. D., Wulff, J. J., and Backer, R. (1951). Reward value of copulation without sex drive reduction. *Journal of Comparative and Physiological Psychology*, *44*, 3–8.

Sheth, B. R., Sandkühler, S., and Bhattacharya, J. (2009). Posterior beta and anterior gamma oscillations predict cognitive insight. *Journal of Cognitive Neuroscience*, *21*, 1269–1279.

Shettleworth, S. J. (2010). Clever animals and killjoy explanations in comparative psychology. *Trends in Cognitive Sciences*, *14*, 477–481.

Shiffrin, R. M., and Schneider, W. (1977). Controlled and automatic human information processing: II. Perceptual learning, automatic attending, and a general theory. *Psychological Review*, *84*, 127–190.

Siegel, S. (1972). Conditioning of insulin-induced glycemia. *Journal of Comparative and Physiological Psychology*, *78*, 233–241.

　(1975). Evidence from rats that morphine tolerance is a learned response. *Journal of Comparative and Physiological Psychology*, *89*, 498–506.

　(1984). Pavlovian conditioning and heroin overdose: reports by overdose victims. *Bulletin of the Psychonomic Society*, *22*, 428–430.

　(2001). Pavlovian conditioning and drug overdose: when tolerance fails. *Addiction Research and Theory*, *9*, 505–513.

　(2005). Drug tolerance, drug addiction, and drug anticipation. *Current Directions in Psychological Science*, *14*, 296–300.

Siegel, S., and Allan, L. G. (1996). The widespread influence of the Rescorla-Wagner model. *Psychonomic Bulletin and Review*, *3*, 314–321.

Siegel, S., Baptista, M. A. S., Kim, J. A., McDonald, R. V., and Weise-Kelly, L. (2000). Pavlovian psychopharmacology: the associative basis of tolerance. *Experimental and Clinical Psychopharmacology*, *8*, 276–293.

Siegel, S., Hinson, R. E., Krank, M. D., and McCully, J. (1982). Heroin "overdose" death: contribution of drug-associated environmental cues. *Science, 216*, 436–437.

Silverman, P. S., and Retzlaff, P. D. (1986). Cognitive stage regression through hypnosis: are earlier cognitive stages retrievable? *International Journal of Clinical and Experimental Hypnosis, 34*, 192–204.

Simon, D., Krawczyk, D. C., and Holyoak, K. J. (2004). Construction of preferences by constraint satisfaction. *Psychological Science, 15*, 331–336.

Simons, D. J., and Levin, D. T. (1998). Failure to detect changes to people during a real-world interaction. *Psychonomic Bulletin and Review, 4*, 644–649.

Simons, D. J., and Rensink, R. A. (2005). Change blindness: past, present, and future. *Trends in Cognitive Sciences, 9*, 16–20.

Skinner, B. F. (1938). *The behavior of organisms.* New York: Appleton-Century-Crofts.
    (1948a). *Walden two.* New York: Macmillan.
    (1948b). "Superstition" in the pigeon. *Journal of Experimental Psychology, 38*, 168–172.
    (1950). Are theories of learning necessary? *Psychological Review, 57*, 193–216.
    (1953). *Science and human behavior.* New York: Macmillan.
    (1957). *Verbal behavior.* New York: Appleton.

Skinner, E. I., and Fernandes, M. A. (2010). Effect of study context on item recollection. *Quarterly Journal of Experimental Psychology, 63*, 1318–1334.

Slamecka, N. J. (1985). Ebbinghaus: some associations. *Journal of Experimental Psychology: Learning, Memory, and Cognition, 11*, 414–435.

Slamecka, N. J., and Graf, P. (1978). The generation effect: delineation of a phenomenon. *Journal of Experimental Psychology: Human Learning and Memory, 4*, 592–604.

Sloman, S. A. (1996). The empirical case for two systems of reasoning. *Psychological Bulletin, 119*, 3–22.

Smith, C. N., Clark, R. E., Manns, J. R., and Squire, L. R. (2005). Acquisition of differential delay eyeblink classical conditioning is independent of awareness. *Behavioral Neuroscience, 119*, 78–86.

Smith, E. E. (1978). Theories of semantic memory. In W. K. Estes (ed.), *Handbook of learning and cognitive processes* (vol. 6, pp. 1–56). Hillsdale, NJ: Erlbaum.

Smith, E. E., Rips, L. J., and Shoben, E. J. (1974). Structure and process in semantic memory: a featural model for semantic decisions. *Psychological Review, 81*, 214–241.

Smith, G. H., and Engel, R. (1968). Influence of a female model on perceived characteristics of an automobile. *Proceedings of the 76th Annual Convention of the American Psychological Association, 3*, 681–682.

Smith, J. D., and Minda, J. P. (1998). Prototypes in the mist: the early epoch of category learning. *Journal of Experimental Psychology: Learning, Memory, and Cognition, 24*, 1411–1436.

Smith, S. M. (1979). Remembering in and out of context. *Journal of Experimental Psychology: Human Learning and Memory, 5*, 460–471.

(1988). Environmental context-dependent memory. In G. M. Davies and D. M. Thomson (eds.), *Memory in context: context in memory* (pp. 13–34). Chichester: Wiley.

Smith, S. M., and Moynan, S. C. (2008). Forgetting and recovering the unforgettable. *Psychological Science, 19*, 462–468.

Solnick, S. J., and Hemenway, D. (1998). Is more always better? A survey on positional concerns. *Journal of Economic Behavior and Organization, 37*, 373–383.

Solomon, R. L., Turner, L. H., and Lessac, M. S. (1968). Some effects of delay of punishment on resistance to temptation in dogs. *Journal of Personality and Social Psychology, 8*, 233–238.

Solso, R. L., and McCarthy, J. E. (1981). Prototype formation of faces: a case of pseudo-memory. *British Journal of Psychology, 72*, 499–502.

Son, L. K. (2010). Metacognitive control and the spacing effect. *Journal of Experimental Psychology: Learning, Memory, and Cognition, 36*, 255–262.

Spanos, N. P., Menary, E., Gabora, N. J., DuBreuil, S. C., and Dewhirst, B. (1991). Secondary identity enactments during hypnotic past-life regression: a sociocognitive perspective. *Journal of Personality and Social Psychology, 61*, 308–320.

Spelke, E. S., Hirst, W. C., and Neisser, U. (1976). Skills of divided attention. *Cognition, 4*, 215–230.

Sperling, G. (1960). The information available in brief visual presentations. *Psychological Monographs, 74* (whole no. 498).

Spiers, H. J., Maguire, E. A., and Burgess, N. (2001). Hippocampal amnesia. *Neurocase, 7*, 357–382.

Squire, L. R. (1987). *Memory and brain.* New York: Oxford University Press.

(1992). Memory and the hippocampus: a synthesis from findings with rats, monkeys, and humans. *Psychological Review, 99*, 195–231.

(2004). Memory systems of the brain: a brief history and current perspective. *Neurobiology of Learning and Memory, 82*, 171–177.

(2009). Memory and brain systems: 1969–2009. *Journal of Neuroscience, 29*, 12,711–12,716.

Standing, L. (1973). Learning 10,000 pictures. *Quarterly Journal of Experimental Psychology, 25*, 207–222.

Standing, L. G., Bobbitt, K. E., Boisvert, K. L., Dayholos, K. N., and Gagnon, A. M. (2008). People, clothing, music, and arousal as contextual retrieval cues in verbal memory. *Perceptual and Motor Skills, 107*, 523–534.

Steblay, N. M. (1997). Social influence in eyewitness recall: a meta-analytical review of lineup instruction effects. *Law and Human Behavior, 21*, 283–298.

Steblay, N. M., Dysart, J., Fulero, S., and Lindsay, R. C. L. (2001). Eyewitness accuracy rates in sequential and simultaneous lineup presentations: a meta-analytic comparison. *Law and Human Behavior, 25*, 459–473.

Stein, B. S., and Bransford, J. D. (1979). Constraints on effective elaboration: effects of precision and subject generation. *Journal of Verbal Learning and Verbal Behavior, 18*, 769–777.

Stevenson, R. J., Boakes, R. A., and Prescott, J. (1998). Changes in odor sweetness resulting from implicit learning of a simultaneous odor-sweetness association: an example of learned synesthesia. *Learning and Motivation, 29,* 113–132.

Stockhorst, U., Wiener, J. A., Klosterhalfen, S., Klosterhalfen, W., Aul, C., and Steingrüber, H.-J. (1998). Effects of overshadowing on conditioned nausea in cancer patients: an experimental study. *Physiology and Behavior, 64,* 743–753.

Strassberg, Z., Dodge, K. A., Pettit, G. S., and Bates, J. E. (1994). Spanking in the home and children's subsequent aggression toward kindergarten peers. *Development and Psychopathology, 6,* 445–461.

Straus, M. A., and Kantor, G. K. (1994). Corporal punishment of adolescents by parents: a risk factor in the epidemiology of depression, suicide, alcohol abuse, child abuse, and wife beating. *Adolescence, 29,* 543–561.

Stuart, R. B. (1967). Behavioral control of overeating. *Behaviour Research and Therapy, 5,* 357–365.

Styles, E. A. (2006). *The psychology of attention* (2nd edn). Hove: Psychology Press.

Suprenant, A. M., and Neath, I. (2009). The nine lives of short-term memory. In A. Thorn and M. Page (eds.), *Interactions between short-term and long-term memory in the verbal domain* (pp. 16–43). Hove: Psychology Press.

Suret, M., and McLaren, I. P. L. (2003). Representation and discrimination on an artificial dimension. *Quarterly Journal of Experimental Psychology, 56,* 30–42.

Sutton, R. S., and Barto, A. G. (1981). Toward a modern theory of adaptive networks: expectation and prediction. *Psychological Review, 88,* 135–170.

Svartdal, F. (1995). When feedback contingencies and rules compete: testing a boundary condition for verbal control of instrumental performance. *Learning and Motivation, 26,* 221–238.

Sweeney, C. A., and Bellezza, F. S. (1982). Use of the keyword mnemonic in learning English vocabulary words. *Human Learning, 1,* 155–163.

Swinnen, S. P., Schmidt, R. A., Nicholson, D. E., and Shapiro, D.C. (1990). Information feedback for skill acquisition: instantaneous knowledge of results degrades learning. *Journal of Experimental Psychology: Learning, Memory, and Cognition, 16,* 706–716.

Talarico, J. M., and Rubin, D. C. (2007). Flashbulb memories are special after all; in phenomenology, not accuracy. *Applied Cognitive Psychology, 21,* 557–578.

Tamai, N., and Nakajima, S. (2000). Renewal of formerly conditioned fear in rats after extensive extinction training. *International Journal of Comparative Psychology, 13,* 137–147.

Tarner, N. L., Frieman, J., and Mehiel, R. (2004). Extinction and spontaneous recovery of a conditioned flavour preference based on calories. *Learning and Motivation, 35,* 83–101.

Taylor, J., and Miller, M. (1997). When timeout works some of the time: the importance of treatment integrity and functional assessment. *School Psychology Quarterly, 12,* 4–22.

Technical Working Group for Eyewitness Evidence (1999). *Eyewitness evidence: a guide for law enforcement* [booklet]. Washington, DC: United States Department of Justice, Office of Justice Programs.

Telegdy, G. A., and Cohen, J. S. (1971). Cue utilization and drive level in albino rats. *Journal of Comparative and Physiological Psychology*, *75*, 248–253.

Terrace, H. S. (1985). Animal cognition: thinking without language. In L. Weiskrantz (ed.), *Animal intelligence* (pp. 113–128). Oxford: Clarendon.

Testa, K. (1996). Church to pay $1 million in false-memory case. *San Jose Mercury News*, *8A*.

Thomas, A. K., and Loftus, E. F. (2002). Creating false memories through imagination. *Memory and Cognition*, *30*, 423–431.

Thomas, G. V. (1981). Contiguity, reinforcement rate, and the law of effect. *Quarterly Journal of Experimental Psychology*, *33B*, 33–43.

Thomas, M. S. C., and McClelland, J. L. (2008). Connectionist models of cognition. In R. Sun (ed.), *Cambridge handbook of computational psychology* (pp. 23–58). Cambridge: Cambridge University Press.

Thorn, A. S. C., and Page, M. P. A. (2009). Current issues in understanding interactions between short-term and long-term memory. In A. Thorn and M. Page (eds.), *Interactions between short-term and long-term memory in the verbal domain* (pp. 1–15). Hove: Psychology Press.

Thorndike, E. L. (1898). Animal intelligence: an experimental study of the associative processes in animals. *Psychological Review Monograph Supplement*, *2(8)*.

(1911). *Animal intelligence.* New York: Macmillan.

(1935). *The psychology of wants, interests, and attitudes.* New York: Appleton-Century-Crofts.

Thyer, B. A., and Birsinger, P. (1994). Treatment of clients with anxiety disorders. In D. K. Granvold (ed.), *Cognitive and behavioral treatment: methods and applications* (pp. 272–284). Pacific Grove, CA: Brooks/Cole.

Tiffany, S. T., Maude-Griffin, P. M., and Drobes, D. J. (1991). Effect of interdose interval on the development of associative tolerance to morphine in the rat: a dose-response analysis. *Behavioral Neuroscience*, *105*, 49–61.

Timberlake, W., and Allison, J. (1974). Response deprivation: an empirical approach to instrumental performance. *Psychological Review*, *81*, 146–164.

Timberlake, W., Wahl, G., and King, D. (1982). Stimulus and response contingencies in the misbehavior of rats. *Journal of Experimental Psychology: Animal Behavior Processes*, *8*, 62–85.

Tinklepaugh, O. L. (1928). An experimental study of representative factors in monkeys. *Journal of Comparative and Physiological Psychology*, *8*, 197–236.

Titchener, E. B. (1915). *A textbook of psychology.* New York: Macmillan.

Tolman, E. C. (1932). *Purposive behavior in animals and men.* New York: Century.

Toth, J. P., and Hunt, R. R. (1999). Not one versus many, but zero versus any: structure and function in the context of the multiple-memory systems debate. In J. K. Foster and M. Jelicic (eds.), *Memory: structure, function or process?* (pp. 232–272). London: Oxford University Press.

Trabasso, T., and Bower, G. H. (1968). *Attention in learning: theory and research*. New York: Wiley.

Traxler, M. A., and Gernsbacher, M. A. (eds.) (2006). *Handbook of psycholinguistics* (2nd edn). Amsterdam: Elsevier.

Treisman, A. (1960). Contextual cues in selective listening. *Quarterly Journal of Experimental Psychology, 12*, 242–248.

Tulley, M., and Chiu, L. H. (1995). Student teachers and classroom discipline. *Journal of Educational Research, 88*, 164–171.

Tulving, E. (1962). Subjective organization in free recall of "unrelated" words. *Psychological Review, 69*, 344–354.

(1968). Theoretical issues in free recall. In T. R. Dixon and D. L. Horton (eds.), *Verbal behavior and general behavior theory* (pp. 2–36). Englewood Cliffs, NJ: Prentice-Hall.

(1972). Episodic and semantic memory. In E. Tulving and W. Donaldson (eds.), *Organization of memory* (pp. 382–403). New York: Academic Press.

(1985). Ebbinghaus's memory: what did he learn and remember? *Journal of Experimental Psychology: Learning, Memory, and Cognition, 11*, 485–490.

(2001). Episodic memory and common sense: how far apart? *Philosophical Transactions of the Royal Society of London, Biological Sciences, 356*, 1505–1515.

(2002). Episodic memory: from mind to brain. *Annual Review of Psychology, 53*, 1–25.

Tulving, E., and Osler, S. (1968). Effectiveness of retrieval cues in memory for words. *Journal of Experimental Psychology, 77*, 593–601.

Tulving, E., and Pearlstone, Z. (1966). Availability versus accessibility of information in memory for words. *Journal of Verbal Learning and Verbal Behavior, 5*, 381–391.

Tulving, E., and Psotka, J. (1971). Retroactive inhibition in free-recall: inaccessibility of information available in the memory store. *Journal of Experimental Psychology, 87*, 1–8.

Tulving, E., and Thomson, D. (1973). Encoding specificity and retrieval processes in episodic memory. *Psychological Review, 80*, 352–373.

Turner, A. M., and Greenough, W. T. (1985). Differential rearing effects on rat visual cortex synapses: I. Synaptic and neuronal density and synapses per neuron. *Brain Research, 329*, 195–203.

Turner, H. A., and Muller, P. A. (2004). Long-term effects of child corporal punishment on depressive symptoms in young adults: potential moderators and mediators. *Journal of Family Issues, 25*, 761–782.

Tversky, A., and Kahneman, A. (1974). Judgment under uncertainty: heuristics and biases. *Science, 185*, 1124–1131.

1981). The framing of decisions and the psychology of choice. *Science, 211*, 453–458.

(1983). Extensional vs. intuitive reasoning: the conjunction fallacy in probability judgment. *Psychological Review, 90*, 293–315.

Ulrich, R. E., and Azrin, N. H. (1962). Reflexive fighting in response to aversive stimulation. *Journal of the Experimental Analysis of Behavior, 5*, 511–520.

Underwood, B. J. (1957). Interference and forgetting. *Psychological Review, 64*, 49–60.

Vadillo, M. A., and Matute, H. (2007). Predictions and causal estimations are not supported by the same associative structure. *Quarterly Journal of Experimental Psychology, 60*, 433–447.

Valentine, T., and Mesout, J. (2009). Eyewitness identification under stress in the London Dungeon. *Applied Cognitive Psychology, 23*, 151–161.

Van Hamme, L. J., and Wasserman, E. A. (1994). Cue competition in causality judgments: the role of nonpresentation of compound stimulus elements. *Learning and Motivation, 25*, 127–151.

Vander Wall, S. B. (1982). An experimental analysis of cache recovery in Clark's nutcracker. *Animal Behaviour, 30*, 84–94.

Vansteenwegen, D., Francken, G., Vervliet, B., De Clercq, A., and Eelen, P. (2006). Resistance to extinction in evaluative conditioning. *Journal of Experimental Psychology: Animal Behavior Processes, 32*, 71–79.

Vargha-Khadem, F., Gadian, D. G., Watkins, K. E., Connelly, A., Van Paesschen, W., and Mishkin, M. (1997). Differential effects of early hippocampal pathology on episodic and semantic memory. *Science, 277*, 376–380.

Verfaellie, M., Koseff, P., and Alexander, M. (2000). Acquisition of novel semantic information in amnesia: effects of lesion location. *Neuropsychologia, 38*, 484–492.

Vermetten, E., and Bremner, J. D. (2003). Olfaction as a traumatic reminder in post-traumatic stress disorder: case reports and review. *Journal of Clinical Psychiatry, 64*, 202–207.

Virués-Ortega, J. (2010). Applied behavior analytic intervention for autism in early childhood: meta-analysis, meta-regression and dose-response meta-analysis of multiple outcomes. *Clinical Psychology Review, 30*, 387–399.

Vohs, K. D., Mead, N. L., and Goode, M. R. (2006). The psychological consequences of money. *Science, 314*, 1154–1156.

Wadden, T. A., Foster, G. D., and Letizia, K. A. (1994). One-year behavioral treatment of obesity: comparison of moderate and severe caloric restriction and the effects of weight maintenance therapy. *Journal of Consulting and Clinical Psychology, 62*, 165–171.

Wagenaar, A. C., and Maldonado-Molina, M. M. (2007). Effects of drivers' license suspension policies on alcohol-related crash involvement: long-term follow-up in 46 states. *Alcoholism: Clinical and Experimental Research, 31*, 1399–1406.

Wagenaar, W. A. (1986). My memory: a study of autobiographical memory over six years. *Cognitive Psychology, 18*, 225–252.

Wagner, A. R., and Brandon, S. E. (1989). Evolution of a structured connectionist model of Pavlovian conditioning (AESOP). In S. B. Klein and R. R. Mowrer (eds.), *Contemporary learning theories: Pavlovian conditioning and the status of learning theory* (pp. 149–189). Hillsdale, NJ: Erlbaum.

(2001). A componential theory of Pavlovian conditioning: applications of a theory. In M. S. Halliday and R. A. Boakes (eds.), *Inhibition and learning* (pp. 301–336). New York: Academic Press.

Wagner, A. R., Rudy, J. W., and Whitlow, J. W. (1973). Rehearsal in animal conditioning. *Journal of Experimental Psychology Monograph*, *97*, 407–426.

Wagner, G. A., and Morris, E. K. (1987). "Superstitious" behavior in children. *Psychological Record*, *37*, 471–488.

Wang, S., and Morris, R. G. M. (2010). Hippocampal-neocortical interactions in memory formation, consolidation, and reconsolidation. *Annual Review of Psychology*, *61*, 49–79.

Ward, P., and Carnes, M. (2002). Effects of posting self-set goals on collegiate football players' skill execution during practice and games. *Journal of Applied Behavior Analysis*, *35*, 1–12.

Warren, R. M. (1970). Perceptual restorations of missing speech sounds. *Science*, *167*, 392–393.

Warren, R. M., and Warren, R. P. (1970). Auditory illusions and confusions. *Scientific American*, *23*, 30–36.

Warren, V. L., and Cairns, R. B. (1972). Social reinforcement satiation: an outcome of frequency or ambiguity? *Journal of Experimental Child Psychology*, *13*, 249–260.

Wasserman, E. A., and Neunaber, D. J. (1986). College students' responding to and rating of contingency relations: the role of temporal contiguity. *Journal of the Experimental Analysis of Behavior*, *46*, 15–35.

Watkins, M. J. (1979). Engrams as cuegrams and forgetting as cue overload: a cueing approach to the structure of memory. In C. R. Puff (ed.), *Memory organization and structure* (pp. 347–372). New York: Academic Press.

Watson, J. B. (1913). Psychology as the behaviorist views it. *Psychological Review*, *20*, 158–177.

Watson, J. B., and McDougall, W. (1929). *The battle of behaviorism*. New York: Norton.

Watson, J. B., and Raynor, R. (1920). Conditioned emotional reactions. *Journal of Experimental Psychology*, *3*, 1–14.

Waugh, N. C., and Norman, D. A. (1965). Primary memory. *Psychological Review*, *72*, 89–104.

Wegner, D. M. (2009). How to think, say, or do precisely the worst thing for any occasion. *Science*, *325*, 48–50.

Weike, A. I., Schupp, H. T., and Hamm, A. O. (2007). Fear conditioning following unilateral temporal lobectomy: dissociation of conditioned startle potentiation and autonomic learning. *Journal of Neurscience*, *25*, 11,117–11,124.

Weingarten, H. P. (1983). Conditioned cues elicit feeding in sated rats: a role for learning in meal initiation. *Science*, *20*, 431–433.

Weinstein, C. E., and Meyer, R. E. (1986). The teaching of learning strategies. In M. Wittrock (ed.), *The handbook of research on teaching* (3rd edn, pp. 315–327). New York: Macmillan.

Weir, A. A. S., Chappell, J., and Kacelnik, A. (2002). Shaping of hooks in New Caledonia crows. *Science*, *297*, 981.

Weiskrantz, L., and Warrington, E. K. (1979). Conditioning in amnesic patients. *Neuropsychologia*, *8*, 281–288.

Weiten, W. (1998). *Psychology: themes and variations* (4th edn). Pacific Grove, CA: Brooks/Cole.

Welch, G. B., and Burnett, C. T. (1924). Is primacy a factor in association formation? *American Journal of Psychology, 35,* 396–401.

Weldon, M. S. (1999). The memory chop shop: issues in the search for memory systems. In J. K. Foster and M. Jelicic (eds.), *Memory: structure, function or process?* (pp. 162–204). London: Oxford University Press.

Weldon, M. S., and Coyote, K. C. (1996). Failure to find the picture superiority effect in implicit conceptual memory tests. *Journal of Experimental Psychology: Learning, Memory, and Cognition, 22,* 670–686.

Wells, G. L., and Bradfield, A. L. (1999). "Good, you identified the suspect": feedback to eyewitnesses distorts their reports of the witnessing experience. *Journal of Applied Psychology, 83,* 360–376.

Wells, G. L., Lindsay, R. C. L., and Ferguson, T. J. (1979). Accuracy, confidence, and juror perceptions in eyewitness identification. *Journal of Applied Psychology, 64,* 440–448.

Wells, G. L., Malpass, R. S., Lindsay, R. C. L., Fisher, R. P., Turtle, J. W., and Fulero, S. M. (2000). From the lab to the police station: a successful application of eyewitness research. *American Psychologist, 55,* 581–598.

Werker, J. F., and Lalonde, C. E. (1988). Cross-language speech perception: initial capabilities and developmental change. *Developmental Psychology, 24,* 672–683.

Wessel, I., and Merckelbach, H. (1998). Memory for threat-relevant and threat-irrelevant cues in spider phobics. *Cognition and Emotion, 12,* 93–104.

White, A. G., and Bailey, J. S. (1990). Reducing disruptive behaviors of elementary physical education students with Sit and Watch. *Journal of Applied Behavior Analysis, 23,* 353–359.

Whitlow, J. W., Jr., and Wagner, A. R. (1984). Memory and habituation. In H. V. S. Peeke and L. Petrinovich (eds.), *Habituation, sensitization, and behavior* (pp. 103–153). New York: Academic Press.

Whittlesea, B. W. A., Jacoby, L. L., and Girard, K. (1990). Illusions of immediate memory: evidence of an attributional basis for feelings of familiarity and perceptual quality. *Journal of Memory and Language, 29,* 716–732.

Wickens, D. D. (1972). Characteristics of word encoding. In A. W. Melton and E. Martin (eds.), *Coding processes in human memory* (pp. 191–215). Washington, DC: Winston.

Wickens, D. D., Born, D. G., and Allen, C. K. (1963). Proactive inhibition and item similarity in short-term memory. *Journal of Verbal Learning and Verbal Behavior, 2,* 440–445.

Wickens, D. D., and Wickens, C. D. (1942). Some factors related to pseudoconditioning. *Journal of Experimental Psychology, 31,* 518–526.

Widrow, G., and Hoff, M. E. (1960). Adaptive switching circuits. *Institute of Radio Engineers, Western Electronic Show and Convention, Convention Record, 4,* 96–194.

Wiens, S., Katkin, E. W., and Öhman, A. (2003). Effects of trial order and differential conditioning on acquisition of differential shock expectancy and skin conductance conditioning to masked stimuli. *Psychophysiology, 40,* 989–997.

Williams, B. A. (1994). Conditioned reinforcement: neglected or outmoded explanatory construct? *Psychonomic Bulletin and Review, 1,* 457–475.

(1997). Varieties of contrast: a review of "Incentive Relativity" by Charles F. Flaherty. *Journal of the Experimental Analysis of Behavior, 68,* 133–141.

Williams, B. A., Preston, R. A., and de Kervor, D. E. (1990). Blocking of the response-reinforcer association: additional evidence. *Learning and Motivation, 21,* 379–398.

Williams, C. D. (1959). The elimination of tantrum behaviors by extinction procedures. *Journal of Abnormal and Social Psychology, 59,* 269.

Williams, D. A., and Hurlburt, J. L. (2000). Mechanisms of second-order conditioning with a backward conditioned stimulus. *Journal of Experimental Psychology: Animal Behavior Processes, 26,* 340–351.

Williams, D. A., Overmier, J. B., and LoLordo, V. M. (1992). A reevaluation of Rescorla's early dictums about Pavlovian conditioned inhibition. *Psychological Bulletin, 111,* 275–290.

Williams, D. E., Kirkpatrick-Sanchez, S., and Iwata, B. A. (1993). A comparison of shock intensity in the treatment of longstanding and severe self-injurious behavior. *Research in Developmental Disabilities, 14,* 207–219.

Williams, D. R., and Williams, H. (1969). Auto-maintenance in the pigeon: sustained pecking despite contingent non-reinforcement. *Journal of the Experimental Analysis of Behavior, 12,* 511–520.

Williams, L. M. (1994a). Recall of childhood trauma: a prospective study of women's memories of child sexual abuse. *Journal of Consulting and Clinical Psychology, 62,* 1167–1176.

(1994b). What does it mean to forget child sexual abuse? A reply to Loftus, Garry, and Feldman (1994). *Journal of Consulting and Clinical Psychology, 62,* 1182–1186.

(1995). Recovered memories of abuse in women with documented childhood sexual victimization histories. *Journal of Traumatic Stress, 8,* 649–674.

Willingham, D. B., Nissen, M. J., and Bullemer, P. (1989). On the development of procedural knowledge. *Journal of Experimental Psychology: Learning, Memory, and Cognition, 15,* 1047–1060.

Wilson, T. D., Lisle, D., Schooler, J., Hodges, S. D., Klaaren, K. J., and LaFleur, S. J. (1993). Introspecting about reasons can reduce post-choice satisfaction. *Personality and Social Psychology Bulletin, 19,* 331–339.

Wilson, T. D., and Schooler, J. W. (1991). Thinking too much: introspection can reduce the quality of preferences and decisions. *Journal of Personality and Social Psychology, 60,* 181–192.

Winkielman, P., Berridge, K. C., and Wilbarger, J. L. (2005). Unconscious affective reactions to masked happy versus angry faces influence consumption behavior and judgements of value. *Personality and Social Psychology Bulletin, 31,* 121–135.

Winograd, T. (1975). Frame representations and the declarative–procedural controversy. In D. G. Bobrow and A. M. Collins (eds.), *Representation and understanding: studies in cognitive science* (pp. 185–210). New York: Academic Press.

Wittgenstein, L. (1953). *Philosophical investigations* (trans. G. E. M. Anscombe). Oxford: Blackwell.

Wolf, M. M., Braukmann, C. J., and Ramp, K. A. (1987). Serious delinquent behavior as part of a significantly handicapping condition: cures and supportive environments. *Journal of Applied Behavior Analysis, 20,* 347–359.

Wolf, M. M., Risley, T. R., and Mees, H. L. (1964). Application of operant conditioning procedures to the behavior problems of an autistic child. *Behavior Research and Therapy, 1,* 305–312.

Wollen, K.A., Weber, A., and Lowry, D. H. (1972). Bizarreness versus interaction of images as determinants of learning. *Cognitive Psychology, 3,* 518–523.

Wolpe, J. (1958). *Psychotherapy by reciprocal inhibition.* Stanford, CA: Stanford University Press.

Wolpe, J., and Lazarus, A. A. (1966). *Behavior therapy techniques.* London: Pergamon.

Wood, N. L., and Cowan, N. (1995). The cocktail party phenomenon revisited: attention and memory in the classic selective listening procedure of Cherry (1953). *Journal of Experimental Psychology: General, 124,* 243–262.

Wood, R., and Flynn, J. M. (1978). A self-evaluation token system versus an external evaluation token system with predelinquent youth. *Journal of Applied Behavior Analysis, 11,* 503–512.

Wood, W., Wong, F. Y., and Chachere, G. (1991). Effects of media violence on viewers' aggression in unconstrained social interaction. *Psychological Bulletin, 109,* 371–383.

Worthen, J. B., and Deschamps, J. D. (2008). Humour mediates the facilitative effect of bizarreness in delayed recall. *British Journal of Psychology, 99,* 461–471.

Wright, D. B., and McDaid, A. T. (1996). Comparing system and estimator variables using data from police lineups. *Applied Cognitive Psychology, 10,* 75–84.

Yates, F. A. (1966). *The art of memory.* London: Routledge & Kegan Paul.

Yerkes, R. M., and Morgulis, S. (1909). The method of Pavlov in animal psychology. *Psychological Bulletin, 6,* 257–273.

Yonelinas, A. P. (2002). The nature of recollection and familiarity: a review of 30 years of research. *Journal of Memory and Language, 46,* 441–517.

Yuille, J., and Cutshall, J. (1986). A case study of eyewitnesses' memory of a crime. *Journal of Applied Psychology, 71,* 291–301.

Zaffy, D. J., and Bruning, J. L. (1966). Drive and the range of cue utilization. *Journal of Experimental Psychology, 71,* 382–384.

Zajonc, R. B. (1968). Attitudinal effects of mere exposure. *Journal of Personality and Social Psychology* [Monograph], *9,* 1–27.

(1998). *Emotions.* In D. T. Gilbert, S. T. Fiske, and G. Lindzey (eds.), *Handbook of social psychology* (4th edn, vol. 1, pp. 591–632). New York: McGraw-Hill.

(2001). Mere exposure: a gateway to the subliminal. *Current Directions in Psychological Science, 10,* 224–228.

Zamble, E., Hadad, G. M., Mitchell, J. B., and Cutmore, T. R. H. (1985). Pavlovian conditioning of sexual arousal: first- and second-order effects. *Journal of Experimental Psychology: Animal Behavior Processes, 11*, 598–610.

Zaragoza, M. S., and Lane, S. M. (1994). Source misattributions and the suggestibility of eyewitness testimony. *Journal of Experimental Psychology: Learning, Memory, and Cognition, 20*, 934–945.

Zener, K. (1937). The significance of behavior accompanying conditioned salivary secretion for theories of the conditioned response. *American Journal of Psychology, 50*, 384–403.

Zentall, T. R., Wasserman, E. A., Lazareva, O. F., Thompson, R. K. R., and Ratterman, M. J. (2008). Concept learning in animals. *Comparative Cognition and Behavior Reviews, 3*, 13–45.

Zhang, Z., and Schumm, J. S. (2000). Exploring effects of the keyword method on limited English proficient students' vocabulary recall and comprehension. *Reading Research and Instruction, 39*, 202–221.

Zucco, G. M., Paolini, M., and Schaal, B. (2009). Unconscious odour conditioning 25 years later: revisiting and extending "Kirk-Smith, Van Toller and Dodd." *Learning and Motivation, 40*, 364–375.

Index

Page numbers in bold are for Glossary entries